Money, Banking, and Financial Markets

Money, Banking, and Financial Markets

Stephen G. Cecchetti
Brandeis University

McGraw-Hill
Irwin

Boston   Burr Ridge, IL   Dubuque, IA   Madison, WI   New York   San Francisco   St. Louis
Bangkok   Bogotá   Caracas   Kuala Lumpur   Lisbon   London   Madrid   Mexico City
Milan   Montreal   New Delhi   Santiago   Seoul   Singapore   Sydney   Taipei   Toronto

McGraw-Hill
Irwin

MONEY, BANKING, AND FINANCIAL MARKETS

Published by McGraw-Hill/Irwin, a business unit of The McGraw-Hill Companies, Inc.,
1221 Avenue of the Americas, New York, NY 10020. Copyright © 2006 by The
McGraw-Hill Companies, Inc. All rights reserved. No part of this publication may be
reproduced or distributed in any form or by any means, or stored in a database or retrieval
system, without the prior written consent of The McGraw-Hill Companies, Inc.,
including, but not limited to, in any network or other electronic storage or transmission,
or broadcast for distance learning.

Some ancillaries, including electronic and print components, may not be available to
customers outside the United States.

This book is printed on acid-free paper.

1 2 3 4 5 6 7 8 9 0 WCK/WCK 0 9 8 7 6 5 4

ISBN 0-07-245269-2

Publisher: *Gary Burke*
Executive sponsoring editor: *Paul Shensa*
Senior developmental editor: *Erin Strathmann*
Senior marketing manager: *Marty Quinn*
Senior media producer: *Kai Chiang*
Senior project manager: *Susanne Riedell*
Senior production supervisor: *Sesha Bolisetty*
Director of design BR: *Keith J. McPherson*
Photo research coordinator: *Lori Kramer*
Photo researcher: *Emily Tietz*
Media project manager: *Lynn M. Bluhm*
Senior supplement producer: *Carol Loreth*
Developer, Media technology: *Brian Nacik*
Cover image: *© L&M Serivces B.V. Amsterdam 20040511 "Rhyme 34" 1934 by Robert Delaumay*
Cover and interior designer: *Jenny El-Shamy*
Typeface: *10.5/12 Goudy*
Compositor: *Precision Graphics Services, Inc.*
Printer: *Quebecor World Versailles Inc.*

Library of Congress Cataloging-in-Publication Data

Cecchetti, Stephen G. (Stephen Giovanni)
  Money, banking, and financial markets / Stephen G. Cecchetti,
    p. cm.
  Includes index.
  ISBN 0-07-245269-2 (alk. paper)
  1. Money. 2. Banks and banking. 3. Finance. 4. Capital market. I. Title.
HG221.C386 2006
332--dc22   2004057946

www.mhhe.com

Dedication

To my father, Giovanni Cecchetti, who argued tirelessly that financial markets are not efficient; and to my grandfather Albert Schwabacher, who patiently explained why inflation is destructive.

About the Author

Stephen G. Cecchetti joined the Brandeis University faculty in 2003 as a Professor of International Economics and Finance at the International Business School. He is also the Director of Research at the Rosenberg Institute for Global Finance at Brandeis. Previously, Professor Cecchetti taught at the New York University Stern School of Business and, for approximately 15 years, was a member of the Department of Economics at The Ohio State University. He has been a Visiting Professor of Economics at Princeton University, Oxford University, the University of Melbourne, and Boston College.

In addition to his academic appointments, Cecchetti's background includes serving as Executive Vice President and Director of Research, Federal Reserve Bank of New York (1997–1999); Editor, *Journal of Money, Credit, and Banking* (1992–2001); Research Associate, National Bureau of Economic Research (1989–present); Board of Editors, *American Economic Review* (1992–1998), and the *Journal of Economic Literature* (1993–present), among others.

He has consulted for various central banks around the world, including the European Central Bank, the Bank of England, the Central Bank of Bolivia, the Bank of Israel, and the Reserve Bank of Australia.

Cecchetti's research interests include inflation and price measurement, monetary policy, macroeconomic theory, economics of the Great Depression, and financial economics. His initial work concentrated on the theoretical basis and empirical plausibility of new Keynesian models of the business cycle that are based on nominal rigidities. More recently, he has developed new measures of core inflation and examined how monetary policy can be used to control aggregate price movements.

He has published over 60 articles in academic and policy journals and since 2000 has been a regular contributor to the *Financial Times*. See www.brandeis.edu/global/news_cecchetti_articles.php for an archive of his recent newspaper columns.

Cecchetti received an SB in Economics from M.I.T. in 1977 and a PhD in Economics from the University of California at Berkeley in 1982.

Preface

For most of the 20th century, defining money and banks was straightforward. Money was currency or a checking account balance; banks were institutions that took deposits and made loans. Then the invention of computers and the resulting revolution in information technology changed everything. Buying dinner used to require cash or checks issued by a local bank. Now diners can pick up the tab for a restaurant meal with a plastic card that debits their brokerage account at a firm whose nearest office may be thousands of miles away. The changes have been so sweeping that if a banker of the 1960s or 1970s were transported to the present day, he or she would hardly recognize our current financial system. The way we use money, financial instruments, financial markets, and financial institutions is completely different from the way our grandparents' generation used them.

Not only do today's money and banks differ from yesterday's, but tomorrow's financial system will surely differ from the current one in ways that are difficult to predict. Thus, students who memorize the operational details of today's financial system are investing in a short-lived asset. My purpose in writing this book is to focus on the *basic functions* served by the financial system, while de-emphasizing its current structure and rules. Learning the economic rationale behind financial tools, rules, and structures is much more valuable than concentrating on the tools, rules, and structures themselves. It is an approach designed to give students the lifelong ability to understand and evaluate whatever financial innovations they may one day confront.

The Core Principles Approach

Toward that end, the entire content of this book is based on five *core principles*. Knowledge of these principles is the basis for learning what the financial system does, how it is organized, and how it is linked to the real economy.

1. Time has value.
2. Risk requires compensation.
3. Information is the basis for decisions.
4. Markets set prices and allocate resources.
5. Stability improves welfare.

These five core principles serve as a framework through which to view the history, current status, and future development of money and banking. They are discussed in detail in Chapter 1; throughout the rest of the text, marginal icons remind students of the principles that underlie particular discussions.

Focusing on core principles has created a book that is both concise and logically organized. This approach does require some adjustments to the traditional methodology used to teach money and banking, but for the most part they are changes in emphasis only. That said, some of these changes have greatly improved both the ease of teaching and the value students draw from the course. Among them are the emphasis on risk; use of the term *financial instrument*; parallel presentation of the Federal Reserve and the European Central Bank; a streamlined, updated section on monetary economics; and the adoption of an integrated global perspective.

Innovations in This Text

In addition to the focus on core principles, this book introduces a series of innovations designed to foster coherence and relevance in the study of money and banking, in both today's financial world and tomorrow's.

Early Introduction of Risk

It is impossible to appreciate how the financial system works without understanding risk. In the modern financial world, virtually all transactions transfer some degree of risk between two or more parties. These risk trades can be extremely beneficial, as they are in the case of insurance markets. But there is still potential for disaster. In 1998, risk-trading activity at Long-Term Capital Management (LTCM) threatened the stability of the international financial system.

Even though risk is absolutely central to an understanding of the financial system, most money and banking books give very little space to the topic. In contrast, this book devotes an entire chapter to defining and measuring risk. Chapter 5 introduces the concept of a risk premium as compensation for risk and shows how diversification can reduce risk. Because risk is central to explaining the valuation of financial instruments, the role of financial intermediaries, and the job of central bankers, the book returns to this concept throughout the chapters.

Emphasis on Financial Instruments

Financial instruments are introduced early in the book, where they are defined based on their economic function. This approach leads naturally to a discussion of the uses of various instruments and the determinants of their value. Bonds, stocks, and derivatives all fit neatly into this framework, so they are all discussed together.

This approach solves one of the problems with existing texts, use of the term *financial market* to refer to bonds, interest rates, and foreign exchange. In its conventional microeconomic sense, the term *market* signifies a place where trade occurs, not the instruments that are traded. This book follows standard usage of the term *market* to mean a place for trade. It uses the term *financial instruments* to describe virtually all financial arrangements, including loans, bonds, stocks, futures, options, and insurance contracts. Doing so clears up the confusion that can arise when students arrive in a money and banking class fresh from a course in the principles of economics.

Parallel Presentation of the Federal Reserve and the European Central Bank

To foster a deep understanding of central banking and monetary policy, the presentation of this material begins with a discussion of the central bank's role and objectives. Descriptions of the Federal Reserve and the European Central Bank follow. By starting on a theoretical plane, students gain the tools they need to understand how all central banks work. They avoid focusing on institutional details that may quickly become obsolete. Armed with a basic understanding of what central banks do and how they do it, students will be prepared to grasp the meaning of future changes in institutional structure.

Another important innovation is the parallel discussion of the two most important central banks in the world, the Federal Reserve and the European Central Bank (ECB). Students of the 21st century are ill-served by books that focus entirely on the U.S. financial system. They need a global perspective on central banking, the starting point for which is a detailed knowledge of the ECB.

Modern Treatment of Monetary Economics

The discussion of central banking is followed by a simple framework for understanding the impact of monetary policy on the real economy. Modern central bankers think and talk about changing the interest rate when inflation and output deviate from their target objectives. Yet traditional treatments of monetary economics employ aggregate demand and aggregate supply diagrams, which relate output to the price level, and discuss inflation in terms of shifts in the AD and AS curves. The resulting development is lengthy and difficult. Because this book skips the ISLM framework, its presentation of monetary economics is several chapters shorter. Only those topics that are most important in a monetary economics course are covered: long-run money growth and inflation and short-run monetary policy and business cycles. This streamlined treatment of monetary theory is not only concise, but more modern and more relevant than the traditional approach. Moreover, it gives students a complete understanding of business-cycle fluctuations.

Integrated Global Perspective

Recent technological advances have dramatically reduced the importance of a bank's physical location, producing a truly global financial system. Twenty years ago money and banking books could afford to focus primarily on the U.S. financial system, relegating international topics to a separate chapter that could be considered optional. But in today's financial world, even a huge country like the United States cannot be treated in isolation. The global financial system is truly an integrated one, rendering separate discussion of a single country's institutions, markets, or policies impossible. This book incorporates the discussion of international issues throughout the text, emphasizing when national borders are important to bankers and when they are not.

Organization

This book is organized to help students understand both the financial system and its economic effects on their lives. That means surveying a broad series of topics, including what money is and how it is used; what a financial instrument is and how it is valued; what a financial market is and how it works; what a financial institution is and why we need it; and what a central bank is and how it operates. More important, it means showing students how to apply the five core principles of money and banking to the evolving financial and economic arrangements that they inevitably will confront during their lifetimes.

Part I: Money and the Financial System. Chapter 1 introduces the core principles of money and banking, which serve as touchstones throughout the book.

Chapter 2 examines money both in theory and in practice. Chapter 3 follows with a bird's-eye view of financial instruments, financial markets, and financial institutions. (Instructors who prefer to discuss the financial system first can cover Chapters 2 and 3 in reverse order.)

Part II: Interest Rates, Financial Instruments, and Financial Markets. Part II contains a detailed description of financial instruments and the financial theory required to understand them. It begins with an explanation of present value and risk, followed by specific discussions of bonds, stocks, derivatives, and foreign exchange. Students benefit from concrete examples of these concepts. In Chapter 7 (The Risk and Term Structure of Interest Rates), for example, students learn how the information contained in the risk and term structure of interest rates can be useful in forecasting. In Chapter 8 (Stocks, Stock Markets, and Market Efficiency), they learn about stock bubbles and how those anomalies influence the economy. And in Chapter 10 (Foreign Exchange), they study the Big Mac index to understand the concept of purchasing power parity. Throughout this section, two ideas are emphasized: that financial instruments transfer resources from savers to investors, and that in doing so, they transfer risk to those best equipped to bear it.

Part III: Financial Institutions. In the next section, the focus shifts to financial institutions. Chapter 11 introduces the economic theory that is the basis for our understanding of the role of financial intermediaries. Through a series of examples, students see the problems created by asymmetric information as well as how financial intermediaries can mitigate those problems. The remaining chapters in Part III put theory into practice. Chapter 12 presents a detailed discussion of banking, the bank balance sheet, and the risk that banks must manage. Chapter 13 provides a brief overview of the financial industry's structure, and Chapter 14 explains financial regulation.

Part IV: Central Banks, Monetary Policy, and Financial Stability. Chapters 15 through 19 survey what central banks do and how they do it. This part of the book begins with a discussion of the role and objectives of central banks, which leads naturally to the principles that guide central bank design. Chapter 16 applies those principles to the Federal Reserve and the European Central Bank. Chapter 17 presents the central bank balance sheet, the process of multiple deposit creation, and the money supply. Chapters 18 and 19 cover operational policy, based on control of both the interest rate and the exchange rate. The goal of Part IV is to give students the knowledge they will need to cope with the inevitable changes that will occur in central bank structure.

Part V: Modern Monetary Economics. The last part of the book covers modern monetary economics. While most books cover this topic in six or more chapters, this one does it in four. This streamlined approach concentrates on what is important, presenting only the essential lessons that students truly need. Chapter 20 sets the stage by exploring the relationship between inflation and money growth. Starting with inflation keeps the presentation simple and powerful, and emphasizes the way monetary policymakers think about what they do. A discussion of aggregate demand, aggregate supply, and the determinants of inflation and output follows. Chapter 21 presents a dynamic aggregate demand curve that integrates monetary policy directly into the presentation. To complete the explanation of business-cycle fluctuations, Chapter 22 introduces short-run and long-run aggregate supply, wrapping up the section with a discussion of the channels of monetary policy transmission and the challenges central bankers face today.

For those instructors who have the time, we recommend closing the course with a rereading of the first chapter and a review of the core principles. What is the future likely to hold for the five parts of the financial system: money, financial instruments, financial markets, financial institutions, and central banks? How do students envision each of these parts of the system 20 or even 50 years from now?

Learning Tools

In a sense, this book is a guide to the principles students will need to critically evaluate and use what they read in the financial press. Reading the newspaper and applying the information it contains require some basic knowledge. Supplying that knowledge is the purpose of the four types of inserts that complement the chapters, providing a break from the more technical material in the body of the text:

Your Financial World inserts provide students with practical information that is based on lessons covered in the chapter. Most chapters contain two of these boxes, each of which examines a personal finance problem that everyone faces. These boxes show students that the concepts taught in the money and banking course are relevant to their everyday lives. Among the topics covered are the importance of saving for retirement, the risk in taking on a variable-rate mortgage, the desirability of owning stocks, and techniques for getting the most out of the financial news.

Applying the Concept sections show how ideas introduced in the chapter can be applied to the world around us. Most describe historical episodes or examine issues relevant to the public policy debate. Subjects include how debt problems in emerging-market countries can create an increase in the demand for U.S. Treasury debt; why Long-Term Capital Management nearly caused a collapse of the world financial system; and what monetary policymakers learned from the Great Depression of the 1930s. Most chapters contain two of these applications.

In the News boxes present articles drawn from *The New York Times*, *The Wall Street Journal*, *The Financial Times*, *The Economist*, and *BusinessWeek*. These readings show how concepts introduced in the chapter are applied in the financial press. Each article is accompanied by a brief analysis that reinforces key concepts. One In the News box appears in each chapter.

Tools of the Trade boxes teach useful skills, including how to read bond and stock tables, how to read charts, and how to do some simple algebraic calculations. Some provide brief reviews of material from the principles of economics course, such as the relationship between the current account and the capital account in the balance of payments. Most chapters contain one of these boxes.

Finally, the end-of-chapter material is divided into three sections:

Key Terms A listing of all the technical terms introduced and defined in the chapter. The key terms are defined in full in the glossary at the end of the book.

Chapter Lessons A list of the key lessons in the chapter. Other textbooks summarize a small number of points at length. This book summarizes a larger number of points, each of them short, clear, and couched in the form of an outline that matches the chapter headings—a format designed to aid student comprehension and retention.

Problems Each chapter contains 15 problems, both conceptual and computational, of varying levels of difficulty. These problems are designed to reinforce the lessons in the chapter.

Organizational Alternatives

While this book greatly streamlines the traditional approach to money and banking, it remains flexible enough to be used in a broad variety of courses. Sixteen to 19 of the book's 23 chapters can be assigned in the following courses:

General Money and Banking Course. Chapters 1–8, 11, 12, 15, 16, 18, and 20–22

This course covers the primary material needed to appreciate the connections between the financial system and the economy.

General Money and Banking Course with International Emphasis. Chapters 1–8, 10, 11, 12, 15–19, and 20

This alternative to the general money and banking course substitutes chapters on foreign exchange and exchange-rate policy for the macroeconomic model included in courses with less international emphasis.

Financial Markets and Institutions. Chapters 1–9, 11–18

The traditional financial markets and institutions course covers money, financial instruments and markets, financial institutions, and central banking. The focus is on Parts II and III of the book.

Monetary Economics and Monetary Policy. Chapters 1–7, 10, 11, 12, 15–23

A course called monetary economics and monetary policy uses the material in Parts II and III as a foundation for understanding the material in Parts IV and V. A half-semester course for students with a background in financial instruments and institutions might cover only Chapters 1–3 and 15–23.

Supplements for Students

Student Study Guide and Workbook

James S. Fackler (University of Kentucky) has written an excellent study guide and workbook for students. It includes descriptions of the major lessons in each chapter, definitions, and practice multiple-choice and essay questions. Detailed answers to the practice test questions are also provided.

Web Site

The book's Web site, www.mhhe.com/economics/cecchetti1e, includes a variety of free content for students, including chapter quizzes, PowerPoint slides, and interactive graphs with related exercises. Instructors may access all the book's major supplements using a special password.

Supplements for Instructors

Instructor's Resources and Solutions Manual

Mary Lesser (Iona College) has collected a broad array of materials for instructors. This manual includes chapter overviews, outlines, and a discussion of how the core principles apply to each chapter. It also addresses concepts students often find difficult, including suggestions for alleviating confusion. Solutions to the problems at the end of each chapter are given. Included as well is helpful advice provided by Stephen Miller (University of Nevada at Las Vegas) on how instructors can easily modify their existing course to take advantage of the approach in this book.

Test Bank

John Nader (Grand Valley State University) has constructed a test bank of 2,300 multiple-choice and 600 short-answer and essay questions. The test bank can be used both as a study guide and as a source for exam questions. It has been computerized to allow for both selective and random generation of test questions.

PowerPoint Slides

Nick Noble (Miami University) has developed a set of PowerPoint slides intended for classroom use. The slides outline the main points in each chapter and reproduce major graphs and charts. This handy, colorful supplement will help to maintain students' interest during lectures.

Acknowledgments

I owe thanks to many more people that I can possibly list, including a large number of academics, central bankers, and financial market participants around the world. A few of these deserve special mention. I would like to thank Robert M. Solow, who set me on the path doing economics as a 20-year-old undergraduate; George A. Akerlof, whose inspiration still guides me, even more than 20 years after he signed my dissertation; William J. McDonough, who gave me the opportunity to watch and ask questions from inside the Federal Reserve; and to Peter R. Fisher, who was my day-to-day guide to what I was seeing at the Fed.

Of my numerous collaborators and colleagues over the years, Nelson Mark (now at the University of Notre Dame) deserves special mention. His encouragement, counsel, and friendship have guided me for more than 15 years. In addition, Mike Bryan of the Federal Reserve Bank of Cleveland has been a constant source of help and encouragement, as have numerous friends throughout the central banking world.

Among all of the professional colleagues who took the time to read early versions of the manuscript, I would like to single out Jim Fackler for his insight and patience. This book is much better for the time he generously devoted to correcting my logical mistakes.

Without all the people at McGraw-Hill/Irwin this book would never have been written. Gary Burke and Paul Shensa first convinced me that I could write this book, and then taught me how. Erin Strathmann worked tirelessly (and daily) to improve the book. Betty Morgan made my sentences and paragraphs readable. And all of the people in production and design turned the words and charts into a beautiful, readable book.

Without students, universities would not exist. And without a class in money and banking to teach, I would not have written this book. I owe a debt to every student who has sat in a classroom with me. Not surprisingly, some students helped more than others. The ones that deserve special mention for the time and effort they put in to helping with the manuscript are: Margaret Mary McConnell of the Federal Reserve Bank of New York, Roisin O'Sullivan of Smith College, Stefan Krause of Emory University, Lianfa Li of China International Capital Corporation, Craig Evers of the Federal Reserve Board, Anne LePard of Brandeis University, and Georgios Karras of University of Illinois, Chicago.

And finally, there is my family; my wife Ruth and our sons Daniel and Ethan. For three years they have put up with my daily routine of writing, rewriting, and rewriting again and again. To them I owe the biggest thanks, and I promise I won't do this again, at least not right away.

Stephen G. Cecchetti
Brandeis University

Chapter Reviewers

Burton Abrams
University of Delaware

Stacie Beck
University of Delaware

Robert Boatler
Texas Christian University

Michael Brandl
University of Texas at Austin

James Butkiewicz
University of Delaware

Ann Bynoe
Pace University

Gabriele Camera
Purdue University

Giorgio Canarella
California State University at Los Angeles

Michael Carter
University of Massachusetts at Lowell

Dong Woo Cho
Wichita State University

Jin W. Choi
DePaul University

Ranjit S. Dighe
State University of New York at Oswego

James Fackler
University of Kentucky

J. Van Fenstermaker
Towson University

Dennis Fixler
University of Wisconsin at Milwaukee

Stuart Glosser
University of Wisconsin at Whitewater

David Hakes
University of Northern Iowa

Joseph Haslag
University of Missouri

Andreas Hauskrecht
Indiana University

Scott Hein
Texas Tech University

Jon A. Hooks
Albion College

Jonathan Jelen
Mercy College

Nancy Jianakoplos
Colorado State University

U. Jin Jhun
State University of New York at Oswego

Theodore Kariotis
George Washington University

Benjamin Kim
University of Nebraska at Lincoln

Ruby Kishan
Southwest Texas State University

Faik Koray
Louisiana State University

Mary Lesser
Iona College

Anthony Lima
California State University at Hayward

Gary Maggs
Saint John Fisher College

Kathryn Marshall
Ohio State University

James McCown
Florida Atlantic University

W. Douglas McMillin
Louisiana State University

Stephen Miller
University of Nevada at Las Vegas

Raoul Minetti
Michigan State University

Ted Muzio
St. John's University (New York)

Jon Nadenichek
California State University at Northridge

John Nader
Grand Valley State University

Ronald Necoechea
Roberts Wesleyan College

John Neri
University of Maryland

Nicholas Noble
Miami University

Rupert Rhodd
Florida Atlantic University

Charles Roussel
Louisiana State University

Joseph Santos
South Dakota State University

Elizabeth Sawyer Kelly
University of Wisconsin at Madison

Frank G. Steindl
Oklahoma State University

Mark Strazicich
University of North Texas

Kristin Van Gaasbeck
California State University Sacramento

John Wassom
Western Kentucky University

Mark Wohar
University of Nebraska at Omaha

King-yuen Yik
University of Michigan

Market Reviews and Surveys

Dean Baim
Pepperdine University

Clare Battista
California Polytechnic State University at San Luis Obispo

Roohi Baveja
University of Michigan

Florin Bidian
University of Minnesota

Michael Brandl
University of Texas at Austin

William Brown
California State University at Northridge

James Butkiewicz
University of Delaware

Jim Campen
University of Massachusetts at Boston

Jen-Chi Cheng
Wichita State University

Nan-Ting Chou
University of Louisville

Meenakshi Dalal
Wayne State College

Bruce Dieffenbach
State University of New York at Albany

Ranjit Dighe
State University of New York at Oswego

Richard Douglas
Bowling Green State University

Michael Dowell
California State University at Sacramento

Marc Fusaro
Northwestern University

Ralph Gamble Jr.
Fort Hays State University

Chris Geiregat
Williams College

Fred Graham
American University

O. David Gulley
Bentley College

W. K. Hannan
Niagara University

Jill Ann Holman
University of Wisconsin at Milwaukee

Daniel Houser
University of Arizona at Tucson

Syed Hyat
Siena College

U Jin Jhun
State University of New York at Oswego

Amir Kia
Carleton University

Benjamin Kim
University of Nebraska at Lincoln

Tony Lowenberg
California State University at Northridge

David Macpherson
Florida State University

James McCown
Oklahoma City University

Cheryl McGaughey
Angelo State University

W. Douglas McMillin
Louisiana State University

Juan Mendoza
State University of New York at Buffalo

Clair Morris Jr.
United States Naval Academy

William Mounts
Mercer University

Jon Nadenichek
California State University at Northridge

Ronald Nate
Brigham Young University at Idaho

Hiranya K. Nath
Sam Houston State University

John Neri
University of Maryland

Rebecca Neumann
University of Wisconsin at Milwaukee

Nicholas Noble
Miami University

Mark Perry
University of Michigan at Flint

Jerrold Peterson
University of Minnesota at Duluth

Manoj Pradhan
State University of New York at Stony Brook

Joseph Santos
South Dakota State University

Daniel Seiver
Miami University

Aldin Shiers
California Polytechnic State University at San Luis Obispo

Richard G. Stahl
Louisiana State University

Richard Tontz
California State University at Northridge

Stan Warren
Niagara University

John C. Wassom
Western Kentucky University

Eugene White
Rutgers University

Mark Witkowski
University of Arkansas at Little Rock

Janet Wolcutt
Wichita State University

Jeffrey Zimmerman
Methodist College

Feature Walkthrough

YOUR FINANCIAL WORLD
Pay Off Your Credit Card Debt as Fast as You Can

Credit cards are extremely useful. They make buying things easy—sometimes too easy. While we all plan to pay off our credit card balances every month, sometimes we just don't have the resources. So we take advantage of the loans the card issuers offer and pay off only part of what we owe. Suddenly we find ourselves deeply in debt.

How fast should you pay off your credit card balance? All the bank or finance company that issued the card will tell you is the minimum you have to pay. You get to decide whether to pay more, and your decision makes a big difference. We can use the present-value concept to figure out your alternatives.

Let's take a typical example. You have a balance of $2,000 and can afford to pay at least $50 per month. How many monthly payments will you need to make to pay off the full debt? What if you paid $60 or $75 per month? To find the answer, use equation (12) for the present value of a fixed series of payments. In this case, the present value is the loan amount, $2,000; the fixed monthly payment is $50, $60, or $75; and the interest rate is whatever your credit card company charges per month. Most credit card companies charge between 10 and 20 percent a year. (The average rate is around 13 percent.) We need to figure out the number of payments, or n in equation (12).[*]

Table 4.4 shows the number of months needed to pay off your $2,000 balance at various interest rates and payment amounts. The first entry tells you that if your credit card company is charging a 10 percent annual interest rate (which is comparatively low), and you pay $50 per month, then you will need to make payments for 48.4 months—just over four years.

Looking at the entire table, you can see the advantage of making big payments. Assume you're paying 15 percent, which is realistic. The table shows that increasing your payment from $50 to $60 will allow you to finish paying off your debt in 42.5 months rather than 54.3 months. In other words, paying $10 more a month will allow you to

Table 4.4	Number of Months to Pay Off a $2,000 Credit Card Debt		
Annual Interest Rate	**Monthly Payment**		
	$50	**$60**	**$75**
10%	48.4	38.9	30.1
12%	50.5	40.3	30.9
15%	54.3	42.5	32.2
20%	62.4	47.0	34.5

finish paying off the loan one full year sooner. And if you can manage to pay $75 a month, you'll be finished 10 months before that.

Looking more closely, you can see that making large payments is much more important than getting a low interest rate. The lesson is: Pay off your debts as fast as you possibly can. Procrastination is expensive.

How fast should you pay off your credit card balance?

SOURCE: © Masterfile

[*]The most straightforward way to do this is to use a spreadsheet to add up the payments until their present value equals the credit card balance. You can also use equation (A-4) in the appendix of this chapter, which can be solved using logarithms.

For a complete listing of titles of chapter features and their page references, refer to the information found on the inside front cover of this text.

Your Financial World

These boxes show students that the concepts taught in the text are relevant to their everyday lives. Among the topics covered are the importance of saving for retirement, the risk in taking on a variable rate mortgage, the desirability of owning stocks, and techniques for getting the most out of the financial news.

YOUR FINANCIAL WORLD
A Guide to Evaluating Risk

Deciding whether a risk is worth taking is extremely difficult, but some simple rules can help. Let's start with the investment described in Table 5.2, where $1,000 yields either $1,400 or $700 with equal probability. If we think about it in terms of gains and losses, this investment offers an equal chance of gaining $400 or losing $300. Should you take the risk? The answer depends on how risk averse you are, but most of us would say no. To see why, let's break the investment down into two parts, the gain and the loss (see Table 5.5).

Taking the gain first, how much would you pay for a 50 percent chance of making $400? Again, the answer depends on your risk aversion, but you surely would pay less than $200, the expected value of such an investment. Let's assume that your answer is $150.

Next, let's turn to the loss. How much would you be willing to pay to avoid a $300 loss altogether? To put it another way, assume that you risk losing $300 and are considering buying insurance against the loss. The insurance company will take the bet for you, losing the $300 in your place if that is the outcome. How much would you be willing to pay an insurance company to avoid taking a 50 percent chance of losing $300? Again, the answer depends on how risk averse you are, but we know that you will pay more than $150, the expected value of the loss, which is $150. (The insurance company would insist on receiving more.) Let's assume you will pay $200 to avoid the loss.

Now we are ready to answer our original question: Is the value of the potential gain sufficient to compensate you for the cost of the potential loss? Subtracting the $200 that you are willing to pay to avoid the $300 loss from the $150 you will pay for the opportunity to gain $400, we get $150 - $200 = -$50, a result less than zero. In short, the potential gain is not big enough to compensate you for the potential loss, so you should not take the risk. In fact, our computation suggests you

Table 5.5	Evaluating the Risk of a $1,000 Investment
A. The Gain	
Payoff	**Probability**
+$400	$\frac{1}{2}$
$0	$\frac{1}{2}$
B. The Loss	
Payoff	**Probability**
$0	$\frac{1}{2}$
−$300	$\frac{1}{2}$

would be willing to pay $50 *not* to make this investment!

Deciding if a Risk Is Worth Taking

1. List all the possible outcomes, or payoffs.
2. Assign a probability to each possible payoff.
3. Divide the payoffs into gains and losses.
4. Ask how much you would be willing to pay to *receive* the gain.
5. Ask how much you would be willing to pay to *avoid* the loss.
6. If you are willing to pay more to receive the gain than to avoid the loss, you should take the risk.

APPLYING THE CONCEPT
ENDING DISCRIMINATION IN LENDING

For many years, banks routinely accepted deposits from households in low-income neighborhoods but refused to lend funds to people in those areas. In this practice, known as *redlining*, loan officers would literally draw a line on a map and lend only to those people who lived on one side of the line. The problem was particularly acute in inner cities, where neither businesses nor individuals could obtain financing for normal activities like building and renovation. Redlining contributed to the decline of inner cities, which became increasingly unpleasant and dangerous places.

To understand the reasons for redlining, imagine that a bank's loan officers are considering loan applications from two neighborhoods, each of which offers a wide variety of loan opportunities. These lenders will make loans in both neighborhoods until, holding the interest rate and other relevant factors fixed, the riskiness of the loans in the two neighborhoods is equal. In this way the bank controls its credit risk. But if one of the neighborhoods offers only high-risk opportunities, all the bank's lending will be funneled into the low-risk neighborhood. That is essentially what happened in the inner cities. From the banker's perspective, redlining was just a way to control credit risk. Default rates were so high in some areas, managers said, that responsible lenders simply did not risk lending there.* Unfortunately, given the racial composition of many high-risk neighborhoods, the policy looked discriminatory even though it may have been color-blind.

Applying the Concept

These sections showcase history and examine issues relevant to the public policy debate. Subjects include how debt problems in emerging market countries can create an increase in the demand for U.S. Treasury debt; why Long-Term Capital Management caused a near collapse of the world financial system; and what monetary policy makers learned from the Great Depression of the 1930s.

IN THE NEWS
David Bowie Becomes a Bond

Washington Post

by Jay Mathews
February 6, 1997

David Bowie, the angular British rock star, has never been afraid to try something new. His stage persona has metamorphosed from Ziggy Stardust to Aladdin Sane to the Thin White Duke, with interesting digressions along the way. He has performed with a succession of bands, from the Kon-rads to the King Bees, to the Lower Third, to Tin Machine.

Now Bowie is the first major artist to turn himself into a bond issue—payable over 10 years at 6.9 percent.

The asset-backed bond—the financial instrument that has put $55 million in Bowie's well-tailored pocket—is a device of rapidly growing popularity that already has helped banks turn home loan payments and credit card receivables into big chunks of cash. But until now no one dared to think the annual income from former hits such as "Space Oddity" or "Let's Dance" might appeal to gray-suited executives looking for stable bond investments.

The bond bonus for Bowie is $55 million immediately, instead of in installments as the records sell, and more money than record companies were offering. What he'll do with the money is unclear, but he seems to have been drawn to the deal by its tax advantages.

The reliability of the revenue stream to pay off the bondholders enabled Bowie to get a favorable interest rate. His success could entice other artists with steady royalty payments to go to market, said David Pullman, the 34-year-old senior vice president at Fahnestock & Co. who designed the deal.

Many rock stars have outsold Bowie in the United States, but his avant-garde image and exotic musical tastes still sell an average 1 million records a year all over the planet, according to his business manager, Bill Zysblat. There also is revenue from 250 songs turned into sheet music, commercials, and background music for elevators, offices, voice mail, and many other uses in an age in which profit sources for art are expanding rapidly.

"It just goes to show you that anything can be securitized," said Craig Moyer, senior fixed-income manager at Meridian Investment Co. in Valley Forge, Pennsylvania, part of CoreStates Financial Corp.

Asset-backed bonds began as a way to help banks turn old-fashioned, slow-moving income sources such as credit card

and car loan payments into big new cash sources that could be reinvested and turned into even more fees and income.

Moyer said Bowie's $55 million deal would be too small to interest most investors because they would be uncertain of finding buyers if they decided to move their money elsewhere. But, he said, he could imagine some clients who would be drawn to the deal, with an interest rate significantly above the 6.4 percent now paid by 10-year Treasury bonds.

Unlike most singer-songwriters, Bowie had kept control of his copyrights and record masters, and the distribution license for his first 25 albums was due to expire in June. He could have signed a new deal, with a substantial advance, but Pullman said he thought he could get more money upfront through a bond sale.

Zysblat agreed to see how big an advance the record companies were offering, while Pullman tested the feasibility of a bond sale. When they met again, Zysblat said, "his numbers were bigger than my numbers."

Record companies who see profits in turning their backlists of CDs and songs into asset-backed bonds have been asking Zysblat for advice, he said. "I tell them I'm not in that business," he said, "but maybe I will be."

SOURCE: Copyright © 1997, The Washington Post, reprinted with permission.

LESSONS OF THE ARTICLE
Virtually anything can be turned into a bond, even the future revenues from the sale of rock music. Here, the revenue from the retail sales of David Bowie's music in all its forms has been turned into an asset-backed security. The benefit to Bowie is that he received a cash payment immediately and shifted the risk that future revenue will be low to the bondholders. Thus buyers of Bowie's bonds must believe that his music will continue to sell well, maintaining the revenue needed to make the promised payments. As it turns out, the entire $55 million bond issue, which had a risk premium of 0.5 percent over U.S. Treasury bonds (6.9 percent minus 6.4 percent), was purchased by a single insurance company. This company realized the bonds offered a type of diversification that is hard to come by, as the risk that David Bowie will become unpopular is surely uncorrelated with almost every other investment out there.

In the News

One article per chapter from major media such as *The New York Times, The Economist, The Financial Times, The Wall Street Journal,* and *BusinessWeek* is featured. These readings show how concepts introduced in the chapter are applied in the financial press. A brief analysis of the article, called "Lessons," reinforces key concepts.

TOOLS OF THE TRADE
Computing Compound Annual Rates

Comparing changes over days, months, years, and decades can be very difficult. If someone tells you that an investment grew at a rate of $\frac{1}{2}$ percent last month, what should you think? You're used to thinking about growth in terms of years, not months. The way to deal with such problems is to turn the monthly rate into a *compound-annual rate.* Here's how you do it.

An investment whose value grows $\frac{1}{2}$ percent per month goes from 100 at the beginning of the month to 100.5 at the end of the month. Remembering to multiply by 100 to convert the decimal into a percentage, we can verify this:

$$100\left(\frac{100.5-100}{100}\right) = 100\left[\left(\frac{100.5}{100}\right)-1\right] = 0.5\%$$

To convert this monthly rate to an annual rate, we need to figure out what would happen if the investment's value continued to grow at a rate of $\frac{1}{2}$ percent per month for the next 12 months. We can't just multiply 0.5 times 12. Instead, we need to compute a 12-month compound rate by raising the one-month rate to the 12th power. Assuming that our index starts at 100 and increases by $\frac{1}{2}$ percent per month, we can use the expression for a compound future value to compute the index level 12 months later. Remembering to convert percentages to their decimal form, so that 0.5 percent is 0.005, we find the result is

$$FV_n = PV(1 + i)^n = 100\,(1.005)^{12} = 106.17,$$

an increase of 6.17 percent. That's the compound annual rate, and it's obviously bigger than the 6 per-

cent result we get from just multiplying 0.5 by 12. The difference between the two answers—the one you get by multiplying by 12 and the one you get by compounding—grows as the interest rate grows. At a 1 percent monthly rate, the compounded annual rate is 12.68 percent.

Another use for compounding is to compute the percentage change per year when we know how much an investment has grown over a number of years. This rate is sometimes referred to as the *average annual rate.* Say that over five years an investment has increased 20 percent, from 100 to 120. What annual increase will give us a 20 percent increase over five years? Dividing by 5 gives the wrong answer because it ignores compounding; the increase in the second year must be calculated as a percentage of the index level at the end of the first year. What is the growth rate that after five years will give us an increase of 20 percent? Using the future-value formula,

$$FV_n = PV(1 + i)^n$$
$$120 = 100\,(1 + i)^5$$

Solving this equation means computing the following:

$$i = \left[\left(\frac{120}{100}\right)^{1/5}\right]-1 = 0.0371$$

This tells us that five consecutive annual increases of 3.71 percent will result in an overall increase of 20 percent. (Just to check, we can compute $(1.0371)^5 = 1.20 = 120/100$.)

Tools of the Trade

These boxes teach useful skills, including how to read bond and stock tables, how to read charts, and how to do some simple algebraic calculations. Some provide brief reviews of material from the principles of economics course, such as the relationship between the current account and the capital account in the balance of payments.

---

es. Income is the stream of earnings over time. Wealth is the value of assets minus liabilities. Money is one of those assets, albeit a very minor one.

Money, in the sense we are talking about, has three characteristics. It is (1) a means of payment, (2) a unit of account, and (3) a store of value. The first of these characteristics is the most important. Anything that is used as a means of payment must be a store of value and thus very likely to become a unit of account. Let's see why this is so.

Means of Payment

The primary use of money is as a **means of payment.** Most people insist on payment in money at the time a good or service is supplied because the alternatives just don't work very well. Barter, in which a good or service is exchanged directly for another good or service, requires that a plumber who needs food find a grocer who needs a plumbing repair. Relying on this "double coincidence of wants" surely causes the economy to run less smoothly. The plumber could pay for his breakfast cereal with a "promise" of plumbing services, which the grocer could then transfer to someone else. But while it would be possible to certify the plumber's trustworthiness, certainly taking payment in money is easier. Money finalizes payments so that buyers and sellers have no further claim on each other. That is money's special role. In fact, so long as a buyer has money, there is nothing more the seller needs to know.

As economies have become more complex and physically dispersed, reducing the likelihood that a seller will have good information about a buyer, the need for money has grown. The increase in both the number of transactions and the number of potential buyers and sellers (the vast majority of whom may never even have seen one another) argues for something that makes payment final and whose value is easily verified. That something is money.

INFORMATION

Unit of Account

Just as we measure length using feet and inches, we measure value using dollars and cents. Money is the **unit of account** that we use to quote prices and record debts. We could also refer to it as a standard of value.

Having a unit of account is

B

Core Principle Marginal Icons

The entire text discussion is organized around the following five core principles: Time has value; risk requires compensation; information is the basis for decisions; markets set prices and allocate resources; and stability improves welfare. Exploring these principles is the basis for learning what the financial system does, how it is organized, and how it is linked to the real economy. They are discussed in detail in Chapter 1; throughout the rest of the text, marginal icons remind students of the principles that underlie particular discussions.

Brief Contents

Contents

Part *III*   Financial Institutions 258

Part V   Modern Monetary Economics   518

Part *I*

Money and the Financial System

Chapter 1

An Introduction to Money and the Financial System

This morning, a typical American college student bought coffee at the local café, paying for it with an ATM card. Then she jumped into her car, on which she carries accident insurance, and drove to the university, which she can afford to attend thanks to her student loan. She may have left her parents' home, which is mortgaged, a few minutes early to avoid construction work on a new dormitory, paid for by bonds issued by the university. Or perhaps she needed to stop at the bookstore to purchase this book, using her credit card, before her first money and banking class began.

Beneath the surface, each financial transaction mentioned in this story—even the seemingly simple ones—is quite complicated. If the café owner and the student use different banks, paying for the coffee will require an interbank funds transfer. The company that insures the student's car has to invest the premiums she pays until they are needed to pay off claims. The student's parents almost surely obtained their home mortgage through a mortgage broker, whose job was to find the mortgage that offered the best interest rate. And the bonds the university issued to finance construction of the new dormitory were created with the aid of an investment bank.

This brief example hints at the complex web of interdependent institutions and markets that underlies the financial transactions we engage in every day. The system is so large, so efficient, and generally speaking so well run that most of us rarely take note of it. But a financial system is like air to an economy: If it disappeared suddenly, everything would grind to a halt. Let's take a closer look at this system.

The Five Parts of the Financial System

The financial system has five parts, each of which plays a fundamental role in our economy. Those parts are money, financial instruments, financial markets, financial institutions, and central banks.

We use the first part of the system, money, to pay for our purchases and to store our wealth. We use the second part, financial instruments, to transfer resources from savers to investors and to transfer risk to those who are best equipped to bear it. Stocks, mortgages, and insurance policies are examples of financial instruments. The third part of our financial system, financial markets, allows us to buy and sell financial instruments quickly and cheaply. The New York Stock Exchange is an example of a financial market. Financial institutions, the fourth part of the financial system, provide a myriad of services, including access to the financial markets and collection of information about prospective borrowers to ensure they are creditworthy. Banks, securities firms, and insurance companies are examples of financial institutions. Finally, central banks, the fifth part of the system, monitor and stabilize the economy. The Federal Reserve System is the central bank of the United States.

While the essential functions that define these five categories endure, their physical form is constantly evolving. *Money* once consisted of gold and silver coins, which were eventually replaced by paper currency, which today is being eclipsed by electronic funds transfers. Methods of accessing means of payment have changed dramatically as well. As recently as 1970, people customarily obtained currency from bank tellers when they cashed their paychecks or withdrew their savings from the local bank. Today, they can get cash from practically any ATM anywhere in the world. To pay their bills, people once wrote checks and put them in the mail, then waited for their monthly bank statements to make sure the transactions had been processed correctly. Today, payments can be made automatically, and account holders can check the transactions at any time on their bank's Web site.

Financial instruments (or securities, as they are often called) have evolved just as much as currency. In the last few centuries, investors could buy individual stocks through stockbrokers, but the transactions were costly. Furthermore, putting together a portfolio of even a small number of stocks and bonds was extremely time consuming; just collecting the information necessary to evaluate a potential investment was a daunting task. As a result, investing was an activity reserved for the wealthy. Today, financial institutions offer people with as little as $1,000 to invest the ability to purchase shares in *mutual funds*, which pool the savings of a large number of investors. Because of their size, mutual funds can construct portfolios of hundreds or even thousands of different stocks and/or bonds.

The markets where stocks and bonds are sold have undergone a similar transformation. Originally, *financial markets* were located in certain coffeehouses and taverns where individuals met to exchange financial instruments. The next step was to create organized markets, like the New York Stock Exchange—trading places specifically dedicated to the buying and selling of stocks and bonds. Today, much of the activity that once occurred at these big-city financial exchanges is handled by electronic networks. Buyers and sellers obtain price information and initiate transactions from their desktop computers or from handheld devices. Because electronic networks have reduced the cost of processing financial transactions, even small investors can afford to participate in them. Just as important, today's financial markets offer a much broader array of financial instruments than those available even 50 years ago.

Financial institutions have changed, as well. Banks began as vaults where people could store their valuables. Gradually, they developed into institutions that accepted deposits and made loans. For hundreds of years, in fact, that was what bankers did. Today, a bank is more like a financial supermarket. Walk in and you will discover a huge assortment of financial products and services for sale, from access to the financial markets to insurance policies, mortgages, consumer credit, and even investment advice.

Finally, *central banks* have changed a great deal. They began as large private banks founded by monarchs for the express purpose of financing wars. For instance, King William of Orange created the Bank of England in 1694 for the express purpose of raising taxes and borrowing to finance a war between Austria, England, and the Netherlands on one side and Louis XIV's France on the other. Eventually, these government treasuries grew into the modern central banks we know today. While only a few central banks existed in 1900, now nearly every country in the world has one, and the central bank has become one of the most

"This is Fluffy, my pet money."

important institutions in government. Central banks control the availability of money and credit to ensure low inflation, high growth, and the stability of the financial system. Because their current mission is to serve the public at large rather than land-hungry monarchs, their operating methods have changed as well. Once the central bank's decisions were shrouded in mystery, but today's policymakers strive for transparency in their operations. Officials at the European Central Bank and the U.S. Federal Reserve—two of the most important central banks in the world—go out of their way to explain the rationale for their decisions.

Though the changing nature of our financial system is a fascinating topic, it poses challenges for both students and instructors. How can we teach and learn about money and banking in a way that will stand the test of time, so that the knowledge we gain won't become outmoded? The answer is that we must develop a way to understand and adapt to the evolutionary structure of the financial system. That means discussing money and banking within a framework of core principles that do not change over time. The next section introduces the five core principles that will guide our studies throughout this book.

The Five Core Principles of Money and Banking

Five core principles will inform our analysis of the financial system and its interaction with the real economy. Once you have grasped these principles, you will have a better understanding not only of what is happening in the financial world today but of changes that will undoubtedly occur in the future. The five principles concern the importance of **Time, Risk, Information, Markets,** and **Stability.**

Core Principle 1: Time Has Value

The first principle of money and banking is that *time has value*. At some very basic level, everyone knows this. If you take a job at the local supermarket, you will almost surely be paid by the hour. An hour's worth of work equals a certain number of dollars. Literally, your time has a price.

On a more sophisticated level, time affects the value of financial transactions. Most loan contracts allow the borrower to spread out the payments over time. If you take out an auto loan, for example, the lender will allow you to make a series of monthly payments over three, four, or even five years. If you add up the payments, you'll discover that the total exceeds the amount of the loan. At an interest rate of six percent, a four-year, $10,000 car loan will require 48 monthly payments of $235 each. That means you will repay a total of $11,280 (48 times $235). The reason your repayments total more than the loan amount is that you are paying interest to compensate the lender for the time during which you use the funds. You are paying rent for the use of the resources.

Interest payments are fundamental to a market economy. In Chapter 4, we will develop an understanding of interest rates and how to use them. Then, throughout the remainder of Part II, we will use the principle that time has value as the starting point in our discussion of the valuation of bonds, stocks, and other financial instruments involving future payments. How much should you be willing to pay for a particular stock or bond? Figuring out what alternative investments are worth, and comparing them, means valuing payments made on different future dates. The same principle applies to the question of how much you must invest today to achieve a particular financial objective in the future. How much of your salary, for example, do you need to save each month to meet your goal of buying a house? The length of time your savings will be earning interest is a key to answering this question.

Core Principle 2: Risk Requires Compensation

The world is filled with uncertainty. More events, both good and bad, *can* happen than *will* happen. Some of the possibilities, such as the likelihood of your home doubling in value after you buy it, are welcome. Other possibilities, such as the chance that you might lose your job and not be able to make your car payments, are distinctly unwelcome. Dealing effectively with **risk** requires that you consider the full range of possibilities in order to eliminate some risks, reduce others, pay someone to assume particularly onerous risks, and just live with what's left. Needless to say, no one will assume your risks for free, which brings us to the second core principle of money and banking: *Risk requires compensation*. In the financial world, compensation is made in the form of explicit payments. That is, investors must be paid to assume risk; the higher the risk, the bigger the required payment.

Car insurance is a common example of paying someone else to shoulder a risk you don't want to take. If your car is wrecked in an accident, you will want to be able to repair it. But beyond that, auto insurance shelters drivers from the possibility of losing all their wealth in the event that they cause an accident in which someone is seriously injured. Although the chances of causing such an accident are quite small, the results can be so serious that, even if the government didn't require it, most of us would voluntarily purchase auto insurance. Driving without it just isn't worth the risk. The insurance company pools the premiums that policyholders pay and invests them. Even though some of the premiums will be spent to settle claims when cars are stolen or damaged by collisions, the chance to make a profit is good. So both the insurance company and the drivers who buy policies are ultimately better off.

Bearing in mind that time has value and risk requires compensation, we can begin to see the rationale behind the valuation of a broad set of financial instruments. For example, a lender will charge a higher interest rate on a loan if there is a chance that the borrower will not repay. We can see this principle when we examine the interest rates on bonds. In chapters 6 and 7, we will study bonds in detail. As we will see, a company that is on the verge of bankruptcy may still be able to issue bonds (called *junk bonds*), but it will have to pay an extremely high interest rate to do so. The reason is that the lender must be compensated for the substantial risk that the company will not repay the loan. Risk requires compensation.

Core Principle 3: Information Is the Basis for Decisions

Most of us collect **information** before making decisions. The more important the decision, the more information we gather. Think of the difference between buying a $5 sandwich and a $10,000 car. You will surely spend more time comparing cars than comparing sandwiches.

What's true for sandwiches and cars is true for finance as well. That is, *information is the basis for decisions*. In fact, the collection and processing of information is the foundation of the financial system. In Chapter 11, we will learn how financial institutions like banks funnel resources from savers to investors. Before a bank makes a loan, a loan officer will investigate the financial condition of the individual or firm seeking it. Banks want to provide loans only to the highest-quality borrowers. Thus, they spend a great deal of time gathering the information needed to evaluate the creditworthiness of loan applicants.

To understand the problem faced by the two parties to any financial transaction, think about a home mortgage. Before making the loan, the mortgage broker examines the applicant's finances and researches the home's value to make sure the applicant can afford the monthly payments and the property is more valuable than the loan.

And before the broker transfers the funds to the seller, the new homeowner must purchase fire insurance. All these requirements arise from the fact that the lender doesn't know much about the borrower and wants to make sure the loan will be repaid.

Information plays a key role in other parts of the financial system as well. In chapters 2 and 3, we'll see that many types of transactions are arranged so that the buyer doesn't need to know anything about the seller. When merchants accept cash, they don't need to worry about the customer's identity. When stocks change hands, the buyer doesn't need to know anything about the seller, or vice versa. Stock exchanges are organized to eliminate the need for costly information gathering, facilitating the exchange of securities. In one way or another, information is the key to the financial system.

Core Principle 4: Markets Set Prices and Allocate Resources

MARKETS

Markets are the core of the economic system. They are the place, physical or virtual, where buyers and sellers meet, where firms go to issue stocks and bonds, and where individuals go to purchase assets. Financial markets are essential to the economy, channeling its resources and minimizing the cost of gathering information and making transactions. In fact, well-developed financial markets are a necessary precondition for healthy economic growth. The better developed a country's financial markets, the faster the country will grow.

The reason for this relationship between markets and growth is that *markets set prices and allocate resources*. Financial markets gather information from a large number of individual participants and aggregate it into a set of prices that signals what is valuable and what is not. Thus, markets are sources of information. By attaching prices to different stocks or bonds, they provide a basis for the allocation of capital.

To see how prices in the financial markets allocate capital, think about a large firm wishing to finance the construction of a new factory costing several hundred million dollars. To raise the funds, the firm can go directly into the financial markets and issue stocks or bonds. The higher the price investors will pay in the market, the more appealing the idea will be, and the more likely it is that the firm will issue securities to raise the capital for the investment.

We will refer to the financial markets throughout much of this book. While our primary focus in Part II will be the nature of financial instruments, we will also study the markets in which those instruments are traded. Chapters 6 through 10 describe the markets for bonds, stocks, derivatives, and foreign currencies.

Importantly, financial markets do not arise by themselves—at least, not the large, well-oiled ones we see operating today. Markets like the New York Stock Exchange, where over 1 billion shares of stock change hands every day, require rules in order to work properly, as well as authorities to police them. Otherwise, they will not function. For people to be willing to participate in a market, they must perceive it as fair. As we will see, this creates an important role for the government. Regulators and supervisors of the financial system make and enforce the rules, punishing people who violate them. When the government protects investors, financial markets work well; otherwise they don't.

Core Principle 5: Stability Improves Welfare

Most of us prefer stable to variable incomes. We like getting raises, but the prospect of a salary cut is not a pleasant one. This brings us to the fifth core principle of money and banking: *Stability improves welfare*. Stability is a desirable quality, not just in our personal lives but in the financial system as a whole.

If you are wondering whether this principle is related to Core Principle 2 (risk requires compensation), you are right. Because volatility creates risk, reducing volatility reduces risk. But while individuals can eliminate many risks on their own (we'll see how when we study financial instruments in Part II), some risks can only be reduced by government policymakers. Business cycle fluctuations are an example of the sort of instability individuals can't eliminate on their own. And though "automatic stabilizers" like unemployment insurance and the income tax system reduce the burden of recessions on individuals, they cannot eliminate an economic slowdown. Monetary policymakers can moderate these downswings by carefully adjusting interest rates. In stabilizing the economy as a whole, they eliminate risks that individuals can't, improving everyone's welfare in the process.

As we will learn in Part IV of this book, stabilizing the economy is a primary function of central banks like the Federal Reserve and the European Central Bank. Officials of these institutions are charged with eliminating inflation and reducing business cycle fluctuations. That is, they work to keep inflation low and stable and to keep growth high and stable. When they are successful, they reduce both the risk that individuals will lose their jobs and the uncertainty that firms face in making investment decisions. Not surprisingly, a stable economy grows faster than an unstable economy. Stability improves welfare.

Throughout the book you will notice icons like this ![TIME icon] in the margin at various points. These will guide you to the core principle that provides the foundation for what is being discussed at that point in the text.

Special Features of This Book

Every chapter of this book contains a series of important elements, beginning with an introduction. The introduction presents real-world examples that lead to the big questions the chapter is designed to answer: What is money? What do banks do? How does the bond market work? What does the Federal Reserve do to prevent financial crises?

The text of each chapter presents the economic and financial theory you need to understand the topics covered. Each chapter also contains a series of inserts that apply the theory. There are four types of insert: Your Financial World, Applying the Concept, In the News, and Tools of the Trade. Here are some guidelines for using them.

Your Financial World

When most people decide to make a major purchase, they begin by collecting information. If they are considering buying a car, they will first try to decide which model is best for them and then work hard to pay the lowest price possible. Even for smaller purchases, like clothes or groceries, people first gather information and then buy.

Financial transactions should be no different from consumer purchases. Become informed first, and then buy. If you're thinking, "That's easier said than done," you're right. The problem is that most people have very little knowledge of the financial system, so they don't know how to start or what kind of information to collect.

That's where Your Financial World comes in. These inserts provide basic guidelines for applying economic theory to the bread-and-butter financial decisions you make nearly every day. Here are some of the questions that are answered in Your Financial World:

- What's the difference between a debit card and a credit card?
- Should you drive your old car for another year or buy a new one?
- How much car and life insurance do you need to buy?
- Should you own stocks?
- Why is inflation bad for everyone?
- What proportion of your current income do you need to save to retire comfortably?

Read these inserts to become informed about the financial system so that you can use it to your advantage. You will be amazed to discover how much is at stake.

Applying the Concept

Each chapter in this book contains a series of applications called Applying the Concept, which show how to put theory into practice. These inserts provide real-world examples of the ideas introduced in the chapter, drawn primarily from history or from relevant public policy debates. Here are some of the questions examined in Applying the Concept:

- Why do interest rates rise when inflation goes up?
- Why does a country's exchange rate suddenly plummet?
- Have government policies successfully ended discrimination in lending?
- Why is it important for central banks to be free of political influence?
- Can monetary policy be used to stabilize the economy?
- What determines inflation?

In the News

One of the primary purposes of this textbook is to help you understand the business news that you read and hear every day. Critically evaluating what you read, hear, and see in the financial news means developing a clear understanding of how the financial system works, as well as reading the news regularly. Like many other skills, critical reading of newspapers and magazines takes practice. You can't just pick up a newspaper and skim through it quickly and efficiently; you need to learn how. Your instructor will make suggestions about what you should read. See Table 1.1 for a list of reliable sources of information on the economy and the financial system.

Given your need to become a skilled consumer of financial information, each chapter in this book closes with an article drawn from the financial press. These stories from *The Wall Street Journal*, the *Financial Times*, the *Economist*, and *BusinessWeek* are reproduced under the heading In the News. Each provides an example of how the

---

Table 1.1   Sources of Economic and Financial News

Sources of Daily News

The Wall Street Journal and www.wsj.com
The Wall Street Journal is the most widely-read business newspaper in the world. Published five days a week and available both in print and on the Internet, the paper provides national and international news of general interest as well as comprehensive coverage of business and finance.

The Financial Times and www.ft.com
The Financial Times is a London-based, English-language newspaper printed daily around the world and updated online 24 hours a day. The newspaper offers comprehensive reporting as well as analysis and commentary on major business, political, financial, and economic events. The *FT*, as it is familiarly known, is written from a distinctly European perspective and contains more detailed coverage of non-U.S. business and financial news than U.S. publications.

Sources of Weekly News

The Economist and www.economist.com
The Economist is a weekly newsmagazine covering global politics, economics, business, finance, and science. Founded in Britain in 1843 to campaign for free trade, it still adheres to the principles of individual freedom and democracy. This publication not only reports the facts but analyzes them and draws policy conclusions. The Finance and Economics section, located roughly three-quarters of the way into each issue, includes detailed stories focused on global economic and financial policy.

BusinessWeek and www.businessweek.com
BusinessWeek is a U.S.-based publication that offers fair and balanced reporting and analysis of top economic, financial, business, and technological issues. The Economic Trends and Business Outlook columns, in particular, often cover central banking, financial markets, and macroeconomic issues.

---

concepts introduced in the chapter are discussed in the real world, and each is followed by a brief summary.

Tools of the Trade

Many chapters in this book include an insert called Tools of the Trade that concentrates on practical knowledge relevant to the chapter. Some of these inserts cover basic skills, including how to read bond and stock tables, how to read charts, and how to do some simple algebraic calculations. Others provide brief reviews of material from principles of economics classes, such as the relationship between the current account and the capital account in the balance of payments. Still other Tools of the Trade inserts address questions such as:

- What is leverage, and how does it affect risk?
- What are hedge funds?
- How does the Federal Reserve buy and sell securities?
- How is a recession defined?

The Organization of This Book

This book is organized into five sections. Each one employs core principles to illuminate a particular part of the financial system and apply economic theory to the world around us. The next two chapters will continue our overview of the financial system. First, we'll study money—what it is and how it is used. We'll see that currency allows transactions to be made anonymously, which reduces the need to gather information. This advantage of currency is related to Core Principle 3: Information is the basis for decisions. In Chapter 3, we'll take a bird's-eye view of financial instruments, financial markets, and financial institutions. At various points in that chapter, we'll refer to the first four core principles.

Part II includes detailed descriptions of financial instruments. We'll study bonds, stocks, and derivatives, as well as exchange rates for foreign currency. The valuation of financial instruments requires a comparison of payments made on different dates as well as an estimate of the risk involved in each instrument. Thus, these chapters focus on Core Principles 1 and 2: Time has value and Risk requires compensation.

Throughout Part II and continuing in Part III, we'll discuss financial markets, whose purpose is to facilitate the buying and selling of financial instruments. No one would buy stocks or bonds if they could not be resold cheaply and easily. Financial markets also provide the information necessary to understand the value and risk that are associated with particular financial instruments. Core Principles 3 and 4 (Information is the basis for decisions and Markets set prices and allocate resources) are both relevant to our discussion of markets.

Part III covers financial institutions, especially banks. Earlier in this chapter (pages 5–6), we emphasized that financial institutions spend a great deal of time collecting and processing information. Without that information, many financial transactions could not take place. This dependence of banks on information is an example of Core Principle 3: Information is the basis for decisions.

Part IV describes central banks, especially the Federal Reserve and the European Central Bank. These institutions exist to stabilize the real economy as well as the financial system. Thus, they embody Core Principle 5: Stability improves welfare. We'll see how central banks manipulate interest rates to stabilize the economy.

Finally, Part V brings together material covered in the first four sections to explain how the financial system influences the real economy. We'll use a macroeconomic model to analyze the mechanism through which central banks influence the economy, paying particular attention to the role of the financial system in determining inflation and growth.

Learning money and banking is going to be hard work. Reading and working through the remaining 22 chapters of this book will take lots of time and energy. But when you are done, you will be armed with the tools you need to understand how the financial system works and why it changes as it does. You will know how to be an informed reader of the financial and economic news and how to put the financial system to use for you. You will understand the various ways that you can pay for your morning coffee and how each one of them works. You will understand the usefulness of bonds and stocks as well as what financial institutions do and how central banks work. You will know how to make sound financial decisions for the rest of your life. Regardless of the career you choose to follow, a solid background in money, banking, and financial markets will help you make sound financial decisions from now on.

Terms

central bank, 2
European Central Bank, 4
Federal Reserve System, 2
financial institution, 2
financial instrument, 2
financial market, 2
financial system, 2

information, 5
markets, 6
money, 2
risk, 5
stability, 7
time, 4

Chapter Lessons

1. A healthy and constantly evolving financial system is the foundation for economic efficiency and economic growth. It has five parts:

   a. Money is used to pay for purchases and to store wealth.

   b. Financial instruments are used to transfer resources and risk.

   c. Financial markets allow people to buy and sell financial instruments.

   d. Financial institutions provide access to the financial markets, collect information, and provide a variety of other services.

   e. Central banks stabilize the economy.

2. The core principles of money and banking are useful in understanding all five parts of the financial system.

   a. Core Principle 1: Time has value.

   b. Core Principle 2: Risk requires compensation.

   c. Core Principle 3: Information is the basis for decisions.

   d. Core Principle 4: Markets set prices and allocate resources.

   e. Core Principle 5: Stability improves welfare.

Problems

1. The United States Treasury borrows money on behalf of the federal government all the time. One type of government borrowing, called a Treasury bill, promises a fixed payment at some number of months in the future. The Treasury receives less for a promise to make a payment of $100 in six months than it does for a promise to make a payment of $100 in three months. Why? Explain how this arrangement illustrates the core principle that time has value.

2. Describe the links among the five components of the financial system and the five core principles of money and banking.

3. Socialists argue that, to reduce the power exerted by the owners of capital, the state should control the allocation of resources. Thus, in a socialist system, the state allocates investment resources. In a market-based capitalist system, financial markets do that job. Which approach do you think works better, and why? Relate your answer to the core principle that markets set prices and allocate resources.

4. Most investment advisers tell their clients to purchase shares in one or more mutual funds rather than to buy individual stocks. They argue that this practice reduces risk. Explain why.

5. Small businesses tend to borrow money from banks. Would you lend directly to a small business? Relate your answer to the third core principle of money and banking: Information is the basis for decisions.

6. Financial innovation has reduced individuals' need to carry cash. Explain how.

7. For many years, people got their mortgages at local banks. Today, a prospective homeowner can get a mortgage through a broker who obtains funds from institutions all over the country. What effect do you think this financial innovation has had on an individual's ability to obtain a mortgage? What effect do you think it has had on interest rates and mortgage fees?

8. Suppose central bankers figure out a way to eliminate recessions. What financial and economic changes would you expect to see? Relate them to the core principle that stability improves welfare.

9. Why is it important that financial markets offer individuals the ability to buy and sell financial instruments quickly and cheaply?

10. When you apply for a loan, you must answer a lot of questions. Why? Why is the set of questions you must answer standardized?

11. What factors determine the premiums individuals pay for automobile insurance? Why would differences in those factors affect the amount of the premiums? Relate your answer to the core principle that risk requires compensation.

12. Try to list the financial transactions you have engaged in over the past week. How might each one have been carried out 50 years ago?

13. Would you expect a college loan to have a higher or lower interest rate than a home mortgage? Why or why not? In your answer, be sure to use one of the core principles of money and banking.

14. Merchants that accept Visa or MasterCard pay the issuer of the card a percentage of the transaction. For example, for each $100 charged on Visa cards, a merchant might receive only $98. Explain both why Visa charges the fee and why the merchant pays it. (You should be able to use at least two core principles in your answer.)

15. The government is heavily involved in the financial system. Explain why.

Chapter 2

Money and the Payments System

The makers of the board game Monopoly print about 50 billion dollars' worth of Monopoly money every year—coincidentally about the same as the amount of new U.S. currency issued in 2002. Every game has bills totaling 15,140 Monopoly dollars. At a cost of about 13 U.S. dollars per set, this "money" would be a good deal if you could buy things other than Boardwalk and Park Place with it. Unfortunately, attempts to pay for groceries, books, or rent with this particular form of money have been unsuccessful.

And that's probably a good thing. Since the mid-1930s, Parker Brothers has sold over 200 million Monopoly games, containing more than 3 trillion Monopoly dollars.[1]

When we pay for our purchases in the real world, we have lots of choices: crisp new $20 bills, credit cards, debit cards, checks, or more complicated electronic methods. Regardless of the choice we make, we are using *money* to buy our food and clothes and pay our bills. To make sure we can do it, thousands of people work through every night, for the payments system really never sleeps. The middle of the night is the busiest time for check-clearing operations. Trucks make pickups and deliveries, and a fleet of leased airplanes flies sacks of paper checks around the country. And the volumes are astounding. The Federal Reserve reports that in 2000 there were 103 billion non-cash payments made in the U.S., 65 percent of which were paper checks. That means something like 250 million paper checks and 150 million electronic payments were processed on an average business day. From the time you put a signed check into an envelope until it returns to you with your bank statement, that small piece of paper travels a long way. If you choose another way to pay, the path of that payment is just as complicated.

Parker Brothers' bestselling board game.

To understand why money is so important to the smooth functioning of the economy and how it improves everyone's well-being, we need to understand exactly what money is. Just why is a $20 bill issued by the U.S. government much more useful than $20 in Monopoly money? Furthermore, to quantify the impact of money on the economy, we need to be able to measure it. Those are the goals of this chapter: to understand what money is, how we use it, and how we measure it.

Money and How We Use It

When people use the word *money* in conversation, they mean many different things. Someone who "makes lots of money" has a high income; a person who "has lots of money" is wealthy. We will use the word *money* in a narrower, specialized sense to mean anything that can readily be used to make economic transactions. Formally defined,

[1]For more fun facts about Monopoly, see www.monopoly.com.

money is *an asset that is generally accepted as payment for goods and services or repayment of debt.* Income, in contrast, is a flow of earnings over time. Wealth is the value of assets minus liabilities. Money is one of those assets, albeit a very minor one.

Money, in the sense we are talking about, has three characteristics. It is (1) a means of payment, (2) a unit of account, and (3) a store of value. The first of these characteristics is the most important. Anything that is used as a means of payment must be a store of value and thus is very likely to become a unit of account. Let's see why this is so.

Means of Payment

The primary use of money is as a means of payment. Most people insist on payment in money at the time a good or service is supplied because the alternatives just don't work very well. Barter, in which a good or service is exchanged directly for another good or service, requires that a plumber who needs food find a grocer who needs a plumbing repair. Relying on this "double coincidence of wants" surely causes the economy to run less smoothly. The plumber could pay for his breakfast cereal with a "promise" of plumbing services, which the grocer could then transfer to someone else. But while it would be possible to certify the plumber's trustworthiness, certainly taking payment in money is easier. Money finalizes payments so that buyers and sellers have no further claim on each other. That is money's special role. In fact, so long as a buyer has money, there is nothing more the seller needs to know.

As economies have become more complex and physically dispersed, reducing the likelihood that a seller will have good information about a buyer, the need for money has grown. The increase in both the number of transactions and the number of potential buyers and sellers (the vast majority of whom may never even have seen one another) argues for something that makes payment final and whose value is easily verified. That something is money.

Unit of Account

Just as we measure length using feet and inches, we measure value using dollars and cents. Money is the unit of account that we use to quote prices and record debts. We could also refer to it as a standard of value.

"I suppose mere promises would not suffice."

Having a unit of account is an incredible convenience. Remember from microeconomics that prices provide the information consumers and producers use to ensure that resources are allocated to their best uses. What matter are the *relative* prices of goods and services. When the price of one product is higher than the price of another, that product is worth more to both producers and consumers. Using dollars makes these comparisons easy. Imagine what would happen if we needed to compute relative prices for each pair of goods. With two goods, we would need only one price. With three goods, we would need three prices. But with 100 goods, we would need 4,950 prices, and with 10,000 goods (substantially less than the 70,000 products in a typical supermarket), we would need nearly 50 million prices.[2] Using money as a yardstick and quoting all prices in dollars certainly is easier.

[2]The general formula is that for n we need $n(n-1)/2$ prices, so for 10,000 goods, the number would be $10,000\,(9,999)/2 = 49,995,000$.

YOUR FINANCIAL WORLD
Don't Worry about Counterfeit Currency

A friend offers you a $100 bill to repay a loan. Because you rarely see $100 bills, you're a bit concerned. How can you tell it's genuine? A $100 bill has a number of security features that you can see quickly without insulting your friend. The three most difficult to counterfeit, and the easiest to see, are a security thread, a watermark, and color-shifting ink. The security thread runs vertically through the bill to the left of Benjamin Franklin's portrait and carries the words "USA 100." The watermark is located to the right of the portrait and is identical to it. And the number 100 in the lower right-hand corner shifts between green and black when you move the bill. All new bills issued in the late 1990s—$5, $10, $20, and $50, as well as $100—have these features.

You don't need to worry about counterfeiting, though. The United States Treasury and the Federal Reserve redesign the notes at least once a decade to stay ahead of the counterfeiters. During 2001, the amount of U.S. currency outstanding increased by over $50 billion, of which less than $50 million was counterfeit. The NexGen notes issued in fall 2003 are even harder to counterfeit than the ones produced in the late 1990s. For more information on the security features built into U.S. currency, visit the Web site of the U.S. Treasury's Bureau of Printing and Engraving (they're the people who print the stuff) at www.moneyfactory.com.

A watermark of Franklin is here.

A security thread with the words "USA 100" runs vertically here.

This number shifts between green and black when you move the bill.

SOURCE: *U.S. Federal Reserve*

Store of Value

For money to function as a means of payment, it has to be a **store of value**, too. That is, if we are going to use money to pay for goods and services, then it must retain its worth from day to day. Sellers are much less likely to accept things that are perishable, like milk or lettuce. So the means of payment has to be durable and capable of transferring purchasing power from one day to the next. Paper **currency** does degrade with use ($1 bills have an average lifetime of 18 months in circulation) but regardless of its physical condition, it is usually accepted at face value in transactions.[3]

Of course, money is not the only store of value. We hold our wealth in lots of other forms—stocks, bonds, houses, even cars. Many of these are actually preferable to

[3]Individuals engaging in dollar transactions outside the United States may accept only dollar bills that are in good condition. Exchanging damaged for new notes usually requires returning them to the United States.

money as stores of value. Some, like bonds, pay higher interest rates than money. Others, like stocks, offer the potential for appreciation in nominal value, which money does not. Still others, like houses, deliver other services over time. Yet we all hold money because money is liquid. Liquidity *is a measure of the ease with which an asset can be turned into a means of payment,* namely money. For example, a bond is much more liquid than a house because it is so much easier and cheaper to sell. The more costly it is to convert an asset into money, the less liquid it is. Because constantly transforming assets into money every time we wished to make a purchase would be extremely costly, we keep some money around.

The Functions of Money

1. Means of payment: Used in exchange for goods and services.
2. Unit of account: Used to quote prices.
3. Store of value: Used to move purchasing power into the future.

APPLYING THE CONCEPT
A PROFESSOR ISSUES CURRENCY

In July 2000, a wealthy Italian academic named Giancinto Auriti printed up his own brand of currency and started distributing it. He called it the *simec.* Anyone who wished could travel to the small southern Italian town where Professor Auriti lived and receive one simec in exchange for one lira (the currency used in Italy before January 1, 2002, when it was replaced by the euro). By mid-August, there were nearly $2 million worth of simecs in circulation.

Why would anyone want this stuff? The answer is that Professor Auriti had promised local merchants that if they brought simecs to him, he would give them two lire to one. That is, he agreed to sell simecs to individuals at par with the lira and redeem them from merchants at double their value. The stores that agreed to accept payment in simecs saw the demand for their products skyrocket.

If your reaction is that something here doesn't add up, you're right. It's fortunate that Professor Auriti is very wealthy, because his experiment was expensive. He claimed he would be able to redeem the simecs merchants turned in using revenue from those just sold, but his plan didn't work. After a brief burst of activity, the number of simecs in circulation began to fall as merchants starting accepting them at a discount. In the end, simecs were not accepted by enough people. They were not the unit of account, and their ability to store value depended on Professor Auriti's promises. On all counts, the simec didn't make very good money, and it hasn't survived. The final reference to it was made in a news report in 2001—the simec lasted about a year.

The Payments System

The payments system is the web of arrangements that allow for the exchange of goods and services, as well as assets, among different people. Because the efficient operation of our economy depends on the payments system, a critical public policy concern is that it functions well. As we will see in Part IV, that is why central banks are directly involved.

Money is at the heart of the payments system. Whether we realize it or not, virtually every transaction we engage in involves the use of money at some point. Let's go through all the possible methods of payment to see how the system works.

Commodity and Fiat Monies

The first means of payment were things with intrinsic value. These commodity monies included everything from silk in China to butter in Norway, whale teeth in Fiji, and salt in Venice. All these things had value even if they were not used as money. The worth of a block of salt, for instance, came from its value as a preservative. But successful commodity monies had other characteristics: They were usable in some form by most people; they could be made into standardized quantities; they were durable; they had high value relative to their weight and size so that they were easily transportable; and they were divisible into small units so that they were easy to trade. For most of human history, gold has been the most common commodity money. It is widely accepted as payment; can be purified and made into standard weight units like coins; and is extremely durable since it does not corrode or tarnish. Moreover, gold is rare (there is only enough in existence to fill about one-third of the Washington Monument with solid gold), so it has high value relative to weight. And it can be cut into smaller pieces without losing its value.

In 1656, a Swede named Johan Palmstruck founded the Stockholm Banco. Five years later he issued Europe's first paper money.[4] At the time, the Swedish currency was copper ingots, which works poorly as money because of its low value per unit of weight. (Today, copper is worth only about 10 cents per ounce, or roughly 1/50 the value of silver and 1/3,000 the value of gold.) Thus, easy-to-handle paper was welcomed, at least at first.

After a few years of printing paper currency, Palmstruck and his sponsor, the King of Sweden, became overly enamored of the new money. The king needed to finance some wars he was fighting, so he convinced Palmstruck to print more and more notes. Since the bills were redeemable on demand for metal, the system worked only as long as people believed there was enough metal sitting in Palmstruck's vaults. As the number of notes increased, Swedes lost confidence in them and started to redeem them for the metal they supposedly stood for. But Palmstruck had issued too many notes, and his bank failed.

Other people tried issuing paper money during the early 1700s. Eventually governments got into the act. In 1775, the newly formed Continental Congress of the United States of America issued "continentals" to finance the Revolutionary War. Twenty years later, revolutionary France issued the "assignat." Lacking any other source of funding for their wars, both governments issued huge quantities of the currencies, and both currencies eventually became worthless.

---

[4]The Chinese were the real monetary pioneers, issuing their first paper currency in the 7th century, 1,000 years before the Europeans.

A Revolutionary War "Continental" issued by the Continental Congress in 1775. The new government of the United States eventually printed $200 million worth, and by 1781 they no longer had any value.

An assignat issued by the French Revolutionary Government in 1793. Faced with the need to finance wars and food shortages, the government eventually printed 40 billion of them and by the late 1790s they were worthless.

The reaction was predictable: People became suspicious of government-issued paper money. But governments need funds and will use all available means to get them. In the United States, the Civil War put pressure on government finances and the two warring parties had little choice but to issue paper money to pay for salaries and supplies. Beginning in 1862, both the Confederate and the Union governments printed and used paper money with no explicit backing. The North's "greenbacks" are still legal tender in the United States, but collectors are the only people who value the Confederate currency.

After the Civil War, the United States reverted to the use of gold as money. Both gold coins and notes backed by gold circulated well into the 20th century. Today, though, we use paper money—high-quality paper, nicely engraved, with lots of special security features. This type of currency is called fiat money, because its value comes from government decree, or *fiat*. Some countries print notes that are durable and attractive, bearing famous works of art in multiple colors. The Australians make their notes out of plastic. But in all cases the money has very little intrinsic worth, and the cost of production is only a small fraction of the face value. The U.S. Treasury's Bureau of Engraving and Printing pays a bit more than 4 cents to print a note, regardless of whether it's a $1 or a $100 bill.

Why are we willing to accept these bills as payment for goods or in settlement of debts? There are two reasons. First, we take them because we believe we can use them in the future; someone else will take them from us. Second, the law says we must accept them. That is, the U.S. government stands behind its paper money. Since the first greenbacks were issued in 1862, all U.S. currency has borne the short and simple phrase "This note is legal tender for all debts, public and private." In practice, this means that private businesses must accept dollar bills as payment. More important, the U.S. government is committed to accepting the currency it has issued in settlement of debts. We will always be able to pay our taxes in dollars. As long as the government stands behind its paper money and doesn't issue too much of it, we will use it. In the end, money is about trust.[5]

---

[5]For a fascinating discussion of why trust is central to money, see Hal Varian, "Why Is That Dollar Bill in Your Pocket Worth Anything?" *New York Times*, January 15, 2004, p. C2, and Mervyn King, "The Institutions of Monetary Policy," *American Economic Review* vol. 94, no. 2 (May 2004).

Checks

Checks are another way of paying for things. Unlike currency, the checks you use to pay your rent and electric bill are not legal tender. In fact, they aren't money at all. A check is just an instruction to the bank to take funds from your account and transfer them to the person or firm whose name you have written in the "Pay to the order of" line. Thus, when you give someone a check in exchange for a good or service, it is not a final payment—at least, not in the same sense as currency. Instead, your check sets in motion a series of transactions that eventually lead to the final payment.

Here are the steps. You hand the check over to a merchant, who then takes it to the bank. Depending on the arrangement, the bank will credit the amount of the check to the merchant's account either immediately or with a short lag. At the end of the day, the bank sends the check through the check-clearing system along with the other 170 million paper checks to be processed that night by shipping them to a check-processing center run by the Federal Reserve or to a private check clearinghouse. (The first check clearinghouses were pubs where bank employees met to have a drink and exchange checks.) At the center, the check is transferred from the bank that sent it in to the bank on which it is written—your bank. The account of the bank presenting the check is credited, and the account of the bank on which the check is written is debited (see Figure 2.1). This is the step that uses *money*.

Finally, on receipt of the check, your bank debits your account and puts it aside with your other canceled checks to return to you at the end of the month.[6] (If the balance in your account is insufficient to cover the check, your bank has a few days to return it to the sending bank, so the transaction isn't actually final until that period has passed.) The whole process is time consuming and expensive. It costs about 75 cents per check.

Recently check volumes have begun to fall, but paper checks are still with us for several reasons. A canceled check is legal proof of payment and, in many states, laws require banks to return checks to customers. Then there is force of habit. Over time, people may get used to receiving bank statements without their checks, but so far not many people have chosen the option.

Electronic Payments

The third and final method of payment is electronic. We are all familiar with credit cards and debit cards. A less common variety is the electronic funds transfer. Credit and debit cards account for some one-third of the 75 trillion or so retail noncash payments made each year in the United States. Checks and other electronic funds transfers account for the rest.

What is the difference between debit cards and credit cards? A debit card works the same way as a check in that it provides the bank with instructions to transfer funds from the cardholder's account directly to a merchant's account. There is usually a charge for this; the processor of the payment takes a fee based on the size of the transaction.

A credit card is a promise by a bank to lend the cardholder money with which to make purchases. When a shopper buys a pair of shoes with a credit card, the shoe store's bank account receives payment immediately, but the money that is used for payment does not belong to the buyer. Instead, the bank that issued the credit card makes

---

[6]In the past, all paper checks were returned to the people who wrote them. In recent years, it has become more and more common to scan them and return printed images of the checks.

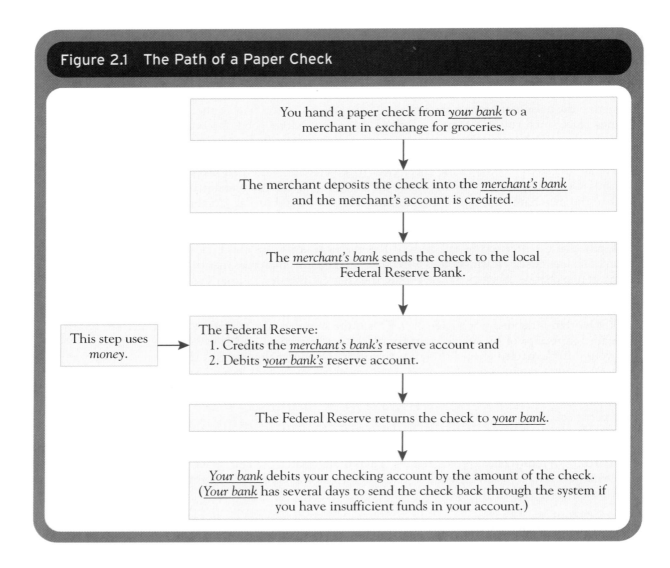

Figure 2.1 The Path of a Paper Check

You hand a paper check from *your bank* to a merchant in exchange for groceries.

The merchant deposits the check into the *merchant's bank* and the merchant's account is credited.

The *merchant's bank* sends the check to the local Federal Reserve Bank.

This step uses *money.* →

The Federal Reserve:
1. Credits the *merchant's bank's* reserve account and
2. Debits *your bank's* reserve account.

The Federal Reserve returns the check to *your bank.*

Your bank debits your checking account by the amount of the check. (*Your bank* has several days to send the check back through the system if you have insufficient funds in your account.)

the payment, creating a loan the cardholder must repay. For this reason, credit cards do not represent money; rather, they represent access to someone else's money.

Electronic funds transfers are movements of funds directly from one account to another. These transactions are used extensively by banks and are becoming increasingly popular for individuals as well.[7] For individuals, the most common form is the **automated clearinghouse transaction (ACH)**, which is generally used for recurring payments such as paychecks and utility bills. Some merchants have started to use them for one-time transactions as well (see Applying the Concept: Writing a Check at Wal-Mart). ACH transactions are just like checks except that they are entirely electronic. Your bank account is debited or credited automatically, and you receive periodic notifications of the activity in your account.

[7]Because paper check clearing is relatively cheap in the United States, Americans are just beginning to appreciate the ease of an electronic funds transfer. In other countries, payment by check is rare, while payment by electronic transfer is common and inexpensive.

YOUR FINANCIAL WORLD
Debit Cards versus Credit Cards

When you go shopping, should you pay with a credit card or a debit card? To decide, you need to understand the difference between the two. First make sure you know which one of your cards is which. Usually an ATM card (the one that you got from the bank when you opened your checking account) is a debit card. But check to make sure.

What's the real difference, from the shopper's point of view? A debit card works just like a check, only faster. When you write a paper check, it usually takes a day or two to go through the system. A debit card transaction goes through right away. The electronic message gets to your bank on the same day, and your account is debited immediately. So, if you want to use your debit card, your account balance has to be higher than the payment you want to make.

A credit card creates a deferred payment. The issuer agrees to make the payment for you, and you repay the debt later. That sounds good, but there's a catch. If you're late paying, there's a late fee. And if you don't pay the entire debt every month, you pay interest on the balance—at what is usually a very high interest rate. If you do pay the entire debt every month, however, there is no late fee and no interest charge. And since you don't pay right away, you get an interest-free loan from the time you make the purchase to the time you pay the balance. If you can pay off your credit cards in full and on time, it's to your advantage to use them.

Credit cards have another advantage over debit cards. They help you to build a credit history, which you'll need when the time comes to buy a car or a house. Because debit cards are just extensions of your bank account, they don't show potential lenders that you are creditworthy. In fact, some businesses, like car rental companies, require their customers to use credit cards for this reason.

Banks use electronic transfers to handle transactions among themselves. The most common method is to send money through a system maintained by the Federal Reserve, called Fedwire. The volume and value of payments made through this system are substantial. On a typical day in 2003, the system completed 500,000 transactions with a total value of about $2.5 trillion.

Retail businesses, together with their banks, are experimenting with a variety of new methods of electronic payment. One is the stored-value card, which looks like a credit or debit card except that it doesn't bear your name. To use one, you go to the bank or ATM machine and put the card into an electronic device that transfers funds from your checking account to your card. Then you take the card to a merchant who has a reader that is capable of deducting funds from the card and depositing them directly into the store's account. The stuff on the card is in fact money, and the system can be set up so that if you lose your card, its current value can be canceled.

So far, these cards have limited usefulness. The New York City Metropolitan Transit Authority and other city transit systems sell stored-value cards, but it's hard to buy anything with them other than subway and bus rides. The same is true of long-distance phone cards and gift cards sold by chain stores like Barnes & Noble. Attempts to implement the stored-value card more broadly haven't worked very well because most merchants lack the hardware to read the cards. And few of us know how to use them.

E-money is another new method of payment. It can be used to pay for purchases on the Internet. You open an account by transferring funds to the issuer of the e-money.

APPLYING THE CONCEPT
WRITING A CHECK AT WAL-MART

When you get to the checkout counter at some Wal-Mart stores, you can pay in a way that isn't available in most other places. If you write out a check, the cashier will scan it and then give it back to you. A moment later you will be asked to sign something that looks like a credit card slip. Then you will get a receipt that looks like a credit card receipt. But you never used a credit card, and you got your check back. What's going on?

Wal-Mart is using a technology called "check conversion," which turns paper checks into ACH transactions. The check itself is not the method of payment; it is just a source of information for a one-time electronic funds transfer, just like the automatic one you may use to pay your electric bill. A machine scans your account number and your bank's routing number and uses them to initiate the one-time transaction.

From Wal-Mart's point of view, this technology is a breakthrough. In 2001, the giant retailer handled a billion checks—about $1\frac{1}{2}$ percent of all the checks written in the United States that year. Imagine how much work it is to keep track of all that paper. Check conversion is not only efficient, since the entire transaction is done at the point of sale, but more secure. The more often a check is handled, the more likely it will be subject to fraud from some unscrupulous employee finding a way to deposit it in his or her own bank account. Ultimately, the cheaper and safer it is to pay for our purchases, the lower the prices of the things we buy.

The format of a typical check in the United States.

Your Name	Your Bank Name	1017
Your Address	Bank address	
	20 ___	$\frac{5\text{-}67}{155}$

PAY TO THE
ORDER OF _____ $

_____ DOLLARS

MEMO _____

⑈⑆⑆⑇⑆⑆⑆⑇⑆ 866 4530 7⑈ 0667

ABA or bank routing number   Account number
always 9 digits and placed
between the "⑆" characters

Then, when you are shopping online, you instruct the issuer to send your e-money to the merchant.

E-money is really a form of private money. It is not issued or guaranteed by the government, so you can't use it to pay your taxes. It's hard to even define what the term *e-money* means. One definition that seems helpful is "monetary value, as represented by a claim on the issuer, which is a) stored on an electronic device, b) issued on receipt of funds, and c) accepted as a means of payment by persons other than the issuer."[8]

But at this point, e-money is questionable at best. Will individuals develop enough trust in e-money to be willing to use it? Will merchants install the expensive equipment to handle it? Who will be allowed to issue e-money? Still, the day may come when you can park your car and pay the parking meter by simply punching a series of numbers into your cell phone that transfers e-money issued by your phone provider to the city government that owns the parking meter.

The Future of Money

Let's speculate about what might happen to money and each of its three functions in the future. As a *means of payment*, it has already undergone big changes. The time is rapidly approaching when safe and secure systems for payment will use virtually no money at all.

We will always need money as a *unit of account* in which to quote values and prices; the efficiency of quoting prices in commonly understood terms isn't going to change. But the question is, how many units of account will we need? Today, many countries have their own currencies, which give rise to their own units of account. In the future, though, there will be little reason to maintain different units of account across different countries. Price systems will be more like systems of weights and measures. Today, there are two commonly used systems of weights and measures: English ounces and yards and metric grams and meters. We will likely see a similar sort of standardization of money and a dramatic reduction in the number of units of account.

Finally, money as a *store of value* is clearly on the way out. With the advances in financial markets, many financial instruments have become highly liquid. They are easily bought and sold and can be converted into a means of payment quickly and cheaply. These instruments and the financial markets in which they trade are the subject of the next chapter. For now, though, we can conclude that in the future, there will almost surely be less and less money.

One caution is in order. As we look into the future and try to discern what will happen to money, we should remember that 150 years ago there was virtually no paper currency in circulation. The first credit card was issued in the early 1950s; the first ATM was installed around 1970. Not until the mid-1990s could we shop via the Internet. Forecasting most of these developments, as well as any other trend in technology, is nearly impossible. After all, who could have predicted even 10 years ago that today we would be able to check our bank balances, buy and sell stocks, and pay our utility bills 24 hours a day, seven days a week from the comfort of our homes?

---

[8]This definition comes from Directive 2000/46 of the European Parliament and the Council of 18 September 2000, "On the Taking Up, Pursuit and Prudential Supervision of the Business of Electronic Money Institutions," *Official Journal of the European Communities*, 275/39, 27 October 2000, http://europa.eu.int/eur-lex/pri/en/oj/dat/2000/l_275/l_27520001027en00390043.pdf.

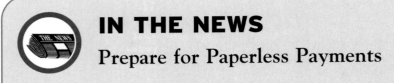

IN THE NEWS
Prepare for Paperless Payments

Financial Times

by Ruth Ann Marshall

December 20, 2002

Greenbacks, pounds, the newly minted euro and even the paper check; all have served us well but increasingly they are being overtaken by new and technologically sophisticated payment options that are more versatile and convenient.

In the US, for example, the use of paper-based payment options such as checks has fallen from 81 per cent of consumer spending in 1990 to 61 percent today.

So far, the evolution of the payment industry looks like this: cash, checks, payment cards (credit, debit, prepaid, payroll) and, on the horizon, radio frequency identification devices and biometric scanners. Where does this leave traditional financial services companies that emphasize paper-based payment options such as cash and checks? How can banks and payment processors chart a course through the technology to remain competitive and retain customers in coming years?

Before getting nostalgic for checks and paper money, it is important to remember that well over 50 per cent of transactions are still paper-based. According to the Federal Reserve, 7 million checks are used daily at points of sale in the US. Consumer payments in the United States last year totaled $5.5 trillion, of which $3.4 trillion was transacted with cash or check. That leaves $2.1 trillion for other forms of payment, of which the fastest-growing segment is debit cards.

Technology and convenience are the primary forces at work to change the nature of payments. The substitution of paper money for precious metal made commercial interactions more efficient. But today, paper itself is a costly inconvenience in the payment process. There is no doubt that technology can present new and paperless ways of paying.

Consider the following. Prepaid or stored-value cards are now widely accepted at retail establishments. Parents can "load" a stored-value card with spending money before sending a college student off to classes. Payroll cards, on which a pay period's worth of salary is stored, take the place of paychecks at some businesses. Cash can be drawn from a payroll card at ATMs, or it can be used as a debit card to make purchases.

Food stamp or government benefit cards are increasingly an alternative option to benefit checks or paper vouchers. Peer-to-peer payment methods are an easy and cost-efficient way for small businesses and Web-sites to accept payments online. Much of the revenue from online auctions, such as eBay, passes through such online payment methods.

continued on next page

Measuring Money

Changes in the amount of money in the economy are related to changes in interest rates, economic growth, and most important, inflation. Inflation is a sustained rise in the general price level—that is, the price of everything goes up more or less at the same time. With inflation, you need more units of money to buy the same basket of goods you bought a month or a year ago. Put another way, inflation makes money less valuable. And the primary cause of inflation is the issuance of too much money. When the Continental Congress issued too much currency to finance the Revolutionary War, the number of continentals people needed to purchase food and shelter rose dramatically. Continentals slowly became less valuable. So the value of the means of payment depends on how much of it is circulating.

To use the insight that money growth is somehow related to inflation, we must be able to measure how much money is circulating. This is no easy task. Let's start with money's primary function, as a means of payment. If that were the definition of money, we would measure the quantity of money as the quantity of currency in circu-

continued from previous page

Recurring payments and electronic bill presenting and payment (EBPP) are also popular. Automated payments for monthly services such as gym membership, or for regular payments such as mortgages, remove the necessity of writing checks all the time. EBPP is a method of securely paying bills online.

On the horizon are more technologically advanced payment options. A chip manufacturer is developing technology that could turn your car into a rolling debit card. A transponder embedded in the vehicle would wirelessly communicate with similar chips at businesses to enable automatic drive-through payments for everything from fast food to petrol. Such systems are used for some toll payments already, such as for the EZ Pass in the United States.

As these payment methods proliferate and offer new opportunities, they are likely to change the role of financial institutions.

Vital to such institutions' future will be their loyal customer base. Traditional financial institutions must find and embrace new ways to retain customers and attract new customers. They must strengthen customer relationships and loyalty by offering new, personalized services.

Orbitz and Travelocity are offering cards that give users $100 discount coupons on airfares they purchase online after charging less than $4,000 on the cards. Financial organizations are putting new payment services and options in place that provide value and differentiation from competitors and give consumers greater choice, control, and convenience.

When it comes to adopting new payment systems, financial institutions can take a lesson from the Internet bust: Do not be seduced by technology for its own sake but do make the appropriate investments. Keep focused on the customer and use technology wisely to increase security and return on investment.

For example, earlier this year shoppers at the Thriftway supermarket chain in West Seattle were among the first in the United States to be able to pay for their purchases with a biometric scan of a finger at the checkout. Customers were excited about the speed and security of the transactions.

The financial institutions and retailers that will succeed will be those that focus closely on the customer, differentiate themselves from the competition, and offer valuable services that fill a need. They will adopt technology-based payment methods that make the business of payment more like a guest experience.

The writer is president of MasterCard North America.

SOURCE: *Reprinted from The Financial Times, 2002 © Ruth Ann Marshall.*

LESSONS OF THE ARTICLE

Technological advances are constantly creating new methods of payment. While their adoption depends on cultural considerations, one thing is for sure: In industrialized countries, currency is becoming less and less necessary for carrying out commercial transactions.

lation—an unrealistically limited measure, since there are many ways to complete transactions (effect final payment) without using currency.

A reasonable alternative would be to consider the functionality of a broad category of financial assets and sort them by their degree of liquidity. That is, we could sort them by the ease with which they can be converted into a means of payment, arranging them along a spectrum from the most liquid (currency) to the least liquid (art, antique cars, and the like). Figure 2.2 shows what our liquidity spectrum would look like.

Once we have our list, we could draw a line and include everything on one side of the line in our measure of money.[9] Over the years, figuring out just where to draw the line has proven very difficult, especially since the introduction of new types of checking accounts. There really is no perfect solution. Instead, we have drawn the line in a number of different places and computed several measures of money, called the **monetary aggregates**: M1, M2, and M3.

---

[9]An alternative to simply drawing a line is to assume that liquidity can be measured by a "liquidity premium" that we can gauge by looking at the asset's price. The more liquid an asset is, the lower the premium, and the more like money the asset is. We can then add the assets together, giving higher weight to those with lower liquidity premiums.

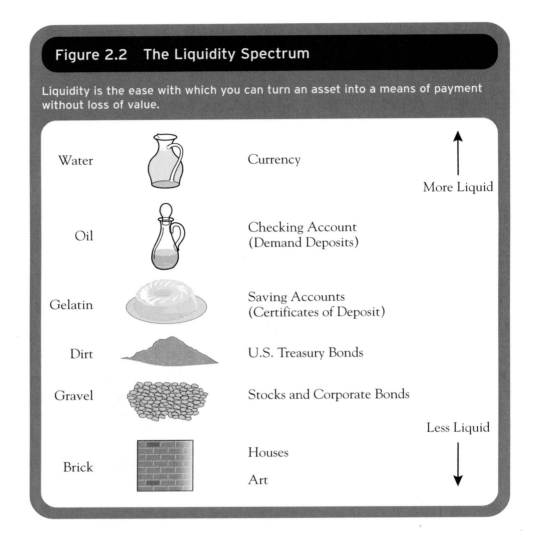

Figure 2.2 The Liquidity Spectrum

Liquidity is the ease with which you can turn an asset into a means of payment without loss of value.

Water	Currency	More Liquid ↑
Oil	Checking Account (Demand Deposits)	
Gelatin	Saving Accounts (Certificates of Deposit)	
Dirt	U.S. Treasury Bonds	
Gravel	Stocks and Corporate Bonds	
Brick	Houses / Art	Less Liquid ↓

Table 2.1 shows the components of the three monetary aggregates as defined by the Federal Reserve, along with the size of each as of August 2004. Let's go through each one to understand how it is constructed. M1, the narrowest definition of money, includes only currency and various deposit accounts on which people can write checks. These are the most liquid assets in the financial system. The components of M1 include **currency in the hands of the public**, which is the quantity of dollar bills outstanding excluding the ones in the vaults of banks; **travelers' checks** issued by travel companies, banks, and credit card companies, which are guaranteed by the issuer and usually work just like cash; **demand deposits** at commercial banks, which are standard checking accounts that pay no interest; and other checkable deposits, which are deposits in checking accounts that pay interest.

M2 equals all of M1 plus assets that cannot be used directly as a means of payment and are difficult to turn into currency quickly. These assets in M2 include small-denomination **time deposits** (less than $100,000) that cannot be withdrawn without advance notice; **savings deposits**, including **money-market deposit accounts**, which pay interest and offer limited check-writing privileges; retail **money-market mutual fund shares**, or shares in funds that collect relatively small sums from individuals, pool them together, and invest them in short-term marketable debt issued by large

Table 2.1   The Monetary Aggregates

Monetary Aggregates	Value as of August 2004 (U.S.$ billions)
M1 = Currency in the hands of the public	686.2
+ Travelers' checks	7.6
+ Demand deposits	315.3
+ Other checkable deposits	328.5
Total M1	1,337.6
M2 = M1	
+ Small-denomination time deposits	794.7
+ Savings deposits including money-market deposit accounts	3415.3
+ Retail money-market mutual fund shares	735.5
Total M2	6,283.1
M3 = M2	
+ Large-denomination time deposits	1,036.3
+ Institutional money-market mutual fund shares	1,104.7
+ Repurchase agreements	516.6
+ Eurodollars	344.5
Total M3	9,285.2

SOURCE: *Board of Governors of the Federal Reserve. These data are published every Thursday in a weekly release called the H.6 (available online at www.federalreserve.gov/releases/H6/).*

corporations. Money-market mutual fund shares can be issued by nonbank financial intermediaries, such as brokerage firms. They do carry check-writing privileges. M2 is the most commonly quoted monetary aggregate, since its movements are most closely related to interest rates and economic growth.

M3 adds to M2 a number of other assets that are important to large institutions but not to individuals. They include large-denomination *time deposits*, which are fixed-maturity accounts with balances of over $100,000 that can often be bought and sold; institutional *money-market mutual fund shares*, which are held by corporations; repurchase agreements (repos), which are overnight loans in which a financial institution or large corporation purchases a U.S. Treasury bill from a bank and agrees to sell it back at a future date at a higher price, which includes the interest; and eurodollars, which are dollar-denominated deposits in foreign banks outside the United States or in foreign branches of United States banks. The portion of eurodollars in M3 is the portion held by U.S. residents.

To clarify what the monetary aggregates mean, let's compare their size to the size of the economy. In spring 2004, nominal U.S. gross domestic product (GDP) was $11.6 trillion. Putting that number into the same units as those used in Table 2.1, that's $11,600 billion. So GDP is nearly 8 and one-half times as large as M1, just under twice as large as M2, and about 30 percent larger than M3.

Which one of the Ms should we use to understand inflation? That's a difficult question whose answer has changed over time. Until the early 1980s, economists

APPLYING THE CONCEPT
WHERE ARE ALL THOSE $100 BILLS?

A quick look at the Federal Reserve's Web site, www.federalreserve.gov, tells us that during the summer of 2004, the public held about $685 billion in United States currency. That's a huge amount. To get some sense of the size of this number, you can divide it by the U.S. population, 290 million, to get roughly $2,350 per person. For a household of four, that's $9,500 in cash. What's even more absurd is that two-thirds of the $625 billion is held in the form of $100 bills, meaning there must be sixteen $100 bills for each United States resident. Clearly, we do not hold all this cash in our wallets or our homes, nor does it fill the cash registers of local businesses. Where are all the $100 bills?

They are outside the country. In many countries, people do not trust their governments to protect the value of the currency they print. They fear the authorities will print too much, creating inflation. And since money is all about trust, if you don't have confidence in your government, you don't want to hold your wealth in the government's money. In many cases, the lack of faith has been warranted. When the Soviet Union collapsed in the early 1990s, the currency issued by the old regime became nearly worthless. The same thing happened in Argentina in the 1980s.

When people stop trusting the local currency, they look for substitutes. The most sought-after is the U.S. dollar bill. Everyone seems to have faith in it. The U.S. Treasury estimates that between two-thirds and three-quarters of U.S. currency is held outside the United States. That's about $500 billion—and most of it is in hundreds!

and policymakers looked at M1. But with the introduction of substitutes for standard checking accounts, especially money-market mutual fund shares, M1 became less useful than M2. These innovations enabled people to shift their balances out of the noninterest-bearing accounts in M1 and into accounts that paid interest. As Table 2.1 shows, demand deposits and other checkable deposits in M1 total about $640 billion, which represents only $5\frac{1}{2}$ percent of GDP. By comparison, the savings deposits, money-market deposit accounts, and retail money-market mutual fund shares in M2 total over $4.1 trillion, representing about 35 percent of GDP. M1 is no longer a useful measure of money.

TIME

Looking at Figure 2.3, you can see that from 1960 to 1980 the growth rates of the three measures of money moved together. After 1980, however, M1 behaved very differently from M2 and M3. Here's what happened. In the late 1970s and early 1980s, inflation climbed to over 10 percent for a few years. Needless to say, people who had money in zero-interest checking accounts were upset. Their money was losing value at a rapid rate. They went looking for ways to get checking services along with interest. Soon financial firms began to offer "money market" accounts that compensated depositors at least in part for inflation. These accounts are part of M2. The movement of funds into the non-M1 portion of M2 meant that the two measures no longer moved together. At same time, the new money market accounts made M2 accounts more liquid. Analysts stopped looking at M1 and began to look at M2.

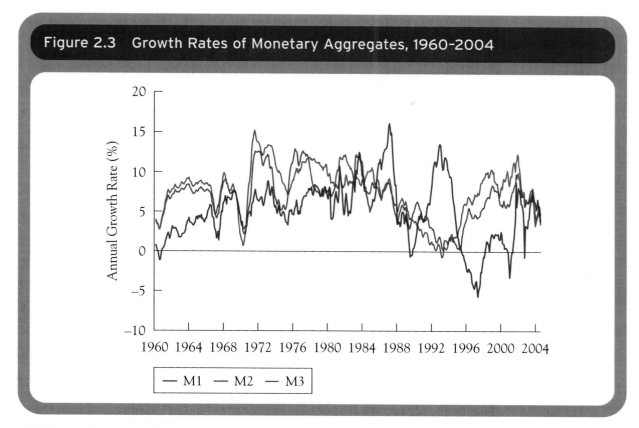

Figure 2.3 Growth Rates of Monetary Aggregates, 1960–2004

SOURCE: *Board of Governors of the Federal Reserve System, Release H.6.*

How useful is M2 in tracking inflation? We already know that when the money supply grows quickly, it produces very high inflation. A cross-country analysis of money growth supports this conclusion. In Turkey, Venezuela, and Ukraine, where in the last half of the 1990s inflation ranged from 30 to 75 percent per year, the money supply grew at comparable rates.[10] By contrast, in the United States, Canada, and Europe, inflation averaged only about 2 percent, and money growth stayed in the range of 6 to 7 percent. Because high money growth means high inflation, controlling inflation means controlling the money supply. Imagine what the inflation rate would be if people could spend the $3 trillion in Monopoly dollars Parker Brothers has printed over the last seven decades!

How useful is money growth in helping us to control moderate inflation? We will address this question at length in Part V of this book. For now, though, let's look at whether money growth helps to forecast inflation.

Figure 2.4 shows inflation on the vertical axis and M2 growth *two years earlier* on the horizontal axis, both for the United States. The solid blue diamonds represent data from 1960 to 1980. Note that, while the relationship is far from perfect in those years, higher money growth was clearly associated with higher inflation two years

[10]From 1995 to 2000, inflation averaged 74 percent, 42 percent, and 30 percent, respectively, in Turkey, Venezuela, and Ukraine. At the same time, a measure of money that is close to U.S. M2 grew at 86, 33, and 36 percent per year. Data for these comparisons come from the International Monetary Fund's *International Financial Statistics.*

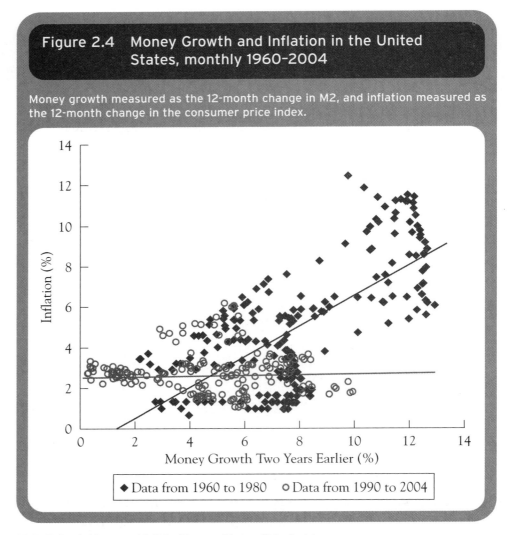

Figure 2.4   Money Growth and Inflation in the United States, monthly 1960–2004

Money growth measured as the 12-month change in M2, and inflation measured as the 12-month change in the consumer price index.

SOURCE: *Board of Governors of the Federal Reserve and Bureau of Labor Statistics.*

later. In fact, the correlation was 0.7.[11] But look at what has happened to the relationship more recently. The hollow beige dots represent data from 1990 to 2004, when there was virtually no relationship at all between the two measures. (The correlation was zero.) Growth in M2 stopped being a useful tool for forecasting inflation.

There are two possible explanations for the fact that M2 no longer predicts inflation. One is that the relationship between the two applies only at high levels of inflation. Figure 2.4 shows that during the period 1960–1980, inflation often rose higher than 5 percent, but from 1990 to 2004, it rarely did. Maybe the relationship between money growth and inflation doesn't exist at low levels of inflation, or it shows up only over longer periods of time. All we really know is that at low levels of money growth, inflation is likely to stay low.

[11]Correlation is a measure of how closely two quantities are related, or change together. The numerical value ranges from +1 to –1. A positive correlation signifies that the two variables move up and down together, while a negative correlation means that they move in opposite directions.

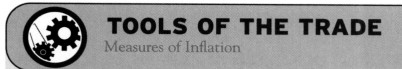

TOOLS OF THE TRADE
Measures of Inflation

Understanding how to measure inflation is central to understanding economics and finance. Most of us keep a close eye on measures like the monthly consumer price index, or CPI, to help gauge the value of our salary increases or the purchasing power of the money we hold.[*] And adjusting interest rates for inflation is critical in making investment decisions. (See Chapter 4.)

While it may be the most commonly used price index, the CPI is not the only gauge of inflation. Three basic types of price indexes are used to measure inflation: fixed-weight indices, deflators, and chain-weight indexes. The CPI is a fixed-weight index. It is designed to answer the question: "How much more would it cost for people to purchase today the same basket of goods and services that they actually bought at some fixed time in the past?" To construct the CPI, government statisticians survey people every few years to measure what they purchased and combine this with monthly information on individual prices. Inflation measured using this index tells us how much more money we need to give someone to restore the purchasing power he or she had in the earlier period when the survey was done.

But adjustments in wages based on fixed-expenditure-weight inflation indexes are known to overcompensate people in an unintended way. This overstatement of inflation is known as *substitution bias*. Since inflation is not uniform, the prices of some products will increase by more than the prices of others. People can escape some of the inflation by *substituting* goods and services that have sustained less inflation for those that have sustained more. By assuming that any substitution makes people worse off, the index *overstates* the impact of price changes.

The second inflation measure, known as a *deflator,* is constructed from national income and product accounts data, such as the gross domestic product (GDP) or the personal consumption expenditure (PCE). Government statisticians compute both *nominal GDP* (the total dollar quantity produced in a given amount of time) and *real GDP* (the measure of the quantity of goods measured at prices in some past "base" year). Growth in nominal GDP can be divided into real growth and inflation, and the deflator is the inflation part. The actual computation of a deflator involves dividing the nominal by the real and looking at the change. Analysis of the deflator is pretty complicated, but in essence it answers the rather convoluted question: "How much more did it cost me to buy what I bought today than it cost me to buy what I bought yesterday?"

The difficulty with a deflator is that the basket of goods is constantly changing. While this may not be a problem when examining adjacent quarters or years, it is a problem if the goal is to compare years that are far apart. Unlike a fixed-weight index, the deflator is known to systematically *understate* inflation by implicitly assuming that substitution never lowers people's standard of living.

The third inflation measure is a *chain-weight index,* which is halfway between the fixed weight and the deflator. It answers the more straightforward question: "How much would it cost for people to purchase today the same basket of goods and services that they actually bought last year?" Statisticians make a chain linking each year to the next, computing the increased cost of living one year at a time. This dramatically reduces either the overstatement of the fixed-weight index or the understatement of the deflator, yielding a more accurate index. For this reason many policymakers, like those at the Federal Reserve, prefer to base their estimates of inflation on the less well-known and somewhat more complex chain-weight index.[†]

[*]In Chapter 4, we will learn about the critical role inflation plays in interpreting the level of interest rates. When inflation is high, interest rates tend to be high as well, to compensate lenders for the decline in the purchasing power of the loans they have made.

[†]For an example, see the Federal Reserve's twice-yearly *Monetary Policy Report to Congress*, which emphasizes a measure of inflation based on something called the "chain-type price index for personal consumption expenditures."

An alternative explanation is that we need a new measure of money that takes into account recent changes in the way we make payments and use money. Once economists have identified the right measure, we'll be able to predict inflation again.

Terms

automated clearinghouse transaction (ACH), 20

checks, 19

commodity monies, 17

credit card, 19

currency, 15

currency in the hands of the public, 26

debit card, 19

demand deposits, 26

electronic funds transfer, 20

e-money, 21

eurodollars, 27

fiat money, 18

gross domestic product (GDP), 27

inflation, 24

liquidity, 16

M1, M2, and M3, 26, 27

means of payment, 14

monetary aggregates, 25

money, 14

money-market deposit accounts, 26

money-market mutual fund shares, 26

payments system, 17

repurchase agreements (repos), 27

savings deposits, 26

store of value, 15

stored-value card, 21

time deposits, 26

travelers' checks, 26

unit of account, 14

wealth, 14

Chapter Lessons

1. Money is an asset that is generally accepted in payment for goods and services or repayment of debts.

   a. Money has three basic uses:

      i. Means of payment

      ii. Unit of account

      iii. Store of value

   b. Money is liquid. Liquidity is the ease with which an asset can be turned into a means of payment.

2. Money makes the payments system work. The payments system is the web of arrangements that allows people to exchange goods and services. There are three broad categories of payments, all of which use money at some stage.

   a. Cash

   b. Checks

   c. Electronic payments

3. In the future, money will be used less and less as a means of payment.

4. To understand the links among money, inflation, and economic growth, we need to measure the quantity of money in the economy. There are three basic measures of money.

   a. M1, the narrowest measure, includes only the most liquid assets.

   b. M2, a broader measure, includes assets not usable as means of payment.

   c. M3, the broadest commonly used measure of money, includes a much higher percentage of illiquid assets than M2.

d. Countries with high money growth have high inflation.

e. In countries with low inflation, money growth is a poor forecaster of inflation.

Problems

1. Order the following commodities by their likely usefulness as money. Explain why each is or is not used as a means of payment.

   a. Shells

   b. Furniture

   c. Oranges

   d. Wine

   e. Treasury bills

2. People who buy lottery tickets often refer to their winnings as "prize money." In what sense are they using the word *money?*

3. The country of Brieonia has an economy that is based largely on farming and agricultural products. The inhabitants of Brieonia use cheese as their money.

   a. Not surprisingly, the Brieonians complain bitterly about the problems that their commodity creates. What are they?

   b. Modern medical science arrives in Brieonia, and doctors begin giving the Brieonians cholesterol tests. The results lead to the recommendation that the Brieonians reduce the amount of cheese they eat. What is the impact of this recommendation on their economy?

   c. As the economy of Brieonia becomes industrialized, what changes in the monetary system would you expect to see, and why?

4. When you make a credit card purchase, the merchant allows you to leave with the goods. Why? Have you made a final payment?

5. Describe at least three ways you could pay for your morning cup of coffee. What are the advantages and disadvantages of each?

6. Explain how money encourages specialization and how specialization improves everyone's standard of living.

7. Prior to the advent of the euro, the members of the European Union had their own currencies. As of 2004, Great Britain, Denmark, and Sweden retained their own currencies, as did the 10 additional countries that joined the EU on May 1 of that year. The remaining 12 countries adopted the euro. What are the advantages of a common currency for someone who is traveling through Europe?

8. What must be the characteristics of a purely electronic substitute for cash if most people are to stop using currency?

9. Using the current level of M2 from the Federal Reserve's Web site, compute the quantity of money divided by the (approximate) population of the United States. Do you think that result is large? Why or why not?

10. Using data from the Federal Reserve's Web site, compute the four-quarter percentage change in M1 and M2 since 1980. Use the data to reproduce Figure 2.3. Comment on the pattern over the last five years. Would it matter which of these two monetary aggregates you looked at?

www.mhhe.com/cecchettile

11. Using data from the Federal Reserve's Web site, update the numbers in Table 2.1.

    a. Comment on the differences between the table you have constructed and the one in the text.

    b. What has happened to the amount of currency outstanding per U.S. citizen? Can you explain the change?

12. Current encryption technology, known as Pretty Good Privacy, is thought to be unbreakable. What would be the impact on the demand for money of a news report that someone had broken the code?

13. Despite the efforts of the U.S. Treasury and the Secret Service, someone discovers a cheap way to counterfeit $100 bills. How will this discovery affect the economy?

14. You open the morning paper and discover that busloads of pickpockets have traveled to your city. How will this affect your desire to carry various forms of money?

15. Over a nine-year period in the 16th century, King Henry VIII reduced the silver content of the British pound to one-sixth its initial value. Why do you think he did so? What do you think happened to the use of pounds as a means of payment? If you held both the old and new pounds, which would you use first? Why?

Chapter 3

Financial Instruments, Financial Markets, and Financial Institutions

Long before formal financial institutions and instruments became common, there were times when people lacked the resources to meet their immediate needs. In the terminology of introductory economics, people's incomes were exceeded by their necessary consumption. When a harvest was poor, they would dip into the reserves stored from previous years or exchange assets like land and livestock for food. But often those measures were insufficient, so communities developed informal financial arrangements that allowed people to borrow or lend among themselves. After a poor harvest, those people with relatively good yields would help those with relatively poor ones. When the tables were turned, help would flow the other way. In some societies, families spread out geographically to facilitate these arrangements. For example, in rural Indian communities, households deliberately married off their daughters to families in different regions to increase the chance that their in-laws would be able to respond in a time of crisis.[1] These informal insurance arrangements ensured that everyone had enough to eat.

While family members and friends still make loans among themselves, the informal arrangements that were the mainstay of the financial system centuries ago have given way to the formal financial instruments of the modern world. Today, the international financial system exists to facilitate the design, sale, and exchange of a broad set of contracts with a very specific set of characteristics. We obtain the financial resources we need from this system in two ways: directly from lenders and indirectly through institutions.

In indirect finance, an institution like a bank stands between the lender and the borrower, borrowing from the lender and then providing the funds to the borrower. Most of us do our borrowing and lending indirectly. If we need a loan to buy a car, we get it from a bank or finance company—that's indirect finance. Once we get the loan, the car becomes one of our assets, and the loan becomes our liability. We all have assets and liabilities. Your assets probably include things of value like a bank account and a computer. If you have a student loan or credit card debt, those are your liabilities.

In direct finance, borrowers sell securities directly to lenders in the financial markets. Governments and corporations finance their activities in this way. These securities become assets for the lenders who buy them and liabilities to the government or corporation that initially sells them. In the next section, we'll look at these financial instruments in more detail so that we can understand exactly how they work.

Financial development is inextricably linked to economic growth. A country's financial system has to grow as its level of economic activity rises, or the country will stagnate. Figure 3.1 plots a commonly used measure of financial activity—the ratio of a broad monetary aggregate to gross domestic product—against real GDP per capita. The resulting correlation should not come as a surprise. There aren't any rich countries that have very low levels of financial development. In fact, the ultimate role of

---

[1]See M. R. Rosenzweig, "Risk, Implicit Contracts, and the Family in Rural Areas of Low-Income Countries," *Economic Journal* 98 (December 1988).

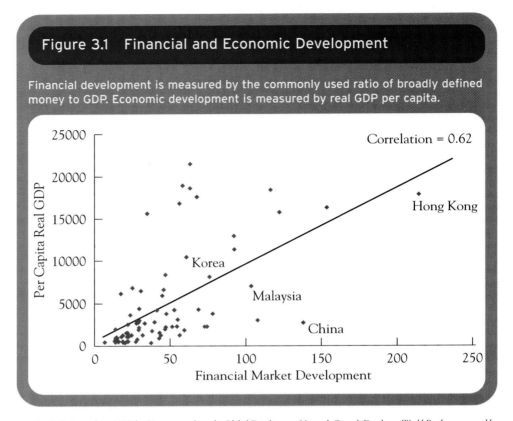

Figure 3.1 Financial and Economic Development

Financial development is measured by the commonly used ratio of broadly defined money to GDP. Economic development is measured by real GDP per capita.

SOURCE: *Data are from 1999 for 81 countries from the Global Development Network Growth Database, World Bank, www.world-bank.org/research/growth.*

the financial system is to facilitate production, employment, and consumption. In a prosperous economy, people have the means to pay for things, and resources flow to their most efficient uses. Savings are funneled through the system so that they can finance investment and allow the economy to grow. The decisions made by the people who do the saving direct the investment.

In this chapter, we will survey the financial system in three steps. First, we'll study *financial instruments*, or *securities*, as they are often called. Stocks, bonds, and loans of all types are financial instruments, as are more exotic agreements like options and insurance. Exactly what are these financial instruments, and what is their role in our economy? Second, we'll look at *financial markets*, such as the New York Stock Exchange and the Nasdaq (National Association of Securities Dealers Automatic Quotations), where investors can buy and sell stocks, bonds, and various other instruments. And finally, we'll look at *financial institutions*—what they are and what they do.

Financial Instruments

A **financial instrument** *is the written legal obligation of one party to transfer something of value, usually money, to another party at some future date, under certain conditions.* Let's dissect this definition to understand it better. First, a financial instrument is a *written legal obligation* that is subject to government enforcement. That is, a person can be compelled to take the action specified in the agreement. The enforceability of the obligation is an important feature of a financial instrument. Without enforcement of the specified terms, financial instruments would not exist.[2]

Second, a financial instrument obligates *one party to transfer something of value, usually money, to another party*. By *party*, we mean a person, company, or government. Usually the financial instrument specifies that payments will be made. For example, if you get a car loan, you are obligated to make monthly payments of a particular amount to the lender. And if you have an accident, your insurance company is obligated to fix your car, though the cost of the repair is left unspecified.

Third, a financial instrument specifies that payment will be made *at some future date*. In some cases, such as a car loan that requires payments, the dates may be very specific. In others, such as car insurance, the payment is triggered when something specific happens, like an accident.

Finally, a financial instrument *specifies certain conditions* under which a payment will be made. Some agreements specify payments only when certain events happen. That is clearly the case with car insurance and with stocks as well. The holder of a stock owns a small part of a firm and so can expect to receive occasional cash payments, called *dividends*, when the company is profitable. There is no way to

know in advance, however, exactly when such payments will be made. In general, financial instruments specify a number of possible contingencies under which one party is required to make a payment to another.

Uses of Financial Instruments

Stocks, loans, and insurance are all examples of financial instruments. Taking them as a group, we can see that they have three functions. Financial instruments can act as a means of payment, and they can also be stores of value. Thus, they offer two of the three uses of money. (Remember from Chapter 2 that money is a means of payment, a unit of account, and a store of value.) But financial instruments have a third function that can make them very different from money: They allow for the trading of risk.

Recall that a means of payment is something that is generally accepted as payment for goods and services or repayment of a debt. It is possible to pay for purchases with financial instruments, even if they don't look much like money. An example is the willingness of employees to accept a company's stock as payment for working. (This means of payment was very popular in the late 1990s, when the stock market was booming.) While we cannot yet pay for groceries with shares of stock, the time may come when we can. For now, although some financial instruments may function as means of payment, they aren't terribly good ones.

---

[2]A myriad of financial arrangements that exist outside the legal system, like loan sharking, are also enforced, but those sorts of obligations are not part of the formal financial system.

Table 3.1 Uses of Financial Instruments

Means of Payment:	Purchase of goods or services.
Store of Value:	Transfer of purchasing power into the future.
Transfer of Risk:	Transfer of risk from one person or company to another.

Having a store of value means that your consumption doesn't need to exactly match your income. For days, months, and years, if necessary, you can spend more than you make, repaying the difference later. Even though most of us are paid weekly or monthly, we eat every day. As stores of value, financial instruments like stocks and bonds are thought to be better than money. Over time, they generate increases in wealth that are bigger than those we can obtain from holding money in most of its forms. These higher payoffs come with higher levels of risk, because the payoffs from holding most financial instruments are generally more uncertain than those that arise from holding money. Nevertheless, many financial instruments can be used to transfer purchasing power into the future.

RISK

The third use of a financial instrument lies in its ability to *transfer risk* between the buyer and the seller. Most financial instruments involve some sort of risk transfer. For example, think of wheat farmers. If one farm has a huge harvest, that farmer does very well. But if everyone's harvest is huge, then prices can plummet and individual farms can lose money. The risk that the harvest will be too good, resulting in low grain prices, is a risk that most individual farmers do not want to take. A *wheat futures contract* allows the farmer to transfer that risk to someone else. A wheat futures contract is a financial instrument in which two parties agree to exchange a fixed quantity of wheat on a prearranged future date at a specified price. By fixing the price at which the crop will be sold well in advance of the harvest, the farmer can forget about what happens in the wheat market because the risk has been transferred to someone else.

Insurance contracts are another example of a financial instrument that transfers risk—in this case, from individuals to an insurance company. Because a car accident can be financially catastrophic, we buy car insurance and transfer the risk to an insurance company. Because insurance companies make similar guarantees to a large group

APPLYING THE CONCEPT
TERRORISM INSURANCE

Private insurance companies paid out over $40 billion in claims following the terrorist attacks of September 11, 2001. The World Trade Center towers alone were insured for over $3 billion—just the buildings, not the contents. Immediately following the attacks, no insurance company would sell terrorism insurance. Building owners who wanted to transfer the risk of financial loss from a future terrorist attack couldn't do it. Needless to say, if large buildings can't be insured, no one will build them.

continued on next page

of people, they have the capacity to shoulder the risk. While the timing of an individual automobile accident is impossible to forecast, a predictable percentage of a large group of drivers will experience accidents over a given period.

Characteristics of Financial Instruments: Standardization and Information

As is obvious from the definition of a financial instrument, these sorts of contracts can be very complex. If you don't believe it, take a look at the fine print in a car insurance policy, a student loan, or even a credit card agreement. Complexity is costly. The more complicated something is, the more it costs to create and the more difficult it is to understand. As a rule, people do not want to bear these costs. Yes, the owner of an oil tanker may be willing to go to the expense of negotiating a specific insurance contract for each voyage a ship makes. The same owner may agree to make premium payments based on the load carried, the distance traveled, the route taken, and the weather expected. But for most of us, the cost of such custom contracts is simply too high.

In fact, people on both sides of financial contracts shy away from specialized agreements. Instead, they use standardized financial instruments to overcome the potential costs of complexity. Because of *standardization*, most of the financial instruments that we encounter on a day-to-day basis are very homogeneous. For example, most mortgages feature a standard application process and offer standardized terms. Automobile insurance contracts generally offer only certain standard options.

Standardization of terms makes sense. If all financial instruments differed in critical ways, most of us would not be able to understand them. Their usefulness would be severely limited. If the shares of Microsoft stock sold to one person differed in a crucial way from the shares sold to someone else, for instance, potential investors might not understand what they were buying. Even more important, the resale and trading of the shares would become virtually impossible, which would certainly discourage anyone from purchasing them in the first place. From this, we conclude that arrangements that obligate people to make payments to one another cannot all be one-of-a-kind arrangements.

Another characteristic of financial instruments is that they communicate *information*, summarizing certain essential information about the issuer. How much do you really want to learn about the original issuer of a financial instrument? Or if you are purchasing an existing instrument, how much do you want to have to know about the person who is selling it to you? Surely, the less you feel you need to know to feel secure

INFORMATION

continued from previous page

The problem was that, since no one had any idea how frequent terrorist attacks would be in the future, insurers couldn't figure out how to price the insurance. So they refused to offer it. While financial instruments can be designed to transfer many types of risk, private markets just weren't up to this particular task.

In the fall of 2002, the U.S. Congress stepped in and agreed to provide the insurance. The federal government routinely provides insurance for natural disasters like hurricanes, earthquakes, and forest fires. These events occur infrequently, are very costly, and are difficult to predict. So the government steps in and spreads the risk over the entire population.

APPLYING THE CONCEPT

HENRY BLODGET AND INVESTOR INFORMATION

The dot-com boom of the 1990s made Henry Blodget a star. After a failed career as a journalist, Blodget had turned to Wall Street. From 1994 to 1999, working for the brokerage giant Merrill Lynch, he built a reputation as one of the best stock analysts in the business. People hung on the words he was paid millions of dollars to utter.

By the end of 2001, however, Blodget was banned from the financial industry, accused of misleading investors with overly optimistic recommendations that he himself did not believe. The dot-com boom had collapsed along with investors' confidence in the information they received from their brokers. Stock analysts everywhere, it seemed, had been less interested in providing accurate information to their retail clients than in pumping up the value of their corporate customers' stocks, especially the dot-coms.

That wasn't the only hit to investor confidence. A flood of accounting scandals forced hundreds of firms to admit that their financial statements were inaccurate. Enron, one of the largest companies in the United States, had used bookkeeping tricks to suggest that its business was growing when it wasn't. WorldCom, a telecommunications giant, had misrepresented

continued on next page

about the transaction, the better. Regardless of whether the instrument is a stock, a bond, a futures contract, or an insurance contract, the holder does not want to have to watch the issuer too closely; continuous monitoring is costly and difficult. Thus, financial instruments are designed to eliminate the expensive and time-consuming process of collecting such information.

A number of mechanisms exist to reduce the cost of monitoring the behavior of the counterparties to a financial arrangement. A counterparty is the person or institution on the other side of a contract. If you obtain a car loan from your local bank, then you are the bank's counterparty and the bank is yours. In the case of a stock or bond, the issuing firm and the investors who hold the instrument are counterparties.

The solution to the high cost of obtaining information on the parties to a financial instrument is to standardize both the instrument and the information provided about the issuer. We can also hire a specialist whom we all trust to do the monitoring. The institutions that have arisen over the years to support the existence of financial instruments provide an environment in which everyone can feel secure about the behavior of the counterparties to an agreement.

In addition to simply summarizing information, financial instruments are designed to handle the problem of *asymmetric information*, which comes from the fact that borrowers have some information they don't disclose to lenders. Instead of buying new ovens, will a bread baker use a $50,000 loan to take an extended vacation in Tahiti? The lender wants to make sure the borrower is not misrepresenting what he or she will do with borrowed funds. Thus, the financial system is set up to gather information on borrowers before giving them resources and to monitor their use of the resources afterwards. These specialized mechanisms were developed to handle the problem of asymmetric information.

continued from previous page

expenses as capital investments, exaggerating the value of its assets. Tyco, an enormous corporation with businesses in electronics, security, health care, and engineering, had concealed loans to top executives. Adelphia Communications, a cable company, had failed to disclose billions of dollars in loans to the company's founders. Investor confidence plummeted, and so did the stock market. When people can't get accurate information about a company, they don't want to invest in it.

Realizing the gravity of the crisis, government regulators began to investigate. By the end of 2002, they had reached an agreement with the largest financial firms involved. Together, the firms paid a fine of $1 billion and agreed to begin purchasing their research information from independent firms. One analyst paid a fine of $15 million; Henry Blodget was fined $4 million.

Many observers thought the fines were too small, given the enormous damage that had been done to the nation's economy. Indeed, when investors make their decisions on the basis of bad information, savings don't flow to the most promising investments. For the financial system to work and make us all better off, investors must have accurate information.

Underlying versus Derivative Instruments

There are two fundamental classes of financial instruments. The first, underlying instruments (sometimes called *primitive securities*), are used by savers/lenders to transfer resources directly to investors/borrowers. Through these instruments, the financial system improves the efficient allocation of resources in the real economy.

The primary examples of underlying securities or instruments are stocks and bonds that offer payments based solely on the issuer's status. Bonds, for example, make payments depending on the solvency of the firm that issued them. Stocks sometimes pay dividends when the issuing corporation's profits are sufficient.

The second class of financial instruments is known as derivative instruments. Their value and payoffs are "derived" from the behavior of the underlying instruments. The most common examples of derivatives are futures and options. In general, derivatives specify a payment to be made between the person who sells the instrument and the person who buys it. The amount of the payment depends on various factors associated with the price of the underlying asset. The primary use of derivatives is to shift risk among investors. We will see some examples in a moment; Chapter 9 discusses derivatives in detail.

A Primer for Valuing Financial Instruments

Why are some financial instruments more valuable than others? If you look at *The Wall Street Journal*, you'll see the prices of many bonds and stocks. They are quite different from each other. Not only that, but from day to day, the prices of an individual bond or stock can vary quite a bit. What makes some financial instruments more valuable than others? What characteristics affect the price someone will pay to buy or sell a financial instrument?

YOUR FINANCIAL WORLD
Disability Income Insurance

People insure their houses so they can rebuild them if they burn down. They insure their cars so they can repair them if they have an accident. And they insure their lives so their families will be financially secure if they die prematurely. But few people insure their most important asset: their ability to produce an income. The biggest risk all of us face is that we will become disabled and lose our earning capacity. Insuring it should be one of our highest priorities.

If you think this advice is alarmist, just look at a few numbers. The odds of a man becoming disabled for 90 days or longer between the ages of 20 and 60 are one in five. For women they're somewhat lower, more like one in seven. In fact, the chance you'll become disabled during your working life is far higher than the chance of your house burning down—which over 40 years is about one in 30.*

Fortunately, you may already have some disability insurance. The government provides some through Social Security; your employer may insure you; and if you're injured on the job and can't work, there is always workers' compensation insurance. But is that enough? You should evaluate what your needs are likely to be. If the disability insurance you already have is not enough, you should buy more. While it isn't very pleasant to think about what would happen if you became disabled, you need to do it. Surely this is one risk you should transfer to someone else.

*The chance of any particular house burning down is 1 in 1,200 in a given year. So there is a 1,199 chance in 1,200 of a house *not* burning down in a particular year. This means that the probability of a house *not* burning down in 40 years is $(1{,}199/1{,}200)^{40} = 0.967$. So the probability of the house burning down is 0.033, which is 1 in 30.

Four fundamental characteristics influence the value of a financial instrument: (1) the *size* of the payment that is promised, (2) *when* the promised payment is to be made, (3) the *likelihood* that the payment will be made, and (4) the *circumstances* under which the payment is to be made. Let's look at each one of these traits.

First, people will pay more for an instrument that obligates the issuer to pay the holder $1,000 than for one that offers a payment of $100. Regardless of any other conditions, this simply must be true: *The bigger the promised payment, the more valuable the financial instrument.*

TIME

Second, if you are promised a payment of $100 sometime in the future, you will want to know when you will receive it. Receiving $100 tomorrow is different from receiving $100 next year. This simple example illustrates a very general proposition: *The sooner the payment is made, the more valuable is the promise to make it.* Time has value because of opportunity cost. If you receive a payment immediately, you have an opportunity to invest or consume it right away. If you don't receive the payment until later, you lose that opportunity.

RISK

The third factor that affects the value of a financial instrument is the odds that the issuer will meet the obligation to make the payment. Regardless of how conscientious and diligent the party who made the promise is, there remains some possibility that the payment will not be made. The impact of this uncertainty on the value of a financial instrument is clear: *The more likely it is that the payment will be made, the more valuable the financial instrument.*

Finally, the value of a financial instrument is affected by the conditions under which a promised payment is to be made. Insurance is the best example. We buy car insurance to receive a payment if we have an accident, so we can repair the car. No

Table 3.2 What Makes a Financial Instrument Valuable?

Size:	Payments that are larger are more valuable.
Timing:	Payments that are made sooner are more valuable.
Likelihood:	Payments that are more likely to be made are more valuable.
Circumstances:	Payments that are made when we need them most are more valuable.

one buys insurance that pays off when good things happen. *Payments that are made when we need them most are more valuable than other payments.*[3]

Examples of Financial Instruments

Let's take a brief look at the most common financial instruments. The best way to organize them is by whether they are used primarily as stores of value or for trading risk.

Financial Instruments Used Primarily as Stores of Value

1. *Bank loans.* A borrower obtains resources from a lender immediately in exchange for a promised set of payments in the future. The borrower, who can be either an individual or a firm, needs funds to make an investment or purchase, while the lender is looking for a way to store value into the future.

2. *Bonds.* Bonds are a form of loan. In exchange for obtaining funds today, a corporation or government promises to make payments in the future. While bond payments are often stated in fixed dollars, they need not be. Unlike most bank loans, most bonds can be bought and sold in financial markets. Like bank loans, bonds are used by the borrower to finance current operations and by the lender to store value.

3. *Home mortgages.* Most people who wish to purchase a home need to borrow some portion of the funds. A mortgage is a loan that is used to purchase real estate. In exchange for the funds, the borrower promises to make a series of payments. The house is collateral for the loan. Collateral is the term used to describe specific assets a borrower pledges to protect the lender's interests in the event of nonpayment. If the payments aren't made, the lender can take the house, a process called *foreclosure*.

4. *Stocks.* The holder of a share of a company's stock owns a small piece of the firm and is entitled to part of its profits. The owner of a firm sells stock as a way of raising funds to enlarge operations as well as a way of transferring the risk of ownership to someone else. Buyers of stocks use them primarily as stores of wealth.

---

[3]This conclusion is related to the principle of declining marginal utility, which you may recall from your study of microeconomics. The idea is that the satisfaction obtained from consumption declines as the level of consumption increases. Each succeeding candy bar brings less pleasure than the last one. Thus, a financial instrument that pays off when marginal utility is high is worth more than one that pays off when marginal utility is low. This means that payoffs that are made when income and wealth are low are more valuable than payoffs that are made when income and wealth are high.

5. *Asset-backed securities.* Asset-backed securities are shares in the returns or payments arising from specific assets, such as home mortgages, student loans, credit card debt, or even movie box-office receipts. Investors purchase shares in the revenue that comes from these underlying assets. The most prominent of these instruments are mortgage-backed securities, which bundle a large number of mortgages together into a pool in which shares are then sold. The owners of these securities receive a share of the payments made by the homeowners who borrowed the funds. Asset-backed securities are an innovation that allows funds in one part of the country to find productive uses elsewhere. Thus, the availability of some sorts of financing no longer depends on local credit conditions.

Financial Instruments Used Primarily to Transfer Risk

1. *Insurance contracts.* The primary purpose of insurance policies is to assure that payments will be made under particular, and often rare, circumstances. These instruments exist expressly to transfer risk from one party to another.

2. *Futures contracts.* A futures contract is an agreement between two parties to exchange a fixed quantity of a commodity (such as wheat or corn) or an asset (such as a bond) at a fixed price on a set future date. A futures contract always specifies the *price* at which the transaction will take place. A futures contract is a type of derivative instrument, since its value is based on the price of some other asset. It is used to transfer the risk of price fluctuations from one party to another.

3. *Options.* Like futures contracts, options are derivative instruments whose prices are based on the value of some underlying asset. Options give the holder the right, but not the obligation, to buy or sell a fixed quantity of the underlying asset at a predetermined price either on a specified date or at any time during a specified period.

These are just a few examples of the most prominent financial instruments. Together, they allow people to buy and sell almost any sort of payment on any date under any circumstances. Thus, they offer the opportunity to store value and trade risk in almost any way that one might want. When you encounter a financial instrument for the first time, try to figure out whether it is used primarily for storing value or for transferring risk. Then try to identify which characteristics determine its value.

Financial Markets

Financial markets are the places where financial instruments are bought and sold. They are the economy's central nervous system, relaying and reacting to information quickly, allocating resources, and setting prices. In doing so, financial markets enable both firms and individuals to find financing for their activities. When they are working well, new firms can start up and existing firms can grow; individuals who don't have sufficient savings can borrow to purchase cars and houses. By ensuring that resources are available to those who can put them to the best use, and by keeping the costs of transactions as low as possible, these markets promote economic efficiency. When financial markets cease to function properly, resources are no longer channeled to their best possible use, and we all suffer.

In this section, we will look at the role of financial markets and the economic justification for their existence. Next, we will examine the structure of the markets and how they are organized. Finally, we will look at the characteristics that are essential for the markets to work smoothly.

The Role of Financial Markets

Financial markets serve three roles in our economic system. They offer savers and borrowers *liquidity*; they pool and communicate *information*; and they allow *risk sharing*. We encountered the concept of liquidity in our discussion of money, where we defined it as the ease with which an asset can be turned into money without loss of value. Without financial markets and the institutional structure that supports them, selling the assets we own would be extremely difficult. Thus, we cannot overstate the importance of liquidity for the smooth operation of an economy. Just think what would happen if the stock market were open only one day a month. Stocks would surely become a less attractive investment. If you had an emergency and needed money immediately, you probably would not be able to sell your stocks in time. Liquidity is a crucial characteristic of financial markets.

Related to liquidity is the fact that financial markets need to be designed in a way that keeps transactions costs—the cost of buying and selling—low. If you want to buy or sell a stock, you have to hire someone to do it for you. The process is complex, and we need not go into it in detail, but you must pay a broker to complete the purchase or sale on your behalf. While this service can't be free, it is important to keep its cost relatively low. The very high trading volumes that we see in the stock market—several billion shares per day in the United States—is evidence that U.S. stock markets have low transactions costs as well as being liquid. (One market in which transactions costs are high is the market for housing. Once you add together everything you pay agents, bankers, and lawyers, you have spent almost 10 percent of the sale price of the house to complete the transaction. The housing market is not very liquid.)

Financial markets pool and communicate information about the issuers of financial instruments, summarizing it in the form of a price. Does a company have good prospects for future growth and profits? If so, its stock price will be high; if not, its stock price will be low. Is a borrower likely to repay a bond? The more likely repayment is, the higher the price of the bond. Obtaining the answers to these questions is time consuming and costly. Most of us just don't have the resources or know-how to do it. Instead, we turn to the financial markets to summarize the information for us so that we can look it up in the newspaper or on the Internet.

Finally, while financial instruments are the means for transferring risk, financial markets are the place where we can do it. The markets allow us to buy and sell risks, holding the ones we want and getting rid of the ones we don't want. As we will see in Chapter 5, a prudent investor holds a collection of assets called a portfolio, which includes a number of stocks and bonds as well as various forms of money. A

Table 3.3   The Role of Financial Markets

Liquidity:	Ensure that owners of financial instruments can buy and sell them cheaply and easily.
Information:	Pool and communicate information about the issuer of a financial instrument.
Risk Sharing:	Provide individuals with a place to buy and sell risks, sharing them with others.

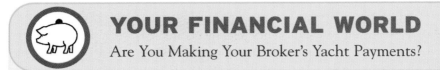

YOUR FINANCIAL WORLD
Are You Making Your Broker's Yacht Payments?

Does your broker drive a fancy car, live in a fancy house, and own a nice yacht? If so, you might want to think about finding another broker. When you have an investment account and trade in stocks and bonds, you are paying someone to do the buying and selling for you, and you need to know how much you are paying. If you are using a no-frills online service, you may be paying only $10 per trade. But if your broker works at a full-service firm and is spending time discussing your investment strategy, you are likely to be paying much more. A $5,000 transaction could be costing you $75. And remember, you pay both when you buy and when you sell. That arrangement gives the broker an incentive to keep you buying and selling, because your trades generate fees. Make sure you invest in a way that gives you the best chance of being the

one to profit. Shop for the broker who offers the services you need at the cheapest prices.

Are your fees funding your investment broker's lavish lifestyle?

SOURCE: © Tropical Stock/IndexStock/Picture Quest.

well-designed portfolio has a lower overall risk than any individual stock or bond. An investor constructs it by buying and selling financial instruments in the marketplace. Without the market, we wouldn't be able to share risk.

The Structure of Financial Markets

There are lots of financial markets and many ways to categorize them. Just take a look at the Money and Investing section of *The Wall Street Journal*. At the bottom of the first page is a market diary with charts and numbers for stocks, global stocks, bonds and interest rates, the U.S. dollar, and commodities. Inside the paper you'll find references to bond markets, credit markets, currency trading, options, futures, and new securities issues. To grasp the overall structure of the various financial markets, we need to group them in some meaningful way—but how?

There are three possibilities. First, we can distinguish between markets where new financial instruments are sold and those where they are resold, or traded. Second, we can categorize the markets by the way they trade financial instruments—whether on a centralized exchange or not. And third, we can group them based on the type of instrument they trade—those that are used primarily as a store of value or those that are used to transfer risk. We'll use the vocabulary that is common as of this writing. Bear in mind that there are no hard and fast rules for the terminology used to describe these markets, so it may change.

Primary versus Secondary Markets A primary financial market is one in which a borrower obtains funds from a lender by selling newly issued securities. Businesses use primary markets to raise the resources they need to grow. Governments use them to finance ongoing operations. Most of the action in primary markets occurs out of public view. While some companies that want to raise funds go directly to the financial markets themselves, most use an investment bank. The bank's analysts examine the company's financial health to determine whether the proposed issue is sound. Assuming that it is, the bank will determine a price and then purchase the securities in preparation for resale to clients. This activity, called *underwriting*, is usually very profitable. Since small investors are not customers of large investment banks, most of us do not have access to these new securities.

Everyone knows about **secondary financial markets**. Those are the markets where people can buy and sell existing securities. If you want to buy a share of stock in IBM or Microsoft, you won't get it from the company itself. Instead, you'll buy it in a secondary market from another investor. The prices in the secondary markets are the ones we hear about in the news.

Centralized Exchanges versus Over-the-Counter Markets   Buying

a stock or bond is not like buying a new pair of shoes. You can't just go into a store, ask for the stock you want, pay for it with your credit card, and walk out with it in a bag. Instead, you have to ask a broker to buy the stock for you in one of the secondary markets. Secondary financial markets are organized in one of two ways. Some, like the New York Stock Exchange and the large exchanges in London and Tokyo, are **centralized exchanges**. Others, like the Nasdaq, are merely electronic networks of dealers who trade with one another from wherever they are sitting. While both types of market allow for the trading of existing financial instruments, they do it in different ways.

Let's start with the New York Stock Exchange (NYSE). The NYSE is a place with an address where trading takes place in person on the floor of the exchange. To get onto the floor and trade, you have to be one of the 1,366 members of the exchange. Membership is very expensive; in recent years single seats have sold for between $1 and $2\frac{1}{2}$ million. Most members are brokerage firms that earn revenue by trading on behalf of their customers. Others are **specialists** who oversee the trading of individual stocks. Every one of the roughly 3,500 stocks traded on the NYSE is assigned to a specialist whose job it is to maintain order in the market for that stock. Roughly 80 percent of the trading in NYSE-listed stocks actually takes place at the exchange itself—and all of that goes through the specialists. (See the Tools of the Trade: Trading in Financial Markets on pages 48–49 for a more detailed description of what specialists do.)

The alternative to a centralized exchange is an **over-the-counter (OTC) market**. These markets are networks of dealers connected electronically. The dealers buy and sell various securities both for themselves and for their customers. Except for stocks sold on organized exchanges, financial instruments are sold in dealer-based markets. The biggest is the Nasdaq, which trades the stocks of roughly 4,000 companies, most of them small. Think of Nasdaq as a large network of dealers, each with a computer screen on which buy and sell orders are posted. The dealers use their computers to match the orders and execute the trades.

A financial market that is organized as an electronic network has both advantages and disadvantages over a physically centralized exchange like the NYSE. One of the big advantages was evident on September 11, 2001. The NYSE building stands only a few blocks from the site of the World Trade Center. When the twin towers fell, the floor of the Exchange became inaccessible. Since its operation depends on the ability of people to gather there, trading stopped and did not restart until Monday, September 17, 2001. Meanwhile, the Nasdaq just kept functioning. The New York dealers shut down, but those located elsewhere in

The trading floor of a stock exchange.

TOOLS OF THE TRADE
Trading in Financial Markets

Trading is what makes financial markets work. No one would ever buy a stock or bond if he or she couldn't sell it. Let's take a brief look at how trading works. For this example, we will focus on the stock market.

Placing an order in a stock market is a bit like going to a fast-food restaurant or a coffee shop. You have to enter your order and wait to be served. Not only that, but the order can be very complicated, and how long you wait depends on both what you ordered and on how many other people are waiting to be served.

If you place an order, it will have a number of important characteristics.

- The stock you wish to trade.
- Whether you wish to buy or sell.
- The size of the order—how many shares you wish to trade.
- The price at which you would like to trade.

You can place either a *market order,* in which case your order is executed at the most favorable price currently available on the other side, or a *limit order,* which places a maximum on the price you wish to pay to buy or a minimum on the price you will accept to sell. Placing a market order means you value speed over price; you want the trade to occur as soon as possible and are willing to pay for the privilege. By contrast, you can specify a time at which the limit order is canceled if it hasn't been filled.

Executing the trade requires finding someone to take the other side. To do this, your broker will send it to an exchange. There are a number of alternatives, including electronic exchanges and physically centralized exchanges. Even though IBM is traded on

the NYSE, you are not required to send an order to buy 100 shares of IBM to the floor of the exchange. You can send it to an electronic network like Instinet. And if you do, you can go to www.island.com and watch the order be placed and executed.

Electronic networks operate in a very simple way. If you want to buy, you enter a bid. If your bid is better than everyone else's, and there is someone willing to sell at or below the price you bid, then you trade immediately. Otherwise, your bid goes into an order book to wait for a seller. On a network like Instinet, customer orders interact automatically following a set of priority rules established by the network. The liquidity in the market is provided by the customers.[*]

For a stock like IBM or GE, the New York Stock Exchange is an alternative place to send the order. If you choose this, the transaction will go through a specialist. The specialist is the person on the floor of the Stock Exchange charged with making a market, ensuring that it is liquid so that people can both buy and sell and that prices aren't overly volatile. The specialist matches the orders as they come in, keeping track of orders that are outstanding. (This is all done electronically.) To make the system work, specialists often buy and sell on their own account.[†]

Specialists are monopolists. Every stock traded on the NYSE has only one. So the specialist gets to see all the orders come in and knows who they come from. Whether an order comes from a large

[*]If you go to www.island.com, you can see the order book. Click on "INET Top 10" and then on one of the ticker symbols. You will be looking at the outstanding buy and sell orders for a given stock. These are all limit orders.

[†]For a detailed discussion of specialists, see Larry Harris, *Trading and Exchanges* (New York: Oxford University Press, 2003).

continued on next page

the country were able to continue. Networks are designed so that if one section shuts down, the rest can continue working, and that is what happened. In a dealer-based market, when one dealer can't trade, someone else is usually waiting to step in.

Electronic markets clearly are not perfect. When dealers are in a hurry or simply get tired, they can push the wrong button, turning a $3 million trade into a $30 million or $300 million trade. Just resting an elbow on a keyboard can initiate unintentional buy and sell orders. And while the systems can be programmed to alert the dealers to likely mistakes, they aren't fail-safe. In contrast, trades executed on the

continued from previous page

Orders to Buy and Sell Microsoft Stock

inet MSFT

GET STOCK
[MSFT] go

LAST MATCH		TODAY'S ACTIVITY	
Price	24.9300	Orders	581
Time	8:25:33	Volume	5,702

BUY ORDERS		SELL ORDERS	
SHARES	PRICE	SHARES	PRICE
1,000	24.9500	1,000	24.9900
1,002	24.9300	10,000	25.0500
200	24.9300	200	25.0800
500	24.9000	300	25.0900
1,000	24.9000	300	25.1200
200	24.8500	1,000	25.1500
1,000	24.8500	1,000	25.1500
50	24.8000	500	25.1600
500	24.7800	3,000	25.1800
100	24.7700	106	25.2000
240	24.7700	33,000	25.2100
600	24.7600	33,000	25.2200
10	24.7500	34,000	25.2300
100	24.7500	33,000	25.2400
250	24.7500	32	25.2500
(162 more)		(290 more)	

As of 8:31:22

(The different colors make it easier to see when the price changes.)

On the left is a screen from the Instinet trading system show-ing the outstanding buy and sell orders from shares of Microsoft stock. At 8:30 a.m. on April 1, 2004, there were a total of 177 buy orders and 305 sell orders outstanding. Looking at this order book, you can see that the highest-priced buy order was for 1,000 shares at $24.95 and the lowest-priced sell order was for 1,000 shares at $24.99. If a market sell order for 1,000 shares were placed, it would be matched with the highest-priced buy order and be exe-cuted at $24.95. An order to sell more than 1,000 shares would be filled at a progressively lower price. Analogously, a market buy order for 1,000 would be executed at $24.99, the lowest-priced sell order for that number of shares.

A quick glance at the order book tells you how much liquidity or *market depth* there is. That is, it tells you how much the price moves as you buy or sell shares in increas-ing quantities.

On the NYSE, it is the job of the specialist to intervene when the gap between the highest buy order price (the *bid*) and the lowest sell order price (the *ask*) becomes large. In essence, their role is to provide buy and sell orders to close the gap, ensuring that prices do not become overly volatile.

The Instinet order book is public, so you can look at it on the Web site. The NYSE order book is proprietary, and the specialist is the only one who can see it continuously.

(usually well-informed) institutional investor or a small (usually less informed) individual investor is information the specialist can use to make profits from his or her own trading activities. The question is whether specialists will survive. Some say they are necessary to maintain liquidity in the market. But others wonder if the advances in technology will eventually make them obsolete.

floor of an exchange are made face to face between two people who write them down for later verification.

In recent years, an alternative to centralized exchanges and dealer networks has arisen in the form of *electronic communications networks,* or *ECNs.* In 2004, there were half a dozen large ECNs with names like Ebrut, Instinet, and Archipelago. Large insti-tutions use these networks to communicate, negotiate, and trade directly with one another, without going through an exchange specialist or an OTC dealer. They do it because it's cheaper.

Debt and Equity versus Derivative Markets   A useful way to think of the structure of financial markets is to distinguish between markets where *debt and equity* are traded and those where *derivative instruments* are traded. Debt markets are the markets for loans, mortgages, and bonds—the instruments that allow for the transfer of resources from lenders to borrowers and at the same time give investors a store of value for their wealth. Equity markets are the markets for stocks. For the most part, stocks are traded in the countries where the companies are based. U.S. companies' stocks are traded in the United States, Japanese stocks in Japan, Chinese stocks in China, and so on. Derivative markets are the markets where investors trade instruments like futures and options, which are designed primarily to transfer risk. To put it another way, in debt and equity markets, actual claims are bought and sold for immediate cash payment; in derivative markets, investors make agreements that are settled later.

Looking at debt instruments in more detail, we can place them in one of two categories, depending on the length of time until the final payment, called the loan's *maturity*. Debt instruments that are completely repaid in less than a year are traded in money markets, while those with a maturity of more than a year are traded in bond markets.

The money market includes the instruments in M3, the monetary aggregate defined in Chapter 2, as well as bonds and loans with a maturity of less than a year. These instruments, called *money market instruments,* have different names and are treated somewhat differently from those with a maturity of more than a year. For example, the United States Treasury issues Treasury bills, which have a maturity of less than one year and are traded in the money market. U.S. Treasury bonds, which are repaid over 10 years or more, are traded in the bond markets. The same distinction can be made for large private corporations, which issue commercial paper when borrowing for short periods and corporate bonds when borrowing for long periods.

Table 3.4   The Structure of Financial Markets

Primary versus Secondary Markets

Primary markets:	Markets where newly-issued securities are sold.
Secondary markets:	Markets where existing securities are traded.

Centralized Exchanges versus Over-the-Counter Markets

Centralized exchanges:	Secondary markets where buyers and sellers meet in a central, physical location.
Over-the-counter markets:	Decentralized secondary markets where dealers stand ready to buy and sell securities electronically.

Debt and Equity versus Derivatives Markets

Debt and equity markets:	Markets where financial claims are bought and sold for immediate cash payment.
Derivatives markets:	Markets where claims based on an underlying asset are traded for payment at a later date.

IN THE NEWS

Regulators to Waive Many Rules to Encourage U.S. Stock Trading

The Wall Street Journal

by Greg Ip and Michael Schroeder

September 17, 2001

WASHINGTON—Financial regulators usually focus on making bankers and Wall Street play by volumes of rules designed to keep the markets safe and fair. But after September 11, 2001, they bent and rewrote many of those rules to ensure that the markets survive.

Three days after terrorists destroyed the World Trade Center and attacked the Pentagon, the Securities and Exchange Commission waived a list of rules to encourage buying at the scheduled reopening of stock markets Monday.

The prohibition on companies' buying their own stock in the first and last 30 minutes of the trading session, designed to prevent manipulation, was waived for as many as 10 days, and companies also could increase daily purchases of their stock to 100 percent of the previous month's daily average volume—up from the normal 25 percent. In addition, corporate insiders such as officers and directors may freely buy their company stock no matter when they last traded. Ordinarily, if insiders trade more frequently than every six months, they must return profits from such trades.

The SEC also waived a prohibition on accounting firms doing the bookkeeping of companies they audit so they can help companies from Manhattan's financial district reconstruct books and records lost in the terrorist attack.

Some of the rule-bending was more low-key. The Federal Reserve, for example, quietly let banks know it would be "very understanding" if they lent to their securities-dealer affiliates, a practice normally restricted by Depression-era laws, officials familiar with that decision said.

Regulators struggled to strike the right balance between ensuring the smooth functioning of a free market and outright government action to prop up the market. Government officials say they have rejected out-of-hand suggestions from listed companies to ban short selling, by which a market participant borrows then sells a stock he doesn't own and then profits by buying it back at a lower price. SEC staff said that would undermine the markets because countless investors' strategies combine buying with short selling, and banning the latter would force those

investors—and their substantial volume—out of the market. In addition, specialists and market makers, who intermediate investors' trades, have to sell short to do their jobs.

"I like markets to operate freely and competitively," SEC Chairman Harvey Pitt said. "I view the SEC actions as facilitating the market—if we were forcing people to buy, that would be intervention."

For example, both SEC and Fed officials said they didn't encourage companies to buy back stock. But the Fed has also used "open-mouth operations" to get banks, brokers, and even phone companies to cooperate in bringing markets back to normalcy.

Both during the 1998 debt-market crisis and Y2K, New York Fed President William McDonough made it clear to bankers that part of their job in times of stress was to keep lending to creditworthy brokers to prevent fears of a liquidity crisis from becoming self-fulfilling.

The Fed also put out a statement shortly after the World Trade Center attack, encouraging banks to lend to disaster-struck companies that had sound credit and work with them on adjusting existing loan terms. "Such practices are consistent with safe and sound banking practice and promote the public interest by assisting in recovery," it said.

Paul Beckett in New York contributed to this article.

LESSONS OF THE ARTICLE

Financial markets are central to our economic system. Following the September 11, 2001, terrorist attacks, the New York Stock Exchange became inaccessible, and other markets were not functioning properly. Alarmed government officials took measures to ensure first that markets would open as soon as possible and then that mechanisms were put in place so that trading could proceed. Without these efforts to get the financial markets up and running, the financial system might quickly have come to a standstill.

APPLYING THE CONCEPT
FINANCIAL DEVELOPMENT REQUIRES
INVESTOR PROTECTION

Investors will provide capital to firms only if they expect to get their money back. For equity holders, this means that they must be able to vote out directors and managers who do not pay them. For creditors, it means they must have the authority to repossess collateral. In addition to having these legal rights, investors must also have confidence that the laws will be enforced.

Disparities in investor protections help us to understand the differences in financial market development across countries.* Figure 3.2 plots the size of each country's equity market against a measure of investor protection in the major industrialized countries. The data clearly show that the better a country's investor protection, the bigger that country's stock market. For example, the United Kingdom has the largest stock market (roughly three times the size of its GDP) and its investor protection is among the best in the world. In contrast, Greece, a country that offers investors very poor protection, has a stock market that is only one-third the size of its GDP. Not surprisingly, where financial markets flourish, firms have no trouble raising the funds they need to grow. It pays to protect investors. In countries that do a poor job of protecting stockholders and bondholders, banks take up much of the slack. Investors lack access to primary financing, so they are forced to go to financial institutions for secondary financing.

*Differences in legal structure and investor protection can explain many economic phenomena. For example, more than 10 percent of U.S. firms with assets over $1 million have incorporated in the state of Delaware, a state with less than one-half of one percent of the country's population. We can explain this anomaly by looking at the development of the legal structure in Delaware and how it differs from that of other states. Originally, large firms were incorporated in New Jersey because that state, in exchange for incorporation fees and franchise taxes, had liberalized its corporation law to allow various mergers and cross-holdings that were not allowed elsewhere. State laws also gave strong powers to corporate directors. (See Christopher Grandy, "New Jersey Corporate Chartermongering, 1875–1929," *Journal of Economic History* 49 (September 1989), pp. 677–92.) Delaware copied New Jersey's statutes and then benefited from changes made to New Jersey's law by Governor Woodrow Wilson in 1913. As this example suggests, economic structure is rooted in legal structure.

continued on next page

Characteristics of a Well-Run Financial Market

Well-run financial markets exhibit a few essential characteristics that are related to the role we ask them to play in our economies. First, these markets must be designed to keep transaction costs low. Second, the information the market pools and communicates must be both accurate and widely available. If analysts do not communicate accurate assessments of the firms they follow, the markets will not generate the correct prices for the firms' stocks. The prices of financial instruments reflect all the information that is available to market participants. Those prices are the link between the financial markets and the real economy, ensuring that resources are allocated to their most efficient uses. If the information that goes into the market is wrong, then the prices will be wrong, and the economy will not operate as effectively as it could.

continued from previous page

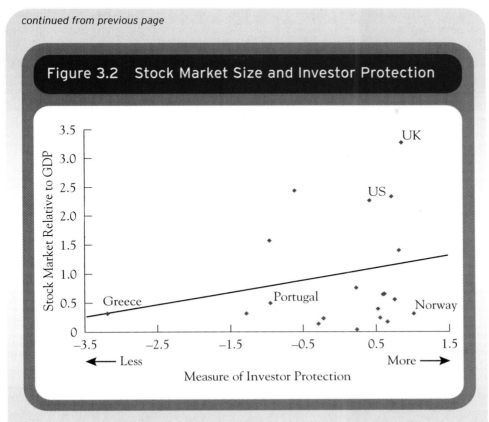

Figure 3.2   Stock Market Size and Investor Protection

SOURCE: *Stock-market size is from the World Bank's World Development Indicators. Investor protection adapted from Table 1 ("Stock Market Size and Investor Protection") from OECD Economics Dept. Working Paper No. 280: "Contributions of Financial Systems to Growth in OECD Countries."*

Finally, investors need protection. For the financial system to work at all, borrowers' promises to pay lenders must be credible. Individuals must be assured that their investments will not simply be stolen. In countries that have weak investor protections, firms can behave deceptively, borrowing when they have no intention of repaying the funds and going unpunished. The lack of proper safeguards dampens people's willingness to invest. Thus, governments are an essential part of financial markets, since they set and enforce the rules of the game. While informal lending networks do develop and flourish spontaneously, they can accommodate only simple, small-scale transactions. Because modern financial markets require a legal structure that is designed and enforced by the government, countries with better investor protections have bigger and deeper financial markets than other countries.

Financial Institutions

Financial institutions are the firms that provide access to the financial markets, both to savers who wish to purchase financial instruments directly and to borrowers who want to issue them. Because financial institutions sit between savers and borrowers, they are also known as *financial intermediaries,* and what they do is known as intermediation. Banks, insurance companies, securities firms, and pension funds are all financial intermediaries. These institutions are essential; any disturbance to the services they provide will have severe adverse effects on the economy.

To understand the importance of financial institutions, think what the world would be like if they didn't exist. Without a bank, individuals and households wishing to save would either have to hold their wealth in cash or figure out some way to funnel it directly to companies that could put it to use. The assets of these household savers would be some combination of government liabilities and the equity and debt issued by corporations. All finance would be direct, with borrowers obtaining funds straight from the lenders.

Such a system would be unlikely to work very well, for a number of reasons. First, individual transactions between saver-lenders and spender-borrowers would likely be extremely expensive. Not only would the two sides have difficulty finding each other, but even if they did, writing the contract to effect the transaction would be very costly. Second, lenders need to evaluate the creditworthiness of borrowers and then monitor them to ensure that they don't abscond with the funds. Individuals are not specialists in monitoring. Third, most borrowers want to borrow for the long term, while lenders favor more liquid short-term loans. Lenders would surely require compensation for the illiquidity of long-term loans, driving the price of borrowing up.

A financial market could be created in which the loans and other securities could be resold, but that would create the risk of price fluctuations. All these problems would restrict the flow of resources through the economy. Financial institutions open up the flow, ensuring that it goes to the most productive investments and increasing the system's efficiency.

The Role of Financial Institutions

Financial institutions reduce transactions costs by specializing in the issuance of standardized securities. They reduce the information costs of screening and monitoring borrowers to make sure they are creditworthy and they use the proceeds of a loan or security issue properly. In other words, financial institutions curb information asymmetries and the problems that go along with them, helping resources flow to their most productive uses.

At the same time that they make long-term loans, financial institutions also give savers ready access to their funds. That is, they issue short-term liabilities to lenders while making long-term loans to borrowers. By making loans to many different borrowers at once, financial institutions can provide savers with financial instruments that are both more liquid and less risky than the individual stocks and bonds they would purchase directly in financial markets.

Figure 3.3 is a schematic overview of the financial system. It shows that there are two types of financial institutions: those that provide brokerage services (top) and those that transform assets (bottom). Broker institutions give households and corporations access to financial markets and direct finance. Institutions that transform assets take deposits and issue insurance contracts to households. They use the proceeds to make loans and purchase stocks, bonds, and real estate. That is their transformation function. Figure 3.4 shows what the balance sheet for such an institution would include.

The Structure of the Financial Industry

In analyzing the structure of the financial industry, we can start by dividing intermediaries into two broad categories called depository and nondepository institutions.

Figure 3.3   Flow of Funds through Financial Institutions

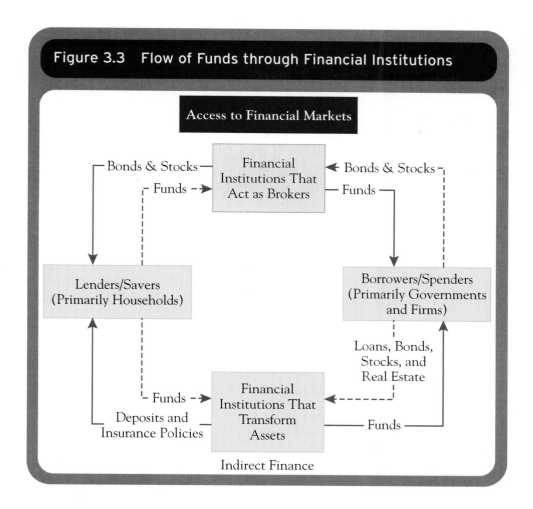

Access to Financial Markets

Depository institutions take deposits and make loans; they are what most people think of as banks, whether they are commercial banks, savings and loans, or credit unions. *Nondepository institutions* include insurance companies, securities firms, mutual fund companies, finance companies, and pension funds. Each of these serves a very different function from a bank. Some screen and monitor borrowers; others transfer and reduce risk. Still others are primarily brokers. Here is a list of the major groups of financial institutions, together with a brief description of what they do.

1. *Depository institutions* (commercial banks, savings banks, and credit unions) take deposits and make loans.
2. *Insurance companies* accept premiums, which they invest in securities and real estate (their assets) in return for promising compensation to policyholders should certain events occur (their liabilities). Life insurers protect against the risk of untimely death. Property and casualty insurers protect against personal injury loss and losses from theft, accidents, and fire.
3. *Pension funds* invest individual and company contributions in stocks, bonds, and real estate (their assets) in order to provide payments to retired workers (their liabilities).

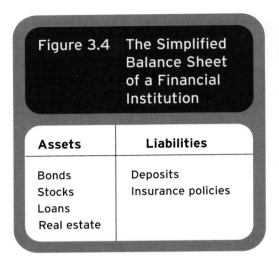

Figure 3.4   The Simplified Balance Sheet of a Financial Institution

Assets	Liabilities
Bonds	Deposits
Stocks	Insurance policies
Loans	
Real estate	

4. *Securities firms* include brokers, investment banks, underwriters, and mutual-fund companies. Brokers and investment banks issue stocks and bonds to corporate customers, trade them, and advise customers. All these activities give customers access to the financial markets. Mutual-fund companies pool the resources of individuals and companies and invest them in portfolios of bonds, stocks, and real estate. Customers own shares of the portfolios, so they face the risk that the assets will change in value. But portfolios are less risky than individual securities, and individual savers can purchase smaller units than they could if they went directly to the financial markets.

5. *Finance companies* raise funds directly in the financial markets in order to make loans to individuals and firms. Finance companies tend to specialize in particular types of loans, such as mortgage, automobile, or certain types of business equipment. While their assets are similar to a bank's, their liabilities are debt instruments that are traded in financial markets, not deposits.

6. *Government-sponsored enterprises* are federal credit agencies that provide loans directly for farmers and home mortgagors. They also guarantee programs that insure loans made by private lenders. The government also provides retirement income and medical care to the elderly through Social Security and Medicare. Pension funds and insurance companies perform these functions privately.

As we continue our study of the relationship between the financial system and the real economy, we will return to the importance of financial institutions, the conduits that channel resources from savers to investors. These intermediaries are absolutely essential to the operation of any economy. When they cease to function, so does everything else. Recall from Chapter 2 that the three measures of money (M1, M2, and M3) include checking deposits, savings deposits, and certificates of deposit, among other things. These are all important liabilities of banks. Because they are very liquid, they are accepted as a means of payment. Clearly, the financial structure is tied to the availability of money and credit. But we are getting ahead of ourselves. Before we study financial institutions, we need to look more closely at financial instruments and financial markets, the subjects of Part II of this book.

YOUR FINANCIAL WORLD
Shop for a Mortgage

Everyone loves a bargain. There are people who will spend hours making sure they pay the lowest price they can for virtually anything they buy. Borrowing shouldn't be any different. When the time comes to buy a house, most of us need to borrow. That is, we need to get a mortgage. Since the mortgage payment will almost surely be your biggest monthly expense, getting the cheapest mortgage you can will save you more than a year's worth of bargain hunting in stores.

There are a number of ways to shop for a mortgage. Any real estate agent can hand you a list of mortgage providers in your area. You can also find Web sites that publish quotes for mortgages. As you look through these lists, you'll notice that many of the firms on them are not banks. Instead, they are *mortgage brokers,* firms that have access to pools of funds earmarked for use as mortgages.

Say, for instance, that a financial firm raises a large amount of financing to be used to make mortgages. A pool of $100 million can finance a thousand $100,000 mortgages. Shares in these pools are sold to investors. If you get a mortgage from one of these firms, it will go into the pool. In 2004, half of the more than $9 trillion in mortgages in the United States was in these mortgage pools.

Should you care whether you get your mortgage from a traditional bank or a mortgage broker? Should you care if your mortgage is pooled and sold off? The answer is no; it should make no difference to you. In fact, chances are that regardless of which option you choose—bank or mortgage broker—you'll make your payments to a company that does nothing but collect them and monitor your compliance. From your point of view, a mortgage is a mortgage. Get the one that suits you best. But shop before you sign on the dotted line. And if you let the various brokers know that you are shopping around, they may start competing for your business and give you a better deal.

Terms

www.mhhe.com/cecchettile

Chapter Lessons

1. Financial instruments are crucial to the operation of the economy.

    a. Financial arrangements can be either formal or informal. Industrial economies are dominated by formal arrangements.

    b. A financial instrument is the written legal obligation of one party to transfer something of value, usually money, to another party at some future date, under certain conditions.

    c. Financial instruments are used primarily as stores of value and means of trading risk. They are less likely to be used as means of payment, although many of them can be.

    d. Financial instruments are most useful when they are simple and standardized.

    e. There are two basic classes of financial instruments: underlying and derivative.

       i. Underlying instruments are used to transfer resources directly from one party to another.

       ii. Derivative instruments derive their value from the behavior of an underlying instrument.

    f. The payments promised by a financial instrument are more valuable

       i. The larger they are.

       ii. The sooner they are made.

       iii. The more likely they are to be made.

       iv. If they are made when they are needed most.

    g. Common examples of financial instruments include

       i. Those that serve primarily as stores of value, including bank loans, bonds, mortgages, stocks, and asset-backed securities.

       ii. Those that are used primarily to transfer risk, including futures and options.

2. Financial markets are essential to the operation of our economic system.

    a. Financial markets

       i. Offer savers and borrowers liquidity so that they can buy and sell financial instruments easily.

       ii. Pool and communicate information through prices.

       iii. Allow for the sharing of risk.

    b. There are several ways to categorize financial markets.

       i. Primary markets that issue new securities versus secondary markets, where existing securities are bought and sold.

       ii. Physically centralized exchanges versus dealer-based electronic systems (over-the-counter markets).

       iii. Debt and equity markets (where instruments that are used primarily for financing are traded) versus derivative markets (where instruments that are used to transfer risk are traded).

   c. A well-functioning financial market is characterized by

      i. Low transactions costs and sufficient liquidity.

      ii. Accurate and widely available information.

      iii. Legal protection of investors against the arbitrary seizure of their property.

3. Financial institutions perform brokerage and asset transformation functions.

   a. In their role as brokers, they provide access to financial markets.

   b. In transforming assets, they provide indirect finance.

   c. Indirect finance reduces transaction and information costs.

   d. Financial institutions, also known as financial intermediaries, help individuals and firms to transfer and reduce risk.

Problems

1. As the end of the month approaches, you realize that you probably will not be able to pay the next month's rent. Describe both an informal and a formal financial instrument that you might use to solve your dilemma.

2. Firms enter into contracts with banks in which, for a fee, the bank agrees to make a loan whenever the firm demands it. These agreements are called lines of credit.

   a. What characteristics of the contract and of the bank would cause the firm to pay more or less for the bank's commitment?

   b. What characteristics of the contract and of the firm would cause the bank to charge more for the commitment?

3. The Chicago Mercantile Exchange has announced the introduction of a financial instrument that is based on rainfall in the state of Illinois. The standard agreement states that for each inch of rain over and above the average rainfall for a particular month, the seller will pay the buyer $1,000. Who could benefit from buying such a contract? Who could benefit from selling it?

4. Most young people face substantial uncertainty about their future incomes. Describe the characteristics of a financial instrument that would allow you to sell your future income risk. Would anyone be willing to buy such a security? Why or why not?

5. Consider an annuity that makes monthly payments for as long as someone lives. Describe what happens to the purchase price of the annuity as

   a. the age of the purchaser goes up.

   b. the size of the monthly payment rises.

   c. the health of the purchaser improves.

6. You are the director of a major art museum with a substantial endowment. You have very few works by European Renaissance artists and would like to purchase some. You know that only a few of these paintings are available at auction each year, so building your collection will be a slow and laborious process. The risk you face is that the prices of the paintings will rise so rapidly that you will run out of resources before you can assemble a collection that meets your standards. Design

a financial instrument that would allow you to transfer this risk to somewhere else. Describe the instrument's properties.

7. Consider the investment returns on holding stock. Which of the following would be more valuable to you, stocks that rise in value when your income rises or stocks that rise in value when your income falls? Why?

8. If you wish to purchase mortgage-backed securities, you will discover an interesting option that results from the fact that borrowers can pay off their mortgages early without incurring a penalty. To understand how it works, imagine that there are 1,000 identical 30-year fixed-rate mortgages in a pool. The asset-backed securities give you the option of the payments that come from the first 200 to be paid off, the next 200, and so on. How will the value of these mortgage-backed securities vary depending on which group you purchase?

9. The foreign exchange market, in which dollars can be exchanged for euros or yen, is an over-the-counter market. Describe the costs and benefits of this form of market organization.

10. Define a primary financial market and explain why very few people ever have any contact with one.

11. *The Wall Street Journal* has a daily listing of what are called *money rates,* or interest rates on short-term securities. Locate it in a recent issue of the paper by looking at the index on page 1 of the Money and Investing section. The most important money rates are the prime rate, the federal funds rate, and the Treasury bill rate. Describe each of these instruments and report the current rate quoted in the paper.

12. Trading on private information is illegal. Why? What would happen to the financial markets if you could trade on information that is not public?

13. You are asked for advice by the government of a small, poorly developed country that wants to increase its rate of economic growth. You notice that the country has no financial markets. What advice would you give?

14. List the six types of financial institutions and describe a transaction you might have that involves each one.

15. The design and function of financial instruments, markets, and institutions are tied to the importance of information. Describe the role of information in each of these three parts of the financial system.

Part *II*

Interest Rates, Financial Instruments, and Financial Markets

Chapter 4

Future Value, Present Value, and Interest Rates

Lenders have been despised for most of history. They make borrowers pay for loans, while just sitting around doing nothing. No wonder people have been vilified for charging interest. No wonder that for centuries, clerics pointed to biblical passages damning interest.[1] Even philosophers like Aristotle weighed in against the practice, calling the "breeding of money from money" unnatural.

After scorning lenders for millennia, today we recognize their service as a fundamental building block of civilization. Credit is one of the critical mechanisms we have for allocating resources. Without it, our market-based economy would grind to a halt. Even the simplest financial transaction, like saving some of your paycheck each month to buy a car, would be impossible. And corporations, most of which survive from day to day by borrowing to finance their activities, would not be able to function. Credit is so basic that we can find records of people lending grain and metal from 5,000 years ago. Credit probably existed before common measures of value, and it predates coinage by 2,000 years.[2]

Despite its early existence and its central role in economic transactions, credit was hard to come by until the Protestant Reformation. By the 16th century views had changed, and interest payments were tolerated if not encouraged, so long as the rate charged was thought to be reasonable. Some historians even point to this shift as a key to the development of capitalism and its institutions. Protestant European countries did develop faster than Catholic ones, at least at first.[3] Since then, credit has exploded, facilitating extraordinary increases in general economic well-being. Yet even so, most people still take a dim view of the fact that lenders charge interest. Why?

The main reason for the enduring unpopularity of interest comes from the failure to appreciate the fact that lending has an opportunity cost. Think of it from the point of view of the lender. People who offer credit don't need to make loans. They have alternatives, and extending a loan means giving them up. While lenders can eventually recoup the sum they lend, neither the time that the loan was outstanding nor the opportunities missed during that time can be gotten back. So interest isn't really "the breeding of money from money," as Aristotle put it; it's more like a rental fee that borrowers must pay lenders to compensate them for lost opportunities.

It's no surprise that in today's world, interest rates are of enormous importance to virtually everyone—individuals, businesses, and governments. They link the present to the future, allowing us to compare payments made on different dates. Interest rates also tell us the future reward for lending today, as well as the cost of borrowing now and repaying later. To make sound financial decisions, we must learn how to calculate and compare different rates on various financial instruments. In this chapter, we'll

---

[1]Even today, the payment of interest is legally prohibited in countries like Iran, which follow the Islamic code of Shariah. In these countries, only payments for risk taking are allowed; debt contracts of the kind we make are banned.

[2]See Sydney Homer, and Richard Sylla, *A History of Interest Rates*, 3rd ed. (New Brunswick, NJ: Rutgers University Press, 1996).

[3]Max Weber makes this argument in his classic work *The Protestant Ethic and the Spirit of Capitalism*, first published in 1905.

explore interest rates using the concepts of future value and present value and then apply those concepts to the valuation of bonds. Finally, we'll look at the relationship between inflation and interest rates.

Valuing Monetary Payments Now and in the Future

To compare the value of payments made on different dates, we need a set of tools called *future value* and *present value*. We'll use them to see how and why the promise to make a payment on one date is more or less valuable than the promise to make a payment on a different date. For example, we already know that if you want to borrow $100 today, your repayment needs to be bigger if you promise to make it in a year than if you promise to make it in a month. But how much more will you have to pay? The answer depends on both the date of payment and the interest rate. For the time being, we're going to assume that we know for sure that you will repay the loan. We'll get to the possibility of default when we study risk in the next chapter.

Future Value and Compound Interest

What is the future value of one dollar deposited in an interest-bearing account today? To answer this question, let's start with a definition: **Future value** *is the value on some future date of an investment made today.* Say that today you invest $100 in a savings account that guarantees 5 percent interest per year. After one year, you'll have $105 (the investment at its present value of $100 plus $5 in interest). So the future value of $100 one year from now at an interest rate of 5 percent is $105. Notice that the same calculation works for a simple loan in which you borrow $100 for one year at 5 percent interest. The amount you will need to repay is $105.

TIME

To generalize this concept so that we can handle different interest rates and initial investments of any size, we can express it mathematically. First we need to convert the percentage interest rate into a decimal, so that 5 percent becomes 0.05. *Note that in this expression, as in all mathematical manipulations in this chapter, the interest rate is expressed in decimal terms.* Now we can express future value as an equation. If the present value of your initial investment is $100 and the interest rate is 5 percent, then the *future value* one year from now is:

$$\underset{\text{Present value of the investment} +}{\$100} \quad \underset{\text{Interest}}{+ \$100 \times (0.05) =} \quad \underset{\text{= Future value in one year}}{\$105} \qquad (1)$$

It is essential to convert all interest rates to decimals before doing any computation. This is consistent with the fact that we quote interest rates as "parts per 100," so 5 percent means 5 parts per 100, or 0.05.

This expression shows us immediately that the higher the interest rate, the higher the future value. If the interest rate were to rise to 6 percent, then the future value of $100 would be $100 + $100 (0.06) = $106. In general, the future value, *FV*, of an investment with a present value, *PV*, invested at an interest rate *i* is

$$FV = PV + PV \times i$$
$$= PV \times (1 + i) \qquad (2)$$

Future value in one year

= Present value of the investment today × (one plus the interest rate)

We can see right away that the higher the interest rate or the amount invested, the higher the future value.

But this example is too simple. Most financial instruments don't make single payments in exactly one year, so we need to figure out what happens when the time to repayment varies. Computing the future value of an investment to be repaid two years from now is straightforward, so let's do that first. But since we quote interest rates on a yearly basis, we need to be careful. Using one-year interest rates to compute the value of an investment that will be repaid more than one year from now requires applying the concept of compound interest, *which is interest on the interest.* If you leave an investment in an interest-bearing account for two years, during the second year you will receive interest not only on your initial investment but also on the interest you earn for the first year.

Getting back to our example, let's say that you leave your $100 deposit in the bank for two years at 5 percent interest per year. The future value of this investment has four parts. The first three are straightforward. They are the initial investment of $100, the interest on that investment in the first year, and the interest on it in the second year. But because you left the interest from the first year in the bank during the second year, it is as if you made a new deposit at the beginning of the second year, and that earns interest too. So the fourth part of the future value is the interest you receive during the second year on the interest you received in the first year. That's compounding. With an initial deposit of $100 and an interest rate of 5 percent, we can add up these four parts to compute your investment's future value in two years.

$$\$100 + \$100(0.05) + \$100(0.05) + \$5(0.05) = \$110.25 \qquad (3)$$

Present value of the initial investment
+ Interest on the initial investment in first year
+ Interest on the initial investment in second year
+ Interest on the interest from first year in second year
= Future value in two years

We can use a small amount of algebra to show that this equals $\$100(1.05)(1.05) = \$100(1.05)^2$. Extending it to three years, four years, or more just means multiplying by (1.05) over and over again. The multiplication takes care of the compounding. Table 4.1 shows the calculations. The final line shows that after 10 years, a deposit

Table 4.1 Computing the Future Value of $100 at 5% Annual Interest

Years into Future	Computation	Future Value
1	$100(1.05)	$105.00
2	$100(1.05)^2$	$110.25
3	$100(1.05)^3$	$115.76
4	$100(1.05)^4$	$121.55
5	$100(1.05)^5$	$127.63
10	$100(1.05)^{10}$	$162.89

with a present value of $100 becomes $162.89. That is, it earns $62.89 in interest. If we had ignored compounding and just multiplied 5 percent by 10 years to get 50 percent, the answer would have been $150. Compounding produced an additional $12.89 in interest over 10 years. To put it as clearly as possible, multiplying the number of years times the annual interest rate gives the *wrong* answer!

Using the computations in Table 4.1, we can derive a general formula for future value.

$$FV_n = PV \times (1 + i)^n \tag{4}$$

Future value in *n* years = Present value of the investment ×
(One plus the interest rate) raised to *n*

So to compute future value, all we need to do is calculate one plus the interest rate (measured as a decimal) raised to the nth power and multiply it by the present value.

Before we go any further, we should stop to consider an important problem. What if you want to put your $100 into a bank for six months, or $2\frac{1}{2}$ years, or any amount of time that is not a round number of years? The answer is that the formula still works. You can compute the future value using equation (4) regardless of whether *n* is a whole number. There is one pitfall, however. *In computing future value, both the interest rate and* n *must be measured in the same time units.* We have been measuring interest rates as the percentage per year, so we were careful to measure *n* in years as well. So, if we want the future value in half of one year, *n* would be $\frac{1}{2}$; if we wanted it in one month, *n* would be 1/12; and if we wanted the future value in one day, *n* would be 1/365.

As you can see, taking advantage of the future-value formula requires an understanding of the transformations needed to convert time from years to months or vice versa. Converting *n* from years to months is easy—everyone knows there are 12 months in a year—but converting the interest rate is harder. If the annual interest rate is 5 percent, what is the interest rate for one month? To figure out the answer, we'll start with the future-value formula, but in months. Remember that compounding means you *cannot* just multiply the monthly interest rate by 12 to get the annual interest rate. Instead, if i^m is the one-month interest rate and *n* is the number of months, then a deposit made for one year will have a future value of $100(1 + i^m)^{12}$. We know that this amount equals $100(1.05)$, so figuring out the answer means equating the two amounts, $(1 + i^m)^{12} = (1.05)$, and raising each side to the one-twelfth power: $(1 + i^m) = (1.05)^{\frac{1}{12}} = 1.0041$. Converting from decimals to a percentage, the one-month interest rate is 0.41 percent. We can handle any mismatch between the time units of *i* and *n* in a similar way (see Tools of the Trade: Computing Compound Annual Rates).

These fractions of percentage points, like 0.41 percent, are so important in discussing interest rates that they have their own name, basis points. A **basis point** is one-one hundredth of a percentage point. That is, one basis point equals 0.01 percent.

You're probably wondering how useful all this discussion of future value really is. To see, consider the following question: If you put $1,000 per year into the bank at 4 percent interest, how much would you have saved after 40 years? The answer is $98,826—more than twice the $40,000 you deposited. Figuring out the exact answer is complicated since we need to add up the future values of forty $1,000 deposits, each made in a different year, but doing so uses the concept of future value. The first $1,000 is deposited for 40 years, so its future value is $1,000(1.04)^{40} = $4,801.02$; the second $1,000 is deposited for 39 years, so its future value is $1,000(1.04)^{39} = $4,616.37$; and so on. The practical implication of this calculation is that buying one less soda or candy bar per day isn't just good for your physical health; it's good for your financial health too.

YOUR FINANCIAL WORLD
How Long Does Your Investment Take to Double?

You invest $100 at 6 percent interest. How long will you need to wait until you have $200? That may seem like a simple question, but compounding makes it difficult. The straightforward (some people would call it "brute force") way to find the answer is to take out your calculator and multiply $100 times 1.06 over and over again, counting how many times it takes to get an answer that is close to $200. If you did that, you would find that after the 12th time, you had reached $201.22. So ignoring the extra $1.22, the answer is that at 6 percent interest, your investment takes 12 years to double.

While the brute force technique works (you can sit there multiplying over and over again), it's clumsy, and it works only for round numbers. Suppose the answer turns out to be $10\frac{1}{2}$ years. How would you figure that out? Fortunately, there is a simpler way called the Rule of 72. If you want to compute the number of years an investment takes to double, divide the annual interest rate (measured as a percent, not decimal) into 72.* So at an

interest rate of 5 percent, we would expect an investment to double in 72/5 = 14.4 years (we can check and see that $1.05^{14.4} = 2.02$). If the interest rate were 8 percent, we would estimate 9 years ($1.08^9 = 2.00$).

The rule of 72 shows the power of compounding. It shows that when the interest rate doubles, the time a $100 investment takes to become $200 is cut in half. That is, while it takes 14.4 years to double at 5 percent interest, it takes only 7.2 years at 10 percent (72/10 = 7.2 and $1.10^{7.2} = 1.99$).

*The rule of 72 is an approximation of the solution to an algebraic problem that requires the use of logarithms. Consider the formula for compound interest, in which the future value after n years is equal to $FV = PV(1 + i)^n$. Setting the present value PV *equal to 1* and the future value FV *equal to 2* and taking logarithms, we get $n = \ln(2)/\ln(1 + i)$. This formula is exact. Next, we use the approximation that $\ln(1 + i) \approx i$ for small i. Substituting this into the equation gives us $n = \ln(2)/i$. The $\ln(2) = 0.693$, so it might seem that we should be using the rule of 69.3. For very low interest rates, we should, but in the range of interest rates we normally see (2 to 15 percent), 72 works better.

Present Value

It's easy to see why future value is important. We often want to know what savings and investments will be worth in the future. But that isn't the only thing we need to know. There is another, somewhat different task that we face with some regularity. We need to be able to figure out how much a payment promised in the future is worth today. Say you agree to make a $225 loan, and the borrower offers to repay you either $100 a year for three years or $125 a year for two years. Which offer should you take? Answering this question means figuring out the current value of the promised payments on the dates when they will be made. To do that, we'll use the concept of present value, sometimes referred to as present discounted value.

TIME

The Definition   We used the term *present value* in our discussion of future value, to mean the initial amount invested or deposited. The way we used the term suggests its technical definition: Present value *is the value today (in the present) of a payment that is promised to be made in the future.* Put another way, present value is the amount that must be invested today in order to realize a specific amount on a given future date. Financial instruments promise future cash payments, so we need to know how to value those payments. Present value is an integral component of the computation of the price of all financial instruments.

To understand the calculation of present value, go back to future value. Remember that at a 5 percent interest rate, the future value one year from now of a $100 investment today is $105 (see equation 1). It follows that at this same 5 percent interest rate, the present value of $105 one year from now is $100. *All we did was invert the future value calculation.*

Reversing the calculation in general terms is just as easy. Start with the fact that the future value of a payment equals the current investment times one plus the interest rate: $FV = PV \times (1 + i)$ (equation 2). Divide both sides of this expression by $(1+i)$ to get an expression for how much we need to invest today to realize the future value one year from today. The result is

$$PV = \frac{FV}{(1+i)} \tag{5}$$

Present value = Future value of the payment divided by (One plus the interest rate)

In our example, we see that

$$\frac{FV}{(1+i)} = \frac{\$105}{(1.05)} = \$100$$

so the present value of $105 one year from now, at a 5 percent interest rate, is indeed $100.

While future value tells us what today's investment will be worth in the future, present value tells us what promised future payments are worth today. This means that the properties of present value mirror those of future value. In the same way that future value *rises* as the interest rate rises, present value *falls* as the interest rate rises. To see this, first look at the calculation of the present value of $105 in one year at an interest rate of 6 percent. The answer is $105/1.06 = $99.06, less than the $100 needed when the interest rate is only 5 percent. *Present value falls as the interest rate rises.*

What happens if the payment is going to be made in two years instead of one? What is the present value of $105 in two years at an interest rate of 5 percent? Again, we can compute the answer using the future-value formula by asking what present value has a future value of $105 in two years at an interest rate of 5 percent. This is the solution to $105 = PV(1.05)^2$. The answer is $PV = \$105/1.05^2 = \$95.24$. We can generalize this process by looking at the future value in n years of an investment today: $FV_n = PV(1 + i)^n$. Dividing both sides of this expression by $(1 + i)^n$, we get the general formula for present value:

$$PV = \frac{FV_n}{(1+i)^n} \tag{6}$$

Present value = Future value of a payment made in n years
divided by (One plus the interest rate) raised to n

From this simple expression, we can deduce three important properties of present value. Present value is higher

1. The higher the future value of the payment, FV_n.
2. The shorter the time until the payment, n.
3. The lower the interest rate, i.

We're going to use equation (6) over and over again. *It is the single most important relationship in our study of financial instruments.* Once we can figure out the present value of any future payment, then we understand the fundamentals of mortgages, credit cards, car loans, and even stocks.

We will spend the rest of this chapter looking at how present value changes when we change the various components of the formula, and how to use it more generally. But before we do, it is important to note one final similarity between present value and future value. Recall that to calculate future value, *n* need not be measured in years. We can do the computation even when *n* is the number of months, so long as the interest rate is measured in months as well. The same is true of present value. So long as we measure *n* and *i* in the same time unit, and the interest rate is expressed as a decimal, the formula works.

How Present Value Changes It is useful to go through each of the three properties of present value, looking at the impact of changing each one: the size of the payment (FV_n), the time until the payment is made (*n*), and the interest rate (*i*). Starting with FV_n, we see that *doubling the future value of the payment, without changing the time of the payment or the interest rate, doubles the present value.* For example, at a 5 percent interest rate, a $100 payment made in two years has a present value of $90.70. Doubling the payment to $200 doubles the present value to $181.40. In fact, increasing or decreasing FV_n by any percentage will change *PV* by the same percentage, in the same direction.

We have already seen that *the sooner a payment is to be made, the more it is worth.* How much more? To see, let's return to the example of a $100 payment at 5 percent interest. How sensitive is the present value of this payment to the time until it is made? Plugging some numbers into the general present-value formula (equation 6), and allowing the time to go from 0 to 30 years, we can construct Figure 4.1, which shows that the present value of the payment is worth $100 if it is made immediately but declines gradually to $23 for a payment made in 30 years.

The rate of decline in the present value is related to the same phenomenon that gives us the rule of 72 (described in Your Financial World: How Long Does Your Investment Take to Double?). Consider this question: At a 5 percent interest rate,

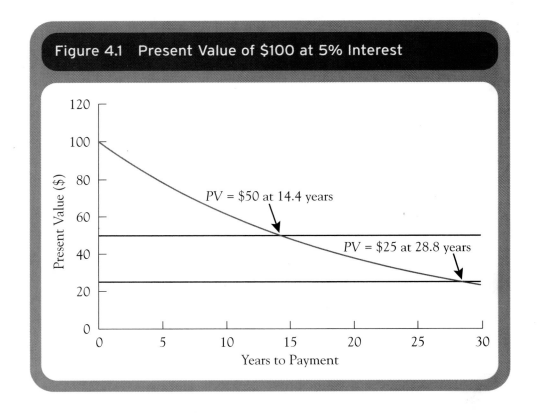

Figure 4.1   Present Value of $100 at 5% Interest

how long into the future must a payment of $100 be made for it to be worth the same as $50 received today? The answer is 14.4 years. That is, at 5 percent interest, the present value of $100 paid in 14.4 years is $50. Note that 14.4 equals 72 divided by 5, so it is also the number of years an investment takes to double in value when the return is 5 percent per year. We can repeat the computation to see that the investment takes 28.8 years to double twice, which tells us that the present value of $100 paid 28.8 years from now is $25. These two points are highlighted in Figure 4.1.

The interest rate is the third important determinant of the present value of a future payment. To see how important it is, let's look at the present value of a $100 payment made 1, 5, 10, and 20 years from now at various interest rates. The general formula (equation 6) allows us to do this series of computations. Table 4.2 shows the numerical results, which are also plotted in Figure 4.2. Note what happens as the interest rate increases—that is, as you read down a column in the table or move to the right in the figure. You can see immediately that *higher interest rates are associated with lower present values, no matter what the size or timing of the payment.* Conversely, lower interest rates are associated with higher present values (see Figure 4.2).

Note, too, that *at any fixed interest rate, an increase in the time until a payment is made reduces its present value.* Read across any row of the table and you will see that as the time increases from 1 to 5 to 10 to 20 years, the present value goes down. In Figure 4.2, the top line, representing the present value of payments made in one year, is higher than the other lines, representing longer payment periods, at all interest rates.

The final lesson to take away from these calculations has to do with how present value changes with both time and the interest rate. Table 4.2 shows what happens to the present value of a payment as the interest rate increases. You can see that if the payment is to be made in one year (column 2), as the interest rate increases from 1 percent to 5 percent, the present value falls from $99.01 to $95.24. This is a drop of $3.77, or just under 4 percent. In fact, for the single payment made in one year, the percentage change in the present value is approximately equal to the percentage point change in the interest rate: A rise of 4 percentage points in the interest rate has caused a decline in present value of 4 percent.

Now look at the present value of a payment that will be made in 10 years (column 4 of Table 4.2). As the interest rate goes from 1 to 5 percent, the present value of a $100 payment 10 years from now falls from $90.53 to $61.39. This is a decline of

Table 4.2   Present Value of a $100 Payment

Interest Rate	Payment due in			
	1 Year	5 Years	10 Years	20 Years
1%	$99.01	$95.15	$90.53	$81.95
2%	$98.04	$90.57	$82.03	$67.30
3%	$97.09	$86.26	$74.41	$55.37
4%	$96.15	$82.19	$67.56	$45.64
5%	$95.24	$78.35	$61.39	$37.69
6%	$94.34	$74.73	$55.84	$31.18
7%	$93.46	$71.30	$50.83	$25.84
8%	$92.59	$68.06	$46.32	$21.45
9%	$91.74	$64.99	$42.24	$17.84
10%	$90.91	$62.09	$38.55	$14.86
11%	$90.09	$59.35	$35.22	$12.40
12%	$89.29	$56.74	$32.20	$10.37
13%	$88.50	$54.28	$29.46	$8.68
14%	$87.72	$51.94	$26.97	$7.28
15%	$86.96	$49.72	$24.72	$6.11

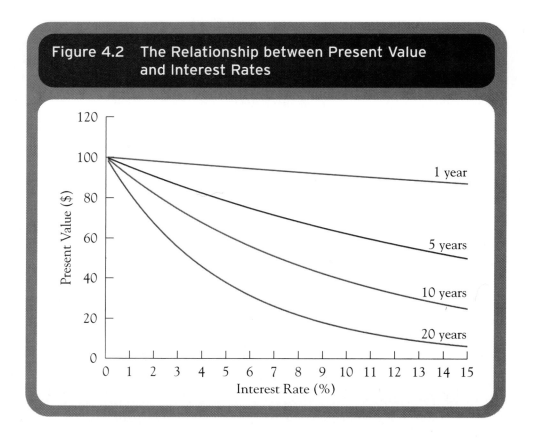

Figure 4.2 The Relationship between Present Value and Interest Rates

$29.14, or more than 30 percent. *Not only does the present value of a future payment fall with the interest rate; the further in the future the promised payment is to be made, the more the present value falls.* As a result, a change in interest rates has a much greater impact on the present value of a payment made far in the future than it has on one to be made soon. Remember this principle because it will be extremely important when we discuss bonds in the next section.

"I'm just glad we got out before interest rates went up again."

TOOLS OF THE TRADE
Computing Compound Annual Rates

Comparing changes over days, months, years, and decades can be very difficult. If someone tells you that an investment grew at a rate of $\frac{1}{2}$ percent last month, what should you think? You're used to thinking about growth in terms of years, not months. The way to deal with such problems is to turn the monthly growth rate into a *compound-annual rate*. Here's how you do it.

An investment whose value grows $\frac{1}{2}$ percent per month goes from 100 at the beginning of the month to 100.5 at the end of the month. Remembering to multiply by 100 to convert the decimal into a percentage, we can verify this:

$$100\left(\frac{100.5-100}{100}\right) = 100\left[\left(\frac{100.5}{100}\right)-1\right] = 0.5\%$$

To convert this monthly rate to an annual rate, we need to figure out what would happen if the investment's value continued to grow at a rate of $\frac{1}{2}$ percent per month for the next 12 months. We can't just multiply 0.5 times 12. Instead, we need to compute a 12-month compound rate by raising the one-month rate to the 12th power. Assuming that our index starts at 100 and increases by $\frac{1}{2}$ percent per month, we can use the expression for a compound future value to compute the index level 12 months later. Remembering to convert percentages to their decimal form, so that 0.5 percent is 0.005, we find the result is

$$FV_n = PV(1 + i)^n = 100 (1.005)^{12} = 106.17,$$

an increase of 6.17 percent. That's the compound annual rate, and it's obviously bigger than the 6 per-

cent result we get from just multiplying 0.5 by 12. The difference between the two answers—the one you get by multiplying by 12 and the one you get by compounding—grows as the interest rate grows. At a 1 percent monthly rate, the compounded annual rate is 12.68 percent.

Another use for compounding is to compute the percentage change per year when we know how much an investment has grown over a number of years. This rate is sometimes referred to as the *average annual rate*. Say that over five years an investment has increased 20 percent, from 100 to 120. What annual increase will give us a 20 percent increase over five years? Dividing by 5 gives the wrong answer because it ignores compounding; the increase in the second year must be calculated as a percentage of the index level at the end of the first year. What is the growth rate that after five years will give us an increase of 20 percent? Using the future-value formula,

$$FV_n = PV(1 + i)^n$$
$$120 = 100 (1 + i)^5$$

Solving this equation means computing the following:

$$i = \left[\left(\frac{120}{100}\right)^{1/5} - 1\right] = 0.0371$$

This tells us that five consecutive annual increases of 3.71 percent will result in an overall increase of 20 percent. (Just to check, we can compute $(1.0371)^5 = 1.20 = 120/100$.)

Some Terminology: Interest Rates and Discount Rates

The interest rate (i) used in the present-value calculation is often referred to as the *discount rate*,[4] in the sense that the present-value calculation involves *discounting*, or reducing future payments to their equivalent value today. Another word that's used for the interest rate is *yield*, the term used to describe the return on holding a bond. For most purposes, the words *interest rate*, *discount rate*, and *yield* all mean the same thing.

---

[4]The word *discount* is used in many contexts in economics and finance, not just those described here. For example, *discount rate* may refer to the interest rate the Federal Reserve charges when it makes loans to commercial banks. The term *discount yield* or *yield on a discount basis* is an interest-rate measure bond dealers use to quote the prices of certain bonds. We will discuss some of these uses later.

YOUR FINANCIAL WORLD
Should You Buy a New Car Now or Wait?

For a long time you've wanted to buy a new car and you know you'll need a loan to do it. You have $4,000 in savings and figure you can afford a monthly payment of $300. A quick check on the Internet tells you that you can get a four-year loan at $6\frac{3}{4}$ percent interest. Payments are $237 a month for each $10,000 you borrow. That is, $10,000 is the present value of $237 per month for 48 months at a monthly interest rate of 0.54581 percent (the monthly rate that equals $6\frac{3}{4}$ percent per year). Since you can afford a $300 payment, you can get a loan of up to $12,658, or (300/237) × $10,000. With a $4,000 down payment, you can afford a car that costs $16,658.

You don't have to buy the car right away, however. You could wait and drive your old car a while longer. What if you wait a year to buy the car? Waiting means you should put $300 per month into the bank along with the $4,000 you already have. At 4 percent interest, at the end of a year you will have $7,838—the future value of the $4,000 plus 12 monthly contributions of $300 each.

For the sake of comparison, let's assume that at the end of the year you look for a three-year loan with a $300 payment. At $6\frac{3}{4}$ percent interest, you can now afford to borrow $9,781. Adding this amount to your savings, you can spend a total of $7,837 + $9,781, or $17,618. So by waiting a year, you'll be able to afford a car that costs about $1,000 more. (That's approximately the 4 percent interest you earned on your $4,000 down payment plus the $6\frac{3}{4}$ percent interest you didn't pay on a $12,658 loan: $160 + $854 = $1,014.)

Should you buy the new car now or wait? It depends on how you feel about the extra $1,000 you will have available to spend if you wait and how much you'll have to pay to repair your old car in the meantime. *

---

*In addition, there is always the possibility that the price of the car will change. It could go up because of general inflation or down as a result of increases in the efficiency of production. If you have reason to believe that the price may change in a particular direction, factor that into your computation.

The idea of an interest rate or discount rate has an important application in individual decision making. We all have to decide how much to save out of our income; some of us save more and some less. One way to describe this difference in saving rates is to say that people who save more of their income than others are more patient. They are more willing to wait, to postpone consumption until the future. And if you are more willing to wait, you don't need to be compensated much to do it. Because the future is almost as important to you as the present, your own personal discount rate must not be very high. If you really like to save, you won't need to be bribed with high interest rates to do it. Thus, people who have a low personal discount rate are more likely to save, while people with a high personal discount rate are more likely to borrow.

We all have a discount rate at which we need to be compensated for postponing consumption and saving a portion of our income. Financial markets offer a return for saving, and that is the interest rate. If the market offers an interest rate that is higher than an individual's personal discount rate, we would expect that person to save. Alternatively, if the market offers an interest rate that is lower than an individual's personal discount rate, we would expect that person to borrow. Just think about what happens when the return you receive for saving goes up—that is, the interest rate rises. You will think harder about spending now because you are being paid more to wait. And the more you're paid to wait, the more waiting you're likely to do. Higher interest rates mean higher saving.

Applying Present Value

All of our examples thus far have focused on computing the present value of a single payment on a given future date. Thinking of present value in this way gives us enormous flexibility. It means that we can compute the present value not just of a single payment but also of any group of payments made on any number of dates. As we saw earlier, to use present value in practice, we need to look at sequences, or streams of payments. And valuing a stream of payments means summing their present values. That is, the value of the whole is the sum of the value of its parts. *Present value is additive.* To see how present value is applied to a stream of payments, we will look at two applications: internal rate of return and the valuation of bonds.

Internal Rate of Return

Imagine that you run a sports equipment factory. As part of your strategic planning, you are considering buying a new machine that makes tennis rackets. The machine costs $1 million and can produce 3,000 rackets a year. If you can sell the rackets for $50 apiece (wholesale), the machine will generate $150,000 in revenue each year. To simplify the analysis, we will assume that the machine is the only necessary input in the production of tennis rackets; that we know the exact amount of revenue it will produce (in reality, that has to be estimated); and that the machine will last for exactly 10 years, during which time it will work perfectly, without requiring any maintenance. At the end of the 10 years, the machine will abruptly cease to operate and will have no resale value. Should you buy the machine?

The answer is: It depends. If you borrow the $1 million to pay for the machine, will the revenue from the machine, $150,000 per year, be enough to cover the payments on the loan? If so and you have something left over, then buying the machine may be a good idea. But if you can't make the payments, then buying the machine is a losing proposition. So you need to figure out whether the machine's revenue will be high enough to cover the payments on the loan you would need to buy it. We'll do this in two steps: First, we'll compute the internal rate of return on your investment in the machine, and second, we'll compare that return to the cost of buying the machine. If the cost is less than the return, then you should buy the machine.

The **internal rate of return** *is the interest rate that equates the present value of an investment with its cost.* For the tennis racket machine, it is the interest rate at which the present value of the revenue from the tennis rackets, $150,000 per year for 10 years, equals the $1 million cost of the machine. To find the internal rate of return, we take the sum of the present value of each of the yearly revenues (we can't take the present value of the total revenue) and equate it with the machine's cost. Then we solve for the interest rate, i:

$$\$1,000,000 = \frac{\$150,000}{(1+i)^1} + \frac{\$150,000}{(1+i)^2} + \ldots + \frac{\$150,000}{(1+i)^{10}} \qquad (7)$$

You can solve this equation using a financial calculator or spreadsheet. The answer, 8.14 percent, is the internal rate of return on your investment. That is, the annual rate of return for investing $1 million in the machine is 8.14 percent. But is that rate of return high enough to justify your investment? That depends on the cost of the $1 million you need to buy the machine.

There are two ways you can come up with the $1 million. You can use your company's retained earnings—the funds you've saved from your past profits. Or you can

Table 4.3	Fixed Annual Payments On a 10-year, $1 million Loan	
Interest Rate		**Payment**
5%		$129,505
6%		$135,868
7%		$142,378
8%		$149,030
9%		$155,820
10%		$162,745

borrow. In the first case, you need to figure out if the machine is more profitable than other ways you might use the funds, just as you might compare interest-bearing investments. The other main use for the retained earnings is to lend it to someone at the same rate at which you could borrow. That is the opportunity cost of your investment. If you borrow the money to buy the machine, you need to know whether you will have a profit left after paying off the loan. Let's assume you're considering borrowing.

Table 4.3 shows the payments you will have to make if you borrow $1 million at various interest rates. To keep the example fairly simple, we'll assume that the loan requires 10 equal payments, one for each year. This type of loan is called a **fixed-payment loan**, and it is exactly the same as a car loan or a mortgage. Using the present-value formula (equation 6), we know that the amount of the loan must equal the present value of the 10 payments. If the interest rate is i, then

$$\$1,000,000 = \frac{Fixed\ payment}{(1+i)} + \frac{Fixed\ payment}{(1+i)^2} + \ldots + \frac{Fixed\ payment}{(1+i)^{10}} \quad (8)$$

$1,000,000 = Present value of 10 equal annual payments at interest rate i.

Using this relationship, we can compute your loan payment at various interest rates,[5] as shown in Table 4.3. As we would expect, when the interest rate rises, the payments rise too.

At what interest rate can you afford a loan to buy the tennis racket machine? Recall that you have $150,000 a year in revenue, and your internal rate of return is 8.14 percent. So as long as the interest rate is 8 percent or less, you know you can cover the payments. But we can answer this question with more precision. To see why, notice that the internal rate of return equation (7) is virtually identical to the loan equation (8). In fact, the internal rate of return is the interest rate at which $150,000 a year for 10 years will exactly cover the loan. So we really needed to do this computation only once to answer the question. You should buy the tennis racket machine if its internal rate of return exceeds the interest rate on the loan you would need to finance it. In general, *an investment will be profitable if its internal rate of return exceeds the cost of borrowing.*

Before we go on, we can use the concept of internal rate of return to answer the question at the beginning of the present-value section: If you agree to make a $225 loan, and the borrower offers to repay either $100 a year for three years or $125 a year for two years, which should you take? The first step in figuring out what to do is to compute the internal rate of return of the two payment streams. For the series of three $100 payments, we need to find the interest rate i that solves

$$\$225 = \frac{\$100}{(1+i)} + \frac{\$100}{(1+i)^2} + \frac{\$100}{(1+i)^3}.$$

The answer is $i = 0.159$, or 15.9 percent.

[5]We can compute these values using the methods described in the appendix to this chapter.

APPLYING THE CONCEPT
RETIREMENT

Everyone wants to retire early. Most people would love to quit work when they turn 40 (that's less than 20 years of work after college) and spend the next 40 years doing whatever they want. In the late 1990s, it looked as if lots of dot-com millionaires had managed to pull it off—at least for a while. But when the Internet bubble burst in 2000, some early retirees discovered that they really couldn't afford retirement. Some had to go back to work. How expensive is early retirement anyway? Very. Let's see how rich you'd need to be to quit working on your 40th birthday.

Here's the problem. Assume that you're going to live to be 85 years old.* Though you're rich, you are willing to live modestly (for a rich person) and spend only $100,000 a year. Remember that you're going to be on vacation 365 days a year and you'll want to put your kids through college, buy new cars, and so on. And you'll still need to pay income taxes, so you won't see all of your income. In short, you'll need $100,000 a year for 45 years.

To figure out how much you need to save by age 40, you can use the present-value concept. Think of the amount you need to invest today to have $100,000 in five years.

$$\$100,000 = PV\,(1 + i)^5$$

Assuming a 4 percent interest rate on your investment (that may seem conservative, but you can't count on much more than that), the answer is

$$PV = \frac{\$100,000}{(1.04)^5} = \$82,193$$

To retire at 40, you need to do this for *each* of the 45 years of your retirement. That is, you need a sequence of $100,000 payments:

$$\frac{\$100,000}{(1.04)^1} + \frac{\$100,000}{(1.04)^2} + \ldots + \frac{\$100,000}{(1.04)^{44}} + \frac{\$100,000}{(1.04)^{45}} = \$2,072,004$$

Retiring at 40 with an income of $100,000 a year means accumulating about $2 million in assets (not counting your house). You can see how someone who retired at age 40 with a few million dollars' worth of Internet stocks might have had to go back to work when the bubble burst and reduced his or her wealth by 75 percent or more.

The point of this discussion is that you need to have significant savings in order to retire. Even if you are willing to work until you are 65 and live on only $50,000 a year, you'll need to amass around $700,000.† A normal retirement is expensive enough. For all but the richest among us, retiring early just is not an option.

*We are assuming the person will die at exactly age 85. In reality, many retirees purchase an annuity that makes payments for as long as they live, providing a form of old-age insurance. We will ignore this complication, since it has only a small effect on our conclusion.

†To see what this requires, recall that earlier in the chapter we computed that if you save $1,000 at an interest rate of 4 percent, after 40 years you will have just under $100,000. To accumulate $700,000 you will need to save slightly more than $7,000 a year for 40 years.

IN THE NEWS

Economic Scene: Pentagon Shows That It Doesn't Always Pay to Take the Money and Run

The New York Times

by Alan B. Krueger

May 24, 2001

Suppose your employer hands you a pink slip and offers you a choice: an annual payment of $8,000 a year for 30 years or a lump sum of $50,000 today. Which would you choose?

This is not just a hypothetical exercise. When it downsized in the early 1990s, the Defense Department offered many military personnel a similar choice. The military also provided pamphlets and counseling to explain how to make the choice wisely. To the surprise of most economists, the affected personnel rarely followed the military's sound advice.

The decision should depend, of course, on how much one values money received today versus tomorrow. A bird

in the hand is worth more today than tomorrow, but how much more? The difference between the value an individual places on a dollar received today as opposed to a year from now is called the discount rate.

Standard economic theory says that if capital markets work perfectly, people will borrow or lend until their discount rate equals the market rate for borrowing or lending. Someone with a low discount rate will save and accumulate interest; someone with a high discount rate will borrow and accumulate debt. This should continue to the point where their personal discount rates equal the market rate.

Thus, with some justification, the military's pamphlet provided calculations of the present value of the annuity payment using a 7 percent discount rate, the interest rate on money-market funds at the time. If the annuity's present value exceeds the value of the lump sum, the annual payment is a better deal.

Mounting evidence indicates that most people put excessive weight on a bird in the hand. That $8,000 annu-

continued on next page

Turning to the alternative, we need to calculate the interest rate that solves

$$\$225 = \frac{\$125}{(1+i)} + \frac{\$125}{(1+i)^2}$$

The answer here is $i = 0.073$, or 7.3 percent.

This means that if you choose the three $100 payments, you will earn 15.9 percent interest on the loan, while if you accept the two $125 payments, the interest rate will be 7.3 percent. Clearly, the three payments are better for you as the lender, but we had to do quite a bit of work to figure it out.

Bonds: The Basics

One of the most common uses of the concept of present value is in the valuation of bonds. A bond is a promise to make a series of payments on specific future dates. It is issued as part of an arrangement to borrow. In essence, the borrower, or seller, gives an IOU to the lender, or buyer, in return for some amount of money. Both governments and corporations need to borrow, so both issue bonds. Because bonds create obligations, they are best thought of as legal contracts that (1) require the borrower to make payments to the lender and (2) specify what happens if the borrower fails to do so.

al payment is worth more than $106,000 if future income is discounted at 7 percent a year—more than double the value of the lump sum. If the discount rate is 10 percent, as high as the interest rate on 30-year fixed-rate mortgages has been the last decade, the promised $8,000 payment is still worth $83,000. The annual payment is a better deal for anyone who can borrow from a bank.

Yet when the military offered essentially this package, three-quarters of enlisted personnel selected the lump sum, according to an article by John Warner of Clemson University and Saul Pleeter of the Defense Department in *The American Economic Review*. The authors also examined a number of other separation packages. The break-even discount rate—or rate that makes the lump sum and annuity payment equivalent—varied from 17 to 20 percent, depending on years of service and salary. Over all, 92 percent of enlisted personnel and 51 percent of officers chose the lump sum.

Because the government could borrow at 7 percent at the time, Mr. Warner and Mr. Pleeter calculate that the Treasury saved $1.7 billion by offering the lump-sum option.

Using a sample of 65,000 departing members of the armed forces, they estimate that the average personal discount rate, taking taxes into account, exceeded 25 percent. Discount rates were higher for the less educated, the young, minorities, and those with dependents; they were lower for officers.

Recognition of this fact helps to explain a number of other phenomena. For instance, the public's penchant for holding high credit card debt—more than $6,000 per household with a credit card—at interest rates near 15 percent a year is also consistent with high discount rates, as are low savings rates. (Indeed, one wonders why the government, which borrows at 5 percent, doesn't offer a credit card to every man, woman, and child at an interest rate of, say, 10 percent. This would help reduce the debt and quench individuals' thirst for fast cash.)

LESSONS OF THE ARTICLE

This article examines a common problem faced by people who are retiring. Should they take a single lump-sum payment or a series of annual payments? Answering this question requires using the concept of present value. The article also describes how most people are extremely impatient, behaving as if their own personal discount rate is extraordinarily high, and how that explains the willingness to borrow at very high interest rates.

TIME

Because there are many different kinds of bonds, to focus our discussion, we'll look at the most common type, a **coupon bond**. Say a borrower who needs $100 "issues" or sells a $100 coupon bond to a lender. The bond issuer is required to make annual payments, called **coupon payments**. The annual amount of those payments (expressed as a percentage of the amount borrowed) is called the **coupon rate**. If the coupon rate is 5 percent, then the borrower/issuer pays the lender/bondholder $5 per year per $100 borrowed. The yearly coupon payment equals the coupon rate times the amount borrowed. The bond also specifies when the issuer is going to repay the initial $100 and the payments will stop, called the **maturity date** or *term to maturity*. The final payment, a repayment of the initial $100 loan, is often referred to as the **principal, face value,** or **par value** of the bond.

Before the advent of computers, an investor buying a bond would receive a certificate with a number of dated coupons attached. To claim the coupon payments, the investor would cut off the coupons and mail them to the bond issuer. At maturity, the investor would redeem the certificate for the final payment. The Reading Railroad Company bond pictured on the next page still has some coupons attached.[6]

---

[6]The bond in the picture is a $1,000 face value 50-year $3\frac{1}{2}$ percent coupon bond issued on May 1, 1945. It promised 100 payments of $17.35, to be made every six months beginning on November 1, 1945, plus a $1,000 final payment on May 1, 1995. The vast majority of bonds pay interest biannually.

A coupon bond issued by the Reading Railroad Company on May 1, 1945. Some of the coupons are still attached to the bond.

You can see that the borrower who issues a bond is promising to make a series of regular interest payments over the life of the bond, plus a final payment on the maturity date. How much should someone be willing to pay for such a contract? The answer comes directly from present value: *The price of a bond is the present value of its payments.* To see how to value a bond, we'll start with repayment of the principal; then we'll add the interest payments.

Valuing the Principal Payment   Valuing the bond's principal, or final payment, is a straightforward application of present value. Let's look at a bond that promises a principal payment of $100 on its maturity date n years in the future. The present value of this payment is

$$P_{BP} = \frac{F}{(1+i)^n} = \frac{\$100}{(1+i)^n} \tag{9}$$

Present value of bond principal (P_{BP}) =
     Principal payment (F) divided by (One plus the interest rate) raised to n.

We can see immediately that the value of the principal payment varies with both the time to maturity and the interest rate. The longer the time until the payment is made—the higher the n—the lower the value of the payment. And the higher the interest rate, i, the lower the value of the payment.

To see how this works, let's start with an interest rate of 6 percent and a final payment of $1,000 to be made in 30 years. If the interest rate is 6 percent, the present value of the final Payment is $\frac{\$1,000}{(1.06)^{30}}$ = \$174.11. Not surprisingly, this promise to make a payment that far in the future is worth only a fraction of the $1,000 principal. Lowering the interest rate, say to 4 percent, would increase the present value of the principal payment to $308.32, but it would still be much less than half of the payment itself.

Valuing the Coupon Payments   What about the coupon payments? This series of equal payments resembles the loan payments we examined in our discussion of internal rate of return. There we computed the sum of a series of equal payments by adding up the present value of each payment. Let's look at this process in more detail, starting with two $10 payments made in consecutive years. Assuming an interest rate of 6 percent, the value of these two payments is

$$\frac{\$10}{1.06} + \frac{\$10}{1.06^2} = \$9.43 + \$8.90 = \$18.33 \qquad (10)$$

Adding additional payments simply means adding more terms. So for five $10 payments made over five consecutive years, the present value is

$$\frac{\$10}{1.06} + \frac{\$10}{1.06^2} + \frac{\$10}{1.06^3} + \frac{\$10}{1.06^4} + \frac{\$10}{1.06^5} = \$9.43 + \$8.90 + \$8.40 + \$7.92 + \$7.47 = \$42.12 \qquad (11)$$

This example highlights two important properties of periodic fixed payments. First, the longer the payments go on—the more of them there are—the higher their total value. Even though the additional payments fall further into the future, the overall present value still grows. Since a long-term bond (one that lasts for 30 years, for instance) has more payments than a short-term maturity bond (one whose final payment is made, say, in five years) the coupon payments on the long-term bond will be worth more than the coupon payments on the short-term bond.

Second, as is always the case in present-value calculations, the higher the interest rate, the lower the present value. Raising the interest rate from 6 to 7 percent, for example, lowers the total value of the five future payments on our short-term bond from $42.12 to $41.00.

We can use the present-value expression to write a general formula for a string of yearly coupon payments made over n years. It is simply the sum of the present value of the payments for each year from one to n years:

$$P_{CP} = \frac{C}{(1+i)^1} + \frac{C}{(1+i)^2} + \frac{C}{(1+i)^3} + \ldots + \frac{C}{(1+i)^n} \qquad (12)$$

Present value of a series of bond coupon payments (P_{CP}) = Sum of yearly coupon payments (C) divided by (one plus the interest rate) raised to the power equal to the number of years from now. This formula is messy, but that's why we have calculators and spreadsheets. (For a derivation of a simpler version of this formula, see the appendix to this chapter.)

Valuing the Coupon Payments plus Principal   To value the yearly coupon payments plus the principal, we can combine equations (9) and (12) as follows:

$$P_{CB} = P_{CP} + P_{BP} = \left[\frac{C}{(1+i)^1} + \frac{C}{(1+i)^2} + \frac{C}{(1+i)^3} + \ldots + \frac{C}{(1+i)^n}\right] + \frac{F}{(1+i)^n} \qquad (13)$$

Present value of coupon bond (P_{CB})

= Present value of yearly coupon payments (P_{CP})

+ Present value of principal payment (P_{BP})

This formula looks complicated because it is. But we can learn two simple facts just by looking at its parts. The value of the coupon bond, P_{CB}, rises when (1) the yearly coupon payments, C, rise, and (2) the interest rate, i, falls. The first of these conclusions follows from the fact that a higher coupon rate means larger payments, and the present value of a larger payment is larger. The second follows directly from the present-value relationship: the higher the interest rate, the lower the present value of any and all future payments.

The fact that lower interest rates mean higher bond prices—and higher interest rates mean lower bond prices—is extremely important. Since bonds promise fixed payments on future dates, the higher the interest rate, the lower their present value. It follows that *the value of a bond varies inversely with the interest rate used to discount the promised payments*.

Real and Nominal Interest Rates

So far we have been computing the present value of future payments using **nominal interest rates**, which are interest rates expressed in current-dollar terms. We did not worry about the possibility that inflation might change the purchasing power of the dollars. Since borrowers and lenders care about the purchasing power of the money they pay out and receive, they care about inflation. So we need to adjust the return on a loan, looking not just at the nominal interest rate but at the inflation-adjusted interest rate, called the **real interest rate**.

Think about a $100 loan made at 5 percent interest rate for one year. The borrower receives $100 at the beginning of the year and repays $105 at the end of the year. If prices go up 5 percent during the year—that is, if inflation is 5 percent—then the $105 returned to the lender at the end of the year will buy exactly what $100 did at the beginning of the year. The lender's inflation-adjusted return is zero. No lender would be happy with a zero return, so no lender is likely to make a loan at a 5 percent nominal interest rate if expected inflation is 5 percent.

The point of this example is that borrowers look at the inflation-adjusted cost of borrowing, while lenders focus on the inflation-adjusted return. *No one cares only about the number of dollars. People also care about what those dollars can buy. In other words, everyone cares about real interest rates.* This is why economists think of the nominal interest rate as having two parts, the real interest rate and expected inflation.

TIME

Say that you want to borrow $100 for one year. You find a lender who is willing to give you a loan, but the two of you need to agree on the interest rate. Both of you care about the inflation rate over the coming year, which will affect the purchasing power of the dollars you will use to repay the loan. But neither of you knows what that rate is going to be, so you need to forecast it to conclude your agreement. That is, the nominal interest rate you agree on must be based on *expected inflation* over the term of the loan, plus the real interest rate you agree on.

YOUR FINANCIAL WORLD

Pay Off Your Credit Card Debt as Fast as You Can

Credit cards are extremely useful. They make buying things easy—sometimes too easy. While we all plan to pay off our credit card balances every month, sometimes we just don't have the resources. So we take advantage of the loans the card issuers offer and pay off only part of what we owe. Suddenly we find ourselves deeply in debt.

How fast should you pay off your credit card balance? All the bank or finance company that issued the card will tell you is the minimum you have to pay. You get to decide whether to pay more, and your decision makes a big difference. We can use the present-value concept to figure out your alternatives.

Let's take a typical example. You have a balance of $2,000 and can afford to pay at least $50 per month. How many monthly payments will you need to make to pay off the full debt? What if you paid $60 or $75 per month? To find the answer, use equation (12) for the present value of a fixed series of payments. In this case, the present value is the loan amount, $2,000; the fixed monthly payment is $50, $60, or $75; and the interest rate is whatever your credit card company charges per month. Most credit card companies charge between 10 and 20 percent a year. (The average rate is around 13 percent.) We need to figure out the number of payments, or *n* in equation (12).*

Table 4.4 shows the number of months needed to pay off your $2,000 balance at various interest rates and payment amounts. The first entry tells you that if your credit card company is charging a 10 percent annual interest rate (which is comparatively low), and you pay $50 per month, then you will need to make payments for 48.4 months—just over four years.

Looking at the entire table, you can see the advantage of making big payments. Assume you're paying 15 percent, which is realistic. The table shows that increasing your payment from $50 to $60 will allow you to finish paying off your debt in 42.5 months rather than 54.3 months. In other words, paying $10 more a month will allow you to

Table 4.4	Number of Months to Pay Off a $2,000 Credit Card Debt		
Annual Interest Rate	**Monthly Payment**		
	$50	**$60**	**$75**
10%	48.4	38.9	30.1
12%	50.5	40.3	30.9
15%	54.3	42.5	32.2
20%	62.4	47.0	34.5

finish paying off the loan one full year sooner. And if you can manage to pay $75 a month, you'll be finished 10 months before that.

Looking more closely, you can see that making large payments is much more important than getting a low interest rate. The lesson is: Pay off your debts as fast as you possibly can. Procrastination is expensive.

How fast should you pay off your credit card balance?

SOURCE: © Masterfile

*The most straightforward way to do this is to use a spreadsheet to add up the payments until their present value equals the credit card balance. You can also use equation (A-4) in the appendix of this chapter, which can be solved using logarithms.

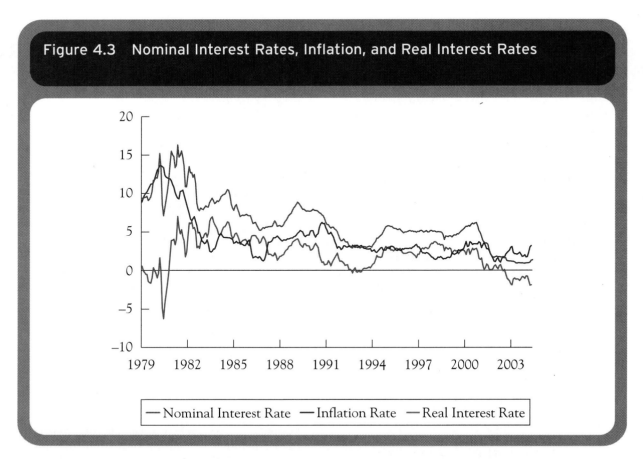

Figure 4.3 Nominal Interest Rates, Inflation, and Real Interest Rates

— Nominal Interest Rate — Inflation Rate — Real Interest Rate

SOURCE: *Three-month Treasury bill rates from the Federal Reserve Board and 12-month inflation rates computed from the Bureau of Labor Statistics Consumer Price Index Research Series. The real interest rate is the nominal rate minus inflation.*

Writing this statement down in the form of an equation is helpful. The nominal interest rate, i, equals the real interest rate, r, plus expected inflation, π^e:[7]

$$i = r + \pi^e \tag{14}$$

This is called the *Fisher equation* after the early 20th-century economist Irving Fisher. It shows that in general, the nominal interest rate is positively related to expected inflation. The higher expected inflation, the higher the nominal interest rate. As we can see in Figure 4.3, the data bear this out. While the relationship is not a tight one, higher nominal interest rates are usually associated with higher inflation. In 1980 and 1981, for example, U.S. interest rates were sky high; the U.S. Treasury had to pay over

[7]This equation is an approximation that works only at low levels of inflation and the real interest rate. The exact relationship among the nominal interest rate, real interest rate, and inflation is $(1 + i) = (1 + r)(1 + \pi^e)$, which equals $(1 + i) = 1 + r + \pi^i + r\pi^e$. The approximation, $i = r + \pi^e$, ignores the cross-term $r\pi^e$, which is usually small. For example, if the real interest rate and the inflation rate are both 5 percent, $r\pi^e$ is 0.25 percent. But when inflation is very high, this cross-term becomes important. If the real interest rate is 5 percent, at zero inflation, a nominal interest rate of 5 percent means that a $100 investment yields $105. But if inflation rises to 100 percent, an investor will require $210 to make the same investment a year later, so the nominal interest rate that results in a 5 percent real return at 100 percent inflation is $(1 + i) = (1 + 0.05)(1 + 1) = 2.1$, which implies an interest rate of 110 percent, not 105 percent. The 5 percent difference comes from the part of the equation that we ignore in the approximation.

APPLYING THE CONCEPT
HIGH INTEREST RATES, LOW INTEREST RATES

Once we realize that the nominal interest rate moves with the expected inflation, big swings in interest rates become less of a mystery. And the fact that the U.S. interest rate is $1\frac{1}{2}$ percent at the same time that the Japanese interest rate is just above zero percent and the Russian interest rate is 13 percent is easier to understand. All we need to do is look at differences in the inflation. In 2004, for example, U.S. prices were rising 1 to 2 percent per year, while Japanese prices were not changing. Russian inflation was an uncomfortable 10 percent per year. The differences in nominal interest rates were almost completely explained by the differences in inflation.

Creditors will lend only if they expect to be compensated. That means the *nominal* interest rate must be greater than inflation so that the *real* interest rate is greater than zero. In low-inflation economies like the United States, Japan, and Germany, the real interest rate occupies a fairly narrow range of 2 to 5 percent.

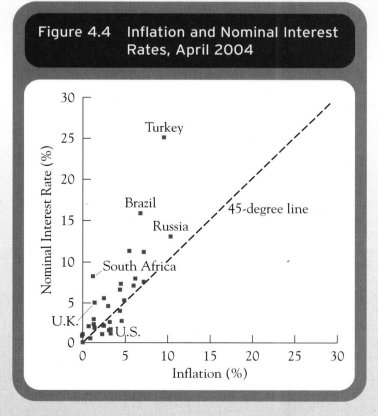

Figure 4.4   Inflation and Nominal Interest Rates, April 2004

SOURCE: *The data come from economic and financial indicators published weekly in the last few pages of* The Economist *magazine.*

continued on next page

continued from previous page

Figure 4.4 shows the nominal interest rate and inflation in 30 countries in August 2004. Note first that high inflation is associated with high nominal interest rates. Second, the vast majority of the points lie above the 45-degree line, meaning that in these countries, the nominal interest rate is higher than inflation. So the ex post real interest rate is positive at an average of 2 percent. Note that the distance of these points from the 45-degree line, which represents the real interest rate, does not vary nearly as much as their distance from the horizontal axis, which represents the nominal interest rate.

15 percent for its short-term borrowing. By 1986, interest rates had dropped to more reasonable levels, close to 5 percent. That's a 10-percentage point move in just five years! The figure shows that as inflation fell, nominal interest rates also fell. In fact, the declines were almost identical. Real interest rates didn't change much during this period.

The term *real interest rate* can cause confusion. The financial markets quote nominal interest rates, the ones that appear in the newspaper and on bank statements.[8] They are "real" in the sense that they are real-life interest rates. When people use the term *interest rate* without qualification, they are referring to the *nominal* interest rate, the one they see every day. We will follow this convention, using the term *interest rate* to mean the nominal rate and the term *real interest rate* to refer to the nominal rate less expected inflation.

Unlike the nominal rates, we cannot directly observe the real interest rate; we have to estimate it. The easiest way to do that is to turn the Fisher equation around, rewriting it as

$$r = i - \pi^e \tag{15}$$

Since we know the nominal interest rate, *i,* measuring the real interest rate means subtracting forecasted inflation. There are a number of sources for these forecasts. Twice a year the Federal Reserve Bank of Philadelphia publishes professional forecasts.[9] Once a month, the Survey Research Center of the University of Michigan computes consumer inflation expectations.

But since forecasts are often wrong, our estimate will usually differ from the real interest rate that occurs. Someone who is making an economically important decision will do so based on the expected real interest rate. Some time later, that person will look back and compute the real interest rate actually paid or received. The first of these is known as the *ex ante* real interest rate, meaning "before the fact." The second, or realized rate, is the *ex post* real interest rate, meaning "after the fact." We can always compute the ex post real interest rate, since we know the nominal interest rate and the level of inflation there actually was. But it is the ex ante real interest rate that we really want to know.

---

[8]One exception is certain bonds whose interest rates are quoted in real, inflation-adjusted terms. We will examine these *indexed* bonds in detail in Chapter 6.

[9]You can find the results of this survey on the bank's Web site, www.phil.frb.org. The Livingston Survey is named after the newspaper columnist Joseph Livingston, who started it in 1946. It summarizes the forecasts of academic, government, and business economists.

Terms

basis point, 65

bond, 76

compound interest, 64

coupon bond, 77

coupon payment, 77

coupon rate, 77

face value, 77

fixed-payment loan, 74

future value, 63

internal rate of return, 73

maturity date, 77

nominal interest rate, 80

par value, 77

present discounted value, 66

present value, 66

principal, 77

real interest rate, 80

rule of 72, 66

Chapter Lessons

1. The value of a payment depends on when it is made.

   a. Future value is the present value of an initial investment times one plus the interest rate for each year you hold it. The higher the interest rate, the higher the future value.

   b. Present value is equal to the value today of a payment made on a future date.

      i. The higher the payment, the higher the present value at a given interest rate.

      ii. The higher the interest rate, the lower the present value of a given payment.

      iii. The longer the time until the payment is made, the lower the present value of a given payment at a given interest rate.

      iv. For a given increase in the interest rate, the present value of a promised payment falls more the farther into the future the payment is to be made.

      v. When computing present value, the interest rate and the time until the payment is to be made must be measured in the same time units.

2. Present value can be used to value any stream of future payments.

   a. The internal rate of return is the interest rate that equates the present value of the future payments or profits from an investment with its current cost.

   b. A coupon bond is a promise to make periodic interest payments and a final principal payment on specific future dates.

      i. The present value of a bond depends on its coupon rate, date of maturity, and the current interest rate.

      ii. The higher the coupon rate, given the maturity and the interest rate, the higher the present value of the bond.

      iii. The price of a bond is inversely related to the interest rate. The higher the price, the lower the interest rate that equates the price with the present value of the promised payments.

3. The real interest rate is the nominal interest rate minus expected inflation. It expresses the interest rate in terms of purchasing power rather than current dollars.

www.mhhe.com/cecchetti1e

Problems

1. Compute the future value of $100 at an 8 percent interest rate five, ten, and fifteen years into the future.

2. Suppose that over the past 20 years the average annual return on investments has been 10.7 percent. For each dollar invested at the beginning of the period, how much money would investors have at the end? What if they had kept the investment for only 10 years? For 30 years?

3. Compute the present value of a $100 investment made six months, five years, and ten years from now at 4 percent interest.

4. You have $1,000 to invest and are considering two options:

   a. 5 percent for two years followed by 7 percent for two years.

   b. 6 percent for four years.

   Which option would you choose? Provide the calculations to justify your answer.

5. You have purchased a $1,000 certificate of deposit (CD) that matures in 10 years. Assuming that interest is paid annually and reinvested, what will be the value of the CD at maturity if the interest rate is 5 percent? What if the interest rate is 10 percent?

2. If the annual interest rate is 5 percent, which of the following has a higher present value?

   a. Two payments of $50, one in six months and the second in twelve months.

   b. One payment of $100 in nine months.

   What if the interest rate is 4 percent? Confirm your answer with calculations.

7. Assuming that the current interest rate is 3 percent, compute the value of a five-year, 5 percent coupon bond with a face value of $1,000. What happens when the interest rate goes to 4 percent?

8. A financial institution offers you a one-year certificate of deposit with an interest rate of 5 percent. You expect inflation to be 3 percent. What is the real return on your deposit?

9. You are a manager in charge of a factory that makes automobile tires. A new production process has been invented, and you want to purchase new machines to take advantage of it.

   a. Describe how you would convince your company's president to purchase the machines.

   b. At the end of the discussion, you conclude that the real rate of return on the investment is 10 percent, so it is worth undertaking. The president responds that in the current financial environment, he cannot borrow for less than 12 percent, so he can't justify the investment. How would you counter this argument?

10. You decide you would like to retire at age 65 and expect to live until you are 85. (Assume there is no chance you will die younger or live longer.) You figure that you can live nicely on $50,000 per year.

    a. Describe the calculation you need to make to determine how much you must save to purchase an annuity paying $50,000 per year for the rest of your life. Assume the interest rate is 7 percent.

the development of modern financial markets is hard to overemphasize. People require compensation for taking risks. Without the capacity to measure risk, we could not calculate a fair price for transferring risk from one person to another, nor could we price stocks and bonds, much less sell insurance. The market for options didn't exist until economists learned how to compute the price of an option using probability theory.

In this chapter, we will learn how to measure risk and assess whether it will increase or decrease. We will also come to understand why changes in risk lead to changes in the demand for particular financial instruments and to corresponding changes in the price of those instruments.

Defining Risk

The dictionary definition of *risk*, the "possibility of loss or injury,"[4] focuses on the perils of putting oneself in a situation in which the outcome is unknown. But this common use of the word doesn't quite fit our purposes because we care about gains as well as losses. We need a definition of risk that focuses on the fact that the outcomes of financial and economic decisions are almost always unknown at the time the decisions are made. Here is the definition we will use:

Risk *is a measure of uncertainty about the future payoff to an investment,* measured over some *time horizon* and *relative to a benchmark.*

This definition has several important elements. First, risk is a *measure* that can be quantified. In comparing two potential investments, we want to know which one is riskier and by how much. All other things held equal, we expect a riskier investment to be less desirable than others and to command a lower price. Uncertainties that are not quantifiable cannot be priced.

TIME

Second, risk arises from *uncertainty about the future.* We know that the future will follow one and only one of many possible courses, but we don't know which one. This statement is true of even the simplest random event—more things can happen than will happen. If you flip a coin, it can come up either heads or tails. It cannot come up both heads and tails or neither heads nor tails; only one of two possibilities will occur.

Third, risk has to do with the *future payoff* of an investment, which is unknown. Though we do not know for certain what is going to happen to our investment, we must be able to list all the possibilities. Imagining all the possible payoffs and the likelihood of each one is a difficult but indispensable part of computing risk.

Fourth, our definition of risk refers to an *investment* or group of investments. We can use the term *investment* very broadly here to include everything from the balance in a bank account to shares of a mutual fund to lottery tickets and real estate.

Fifth, risk must be measured over some *time horizon.* Every investment has a time horizon. We hold some investments for a day or two and others for many years. In most cases, the risk of holding an investment over a short period is smaller than the risk of holding it over a long one, but there are important exceptions to the rule that we will discuss later.[5]

Finally, risk must be measured *relative to a benchmark* rather than in isolation. If someone tells you that an investment is risky, you should immediately ask: "Relative to what?" The simplest answer is "Relative to an investment with no risk at all," called a *risk-free investment.* But there are other possibilities, often more appropriate. For example, in considering the performance of a particular investment advisor or money manager, a good benchmark is the performance of a group of experienced

---

[4]*Merriam-Webster's Collegiate Dictionary,* 11th ed. (Springfield, MA: Merriam-Webster, Inc., 2003).

[5]In Chapter 8 we will consider evidence that holding stock for one year is riskier than holding it for 20 years.

APPLYING THE CONCEPT
IT'S NOT JUST EXPECTED RETURN THAT MATTERS

Your life seems to be going well. You enjoy your job, and it pays well enough that you can put a little aside each month. You can't resist the dollar-for-dollar match your employer is offering on contributions to your retirement account, so you're slowly building up some long-term savings. But every so often, you wonder if you're saving enough. One day you go home and fire up the financial planning program on your computer, just to check.

Going through the retirement planner, you enter all the standard information: your age now and when you hope to retire; your salary and the value of all your assets; the monthly contribution to your retirement account and the monthly income you want at retirement. When you finish, the program asks what rate of return to assume. That is, how fast do you expect your savings to grow from now until your retirement? Following the suggestion on the screen and adjusting for inflation, you enter 7 percent, which is the average *real* return on the stock market over the last 75 years.* The light flashes green, signaling that you're on track to meet your financial goals. But are you?

---

*Inflation complicates computations over very long time periods. Price increases of 2 or 3 percent per year may not seem like much, but over 40 years they add up. At 2 percent inflation, prices double every 36 years. The simplest approach is to ignore inflation and measure income, wealth, and savings in current dollars. Then use a real rate of interest to compute future and present value.

continued on next page

investment advisors or money managers. If you want to know the risk associated with a specific investment strategy, the most appropriate benchmark would be the risk associated with other strategies.

Now that we know what risk is, how do we measure it? We use some rudimentary tools of probability theory, as we will see in the next section.

Measuring Risk

Armed with our definition of risk, we are now ready to quantify and measure it. In this section we will become familiar with the mathematical concepts useful in thinking about random events. We have already used some of these concepts. Recall from the last chapter that the *real* interest rate equals the *nominal* interest rate minus *expected* inflation. Without the proper tools, we weren't able to be explicit about what the term *expected inflation* means. The same is true of the term *expected return*. We see now that the best way to think about expected inflation and expected return is as the average or best guess—the *expected value*—of inflation, or the investment's return out of all the possible values.

Possibilities, Probabilities, and Expected Value

Probability theory tells us that in considering any uncertainty, the first thing we must do is to *list all the possible outcomes* and then *figure out the chance of each one occurring*. When you toss a coin, what are all the *possible* outcomes? There are two and only two.

continued from previous page

Maybe. The program did a series of future- and present-value calculations like the ones described in Applying the Concept: Retirement in Chapter 4. The green light means that if the assumptions you entered are valid, your saving rate is sufficient. That is, *if* your savings grow at 7 percent (adjusted for inflation), you'll be okay. So you need to decide whether you think 7 percent is a reasonable number. While it might be your best guess for the return (that's the *expected return*) over the next few decades, it is surely not the only possibility. You have very little sense of what the average return will be between now and the time that you retire.

To get a 7 percent expected return, you will have to take risk. And risk means that you could end up with less. What if your investment return is only 4 percent per year? Over 40 years that's an enormous difference. At 7 percent annual growth, one dollar today is worth nearly $15 in 40 years, and if you can save $1,000 per year you'll have over $200,000 saved up. Reducing the growth rate to 4 percent means that the future value of a dollar 40 years from now falls to less than $5. The lower return means that with the same $1,000 per year savings, you're left with less than $100,000 after 40 years.[†] You'll have to save twice as much to meet the same goal. Now that's risk!

You need to know what the possibilities are and how likely each one is. Only then can you assess whether your retirement savings plan is risky or not.

[†]These numbers are based on future-value calculations. If you save $1,000 per year, after 40 years you will have $1,000 \times (1.07)^{40} + \$1,000 \times (1.07)^{39} + \ldots + \$1,000 \times (1.07)^2 + \$1,000 \times (1.07) = \$213,610$.

The coin can come down either heads or tails. What is the *chance* of each one of these two outcomes occurring? If the coin is fair, it will come down heads half the time and tails the other half; that's what we mean by *fair*. If we tossed a fair coin over and over again, thousands of times, it would come down heads half the time and tails the other half. But for any individual toss, the coin has an equal chance of coming down heads or tails. To quantify this statement, we can say that the *probability* that the coin will come up heads is one-half.

Probability is a measure of the likelihood that an event will occur. It is always expressed as a number between zero and one. The closer the probability is to zero, the *less* likely it is that an event will occur. If the probability is exactly zero, we are sure that the event will *not* happen. The closer the probability is to one, the *more* likely it is that an event will occur. If the probability is exactly one, the event *will* definitely occur.

Some people prefer to think of random outcomes in terms of frequencies rather than probabilities. Instead of saying that the probability of a coin coming down heads is one-half, we could say that the coin will come down heads once every two tosses on average. Probabilities can always be converted into frequencies in this way.

To grasp these concepts, it is helpful to construct a table. The table lists everything that can happen (all the possibilities) together with their chances of occurring (their probabilities).[6] Let's start with a single coin toss. Table 5.1 lists the possibilities— heads or tails—and the probabilities, both equal to one-half.

[6]In the language of probability and statistics, the first step is to construct the probability distribution for the possible outcomes.

Table 5.1 A Simple Example: All Possible Outcomes of a Single Coin Toss

Possibilities	Probability	Outcome
#1	$\frac{1}{2}$	Heads
#2	$\frac{1}{2}$	Tails

In constructing a table like this one, we must be careful to list *all* possible outcomes. In the case of a coin toss, we know that the coin can come down only two ways, heads or tails. We know that one of these outcomes *must* occur. We just don't know which one.

One important property of probabilities is that we can compute the chance that one *or* the other event will happen by adding the probabilities together. In the case of the coin flip there are only two possibilities; the probability that the coin will come up either heads or tails must be one. If the table is constructed correctly, then, *the values in the probabilities column will sum to one*.

Let's move from a coin toss to something a bit more complicated: an investment that can rise or fall in value. Assume that for $1,000 you can purchase a stock whose value is equally likely to fall to $700 or rise to $1,400. We'll refer to the amount you could get back as the investment's **payoff**. Following the procedure we used to analyze the coin toss, we can construct Table 5.2. Again we list the possibilities and the probability that each will occur, but we add their payoffs (column 3).[7]

We can now go a step further and compute what is called the **expected value** of the investment. We are familiar with the idea of expected value as the **average** or most likely outcome. The expected value is also known as the **mean**. After listing all of the possible outcomes and the probabilities that they will occur, we compute the expected value as the sum of their probabilities times their payoffs. (Another way to say this is that the expected value is the probability-weighted sum of the possible outcomes.)

Computing the expected value of the investment is straightforward. In Table 5.2, the first step is to take the probabilities in the second column and multiply them by their associated payoffs in the third column. The results are in the fourth column. Summing them, we get

$$\text{Expected value} = \tfrac{1}{2}\,(\$700) + \tfrac{1}{2}\,(\$1,400) = \$1,050$$

which appears at the bottom of the table.

---

[7]As you go through the examples in the chapter, be aware that it is often very difficult to estimate the probabilities needed to do the risk computations. The best way to do it is often to look at history. Investment analysts usually estimate the possibilities and probabilities from what happened in the past.

Table 5.2 Investing $1,000: Case 1

Possibilities	Probability	Payoff	Payoff × Probability
#1	$\frac{1}{2}$	$700	$350
#2	$\frac{1}{2}$	$1,400	$700
Expected Value = Sum of (Probability times Payoff) = $1,050			

The expected value of an investment is a very useful concept, but it can be difficult at first. The problem is that if we make this investment only once, we will obtain either $700 or $1,400, not $1,050. In fact, regardless of the number of times we make this particular investment, the payoff will *never* be $1,050. But what would happen if we were to make this investment 1 million times? About 500,000 of those times the investment would pay off $1,400 and the other 500,000 times it would pay off $700. (Notice that we just converted the probabilities into frequencies.) So the *average* payoff from the 1 million investments would be

$$\frac{500,00}{1,000,000}(\$700) + \frac{500,00}{1,000,000} = (\$1,400) = \$1,050 \text{ (the expected value).}$$

While the world of casino gambling may offer simple bets with just two outcomes, the financial world rarely does. To make the example more realistic, let's double the number of possibilities and look at a case in which the $1,000 investment might pay off $100 or $2,000 in addition to $700 or $1,400. Table 5.3 shows the possibilities, probabilities, and payoffs. We'll assume that the two original possibilities are the most likely; the two new possibilities are much less likely to occur. Note that the probabilities sum to one: 0.1 + 0.4 + 0.4 + 0.1 = 1. Again, we could convert the probabilities to frequencies, so that 0.4 means 4 out of 10. And again, we can compute the expected value by multiplying each probability times its associated payoff and then summing them. So $100 would be the payoff one out of every 10 times, $700 the payoff four out of every 10 times, and so on. To compute the expected value, we would find the average of these 10 investments: $100 + $700 + $700 + $700 + $700 + $1,400 + $1,400 + $1,400 + $1,400 + $2,000 = $10,500; and $10,500/10 = $1,050. Once again the expected value is $1,050.

Because the expected value of this $1,000 investment is $1,050, the expected gain is $50. But most people don't discuss investment payoffs in terms of dollars; instead, they talk about the percentage return. Expressing the return as a percentage allows investors to compute the gain or loss on the investment regardless of the size of the initial investment. In this case, the **expected return** is $50 on a $1,000 investment, or 5 percent. Note that the two $1,000 investments we just discussed are not distinguishable by their expected return, which is 5 percent in both cases. Does that mean an investor would be indifferent between them? Even a casual glance suggests that the answer is no because the second investment has a wider range of payoffs than the first.

Table 5.3   Investing $1,000: Case 2

Possibilities	Probability	Payoff	Payoff × Probability
#1	0.1	$100	10
#2	0.4	$700	280
#3	0.4	$1,400	560
#4	0.1	$2,000	200

Expected Value = Sum of (Probability times Payoff) = $1,050

The highest payoff is higher and the lowest payoff lower than for the first investment. So the two investments carry different levels of risk. The next section discusses measures of risk.

One last word on expected values. Recall from the last chapter that to compute the real interest rate, we need a measure of *expected inflation*. One way to calculate expected inflation is to use the technique we just learned. That is, list all the possibilities for inflation, assign each one a probability, and then calculate the expected value of inflation.

Measures of Risk

Most of us have an intuitive sense of risk and its measurement. For example, we know that walking on a sidewalk is usually a safe activity. But imagine that one day as you are strolling along, you come upon a three-foot hole in the sidewalk. The only way across is to jump over it. If the hole is just a few inches deep, it won't stop you. But the deeper it is, the greater the risk of jumping across because the greater the range of injuries you could sustain. We all have an intuitive sense that the wider the range of

YOUR FINANCIAL WORLD
Choosing the Right Amount of Car Insurance

Car insurance is expensive, especially for young drivers. That should be no surprise, since the younger you are, the more likely you are to have an accident. Only about one in seven drivers is under 25 years old, but more than one quarter of the 10 million accidents that happen each year involve a driver between 16 and 24. Men are worse risks than women. It's hard to fault insurance companies for charging higher premiums to drivers who are more likely than others to file claims.

While you must have some insurance—most states require that you have *liability insurance*, to pay for damage and injuries to others if you cause an accident—you do have some choices. The most important choice is whether or not to buy collision insurance, which pays for damage to your car when the accident is your fault. If you go without it, you'll have to pay for the repairs if you cause a crash.

There is no easy way to figure out how much collision insurance to buy, but there are a few things to think about when you make your decision. First, how much is your car worth? If you do have an accident, the insurance company doesn't promise to fix your car regardless of the costs. Instead, the company will pay you what it is worth.

So if your car is old and you crash, the odds are you'll get a check, not a repaired car. Buying collision insurance on old cars is rarely worth it.

What should you do if you have a new car? Here the question is not whether to buy collision insurance but how much. The choice is in something called a *deductible*, the amount you pay for the repair after a crash. If you have a $250 deductible, you'll pay the first $250 and the insurance company will pay the rest. The higher your deductible is, the lower your insurance premium will be.

To see how much your premium can vary, let's look at an example: a 19-year-old male driving a new Saturn (a four-door sedan that cost around $13,000 in 2004). A college student living away from home, he has a good driving record and a good student discount. With a $250 collision deductible, his insurance costs about $2,400 per year. Raising the deductible to $500 would lower the premium by $150 per year, to around $2,250. Can $250 worth of extra insurance possibly be worth paying an extra $150 a year? Only if the driver expects to have an accident once every 20 months. Ideally he won't, so the extra insurance isn't worth paying for.

outcomes, the greater the risk. That's why the investment that has four possible payoffs (Table 5.3) seems riskier than the one with two possible payoffs (Table 5.2).

Thinking about risk in terms of the range of possible outcomes is straightforward. The best way to do it is to start with something that has no risk at all—a sidewalk without a hole in it or an investment with only one possible payoff. We will refer to a financial instrument with no risk at all as a risk-free investment or risk-free asset. A risk-free asset *is an investment whose future value is known with certainty and whose return is the risk-free rate of return.*[8] The payoff that you will receive from such an investment is guaranteed and cannot vary. For instance, if the risk-free return is 5 percent, a $1,000 risk-free investment will pay $1,050, its expected value, with certainty. If there is a chance that the payoff will be either more or less than $1,050, the investment is risky.

Let's compare this risk-free investment with the first investment we looked at, the one in which $1,000 had an equal chance of turning into $1,400 or $700 (see Table 5.2). That investment had the same expected return as the risk-free investment, 5 percent. The difference is that the payoff wasn't certain, so risk was involved. What caused the risk was the increase in the spread of the potential payoffs. The larger the spread, the higher the risk.

These examples suggest that we can measure risk by quantifying the spread among an investment's possible outcomes. We will look at two such measures. The first is based on a statistical concept called the *standard deviation* and is strictly a measure of spread. The second, called *value at risk,* is a measure of the riskiness of the worst case. When the hole in the sidewalk gets deep enough, you risk being killed if you fall in.

"Come on, Louis. No risk, no reward."

Variance and Standard Deviation   The variance is defined as the probability-weighted average of the squared deviations of the possible outcomes from their expected value. To calculate the variance of an investment, you can compute the expected value and then subtract it from each of the possible payoffs. Then you square each of the results, multiply it by its probability, and add up the results. In the example of the $1,000 investment that pays either $700 or $1,400, the steps are

1. Compute the expected value: $(\$1,400 \times \frac{1}{2}) + (\$700 \times \frac{1}{2}) = \$1,050$.
2. Subtract this from each of the possible payoffs:
   $\$1,400 - \$1,050 = \$350$
   $\$700 - \$1,050 = -\$350$
3. Square each of the results: $\$350^2 = 122,500$ dollars^2 and $(-\$350)^2 = 122,500$ dollars^2
4. Multiply each result times its probability and add up the results:
   $\frac{1}{2}[122,500$ dollars$^2] + \frac{1}{2}[122,500$ dollars$^2] = 122,500$ dollars^2

Writing this procedure more compactly, we get

$$\text{Variance} = \tfrac{1}{2}(\$1,400 - \$1,050)^2 + \tfrac{1}{2}(\$700 - \$1,050)^2$$
$$= 122,500 \text{ dollars}^2$$

---

[8]In most financial markets, no truly risk-free asset exists, so the risk-free rate of return is not directly observable. Regardless of our inability to measure it exactly, the risk-free rate of return remains a useful concept.

The **standard deviation** is the square root of the variance,[9] or

$$\text{Standard deviation} = \sqrt{Variance} = \sqrt{122{,}500\ dollars^2} = \$350$$

The standard deviation is more useful than the variance because it is measured in the same unit as the payoffs: dollars. (Variance is measured in dollars squared.) That means that we can convert the standard deviation into a percentage of the initial investment of $1,000, or 35 percent. This calculation provides a baseline against

[9]Note that we first find squared deviations of individual outcomes from the expected value. That's the variance. We square the differences when calculating the variance so that payoffs above and below the expected payoff don't cancel each other out. We then take the square root of the variance to get the standard deviation. This gives us a measure of the average difference between the possible payoffs in a way that treats those above and below the expected value equally.

TOOLS OF THE TRADE
The Impact of Leverage on Risk

"Funds Use Leverage to Magnify Returns, But Risks Grow Too" read a headline in *The Wall Street Journal* (November 1, 2002). What is leverage, and how does it affect risk and return? Leverage is the practice of borrowing to finance part of an investment. Common examples of leverage are borrowing to buy stock (called a *margin loan*) and borrowing to acquire a house (called a mortgage).[*] In the case of a margin loan, an investor borrows from a brokerage firm to increase the quantity of stock purchased.

To understand the effects of leverage, let's look at an investment of $1,000 with an expected return of 5 percent (a gain of $50) and a standard deviation of 35 percent ($350). That's the example in Table 5.2. What if in addition to investing $1,000 of your own, you borrow $1,000 and invest a total of $2,000? This investment strategy changes the risk involved. The reason is that the lender wants to be repaid the $1,000 loan regardless of how much your investment returns. If the investment's payoff is high, your $2,000 investment will increase in value to $2,800. After repaying the $1,000 loan, you will be left with $1,800—an increase of $800 over your initial investment of $1,000. If your investment falls in value, the $2,000 will become $1,400. After repaying the $1,000 loan, you will be left with $400—a loss of $600.

Since these two results are equally likely, the expected value of your leveraged investment is $\frac{1}{2}(\$1{,}800) + \frac{1}{2}(\$400) = \$1{,}100$. Your expected gain—

[*]Corporate borrowing through the issuance of bonds is another form of leverage. As we will see in Chapter 8, this type of leverage affects the risk of owning a firm's equity or stock.

the difference between your investment of $1,000 and its expected value of $1,100–is now $100 and your expected return is 10 percent. That's double the expected return from your investment of $1,000 without any borrowing–double what it would be without leverage. So we have part of the answer to our question: *Leverage increases the expected return.*

$$\text{St. dev.} = \sqrt{\frac{1}{2}(1{,}800 - 1{,}100)^2 + \frac{1}{2}(400 - 1{,}100)^2} = \$700$$

But what about risk? To figure it out, let's calculate the standard deviation of your leveraged investment.

The standard deviation has doubled too–*twice the expected return at twice the risk!*

We can repeat these calculations for any amount of leverage we want. For example, homebuyers commonly pay 20 percent of the price of a house with their savings and borrow the remaining 80 percent. Since mortgage lenders expect to be repaid, changes in the price of the house become gains or losses to the owner. Say you buy a $100,000 house by borrowing $80,000 and paying $20,000 from your savings, often called your *equity*. A 10 percent increase in your home's value would raise the price to $110,000. Subtracting the $80,000 you borrowed, your $20,000 down payment would become $30,000, a 50 percent increase. On the other hand, if your home's value fell by 10 percent, you would *lose* half your $20,000 down payment. *Leverage magnifies the effect of price changes* (see Figure 5.1).

which we can measure the risk of alternative investments. Given a choice between two investments with the same expected payoff, most people would choose the one with the lower standard deviation. A higher-risk investment is less desirable.

Let's compare this two-payoff investment with the one that has four possible payoffs (Table 5.3). We already concluded that the second investment is riskier, since the payoffs are more spread out. But how much riskier is it? To answer this question, let's compute the standard deviation:

$$\text{St. dev.} = \sqrt{0.1(100-1{,}050)^2 + 0.4(1{,}400-1{,}050)^2 + 0.4(700-1{,}050)^2 + 0.1(2{,}000-1{,}050)^2}$$
$$= \sqrt{0.1(950)^2 + 0.4(350)^2 + 0.4(350)^2 + 0.1(950)^2}$$
$$= \$528$$

We can use these examples to develop a formula for the impact of leverage on the expected return and standard deviation of an investment. If you borrow to purchase an asset, you increase both the expected return and the standard deviation by a leverage ratio of

$$\text{Leverage ratio} = \frac{\text{Cost of investment}}{\text{Owner's contribution to the purchase}}$$

where the "Owner's contribution to the purchase" in the denominator is just the cost of investment minus the amount borrowed. If the expected return and standard deviation of the unleveraged investment are 5 percent and 35 percent (as in our first example), then borrowing half and contributing half means that for each dollar invested, the buyer is contributing 50 cents. The formula tells us that the leverage ratio is 1/0.5, which equals 2. Thus the investment's expected return is 2 × 5 percent = 10 percent, and its standard deviation is 2 × 35 percent = 70 percent. And if the homeowner borrows 80 percent of the purchase price of the house, his or her contribution is 20 percent, so the leverage ratio is $\frac{1}{(1-80/100)} = \frac{1}{0.2} = 5$ times what it would be for someone who could buy the house outright, with no mortgage.

We have focused on the impact of leverage on risk, but leverage has at least as big an impact on value at risk. Note that for the $1,000 investment without leverage in Table 5.2, the worst case was a loss of $300, or 30 percent, half the time. If an investor borrowed 90 percent of the funds needed to make the investment, half the time the investor would lose not only the entire $100 invested but an additional $200 of borrowed funds as well. *Leverage compounds the worst possible outcome.*

Figure 5.1   The Effect of Leverage on Risk and Return

To understand leverage, picture a set of two gears, one large and one small. The movement in the price of the leveraged investment is measured by the number of revolutions in the big gear. The investor's risk and return are measured by the number of revolutions in the small gear. The bigger the big gear, the more times the small gear goes around with each revolution of the big gear. That's leverage.

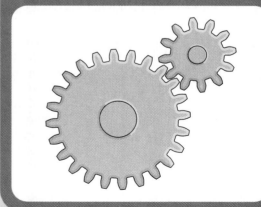

This result is much higher than the $350 standard deviation of the first investment, which has only two possible payoffs. Since the two investments have the same expected value, the vast majority of people would prefer the first. *The greater the standard deviation is, the higher the risk.*

Value at Risk   Standard deviation is the most common measure of financial risk, and for most purposes it is adequate. But in some circumstances we need to take a different approach. Sometimes we are less concerned with the spread of possible outcomes than with the value of the worst outcome. For example, no one wants the local bank to close its doors. Neither the depositors nor the government regulators care how well or badly the bank's shareholders fare as long as they do well enough to keep the doors open. The concept used to assess this sort of risk is called value at risk (VaR).

Let's assume you are considering buying a house. In going through your finances, you conclude that you can afford a monthly mortgage payment of $750 per month and not a dollar more. You find a nice house and a mortgage lender who is willing to lend you $100,000 to buy it. You expect to complete the purchase transaction and move in within six months.

Now assume that the current mortgage interest rate is 7 percent, yielding a $651 monthly payment that is well within your budget. But over the next six months, interest rates could go up or down. A decline in interest rates reduces your monthly payment, but a rise in rates increases it. This creates a risk for you. If interest rates rise high enough, the required monthly payment might exceed your budget.

Realizing your predicament, the mortgage company offers you a sort of insurance policy. It will commit to financing your mortgage at a fixed rate of 8 percent, or one percentage point above the current market rate. The alternative is to wait and take the interest rate that prevails in six months when you actually get the loan. What should you do?

To decide, start by listing the possibilities and their associated probabilities—that is, the possible interest rates and the likelihood that each one will occur. Let's assume that the rate could stay the same, rise to 10 percent, or fall to 6 percent. There is a 0.50 probability that it will stay at 7 percent, a 0.25 probability that it will rise to 10 percent, and a 0.25 probability that it will fall to 6 percent. Each of these possibilities implies a monthly payment on a 30-year, $100,000 fixed loan (see Table 5.4). The 10 percent loan means a payment of $846 (too high) and the 8 percent loan requires a monthly payment of $714.[10] Should you accept the risk of interest-rate fluctuations or take the insurance and lock in the interest rate at 8%?

The fixed rate of 8 percent is insurance against a risk, but the risk of what? We could compute the standard deviation of the monthly payment under both cases (and you should do that as an exercise). But without picking up a calculator, we know that the standard deviation of the payment associated with the 8 percent rate is zero and the standard deviation of the fluctuating rate is greater than zero. With a calculator we can figure out that the expected value of the interest rate is 7.5 percent. But what does that tell us?

In this case, the computation of the expected value and standard deviation does not seem to get at the heart of the problem. The reason is that it doesn't take proper account of the worst case, when the interest rate rises to 10 percent and your required monthly payments climb to $846 per month—well beyond your $750 budget. If that happens, you don't just lose the $132 per month difference between the guaranteed 8 percent payment and the 10 percent payment. You lose the house!

---

[10]As a rule, on a long-term mortgage, the monthly payments will approximate the interest alone. For instance, if we take a 10 percent, 30-year mortgage and compute the monthly interest rate, we get 0.797 percent. Paying the monthly interest costs $797, just $49 less than the full payment of $846.

Table 5.4   Monthly Payments on a $100,000 Mortgage

Interest Rate	Approximate Monthly Payment	Probability
10%	$846	0.25
8%	$714	—
7%	$651	0.50
6%	$589	0.25

Monthly payments on a 30-year, $100,000 fixed-rate mortgage at various interest rates.

APPLYING THE CONCEPT
GOVERNMENT-RUN LOTTERIES

Governments use lotteries to finance a range of activities, including public schools and the arts. But for lotteries to remain profitable, the people who run them must keep a large percentage of the revenue. State-run lotteries commonly pay out only 60 percent of the revenue they receive. That is, for each $1 bet on the lottery, the government pays out 60 cents. The expected value of a $1 lottery ticket is 60 cents.

Lotteries, then, are a risky investment. And since people generally don't like risk, you would think that the government would have to pay a premium to get people to play. Instead, the opposite is true. Millions of people pay good money for a very small chance to win big. As the jackpots grow larger, the lines of those waiting to buy tickets grow longer and longer. How can we explain this puzzle?

One answer is that playing the lottery is a form of entertainment, like going to the movies. But that doesn't really seem to explain it. We can use the concept of value at risk to provide a more coherent explanation. Compare paying $1 for a chance to win $1 million with paying $10,000 for a chance to win $10 billion. We see people spending $1 but not $10,000 for lottery tickets. The reason is that the risk of losing $1 is inconsequential, but the potential gain of $1 million is significant. The risk of losing $10,000, however, would loom large even compared to a payoff of $10 billion. Value-at-risk calculation tells us that the $1 lottery isn't very risky, and that's why people play.*

*Before you run out and buy a lottery ticket, think about the lottery's advertising. The people who run lotteries are allowed to advertise that they are paying a jackpot of, say, $10 million, when they are really promising to pay $500,000 per year for 20 years. At a 6 percent interest rate, the present value of 20 payments of $500,000 per year is about $6 million, not $10 million. If private companies tried to advertise that way, they would probably get into trouble.

This example highlights the fact that sometimes risk should be measured by the value of the worst case rather than by expected value and standard deviation. Value at Risk, which measures risk as the maximum potential loss, is more appropriate in a case like this. VaR is the answer to the question: How much will I lose if the worst possible disaster occurs? In the $1,000 investment summarized in Table 5.2, the worst case was a loss of $300. In the more complex $1,000 investment, summarized in Table 5.3, the value at risk was $900, the most you could possibly lose. In the mortgage example (Table 5.4), the value at risk is the house: If the payment increases to more than $750 a month, you can't make the payments on your loan. If that happens, you will be forced to sell the house and move.

A more sophisticated value-at-risk analysis would include a time horizon and probabilities. In fact, the formal definition of value at risk is *the worst possible loss over a specific time horizon, at a given probability*. For the mortgage example, the time horizon is the six months over which the interest rate can move, and the probability that the worst case will actually occur is 0.25. VaR is a measure of risk that we will find very useful in discussing the management and regulation of financial institutions. Bank managers and regulators work hard to ensure that financial collapse is an extremely remote possibility, and to do it they employ the concept of value at risk.

Risk Aversion, the Risk Premium, and the Risk-Return Trade-off

RISK

The implication of our discussion so far is that most people don't like risk and will pay to avoid it. While some people enjoy risky activities like skydiving and car racing, most of us are more careful. And while some people gamble large sums, most of us don't because we can't sustain large losses comfortably. In fact, the reason we buy insurance is that we want someone else to take the risk. Insurance is an interesting case; remember, for an insurance company to make a profit, it must charge more than it expects to pay out. Thus, insurance premiums are higher than the expected value of the policyholder's losses. We pay to avoid risks because most of us are *risk averse*.

To understand risk aversion, imagine that you are offered a single chance to play a game in which a fair coin will be tossed. If it comes up heads you will win $1,000; if it comes up tails, you will get nothing. How much would you be willing to pay to play the game just once? The expected value of the game is $500—that is, on average, the game yields $500—but you may play only one time. Would you pay $500 to play the game? If so, you are **risk neutral**. Most people would not play the game at $500, though they would at less than that amount. These people are **risk averse**.

Because the coin toss is similar to an investment, we can apply the same logic to investor behavior and conclude that *a risk-averse investor will always prefer an investment with a certain return to one with the same expected return but any amount of uncertainty.* (A risk-neutral person wouldn't care as long as the expected return is the same.) A risk-free investment with a guaranteed return is clearly preferable to a risky investment with the same expected return but an uncertain outcome. In the case of the coin toss, most people would take $500 with certainty rather than risk tossing the coin and getting double or nothing.

"I'm sorry, but you don't get frequent flyer miles for regularly investing in high risk securities."

One result of this desire to avoid risk is that investors require compensation for taking risk. That's the flip side of buying insurance. When we buy insurance, we pay someone else to take our risks, so it makes sense that if someone wants us to take on a risk, we need to be paid to do it. A risky investment, then, must have an expected return that is higher than the return on a risk-free asset. In economic terms, it must offer a risk premium. In general, *the riskier an investment (the higher the compensation investors require for holding it), the higher the risk premium* (see Figure 5.2).

By extension, if riskier investments have higher risk premiums, they must have higher expected returns. Thus, there is a trade-off between risk and expected return; you can't get a high return without taking considerable risk. So if someone tells you he or she made a big return on an investment, you should suspect that it was a very risky investment. No risk, no reward!

Sources of Risk: Idiosyncratic and Systematic Risk

Risk is everywhere. It comes in many forms and from almost every imaginable place. In most circumstances the sources of risk are obvious. For drivers, it's the risk of an accident; for farmers, the risk of bad weather; for investors, the risk of fluctuating stock prices. Regardless of the source, however, we can classify all risks into one of two groups: (1) those affecting a small number of people but no one else and (2) those

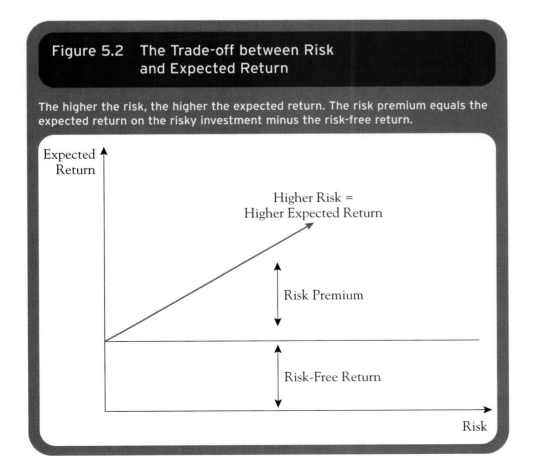

Figure 5.2   The Trade-off between Risk and Expected Return

The higher the risk, the higher the expected return. The risk premium equals the expected return on the risky investment minus the risk-free return.

How much risk should you tolerate? Figuring that out isn't easy, but there are a few ways to get some sense of the right level of risk for you. First, there are risk quizzes, short sets of questions financial advisers give their clients to determine the level of risk they can live with. For instance, "What would you do if a month after you invest in the stock market, the value of your stocks suddenly falls by 20 percent?" Answers might include "Sell right away," "Nothing," and "Buy more." Taking such a quiz is a useful first step, so you might want to try the one in Appendix 5A.

But don't stop there. Even if you are willing to take risks, that doesn't mean you should. You may not have time to make back the losses you might suffer. Think about the difference between a 25-year-old and a 60-year-old both saving for their retirement. Which one of these people can afford to suddenly lose a quarter of her savings? Obviously, it is the 25-year-old. If a 60-year-old loses a quarter of her retirement savings, it's a disaster! Likewise, if you're saving to buy a car or a home, the sooner you are planning to make the purchase, the less you can afford to lose what you have. Always ask yourself: How much can I stand to lose? The longer your time horizon (and the wealthier you are), the more risk you can tolerate.

affecting everyone. We'll call the first of these idiosyncratic or *unique risks* and the second systematic or *economywide risks*.[11]

To understand the difference between idiosyncratic and systematic risk, think about the risks facing General Motors stockholders. Why would the value of GM's stock go up or down? There are two reasons. First, there is always the risk that GM will lose its position as the largest producer of cars and trucks in the world. The fact is, DaimlerChrysler, Ford, and Toyota are working every day to take away some of GM's business. So GM may do poorly compared to its competition, and its market share may shrink (see Figure 5.3). This risk is unique to GM because if GM does poorly, someone else must be doing better. Idiosyncratic risk affects specific firms, not everyone.

The second risk GM's stockholders face is that the entire auto industry will do poorly (see Figure 5.3). This is systematic, economywide risk. If idiosyncratic risk is a change in the *share* of the auto-market pie, systematic risk is a change in the *size* of the pie. It is the risk that everyone will do poorly at the same time. Sales of cars and trucks could simply collapse for reasons that are completely unrelated to any individual company's performance.

We can apply the concept of idiosyncratic and systematic risk to the entire economy. Surely some events will affect firms like GM and Ford in one way and other firms in another way. An example would be a change in the price of oil. History tells us that when oil prices rise, auto sales fall and the automobile industry suffers. But higher oil prices improve the profits of firms that supply energy, such as ExxonMobil, Shell, and Texaco. An oil price change that is bad for GM is good for the oil companies. Looking at the economy as a whole, this is an idiosyncratic risk.

Not all idiosyncratic risks are balanced by opposing risks to other firms or industries. Some unique risks are specific to one person or company and no one else. The risk that two people will have an automobile accident is unrelated to whether anyone else has one. We include these completely independent risks in the category of idiosyncratic risks.

[11]These are also sometimes referred to as *specific* and *common risks*.

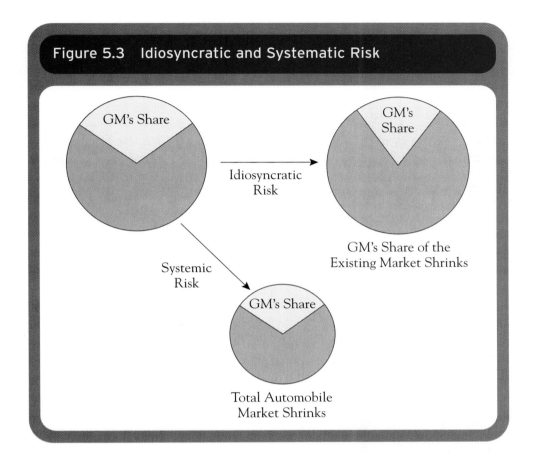

Figure 5.3   Idiosyncratic and Systematic Risk

Systematic risks affect *all* firms and individuals in the entire economy. They are economywide risks that come from changes in general economic conditions that have an impact on everyone. Macroeconomic factors, such as swings in consumer and business confidence brought on by changes in the political climate or in the global economic conditions, are the source of systematic risks.

Reducing Risk through Diversification

When George T. Shaheen left his $4 million-a-year job overseeing 65,000 employees of a large management consulting firm to become chief executive of the Webvan Group, he may not have realized how much of a risk he was taking. He thought Webvan would change the way people bought their groceries. Consumers would order their cereal, milk, apples, and ice cream over the Internet, and Webvan would deliver to their door. In November 1999, just a few months after Mr. Shaheen joined the company, his stock in Webvan was worth more than $280 million. But by April 2001, his shares were worth a paltry $150,000 and Mr. Shaheen had left the company. On July 10, 2001, Webvan collapsed and stockholders were left with nothing.

What happened to Webvan and its plan to change the way people shop? Maybe people actually like getting out of the house and going to the grocery store. But this story is about more than shopping; it's also about risk. Shaheen took on so much risk that a single big loss wiped him out. Traders in the financial markets call this experience

YOUR FINANCIAL WORLD
A Guide to Evaluating Risk

Deciding whether a risk is worth taking is extremely difficult, but some simple rules can help. Let's start with the investment described in Table 5.2, where $1,000 yields either $1,400 or $700 with equal probability. If we think about it in terms of gains and losses, this investment offers an equal chance of gaining $400 or losing $300. Should you take the risk? The answer depends on how risk averse you are, but most of us would say no. To see why, let's break the investment down into two parts, the gain and the loss (see Table 5.5).

Taking the gain first, how much would you pay for a 50 percent chance of making $400? Again, the answer depends on your risk aversion, but you surely would pay less than $200, the expected value of such an investment. Let's assume that your answer is $150.

Next, let's turn to the loss. How much would you be willing to pay to avoid a $300 loss altogether? To put it another way, assume that you risk losing $300 and are considering buying insurance against the loss. The insurance company will take the bet for you, losing the $300 in your place if that is the outcome. How much would you be willing to pay an insurance company to avoid taking a 50 percent chance of losing $300? Again, the answer depends on how risk averse you are, but we know that you will pay more than the expected value of the loss, which is $150. (The insurance company would insist on receiving more.) Let's assume you will pay $200 to avoid the loss.

Now we are ready to answer our original question: Is the value of the potential gain sufficient to compensate you for the cost of the potential loss? Subtracting the $200 that you are willing to pay to avoid the $300 loss from the $150 you will pay for the opportunity to gain $400, we get $150 − $200 = −$50, a result less than zero. In short, the potential gain is not big enough to compensate you for the potential loss, so you should not take the risk. In fact, our computation suggests you would be willing to pay $50 *not* to make this investment!

Table 5.5 Evaluating the Risk of a $1,000 Investment	
A. The Gain	
Payoff	Probability
+$400	$\frac{1}{2}$
$0	$\frac{1}{2}$
B. The Loss	
Payoff	Probability
$0	$\frac{1}{2}$
−$300	$\frac{1}{2}$

Deciding if a Risk Is Worth Taking

1. List all the possible outcomes, or payoffs.
2. Assign a probability to each possible payoff.
3. Divide the payoffs into gains and losses.
4. Ask how much you would be willing to pay to *receive* the gain.
5. Ask how much you would be willing to pay to *avoid* the loss.
6. If you are willing to pay more to receive the gain than to avoid the loss, you should take the risk.

"blowing up." Surely Shaheen could have done something to protect at least a portion of his phenomenal wealth from the risk that it would suddenly disappear. But what?

Cervantes answered this question in *Don Quixote* in 1605: "It is the part of a wise man to keep himself today for tomorrow, and *not to venture all his eggs in one basket* [emphasis added]." In today's terminology, risk can be reduced through diversification, the principle of holding more than one risk at a time. Though it may seem counterintuitive, holding several different investments can reduce the overall risk an investor bears. A combination of risky investments is often less risky than any one individual investment. There are two ways to diversify your investments. You can *hedge* risks or you can *spread* them among the many investments. Let's discuss hedging first.

Hedging Risk

Hedging is the strategy of reducing overall risk by making two investments with opposing risks. When one does poorly, the other does well, and vice versa. So while the payoff from each investment is volatile, together their payoffs are stable.

Consider the risk an investor faces from a potential change in the price of oil. Increases in the price of oil are bad for most of the economy, but they are good for oil companies. So an investor might buy stock in both General Electric (GE), maker of everything from lightbulbs to dishwashers and jet engines, and Texaco, a large oil company. For the sake of our example, let's assume that oil prices have an equal chance of rising or falling. When they rise, owners of Texaco stock receive a payoff of $120 for each $100 they invested. When oil prices fall, Texaco's shareholders just get their $100 investment back. The reverse is true for GE. When oil prices fall, owners of GE stock get $120 for each $100 they invested; when oil prices rise, they get $100.

Table 5.6 summarizes these relationships.

Let's compare three strategies for investing $100, given the relationships shown in the table:

Table 5.6	Payoffs on Two Separate Investments of $100		
	Payoff from Owning Only		
Possibility	**GE**	**Texaco**	**Probability**
Oil prices rise	$100	$120	$\frac{1}{2}$
Oil prices fall	$120	$100	$\frac{1}{2}$

1. Invest $100 in GE.
2. Invest $100 in Texaco.
3. Invest half in each company: $50 in GE and $50 in Texaco.

Regardless of whether you invest $100 in GE or Texaco, the expected payoff is $\frac{1}{2}\$120 + \frac{1}{2}\$100 = \$110$; and the

$$\text{Standard deviation of the payoff} = \sqrt{\frac{1}{2}(\$120 - \$110)^2 + \frac{1}{2}(\$100 - \$110)^2} = \$10$$

But what about the third option? What if you split your $100 and put half in GE and half in Texaco? Since $50 is half the size of your initial investment, the payoff is half as big as well—a $50 investment in either stock pays off either $60 or $50. But the important point about this strategy is that it reduces your risk (see Table 5.7). When oil prices go up, Texaco does well but GE does badly. When oil prices fall, the reverse happens. Regardless of whether oil prices go up or down, you will get back $110 on your $100 investment. Investing $50 in each stock ensures your payoff. Hedging—splitting your investment between two stocks with different payoff patterns—has eliminated your risk entirely.

Could George Shaheen have hedged the risk of owning so much Webvan stock? To do it, he would have had to find a company whose stock price would rise when Webvan's

Table 5.7 Results of Possible Investment Strategies: Hedging Risk Initial Investment = $100		
Investment Strategy	**Expected Payoff**	**Standard Deviation**
GE only	$110	$10
Texaco only	$110	$10
$\frac{1}{2}$ and $\frac{1}{2}$	$110	$0

fell. That would have been difficult, since Webvan's business concept was new and untested. But Shaheen did have another option.

Spreading Risk

Because investments don't always move predictably in opposite directions, you can't always reduce risk through hedging. Fortunately, there is another way. You can simply **spread risk** around—and that's what George Shaheen should have done. To spread your risk, all you need to do is find investments whose payoffs are unrelated. Let's replace Texaco with Microsoft and assume that GE and Microsoft's payoffs are independent of each other. So we toss a coin once to see if GE does well or badly, and then we toss it a second time to see how Microsoft does. As before, a $100 investment in either company pays off either $120 or $100 with equal probability.

Again, we'll consider three investment strategies: (1) GE only, (2) Microsoft only, and (3) half in GE and half in Microsoft. The expected payoff on each of these strategies is the same: $110. For the first two strategies, $100 in either company, the standard deviation is still $10, just as it was before. But for the third strategy, $50 in GE and $50 in Microsoft, the analysis is more complicated. There are four possible outcomes, two for each stock.

To solve the problem, we need to create a table showing all the possibilities, their probabilities, and the associated payoffs (see Table 5.8). We're familiar with possibilities 2 and 3, in which one stock pays off but the other one doesn't, just as in the GE/Texaco example. But possibilities 1 and 4 are new. To assess how risky this investment is, we need to compute its expected payoff and standard deviation of the payoff. The expected payoff is $\frac{1}{4}\$120 + \frac{1}{4}\$110 + \frac{1}{4}\$110 + \frac{1}{4}\$100 = \$110$. Using the information in the table, we can compute the standard deviation of the payoff.

St. dev. of payoff =

$$\sqrt{\frac{1}{4}(\$120-\$110)^2 + \frac{1}{4}(\$110-\$110)^2 + \frac{1}{4}(\$110-\$110)^2 + \frac{1}{4}(\$100-\$110)^2}$$

$$= \sqrt{\frac{1}{4}(\$10)^2 + \frac{1}{4}(\$0)^2 + \frac{1}{4}(\$0)^2 + \frac{1}{4}(\$10)^2}$$

$$= \sqrt{50(\text{dollars})^2} = \$7.1$$

Table 5.8   Payoffs from Investing $50 in Each of Two Stocks
Initial Investment = $100

Possibilities	GE	Microsoft	Total Payoff	Probability
#1	$60	$60	$120	$\frac{1}{4}$
#2	$60	$50	$110	$\frac{1}{4}$
#3	$50	$60	$110	$\frac{1}{4}$
#4	$50	$50	$100	$\frac{1}{4}$

Table 5.9 summarizes the results so that we can compare the three investment strategies. As we have already noted, they all have the same expected payoff, but the strategy of investing in both stocks has a lower standard deviation. By spreading your investment among independently risky investments, you have lowered your overall risk.

Measures of risk other than standard deviation will give us the same result. When you split your investment between the two stocks, 75 percent of the time the payoff is $110 or higher; only 25 percent of the time is the payoff $100. For most people, that prospect is more appealing than a 50 percent probability of getting $100 and a 50 percent probability of getting $120, the odds an investor faces in holding only one stock.

In the real world, there is no reason for an investor to stop diversifying at two stocks. The more independent sources of risk you hold in your portfolio, the lower your overall risk. Using the same numbers in this example—a payoff of either $100 or $120 per $100 investment, with equal probability—we can increase the number of stocks from two to three to four, and the standard deviation of a $100 investment will fall from $7.1 to $5.8 to $5.0. As we add more and more independent sources of risk, the standard deviation becomes negligible. (Appendix 5B explains the algebra behind this statement.)

In summary, spreading the risk is a fundamental investment strategy. As Cervantes put it (and George Shaheen learned), never put all your eggs in one basket. If Shaheen had sold his Webvan stock and invested the proceeds in a portfolio composed of many stocks representative of the stock market as a whole, he would probably still have most of his $280 million.[12] Diversification really works.

Diversification through the spreading of risk is the basis for the insurance business. A large automobile insurer writes millions of policies. It counts on the fact that not everyone will have accidents at the same time, for the risk of any one policyholder

Table 5.9   Results of Possible Investment Strategies: Spreading Risk
Initial Investment = $100

Investment Strategy	Expected Payoff	Standard Deviation
GE only	$110	$10
Microsoft only	$110	$10
$\frac{1}{2}$ and $\frac{1}{2}$	$110	$7.1

[12]Shaheen may not have been able to sell all his stock because of restrictions on sales by company executives. But he surely could have sold some of it and invested the proceeds more prudently.

IN THE NEWS
A Poor Retirement

Financial Times

by Andrew Hill and Elizabeth Wine

December 12, 2001

Enron had thousands of employees, customers, creditors, and shareholders, all of whom have been hit by the energy trader's abrupt collapse into bankruptcy 10 days ago.

But the broadest impact of the company's demise is likely to be felt by millions of working Americans who hold defined-contribution retirement savings accounts, called 401(k)s after the paragraph of the U.S. tax code that brought them into being in the early 1980s.

Under the 401(k) system, companies provide employees with a menu of investment options, generally including several choices of stock and bond mutual funds, as well as money-market funds. Frequently, companies will also offer their own stock for purchase by employees. Workers set aside a percentage of their salary each month to purchase assets for their 401(k) accounts.

Even before the Enron debacle, the benefits of 401(k)s had been called into question. William Bernstein, a principal at an investment management firm, says that high fees, a lack of understanding, and low long-term returns mean that most employees investing through 401(k)s are bound to be disappointed. "I think for the average person, 401(k)s are going to be bad and for a significant minority of people—20 to 30 percent—they are going to be very, very bad," he says.

Enron's plan suffered from particular flaws. The $2.1 billion plan offered employees 18 investment options, including a range of mutual funds and its own stock, but by the end of 2000, 60 percent of the plan was invested in Enron shares—a far higher proportion than most investors would consider prudent diversification. The allocation to Enron rose that high at least partly because Enron matched employee contributions to their own retirement accounts with company stock rather than cash.

Much of the blame for that lack of diversification falls squarely on the shoulders of Enron employees, who were not forced to choose Enron stock. But the problem was compounded by Enron "locking down" its 401(k) plan. Between October 17 and November 19, just as the crisis of confidence in the energy trader became more acute, the company stopped employees from selling Enron shares out of their plan.

Enron shares were priced at $32.20 on October 17, already a fraction of their peak of more than $80 last year. By November 19, the stock had dropped 71 percent to $9.06. With the company in bankruptcy, the shares now trade at less than a dollar.

crashing is independent of the risk of another policyholder crashing. If it writes enough policies, the company can expect a predictable number of accident claims each year. Just as when you toss a coin a million times, you know it will turn up heads 500,000 times and tails 500,000 times, assembling a large enough pool of independent risks isn't risky.

Terms

Enron was not alone in offering to match employee contributions with stock instead of cash. About 2,000 U.S. companies do so. That represents only 0.5 percent of 401(k) plans, but the practice affects a greater proportion of workers because the companies are among the biggest and oldest in the U.S. Many of the Fortune 500 companies run their plans in this manner.

Among 140 of the largest companies, the average allocation to company stock in the 401(k) plan is about 35 percent, according to the Committee on the Investment of Employee Benefit Assets, a group of corporate pension plan sponsors. At General Electric, for example, 75 percent of the defined-contribution plan consists of GE stock. About 78 percent of Coca Cola's plan is invested in the company's shares.

[W]hen it comes to taking away or restricting existing investment choices, politicians are cautious. Senator Jeff Bingaman, a Democrat from New Mexico, says retirement policy cannot be "based on the assumption that it is always going to be a sunny day" in the markets but at the same time he strongly believes in "the ability and intelligence of employees to invest their own money" in 401(k)s. David Wray, president of the Profit Sharing/401(k) Council of America (PSCA), a trade association of 1,200 companies that sponsor such plans, concurs: "This is about the long term, it isn't about getting rich in the short term or disappearing because you have a temporary downturn."

That does not convince former Enron employees such as Cregg Lancaster, a 43-year-old father of two, who has lost $100,000 in 401(k) retirement savings as well as his job. "Long-term I'm confident but it's just getting through [to] that long term," he says. Mr Lancaster did not consider selling stock from his 401(k) because it was money he had set aside for retirement. Enron seemed a solid company and a favorite of Wall Street.

It does not yet seem likely that the bankruptcy of Enron will lead to a fundamental restructuring of the U.S. retirement savings system. But whatever the impact, it has taught at least one important lesson to holders of 401(k) plans: retirement nest eggs can go down as well as up.

SOURCE: Copyright © 2001 by *The Financial Times*. Reprinted with permission.

LESSON OF THE ARTICLE

Don't put all of your eggs in one basket; diversify. Diversification is especially important for retirement savings. But Enron employees lost more than just their investment in Enron stock. They lost their jobs, too. Almost every aspect of their financial well-being was tied up in the same company. The real lesson is that you shouldn't buy stock in the company you work for. If the company goes bankrupt, as Enron did, you're in bad enough shape. You don't want your savings to go down the drain along with your job.

Chapter Lessons

1. Risk is a measure of uncertainty about the possible future payoffs of an investment. It is measured over some time horizon, relative to a benchmark.

2. Measuring risk is crucial to understanding the financial system.

   a. To study random future events, start by listing all the possibilities and assign a probability to each. Be sure the probabilities add to one.

b. The expected value is the probability-weighted sum of all possible future outcomes.

c. A risk-free asset is an investment whose future value, or payoff, is known with certainty.

d. Risk increases when the spread (or range) of possible outcomes widens but the expected value stays the same.

e. One measure of risk is the standard deviation of the possible payoffs.

f. A second measure of risk is value at risk, the worst possible loss over a specific time horizon, at a given probability.

3. A risk-averse investor

a. Always prefers a certain return to an uncertain one with the same expected return.

b. Requires compensation in the form of a risk premium in order to take risk.

c. Trades off between risk and expected return: the higher the risk, the higher the expected return risk-averse investors will require for holding an investment.

4. Risk can be divided into idiosyncratic risk, which is specific to a particular business or circumstance, and systematic risk, which is common to everyone.

5. There are two types of diversification:

a. Hedging, in which investors reduce risk by making investments with offsetting payoff patterns.

b. Spreading, in which investors reduce risk by making investments with independent payoff patterns.

Problems

1. Consider a game in which a coin will be flipped three times. For each heads you will be paid $100. Assume that the coin has a two-thirds probability of coming up heads.

a. Construct a table of the possibilities and probabilities in this game.

b. Compute the expected value of the game

c. How much would you be willing to pay to play this game?

d. Consider the effect of a change in the game so that if tails comes up twice in a row, you get nothing. How would your answers to the first three parts of this question change?

2. Begin with the $1,000 investment depicted in Table 5.2.

a. Recompute the payoff and the payoff times the probability as percentages rather than dollars. Then compute the expected value and standard deviation of the percentage return.

b. Repeat this exercise using the investment in Table 5.3.

3. An investor is boasting about his ability to obtain a better return than everyone else's. Using the tools in this chapter, how would you explain his performance?

4. You are the founder of IGRO, an Internet firm that delivers groceries.

a. Describe the idiosyncratic and systematic risks your company faces.

b. As founder of the company, you own a significant portion of the firm, and your personal wealth is highly concentrated in IGRO shares. What risks do you face, and how should you try to reduce them?

5. Assume that the economy can experience high growth, normal growth, or recession. You expect the following stock-market returns for the coming year under these conditions.

State of the Economy	Probability	Return
High Growth	0.2	+30%
Normal Growth	0.7	+12%
Recession	0.1	−15%

   a. Compute the expected value of a $1,000 investment both in dollars and as a percentage over the coming year.

   b. Compute the standard deviation of the return as a percentage over the coming year.

   c. If the risk-free return is 7 percent, what is the risk premium for a stock-market investment?

6. You can save $5,000 per year from your salary and currently have $15,000 in savings. One year from now you hope to purchase a house for $100,000. To obtain a mortgage you can afford, you will need a down payment equal to 20 percent of the purchase price of the house. You have two possible investments available. The first is a risk-free bond that pays 5 percent; the second is the stock-market investment described in problem 5. How would you decide which investment to make?

7. An investment advisor offers you an opportunity to buy a financial instrument with the following payoffs.

State of the Economy	Probability	Return
High Growth	0.2	−10%
Normal Growth	0.7	+4%
Recession	0.1	+8%

Assuming that you also have available the opportunity in problem 5, is this investment valuable to you? Why or why not?

8. You are a typical American investor. An insurance broker calls and asks if you would be interested in an investment with a high payoff if the annual Indian monsoons are less damaging than normal. If damage is high, you will lose your investment. On calculating the expected return, you realize that it is roughly the same as that of the stock market. Is this opportunity valuable to you? Why or why not?

9. Among the many consequences of Enron's bankruptcy in 2001 was the loss of savings Enron employees suffered. Roughly 47 percent of employee pension funds

were invested in Enron stock. Why was this investment so risky? How could the risk have been reduced?

10. In Table 5.4, what interest rate is consistent with your $750 threshold? That is, what maximum interest rate will you accept to insure against the possibility of interest rates and payments rising above your means?

11. Car insurance companies eliminate risk (or come close) by selling a large number of policies. Explain how they do this.

12. One morning you are intrigued by an e-mail offering you income insurance. A company has formed to guarantee college students a fixed income for the rest of their lives. As payment, you have to agree to give them your salary. Is this the sort of insurance people are likely to buy? Will the company be able to stay in business?

13. Mortgages increase the risk faced by homeowners.

    a. Explain how.

    b. What happens to the homeowner's risk as the down payment on the house rises from 10 percent to 50 percent?

14. Banks pay substantial amounts to monitor the risks that they take. One of the primary concerns of a bank's risk managers is to compute the value at risk. Why is value at risk so important for a bank (or any financial institution)?

15. How much would you be willing to pay for the investment described in Table 5.3? Explain why it is more or less than $1,050.

Appendix 5A

A Quick Test to Measure Your Risk Tolerance[*]

The following quiz is adapted from one prepared by the T. Rowe Price group of mutual funds. It can help you figure out how comfortable you are with varying degrees of investment risk. Other things being equal, your risk tolerance is a useful guide for deciding how heavily you should weight your portfolio toward low- or high-risk investments.

1. You are the winner of a TV game show. Which prize would you choose?
   - $2,000 cash (1 point).
   - A 50 percent chance to win $4,000 (3 points).
   - A 20 percent chance to win $10,000 (5 points).
   - A 2 percent chance to win $100,000 (9 points).

2. You are down $500 in a poker game. How much more would you be willing to bet to win the $500 back?
   - $500 (6 points).
   - $250 (4 points).
   - $100 (2 points).
   - Nothing. You'll cut your losses and quit now (1 point).

3. A month after you invest in a stock, it suddenly goes up 15 percent. With no further information, what would you do?
   - Hold it, hoping for further gains (3 points).
   - Sell it and take your gains (1 point).
   - Buy more. It will probably go higher (4 points).

4. Your investment suddenly goes down 15 percent. Its fundamentals still look good. What would you do?
   - Buy more. If it looked good at the original price, it looks even better now (4 points).
   - Hold on and wait for it to come back (3 points).
   - Sell it to avoid losing even more (1 point).

5. You are a key employee in a start-up company. You can choose one of two ways to take your year-end bonus. Which would you pick?
   - $1,500 cash (1 point).
   - Company stock options that could bring you $15,000 next year if the company succeeds but will be worthless if it fails (5 points).

Your score: _____

[*]From Jack Kapoor, Les Dlabay, Robert J. Hughes, *Personal Finance* (New York: McGraw-Hill, 2004).

www.mhhe.com/cecchettile

Scoring

5–18 points: You are a conservative investor. You prefer to minimize financial risks. The lower your score, the more cautious you are. When you choose investments, look for high credit ratings, well-established records, and an orientation toward stability. In stocks, bonds, and real estate, focus on income.

19–30 points: You are a less conservative investor. You are willing to take more chances in pursuit of greater rewards. The higher your score, the bolder you are and the more risk you are willing to take. You may want to consider bonds with higher yields and lower credit ratings, the stocks of newer companies, and real estate investments that use mortgage debt.

Appendix 5B

The Mathematics of Diversification

With a small amount of mathematics, we can show how diversification reduces risk. Let's begin with two investments in GE and Texaco. We'll label the payoffs to these investments x and y. If x is the payoff to buying GE stock, then it must equal either $120 or $100, each with a probability of one-half (see Table 5.6). Then y is the payoff to buying Texaco stock.

Hedging Risk

In the chapter, we considered splitting our investment between GE and Texaco. If x and y are the payoff from holding GE and Texaco, respectively, then the payoff on the investment is

$$\text{Investment payoff} = \tfrac{1}{2}x + \tfrac{1}{2}y \qquad (A1)$$

What is the variance of this payoff? (Since the standard deviation is the square root of the variance, the two must move together—a lower variance means a lower standard deviation—so we can skip the standard deviations.) In general, the variance of any weighted sum $ax + by$ is

$$\text{Var}(ax + by) = a^2\text{Var}(x) + b^2\text{Var}(y) + 2ab\,\text{Cov}(x,y), \qquad (A2)$$

where Var is the variance and Cov is the covariance. While the variance measures the extent to which each payoff moves on its own, the covariance measures the extent to which two risky assets move together. If the two payoffs rise and fall together, then the covariance will be positive. If one payoff rises while the other falls, then the covariance will be negative.

It is useful to express these quantities symbolically. Assume that p_i is the probability associated with a particular outcome x_i. Then the expected value of x is the probability-weighted sum of the possible outcomes.

$$\text{Expected value of } x = E(x) = \bar{x} = \sum_i p_i x_i. \qquad (A3)$$

As described in the chapter (page 97), the variance of x is the probability-weighted sum of the squared deviations of x from the expected value.

$$\text{Variance of } x = \text{Var}(x) = \sigma_x^2 = \sum_i p_i(x_i - \bar{x})^2. \qquad (A4)$$

The covariance of x and y is defined analogously as

$$\text{Covariance of } x \text{ and } y = \text{Cov}(x,y) = \sigma_{x,y} = \sum_i p_i\,(x_i - \bar{x})\,(y_i - \bar{y}). \qquad (A5)$$

In our GE/Texaco examples $a = b = \tfrac{1}{2}$, so

$$\text{Var(Investment payoff)} = \tfrac{1}{4}\text{Var}(x) + \tfrac{1}{4}\text{Var}(y) + \tfrac{1}{2}\text{Cov}(x,y) \qquad (A6)$$

We know from Table 5.7 that the expected payoff to GE and Texaco is $110 each and the standard deviation is $10 as well. The variance is the standard deviation squared, so it is 100. What about the covariance? We can compute it easily from Table 5.6:

$$\text{Cov(Payoff on GE and Texaco)} = \tfrac{1}{2}(100-110)(120-110) + \tfrac{1}{2}(120-110)(100-110) = -100 \qquad \text{(A7)}$$

Substituting this value into the formula for the variance of the investment payoff, we get

$$\text{Var(Investment payoff)} = \tfrac{1}{4}(100) + \tfrac{1}{4}(100) - \tfrac{1}{2}(100) = 0 \qquad \text{(A8)}$$

The fact that the covariance is negative means that the variance, or risk, in a portfolio containing both GE and Texaco stock is lower than the risk in a portfolio containing one or the other. The stocks act as hedges for each other.

Spreading Risk

Showing how spreading reduces risk is a bit more complex. Let's consider spreading our investment between GE and Microsoft. Again, the variance of the investment payoff depends on the variances of the individual stock payoffs and on their covariance. But here we must assume that the covariance between the GE and Microsoft payoffs is zero. That is, they are independent of each other. As before, each stock has a variance of 100, so the variance of a portfolio that is split half and half is

$$\text{Var(Investment payoff)} = \tfrac{1}{4}(100) + \tfrac{1}{4}(100) = 50, \qquad \text{(A9)}$$

and the standard deviation is 7.1 (see Table 5.9).

This result suggests that individual stocks or groups of stocks with independent payoffs are potentially valuable, as they will reduce risk. Let's consider an arbitrary number of independent investments, each with the same individual variance. What is the variance of an equally weighted portfolio of these investments? Assume that the number of investments is n, each with the same expected payoff, $\bar{x}$, and the same variance, σ_x^2. We hold $1/n$ of our portfolio in each stock, so the expected payoff is

$$\text{Expected payoff} = \frac{1}{n}\sum_{i=1}^{n} x_i = \bar{x} \qquad \text{(A10)}$$

Since the payoff on each stock is independent of all the rest, the covariances are all zero. So the variance is

$$\text{Variance of payoff} = \left(\frac{1}{n}\right)^2 \sum_{i=1}^{n} \sigma_x^2 = \frac{\sigma_x^2}{n} \qquad \text{(A11)}$$

That is, the variance of the payoff on a portfolio of n independent stocks is the variance divided by n. Most important, as n increases, the variance declines, so when the value of n is very large, the variance is essentially zero.

In summary, spreading exposure to risk among a wide range of independent risks reduces the overall risk of a portfolio. As we saw in this chapter, this is the strategy that insurance companies use. While the payoff to an individual policyholder is highly uncertain, the payoffs to a large group of policyholders are almost unrelated. By selling millions of insurance policies, the company reduces the payoffs it must make and simply pays the expected value.

Chapter 6

Bonds, Bond Prices, and the Determination of Interest Rates

Virtually any financial arrangement involving the current transfer of resources from a lender to a borrower, with a transfer back at some time in the future, is a form of bond. Car loans, home mortgages, even credit card balances all create a loan from a financial intermediary to an individual making a purchase—just like the bonds governments and large corporations sell when they need to borrow.

When companies like General Motors, AT&T, or General Electric need to finance their operations, they sell bonds. When the U.S. Treasury or a state government needs to borrow, it sells bonds. And they do it billions of dollars at a time. In 2003 alone, U.S. corporations raised $750 billion through bonds, adding to the nearly $13 trillion they had already borrowed. Federal, state, and local American governments have more than $11 trillion in outstanding debt as well.[1] The ease with which individuals, corporations, and governments borrow is essential to the functioning of our economic system. Without this free flow of resources through the bond markets, the economy would grind to a halt.

"The name's Bond. Duane Bond."

Historically, we can trace the concept of using bonds to borrow to monarchs' almost insatiable appetite for resources. To maintain lavish lifestyles, fight wars, and explore the globe, kings, princes, and other rulers drew on every available source of financing. Even with these incentives, after thousands of years of civilization only a few possibilities had been developed: outright confiscation; taxation, which is a mild form of confiscation; debasement of currency, in which people are required to exchange their coins for ones that weigh less—in effect, a tax on currency; and borrowing. Monarchs who borrowed directly from international bankers frequently defaulted or failed to make the loan payments they had promised. Between 1557 and 1696, the various kings of Spain defaulted 14 times. With that track record, it's no wonder they had to pay interest rates close to 40 percent.

The Dutch invented modern bonds to finance their lengthy war of independence against those same Spanish kings who defaulted on loans in the 16th and 17th centuries. Over the next two centuries, the British refined the use of bonds to finance

---

[1]These numbers come from the *Flow of Funds Accounts of the United States,* published quarterly by the Federal Reserve Board. For U.S. corporations, the new borrowing is the sum of Table F2 line 19, "Credit Market Borrowing by Nonfinancial Business," plus Table F3 line 6, "Credit Market Borrowing by Private Financial Sectors," and includes commercial paper as well as long-term bonds. The quantities outstanding are the equivalent values from Tables L2 and L3. For the government, the numbers are the sum of Table L2 lines 2 and 23 plus Table L3 line 2; these include debt issued by government-sponsored entities.

government activities. The practice then spread to other countries. Alexander Hamilton, the first Secretary of the U.S. Treasury and the man whose face appears on the $10 bill, brought bonds to the United States. One of Hamilton's first acts after the formation of the U.S. Treasury in 1789 was to consolidate all the debt remaining from the Revolutionary War. This resulted in the first U.S. government bonds. While the depth and complexity of bond markets have increased in modern times, many of their original features remain.

If we want to understand the financial system, particularly the bond market, we must understand three things. The first is the relationship between bond prices and interest rates (yet another application of present value). The second is that supply and demand in the bond market determine the price of bonds. The third is why bonds are risky. Let's get started.

Bond Prices

A standard bond specifies the fixed amounts to be paid and the exact dates of the payments. *How much should you be willing to pay for a bond?* The answer depends on the bond's characteristics. We will look at four basic types:

1. *Zero-coupon bonds*, which promise a single future payment, such as a U.S. Treasury bill.
2. *Fixed-payment loans*, such as conventional mortgages.
3. *Coupon bonds*, which make periodic interest payments and repay the principal at maturity. U.S. Treasury bonds and most corporate bonds are coupon bonds.
4. *Consols*, which make periodic interest payments forever, never repaying the principal that was borrowed. (There aren't many examples of these.)

Let's see how each of these bonds is priced. To keep the analysis simple, we'll ignore risk for now.

Zero-Coupon Bonds

U.S. Treasury bills (commonly known as T-bills) are the most straightforward type of bond. Each T-bill represents a promise by the U.S. government to pay $100 on a fixed future date. There are no coupon payments, which is why T-bills are known as zero-coupon bonds. They are also called pure discount bonds, since the price is less than their face value—they sell at a discount. This isn't a discount in the sense of a markdown at a clothing store, however. If a $100 face value T-bill sells for $96, the $4 difference is the interest, the payment to the lender for making the loan.

Since a Treasury bill makes a single payment on a future date, its price is just the present value of that payment:

$$\text{Price of \$100 face value zero-coupon bond} = \frac{\$100}{(1+i)^n} \tag{1}$$

where i is the interest rate expressed in decimal form and n is the time until the payment is made, measured in the same time units as the interest rate. Suppose the annual interest rate is 4 percent. What is the price of a one-year T-bill? To figure out the answer, take the present value formula, set i at 0.04 and n at 1, and then compute the price:

$$\text{Price of one-year Treasury bill} = \frac{\$100}{(1+0.04)} = \$96.15 \tag{2}$$

The U.S. Treasury doesn't issue T-bills with a maturity of more than one year; six-month T-bills are much more common. At an annual interest rate of 4 percent, what is the price of such a zero-coupon bond? We can use the present-value formula, again, but this time we have to be careful. Recall that we need to measure i and n in the same unit. Since i is the interest rate for one year, we need to measure n in years, and since six months is half a year,

TIME

$$\text{Price of a six - month Treasury bill} = \frac{\$100}{(1+0.04)^{1/2}} = \$98.06 \qquad (3)$$

As you can see, the price of a six-month Treasury bill is higher than that of a one-year T-bill. The shorter the time until the payment is made, the more we are willing to pay for it now. If we go on to compute the price of a three-month T-bill, setting n at 0.25 (one-fourth of a year), we find the answer is $99.02.

Equation (1) shows that for a zero-coupon bond, the relationship between the price and the interest rate is the same as the one we saw in our discussion of present value. When the price moves, the interest rate moves with it, albeit in the opposite direction. Thus we can compute the interest rate from the price using the present-value formula. For example, if the price of a one-year T-bill is $96, then the interest rate is $i = \frac{\$100}{\$96} - 1 = 0.0417$, or 4.17 percent.

Fixed-Payment Loans

Home mortgages and car loans are called *fixed-payment loans* because they promise a fixed number of equal payments at regular intervals. These loans are *amortized*, meaning that the borrower pays off the principal along with the interest over the life of the loan. Each payment includes both interest and a portion of the principal. Pricing these sorts of loans is straightforward using the present-value formula: The value of the loan today is the present value of all the payments. If we assume that the annual interest rate is i (measured as a decimal) and that the loan specifies n payments, then

$$\begin{array}{l}\text{Value of a fixed-} \\ \text{payment loan}\end{array} = \frac{\text{Fixed payment}}{(1+i)} + \frac{\text{Fixed payment}}{(1+i)^2} + \ldots + \frac{\text{Fixed payment}}{(1+i)^n} \qquad (4)$$

Using this formula is complicated, so we won't go any further.[2] But when lenders figure out your monthly payment for a car loan or home mortgage, this is how they do it.

Coupon Bonds

Recall from Chapter 4 that the issuer of a coupon bond promises to make a series of periodic interest payments called coupon payments, plus a principal payment at maturity. So we can value a coupon bond using (you guessed it) the present-value formula. The price of the coupon bond is

$$P_{CB} = \left[\frac{\text{Coupon payment}}{(1+i)^1} + \frac{\text{Coupon payment}}{(1+i)^2} + \ldots + \frac{\text{Coupon payment}}{(1+i)^n} \right] + \frac{\text{Face value}}{(1+i)^n} \qquad (5)$$

The right side of this equation has two parts. The first part, in brackets, looks just like the fixed-payment loan—and it is, with the important exception that it represents only the interest. The second part, on the far right, looks just like a zero-coupon bond, and it is. It represents the value of the promise to repay the principal at maturity.

[2]The appendix to Chapter 4 shows the computations required to find the price of a finite stream of payments. Spreadsheets and financial calculators have built-in functions to perform this task.

YOUR FINANCIAL WORLD
Are You Making an Interest-Free Loan to the IRS?

If you receive a tax refund, you are making an interest-free loan to the IRS. And while most people are happy to get a refund, they shouldn't be. When you work, your employer takes a portion of your wages from every paycheck and sends it to the Internal Revenue Service (IRS) at the U.S. Treasury. This process is called *withholding*. The government requires withholding to lower the risk that individuals won't pay the full amount they owe for the year when income tax comes due on April 15.

If you get a tax refund, the government has been holding more of your salary than necessary. Most people fail to consider that by allowing extra withholding, they have forgone a variety of other uses for their funds. Add to this the fact that the government's refund checks do not include interest and you need to spend time filling out forms to

get your money back, and it becomes clear that tax refunds are not such a good deal after all. Of course, the government likes receiving interest-free loans from taxpayers, so the tax withholding system is designed to make it much easier for people to overpay than to underpay.

For those who have difficulty saving, either because they are on a tight budget or because they simply aren't disciplined in their spending habits, overpaying taxes and "letting the IRS save for you" may make sense. But many people would benefit from reducing their tax withholding and putting that same amount in an interest-bearing bank account instead. To find out how to do this, go to the IRS Web site at www.irs.gov. The site includes a withholding calculator that can help you to stop making interest-free loans to the government.

Consols

Another type of bond offers only periodic payments. That is, the borrower pays only interest, never repaying the principal. These loans, called consols or perpetuities, are like coupon bonds whose payments last forever. Because governments are really the only borrowers that can credibly promise to make payments forever, there are no privately issued consols. You won't be surprised to learn that the price of a consol is the present value of all the future interest payments. The fact that the number of payments is infinite complicates things. But we can derive a formula for the price of a consol that makes a coupon payment every year forever.[3] At interest rate i,

$$P_{Consol} = \frac{\text{Yearly coupon payment}}{i} \qquad (6)$$

The price of a consol equals the annual coupon payment divided by the interest rate. So at an interest rate of 5 percent, a consol that promises $1 per year forever

---

[3]You may find it troubling that you can add up an infinite number of payments and get a finite number. To see why this works, notice that as the number of years at which the terminal payment occurs increases, $1/(1 + i)^n$ grows very small. After 100 years, at an interest rate of 5 percent, it is 0.008. So the present value of $1 promised in 100 years is less than one cent. We could just ignore the payments that come after this and get virtually the same answer. To derive the expression for the price of a consol, use the techniques from Appendix 4. Start by calling C the coupon payment and writing the price as the sum of the present value of the (infinite) number of payments $P_{Consol} = \frac{C}{(1+i)} + \frac{C}{(1+i)^2} + \frac{C}{(1+i)^3} + \cdots$. Next, multiply this expression by $[1/(1 + i)]$ to get

$\frac{1}{(1+i)} P_{Consol} = \frac{C}{(1+i)^2} + \frac{C}{(1+i)^3} + \frac{C}{(1+i)^4} + \cdots$. Then subtract this expression from the original, which gives

$P_{Consol} - \frac{1}{(1+i)} P_{Consol} = \frac{C}{(1+i)}$. Solving for the price yields equation (6).

would sell for $20. If the interest rate changes to 4 percent, the price rises to $25. Again, the interest rate and the price move in opposite directions.

Bond Yields

Now that we know how to calculate a bond price given the interest rate, we need to move in the other direction and calculate the interest rate, or the return to an investor, implicit in the bond's price. Doing so means combining information about the promised payments with the price to obtain what is called the *yield*—a measure of the cost of borrowing and the reward for lending. When people talk about bonds they use the terms *yield* and *interest rate* interchangeably, so we will too.

Yield to Maturity

The most useful measure of the return on holding a bond is called the yield to maturity, or the yield bondholders receive if they hold the bond to its maturity when the final principal payment is made. Take a $100 face value 5 percent coupon bond with one year to maturity. At maturity, the owner of this bond receives a coupon payment of $5 plus a principal payment of $100.[4] Using the formula from equation (5), we know that the price of the bond is

$$\text{Price of one-year 5 percent coupon bond} \ = \frac{\$5}{(1+i)} + \frac{\$100}{(1+i)} \qquad (7)$$

The value of i that solves this equation is the *yield to maturity*. Remembering that present value and interest rates move in opposite directions, we can conclude the following:

1. If the price of the bond is $100, then the yield to maturity equals the coupon rate. (Recall from Chapter 4 that the coupon rate is the ratio of the annual coupon payments to the face value of the bond.)
2. Since the price rises as the yield falls, when the price is *above* $100, the yield to maturity must be *below* the coupon rate.
3. Since the price falls as the yield rises, when the price is *below* $100, the yield to maturity must be *above* the coupon rate.

Looking at the one-year 5 percent coupon bond, we can see right away that if the yield to maturity is 5 percent, then $\frac{\$5}{(1+0.05)} + \frac{\$100}{(1+0.05)} = \frac{\$105}{1.05} = \$100$. That's the first point. Now look at what happens when yield to maturity falls to 4 percent. The price becomes $\frac{\$5}{(1+0.04)} + \frac{\$100}{(1+0.04)} = \frac{\$105}{1.04} = \$100.96$. That's the second point. If the yield to maturity rises to 6 percent, then the price falls to $\frac{\$5}{(1+0.06)} + \frac{\$100}{(1+0.06)} = \$99.06$. That's the third point. You can try this process with a more complicated bond—say, one with 10 years to maturity that makes more than just one coupon payment—and get exactly the same results.

The fact that the return on a bond depends on the price you pay for it really isn't that mysterious. If you pay $95 for a $100 face value bond, for example, you will receive both the interest payments and the increase in value from $95 to $100. This rise in value, referred to as a capital gain, is part of the return on your investment. So when the price of the bond is below the face value, the return is above the coupon rate. When the price is above the face value, the bondholder incurs a capital loss and the bond's yield to maturity falls below its coupon rate.

---

[4]Most bonds offer two semiannual payments, each equal to half the annual coupon. We will ignore this complication.

Current Yield

Current yield is a commonly used, easy-to-compute measure of the proceeds the bond-holder receives for making a loan. It is the yearly coupon payment divided by the price:

$$\text{Current yield} = \frac{\text{Yearly coupon payment}}{\text{Price paid}} \tag{8}$$

Looking at this expression, we can see that the current yield measures that part of the return from buying the bond that arises solely from the coupon payments. It ignores the capital gain or loss that arises when the price at which the bond is purchased differs from its face value. So if the price is below par, the current yield will be below the yield to maturity.

Let's return to the one-year 5 percent coupon bond and assume that it is selling for $99. The current yield is easy to calculate as $\frac{5}{99}$ = 0.0505, or 5.05 percent. The yield to maturity for this bond is the solution to $\frac{\$5}{(1+i)} + \frac{\$100}{(1+i)}$ = $99, which is 6.06 percent. The point is that if you buy the bond for $99, one year later you get not only the $5 coupon payment but also a guaranteed $1 capital gain, so that your total compensation is $6.

We can repeat these calculations for a case in which the bond is selling for $101. The current yield in that case is $\frac{5}{101}$ = 0.0495, or 4.95 percent, and the yield to maturity is $\frac{\$5}{(1+i)} + \frac{\$100}{(1+i)}$ = $101, or 3.96 percent.

Putting all this together, we see the relationship between the current yield and the coupon rate. Again, it comes from the fact that current yield moves in the opposite direction from the price: it falls when the bond's price goes up and rises when the price goes down. So when the price equals the face value of the bond, the current yield and coupon rate are equal. When the price rises above the face value, the current yield falls below the coupon rate. And when the price falls below the face value, the current yield rises above the coupon rate.

Table 6.1 summarizes the relationships among the price, coupon rate, current yield, and yield to maturity. We know that when the bond price is less than face value, the current yield and the yield to maturity are both higher than the coupon rate. But since the yield to maturity takes account of the capital gain the bondholder receives, while the current yield does not, the yield to maturity must be even higher than the current yield. When the price is above the face value, the yield to maturity is lower than the current yield, which is lower than the coupon rate.

Holding Period Returns

We have emphasized that if you buy a bond whose yield to maturity deviates from the coupon rate, the price will not be the face value. Similarly, the return from holding a

---

Table 6.1   Relationship among a Bond's Price and Its Coupon Rate, Current Yield, and Yield to Maturity

- *Bond price < Face value:* Coupon rate < Current yield < Yield to maturity
- *Bond price = Face value:* Coupon rate = Current yield = Yield to maturity
- *Bond price > Face value:* Coupon rate > Current yield > Yield to maturity

bond need not be the coupon rate. For example, if you pay $95 for a one-year 6-percent coupon bond, one year later you will get both the $6 coupon payment and the $5 difference between the purchase price and the $100 face value at maturity. But this example is really too simple, since it assumes that the investor holds the bond to maturity. Most holders of long-term bonds plan to sell them well before they mature. And since the price of the bond may change between the time of the purchase and the time of the sale, the return to buying a bond and selling it before it matures—the holding period return—can differ from the yield to maturity.

Take an example in which you pay $100 for a 10-year, 6-percent coupon bond with a face value of $100. You intend to hold the bond for one year. That is, you are going to buy a 10-year bond and then a year later, you'll sell a 9-year bond. What is your return from holding this bond? If the interest rate doesn't change (that is, it stays at 6 percent) your return will be $\frac{\$6}{\$100}$ = 0.06, or 6 percent. But if the interest rate changes, calculating your return becomes more complicated. Say that over the year you hold the bond, the interest rate falls from 6 to 5 percent. That is, the yield to maturity falls to 5 percent. Using equation (5), we can figure out that you have bought a 10-year bond for $100 and sold a 9-year bond for $107.11. What is your one-year holding period return on the initial $100 investment? It has two parts: the $6 coupon payment and the $7.11 capital gain (the difference between the price at which you bought the bond and the price at which you sold it). So the holding period return is

$$\text{One-year holding period return} = \frac{\$6}{\$100} + \frac{\$107.11 - \$100}{\$100} = \frac{\$13.11}{\$100} = 0.1311 \qquad (9)$$

$$= 13.11 \text{ percent}$$

Obviously, bond prices can go down as well as up. Consider what happens if the yield to maturity rises to 7 percent so that the price falls to $93.48. Now the one-year holding period return is

$$\text{One-year holding period return} = \frac{\$6}{\$100} + \frac{\$93.48 - \$100}{\$100} = \frac{-\$.52}{\$100} = -0.0052 \qquad (10)$$

$$= -0.52 \text{ percent}$$

The coupon payment still represents a 6 percent return, but the capital loss from the price movement is 6.52 percent. The one-year holding period return is negative, as overall there is a small loss.

To generalize these examples, look at equations (9) and (10) and notice that the one-year holding period return is the sum of the yearly coupon payment divided by the price paid for the bond, and the change in the price (price sold minus price paid) divided by the price paid:

$$\text{Holding period return} = \frac{\text{Yearly coupon payment}}{\text{Price paid}} + \frac{\text{Change in price of bond}}{\text{Price paid}} \qquad (11)$$

The first part on the right-hand side of this equation is the current yield (equation 8). The second part is the capital gain. So the holding period return is

$$\text{Holding period return} = \text{Current yield} + \text{Capital gain} \qquad (12)$$

Whenever the price of a bond changes, there is a capital gain or loss. The greater the price change, the more important a part of the holding period return the capital gain or loss becomes. The potential for interest-rate movements and changes in bond prices

TOOLS OF THE TRADE
Reading the Bond Page

Every day *The Wall Street Journal* lists the previous day's closing prices and yields for a wide variety of bonds, including U.S. Treasury bills and bonds and corporate bonds. The data in Table 6.2 are taken from the *Market Data Center* at www.wsj.com and are also available in the *Money & Investing* section of the print edition. Let's see how to read this information.

Table 6.2 Sample Bond Quotations

U.S. Government Bonds and Notes

Rate	Maturity Mo/Yr	Bid	Asked	Chg	Asked Yield
7.500	Feb 05n	102:27	102:28	−1	1.67
6.500	Oct 06n	108:09	108:10	2	2.52
2.625	May 08n	98:13	98:14	5	3.06
3.250	Jan 09n	99:29	99:30	6	3.26
5.750	Aug 10n	111:08	111:09	8	3.64
4.000	Feb 14n	98:13	98:14	9	4.20
10.375	Nov 09	102:09	102:10	−1	0.91
10.625	Aug 15	154:13	154:14	13	4.34
5.375	Feb 31	105:07	105:08	15	5.01

U.S. Treasury Bills

Maturity	Days to Mat.	Bid	Asked	Chg	Ask Yield
Aug 19 04	5	1.33	1.32	0.03	1.34
Oct 21 04	68	1.39	1.38	−0.01	1.40
Dec 09 04	117	1.52	1.51	. . .	1.54
Feb 10 05	180	1.68	1.67	−0.02	1.71

U.S. Treasury Strips

Maturity	Type	Bid	Asked	Chg.	Asked Yield
Aug 05	np	98:04	98:04	1	1.91
Nov 09	bp	82:20	82:20	8	3.68
Nov 14	ci	62:26	62:26	10	4.59

Corporate Bonds

Company	Coupon	Maturity	Last Price	Last Yield	Estimated Spread
General Motors (GM)	8.375	Jul 15 2033	104.831	7.945	293
Wal-Mart (WMT)	6.875	Aug 10 2009	113.138	3.942	54
Bear Stearns (BSC)	4.500	Oct 28 2010	100.316	4.440	106

Representative over-the-counter quotations based on transactions of $1 million or more. U.S. Treasury bond, note, and bill quotes are for midafternoon. Source: *The Wall Street Journal*, August 16, 2004, various pages in Section C.

U.S. Government Bonds and Notes

In recent years the Treasury of the United States has issued over 150 different coupon-bearing instruments. Table 6.2 shows just a few. We'll read across the table from left to right.

Rate. Column 1 reports the coupon rate that a note or bond pays. The rate of 6.500 for Bond A means that the holder will receive two semiannual payments of $3.250 for each $100 of face value held.

Maturity. Column 2 shows the date on which the principal and final interest payment are paid. The U.S. Treasury makes payments on the 15th of the month, so the owner of an Aug 10 bond will receive payment on August 15, 2010. The *n* following the date of Bond B signifies that it is a U.S. Treasury note, meaning that it had a somewhat shorter maturity than a bond when issued.[*] (The only difference between U.S. Treasury bonds and notes is their time to maturity when they are issued. Notes mature in more than one and not more than 10 years. Bonds mature more than 10 years from their issue date.)

Bid and Asked. Bond dealers are usually ready to buy or sell as long as you're willing to meet their price. Column 3 is the price at which the dealers are willing to buy—they're *bidding*—and Column 4 is the price at which they are willing to sell—they're *asking*. These prices are for each $100 of face value and are quoted in 32nds, not in standard decimal form. For Bond A, the bid of 108:09 means that an investor can sell each $100 of face value for $108 + 9/32, or $108.28. The difference between the bid and the ask prices represents the *spread,* which can be thought of as a fee the dealer charges for the service of buying and selling the bond.

Chg. Column 5 shows the change since the previous day in the bid price of the bond, measured in 32nds.

Asked Yield. Column 6 shows the yield to maturity computed using the ask price. If investors purchased the bond at the ask price, this is the yield to maturity they would receive.[†]

U.S. Treasury Bills

The first two column headings for bills differ from the ones for bonds because there is no coupon rate. (These are all zero-coupon bonds.) Instead, the first column in this section reports the maturity date when the payment will be made; the second column indicates the number of days to maturity. The bid and asked columns show yields rather than prices, so the ask is less than the bid, and are quoted on what is called the yield on a discount basis. For a U.S. Treasury bill with a purchase price of P and a face value of F, maturing in t days, the yield on a discount basis[††] is $\frac{(F - P)}{F} \times \frac{360}{t}$. So on the short-maturity T-bill (the one with five days to maturity that is labeled "C"), the ask price is the solution to $\frac{(100 - P)}{100} \times \frac{360}{5} = 0.0132$, or 99.98167.

The "Chg" column shows the change in the "Asked" yield, usually measured in basis points. (Recall that a *basis point* is one one-hundredth of a percentage point. The changes of 0.03 in the table is an increase of 3 basis points.) The column labeled "Ask Yield" shows the yield to maturity computed from the ask price.

U.S. Treasury Strips

In valuing a bond, we treated the coupon payments and the principal payment separately: see equation (5). Just because bond issuers sell both

---

[*]In the past, listings included bonds with two maturity dates. In those cases, the maturity column would read something like "May 06–11," signifying that the bond is **callable**. That is, the U.S. Treasury has an option to repay the bond as early as May 2006 but must repay no later than May 2011.

[†]The yield published in the financial press is actually a *bond-equivalent yield*, which is twice the yield to maturity, computed on a semiannual basis. It differs from the yield to maturity in that it ignores the within-year compounding implied in the present-value formulas of Chapter 5. For low interest rates, the differences are very small.

[††]The yield on a discount basis differs from the yield to maturity in two ways. First, the yield on a discount basis is computed as if a year is 360 days long, while the yield to maturity is computed on a full 365-day year. Second, in the yield on a discount basis, the return on holding the Treasury bill, the face-value payment minus the price, is computed as a percentage of the face value rather than as a percentage of the price paid. In the yield to maturity the latter method, which is a natural measure on the return to the initial investment, is used.

continued on next page

continued from previous page

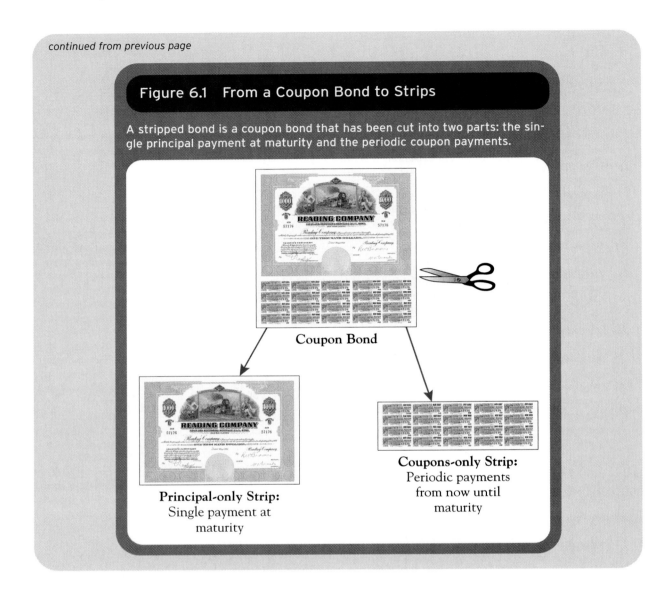

Figure 6.1 From a Coupon Bond to Strips

A stripped bond is a coupon bond that has been cut into two parts: the single principal payment at maturity and the periodic coupon payments.

Coupon Bond

Principal-only Strip:
Single payment at maturity

Coupons-only Strip:
Periodic payments from now until maturity

creates risk. The longer the term of the bond, the greater those price movements and the associated risk can be, as we'll see in more detail in the last section of this chapter.

The Bond Market and the Determination of Interest Rates

Now that we understand the relationship between bond prices and various measures of interest rates, we need to figure out how bond prices are determined and why they change. The best way to do that is to look at bond supply, bond demand, and equilibrium prices in the bond market. Once we understand how the bond market determines bond prices, we can figure out why the prices change.

continued from previous page

together does not mean the financial markets need to trade them that way. This realization has led to the creation of stripped bonds, in which the two parts are separated. In the same way that a property owner can sell the air rights above a building separately from the building itself, an owner can strip U.S. Treasury bonds and sell the principal and the coupon payments separately. (Figure 6.1 shows how the Reading Railroad bond first pictured in Chapter 4 could be stripped.)

The price of each piece is reported daily. These prices represent the cost of purchasing a U.S. Treasury promise to make the payment of $100 of either principal or coupon interest on the maturity date with no intervening payments. That is, these are zero-coupon or pure discount bonds like U.S. Treasury bills, just with longer maturities. The designations *np, bp,* and *ci* in column 2 show whether the price is for payment of the note principal, the bond principal, or the coupon interest.

Corporate Bonds

The Wall Street Journal regularly lists the most actively traded corporate bonds from the previous day. Column 1 of the table shows the name of the firm that issued the bond—on this day, General Motors (GM), Wal-Mart (WMT), and Bear Stearns (BSC). Column 2 reports the coupon rate, and Column 3 shows the date on which the bond matures. Column 4 states the last traded price and Column 5 reports the yield computed at that price. Differences in the yields arise both from differences in maturity and from differences in risk ratings. The final column is the spread (measured in basis points) between the price at which a dealer is willing to buy and the price at which a dealer (often the same one) is willing to sell. The spread provides information about market liquidity. The lower the spread, the more liquid the market.[§]

[§]Recall that the more liquid a financial instrument is, the cheaper and easier it is to sell and convert into another instrument. The smaller the spread in the market, the cheaper it is to buy and sell a bond.

"Your pot o' gold is doing nothing for you sitting at the end of the rainbow. At the very least, you should put it in a no-risk interest-bearing account."

To keep the analysis simple, we need to make a few choices about how to proceed. First, we'll restrict the discussion to the market for existing bonds at a particular time, called the *stock of bonds*. (We could look at what causes the changes in the quantity of bonds outstanding—the *flow*—but that would complicate matters.) Second, we are going to talk about *bond prices* rather than interest rates. Since a bond's price, together with its various characteristics, determines its yield, it really doesn't matter whether we talk about yields (interest rates) or bond prices. Once we know the price, we know the yield. Finally, we're going to consider the *market for a one-year zero-coupon bond* (one that makes no coupon payments) with a face value of $100.

If we assume the investor is planning to purchase a one-year bond and hold it to maturity—they have a one-year **investment horizon**—then the holding period return equals the bond's yield to maturity, and both are determined directly from the price. The present-value formula shows that the relationship between the price and the yield on such a bond is simply $P = \frac{\$100}{(1+i)}$, so $i = \frac{\$100 - P}{P}$.

For example, if a bond sells for $95, then the yield is $i = \frac{\$5}{\$95} = 0.0526$, or 5.26 percent.

Bond Supply, Bond Demand, and Equilibrium in the Bond Market

How are bond prices (and bond yields) determined? Not surprisingly, by supply and demand. Some investors are supplying bonds, while others are demanding them. The *bond supply curve* is the relationship between the price and the quantity of bonds people are willing to sell, all other things being equal. The higher the price of a bond, the larger the supply will be for two reasons. From investors' point of view, the higher the price, the more tempting it is to sell a bond they currently hold. From the point of view of companies seeking finance for new projects, the higher the price at which they can sell bonds, the better. Taking our example of a $100 one-year zero-coupon bond, the supply will be higher at $95 than it will be at $90, all other things being equal. This means that *the bond supply curve slopes upward*.

MARKETS

The *bond demand curve* is the relationship between the price and quantity of bonds that investors demand, all other things being equal. As the price falls, the reward for holding the bond rises, so the demand goes up. That is, the lower the price potential bondholders must pay for a fixed-dollar payment on a future date, the more likely they are to buy a bond. Again, think of the zero-coupon bond promising to pay $100 in one year. That bond will attract more demand at $90 than it will at $95, all other things being equal. Thus, *the bond demand curve slopes downward*. Since the price of bonds is inversely related to the yield, the demand curve implies that the higher the demand for bonds, the higher the yield.

Equilibrium in the bond market is the point at which supply equals demand—point E in Figure 6.2. As is always the case with supply and demand analysis, we need to explain how the market adjusts when the price deviates from the price that equates supply and demand—point P_0 in Figure 6.2. Let's look briefly at the two possibilities: either the price is too high or the price is too low. If bond prices start out above the equilibrium point, somewhere greater than P_0, supply will exceed demand. That is, excess supply means that suppliers cannot sell the bonds they want to at the current price. To make the sale, they will start cutting the price. The excess supply will put downward pressure on the price until supply equals demand.

When the price is below the equilibrium point, demand will exceed supply. Those people who wish to buy bonds cannot get all they want at the prevailing price. Their reaction is to start bidding up the price. Excess demand continues to put upward pressure on the price until the market reaches equilibrium.

So far, so good. But to really understand how bond prices (and bond yields) change over time, we need to learn what determines the location of the supply and demand curves. Over time they shift around, leading to changes in the equilibrium prices. As we discuss the causes of such shifts in the following section, make sure you remember the distinction between moving *along* a supply or demand curve and *shifting* a curve. When the demand or supply changes because of a change in the price, it produces a movement along the curve. But when the quantity demanded or supplied at a given price changes, it shifts the entire curve. More important, in the bond market, a shift in either the supply or the demand curve changes the price of bonds, so it changes the yield as well.

Figure 6.2   Supply, Demand, and Equilibrium in the Bond Market

The supply of bonds from borrowers slopes up and the demand for bonds from lenders slopes down. Equilibrium in the bond market is determined by the intersection of supply and demand.

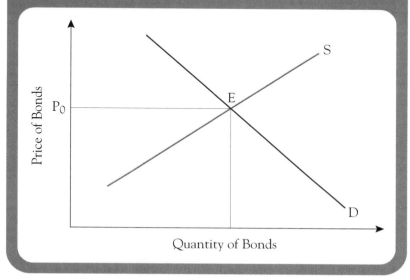

Factors That Shift Bond Supply

What changes the *supply* of bonds at a given price, shifting the supply curve? We can identify three factors: changes in government borrowing, in general business conditions, and in expected inflation. Let's look at these one at a time.

Changes in Government Borrowing   The government's need to issue bonds affects the supply of bonds out there. Both changes in tax policy and adjustments in fixed spending can affect a government's need to borrow. Regardless of the reason, *any increase in the government's borrowing needs increases the quantity of bonds outstanding, shifting the bond supply curve to the right.* The result is an increase in quantity of the bonds supplied at every price (see Figure 6.3). Since the demand curve stays where it is (remember, we're holding everything else constant), the increase in supply drives the price down. The added supply of U.S. government bonds has reduced prices, raising interest rates.

Changes in General Business Conditions   During business-cycle expansions, when general business conditions are good, investment opportunities abound, prompting firms to increase their borrowing. As the amount of debt in the economy rises, the quantity of bonds outstanding goes up. So *as business conditions improve, the bond supply curve shifts to the right,* forcing bond prices down and interest rates up. Again, Figure 6.3 shows what happens. This connection between general business

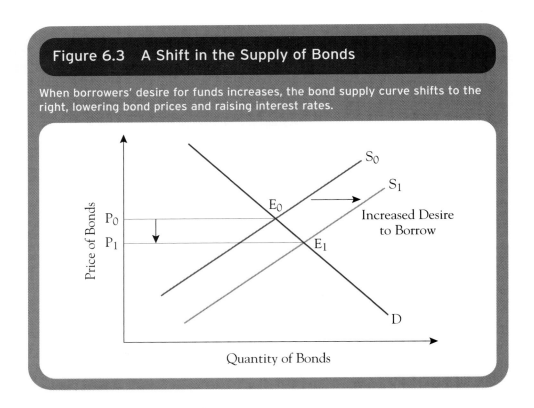

Figure 6.3 A Shift in the Supply of Bonds

When borrowers' desire for funds increases, the bond supply curve shifts to the right, lowering bond prices and raising interest rates.

conditions and the supply of bonds also helps explain how weak economic growth can lead to rising bond prices and lower interest rates.

Changes in Expected Inflation Bond issuers care about the *real* cost of borrowing—the cost of the loan taking inflation into account. At a given *nominal* interest rate, higher expected inflation means a lower *real* interest rate. And at a lower real interest rate, fewer real resources are required to make the payments promised by a bond. So when expected inflation rises, the cost of borrowing falls and the desire to borrow rises. Figure 6.3 shows that *an increase in expected inflation shifts the bond supply curve to the right*. Higher expected inflation increases the bond supply, reducing bond prices and raising the nominal interest rate.

Table 6.3 summarizes the factors that increase bond supply. Before moving on to shifts in the demand for bonds, we should mention that there is one other factor that shifts the bond supply: changes in corporate taxation. Because such changes in the tax code require government legislation, they don't occur very often. But when they do, they can affect the economywide supply of bonds. Corporations pay taxes on their profits, just as individuals pay taxes on their income, so they are concerned with after-tax profits. Governments often create special tax subsidies that make corporate investments less costly. These tax incentives increase the supply of bonds because they raise the after-tax profitability of investing in new equipment purchased with funds raised from selling bonds. Like the other three factors we have considered, government tax incentives increase bond supply, shift the supply curve to the right, and lower the price of bonds.

Table 6.3   Factors That Increase Bond Supply, Lower Bond Prices, and Raise Interest Rates

Change	Effect on Bond Supply, Bond Prices, and Interest Rates
An increase in the government's desired expenditure relative to its revenue	Bond supply shifts to the right, Bond prices ↓, and interest rates ↑
An improvement in general business conditions	Bond supply shifts to the right, Bond prices ↓, and interest rates ↑
An increase in expected inflation, reducing the real cost of repayment	Bond supply shifts to the right, Bond prices ↓, and interest rates ↑

YOUR FINANCIAL WORLD
Interest-Only Mortgages

Your job has been transferred to the San Francisco Bay Area, so you're moving. The idea of living in California appeals to you, but your enthusiasm is tempered by the fact that housing there is extremely expensive. Even a modest home costs $500,000. How are you going to afford a place to live? Then you stumble on an intriguing kind of mortgage. Like many mortgages, it runs for 30 years and has a fixed interest rate, but for the first five years, you pay only interest. Say you need to borrow $400,000. At an interest rate of 6 percent, your payments for the first five years will be $1,947 a month. That's a lot of money, but you're making a good salary, so you can manage it. You are especially tempted since if you got a regular 30-year, fixed-rate mortgage at 6 percent, which would require you to pay some of the principal down from the start of the loan, the monthly payments would be $2,357, which you can't afford.*

Should you try the interest-only option? As usual, there is no hard and fast answer to such questions. But before you sign on the dotted line,

you need to figure out what will happen to your payments after the first five years. In a conventional mortgage, the payments will stay at $2,357 a month. With the interest-only mortgage, the payments will go up, because you have to start paying off the principal. The interest-only mortgage then becomes a 25-year, fixed rate, 6-percent mortgage with payments of $2,538 a month. Either you could start paying that amount or you could refinance and get a new 30-year mortgage at whatever the interest rate happens to be. This second option involves interest-rate risk. If the interest rate has gone up by even one percentage point, you will pay $2,772 a month (the monthly payment on a 7 percent, 25-year, fixed-rate mortgage).

Unless the interest rate drops after you buy your house, once you hit the five-year mark with an interest-only mortgage, your payments are likely to go up significantly, regardless of whether you keep your current mortgage or refinance. Unless your salary rises quickly in those first five years, you risk not being able to make the new higher payments. But if this is a risk you're willing to take, then an interest-only mortgage may be for you.

*This computation uses the formula in Appendix 4 and assumes that the monthly interest rate can be computed from $(1.06)^{1/12}$.

Factors That Shift Bond Demand

Now we move on to bond demand. Six factors shift the *demand* for bonds at a given price: wealth, expected inflation, the expected return on stocks and other assets, expected interest rates, risk, and the liquidity of bonds.

Wealth   The more rapidly the economy grows, the wealthier individuals become. As their wealth increases, they increase their investment in stocks, bonds, real estate, and art. Thus, *increases in wealth shift the demand for bonds to the right,* raising bond prices and lowering yields (see Figure 6.4). This is what happens in a business-cycle expansion. In a recession, as wealth falls, the demand for bonds falls with it, lowering bond prices and raising interest rates.

Expected Inflation   Changes in expected inflation alter investors' willingness to purchase bonds with fixed-dollar payments. A decline in expected inflation means that the payments promised by the bond's issuer have a higher value than borrowers originally thought, so the bond will become more attractive. *This fall in expected inflation shifts the bond demand curve to the right,* increasing demand at each price and lowering the yield, as shown in Figure 6.4. In short, the higher real return on the bond increases the willingness of would-be lenders to buy it at any given price. Note that the decline in expected inflation has reduced the nominal interest rate that investors require in order to make a loan.

Expected Returns and Expected Interest Rates   An investor's desire to hold any particular financial instrument depends on how its return compares to those of alternative instruments. Bonds are no different. *If the return on bonds rises relative to*

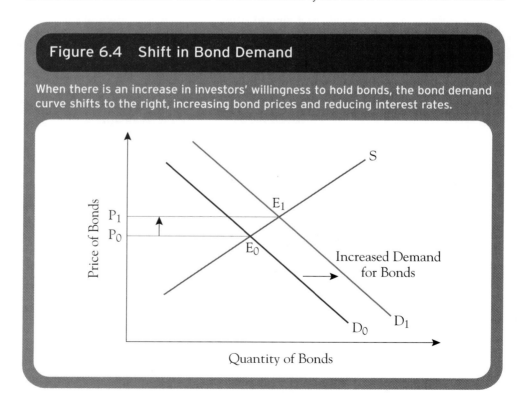

Figure 6.4   Shift in Bond Demand

When there is an increase in investors' willingness to hold bonds, the bond demand curve shifts to the right, increasing bond prices and reducing interest rates.

the return on alternative investments, the demand for bonds will rise. This leads us to conclude that bond prices are connected to the stock market. Investors see bonds as an alternative to stocks, so when the stock market drops, they shift their portfolios into bonds, increasing demand, driving prices up and interest rates down.

Similarly, when interest rates are expected to change, bond prices change immediately. Recall that the holding period return on a bond depends on the coupon payment plus the capital gain or loss. When interest rates fall, bond prices rise, creating a capital gain. Whenever interest rates are expected to fall, then bond prices are expected to rise, creating an expectation of a capital gain. This makes bonds more attractive. Knowing that bonds are a good investment, investors increase their demand immediately, driving bond prices up. So *an increase in the expected return on a bond, relative to the return on alternatives, shifts bond demand to the right.*

Risk Relative to Alternatives   On May 13, 2002, a headline in *The Wall Street Journal* read "Japan Gets Irate at Having Its Risk Compared to Botswana." What's going on here? Japan is the second largest economy in the world, with a population of more than 125 million and a GDP of $3.5 trillion. Botswana is a landlocked country in Southern Africa with a population of 1.5 million people and a GDP of $13.5 billion.

The problem was that investors had two reasons to question Japan's budget outlook. First, the current fiscal deficit was a very high 7 percent of GDP. Second, over the next few decades, the Japanese government would have to find a way to meet its promises to make pension payments to the growing number of retirees. Together these created the perception that Japan's bonds were risky, which meant that investors would be less interested in holding them.

Remember that investors require compensation for risk, which means that when a bond becomes more or less risky, the demand for the bond changes. The less risky the bond, the higher the price investors are willing to pay for it, all other things being equal. From this we can conclude that *if a bond becomes less risky relative to alternative investments, the demand for the bond shifts to the right.* The reason Japan was irate was because the price of its bonds would be lower, so its borrowing costs would be higher.

Liquidity Relative to Alternatives   Liquidity measures how easily and cheaply investors can convert one financial instrument into another. A liquid asset is something investors can sell without a large loss in value. Investors like liquidity; the more liquid a bond, the higher the demand for it, all other things being equal. So if a bond's liquidity changes, demand for it changes, too.

During the financial crisis in the fall of 1998, for example, the bonds issued by emerging-market governments in Latin America and Eastern Europe became virtually impossible to sell. For all practical purposes, the market for them disappeared. When a buyer could be found, prices were severely depressed. Who wants to buy a bond that is difficult to sell? Liquidity matters. The less liquid a bond is, the lower the demand for it, and the lower the price. So *when a bond becomes more liquid relative to alternatives, the demand curve shifts to the right.*

Understanding Changes in Equilibrium Bond Prices and Interest Rates

Before we continue, let's look again at how bond prices and interest rates move in response to changes in expected inflation and a change in general business conditions.

Table 6.4   Factors That Increase Bond Demand, Raise Bond Prices, and Lower Interest Rates

Change	Effect on Bond Demand
An increase in wealth increases demand for all assets, including bonds.	Bond demand shifts to the right, bond prices ↑, and interest rates ↓
A reduction in expected inflation makes bonds with fixed nominal payments more desirable.	Bond demand shifts to the right, bond prices ↑, and interest rates ↓
An increase in the expected return on the bond relative to the expected return on alternatives makes bonds more attractive.	Bond demand shifts to the right, bond prices ↑, and interest rates ↓
A decrease in the expected future interest rate makes bonds more attractive.	Bond demand shifts to the right, bond prices ↑, and interest rates ↓
A fall in the riskiness of the bond relative to the riskiness of alternatives makes bonds more attractive.	Bond demand shifts to the right, bond prices ↑, and interest rates ↓
An increase in the liquidity of the bond relative to the liquidity of alternatives makes bonds more attractive.	Bond demand shifts to the right, bond prices ↑, and interest rates ↓

APPLYING THE CONCEPT
WHEN RUSSIA DEFAULTED

The idea that risk matters to bond investors is not just a textbook theory. On numerous occasions, investors' concerns about increased risk in certain areas of the globe have led to a significant shift in demand for U.S. Treasury bonds. A noteworthy example occurred in August 1998, when the Russian government failed to make the payments on some bonds held by foreign investors. That is, the Russian government defaulted. Suddenly, no one wanted to hold Russian debt. More important, people lost confidence in the debt issued by all emerging market countries, including Brazil, Argentina, Turkey, and Thailand. After dumping anything that looked at all risky, investors went looking for a safe place to put the proceeds.

Since the safest assets around are U.S. Treasury bonds, that is what they bought. The perception during this episode was that the riskiness of U.S. Treasury bonds had fallen relative to the riskiness of virtually everything else. The result was an increase in the price of U.S. Treasury bonds and a decline in their yield. At the same time, the prices of the more risky alternatives fell and their yields rose.

The data in Figure 6.5 show what happened. After the default (at the vertical line in the figure), the price of U.S. Treasury bonds rose by roughly 10 percent while the price of Brazilian bonds fell by more than one-third. Even though it was a half a world away from Russia, investors' demand for Brazilian bonds plummeted. Meanwhile, demand for the safe U.S. Treasury debt went up.

Recall that expected inflation affects both bond supply and bond demand. An increase in expected inflation reduces the real cost of borrowing, shifting bond *supply* to the *right*. But at the same time, this increase in expected inflation lowers the real return on lending, shifting bond *demand* to the *left*. These two effects reinforce each other, lowering the price of the bond and raising the interest rate (see Figure 6.6).

We also saw that changes in business conditions affect both the supply and the demand for bonds. A business-cycle downturn reduces business investment opportunities, shifting the bond *supply* to the left, and reduces wealth, shifting bond *demand* in the same direction. When both curves shift in the same direction, the price can rise or fall. The theory does not give us an unambiguous prediction. In cases like this, we can look for regular movements in the data to help resolve the question. In this case we know that in recessions, interest rates tend to fall, so prices should increase (see Figure 6.7).

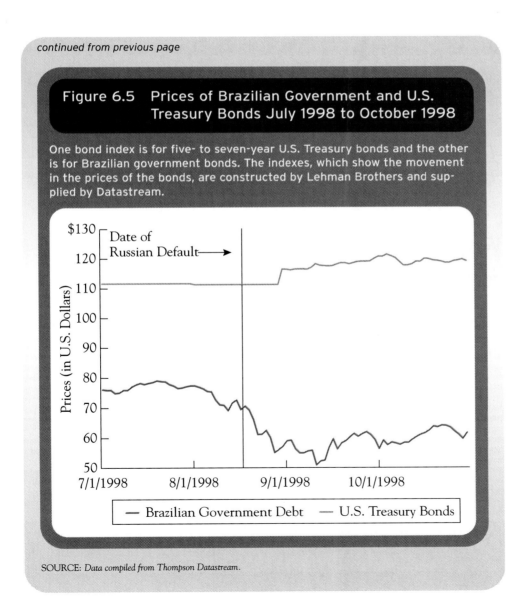

continued from previous page

Figure 6.5   Prices of Brazilian Government and U.S. Treasury Bonds July 1998 to October 1998

One bond index is for five- to seven-year U.S. Treasury bonds and the other is for Brazilian government bonds. The indexes, which show the movement in the prices of the bonds, are constructed by Lehman Brothers and supplied by Datastream.

SOURCE: *Data compiled from Thompson Datastream.*

Figure 6.6 Equilibrium in the Bond Market: The Effect of an Increase in Expected Inflation

An increase in expected inflation increases bond supply from S_0 to S_1 by lowering the real cost of borrowing. At the same time, it reduces bond demand from D_0 to D_1 by reducing the real interest rate bondholders receive. These two effects reinforce each other, lowering the bond's price from P_0 to P_1 and increasing the interest rate.

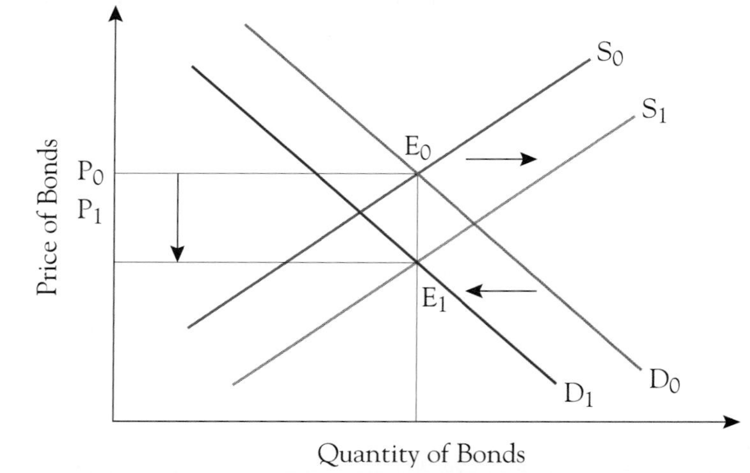

Why Bonds Are Risky

"Bonds Look Attractive Now but They Come with Risks"

—*The Wall Street Journal*, July 26, 2002

RISK

How can bonds be risky? They are promises to make fixed payments on future dates. Where is the risk in that? The fact is that the return an investor receives for holding a bond is far from riskless. Bondholders face three major risks. Default risk is the chance that the bond's issuer may fail to make the promised payment. Inflation risk means an investor can't be sure of what the real value of the payments will be, even if they are made. And interest-rate risk arises from a bondholder's investment horizon, which may be shorter than the maturity of the bond. If the interest rate changes between the time the bond is purchased and the time it is sold, the investor could suffer a capital loss (see Figure 6.8).[5]

We'll look at each of these sources of risk separately, using the tools for understanding risk introduced in Chapter 5. Remember that risk arises from the fact that an

[5]Beyond these three primary sources of risk, the buyer of a bond faces a number of more subtle risks. For example, liquidity risk is the possibility that the investor will experience difficulty selling a bond before it matures. An investor who buys a bond denominated in a foreign currency faces the risk of changes in the exchange rate. A bond may promise payments in euros, say, which must be converted into dollars before they can be used or reinvested.

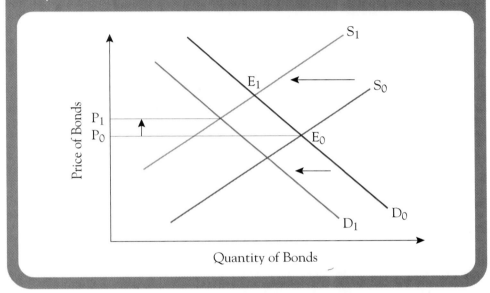

Figure 6.7   Equilibrim in the Bond Market: The Effect of a Business-Cycle Downturn

Interest rates tend to fall during business-cycle downturns. The combination of reduced investment opportunities for businesses, which shifts the bond supply curve to the left from S_0 to S_1, and a decline in household wealth, which shifts the bond supply curve to the left from D_0 to D_1, causes an increase in bond prices and a drop in the interest rate.

investment has many possible payoffs during the horizon for which it is held. So in looking at the risk a bondholder faces, we need to ask what the possible payoffs are and how likely each one is to occur. As we do, we will be looking at the impact of risk on the bond's return relative to the risk-free rate. That is, we will try to figure out how certain risks affect the premium investors require over the risk-free return. Once again, *risk requires compensation.*

Default Risk

There is no guarantee that a bond issuer will make the promised payments. While we might ignore default risk in thinking about U.S. Treasury bonds, we cannot do so when discussing bonds issued by private corporations. When corporations fail to meet their payments, what happens to the price of their bonds?

To figure out the answer, let's list all the possibilities and payoffs that might occur, along with their probabilities. We can then calculate the expected value of the promised payments, from which we can compute the bond's price and yield. Suppose, for example, that the one-year risk-free interest rate is 5 percent. Flim.com, an Internet

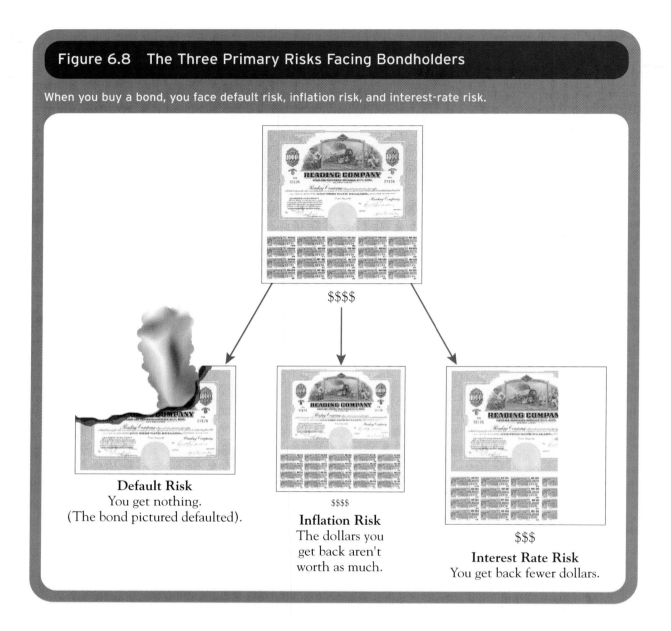

Figure 6.8 The Three Primary Risks Facing Bondholders

When you buy a bond, you face default risk, inflation risk, and interest-rate risk.

$$$$

Default Risk
You get nothing.
(The bond pictured defaulted).

$$$$

Inflation Risk
The dollars you
get back aren't
worth as much.

$$$

Interest Rate Risk
You get back fewer dollars.

firm hoping to market its own brand of e-cash called "Flam,"[6] has issued one-year, 5 percent coupon bonds with a face value of $100. This represents a promise to pay $105 in one year. What is the price of this bond?

If Flim.com were risk free, and lenders were certain they would be paid back, the price of the bond would be computed as the present value of the $105 payment, calculated using the 5 percent risk-free interest rate.

$$\text{Price of Flim.com bond if it is risk free} = \frac{\$100 + \$5}{1.05} = \$100 \qquad (13)$$

[6]This example is not farfetched. In the 1990s a company called flooz.com tried to issue e-money called "flooz."

> ### Table 6.5   Expected Value of Flim.com Bond Payment
>
> | Possibilities | Payoff | Probability | Payoff × Probabilities |
> |---|---|---|---|
> | Full payment | $105 | 0.90 | $94.50 |
> | Default | $0 | 0.10 | $0 |
> | Expected Value = Sum of Payoffs times Probabilities = $94.50 | | | |

But unlike the U.S. Treasury, Flim.com may not make the payments. People might be unwilling to use Flam, so Flim.com could default. Suppose there is a 0.10 probability (one chance in ten) that Flim.com will go bankrupt before paying bondholders their $105. To simplify the example, we will assume that in the case of default, the bondholders get nothing. This means that there are two possible payoffs, $105 and $0 (see Table 6.5).

Table 6.5 shows that the expected value of the payment on this bond is $94.50. But even if the payment is made, it will be made one year from now, which means that the price we would be willing to pay for the bond today must be the present value of the future payment. Using the risk-free interest rate for this computation, we find that

$$\text{Expected present value of Flim.com bond payment} = \frac{\$94.50}{1.05} = \$90 \qquad (14)$$

So the bond will sell for $90. What yield to maturity does this price imply? If the promised payment is $105, the promised yield to maturity is

$$\text{Promised yield on Flim.com bond} = \frac{\$105}{\$90} - 1 = 0.1667 \qquad (15)$$

Converting the decimal to a percentage, we get an interest rate of 16.67 percent.[7] Since the default-risk premium is the promised yield to maturity minus the risk-free rate, it is 16.67 percent – 5 percent = 11.67 percent.

In calculating the default-risk premium on Flim.com's bond, we computed the expected value of holding the bond—the yield at which the bond is a fair bet. But we know that risk-averse investors require some compensation for bearing risk. The more risk, the greater the compensation they demand. Only a risk-neutral investor would be willing to pay $90 for this bond. Any risk premium will drive the price down below $90 and push the yield to maturity above 16.67 percent.

This example shows that the higher the default risk, the higher the probability that the bondholders will not receive the promised payments. Risk reduces the expected value of a given promise, lowering the price an investor is willing to pay and raising the yield. The higher the default risk, the higher the yield.

---

[7]This set of calculations could have been done in reverse. Given the yield of 16.67 percent and the characteristics of the bond, it is straightforward to compute the probability of default as 10 percent.

APPLYING THE CONCEPT
RISKY TRUCK-SCHOOL STUDENT LOANS

You can find default risk in some strange places. On November 11, 2002, the Credit Markets column of *The Wall Street Journal* told the story of 90,000 student loans valued at more than $500 million.* The loans, made to students at truck-driving schools, had been bundled together and bonds had been issued, backed by payments on the loans. These are *asset-backed securities*, as described in Chapter 3. Unfortunately, by 2002, a staggering 70 percent of the student loans included in this investment were in default, guaranteeing that someone involved in this particular investment was going to take a hit. Interestingly, that someone turned out not to be the people who bought the securities backed by the loans, but the company that had insured the loans.

What is surprising is that anyone was willing to insure these loans in the first place. Think about it: How do you find a truck driver who stops paying you back in order to demand repayment? Most of the time truck drivers are on the road. Sometimes you don't need mathematical formulas to see risk. You just need a bit of common sense.

*See Christine Richard and David Feldheim, "Truck-School Loans Get Lost as Royal Indemnity Files Suit," *The Wall Street Journal*, November 11, 2002.

Inflation Risk

With few exceptions, bonds promise to make fixed-dollar payments. That is, a $100 face value, one-year bond at 5 percent is a promise to make a $105 payment in one year. If this promise comes from the government (and therefore is free of default risk), the bondholder can be sure of receiving the $105 payment. Still, there is a risk of inflation. Remember that what you care about is the purchasing power of the money, not the number of dollars. In other words, bondholders are interested in the *real interest rate*, not just the nominal interest rate. And they don't know how much inflation rate there will be.

Let's look at an example that shows how inflation risk affects the interest rate. To begin with, think about the interest rate as having three components: the real interest rate, expected inflation, and a compensation for inflation risk. Suppose the real interest rate is 3 percent but we are unsure how much inflation there will be. It could be either 1 percent or 3 percent with equal probability (see case I in Table 6.6). Expected inflation is 2 percent, with a standard deviation of 1.0 percent. This means the nominal interest rate should equal the 3 percent real interest rate plus the 2 percent expected inflation plus the compensation for inflation risk. The greater the inflation risk, the larger the compensation for it will be.

In cases II and III, expected inflation is the same (2 percent) but the standard deviation is lower, since we are more certain that inflation will be close to its expected value. That is, case III is less risky than case II, which is less risky than case I. Since risk requires compensation, we would expect the interest rate to be highest in case I and lowest in case III. While we may not see this distinction much in the United States or Europe, where inflation is stable, emerging-market countries can go through periods when increases in inflation risk substantially drive up nominal interest rates.

Table 6.6   Inflation Risk

| Inflation | Probabilities | | |
	Case I	Case II	Case III
1 percent	0.50	0.25	0.10
2 percent	–	0.50	0.80
3 percent	0.50	0.25	0.10
Expected inflation	2 percent	2 percent	2 percent
Standard deviation	1.0 percent	0.71 percent	0.45 percent

YOUR FINANCIAL WORLD
Bonds Guaranteed to Beat Inflation

Inflation creates risk that the nominal return you receive on a bond won't be worth as much as you expected. If a bond pays a 6 percent yield but inflation is also 6 percent, then the real return is zero! What can you do? You could accept the inflation risk, buy a regular bond, and hope for the best. But that's not always appealing.

Fortunately, there are alternatives. One is to buy a type of U.S. Treasury bond that compensates you for inflation. This inflation-indexed bond is structured so that the government promises to pay you a fixed interest rate plus the change in the consumer price index (the CPI). For instance, if you buy a $1,000 bond with an interest rate of 3 percent plus inflation, and the CPI rises 2 percent, you will get 3 + 2 = 5 percent. If inflation jumps to 5 percent, then you'll get 3 + 5 = 8 percent. Regardless of what inflation turns out to be, you get 3 percent more, so there is no inflation risk. And since the U.S. Treasury issues these bonds, there is no default risk.

The U.S. Treasury sells two types of bonds that are guaranteed to beat inflation, Series I savings bonds and Treasury Inflation Protection Securities (*TIPS*). But while you can buy a savings bond with as little as $50, you'll need $1,000 to start buying TIPS. Series I savings bonds have a long list of rules about how many can be purchased and how long they need to be held. You can learn about these bonds on the Web site of the Bureau of Public Debt at www.publicdebt.treas.gov. You can buy and sell TIPS in financial markets, or you can buy them directly from the U.S. Treasury through Treasury Direct (see Your Financial World in Chapter 16).

SOURCE: *Courtesy of the Bureau of the Public Debt U.S. Department of Treasury.*

Interest-Rate Risk

To explain interest-rate risk, we'll focus on a U.S. Treasury bond and assume that we know how much inflation there will be, so there is no default or inflation risk. Interest-rate risk arises from the fact that investors don't know the holding period yield of a long-term bond. Remember that when interest rates change, bond prices move; the longer the term of the bond, the larger the price change for a given change in the interest rate. Now think about what happens if you have a short investment

IN THE NEWS
David Bowie Becomes a Bond

Washington Post

by Jay Mathews

February 6, 1997

David Bowie, the angular British rock star, has never been afraid to try something new. His stage persona has metamorphosed from Ziggy Stardust to Aladdin Sane to the Thin White Duke, with interesting digressions along the way. He has performed with a succession of bands, from the Kon-rads to the King Bees, to the Lower Third, to Tin Machine.

Now Bowie is the first major artist to turn himself into a bond issue—payable over 10 years at 6.9 percent.

The asset-backed bond—the financial instrument that has put $55 million in Bowie's well-tailored pocket—is a device of rapidly growing popularity that already has helped banks turn home loan payments and credit card receivables into big chunks of cash. But until now no one dared to think the annual income from former hits such as "Space Oddity" or "Let's Dance" might appeal to gray-suited executives looking for stable bond investments.

The bond bonus for Bowie is $55 million immediately, instead of in installments as the records sell, and more money than record companies were offering. What he'll do with the money is unclear, but he seems to have been drawn to the deal by its tax advantages.

The reliability of the revenue stream to pay off the bondholders enabled Bowie to get a favorable interest rate. His success could entice other artists with steady royalty payments to go to market, said David Pullman, the 34-year-old senior vice president at Fahnestock & Co. who designed the deal.

Many rock stars have outsold Bowie in the United States, but his avant-garde image and exotic musical tastes still sell an average 1 million records a year all over the planet, according to his business manager, Bill Zysblat. There also is revenue from 250 songs turned into sheet music, commercials, and background music for elevators, offices, voice mail, and many other uses in an age in which profit sources for art are expanding rapidly.

"It just goes to show you that anything can be securitized," said Craig Moyer, senior fixed-income manager at Meridian Investment Co. in Valley Forge, Pennsylvania, part of CoreStates Financial Corp.

Asset-backed bonds began as a way to help banks turn old-fashioned, slow-moving income sources such as credit card and car loan payments into big new cash sources that could be reinvested and turned into even more fees and income.

Moyer said Bowie's $55 million deal would be too small to interest most investors because they would be uncertain of finding buyers if they decided to move their money elsewhere. But, he said, he could imagine some clients who would be drawn to the deal, with an interest rate significantly above the 6.4 percent now paid by 10-year Treasury bonds.

Unlike most singer-songwriters, Bowie had kept control of his copyrights and record masters, and the distribution license for his first 25 albums was due to expire in June. He could have signed a new deal, with a substantial advance, but Pullman said he thought he could get more money upfront through a bond sale.

Zysblat agreed to see how big an advance the record companies were offering, while Pullman tested the feasibility of a bond sale. When they met again, Zysblat said, "his numbers were bigger than my numbers."

Record companies who see profits in turning their backlists of CDs and songs into asset-backed bonds have been asking Zysblat for advice, he said. "I tell them I'm not in that business," he said, "but maybe I will be."

SOURCE: *Copyright © 1997, The Washington Post, reprinted with permission.*

LESSONS OF THE ARTICLE

Virtually anything can be turned into a bond, even the future revenues from the sale of rock music. Here, the revenue from the retail sales of David Bowie's music in all its forms has been turned into an asset-backed security. The benefit to Bowie is that he received a cash payment immediately and shifted the risk that future revenue will be low to the bondholders. Thus buyers of Bowie's bonds must believe that his music will continue to sell well, maintaining the revenue needed to make the promised payments. As it turns out, the entire $55 million bond issue, which had a risk premium of 0.5 percent over U.S. Treasury bonds (6.9 percent minus 6.4 percent), was purchased by a single insurance company. This company realized the bonds offered a type of diversification that is hard to come by, as the risk that David Bowie will become unpopular is surely uncorrelated with almost every other investment out there.

horizon. If you buy a long-term bond, you will need to sell the bond before it matures, so you have to worry about what will happen if the interest rate changes.

Whenever there is a mismatch between your investment horizon and a bond's maturity, there is interest-rate risk. Because the prices of long-term bonds can change dramatically, this can be an important source of risk. Table 6.2 (in Tools of the Trade) showed that as of August 2004, the Aug 15 10.625 bond, which matures in 2015, was trading for over $154 per $100 face value. When it was issued as a 30-year bond in August 1985, this bond had a price of $99.686 per $100 face value.[8] An investor who bought the bond when it was originally issued and sold it in August 2004 would have experienced a more than 50 percent capital gain. By comparison, by August 2004 a purchaser of the May 08 2.625 note, issued as a 4-year 11-month note on June 16, 2003, at a price of $102.437, had suffered a capital loss, as the bond was currently priced at $98.14 per $100 face value.

The lesson is that any move in interest rates changes the price of a bond. For investors with holding periods shorter than the maturity of the bond, the potential for a change in interest rates creates risk. The more likely interest rates are to change during the bondholder's investment horizon, the larger the risk of holding a bond.

Table 6.7   What Makes Bonds Risky?

1. *Default risk:* The issuer may not make the promised payments.
2. *Inflation risk:* Inflation may turn out to be higher than expected, reducing the real return on holding the bond.
3. *Interest-rate risk:* Interest rates may rise between the time a bond is purchased and the time it is sold.

[8]The U.S. Treasury auctions its bonds, so the original selling price is not the exact par value of the bond. To see the original auction prices, go to www.publicdebt.treas.gov.

Terms

www.mhhe.com/cecchetti1e

Chapter Lessons

1. Valuing bonds is an application of present value.

    a. Pure discount or zero-coupon bonds promise to make a single payment on a predetermined future date.

    b. Fixed-payment loans promise to make a fixed number of equal payments at regular intervals.

    c. Coupon bonds promise to make periodic interest payments and repay the principal at maturity.

    d. Consols (perpetuities) promise to make periodic coupon payments forever.

2. Yields are measures of the return on holding a bond.

    a. The yield to maturity is a measure of the interest rate on a bond. To compute it, set the price of the bond equal to the present value of the payments.

    b. The current yield on a bond is equal to the coupon rate divided by the price.

    c. Holding period returns are equal to the sum of the current yield and any capital gain or loss arising from a change in a bond's price.

    d. When the price of a bond is above its face value, the coupon rate is greater than the current yield, which is higher than the yield to maturity.

3. Bond prices (and bond yields) are determined by supply and demand in the bond market.

    a. The higher the price, the larger the quantity of bonds supplied.

    b. The higher the price, the smaller the quantity of bonds demanded.

    c. The supply of bonds rises when

        i. Governments need to borrow more.

        ii. General business conditions improve.

        iii. Expected inflation rises.

    a. The demand for bonds rises when

        i. Wealth increases.

        ii. Expected inflation falls.

        iii. The expected return, relative to other investments, rises.

        iv. The expected future interest rate falls.

        v. Bonds become less risky relative to other investments.

        vi. Bonds become more liquid relative to other investments.

4. Bonds are risky because of

    a. Default risk: the risk that the issuer may fail to pay.

    b. Inflation risk: the risk that the inflation rate may be more or less than expected, affecting the real value of the promised nominal payments.

    c. Interest-rate risk: the risk that the interest rate may change, causing the bond's price to change.

Problems

1. Consider a U.S. Treasury bill with 270 days to maturity. If the annual yield is 3.8 percent, what is the price?

2. Which of these $100 face value bonds will have a higher yield to maturity? Why?

   a. 6 percent coupon bond selling for $85

   b. 7 percent coupon bond selling for $100

   c. 8 percent coupon bond selling for $115

3. You are considering purchasing a consol that promises annual payments of $4.

   a. If the current interest rate is 5 percent, what is the price of the consol?

   b. You are concerned that the interest rate may rise to 6 percent. Compute the percentage change in the price of the consol and the percentage change in the interest rate. Compare them.

   c. Your investment horizon is one year. You purchase the consol when the interest rate is 5 percent and sell it a year later, following a rise in the interest rate to 6 percent. What is your holding period return?

4. In a recent issue of *The Wall Street Journal*, locate the prices and yields on U.S. Treasury issues. For one bond selling above par and one selling below par (assuming they both exist), compute the current yield and compare it to the coupon rate and the ask yield printed in the paper.

5. There is considerable concern that the government of Transaxia, an emerging economy in Eastern Europe, will default on its debt. Some years ago it issued 8 percent coupon bonds that now have one year to maturity. Looking at the market, you find that the yield on these bonds is 24 percent. If the current risk-free interest rate is 5 percent, and assuming that investors do not demand a risk premium for holding Transaxian bonds, what is the probability that the Transaxians will default?

6. The Transaxians do, in fact, default. As a result, investors become more attuned to the chances that other small emerging-market economies may default and immediately move to reduce their exposure to them. Describe the consequences of this increase in risk aversion for the prices of both low-risk bonds and riskier emerging-market bonds.

7. A 10-year zero-coupon bond has a yield of 6 percent. Through a series of unfortunate circumstances, expected inflation rises from 2 percent to 3 percent.

   a. Compute the change in the price of the bond.

   b. Suppose that expected inflation is still 2 percent but the probability that it will move to 3 percent has risen. Describe the consequences for the price of the bond.

8. Assume that forecasts for the U.S. economy have taken a sudden turn for the worse. Everyone had expected healthy growth of 3 to 4 percent in the coming year, but now a recession is predicted, with output contracting by as much as 2 percent. Officials expect unemployment to rise and corporate profits to plummet. Describe the consequences for prices and interest rates for both government and private-sector bonds. Consider both the supply and demand effects. Use graphs to support your answer.

9. What impact would a stock-market collapse have on bonds? Why?

10. The government proposes cutting taxes on investment by implementing a credit for investment in information technology equipment. The proposal would reduce government tax revenues. Describe the likely impact on the bond market.

11. Other musicians, among them Rod Stewart, James Brown, and Dusty Springfield, have issued bonds similar to those created by David Bowie (as described in the article in the chapter). What is likely to make such bond issues successful?

12. Use supply and demand in the bond market to explain each of the following news headlines. Show in a diagram what shifts and explain why.

    a. "Treasury prices fell for the sixth time in seven sessions as investors made room for new debt issues."

    b. "Government bonds continued their month-long rise as data indicated the U.S. economy is still progressing, but at a moderate pace."

    c. "U.S. Treasurys rise sharply as stocks take dive."

    d. "Treasury prices are rising on expected future rate cut."

    e. "Illiquidity is crippling bond world."

13. As you read the morning paper, you come across an ad for a bond mutual fund, a fund that pools the investments from a large number of people and then purchases bonds, giving the individuals "shares" in the fund. The company claims the fund has had a return of $13\frac{1}{2}$ percent over the last year. But you remember that interest rates have been pretty low, 5 percent at most. A quick check of the numbers in the business section you're holding tells you that your recollection is correct. Explain the logic behind the mutual fund's claim in the ad.

14. Your Financial World: Interest-Only Mortgages describes the monthly payments a person would have to make under various circumstances. Show how to derive the results in parts a–c if you borrow $400,000 at an annual interest rate of 6 percent:

    a. An interest-only mortgage requires a payment of $1,947 a month.

    b. A 30-year, fixed-rate mortgage requires 360 equal payments of $2,357.

    c. A 25-year, fixed-rate mortgage requires 300 equal payments of $2,538.

    Note: To answer these questions, you will need to compute the monthly compound interest rate and use the formulas in Appendix 4.

15. At the dinner table, your father is extolling the benefits of investing in bonds. He insists that as a conservative investor he will make only investments that are safe, and what could be safer than a bond, especially a U.S. Treasury bond? What accounts for his view of bonds? Explain why you think it is right or wrong.

Chapter 7

The Risk and Term Structure of Interest Rates

On October 5, 1998, William McDonough, president of the Federal Reserve Bank of New York, declared "I believe that we are in the most serious financial crisis since World War II."[1] Since August 17, when the Russian government had defaulted on some of its bonds, deteriorating investor confidence had increased volatility in the financial markets. Bond markets were the hardest hit; as lenders re-evaluated the relative risk of holding different bonds, some prices plummeted while others soared. This simultaneous increase in some interest rates and decline in others—a rise in what are called **interest-rate spreads**—was a clear sign to McDonough that the substantial stress the financial markets were experiencing could easily spread to the wider economy, affecting everyone.

Changes in bond prices can have a pronounced effect on the welfare of individual corporations. The case of General Electric, one of the largest companies in the world, provides an instructive example. GE borrows to maintain and expand its business by issuing bonds that take as long as 30 years to mature. The company also sells **commercial paper**, which is short-term debt that must be repaid in less than a year. In March 2002, information slowly emerged that GE might need to increase its borrowing significantly, adding to its existing $250 billion in long- and short-term debt. This prospect led investors to question GE's financial condition and its ability to repay what it owed. Despite the fact that GE is a very large corporation, its borrowing pattern meant it would have to raise substantial funds quickly to meet obligations to creditors. The result was an increase in the perceived risk of GE's bonds and a corresponding decline in their price.

These examples highlight the need to understand the differences among the many types of bonds that are sold and traded in financial markets. What was it about the movement in the prices of different bonds that Mr. McDonough found so informative? How did information about the issuance of one sort of debt affect investors' willingness to lend to GE? To answer these questions, we will study the differences among the multitude of bonds in the world. We will see that these bonds differ in two crucial respects: the identity of the issuer and the time to maturity. This chapter will examine how each of these affects the price of a bond and then use our knowledge to interpret fluctuations in a broad variety of bond prices.

Ratings and the Risk Structure of Interest Rates

Default is one of the most important risks a bondholder faces. Not surprisingly, the risk that an issuer will fail to make a bond's promised payments varies substantially from one borrower to another. The risk of default is so important to potential investors that

---

[1] Mr. McDonough's job was to monitor financial market developments for the Federal Reserve System, to devise government reaction to such financial crises, and to formulate policies that prevented crises. As we will see in our discussion of the structure of the Federal Reserve System in Chapter 16, the Federal Reserve Bank of New York is the largest of the 12 regional banks in the Federal Reserve System. The president of that bank plays a special role as the eyes and ears of the government in world financial markets.

independent companies have come into existence to evaluate the creditworthiness of potential borrowers. These firms, sometimes called rating agencies, estimate the likelihood that a corporate or government borrower will make a bond's promised payments. Let's look at these companies and the information that they produce.

Bond Ratings

SOURCE: *Courtesy of Standard & Poor's.*

The best-known bond rating services are Moody's and Standard & Poor's.[2] These companies monitor the status of individual bond issuers and assess the likelihood that a lender/bondholder will be repaid by a borrower/bond issuer. Companies with good credit—those with low levels of debt, high profitability, and sizable amounts of cash assets—earn high bond **ratings**. A high rating suggests that a bond issuer will have little problem meeting a bond's payment obligations.

Table 7.1 reports the rating systems of Moody's and Standard & Poor's. As you can see, they are very similar. Both systems are based on letters and bear a broad similarity to the rankings in minor-league baseball. Firms or governments with an exceptionally strong financial position carry the highest ratings and are able to issue the highest-rated bonds, Triple A. The U.S. Government, the Tennessee Valley Authority (TVA), and General Electric are all examples of entities with Aaa bond ratings.

Aaa bonds are considered **investment-grade bonds**, meaning they have a very low risk of default. This category, which includes the top four ratings (see Table 7.1) is reserved for most government issuers as well as the corporations that are among the most financially sound.[3] At this writing, Citigroup, BellSouth Telecommunications, and Taiwan all have Aa ratings; Ameritech, IBM, Oracle, Disney, and Korea have A ratings; and AOL TimeWarner, GM, and Mexico have Baa ratings.

The distinction between investment-grade and speculative, noninvestment-grade bonds is an important one. A number of regulated institutional investors, among them some insurance companies, pension funds, and commercial banks, are not allowed to invest in bonds that are rated below Baa on Moody's scale or BBB on Standard & Poor's scale.[4]

Bonds issued by Gap, Omnipoint, and the country of Bolivia are in the next two rating categories, Ba and B. These companies and countries may have difficulty meeting their bond payments but are not at risk of immediate default. The final category in Table 7.1, highly speculative bonds, includes debts that are in serious risk of default. Enron, which declared bankruptcy in the fall of 2001, is an example.

Both speculative grades, those below Moody's Baa or Standard & Poor's BBB, are often referred to as **junk bonds** or sometimes more politely as *high-yield bonds* (a reminder that to obtain a high yield, investors must take a large risk).[5] There are two types of junk bonds. The first type, called **fallen angels**, were once investment-grade bonds, but their issuers fell on hard times. The second are cases in which little is known about the risk of the issuer.

---

[2]Duff & Phelps, Fitch IBCA is a third, less well-known bond rating company.

[3]Government debt ratings are important, as they generally create a ceiling on the ratings for private companies in that country.

[4]Restrictions on the investments of financial intermediaries, such as insurance companies, are a matter for state regulators. There is no comprehensive reference for all of the legal restrictions that force financial firms to sell bonds whose ratings fall below Baa. In many cases, such as those of bond mutual funds, the restrictions are self-imposed.

[5]*Junk bond* is really an informal term meaning a highly speculative security that has a low rating. While most people use the term to refer to bonds that are below investment grade, it has no exact definition.

Table 7.1   A Guide to Bond Ratings

	Moody's	Standard & Poor's	Description
Investment Grade	Aaa	AAA	Bonds of the best quality with the smallest risk of default. Issuers are exceptionally stable and dependable.
	Aa	AA	High quality, with slightly higher degree of long-term risk.
	A	A	High-medium quality, with many strong attributes, but somewhat vulnerable to changing economic conditions.
	Baa	BBB	Medium quality, currently adequate but perhaps unreliable over the long term.
Noninvestment, Speculative Grade	Ba	BB	Some speculative element, with moderate security but not well safeguarded.
	B	B	Able to pay now but at risk of default in the future.
Highly speculative	Caa	CCC	Poor quality, clear danger of default.
	Ca	CC	Highly speculative quality, often in default.
	C	C	Lowest-rated, poor prospects of repayment though may still be paying.
		D	In default.

SOURCE: *From The Wall Street Journal Guide to Money & Investing by Kenneth M. Morris and Virginia B. Morris. Copyright: 2004 by Lightbulb Press Inc., and Dow Jones & Co., Inc. For a more detailed definition of ratings, see Moody's Web site, www.moodys.com/moodys/cust/ratingdefinitions/rdef.asp., or Standard & Poor's Web site, www.standardandpoors.com/ResourceCenter/RatingsDefinitions.html.*

WorldCom, the telecommunications giant, was one company whose bond rating fluctuated between investment grade and junk. When it began issuing bonds in 1997, the firm was below investment grade (Moody's Ba). WorldCom saw its rating rise for several years, until it peaked as a Moody's A from mid-1999 to the end of 2001. Taking advantage of this investment-grade rating, WorldCom issued $11.8 billion worth of bonds in May 2001. Just one year later, WorldCom's rating dropped back to where it started, Ba, and its 10-year bonds were trading for 44 cents on the dollar, less than half of their initial prices. By mid-2002, as the company filed for bankruptcy, its bonds had fallen one more notch to B.

Material changes in a firm's or government's financial conditions precipitate changes in its debt ratings. The rating services are constantly monitoring events and announcing modifications to their views on the creditworthiness of borrowers. If a particular business or country encounters problems (as occurs with some frequency), Moody's and Standard

Table 7.2 Commercial Paper Ratings

	Moody's	Standard & Poor's	
Investment or Prime Grade	P-1	A-1+, A-1	Strong likelihood of timely repayment.
	P-2	A-2	Satisfactory degree of safety for timely repayment.
	P-3	A-3	Adequate degree of safety for timely repayment.
Speculative, Below Prime Grade		B, C	Capacity for repayment is small relative to higher-rated issuers.
Defaulted		D	

SOURCE: *Based on Thomas K. Hahn, "Commercial Paper," Instruments of the Money Market, Chapter 9, Federal Reserve Bank of Richmond, 1998.*

& Poor's will lower that issuer's bond rating in what is called a **ratings downgrade**. Typically, an average of 5 to 7 percent of bonds that begin a year in an investment-grade category—Aaa to Baa—have their ratings downgraded to one of the noninvestment grades. The WorldCom downgrade in May 2002 reflected the agencies' view that the company had too much debt and (given the dismal state of the telecommunications industry at the time) little opportunity to reduce it. **Ratings upgrades** occur as well. Roughly 7 percent of Aa-rated bonds are upgraded to Aaa each year.[6]

Commercial Paper Ratings

Commercial paper is a short-term version of a bond. Both corporations and governments issue commercial paper. Because the borrower offers no collateral, this form of debt is **unsecured**. So only the most creditworthy companies can issue it.[7] Nevertheless, in 2004 there was over $1.3 trillion of commercial paper outstanding in the United States. Financial companies, such as Merrill Lynch and GE Capital (the financing arm of General Electric), issue the vast majority of it.

Like a U.S. Treasury bill, commercial paper is issued on a discount basis, as a zero-coupon bond that specifies a single future payment with no associated coupon payments. For legal reasons, commercial paper usually has a maturity of less than 270 days.[8] Roughly one-third of all commercial paper is held by money-market mutual funds (MMMFs), which require very short-term assets with immediate liquidity. Most

---

[6]Leland E. Crabbe, "A Framework for Corporate Bond Strategy," *Journal of Fixed Income*, June 1995, reports a Moody's study of bond ratings over the period 1970–1993.

[7]Recall that collateral is something of value pledged by the borrower that the lender could sell if the loan is not repaid.

[8]As described in detail by Thomas K. Hahn, "Commercial Paper," *Instruments of the Money Market* (Federal Reserve Bank of Richmond, 1998), Chapter 9, commercial paper is exempt from the securities registration requirement of the Securities Act of 1933. Registration is time consuming and expensive. But Section 3(a) (3) of the 1933 Act exempts securities with less than 270 days to maturity as long as they meet certain requirements.

APPLYING THE CONCEPT
THE DAY GENERAL ELECTRIC WENT TOO FAR

On March 19, 2002, Bill Gross lost patience with GE and its financing company, GE Capital. If one of us became angry with a company that has 300,000 employees and annual sales of $125 billion, no one would care. But Gross was different. He manages a $52 billion portfolio of bonds and commercial paper for the Pacific Investment Management Company (PIMCO). When Bill Gross got angry with GE, he sold $1 billion worth of GE's commercial paper.

What irritated Mr. Gross was the manner in which GE was borrowing. At the end of 2001, GE had a whopping $80 billion in AAA-rated long-term bonds outstanding, plus $161 billion in short-term borrowings, including $117 billion of A-1/P-1 commercial paper. Then in mid-March 2002, GE issued a record $11 billion worth of 3-year, 5-year, and 30-year bonds. Everything was fine until a week later, when the company unexpectedly announced that it might need another $50 billion in short-term borrowing. The prospect that GE might issue even more debt sent bond prices down.

It is easy to see what made Mr. Gross upset. He saw himself as a significant investor in GE who deserved to get timely information about future financing plans. After a record-sized $11 billion bond sale, it is not very nice to your investors to go back and say that you may need more soon. But more than that, Mr. Gross was unhappy with GE's reliance on short-term financing. Why, he wondered, did the company have to borrow so much in the commercial paper market? GE's management responded by promising to reduce the company's short-term debt from over half of total borrowing to about one-third.

commercial paper is issued with a maturity of 5 to 45 days and is used exclusively for short-term financing.

The rating agencies rate the creditworthiness of commercial paper issuers in the same way as bond issuers. Again, Moody's and Standard & Poor's have parallel rating schemes that differ solely in their labeling (see Table 7.2). By some estimates, 90 percent of issuers carry Moody's P-1 rating and another 9 percent are rated P-2—the P stands for **prime-grade commercial paper**. Speculative-grade commercial paper does exist, but not because it was originally issued as such.[9]

The Impact of Ratings on Yields

Bond ratings are designed to reflect default risk: The lower the rating, the higher the risk of default. We know investors require compensation for risk, so everything else held equal, the lower a bond's rating, the lower its price and the higher its yield. From

[9]For an in-depth survey of commercial paper, see either Thomas K. Hahn, "Commercial Paper," *Instruments of the Money Market* (Federal Reserve Bank of Richmond, 1998), Chapter 9 (available at www.rich.frb.org/pubs/instruments/ch9.html) or Dusan Stojanovic and Mark D. Vaugh, "The Commercial Paper Market: Who's Minding the Shop?" *The Regional Economist* (Federal Reserve Bank of St. Louis, April 1998), pp. 5–9 (available at www.stls.frb.org/publications/re/1998/b/index.html).

Figure 7.1 The Effect of an Increase in Risk on Equilibrium in the Bond Market

Increased risk reduces the demand for the bond at every price, shifting the demand curve to the left from D_0 to D_1. The result is a decline in the equilibrium price and quantity in the market. Importantly, the price falls from P_0 to P_1, so the yield on the bond must rise.

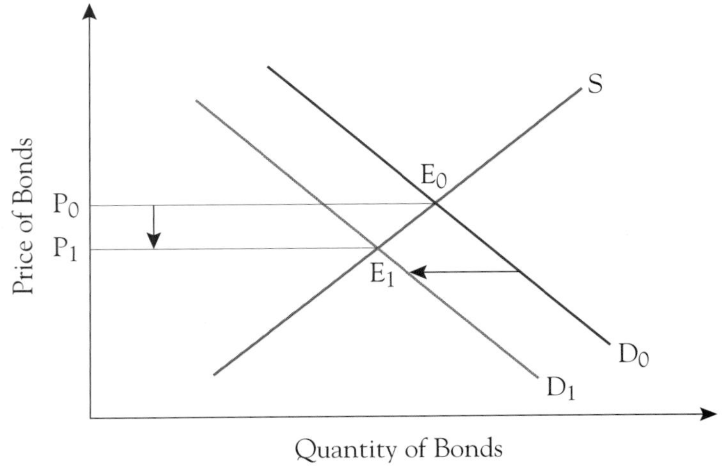

Chapter 6 we know that we can think about changes in risk as shifts in the demand for bonds. Increases in risk will reduce investor demand for bonds at every price, decreasing the equilibrium price and increasing the yield (see Figure 7.1).

The easiest way to understand the quantitative impact of ratings on bond yields is to compare different bonds that are identical in every way except for the issuer's credit rating. U.S. Treasury issues are the natural standard of comparison[10] because they are the closest to being risk free. This is why they are commonly referred to as **benchmark bonds**, and the yields on other bonds are measured in terms of the **spread over Treasuries**.

We can think of any bond yield as the sum of two parts: the yield on the benchmark U.S. Treasury bond plus a default-risk premium, sometimes called a **risk spread**.

$$\text{Bond yield} = \text{U.S. Treasury yield} + \text{Default risk premium} \qquad (1)$$

If bond ratings properly reflect the probability of default, then the lower the rating of the issuer, the higher the default-risk premium in equation (1). This way of thinking about bond yields provides us with a second insight: When Treasury yields move, all other yields move with them.

These two predictions—that interest rates on a variety of bonds will move together and that lower-rated bonds will have higher yields—are both borne out by the data. To

---

[10]Over the course of history many governments have defaulted on their bonds. There is always a remote possibility that the U.S. Treasury will do the same, but if so, investors will probably have bigger problems to worry about than the government's failure to meet its financial obligations.

Figure 7.2 Comparing Long-Term Interest Rates

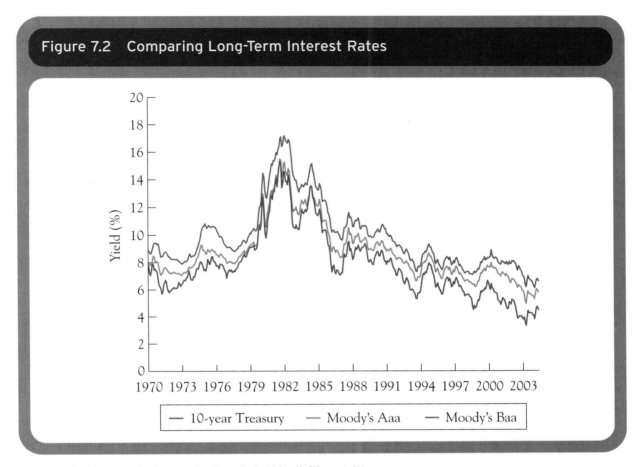

SOURCE: *Federal Reserve Board of Governors, http://research.stlouisfed.org/fred2/categories/22.*

see this, let's look at a plot of the **risk structure of interest rates**. Figure 7.2 shows the estimated yield to maturity for long-term bonds with three different ratings: 10-year U.S. Treasury, Moody's Aaa rated, and Moody's Baa long-term bonds. As you can see from the figure, all of these yields move together. When the U.S. Treasury yield goes up or down, the Aaa and Baa yields do too. While the default-risk premiums do fluctuate, changes in the U.S. Treasury yield account for most of the movement in the Aaa and Baa bond yields. Furthermore, the yield on the higher-rated U.S. Treasury bond is consistently the lowest.[11] In fact, over the 34 years from 1970 to 2004, the 10-year U.S. Treasury bond yield has averaged almost a full percentage point below the average yield on Aaa bonds and two percentage points below the average yield on Baa bonds.

How important is one or two percentage points in yield? To see, we can do a simple computation. At an interest rate of 5 percent, the present value of a $100 payment made 10 years from now is $61.39. If the interest rate rose to 7 percent, the

[11]This statement holds for every month but two in the figure. In those months, the Aaa bonds had a lower yield than the 10-year Treasury bonds did. The reason is that for the corporate bond data from Moody's, the time to maturity varies more than it does for Treasury issues; on occasion, these private sector bonds are less than 10 years to maturity, on average. And, as we will see later in the chapter, shorter maturity bonds usually have a lower yield to maturity.

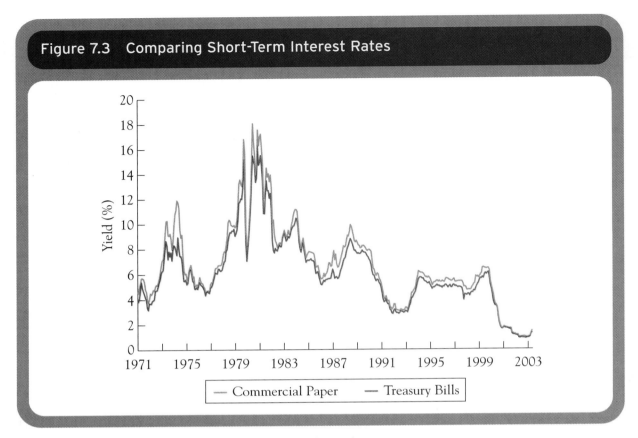

Figure 7.3 Comparing Short-Term Interest Rates

SOURCE: *Federal Reserve Board of Governors, http://research.stlouisfed.org/fred2/categories/22.*

value of this same promise would decline to $50.83. So a two-percentage point increase in the yield, from 5 percent to 7 percent, lowers the value of the promise of $100 in 10 years by 17 percent!

From the viewpoint of the borrower, an increase in the interest rate from 5 percent to 7 percent means paying $7 rather than $5 per year for each $100 borrowed. That is a 40 percent difference. Clearly, ratings are crucial to corporations' ability to raise financing. Whenever a company's bond rating declines, the cost of funds goes up, impairing the company's ability to finance new ventures.[12]

What is true for long-term bond yields is true for short-term bond yields; they move together, and lower ratings imply higher yields. Compare the yields on three-month U.S. Treasury bills with those on A-1/P-1 commercial paper of the same maturity (see Figure 7.3). The two yields clearly move together, and the U.S. Treasury bill yield is always lower than the yield on commercial paper. From 1971 to 2004, the spread of commercial paper over U.S. Treasury bills averaged about six-tenths of one percentage point, or roughly 60 *basis points*. (Recall from Chapter 6 that a basis point is one one-hundredth of a percentage point, or 0.01 percent.)

[12]The same is true for individuals. Consider the impact on the monthly payments required to service a thirty-year, $100,000 mortgage. At an interest rate of 5 percent, payments would be approximately $530 per month. If the interest rate were to increase to 7 percent, the required monthly payments would rise to more than $650. You can compute these amounts using the formulas in Appendix 4.

YOUR FINANCIAL WORLD
Your Credit Rating

Companies aren't the only ones with credit ratings; you have one, too. Have you ever wondered how someone decides whether to give you a loan or a credit card? The answer is that there are companies keeping track of your financial information. They rate your creditworthiness, and they know more about you than you might think. Credit-rating companies know all about your credit cards, your car loan or mortgage (if you have one), and whether you pay your bills on time. All of this information is combined in something called a *credit score*. If you have low levels of debt and pay your bills on time, you have a high credit score.

You care about your credit score; here's why. Lenders use credit scores to calculate the interest rate they charge on a loan. With a top credit score, a four-year, $10,000 car loan might have an interest rate of 6 3/4 percent and monthly payments of $237. But if your credit score was low, because you missed a payment on a credit card or paid your utility bill late, then the interest rate could be as high as 16 percent, which would mean monthly payments $40 higher. The same principle applies to home mortgages; the better your credit score, the lower the interest rate. It pays to pay all your bills on time.*

*Ironically, someone who has never had a credit card and never owed anyone any money has no credit history at all and so will have a low credit score. You cannot start too soon in creating a record as a good credit risk. For a modest fee, the credit-scoring companies will release your credit score to you via the Internet.

The lesson is clear; investors must be compensated for assuming risk. The less creditworthy the borrower, the higher the risk of default, the lower the borrower's rating, and the higher the cost of borrowing. And the lower the rating of the bond or commercial paper, the higher the yield.

Michael Milken and the History of Junk Bonds

"Junk" is the label customarily attached to the lowest-grade bonds, those with the highest risk of default. But many people prefer to identify such bonds—those with ratings below BBB—as *high-yield bonds*, reflecting the fact that their promised yields are substantially higher than those of investment-grade bonds. Junk bonds, and the way the market for them developed, reveal much about the way the financial world operates, so let's pause for a moment to consider their history.

The modern history of junk bonds is the history of the financier Michael Milken and the investment bank he worked for, Drexel Burnham Lambert. Before Milken, junk bonds were exclusively fallen angels—that is, bonds that had been downgraded. Thanks to him, the term junk bond is more inclusive today.

Folklore has it that as an MBA student, Milken came upon a series of books about corporate bonds written in the 1940s.[13] After reading them, Milken concluded that the fallen angels were underpriced. He believed their high yields were not justified by their default rates, so an investor who purchased a well-diversified portfolio of low-grade, speculative bonds

Michael Milken

SOURCE: ©*Trapper Frank*/ CORBIS SYGMA

[13]These books, which haven't been in print for decades, included *Corporate Bond Quality and Investor Experience* and *Corporate Bonds: Quality and Investment Performance*.

could obtain a better return than a buyer of investment-grade bonds. That is, if fewer issuers defaulted than the price of the bonds implied, an investor could generate a high return through diversification.

After graduating in 1970, Milken went to work for what was then Drexel Harriman Ripley, a staid New York investment bank. He convinced the firm to allow him to start trading bonds that were below investment grade. One of the major problems with the market for junk bonds had been the difficulty and expense associated with buying or selling them. Because there was no *liquid* market[14] for them, institutional investors—insurance companies, pension funds, commercial banks, and the like—were hesitant to buy junk bonds. In effect, Milken made a market in low-grade bonds by offering to buy and sell them. His operation could quote prices for a broad array of high-yield securities on short notice. In addition to creating a market for junk bonds, Milken began to purchase them for Drexel's own account. When the value of the bonds rose, the firm—and Milken—profited.

Having created a market for junk bonds and a base of customers willing to hold them, Milken took the next logical step. In April 1977 he began to sell bonds that carried speculative ratings from their inception, called *original-issue high-yield bonds*. Over the next decade, Milken and Drexel raised funds for a broad array of companies, including MCI, Mirage Resorts, and Warner Communications (now part of AOL Time Warner). Their junk-bond issues, ranging from several million to several billion dollars, provided financing to firms that couldn't get it elsewhere.

Until 1984, Milken's operation was restricted to financing existing businesses that were in poor financial condition. Then Milken began to raise financing for a new phenomenon, hostile corporate takeovers. Before 1984, the managers and board of directors of a large company had been insulated from the threat of a buyout or takeover because of the company's size. Who, after all, could raise several billion dollars to buy an entire oil or tobacco company? But with his base of customers, Milken could do just that. He began issuing junk bonds to create war chests for use in takeovers of companies that were thought to be underperforming. The idea was to buy all the company's stock and then replace its management with more capable people. Since these purchases were made with mostly borrowed money, they were called *leveraged buyouts*, or LBOs. By improving the operation of individual firms, LBOs (or the threat of them) are thought to make the economy more efficient.

Milken made enormous amounts of money in this way for his firm (by then called Drexel Burnham Lambert), his colleagues, and himself. In 1986 alone, he is reported to have been paid $550 million.

By the late 1980s Milken's massive wealth, together with his financing of LBOs, had attracted the attention of journalists. Many of the companies whose takeovers he had financed had been reorganized by the new owners. To meet the high interest payments required by the debt issued to buy out these companies, the new managers often had to run their businesses to maximize short-term cash flow rather than long-term viability. Soon critics were asking questions about Milken's practices. Should his customers—insurance companies, pension funds, and banks—be holding speculative-grade debt? Did Milken force companies for whom he had issued junk bonds to purchase new issues under the threat that he might stop making a market in their debt if they did not? Did he engage in illegal trading schemes?

Finally, in 1989, Milken was indicted for securities fraud. He pleaded guilty to six felonies, for which he received a 10-year prison sentence, was fined $1.1 billion, and

---

[14]The larger the volume of trading in any individual financial instrument, the cheaper any individual transaction. If a financial instrument is traded only rarely, an investor will have to pay a high fee to buy it or sell it.

was barred for life from working in the securities industry. In all, he spent three years in prison.[15] But the tale of junk bonds did not end with his convictions. Low-grade debt turned out to be just as risky as people thought. According to one well-known study, one-third of the bonds issued in 1977 and 1978 had gone into default 10 years later.[16] During the recession of 1990–1991, the risk premium on these bonds rose to about 9 percentage points, and their holders suffered large capital losses. Drexel Burnham Lambert, a particularly heavy investor, went bankrupt.

We can take away three important lessons from the history of junk bonds:

MARKETS

- The market in which junk bonds are bought and sold survived the person who created it.
- The ability of less creditworthy firms to obtain funds by issuing high-yield bonds has surely improved the functioning of the financial system.
- New financial instruments, and the markets in which they are traded, can come into existence and prosper if they improve the allocation of economic resources.

Differences in Tax Status and Municipal Bonds

Default risk is not the only factor that affects the return on a bond. The second important thing is taxes. Bondholders must pay income tax on the interest income they receive from owning privately issued bonds, but government bonds are different. These are taxable bonds. In contrast, the coupon payments on bonds issued by state and local governments, called municipal or tax-exempt bonds, are specifically exempt from taxation.[17]

The general rule in the United States is that the interest income from bonds issued by one government is not taxed by another government, although the issuing government may tax it. The interest income from U.S. Treasury securities is taxed by the federal government, which issued them, but not by state or local governments. In the same way, the federal government is precluded from taxing interest on municipal bonds. In an effort to make their bonds even more attractive to investors, however, state and local governments usually choose not to tax the interest on their own bonds, exempting it from all income taxes.

How does a tax exemption affect a bond's yield? Bondholders care about the return they actually receive, after tax authorities have taken their cut. If investors expect to receive a payment of $6 for holding a bond but know they will lose $1.80 of it in taxes, they will act as if the return on the investment is only $4.20. That is, investors base their decisions on the *after-tax yield*.

Calculating the tax implications for bond yields is straightforward. Consider a one-year $100 face value taxable bond with a coupon rate of 6 percent. This is a promise to pay $106 in one year. If the bond is selling at par, at a price of $100, then the yield

[15]Two of the most comprehensive books about Michael Milken, Drexel Burnham Lambert, and the development of the junk-bond market are Connie Bruck's *The Predator's Ball: The Inside Story of Drexel Burnham and the Rise of the Junk Bond Raiders* (NY: Simon and Schuster, 1988) and James B. Stewart's *Den of Thieves* (NYL Simon and Schuster, 1991).

[16]See Paul Asquith, David W. Mullins Jr., and Eric D. Wolf, "Original Issue High Yield Bonds: Aging Analyses of Defaults, Exchanges, and Calls," *Journal of Finance*, September 1989, 923–952.

[17]Municipal bonds come in two varieties. Some are general-obligation bonds backed by the taxing power of the governmental issuer. Others are revenue bonds issued to fund specific projects; these are backed by revenues from the project or operator.

YOUR FINANCIAL WORLD
Which Bond Is Best For You?

Chances are that you receive some kind of interest payment, and the unpleasant truth is that you have to pay taxes on it. (If you don't, the Internal Revenue Service will hunt you down.) The importance of considering taxes when you are making investment decisions is hard to understate. If you have plans to invest in a bond, then you should compare the bonds that are available and take the trouble to learn about their tax implications.

Here are a few things to keep in mind when making such comparisons:

- Everyone who taxes you—the federal government, plus your state and local governments, if applicable—taxes the interest on bonds issued by private corporations.
- Only the Internal Revenue Service, not state and local tax authorities, taxes interest

payments made by the U.S. Treasury. So, if a certificate of deposit and a U.S. Treasury or savings bond carry the same time to maturity and the same interest rate, you should buy the Treasury bond; it will give you a better yield after taxes.*

- Municipal bonds are worth buying if your income tax rate is high.
- Never buy tax-exempt bonds for a retirement account (like an IRA) since the interest income from those accounts is not taxed anyway.
- When tax rates change, the investment that is best for you will change, too.

*Don't think that you can't buy U.S. Treasury bonds. If you do it directly, through *Treasury Direct,* you can start with as little as $1,000. (See www.publicdebt.treas.gov/)

to maturity is 6 percent. From the point of view of the government issuers, the bondholder receives $6 in taxable income at maturity. If the tax rate is 30 percent, the tax on that income is $1.80, so the $100 bond yields $104.20 after taxes. In other words, at a 30 percent tax rate, a 6 percent taxable bond yields the equivalent of 4.2 percent.

This same calculation works for any interest rate and any bond, which allows us to derive a relationship between the yields on taxable and tax-exempt bonds. The rule is that the yield on a tax-exempt bond equals the taxable bond yield times one minus the tax rate:

$$\text{Tax-exempt bond yield} = (\text{Taxable bond yield}) \times (1 - \text{Tax rate}). \qquad (2)$$

For an investor with a 30 percent tax rate, then, we can compute the tax-exempt yield on a 10 percent bond by multiplying 10 percent times $(1 - 0.3)$, or 7 percent. Overall, the higher the tax rate, the wider the gap between the yields on taxable and tax-exempt bonds.

The Term Structure of Interest Rates

A bond's tax status and rating aren't the only factors that affect its yield. In fact, bonds with the same default rate and tax status but different maturity dates usually have different yields. Why? The answer is that long-term bonds are like a composite of a series of short-term bonds, so their yield depends on what people expect to happen in years to come. In this section, we will develop a framework for thinking about *future interest rates.*

The relationship among bonds with the same risk characteristics but different maturities is called the **term structure of interest rates**. A plot of the term structure, with the yield to maturity on the vertical axis and the time to maturity on the horizontal axis, is called the **yield curve**. *The Wall Street Journal's* daily credit market column, in the Money & Investing section (Section C), includes a plot of the yield curve for U.S. Treasury issues like the one shown in Figure 7.4.

In studying the term structure of interest rates, we will focus our attention on Treasury yields; see Figure 7.5. Comparing information on 3-month (the orange line) and 10-year (the green line) Treasury issues, we can draw three conclusions:

1. *Interest rates of different maturities tend to move together.* The bulk of the variation in short- and long-term interest rates is in the same direction. That is, the orange and green lines clearly move together.

2. *Yields on short-term bonds are more volatile than yields on long-term bonds.* The orange line moves over a much broader range than the green line.

3. *Long-term yields tend to be higher than short-term yields.* The green line usually, *but not always*, falls above the orange line.

Default risk and tax differences cannot explain these relationships. What can? We will examine two explanations, the expectations hypothesis and the liquidity premium theory.

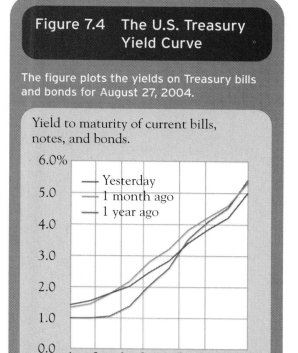

Figure 7.4 The U.S. Treasury Yield Curve

The figure plots the yields on Treasury bills and bonds for August 27, 2004.

SOURCE: *Data compiled from The Board of Governors of the Federal Reserve System.*

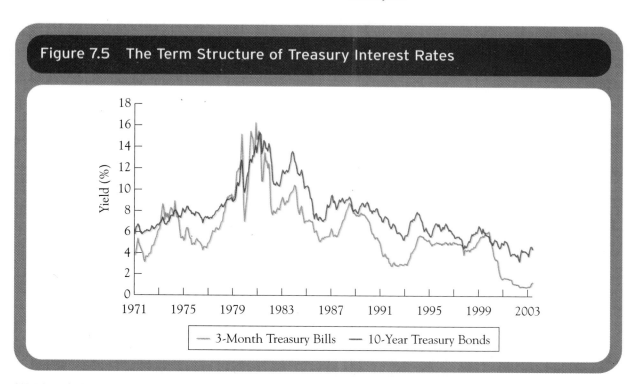

Figure 7.5 The Term Structure of Treasury Interest Rates

The Expectations Hypothesis

Over the years, economists have proposed and discarded numerous theories to explain the term structure of interest rates. We can benefit from this history, and ignore all the less useful ones. The first one we will focus on, called the **expectations hypothesis**, is straightforward and intuitive. If we think about yields as the sum of a risk-free interest rate and a risk premium, the expectations hypothesis focuses on the first of those elements. It begins with the observation that the risk-free interest rate can be computed, assuming there is no uncertainty about the future. That is, we know not just the yield on bonds available today but the yields that will be available on bonds next year, the year after that, and so on.

To understand the implications of this statement, think about an investor who wishes to purchase a bond and hold it for two years. Since there is no uncertainty, the investor knows the yield today on a bond with two years to maturity, as well as the yields on a one-year bond purchased today and on a second one-year bond purchased one year from now. Being sure about all of these, the investor will be indifferent between holding the two-year bond and holding a series of two one-year bonds. *Certainty means that bonds of different maturities are perfect substitutes for each other.* This is the essence of the expectations hypothesis.

To see how this works, assume that the current one-year interest rate is 5 percent. The expectations hypothesis implies that the current two-year interest rate should equal the average of 5 percent and the one-year interest rate one year in the future. If that future interest rate is 7 percent, then the current two-year interest rate will be $(5 + 7)/2 = 6\%$.[18]

According to the expectations hypothesis, then, when interest rates are expected to rise in the future, long-term interest rates will be higher than short-term interest rates. In other words, the yield curve will slope up (see Figure 7.6). (Analogously, the expectations hypothesis implies that if interest rates are expected to fall, the yield curve will slope down. We will return to this shortly.)

If bonds of different maturities are perfect substitutes for each other, then we can construct investment strategies that must have the same yields. Let's look at the investor with a two-year horizon. Two possible strategies are available to this investor:

A. Invest in a two-year bond and hold it to maturity. We will call the interest rate associated with this investment i_{2t} ("i" stands for the interest rate, "2" for two years, and "t" for the time period, which is today). Investing one dollar in this bond will yield $(1 + i_{2t})(1 + i_{2t})$ two years later.

B. Invest in two one-year bonds, one today and a second when the first one matures. The one-year bond purchased today has an interest rate of i_{1t} ("1" stands for one year). The one-year bond purchased one year from now has an interest rate of i_{t+1}^e, where the "$t+1$" stands for one time period past period t, or next year. The "e," which stands for *expected*, indicates that this is the one-year interest rate investors *expect* to obtain one year ahead. Since we are assuming that the future is known, this expectation is certain to be correct. A dollar invested using this strategy will return $(1 + i_{1t})(1 + i_{t+1}^e)$ in two years.

---

[18]As we will see in footnote 19, the exact computation would be $\sqrt{(1.05)(1.07)} = 1.05995$, which is close enough to 6 percent that we can ignore the difference.

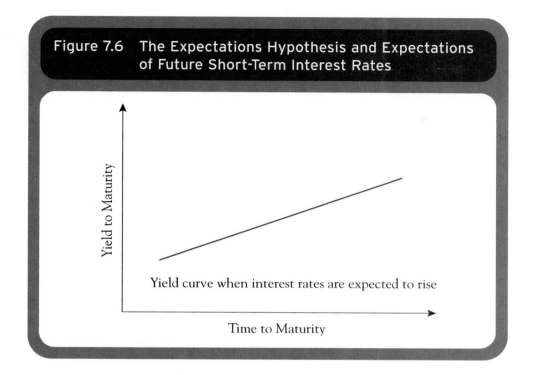

Figure 7.6   The Expectations Hypothesis and Expectations of Future Short-Term Interest Rates

Yield to Maturity

Yield curve when interest rates are expected to rise

Time to Maturity

The expectations hypothesis tells us that investors will be indifferent between these two strategies. (Remember, the bonds are perfect substitutes for each other.) Indifference between strategies A and B means that they must have the same return, so

$$(1 + i_{2t})(1 + i_{2t}) = (1 + i_{1t})(1 + i^e_{t+1}) \qquad (3)$$

Expanding (3) and taking an approximation that is very accurate, we can write the two-year interest rate as the average of the current and future expected one-year interest rates:[19]

$$i_{2t} = \frac{i_{1t} + i^e_{1t+1}}{2} \qquad (4)$$

For a comparison between a three-year bond and three one-year bonds, we get

$$i_{3t} = \frac{i_{1t} + i^e_{1t+1} + i^e_{1t+2}}{3}, \qquad (5)$$

where the notation i_{3t} stands for a three-year interest rate and i^e_{1t+2} for the expected one-year interest rate two years from now.

The general statement of the expectations hypothesis is that the interest rate on a bond with n years to maturity is the average of n expected future one-year interest rates:

$$i_{nt} = \frac{i_{1t} + i^e_{1t+1} + i^e_{1t+2} + \ldots + i^e_{1t+n-1}}{n}. \qquad (6)$$

[19]Expanding (3) gives us $2i_{2t} + i^2_{2t} = i_{1t} + i^e_{1t+1} + (i_{1t})(i^e_{1t+1})$. The squared term on the left-hand side and the product term on the right-hand side of this equation are small, and their difference is even smaller. Using the example of 5 percent and 7 percent for the one-year interest rates, we can see that ignoring the two product terms means ignoring $((.06)^2 - (.05^* .07))/2 = (0.0036 - 0.0035)/2 = 0.00005$, an error of 0.005 percent.

What are the implications of this mathematical expression? Does the *expectations hypothesis of the term structure of interest rates* explain the three observations we started with? Let's look at each one.

1. The expectations hypothesis tells us that long-term bond yields are all averages of expected future short-term yields—the same set of short-term interest rates—so *interest rates of different maturities will move together*. From equation (6) we see that if the current one-year interest rate, i_{1t}, changes, all the yields at higher maturities will change with it.

2. The expectations hypothesis implies that *yields on short-term bonds will be more volatile than yields on long-term bonds*. Because long-term interest rates are averages of a sequence of expected future short-term rates, if the current 3-month interest rate moves, it will have only a small impact on the 10-year interest rate. Again, look at equation (6).[20]

3. The expectations hypothesis *cannot* explain why *long-term yields are normally higher than short-term yields*, since it implies that the yield curve slopes upward only when interest rates are expected to rise. To explain why the yield curve normally slopes upward, the expectations hypothesis would suggest that interest rates are normally expected to rise. But as the data in Figure 7.5 show, interest rates have been trending downward for the past 20 years, so anyone constantly forecasting interest-rate increases would have been sorely disappointed.

The expectations hypothesis has gotten us two-thirds of the way toward understanding the term structure of interest rates. By ignoring risk and assuming that investors view short- and long-term bonds as perfect substitutes, we have explained why yields at different maturities move together and why short-term interest rates are more volatile than long-term rates. But we have failed to explain why the yield curve normally slopes upward. To understand this, we need to extend the expectations hypothesis to include risk. After all, we all know that long-term bonds are riskier than short-term bonds. Integrating this observation into our analysis will give us the *liquidity premium theory* of the term structure of interest rates.

The Liquidity Premium Theory

Throughout our discussion of bonds, we emphasized that even default-free bonds are risky because of uncertainty about inflation and future interest rates. What are the implications of these risks for our understanding of the term structure of interest rates? The answer is that risk is the key to understanding the *slope* of the yield curve. The yield curve's upward slope is explained by the fact that long-term bonds are riskier than short-term bonds. Bondholders face both inflation and interest-rate risk. The longer the term of the bond, the greater both types of risk.

The reason for the increase in inflation risk over time is clear-cut. Remember that bondholders care about the purchasing power of the return—the *real* return—they receive from a bond, not just the nominal dollar value of the coupon payments. Computing the real return from the nominal return requires a forecast of future inflation, or *expected* future inflation. For a three-month bond, an investor need only be concerned with inflation over the next three months. For a 10-year

---

[20]Take a simple example in which the one-year and two-year interest rates, i_{1t} and i_{2t}, are both 5 percent. If the one-year interest rate increases to 7 percent, then the two-year interest rate will rise to 6 percent. The two move together, and the short-term rate is more volatile than the long-term rate.

RISK

bond, however, computation of the real return requires a forecast of inflation over the next decade.

In summary, uncertainty about inflation creates uncertainty about a bond's real return, making the bond a risky investment. The further we look into the future, the greater the uncertainty about inflation. We are more uncertain about the level of inflation several years from now than about the level of inflation a few months from now, which implies that *a bond's inflation risk increases with its time to maturity*.[21]

What about interest-rate risk? Interest-rate risk arises from a mismatch between the investor's investment horizon and a bond's time to maturity. Remember that if a bondholder plans to sell a bond prior to maturity, changes in the interest rate (which cause bond prices to move) generate capital gains or losses. The longer the term of the bond, the greater the price changes for a given change in interest rates and the larger the potential for capital losses.

Since some holders of long-term bonds will want to sell their bonds before they mature, interest-rate risk concerns them. These investors require compensation for the risk they take in buying long-term bonds. As in the case of inflation, the risk increases with the term to maturity, so the compensation must increase with it.

What are the implications of including risk in our model of the term structure of interest rates? To answer this question, we can think about a bond yield as having two parts, one that is risk free and another that is a risk premium. The expectations hypothesis explains the risk-free part, and inflation and interest-rate risk explain the risk premium. Together they form the liquidity premium theory of the term structure of interest rates. Adding the risk premium to equation (6), we can express this theory mathematically as

$$i_{nt} = rp_n + \frac{i_{1t} + i^e_{1t+1} + i^e_{1t+2} + \ldots + i^e_{1t+n-1}}{n}, \qquad (8)$$

where rp_n is the risk premium associated with an n-year bond. The larger the risk, the higher the risk premium, rp_n, is. Since risk rises with maturity, rp_n increases with n, the yield on a long-term bond includes a larger risk premium than the yield on a short-term bond.

Can the liquidity premium theory explain all three of our conclusions about the term structure of interest rates? The answer is yes. Like the expectations hypothesis, the liquidity premium theory predicts that *interest rates of different maturities will move together* and that *yields on short-term bonds will be more volatile than yields on long-term bonds*. And by adding a risk premium that grows with time to maturity, it explains why *long-term yields are higher than short-term yields*. Since the risk premium increases with time to maturity, the liquidity premium theory tells us that the yield curve will normally slope upward; only rarely will it lie flat or slope downward. (A flat yield curve means that interest rates are expected to fall; a downward-sloping yield curve suggests that the financial markets are expecting a significant decline in interest rates.)

---

[21]Historically, the long-term inflation rate has surely been more uncertain than the short-term inflation rate. But the extent of the increased uncertainty and risk has depended on the behavior of the central bank. We will discuss this topic in more detail in Part IV.

TOOLS OF THE TRADE
Reading Charts

A picture can be worth a thousand words, but only if you know what it represents. To decode charts and graphs, use these strategies:

1. *Read the title of the chart.* This point may seem trivial, but titles are often very descriptive and can give you a good start in understanding a chart.

2. *Read the label on the horizontal axis.* Does the chart show the movements in a stock price or in the interest rate over minutes, hours, days, weeks, months, or years? Are the numbers spaced evenly?

   Look at Figure 7.7, a sample of the Treasury yield curve that appears in *The Wall Street Journal* every day. The horizontal axis extends from three months to 30 years, but the increments are not evenly spaced. In fact, a distance that starts out as three months on the left-hand corner becomes over 10 years at the far right. The axis is drawn in this way for two reasons. First, it focuses the reader's eye on the shorter end of the yield curve. Second, the telescoped axis narrows so that it takes up less space.

   Interestingly, this particular yield curve shows a slight downward slope from three months to one year, followed by a steep upward slope. This pattern suggests that investors expected interest rates to decline sharply for the next year and then rise after that, which is exactly what happened.

3. *Read the label on the vertical axis.* What is the range of the data? This is a crucial piece of information, since most charts are made to fill the space available. As a result, small movements can appear to be very large. Compare the two charts on page 167 of inflation that follow. The first shows the percentage change in the consumer price index from 1989 to 2001; the second shows the same data starting seven years later, in 1996.

   In the first chart, the vertical axis ranges from 0 percent to 8 percent; in the second chart, it covers only 0 to 4 percent. To fill the second chart visually, the artist changed the vertical scale.

   Looking quickly at these two charts can be misleading. Without noticing the difference in their vertical scale, we could conclude that the increase in inflation from 1999 to 2000 was at least as dramatic as the decline in inflation during 1991. But on closer inspection, we see that from 1999 to 2000 inflation rose from $1\frac{1}{2}$ percent to $3\frac{1}{2}$ percent, while in 1991 it fell from 6 percent to just over 2 percent. A proper reading of the charts leads to the correct conclusion that the decline in 1991 was twice as large as the increase in 1991–2000.

Figure 7.7 Treasury Yield Curve

April 23, 2001

(Yield curve chart with vertical axis from 3.00% to 6.00% in 0.50 increments, horizontal axis showing maturities: 3 mos., 6, 1 yr., 2, 5, 10, 30. Three lines shown: Friday, 1 week ago, 4 weeks ago)

continued on next page

continued from previous page

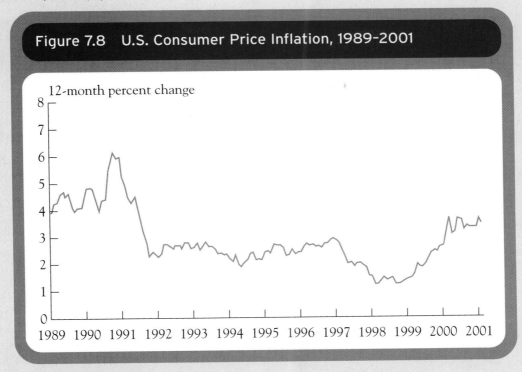

Figure 7.8   U.S. Consumer Price Inflation, 1989–2001

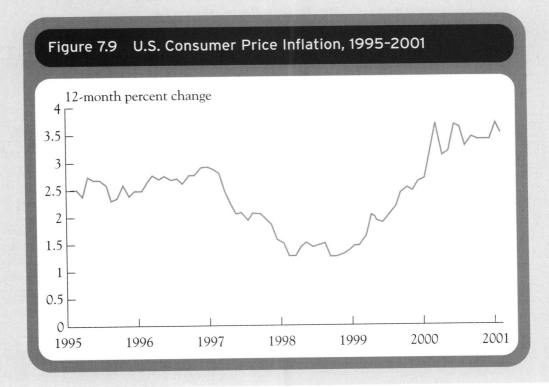

Figure 7.9   U.S. Consumer Price Inflation, 1995–2001

The Information Content of Interest Rates

The risk and term structure of interest rates contain useful information about overall economic conditions. These indicators are helpful in evaluating both the present health of the economy and its likely future course. Risk spreads provide one type of information, the term structure another. In the following sections we will apply what we have just learned about interest rates to recent U.S. economic history and show how forecasters use these tools.

Information in the Risk Structure of Interest Rates

When the overall growth rate of the economy slows or turns negative, it strains private businesses, increasing the risk that corporations will be unable to meet their financial obligations. The immediate impact of an impending recession, then, is to raise the risk premium on privately issued bonds. Importantly, though, an economic slowdown or recession does not affect the risk of holding government bonds.

The increased risk of default is not the same for all firms. The impact of a recession on companies with high bond ratings is usually small, so the spread between U.S. Treasuries and Aaa-rated bonds of the same maturity is not likely to move by much. But for issuers whose finances were precarious prior to the downturn, the effect is quite different. Those borrowers who were least likely to meet their payment obligations when times were good are even less likely to meet them when times turn bad. There is a real chance that they will fail to make interest payments. Of course, firms for whom even the slightest negative development might mean disaster are the ones that issue low-grade bonds. The lower the initial grade of the bond, the more the default-risk premium rises as general economic conditions deteriorate. The spread between U.S. Treasury bonds and junk bonds widens the most.

Figure 7.10A shows annual GDP growth over three decades superimposed on shading that shows the dates of recessions. (We'll learn more about recession dating in Chapter 22.) Notice that during the shaded periods, growth is usually negative. In Figure 7.10B, GDP growth is drawn as the lighter, orange line and the darker, maroon line is the spread between yields on Baa-rated bonds and U.S. Treasury bonds. Note that the two lines move in opposite directions. (The correlation between the two series is –0.45.) That is, when the risk spread rises, output falls. The risk spread provides a good measure of general economic activity, and since financial markets operate every day, this information is available well before GDP data, which is published only once every three months.[22]

Information in the Term Structure of Interest Rates

Like information on the risk structure of interest rates, information on the term structure—particularly the slope of the yield curve—helps us to forecast general economic conditions. Recall that according to the expectations hypothesis, the long-term interest rates contain information about expected future short-term interest rates. And according to the liquidity premium theory, the yield curve usually slopes upward.

---

[22]For an extended discussion of how to use the spread between investment-grade and junk bonds as an indicator of business-cycle activity, see Mark Gertler and Cara Lown, "The Information in the High Yield Bond Spread for the Business Cycle: Evidence and Some Implications," *Oxford Review of Economic Policy* 15, no. 3 (Autumn 1999), pp. 132–150.

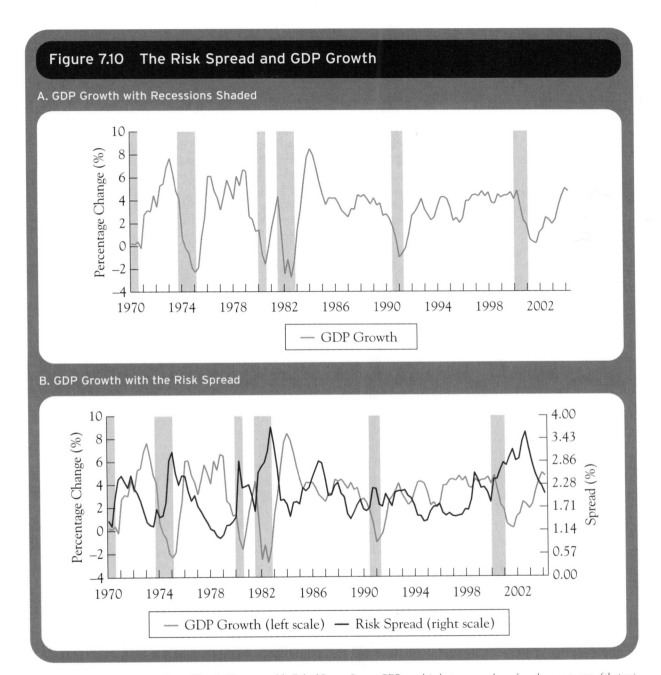

Figure 7.10   The Risk Spread and GDP Growth

A. GDP Growth with Recessions Shaded

— GDP Growth

B. GDP Growth with the Risk Spread

— GDP Growth (left scale)   — Risk Spread (right scale)

SOURCE: *Bureau of Economic Analysis and Board of Governors of the Federal Reserve System. GDP growth is the percentage change from the same quarter of the previous year, while the yield spread is the (rescaled) difference between the average yield on Baa and 10-year U.S. Treasury bonds during the quarter.*

APPLYING THE CONCEPT
THE FLIGHT TO QUALITY

Standing in the middle of an open field during a thunderstorm is a good way to get hurt, so few people do it. Instead, they take shelter. Investors do exactly the same thing during financial storms; they look for a safe place to put their investments until the storm blows over. In practical terms, that means selling risky investments and buying the safest instruments they can: U.S. Treasury bills, notes, and bonds. An increase in the demand for government bonds coupled with a decrease in the demand for virtually everything else is called a **flight to quality**. When it happens, there is a dramatic increase in the difference between the yields on safe and risky bonds—the *risk spread* rises.

When the government of Russia defaulted on its bonds in August 1998, the shock set off an almost unprecedented flight to quality. Yields on U.S. Treasuries plummeted, while those on corporate bonds rose. Risk spreads widened quickly; the difference between U.S. Treasury bill and commercial paper rates more than doubled, from its normal level of half a percentage point to over one percentage point. The debt of countries with emerging markets was particularly hard hit.

This flight to quality was what William McDonough called "the most serious financial crisis since World War II" (see the opening of this chapter). Because people wanted to hold only U.S. Treasury securities, the financial markets had ceased to function properly. McDonough worried that the problems in the financial markets would spread to the economy as a whole. Fortunately for all of us, they didn't.

The key term in this statement is *usually*. On rare occasions, short-term interest rates exceed long-term yields. When they do, the term structure is said to be *inverted*, and the yield curve slopes downward.

An **inverted yield curve** is a valuable forecasting tool because it predicts a general economic slowdown. Since the yield curve slopes upward even when short-term yields are expected to remain constant—it's the average of expected future short-term interest rates plus a risk premium—an inverted yield curve signals an expected fall in short-term interest rates. If interest rates are comparatively high, they serve as a brake on real economic activity. As we will see in Part IV, monetary policymakers adjust short-term interest rates in order to influence real economic growth and inflation. When the yield curve slopes downward, it indicates that policy is *tight* because policymakers are attempting to slow economic growth and inflation.

Careful statistical analysis confirms the value of the yield curve as a forecasting tool.[23] Figure 7.11 shows GDP growth and the slope of the yield curve, measured as the difference between the 10-year and 3-month yields—what is called a **term spread**. Figure 7.11A shows GDP growth (as in Figure 7.10) together with the contempora-

[23]See Arturo Estrella and Frederic S. Mishkin, "The Yield Curve as a Predictor of U.S. Recessions," Federal Reserve Bank of New York, *Current Issues in Economics and Finance* 2, no. 7 (June 1996); and Michael Dotsey, "The Predictive Content of the Interest Rate Term Spread for Future Economic Growth," Federal Reserve Bank of Richmond *Economic Quarterly* 84, no. 3 (Summer 1998), pp. 31–51.

Figure 7.11   The Term Spread and GDP Growth

A. Current Term Spread and GDP Growth

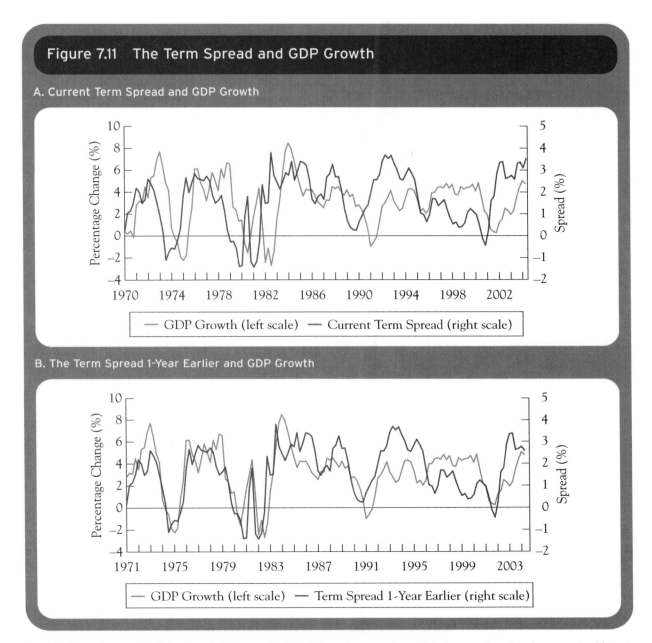

B. The Term Spread 1-Year Earlier and GDP Growth

SOURCE: *Bureau of Economic Analysis and Board of Governors of the Federal Reserve System. GDP growth is the percentage change from the same quarter of the previous year, while the term spread is the difference between the average yield on 10-year U.S. Treasury bond and a 3-month U.S. Treasury bill during the quarter. In panel B, the spread is lagged one year.*

neous term spread (the growth and the term spread at the same time). Notice that when the term spread falls, GDP growth tends to fall somewhat later. In fact, when the yield curve becomes inverted, the economy tends to go into a recession roughly a year later. Figure 7.11B makes this clear. At each point, GDP growth in the current year (e.g., 1990) is plotted against the slope of the yield curve *one year earlier* (e.g., 1989). The two lines clearly move together; their correlation is +0.58. What the data

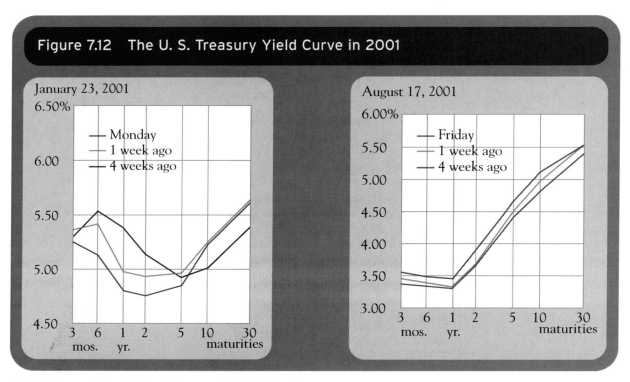

Figure 7.12   The U. S. Treasury Yield Curve in 2001

January 23, 2001

— Monday
— 1 week ago
— 4 weeks ago

August 17, 2001

— Friday
— 1 week ago
— 4 weeks ago

SOURCE: *Data compiled from The Board of Governors of the Federal Reserve System.*

show is that when the term spread falls, GDP growth tends to fall one year later. The yield curve is a valuable forecasting tool.

An example illustrates the usefulness of this information. In the left-hand panel of Figure 7.12, we can see that on January 23, 2001, the yield curve sloped downward from 3 months to 10 years, then upward for maturities to 30 years. This pattern indicated that interest rates were expected to fall over the next few years. Eight months later, after monetary policy had eased and the U.S. economy had slowed substantially, the Treasury yield curve sloped upward again (see the right-hand panel of Figure 7.12). At that point, growth was at a virtual standstill, and policymakers were doing everything they could to get the economy moving again. They had reduced interest rates by more than 3 percentage points over a period of less than nine months. Thus, investors expected little in the way of short-term interest-rate reductions. This prediction turned out to be wrong, however; interest rates kept falling after the terrorist attacks of September 11, 2001. They continued to fall through the remainder of 2001 as the economy went into a mild recession.

We started this chapter by asking why different types of bonds have different yields and what it is we can learn from those differences. After a bit of work, we can now see that differences in both risk and time to maturity affect bond yields. The less likely the issuer is to repay or the longer the time to maturity, the riskier a bond and the higher its yield. Even more importantly, both increases in the risk spread and an inverted yield curve suggest troubled economic times ahead.

IN THE NEWS

The Future is in Bonds: Put down those tea leaves; the bond market is the best soothsayer we have.

FORTUNE

by Lee Clifford

Monday, May 14, 2001

When Cisco CEO John Chambers announced in late April 2001 that he wouldn't meet sales and profit targets for the fiscal third quarter, he compared the brutal slowdown of 2000–2001 to an unforeseeable 100-year flood. "We never built models to anticipate something of this magnitude," he said.

If Chambers had paid attention to the bond markets, he might have had time to build a life-saving ark. While Cisco and others were ramping up production, bond strategists were obsessing over a phenomenon called an "inverted yield curve," which appeared at the beginning of 2000. (The rare occurrence, in which short-term Treasury bond yields move higher than long-term yields, portends a weakening economy.)

As an experience, bond analysis ranks right up there with, say, getting hit over the head with a shovel—it's painful and leaves you feeling a bit shell-shocked. Nonetheless, investors are realizing the importance of the bond market as an economic barometer. Economists say that more often than not, the yield curve predicts changes in the economy.

Months before major companies began toying with declaring bankruptcy to escape their obligations, Wall Street analysts concluded that they were carrying crushing debt loads and started predicting their demise. "The bond market was ahead of everyone in saying the economy is weak and that the Fed is going to have to ease aggressively," says William Dudley, chief U.S. economist at Goldman Sachs.

So what are bonds saying now in the spring of 2001? Some encouraging things, it turns out. First off, the same yield curve that called the slowdown reversed course in December and is now anticipating economic growth. "The curve hasn't been this steep since 1998," says John Lonski, chief economist at Moody's. (In fact, long-term bonds have experienced a selloff because traders fear that once the economy picks up, inflation will rise—but that's another story.) This turnaround is only good news, says Tony Crescenzi, chief bond market strategist at brokerage Miller Tabak & Co. "Bond yields rise prior to improvements in the economy. It's almost universal."

The high-yield, or junk-bond, markets—often the only place companies with bad credit can go for financing and thus a good gauge of the market's appetite for risk—are also looking up, at least in terms of liquidity. The markets, which all but dried up at the end of last year, have started to improve. Among other indicators, mortgage applications and refinancings—a way that bond analysts measure how quickly consumers are responding to the Fed's lower interest rates—are also trending sharply upward.

Some important sectors are also showing signs of improvement. High-yield spreads (the difference between the interest rate that companies are charged on their junk bonds and what Treasuries pay) in industries like automotive supplies, building materials, retail, finance, insurance, and health care have narrowed since the year began, meaning debt investors are growing less leery of them. Evidence, says Lonski, "that in those sectors, the worst may have passed."

The bond market's outlook could change if the Federal Reserve doesn't deliver on expectations; bond watchers are counting on Federal Reserve Board Chairman Alan Greenspan to cut interest rates by 50 basis points in the next two months, according to Ken Hackel, Merrill Lynch's chief U.S. fixed-income strategist. "The bond markets have decided that Greenspan will prevent Armageddon," says Paul McCulley, managing director at PIMCO. The most bullish strategists see the broader economy beginning to rebound as early as the end of the summer—anticipating improved earnings in the fourth quarter of this year or the first quarter of 2002. A ways off, but nothing like a 100-year flood. "Stock investors should be comforted by what bond investors are seeing," says Crescenzi. That's one way to put it. Or there's McCulley's take: "We won't go to hell twice," he says. "But we may just have to stay in purgatory a bit longer."

LESSONS OF THE ARTICLE

The yield curve predicts changes in the economy. Business decision makers, Wall Street analysts, and government policymakers all look to the bond market for information on future economic developments. In particular, increases in the risk premium on certain bonds often serve as early warning signs of general economic problems.

Terms

benchmark bond, 154

commercial paper, 149

expectations hypothesis of the term structure, 162

fallen angel, 150

flight to quality, 170

interest-rate spread, 149

inverted yield curve, 170

investment-grade bond, 150

junk bond, 150

liquidity premium theory of the term structure, 165

municipal bonds, 159

prime-grade commercial paper, 153

rating, 150

ratings downgrade, 152

ratings upgrade, 152

risk spread, 154

risk structure of interest rates, 155

spread over Treasuries, 154

taxable bond, 159

tax-exempt bond, 159

term spread, 170

term structure of interest rates, 160

unsecured, 152

yield curve, 160

Chapter Lessons

1. Bond ratings summarize the likelihood that a bond issuer will meet its payment obligations.

   a. Highly rated investment-grade bonds are those with the lowest risk of default.

   b. If a firm encounters financial difficulties, its bond rating may be downgraded.

   c. Commercial paper is the short-term version of a privately issued bond.

   d. Junk bonds are high-risk bonds with very low ratings. Firms that have a high probability of default issue these bonds.

   e. Investors demand compensation for default risk in the form of a risk premium. The higher the risk of default, the lower a bond's rating, the higher its risk premium, and the higher its yield.

2. The history of the junk-bond market teaches us that new financial instruments and markets will survive when they improve the allocation of economic resources.

3. Municipal bonds are usually exempt from income taxes. Since investors care about the after-tax returns on their investments, these bonds have lower yields than bonds whose interest payments are taxable.

4. The term structure of interest rates is the relationship between yield to maturity and time to maturity. A graph with the yield to maturity on the vertical axis and the time to maturity on the horizontal axis is called the yield curve.

   a. Any theory of the term structure of interest rates must explain three facts:

      i. Interest rates of different maturities move together.

      ii. The yields on short-term bonds are more volatile than the yields on long-term bonds.

      iii. Long-term yields are usually higher than short-term yields.

   b. The expectations hypothesis of the term structure of interest rates states that long-term interest rates are the average of expected future short-term interest rates. This hypothesis explains only the first two facts about the term structure of interest rates.

c. The liquidity premium theory of the term structure of interest rates, which is based on the fact that long-term bonds are riskier than short-term bonds, explains all three facts in 4a.

5. The risk structure and the term structure of interest rates both signal financial markets' expectations of future economic activity. Specifically, the likelihood of a recession will be higher when

a. The risk spread, or the range between low- and high-grade bond yields, is growing.

b. The yield curve slopes downward, or is inverted, so that short-term interest rates are higher than long-term interest rates.

Problems

1. During a recession, all businesses encounter difficulties at the same time. What would you expect to happen to bond ratings during such an episode?

2. Suppose your marginal federal income tax rate is 36 percent. What is your after-tax return from holding a one-year corporate bond with a yield of 9 percent? What is your after-tax return from holding a one-year municipal bond with a yield of 5 percent? How would you decide which bond to hold?

3. The U.S. Congress is considering cutting the highest federal income tax rate from 36 percent to 28 percent. Explain the impact such a move would be likely to have on the price and yield of tax-exempt municipal bonds. If you were the mayor of your city, how would you react to the proposed change in tax rate?

4. Over the years, income tax rates have changed dramatically. In 1981, the highest tax rate was reduced from 70 percent to less than 40 percent. What impact do you think this reduction had on the difference between the yields on U.S. Treasury bonds and municipal bonds? Using the data available on the Federal Reserve's Web site, compare the return on "Over 10 year (long-term)" Treasury bonds with the return on "State and Local" bonds around the time of the tax code change to determine the movement in the spread.

5. Suppose that the interest rate on one-year bonds is 4 percent today and is expected to be 5 percent one year from now and 6 percent two years from now. Using the expectations hypothesis, compute the yield curve for the next three years.

6. You have $1,000 to invest over an investment horizon of three years. The bond market offers various options. You can buy (a) a sequence of three one-year bonds; (b) a three-year bond; or (c) a two-year bond followed by a one-year bond. The current yield curve tells you that the one-year, two-year, and three-year yields to maturity are 3.5 percent, 4.0 percent, and 4.5 percent respectively. You expect that one-year interest rates will be 4 percent next year and 5 percent the year after that. Assuming annual compounding, compute the return on each of the three investments. Discuss which one you would choose.

7. In the winter of 1994 the yield curve sloped upward, but the Federal Reserve Board was concerned that the economy might be overheating. In response, the Board raised short-term interest rates a number of times. At first the yield curve simply shifted upward in a roughly parallel movement. Eventually it began to flatten, at

www.mhhe.com/cecchettile

which point interest rates stopped rising. Using the expectations hypothesis, explain what happened.

8. During the 1990s, the Japanese economy stagnated. For most of the decade, there was virtually no economic growth and prices actually fell. The yield curve went from close to zero at short maturities to rates of $1\frac{1}{4}$ to $1\frac{1}{2}$ percent at the long end. When the Japanese economy finally begins to improve, what do you expect will happen to the yield curve? Why?

9. As economic conditions improve in countries with emerging markets, the cost of borrowing funds there tends to fall. Explain why.

10. When emerging markets countries have financial problems, yields on U.S. Treasury issues tends to fall. Can you explain this phenomenon? What would happen to the risk spread under such circumstances, and how would you use that information?

11. As a result of problems with the tires on the Ford Explorer (an SUV), the Ford Motor Company faced the possibility of a downgrade in its commercial paper rating, from A-1/P-1 to A-2/P-2. The spread between the two ratings is roughly half a percentage point. If Ford needed to issue $1 billion of commercial paper in order to maintain its operations, how much would this ratings downgrade cost the company?

12. Since short-term interest rates are usually lower than long-term rates, some people have suggested that issuing long-term bonds makes very little sense. Analyze this assertion.

13. Suppose the risk premium on bonds increases. How would the change affect your forecast of future economic activity? Why?

14. The Japanese population is aging more rapidly than that of most other countries, so the ratio of working-age people to retirees is falling. Many years ago, the government promised Japanese citizens a retirement income—a pledge that is likely to strain Japanese finances for years to come. How would you expect this population trend to affect the credit rating of the Japanese government's bonds? Why?

15. Go to the Federal Reserve Board's Web site (www.federalreserve.gov) and click first on Research and Data, then on Statistical Data and Releases. Compute the spread between the yield on three-month commercial paper and three-month Treasury bills sold on the secondary market. Looking at the data for the last few years, can you infer anything interesting from the movements in the spread?

Chapter 8

Stocks, Stock Markets, and Market Efficiency

Stocks play a prominent role in our financial and economic lives. For individuals, they provide a key instrument for holding personal wealth as well as a way to diversify, spreading and reducing the risks that we face. Importantly, diversifiable risks are risks that are more likely to be taken. By providing individuals with a way to transfer risk, stocks provide a type of insurance enhancing our ability to take risk.[1]

For companies, they are one of several ways to obtain financing. Beyond that, though, stocks and stock markets are one of the central links between the financial world and the real economy. Stock prices are fundamental to the functioning of a market-based economy. They tell us the value of the companies that issued the stocks and, like all other prices, they allocate scarce investment resources. The firms deemed most valuable in the marketplace for stocks are the ones that will be able to obtain financing for growth. When resources flow to their most valued uses, the economy operates more efficiently.

Mention of the stock market provokes an emotional reaction in many people. They see it as a place where fortunes are easily made or lost, and they recoil at its unfathomable booms and busts. During one infamous week in October 1929, the New York Stock Exchange lost over 25 percent of its value—an event that marked the beginning of the Great Depression. In October 1987, prices fell nearly 30 percent in one week, including a record decline of 20 percent in a single day. Crashes of this magnitude have become part of the stock market's folklore, creating the popular impression that stocks are very risky.

In the 1990s, stock prices increased nearly fivefold and Americans forgot about the "black Octobers." By the end of the decade, many people had come to see stocks as almost a sure thing; you could not afford not to own them. In 1998, nearly half of all U.S. households owned some stock, either directly or indirectly through mutual funds and managed retirement accounts.

When the market's inexorable rise finally ended, the ensuing decline seemed more like a slowly deflating balloon than a crash. From January 2000 to the week following the terrorist attacks of September 11, 2001, the stock prices of the United States' biggest companies, as measured by the Dow Jones Industrial Average, fell more than 30 percent. While many stocks recovered much of their loss fairly quickly, a large number did not. During the same period, the Nasdaq Composite index fell 70 percent, from 5,000 to 1,500; by summer 2004, it still remained below 2,000. Since the Nasdaq tracks smaller, newer, more technologically oriented companies, many observers dubbed this episode the "Internet bubble."

Contrary to popular mythology, stock prices tend to rise steadily and slowly, collapsing only on those rare occasions when normal market mechanisms are out of alignment. For most people the experience of losing or gaining wealth suddenly is

---

[1]This point was central to our discussions of risk in Chapter 5. Our ability to diversify risk either through the explicit purchase of insurance or through investment strategies means that we do risky things that we otherwise would not do.

more memorable than the experience of making it gradually. By being preoccupied with the potential short-term losses associated with crashes, we lose sight of the gains we could realize if we took a longer-term view. The goal of this chapter is to try to make sense of the stock market—to show what fluctuations in stock value mean for individuals and for the economy as a whole and look at a critical connection between the financial system and the real economy. We will also explain how it is that things sometimes go awry, resulting in bubbles and crashes. First, however, we need to define the basics: what stocks are, how they originated, and how they are valued.

The Essential Characteristics of Common Stock

Stocks, also known as common stock or equity, are shares in a firm's ownership. A firm that issues stock sells part of itself, so that the buyer becomes a part owner. Stocks as we know them first appeared in the 16th century. They were created to raise funds for global exploration. Means had to be found to finance the dangerous voyages of explorers such as Sir Francis Drake, Henry Hudson, and Vasco de Gama. Aside from kings and queens, no one was wealthy enough to finance these risky ventures alone. The solution was to spread the risk through *joint-stock companies*, organizations that issued stock and used the proceeds to finance several expeditions at once. In exchange for investing, stockholders received a share of the company's profits.

These early stocks had two important characteristics that we take for granted today. First, the shares were issued in *small denominations*, allowing investors to buy as little or as much of the company as they wanted; and second, the shares were *transferable*, meaning that an owner could sell them to someone else. Today, the vast majority of large companies issue stock that investors buy and sell regularly. The shares normally are quite numerous, each one representing only a small fraction of a company's total value. The large number and small size of individual shares—prices are usually below $100 per share—make the purchase and sale of stocks relatively easy.

Until recently, all stockowners received a certificate from the issuing company. Figure 8.1, on the left, shows the first stock certificate issued by the Ford Motor Company in 1903, to Henry Ford. The right-hand side of the figure shows a more recent stock certificate issued by the World Wrestling Federation (WWF), renamed World Wrestling Enterprises (WWE). The WWE is the media and entertainment company that produces the wrestling events involving characters like The Rock and Hulk Hogan. The former governor of Minnesota, Jesse Ventura, worked for the WWF before entering politics.

Today, most stockholders no longer receive certificates; the odds are that you will never see one. Instead, the information they bear is computerized, and the shares are registered in the names of brokerage firms that hold them on investors' behalf. This procedure is safer, since computerized certificates can't be stolen. It also makes the process of selling the shares much easier.

The ownership of common stock conveys a number of rights. First and most importantly, a stockholder is entitled to participate in the profits of the enterprise. Importantly, however, the stockholder is merely a residual claimant. If the company runs into financial trouble, only after all other creditors have been paid what they are owed will the stockholders receive what is left, if anything. Stockholders get the leftovers!

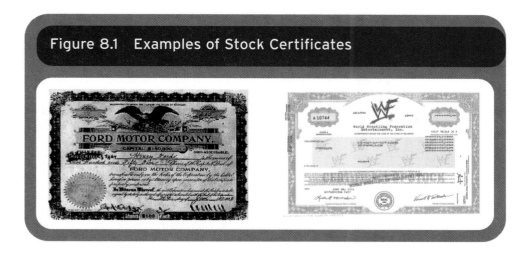

Figure 8.1   Examples of Stock Certificates

To understand what being the residual claimant means, let's look at the case of a software manufacturer. The company needs a number of things to make it run. The list might include rented office space, computers, programmers, and some cash balances for day-to-day operations. These are the *inputs* into the production of the company's software *output*. If we took a snapshot of the company's finances on any given day, we would see that the firm owes payments to a large number of people, including the owner of the office space it rents, the programmers that work for it, the supplier of its computers, and the bondholders and bankers who have lent the firm resources. The company uses the revenue from selling its software to pay these people. After everyone has been paid, the stockholders get the rest of the revenue. In some years, the company does well and there are funds left over, so the stockholders do well. But when the firm does poorly, the stockholders may get nothing. If the firm performs really poorly, failing to sell enough software to cover its obligations, it can go bankrupt and cease operating entirely. In that case, the stockholders lose their entire investment.

The possibility of bankruptcy brings up an interesting question. What happens if a company's revenue is insufficient to cover its obligations to nonstockholders? What if its revenue is too small to pay the landlord, the programmers, the supplier of the computers, and the bondholders and other lenders? It would appear that the stockholders' promised participation in the firm's profits would yield a liability rather than a payment. If the company does very poorly, will the stockholders have to pay the firm's creditors?

An arrangement in which the stockholders are held liable for the firm's losses is very unappealing and would surely discourage people from buying stock. Stockholders bore that risk until the early 19th century. It ended with the introduction of the legal concept of limited liability.[2] Limited liability means that, even if a company fails completely, the maximum amount that shareholders can lose is their initial investment. *Liability* for the company's losses is *limited* at zero, meaning that investors can never lose more than they have invested. Clearly, buying stock is much more attractive if you know that your maximum potential loss is the price you pay for the stock in the first place.

Beyond participating in the firm's profits, owners of common stock are entitled to vote at the firm's annual meeting. Though managers supervise a firm's day-to-day activities, the shareholders elect the board of directors, which meets several times per year

[2]The United States passed the first general law granting limited liability to manufacturing companies in 1811.

to oversee management. Ultimately, the shareholders' ability to dislodge directors and managers who are performing poorly is crucial to their willingness to purchase shares.[3] This ability to elect and remove directors and managers varies with a country's legal structure. In places where shareholders' legal rights are weak, stock ownership is less appealing, and equities are a less important form of corporate financing.

Today, stock ownership is immensely popular. Investors want to own stocks and companies want to issue them. Over the past century, markets have developed in which people buy and sell billions of shares every day. This thriving financial trade is possible because

- An individual share represents only a small fraction of the value of the company that issued it.
- A large number of shares are outstanding.
- Prices of individual shares are low, allowing individuals to make relatively small investments.
- As residual claimants, stockholders receive the proceeds of a firm's activities only after all other creditors have been paid.
- Because of limited liability, investors' losses cannot exceed the price they paid for the stock.
- Shareholders can replace managers who are doing a bad job.

Measuring the Level of the Stock Market

Stocks are one way in which we choose to hold our wealth. When stock values rise, we get richer; when they fall, we get poorer. These changes affect our consumption and saving patterns, causing general economic activity to fluctuate. We need to understand the dynamics of the stock market, both to manage our personal finances and to see the connections between stock values and economic conditions. From a macroeconomic point of view, we need to be able to measure the level of fluctuation in all stock values. We will refer to this concept as the *value* of the stock market and to its measures as stock-market indexes.

You are probably familiar with price indexes, like the consumer price index, and output indexes, like industrial production and real gross domestic product. The purpose of an index number is to give a measure of scale so that we can compute percentage changes. The consumer price index, for example, is not measured in dollars. Instead, it is a pure number. In June 2004, the value of the Consumer Price Index for All Urban Consumers was 189.4, which isn't very interesting on its own. If, however, you know that 12 months earlier, in June 2003, the same CPI index was 183.5, then you can figure out that prices rose 3.2 percent over a 12-month period—that's the percentage change in the index.

Stock-market indexes are the same. They are designed to give us a sense of the extent to which things are going up or down. Saying that the Dow Jones Industrial Average is at 10,000 doesn't mean anything on its own. But if you know that the Dow index rose from 10,000 to 11,000, that tells you that stock prices (by this measure) went up 10 percent. As we will see, stock indexes can tell us both how much the value of an average stock has changed and how much total wealth has gone up or down. Beyond that, stock

---

[3]Managers and directors may have different priorities and objectives from shareholders. While the firm's owners would like to see the value of their investment increase, managers may be more interested in ensuring that they retain their jobs.

indexes provide benchmarks for performance of money managers, allowing us to measure whether a particular manager has done better or worse than "the market" as a whole.

A quick look at the financial news reveals a number of stock-market indexes, covering both domestic stocks and stocks issued by firms in foreign countries. Our goal in this section is to learn what these are and, more important, what question each is designed to answer. We will start with a detailed discussion of the two most important U.S. indexes, the *Dow Jones Industrial Average* and the *Standard & Poor's 500 Index*. A brief description of other indexes and a short history of the performance of the U.S. stock market will follow.

The Dow Jones Industrial Average

The first, and still the best known, stock market index is the Dow Jones Industrial Average (DJIA). Created by Charles Dow in 1884, the DJIA began as an average of the prices of 11 stocks. Today, the index is based on the stock prices of 30 of the largest companies in the United States. The DJIA measures the value of purchasing a single share of each of the stocks in the index. That is, adding up the per-share prices of all 30 stocks and dividing by 30 yields the index. The percentage change in the DJIA over time is the percentage change in the sum of the 30 prices. Thus, the DJIA measures the return to holding a portfolio of a single share of each stock included in the average.

The Dow Jones Industrial Average is a price-weighted average. Price-weighted averages give greater weight to shares with higher prices. To see how this works, take the example of an index composed of just two companies, one with an initial price of $50 and the other with an initial price of $100. The purchase of two shares of stock, one from each company, would cost $150. Now consider the effect of a 15 percent increase in the price of the first stock. It raises the value of the two-stock portfolio by $7.50, or 5 percent, to $157.50. Yet a 15 percent increase in the value of the second stock raises the value of the portfolio by $15, or 10 percent, to $165. The behavior of higher-priced stocks, then, dominates the movement of a price-weighted index like the DJIA.[4]

Since Charles Dow first created his index of 11 stocks, nine of which were railroad stocks, the structure of the U.S. economy has changed markedly. At various times, steel, chemical, and automobile stocks have dominated the DJIA. The index now includes the stocks of information technology firms, such as Microsoft and Intel, as well as of retailing firms, such as Wal-Mart and Home Depot. General Electric is the only one of the original 11 stocks that remains in the index.[5]

The Standard & Poor's 500 Index

The Standard & Poor's 500 Index differs from the Dow Jones Industrial Average in two major respects. First, it is constructed from the prices of many more stocks. Second, it uses a different weighting scheme. As the name suggests, the S&P 500 Index is based on the value of 500 firms, the largest firms in the U.S. economy. And unlike the DJIA, the S&P 500 tracks the total value of owning the entirety of those firms. In the index's calculation, each firm's stock price receives a weight equal to its total market value. Thus, the S&P 500 is a value-weighted index. Unlike the DJIA, in which higher-priced stocks carry more weight, larger firms are more important in the S&P 500.

---

[4]You may wonder how the DJIA has climbed to over 10,000 if it is the average of 30 stock prices, all of which are less than $200 per share. The answer is that the averaging process takes account of stock splits and the companies included in the index change periodically.

[5]For a detailed description of the history and current composition of the DJIA, see www.djindexes.com/downloads/DJIA_Hist_Comp.pdf.

To see this, we can return to the two companies in our last example. If the firm whose stock is priced at $100 has 10 million shares outstanding, all its shares together—its total market value, or market capitalization—are worth $1 billion. If the second firm—the one whose shares are valued at $50 apiece—has 100 million shares outstanding, its market capitalization is $5 billion. Together, the two companies are worth $6 billion.

Now look at the effect of changes in the two stocks' prices. If the first firm's per-share price rises by 15 percent, its total value goes up to $1.15 billion, and the value of the two companies together rises to $6.15 billion—an increase of $2\frac{1}{2}$ percent. (Remember that in the last example, the price-weighted DJIA rose by 10 percent.) Contrast that with the effect of a 15 percent increase in the price of the second stock, which raises the total value of that firm to $5.75 billion. In this case, the value of the two firms together goes from $6 billion to $6.75 billion—an increase of $12\frac{1}{2}$ percent. (In the last example, the price-weighted DJIA rose only 5 percent.)

Clearly, price-weighted and value-weighted indexes are very different! A price-weighted index gives more importance to stocks that have high prices, while a value-weighted index gives more importance to companies with a high market value. Price per se is irrelevant.

Neither price weighting nor value weighting is necessarily the best approach to constructing a stock price index. The S&P 500 is neither better nor worse than the DJIA. Rather, the two types of index simply answer different questions. Changes in a price-weighted index like the DJIA tell us the change in the value of a portfolio composed of a single share of each of the stocks in the index. This tells us the change in the price of a typical stock. Changes in a value-weighted index tell us the return to holding a portfolio of stocks weighted in proportion to the size of the firms. Thus, they accurately mirror changes in the economy's overall wealth.

Other U.S. Stock Market Indexes

Besides the S&P 500 and the DJIA, the most prominent indexes in the United States are the Nasdaq Composite index, or Nasdaq for short, and the Wilshire 5000. The Nasdaq is a value-weighted index of over 5,000 companies traded on the over-the-counter (OTC) market through the National Association of Securities Dealers Automatic Quotations (Nasdaq) service. The Nasdaq Composite is composed mainly of smaller, newer firms and in recent years has been dominated by technology and Internet companies. The Wilshire 5000 is the most broadly based index in use. It covers all publicly traded stocks in the United States, including all the stocks on the New York Stock Exchange, the American Stock Exchange, and the OTC, which together total more than 6,500 (contrary to the index's name). Like the Nasdaq and the S&P 500, the Wilshire 5000 is value-weighted. Because of its great breadth, this index is the best measure of overall market wealth.

World Stock Indexes

Every major country in the world has a stock market, and each of these markets has an index. Most are value-weighted indexes like the S&P 500. Listings of other countries' stock indexes are in newspapers such as *The Wall Street Journal* or the *Financial Times*, as well as online at Web sites such as www.bloomberg.com (see Table 8.2).

YOUR FINANCIAL WORLD
Reading Stock Indexes in the Business News

Each morning, the business news brings reports of the prior day's changes in all the major stock-market indexes. Table 8.1, reproduced from *The Wall Street Journal* of September 10, 2004, is an example of this sort of summary.* It includes a number of indexes besides the DJIA, the S&P 500, the Nasdaq Composite, and the Wilshire 5000. Some of them cover firms of a particular size. For example, Standard & Poor's MidCap index covers 400 medium-size firms; its SmallCap index covers 600 small firms. And the Russell 2000 tracks the value of the smallest two-thirds of the 3,000 largest U.S. compa-

nies. Other indexes cover a particular sector or industry. Note that Dow Jones publishes indexes for transportation and utilities; the Nasdaq has special indexes for insurance, banking, computers, and telecommunications. Many more indexes are published, all of them designed for specific functions. When you encounter a new index, make sure you understand both how it is constructed and what it is designed to measure.

*This particular table comes from the Market Data Center on *The Wall Street Journal*'s Web site.

Table 8.1   U.S. Stock Market Indexes

Dow Jones Averages	Daily					12-Month					
	High	Low	Close	Net Chg	% Chg	High	Low	Chg	% Chg	From 12/31	% Chg
30 Industrial	10,337.33	10,269.49	10,289.10	−24.26	−0.24	10,737.70	9,275.06	829.34	8.77	−164.82	−1.58
20 Transportation	3,207.11	3,182.10	3,198.81	5.02	0.16	3,204.31	2,663.83	458.74	16.77	186.76	6.21
15 Utilities	293.12	290.66	292.12	1.37	0.47	293.56	243.47	48.14	19.73	25.22	9.45
65 Composite	3,082.60	3,065.89	3,072.81	0.02	0.00	3,080.79	2,691.35	348.47	12.79	72.06	2.40
New York Stock Exchange											
NYSE Composite	6,556.21	6,517.10	6,544.31	10.22	0.16	6,780.03	5,644.03	809.80	14.12	140.01	1.61
NYSE Financial	6,831.77	6,761.68	6,786.05	−15.20	−0.22	7,109.18	5,834.41	951.64	16.31	109.63	1.64
NYSE Healthcare	5,943.51	5,897.00	5,901.54	−29.01	−0.49	6,227.42	5,308.67	435.77	7.97	−24.43	−0.41
NYSE Energy	7,172.93	7,043.27	7,163.08	77.29	1.09	7,163.08	5,366.64	1,669.49	30.39	842.03	13.32
Standard & Poor's											
500 Index	1,121.30	1,113.62	1,118.38	2.11	0.19	1,157.76	995.97	101.96	10.03	6.46	0.58
400 MidCap	587.93	582.54	586.68	4.14	0.71	616.70	508.47	68.21	13.16	10.67	1.85
600 SmallCap	287.48	283.25	286.87	3.62	1.28	296.35	234.33	41.32	16.83	16.45	6.08
1500 Index	250.17	248.36	249.53	0.68	0.27	258.12	221.12	23.80	10.54	2.22	0.90
Nasdaq Stock Market											
NASDAQ Composite	1,875.39	1,849.37	1,869.65	19.01	1.03	2,153.83	1,752.49	23.56	1.28	−133.72	−6.67
Nasdaq 100	1,396.55	1,373.37	1,391.53	14.76	1.07	1,553.66	1,303.70	40.73	3.02	−76.39	−5.20
Industrials	1,569.59	1,554.29	1,565.83	5.89	0.38	1,740.89	1,397.91	122.56	8.49	−37.84	−2.36
Insurance	3,056.99	3,040.48	3,056.29	7.84	0.26	3,085.12	2,585.23	416.71	15.79	256.15	9.15
Bank	2,982.86	2,957.90	2,979.47	22.79	0.77	3,010.86	2,592.05	356.71	13.60	80.29	2.77
Biotechnology	709.95	699.86	706.80	3.25	0.46	845.11	622.19	−73.12	−9.38	−17.34	−2.39
Computer	806.17	791.04	802.75	12.91	1.63	1,012.13	768.60	−65.85	−7.58	−132.15	−14.14
Telecom	176.59	173.40	176.15	2.70	1.56	204.89	154.73	17.53	11.05	−7.42	−4.04
Others											
Russell 2000	567.73	557.79	566.18	8.39	1.50	606.39	485.29	58.75	11.58	9.27	1.66
Wilshire 5000	10,919.16	10,827.26	10,880.00	32.85	0.30	11,314.42	9,646.46	1,026.89	10.42	80.37	0.74

SOURCE: The Wall Street Journal, *Friday, September 10, 2004. Reprinted by permission of* The Wall Street Journal, *Copyright © 2004 Dow Jones & Company, Inc. All Rights Reserved Worldwide.*

Table 8.2 World Stock Markets

Country	Index Name	Index Level 9/2001	Change from 2001 Peak	Change over the year
Argentina	General	11,213.7	–7,250.4	–39%
Australia	All Ordinaries	2,941.6	–483.6	–14%
Brazil	Bovespa	10,404.7	–7,484.4	–42%
Britain	FTSE 100	4,763.7	–1,570.8	–25%
Canada	Toronto 300 Comp.	6,669.4	–2,679.0	–29%
France	CAC 40	4,013.2	–1,985.3	–33%
Germany	DAX	4,184.5	–2,610.5	–38%
Hong Kong	Hang Seng	9,600.8	–6,563.2	–41%
Italy	MibTel General	19,877.0	–11,271.0	–36%
Japan	Nikkei 225	9,696.5	–4,833.0	–33%
Mexico	IPC All-Shares	5,306.1	–1,662.8	–24%
Singapore	Straits Times	1,310.9	–480.4	–27%
United States	S&P 500	1,018.6	–355.1	–26%

SOURCE: *World Stock Markets*, Financial Times, *September 28, 2001, p. B45. Reprinted by permission of* The Wall Street Journal, *Copyright © 2004 Dow Jones & Company, Inc. All Rights Reserved Worldwide.*

Table 8.2 gives some sense of the behavior of stock markets during 2001. The index levels (column 3) don't mean much, since the indexes themselves aren't comparable. No one would think that the Brazilian stock exchange was bigger than the New York Stock Exchange, even though the Bovespa index stood over 10,000 when the S&P 500 was just over 1,000. Instead, we need to focus on the percentage changes in these indexes (column 5). A 100-point move in the Singapore Straits Times index, with a level of 1,300, would be much more significant than a 100-point move in the Japanese Nikkei, with a level of almost 10,000. But percentage change isn't everything (see the Tools of the Trade box).

Table 8.2 also shows that when the U.S. stock market fell in 2001, all the rest followed. The year 2001 was bad for stocks everywhere—a year of worldwide recession in which technology stocks collapsed and terrorists destroyed the World Trade Center in New York City. From the table, we can see that Australia experienced a decline in stock prices of only 14 percent, but the value of the shares in some other countries fell 40 percent or more.

Valuing Stocks

People differ on how stocks should be valued. Some believe they can predict changes in a stock's price by looking at patterns in its past price movements. Because these people study charts of stock prices, they are called *chartists*. Other investors, known as *behavioralists*, estimate the value of stocks based on their perceptions of investor psychology and behavior. Still others estimate stock values based on a detailed study of companies' financial statements. In their view, the value of a firm's stock depends both on its current assets and on estimates of its future profitability—what they call the *fundamentals*. Thus, the fundamental value of a stock is based on the timing and uncertainty of the returns it brings.

We can use our toolbox for valuing financial instruments to compute the fundamental value of stocks. Based on the size and timing of the promised payments, we can use the present-value formula to assess how much a stock is worth in the absence of any risk. Then, realizing that the payments are uncertain in both their size and timing, we can adjust our estimate of the stock's value to accommodate those risks. Together, these two steps give us the fundamental value.

The chartists and behavioralists question the usefulness of fundamentals in understanding the level and movement of stock prices. They focus instead on estimates of the deviation of stock prices from those fundamental values. These deviations can create short-term bubbles and crashes, which we'll take up later in the chapter. First, though, let's use some familiar techniques to develop an understanding of basic stock valuation.

Fundamental Value and the Dividend-Discount Model

Like all financial instruments, a stock represents a promise to make monetary payments on future dates, under certain circumstances. With stocks, the payments are usually in the form of dividends, or distributions made to the owners of a company when the company makes a profit.[6] If the firm is sold, the stockholders receive a final distribution that represents their share of the purchase price.

Let's begin with an investor who plans to buy a stock today and sell it in one year. The principle of present value tells us that the price of the stock today should equal the present value of the payments the investor will receive from holding the stock. This is equal to the selling price of the stock in one year's time plus the dividend payments received in the interim. Thus, the current price is the present value of next year's price plus the dividend. If P_{today} is the purchase price of the stock, $P_{next\ year}$ is the sale price one year later, and $D_{next\ year}$ is the size of the dividend payment, we can write this expression as

TIME

$$P_{today} = \frac{D_{next\ year}}{(1+i)} + \frac{P_{next\ year}}{(1+i)}, \tag{1}$$

where i is the interest rate used to compute the present value (measured as a decimal).

What if the investor plans to hold the stock for two years? To figure out the answer, start by using present value to calculate that the price next year equals the value next year of the price in two years plus next year's dividend payment. Using the logic and notation from equation (1), this is

$$P_{next\ year} = \frac{D_{in\ two\ years}}{(1+i)} + \frac{P_{in\ two\ years}}{(1+i)}. \tag{2}$$

Substituting this into equation (1), we get that the current price is the present value of the price in two years plus two dividend payments, one each year, or

$$P_{today} = \frac{D_{next\ year}}{(1+i)} + \frac{D_{in\ two\ years}}{(1+i)^2} + \frac{P_{in\ two\ years}}{(1+i)^2}. \tag{3}$$

Extending this formula over an investment horizon of n years, the result is

$$P_{today} = \frac{D_{next\ year}}{(1+i)} + \frac{D_{in\ two\ years}}{(1+i)^2} + \ldots + \frac{D_{n\ years\ from\ now}}{(1+i)^n} + \frac{P_{n\ years\ from\ now}}{(1+i)^n}. \tag{4}$$

That is, the price today is the present value of the sum of the dividends plus the present value of the price at the time the stock is sold n years from now.

[6]To be precise, not all profits are distributed to shareholders. Some of these "earnings" are retained by the firm and used to increase its size. A firm may also use profits to buy back its own stock, thereby increasing the value of the remaining shares. We will ignore these complications.

At this point, you may be asking: What about companies that do not pay dividends? How do we figure out their stock price? The answer is that we estimate when they will start paying dividends and then use the present-value framework. From (4) you can see that there is no reason all of the dividends need to be positive. Some of them can be zero, and we can still do the calculation. So if we figure that the company will start paying dividends in 10 years, we just set the first 9 years' worth of dividends equal to zero, and compute the present discounted value of dividend payments starting in year 10.

Returning to our baseline case, looking at the messy equation (4) we can see that unless we know something more about the annual dividend payments, we are stuck. To proceed, we will assume that dividends grow at a constant rate of g per year. That is, the dividend next year will equal the dividend today multiplied by one plus the growth rate:

$$D_{\text{next year}} = D_{\text{today}} (1 + g). \qquad (5)$$

TOOLS OF THE TRADE
Beware Percentage Changes

On Friday, April 20, 2001, an article titled "Will Beaten-Up Funds Rise Again?" appeared in *The Wall Street Journal*. The story noted that money managers whose funds had lost significant value during the market declines of the early 1970s went on to become the stars of the next decade. One fund, called the American Heritage Fund, declined in value more than 75 percent during the 21 months from December 1972 through September 1974. Over the next 10 years, from the end of 1974 to the end of 1984, the same fund rose 250 percent. The implication of the story was that, while the fund was hard hit in 1973 and 1974, it later recouped its losses and went on to post large gains. But did it really?

To see how well the fund actually did, imagine that you made a $100 investment in American Heritage in December 1972 and sold it in December 1984. What kind of return would you have realized? First, by September 1974, your $100 would have shrunk to $23.20. Over the next 10 years, you would have received a cumulative return of 250 percent on this sum, or a total of $58. When you sold your shares in the American Heritage Fund at the end of 1984, you would have realized $81.20. That is, over the 12 years beginning at the end of 1972, you would have lost $18.80! In comparison, if you had invested $100 in the S&P 500 Index in December 1972, you would have sustained a loss of 42.6 percent followed by a gain of 298 percent. At the end of 1984, you would have had $228.45.

Sometimes investment reports imply that it is possible to evaluate a fund's overall performance simply by adding the percentage loss over one period to a subsequent percentage gain. But, as this example suggests, nothing could be further from the truth. Another *Wall Street Journal* story, published on May 18, 2001, under the headline "Doing the Math: Tech Investors' Road to Recovery Is Long," makes exactly that point. The article included an illuminating figure (Figure 8.2).

As the accompanying story explained, an investment in the Profunds UltraOTC fund had gained 95.6 percent after a 94.7 percent decline. As the graph shows, the initial $10,000 investment was still worth only about $1,000, even after the huge gain.

What percentage increase will bring an investment in the Profunds UltraOTC fund back to its original level? The easiest way to answer this question is to compute a general formula for percentage increase required to bring a losing investment back to its original value. If d is the initial *decline* in the value of a $100 investment, then $(100 - d)$ is left. What percentage increase in $(100 - d)$ will return the investment to a value of 100? Recall that the percentage change is just the end value, which is $100 minus the initial value $(100 - d)$, divided by the initial value, and multiplied by 100 (so that the answer is a percentage). Putting this all together, we get the formula we are looking for:

Percentage increase required
to return to original value =

$$100 \times \frac{100 - (100 - d)}{(100 - d)} = 100 \times \frac{d}{(100 - d)}$$

As long as the growth rate remains constant, all we need to do is multiply by $(1 + g)$ to compute future dividends. Following the procedure for computing present value in n years, we can see that the dividend n years from now will be

$$D_{n \text{ years from now}} = D_{today} (1 + g)^n. \tag{6}$$

Using equation (6), we can rewrite the price equation (4) as

$$P_{today} = \frac{D_{today}(1+g)}{(1+i)} + \frac{D_{today}(1+g)^2}{(1+i)^2} + \cdots + \frac{D_{today}(1+g)^n}{(1+i)^n} + \frac{P_{n \text{ years from now}}}{(1+i)^n}. \tag{7}$$

Even if we know the dividend today, D_{today}, and the interest rate, i, as well as an estimate of the dividend growth rate, g, we still can't compute the current price, P_{today}, unless we know the future price, $P_{n \text{ years from now}}$. We can solve this problem

What happens to this formula as d increases? For very small losses, such as 1 percent to 5 percent, the percentage increase needed is nearly the same as the loss. But as d increases, the required percentage increase climbs rapidly. While a 10 percent decline requires an 11.1 percent increase to return to the initial level, a 90 percent decline requires a 900 percent increase. At the level of the Profunds UltraOTC fund—a 95 percent decline—investors need a 1,900 percent increase just to return to the level at which they started!

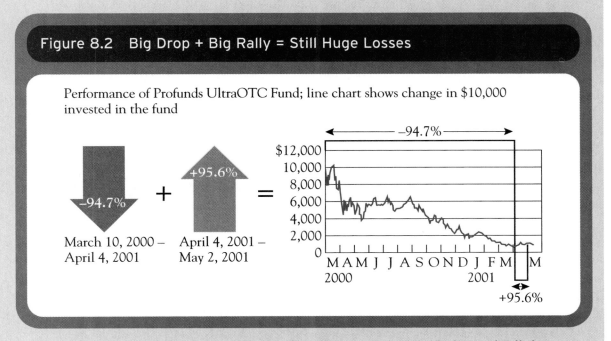

Figure 8.2   Big Drop + Big Rally = Still Huge Losses

Performance of Profunds UltraOTC Fund; line chart shows change in $10,000 invested in the fund

−94.7%
March 10, 2000 – April 4, 2001

+95.6%
April 4, 2001 – May 2, 2001

by assuming that the firm pays dividends forever. This assumption turns the stock into something like a consol—the strange bond that makes fixed coupon payments forever and never repays the principal.[7] It allows us to convert equation (6) into the following simple formula:[8]

$$P_{today} = \frac{D_{today}}{i - g}.$$

(8)

This relationship is the dividend-discount model. Using the concept of present value, together with the simplification that the firm's dividends will grow at a constant rate g, we have discovered that the "fundamental" price of a stock is simply the current dividend divided by the interest rate, minus the dividend growth rate. The model tells us that stock prices should be high when dividends (D_{today}) are high, when dividend growth (g) is rapid (that is, when g is large), or when the interest rate (i) is low. (In using the dividend-discount model, we will need to remember to write both i and g as decimals—numbers like 0.03 and 0.05.)

The dividend-discount model is simple and elegant, but we have ignored risk in deriving it. Stock prices change constantly, making investors' returns uncertain. Where does this risk come from, and how does it affect a stock's valuation? We turn now to an analysis of risk.

Why Stocks Are Risky

Recall that stockholders are the firm's owners, so they receive the firm's profits. But their profits come only after the firm has paid everyone else, including bondholders. It is as if the stockholders bought the firm by putting up some of their own wealth and borrowing the rest. This borrowing creates *leverage*, and leverage creates risk. (See the Tools of the Trade box in Chapter 5.)

A simple example will show what happens. Imagine a software business that needs only one computer. Say the computer costs $1,000 and the purchase can be financed by any combination of stock (equity) and bonds (debt).[9] If the interest rate on bonds is 10 percent, for each $100 borrowed the firm must pay $10 in interest. Finally, assume that the company, which produces software, earns $160 in good years and $80 in bad years, with equal probability.

Table 8.3 shows what happens to the company's equity returns as its level of debt changes. The more debt, the more leverage and the greater the owners' risk (as measured

---

[7]Since neither the consol nor the stock has a maturity date, it makes sense that they would be formally the same.

[8]To compute equation (8), begin by noticing that if we change notation slightly so that P_j and D_j are the price and dividend in year j, then the original pricing equation (4) can be rewritten as an infinite sum, so that

$P_0 = \sum_{i=1}^{\infty} \frac{D_j}{(1+i)_i}$. Substituting in the expression for the dividend growth rate, $D_j = (1+g)^j$, this gives us

$P_0 = \sum_{t=1}^{\infty} \frac{D_0(1+g)^t}{(1+i)^t}$. This expression looks exactly like the one for a consol, with the current dividend in place of the coupon payment and an interest rate equivalent to $(1 + i^*) = (1 + i)/(1 + g)$. That is, we can write it as

$P_0 = \sum_{t=1}^{\infty} \frac{D_0}{(1+i^*)^t}$. So long as both the interest rate and the dividend growth rate are relatively small, we can

approximate this as $(1 + i^*) \approx (1 + i - g)$, and so $P_0 = \sum_{t=1}^{\infty} \frac{D_0}{(1+i-g)^t}$. So long as g is smaller than i, so i^* is

positive, this sum will not explode, so we can use the techniques in Appendix 4 to give us the solution that is equation (8).

[9]For the sake of simplicity, we will ignore the fact that computers become obsolete and are replaced every few years.

Table 8.3   Returns Distributed to Debt and Equity Holders under Different Financing Assumptions

Percent Equity (%)	Percent Debt (%)	Required Payments on 10% Bonds ($)	Payment to Equity Holders ($)	Equity Return (%)	Expected Equity Return (%)	Standard Deviation of Equity Return
100%	0	0	$80–$160	8–16%	12%	4%
50%	50%	$50	$30–$110	6–22%	14%	8%
30%	70%	$70	$10–$90	$3\frac{1}{3}$–30%	$16\frac{2}{3}$%	$13\frac{1}{3}$%
20%	80%	$80	$0–$80	0–40%	20%	20%

Firm requires a $1,000 capital investment that can be financed by either stock (equity) or 10% bonds (debt). Revenue is either $80 or $160, with equal probability.

by the standard deviation of the equity return). As the proportion of the firm financed by equity falls from 100 percent to 20 percent, the expected return to the equity holders rises from 12 percent to 20 percent, but the associated risk rises substantially as well.

If the firm were only 10 percent equity financed, the stockholders' limited liability could come into play. Issuing $900 worth of bonds would mean incurring an obligation to make $90 in interest payments. If business turned out to be bad, the firm's revenue would be only $80—not enough to pay the interest. Without their limited liability, the common stockholders, who are the firm's legal owners, would be liable for the $10 shortfall. Instead, the stockholders would lose only their initial $100 investment, and no more, and the firm goes bankrupt.

Stocks are risky, then, because the shareholders are residual claimants. Because they are paid last, they never know for sure how much their return will be. Any variation in the firm's revenue flows through to them dollar for dollar, making their returns highly volatile.[10] In contrast, bondholders receive fixed nominal payments and are paid before the stockholders in the event of a bankruptcy.

Risk and the Value of Stocks

Stockholders require compensation for the risk they face; the higher the risk, the greater the compensation. To integrate risk into stock valuation, we will return to the simple question we asked earlier: How will investors with a one-year investment horizon value a stock? Our initial answer was that the stock price equals the present value of the price of the stock in one year's time plus the dividend payments received in the interim. From this statement, we derived the dividend-discount model. But once we recognize the risk involved in buying stock, the answer to our question must change. The new answer is that an investor will buy a stock with the idea of obtaining a certain return, which includes compensation for the stock's risk.

RISK

[10]This example brings up an interesting point concerning the interpretation of profit reports in the financial press. Most firms carry high fixed expenses, including fixed payroll payments. Because adjusting them is difficult over the short term, fluctuations in a firm's revenue become fluctuations in its profits. Thus, news reports often show wild fluctuations in "accounting" profits. Changes of 50 percent or more are common during business-cycle downturns and recoveries.

Here is how the process works. Buying the stock for an initial price P_{today} entitles the investor to a dividend $D_{next\ year}$ plus the proceeds from the sale of the stock one year later, at price $P_{next\ year}$. The return from the purchase and subsequent sale of the stock equals the dividend plus the difference in the price, both divided by the initial price:

$$\text{Return to holding stock for one year} = \frac{D_{next\ year}}{P_{today}} + \frac{P_{next\ year} - P_{today}}{P_{today}}. \tag{9}$$

Since the ultimate future sale price is unknown, the stock is risky and the investor will require compensation in the form of a risk premium. We will think of the required return as the sum of the risk-free interest rate and the risk premium (sometimes called the *equity risk premium*). Recall from earlier chapters that we can think of the risk-free rate as the interest rate on a U.S. Treasury security with a maturity of several months. Such an instrument has virtually no default risk, since the government isn't going to collapse, and it has almost no inflation risk, since inflation is highly persistent and so is unlikely to change over a year or so. In addition, there is very little price risk, since interest rates normally don't move quickly and suddenly either.[11] Dividing the required stock return into its two components, we can write

$$\text{Required stock return } (i) = \text{Risk-free return } (rf) + \text{Risk premium } (rp) \tag{10}$$

Combining this equation with our earlier analysis is straightforward. All we need to do is recognize that the interest rate used for the present-value calculation in the dividend-discount model, equation (8), is the sum of the risk-free return and a risk premium. Using this insight, we can rewrite equation (8) as

$$P_{today} = \frac{D_{today}}{rf + rp - g}. \tag{11}$$

Looking at equation (11), we can see that the higher the risk premium investors demand to hold a stock, the lower its price. Similarly, the higher the risk-free return, the lower the stock's price. (See Table 8.4 for a summary.)

---

[11]TIPS (Treasury Inflation Protection Securities), mentioned in Chapter 6, are a ready source of a risk-free interest rate that is adjusted for inflation. TIPS let us measure the risk-free real interest rate directly in financial markets.

Table 8.4 Implications of the Dividend-Discount Model with Risk

Stock Prices Are High When

1. Current dividends are high (D_{today} is high).
2. Dividends are expected to grow quickly (g is high).
3. The risk-free rate is low (rf is low).
4. The risk premium on equity is low (rp is low).

APPLYING THE CONCEPT
CAN WE JUSTIFY CURRENT STOCK PRICES?

The S&P 500 Index finished the year 2003 at just over 1,100. Was this level warranted by fundamentals? To check, we can use the dividend-discount formula in equation (11). First, we need to fill in a few numbers. The sale of Treasury index securities (TIPS) tells us that the (long-term) risk-free real interest rate is about 2 percent, or $rf = 0.02$. Historical information suggests a risk premium of about 4 percent, or $rp = 0.04$, and a dividend growth rate of around 2 percent, or $g = 0.02$. Finally, we need an estimate of dividends. The owner of a $1,000 portfolio of the S&P 500 stocks would have received roughly $30 in dividends during 2003.* Substituting this information into equation (11) gives us a price of $P_{today} = \$750$:

$$P_{today} = \frac{\$30}{0.02 + 0.04 - 0.02} = \$750 \qquad (12)$$

Actual stock prices were substantially higher than this simple calculation suggests they should have been. How can we explain this discrepancy? At least one of our assumptions must be wrong, and the most likely candidate is the risk premium. If investors were demanding a lower risk premium in 2003 than in earlier years, that would explain why stock prices were high. We can compute the value of rp that would be consistent with a level of 1,100 on the S&P 500 index, $P_{today} = 1,100$, as follows:

$$1,100 = \frac{30}{(0.02 + rp) - 0.02} \qquad (13)$$

The answer is approximately 2.75 percent. Thus, we can explain recent price levels in the stock market if we assume that the risk premium on equity is below 3 percent—more than a full percentage point below its historical average level. If our assumption is correct, stock prices are high because the risk premium is low.

*This amount is adjusted for the fact that companies commonly buy back some of their shares as a complement to paying dividends. The practice drives up the price of the stock, creating capital gains for investors. Since capital gains are taxed at a lower rate than dividends, investors prefer buybacks to dividends, and firms oblige.

The Theory of Efficient Markets

Stock prices change nearly continuously. Why? One explanation starts in the same place as the dividend-discount model and is based on the concept of fundamental value. When fundamentals change, prices must change with them.

This line of reasoning gives rise to what is commonly called the theory of efficient markets. The basis for the theory of efficient markets is the notion that the prices of all financial instruments, including stocks, reflect all available information. As a result, markets adjust immediately and continuously to changes in fundamental values. If the theory of efficient markets is correct, the chartists are doomed to failure.

The theory of efficient markets implies that stock price movements are unpredictable. If they weren't—if you could accurately forecast that the price of a stock was going to rise tomorrow—you would immediately buy as many shares of the stock as possible. Your action would increase demand for the stock, driving its price up today. In other words, the fact that you think stock's price will rise tomorrow makes it rise today.[12] When markets are efficient, the prices at which stocks currently trade reflect all available information, so future price movements are unpredictable.

If no one can predict stock price movements, then what good is investment advice? Not much! If the theory of efficient markets is correct, no one can consistently beat the market average. This means that active portfolio management—buying and selling stocks based on someone's advice—will not yield a higher return than that of a broad stock-market index—the market average—year after year.

There is quite a bit of evidence to support the view that stock price changes are unpredictable and that professional money managers cannot beat an index like the S&P 500 with regularity. On average, the return on managed portfolios is about 2 percent less than average stock-market returns. But we do see managers who at least claim to exceed the market average year after year.[13] How can this be? There are four possibilities: (1) They have private information, which is illegal; (2) they are taking on risk, which brings added compensation but means that at times, returns will be extremely poor; (3) they are lucky; or (4) markets are not efficient.

It is intriguing to think that high (or low) investment returns could simply be the result of chance. To understand why this is so, consider the following parable, which appears in Peter Bernstein's book *Capital Ideas*.[14] Suppose that 225 million people all join in a coin-tossing contest. On the first day, each person finds a partner and they each bet a dollar on the coin toss. The winner gets $2 and the loser leaves the game. Each day the coin toss is repeated, with the losers turning their dollars over to the winners, who then stack their winnings on the next day's toss. The laws of chance tell us that, after 10 flips on 10 consecutive mornings, only 220,000 people will still be in the contest, and each will have won a little more than $1,000. Then the game heats up. Ten days later, after 20 tosses, only 215 people will still be playing, and each will have nearly $1,050,000. These winners had no special knowledge. No skill was involved in their accumulation of high returns, just pure chance.

You may be asking what this has to do with investment and efficient markets. The answer is that when there are lots of people placing bets—and there surely are a large number of investors trying to gain advantages in the stock market—there will be a fair number of people who do well just by pure chance. And the problem with the stock market is that the number of people who "win" is about the same as the number we would expect to be lucky.

Investing in Stocks for the Long Run

Stocks appear to be risky, yet many people hold a substantial proportion of their wealth in the form of stock. We can reconcile our perception of risk with observed behavior in two ways. Either stocks are not that risky, or people are not that averse to

---

[12]If you felt sure that a stock's price was going to fall, you could take advantage of your forecast by using a strategy called *short selling*. You would borrow shares and sell them with the idea of buying them back at a lower price in the future. This tactic increases the supply of shares for sale, driving the stock's price down.

[13]Remember that someone owns every share in the stock market, so above-average returns to one person must be matched by below-average returns to someone else.

[14]Peter Bernstein. *Capital Ideas: The Improbable Origins of Modern Wall Street* (New York: Free Press, 1993).

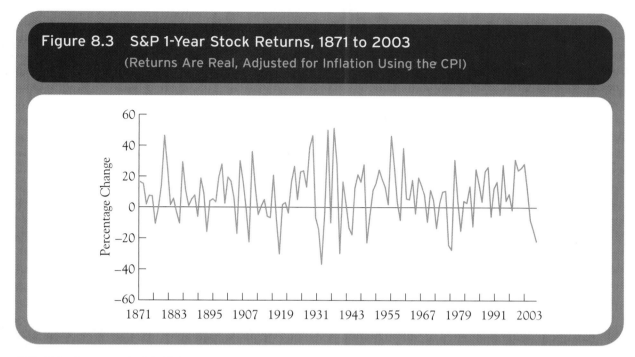

Figure 8.3   S&P 1-Year Stock Returns, 1871 to 2003
(Returns Are Real, Adjusted for Inflation Using the CPI)

SOURCE: *http://www.econ.yale.edu/~shiller/. Reprinted with permission from author.*

the risk and so do not require a large risk premium to hold stocks. Which of these explanations is more plausible?

To get a sense of the risk in holding stock, we can look at the one-year return on the S&P 500 Index for each of the past 130 years. Figure 8.3 plots the one-year real return to holding this portfolio (including dividend payments and adjusted for inflation using the consumer price index). The average real return over 130 years exceeded 8.5 percent per year.

In looking at the figure, remember to check the axis labels. Start by noting that the scale on the vertical axis goes from –60 percent to +60 percent, a huge range. The minimum return was nearly –40 percent (in 1932), and the maximum was more than +50 percent (in 1936). Over the last 50 years the range has narrowed, to a maximum annual return of 46 percent (in 1955) and a minimum of –27 percent (in 1975). Nearly half the time, the return on holding stocks has been either less than zero (negative) or above 25 percent (substantially positive). The graph certainly gives the impression that prices fluctuate wildly and that holding stocks is extremely risky.

A decade or so ago, though, Professor Jeremy Siegel of the University of Pennsylvania's Wharton School wrote a book titled *Stocks for the Long Run*,[15] in which he suggested that investing in stocks is risky only if you hold them for a short time. If you buy stocks and hold them for long enough, they really are not very risky.

To see Professor Siegel's point, we can look at the return to holding stocks for 25 years instead of one (see Figure 8.4). The smooth green line shows the average annual return from investing in the S&P 500 for a 25-year period, while the choppy beige

[15]Jeremy J. Siegel. *Stocks for the Long Run: A Guide to Selecting Markets for Long-Term Growth* (Chicago: Richard D. Irwin, 1994).

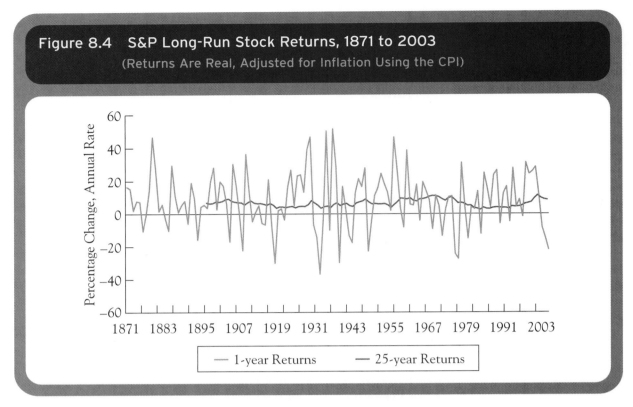

Figure 8.4 S&P Long-Run Stock Returns, 1871 to 2003
(Returns Are Real, Adjusted for Inflation Using the CPI)

SOURCE: *http://www.econ.yale.edu/~shiller/*. *Reprinted with permission from author.*

line shows the one-year return in Figure 8.3. We can see immediately that the green line is much smoother and fluctuates over a much smaller range—and it never dips below zero. In fact, the *minimum* average annual return over 25 years is a substantial 4.7 percent, while the maximum is 16.6 percent. Changing these nominal rates to real, inflation-adjusted rates simply lowers their level by about 2 percent. Siegel's point is that if you buy stocks and hold them for the long run—25 years or so—your investment is not very risky.

That was not the end of Professor Siegel's analysis. His next step was to compare the returns from holding bonds with those from holding stock. The results were startling. Siegel reported that, between 1871 and 1992, there was no 30-year period when bonds outperformed stocks. In other words, when held for the long term, *stocks are less risky than bonds!*

For many people, investing in stock is a way of saving for retirement, so their investment horizon is very long. Professor Siegel's calculations tell us that our retirement savings should be invested in stock and that we shouldn't worry about year-to-year fluctuations in their value.[16]

[16]For a more sobering view of the stock market rise of the late 1990s, see Robert J. Shiller, *Irrational Exuberance* (Princeton, NJ: Princeton University Press, 2000).

YOUR FINANCIAL WORLD
Should You Own Stocks?

Should you own stocks? The answer is yes, especially if you are young! Many people shy away from stocks and invest in bonds (or other interest-bearing assets). But remember that bonds are risky, too—even U.S. Treasury bonds carry interest-rate risk and inflation risk. Though stocks may look risky, history suggests that a well-diversified portfolio of stocks held over the long term is not. The real question is *how* to buy stock.

There are five issues to think about when buying stock: affordability, liquidity, diversification, management, and cost. Prepackaged portfolios called mutual funds address all these issues in one way or another. The problem is that there are literally thousands of mutual funds. So, how do we choose? Here are some points to keep in mind:

1. *Affordability*. Most mutual funds allow a small initial investment. You can start with as little as $1,000.

2. *Liquidity*. In an emergency, you may need to withdraw resources quickly. Make sure you can withdraw your investment easily if you need to.

3. *Diversification*. The vast majority of mutual funds are much more diversified than any individual portfolio of stocks. Even so, it is important to check before you buy.

4. *Management*. Mutual funds offer the advantage of professional management. You do need to be careful, as funds in which people make the decisions, so-called managed funds, tend to perform worse than index funds, which are designed to mimic stock market indexes like the S&P 500.

5. *Cost*. Mutual fund managers charge fees for their services. The fees for managed funds run about $1\frac{1}{2}$ percent per year, compared to $\frac{1}{2}$ percent or less for index funds. This is a significant difference. Over 20 years, an investment of $10,000 with an average annual return of 8 percent will amount to $46,610. If you pay a 1 percent fee, so that the return averages only 7 percent, the value of the investment drops to $38,697, or $7,913 less.

Taken together, these considerations persuade many people to invest in index funds. Index funds are affordable and liquid, they offer excellent diversification, and they tend to be cheap. Don't take my word for it; always ask before you invest.

The Stock Market's Role in the Economy

The stock market plays a crucial role in every modern capitalist economy. The prices determined there tell us the market value of companies, which guides the allocation of resources. Firms with a high stock-market value are the ones investors prize, so they have an easier time garnering the resources they need to grow. In contrast, firms whose stock value is low have difficulty financing their operations.

So long as stock prices accurately reflect fundamental values, this resource allocation mechanism works well. The signals are accurate, and investment resources flow to their most socially beneficial uses. But at times, stock prices deviate significantly from the fundamentals and move in ways that are difficult to attribute to changes in the real interest rate, the risk premium, or the growth rate of future dividends.

While many economists believe that markets are always efficient and that prices never deviate from fundamental values, it is worth entertaining the possibility that shifts in investor psychology may distort prices. The fact is, both euphoria and depression are contagious, so when investors become unjustifiably exuberant about the market's future prospects, prices rise regardless of the fundamentals. Such mass enthusiasm creates bubbles, persistent and expanding gaps between actual stock prices and

IN THE NEWS

Don't Just Analyze the Market, Analyze the Investor: "Behaviorist" fund managers make hay by studying quirky sentiments

Wall Street Column
BusinessWeek

by Mara Der Hovanesian

May 21, 2001

The market is one big head case. After the tear and tumble of Internet stocks, who can deny how intensely the power of suggestion works on investors? They're seduced by the markets, from tulips to technology. Seasons and days of the week sway them to buy or sell a stock. Academics have come up with a slew of diagnoses to explain their neuroses. And from that, a new breed of money manager has emerged—one who capitalizes on investor quirks.

"I can't outguess [billionaire investment wizard] Warren Buffett, but I can stay one step ahead of the American multitudes," says Harvard University's Richard J. Zeckhauser, a behavioral economist who runs seminars on the topic. "Stock patterns emerge from common human behavior."

Wall Street traditionalists bank their bucks on such market data as earnings estimates, price-earnings ratios, and revenue growth. They subscribe to theories that say markets behave efficiently. Not so, say behavioral economists, whose ideas gained credibility in the 1990s. They maintain that the emotional baggage of investors can make markets go haywire, though reality eventually sets in. The ability to spot irrationality allows these managers to profit from market imperfections, betting that investors will return to their senses. And there's a lot investors can learn from these pros about how to keep their heads straight when investing.

One example of fear overpowering reason: Think back to November [2000] when recession jitters began. Prospects for retailers looked bleak, and stocks like Best Buy Inc. got hit. It fell to $22 from $55—a buy signal for behavioral manager David Dreman, chief investment officer of Dreman Value Management LLC, which oversees $5.7 billion. "You buy when the solid companies get knocked down too cheap," he says. Once investors saw the error of their ways, they bid Best Buy back up to a current $53. The stock stars in the 48.6 percent one-year return for the Scudder-Dreman High Return Fund.

On Autopilot.

Behaviorists say investors tend to latch on to extremes, too. Down or up trends are etched in their minds as certainties,

those warranted by the fundamentals. These bubbles inevitably burst, creating crashes. This phenomenon is one explanation for the very jagged pattern in stock returns—the large gains followed by equally large losses—shown in Figure 8.2.[17]

Investors surely care about the large gains and losses they see when stock prices rise or fall serendipitously. But they are not the only ones who should be concerned. Bubbles affect all of us because they distort the economic decisions companies and consumers make. Here is what happens to companies. When their stock prices rise, financing becomes easier to obtain. They can sell shares and use the proceeds to fund new business opportunities. In the feeding frenzy of a bubble, companies can sell shares for prices that are too high, so financing new investments becomes too easy. It is not much of a challenge to identify high-technology companies that raised staggering sums in the equity markets in the late 1990s, only to crash and burn several years

---

[17]The fact that large declines tend to be followed by equally large increases is what makes stocks less risky when held over a long period, as Professor Siegel noticed.

rather than mere probabilities. Take Cisco Systems Inc. The stock zoomed for years, delivering double-digit returns. Investors got used to it, and expected history to repeat itself. [In 2000], when the stock began to fall as evidence emerged that business was shaky, many investors went into denial, refusing to let go. "Investors have extrapolated Cisco's past performance too far into the future," says Josef Lakonishok, chief investment officer of LSV Asset Management. He is a behavioral finance professor at the University of Illinois who launched LSV in 1994 and now manages $7.5 billion for the likes of Caterpillar and Stanford.

Far too often, analysts—and investors who follow them—exhibit "anchoring" behavior. They get attached to inaccurate price targets and ignore evidence that they might be wrong. One might say that UBS/PaineWebber's analyst Walter Piecyk had a problem with anchoring: In December, 1999, Piecyk's "buy" rating for Qualcomm Inc. caused the telecom stock to jump 30 percent in one day. At the time, the stock was trading at $659, a 52-week high. Piecyk held onto a $1,000 target for months despite the fact that the company was having problems. After a 4-for-1 stock split, shares now trade for $59, or a presplit price of $236. "We look for stocks where the analysts are anchored on their own prior forecasts and overconfident in their ability to predict the future," says Richard H. Thaler, a University of Chicago economist and partner at Fuller & Thaler Asset Management Inc., which manages $1.4 billion. Thaler doesn't forecast the market and has never owned Qualcomm: "We just try to forecast the errors of others."

Future Shock.

Stereotyping a company makes investors think it can't win. If a stock has been a dog for ages, they're conditioned to expect the worst and miss turnarounds. Thaler's $140 million Behavioral Growth Fund buys companies to which the market "underreacts." One of its top 10 holdings, Oakley Inc., which makes athletic wear, is in the portfolio for an average cost of $11. While it languished for a while, new footwear lines and eyeglass designs eventually improved the bottom line. Earnings were double analysts' 2000 estimates. "This company slipped a number of years ago, and it was hardwired into investors' heads," says Thaler fund manager Fred Stanske. "It came back from the dead." Once investors got the picture, they bid up the stock, doubling Stanske's investment.

LESSONS OF THE ARTICLE
Some money managers believe that markets are inefficient. Instead of being cold, calculating, and rational, people let their emotions get the better of them. Not only that, but people tend to think similar thoughts about stocks and take similar actions. Sentiment is contagious; it can drive stock prices away from fundamentals in a way that behavioralists believe they can exploit for a profit.

later. They spent the funds they raised on investments in equipment and buildings that turned out later to be worth nothing, to them or anyone else.[18]

The consequences of such a bubble are not innocuous. The companies whose stock prices rise the most can raise financing the most easily. The result is that they invest too much. Meanwhile, firms in businesses that are not the objects of investor euphoria have a more difficult time raising financing, so they invest too little. The distortions can be large, and recovery can be slow, especially since companies find it almost impossible to find financing for new projects after the bubble bursts.

The impact of stock price bubbles on consumer behavior is equally damaging. Rising equity prices increase individual wealth. The richer we become, the more income we spend and the less we save. Unjustifiably high stock prices lead us to buy luxury cars, large houses, and extravagant vacations, which fuels a boom in economic activity.

[18]Stories about the Internet boom of the late 1990s, together with data on stock prices and market values of firms, are collected in John Cassidy's *Dot.con: How America Lost Its Mind and Money in the Internet Era* (New York: HarperCollins, 2002).

People begin to think they will not need to work as long before they retire. After all, the stock market has made them wealthy, and rich people don't need to work.

The euphoria can't last. When the bubble eventually bursts, individuals are forced to reevaluate their wealth. People discover that their houses and mortgages are too large for their paychecks and their investment accounts are only a shadow of what they once were. Now they need to work harder than ever just to keep up, and their plans for an early retirement are a distant memory. That's not all. Firms that geared up to produce luxury goods for rich shoppers are in trouble. Their wealthy customers disappeared when the bubble burst, and now they are stuck with products people can't afford to buy.

If bubbles result in real investment that is both excessive and inefficiently distributed, crashes do the opposite. The shift from overoptimism to excessive pessimism causes a collapse in investment and economic growth. Normally, the stock market works well and investment funds flow to their most beneficial uses. Occasionally the process goes awry and stock prices move far from any reasonable notion of fundamental value. When these bubbles grow large enough, especially when they lead to crashes, the stock market can destabilize the real economy.

APPLYING THE CONCEPT
WHAT WAS THE INTERNET BUBBLE ALL ABOUT?

During the late 1990s, the stock prices of many new high-technology companies, commonly referred to as *dot-coms,* rose rapidly and then crashed. VA Linux was a representative example. The company's claim to fame was its Unix-based operating system for Web and database servers, which it gave away for free. On the first day of public trading in December 1999, the stock opened at $300 per share. A little over a year later, it was trading at just $5 a share. Other examples are easy to find. In fact, the Nasdaq Composite Index, which is composed of numerous small start-ups as well as large information technology (IT) firms, doubled in value from September 1999 to March 2000, then fell by 70 percent over the next year.

Good things did come from the Internet bubble. One was a change in the way new companies obtain financing. Before 1995, the only funding new companies could get was from people called *venture capitalists,* who specialized in the very high-risk business of financing new companies—that is, new ventures. But venture capitalists parted with their resources reluctantly, and only when they were promised extremely high rates of return. By the late 1990s, start-up companies could bypass the venture capitalists and go directly to the capital markets to raise funds. Individual investors could diversify their portfolios in a way that had not been possible a few years before.

The drawbacks of the Internet bubble outweighed the advantages, however. Not only did people who bought these stocks at their peaks incur substantial losses, but the artificially inflated prices also created the mistaken impression that the investments were worthwhile. The boom in stock prices was mirrored by overinvestment in the companies. By 2001, warehouses were piled high with practically new computers left behind by bankrupt dot-com companies. The distortions caused by unjustifiably high stock prices had warped investors' decisions, leaving many worthwhile projects unfunded—an outcome that was bad for everyone.

Terms

Chapter Lessons

1. Stockholders own the firms in which they hold shares.
    a. They are residual claimants, which means they are last in line after all other creditors.
    b. They have limited liability, so their losses cannot exceed their initial investments.
2. There are two basic types of stock-market index.
    a. The Dow Jones Industrial Average is a price-weighted index.
    b. The S&P 500 is a value-weighted index.
    c. For every stock market in the world, there is a comprehensive index that is used to measure overall performance.
3. There are several ways to value stocks.
    a. Some analysts examine patterns of past performance; others follow investor psychology.
    b. The fundamental value of a stock depends on expectations for a firm's future profitability.
    c. To compensate for the fact that stocks are risky investments, investors in stock require a risk premium.
    d. The dividend-discount model is a simple way to assess fundamental value. According to this model, stock prices depend on the current level of dividends, the growth rate of dividends, the risk-free interest rate, and the equity risk premium.
    e. According to the theory of efficient markets, stock prices reflect all available information.
    f. If markets are efficient, then stock price movements are unpredictable, and investors cannot systematically outperform a comprehensive stock market index like the S&P 500.
4. Stock investments are much less risky when they are held for long periods than when they are held for short periods.
5. Stock prices are a central element in a market economy, because they ensure that investment resources flow to their most profitable uses. When occasional bubbles and crashes distort stock prices, they can destabilize the economy.

Problems

1. Explain why being a residual claimant makes stock ownership risky.

2. Why might some firms find it easier than others to issue stock?

3. Check the business section of a recent newspaper to find the current level of each of the following indexes, along with their change over the last 12 months:

   a. Dow Jones Industrial Average

   b. Standard & Poor's 500 Index

   c. Nasdaq Composite

   d. Wilshire 5000

   Comment on what you found, including the differences among the indexes.

4. You open the morning paper and note that the Dow Jones Industrial Average rose while the Standard & Poor's 500 Index fell. Explain how these two indexes can move in opposite directions.

5. A stock that sells for $100 entitles you to a dividend payment of $4. You estimate that the growth rate of the firm's dividends is about 2 percent per year and that the risk-free rate is $3\frac{1}{2}$ percent. What is the risk premium suggested by the price of this stock? Does it strike you as high or low? How would your answer change if the stock price were $150 instead of $100?

6. As you flip through *The Wall Street Journal* you notice advertisements by investment firms wanting to sell you their products. Common among all of the ads is the claim that the firm has a track record of performing above average. Explain how they can all be above average. Is this inconsistent with the efficient markets theory?

7. Return to the example summarized in Table 8.3, in which a firm purchases a $1,000 computer. Assume that the firm has only 20 percent equity outstanding, so it needs an $800 loan. Managers expect revenue of $200 in good times and $100 in bad times. Compute the percentage change in revenue and profits (revenue minus interest payments) if revenue is $200 in the first year and $100 in the second year. Then compute the return to the stockholders in each year.

8. Using the dividend-discount model, construct some simple examples to show why stock prices go up when the required risk premium on stocks goes down. What do your examples suggest about the practice of using recent history to predict future stock returns?

9. Explain why an investment portfolio composed of all the stocks in the Standard & Poor's 500 Index is less risky than an investment portfolio composed of 20 stocks chosen randomly.

10. One possible investment strategy is to identify those money managers who realized the best returns over the last year and invest in their funds. Evaluate such a strategy in light of the efficient markets theory.

11. If Professor Siegel is correct that stocks are less risky than bonds, then the risk premium on stock should be zero. Assuming that the risk-free interest rate is $3\frac{1}{2}$ percent, the growth rate of dividends is 2 percent, and the current level of dividends is $30, use the dividend-discount model to compute the level of the S&P 500 that is warranted by the fundamentals. Compare the result to the current S&P 500 level and comment on it.

12. In March 2002, General Electric announced plans to sell billions of dollars worth of bonds. (See Applying the Concept: The Day General Electric Went Too Far in Chapter 7.) What do you think the likely impact was on the price of GE stock? Why?

13. The financial press tends to become excited when the Dow Jones Industrial Average rises or falls sharply. After a particularly steep rise or fall, newspapers may publish tables ranking the day's results with other large advances or declines. What do you think of such reporting? If you were asked to construct a table of the best and worst days in stock-market history, how would you do it? Why would you use your approach?

14. For 14 years, from 1988 through 2002, *The Wall Street Journal* ran a competition in which investment professionals competed against a portfolio of stocks created by editors throwing darts at the newspaper's stock tables. What would the theory of efficient markets suggest about the likely outcome of the contest? In formulating the competition, *Journal* editors asked four stock pickers to pick one stock apiece and then chose a competing portfolio by throwing four darts. What do you think the result of the competition was?

15. You are reading the newspaper over your morning coffee when you come across an ad for a mutual fund trumpeting returns far exceeding those of the S&P 500 over the past five years. The ad claims that the fund's return averaged 15 percent while the S&P 500 averaged only 10 percent. What might explain this difference in returns? How would you use data from a period in which the market was falling to test your hypothesis?

Chapter 9

Derivatives: Futures, Options, and Swaps

In recent years, stories detailing the abuse of derivatives have filled the pages of the business press. Derivatives were at the bottom of the scandal that engulfed Enron immediately after it declared bankruptcy in November 2001. As we have learned since then, Enron engaged in a variety of financial transactions whose express purpose was to give the appearance of low debt, low risk, and high profitability. This sleight of hand kept the stock price high and made shareholders happy, so no one complained. In fact, no one even looked. But eventually the day of reckoning came, and the company collapsed.

Financial derivatives were also linked to the collapse of Long-Term Capital Management (LTCM), a Connecticut-based hedge fund, in fall 1998. On a single day in August 1998, LTCM lost an astounding $553 million. By late September, the fund had lost another $2 billion. That left LTCM with over $99 billion in debt and $100 billion in assets. With loans accounting for 99 percent of total assets, repayment was nearly impossible. LTCM also had significant derivatives positions that did not show up on the balance sheet as assets or liabilities. These off-balance-sheet arrangements, which carried even more risk, were the primary cause of the fund's stunningly swift losses.

If derivatives are open to abuse, why do they exist? The answer is that, when used properly, derivatives are extremely helpful financial instruments. They can be used to reduce risk, allowing firms and individuals to enter into agreements that they otherwise wouldn't be willing to accept. Derivatives can also be used as insurance. For example, in winter 1998, a snowmobile manufacturer named Bombardier offered a $1,000 rebate to buyers should snowfall in 44 cities total less than half what it had averaged over the preceding three years. Sales rose 38 percent. The existence of "weather derivatives" enabled Bombardier to undertake this risky marketing strategy. Paying the rebates would have bankrupted the company, but Bombardier purchased derivatives that would pay off if snowfall were low. By using this unorthodox form of insurance, Bombardier transferred the risk to someone else.

What exactly are derivatives, and why are they so important? Though they play a critical role in our financial well-being, most people barely know what they are. This chapter will provide an introduction to the uses and abuses of derivatives.

The Basics: Defining Derivatives

To understand what derivatives are, let's begin with the basics. A derivative is a financial instrument whose value depends on—is *derived* from—the value of some other financial instrument, called the *underlying asset*. Some common examples of underlying assets are stocks, bonds, wheat, snowfall, and stock market indexes like the S&P 500.

A simple example of a derivative is a contractual agreement between two investors that obligates one to make a payment to the other, depending on the movement in interest rates over the next year. This type of derivative is called an interest-rate *futures contract*. Such an arrangement is quite different from the outright purchase of a bond for two reasons. First, derivatives provide an easy way for investors to profit from price declines. The purchase of a bond, in contrast, is a bet that its price will rise.[1] Second, and more important, in a derivatives transaction, one person's loss is always another person's gain. Buyer and seller are like two people playing poker. How much each player wins or loses depends on how the game progresses, but the total amount on the table doesn't change.

While derivatives can be used to *speculate*, or gamble on future price movements, the fact that they allow investors to manage and reduce risk makes them indispensable to a modern economy. Bombardier used a derivative to hedge the risk of having to pay rebates in the event of low snowfall (we discussed hedging in Chapter 5). As we will see, farmers use derivatives regularly, to insure themselves against fluctuations in the market prices of their crops. Risk can be bought and sold using derivatives. Thus, *the purpose of derivatives is to transfer risk from one person or firm to another.*

"*At the Hawescroft School we've de-emphasized singing and drawing and emphasized stocks and derivatives.*"

Source: © 2004 Peter Steiner from cartoonbank.com. All Rights Reserved.

When people have the ability to transfer risks, they will do things that they wouldn't do otherwise. Think of a wheat farmer and a bread baker. If he or she cannot insure against a decline in the price of wheat, the farmer will plant fewer acres of wheat. And without a guarantee that the price of flour will not rise, the baker will build a smaller bakery. Those are prudent responses to the risks created by price fluctuations. Now introduce a mechanism through which the farmer and the baker can guarantee the price of wheat. As a result the farmer will plant more and the baker will build a bigger bakery. Insurance is what allows them to do it! Derivatives provide that insurance. In fact, by shifting risk to those most able to bear it, derivatives increase the risk-carrying capacity of the economy as a whole, improving the allocation of resources and increasing the level of output.

While derivatives allow individuals and firms to manage risk, they also allow them to conceal the true nature of certain financial transactions. In the same way that stripping a coupon bond separates the coupons from the principal payment, buying and selling derivatives can unbundle virtually any group of future payments and risks. A company that hesitates to issue a coupon bond for fear analysts will frown on the extra debt can instead issue the coupon payments and the principal payment as individual zero-coupon bonds, using derivative transactions to label them something other than borrowing. Thus, if stock-market analysts penalize companies for obtaining funding in certain ways, derivatives (as we will see) allow the companies to get exactly the same resources at the same risk but under a different name.

Derivatives may be divided into three major categories: forwards and futures, options, and swaps. Let's look at each one.

Forwards and Futures

Of all derivative financial instruments, forwards and futures are the simplest to understand and the easiest to use. A **forward**, or forward contract, *is an agreement between*

---

[1]Investors can bet that prices will fall using a technique called *short selling*. The investor borrows an asset from its owner for a fee, sells it at the current market price, and then repurchases it later. The short seller is betting that the price of the asset will fall between the time it is sold and the time it is repurchased.

Trading pit at the New York Mercantile Exchange in New York City that appeared in the movie *Trading Places* with Eddie Murphy and Dan Aykroyd.

SOURCE: © *Reuters/CORBIS.*

a buyer and a seller to exchange a commodity or financial instrument for a specified amount of cash on a prearranged future date. Forward contracts are private agreements between two parties. Because they are customized, forward contracts are very difficult to resell to someone else.

To see why forward contracts are difficult to resell, consider the example of a yearlong apartment lease, in which the renter agrees to make a series of monthly payments to the landlord in exchange for the right to live in the apartment. Such a lease is a sequence of 12 forward contracts. Rent is paid in predetermined amounts on prearranged future dates in exchange for housing. While there is some standardization of leases, a contract between a specific renter and a specific landlord is unlike any other rental contract. Thus, there is no market for the resale or reassignment of apartment rental contracts.

In contrast, a **future***, or* futures contract*, is a forward contract that has been standardized and sold through an organized exchange.* A futures contract specifies that the seller—who has the short position—will deliver some quantity of a commodity or financial instrument to the buyer—who has the long position—on a specific date, called the *settlement* or *delivery* date, for a predetermined price. No payments are made initially when the contract is agreed to. The seller/short position benefits from declines in the price of the underlying asset, while the buyer/long position benefits from increases.[2]

Take the U.S. Treasury bond futures contract that trades on the Chicago Board of Trade. The contract specifies the delivery of $100,000 face value worth of 10-year, 6 percent coupon U.S. Treasury bonds at any time during a given month, called the *delivery* month.[3] Table 9.1 shows the prices and trading activity for this contract on April 15, 2004. The fact that the contract is so specific means there is no need for negotiation. And the existence of the exchange creates a natural place for people who are interested in a particular futures contract to meet and trade. Historically, exchanges have been physical locations, but with the Internet came online trading of futures. In recent years, firms have created virtual futures markets for a wide variety of products, including energy, bandwidth, and plastics.

One more thing is needed before anyone will actually buy or sell futures contracts: assurance that the buyer and seller will meet their obligations. In the case of the U.S. Treasury bond futures contract, the buyer must be sure the seller will deliver the bond, and the seller must believe that the buyer will pay for it. Market participants have found an ingenious solution to this problem. Instead of making a bilateral arrangement, the two parties to a futures contract each make an agreement with a clearing corporation. The clearing corporation, which operates like a large insurance company, is the counterparty to both sides of a transaction, guaranteeing that they will meet their obligations. This arrangement reduces the risk buyers and sellers face.

Margin Accounts and Marking to Market

To reduce the risk it faces, the clearing corporation requires both parties to a futures contract to place a deposit with the corporation itself. This practice is called posting

---

[2]The term *short* refers to the fact that one party to the agreement is obligated to deliver something, whether or not he or she currently own it. The term *long* signifies that the other party is obligated to buy something at a future date.

[3]The seller of a U.S. Treasury bond futures contract need not deliver the exact bond specified in the contract. The Chicago Board of Trade maintains a spreadsheet of conversion factors to use in adjusting the quantity (face value) when delivery of some other bond is made. While these particular futures allow for delivery at any time during the delivery month, other futures may require delivery on a specific day.

Table 9.1 Interest-Rate Futures

Treasury Bond Futures (CBT) – $100,000; pts 32nds of 100%

(1)	(2)	(3)	(4)	(5)	(6)	(7)	(8)	(9)
						Lifetime		Open Interest
	Open	High	Low	Settle	Change	High	Low	
June 04	108–09	108–21	107–20	107–25	–10	116–15	104–00	454,886
Sept 04	106–31	107–05	106–11	106–12	–10	114–30	101–25	18,919

Using the Table

This table reports information on a contract for delivery of $100,000 face value worth of 10-year 6 percent coupon U.S. Treasury Bonds.

Column 1 reports the month when the contract requires delivery of the bonds from the short position/seller to the long position/buyer.

Column 2. "Open" is the price quoted when the exchange opened on the morning of April 15, 2004. This need not be the same as the price at the preceding afternoon's close. The price, 108-09, is quoted in 32nds and represents the cost of $100 face value worth of the 10-year 6 percent coupon U.S. Treasury bonds.

Columns 3 and 4. "High" and "Low" are the highest and lowest prices posted during the trading day.

Column 5. "Settle" is the closing or settlement price at the end of the trading day. This is the price used for marking to market.

Column 6. "Change" is the change in the closing price, measured in 32nds, from the preceding day's closing price.

Columns 7 and 8. "Lifetime High" and "Lifetime Low" are the highest and lowest prices over the life of the contract.

Column 9. "Open Interest" is the number of contracts outstanding, or open. For contracts near expiration, this number is often quite large. Most of the time, contract sellers repurchase their positions rather than delivering the bonds, a procedure called *settlement by offset.*

SOURCE: The Wall Street Journal, *April 16, 2004, p. C12. Reprinted by permission of* The Wall Street Journal, *Copyright © 2004 Dow Jones & Company, Inc. All Rights Reserved Worldwide.*

margin in a *margin account.* The margin deposits guarantee that when the contract comes due, the parties will be able to meet their obligations. But the clearing corporation does more than collect the *initial margin* when a contract is signed. It also posts daily gains and losses on the contract to the margin accounts of the parties involved.[4] This process is called *marking to market.*

Marking to market is analogous to what happens during a poker game. At the end of each hand, the amount wagered is transferred from the losers to the winner. In financial parlance, the account of each player is marked to market. Alternative methods of accounting are too complicated, making it difficult to identify players who should be excused from the game because they have run out of resources. For similar reasons, the clearing corporation marks futures accounts to market every day. Doing so ensures that sellers always have the resources to make delivery and that buyers always can pay. As in poker, if someone's margin account falls below the minimum, the clearing corporation will sell the contracts, ending the person's participation in the market.

An example will help you understand how marking to market works. Take the case of a futures contract for the purchase of 1,000 ounces of silver at $7 per ounce. The contract specifies that the buyer of the contract, the long position, will pay $7,000 in

[4]On April 15, 2004, the June 2004 U.S. Treasury bond futures contract in Table 9.1 fell 10/32 per $100 face value worth of bonds. A single contract covers 1,000 times that amount, so the value of each contract fell by ($10/32)(1000) = $312.50. Marking to market means that, at the end of the day for each outstanding contract, the clearing corporation credited the short position/seller $312.50 and debited the long position/buyer $312.50.

exchange for 1,000 ounces of silver. The seller of the contract, the short position, receives the $7,000 and delivers the 1,000 ounces of silver. We can think about this contract as guaranteeing the long position the ability to buy 1,000 ounces of silver for $7,000 and guaranteeing the short position the ability to sell 1,000 ounces of silver for $7,000. Now consider what happens when the price of silver changes. If the price rises to $8 per ounce, the seller needs to give the buyer $1,000 so that the buyer pays only $7,000 for the 1,000 ounces of silver. By contrast, if the price falls to $6 an ounce, the buyer of the futures contract needs to pay $1,000 to the seller to make sure that the seller receives $7,000 for selling the 1,000 ounces of silver. Marking to market is the transfer of funds at the end of each day that ensures the buyers and sellers get what the contract promises.

Hedging and Speculating with Futures

Futures contracts allow the transfer of risk between buyer and seller. This transfer can be accomplished through hedging or speculation. Let's look at *hedging* first. Say a government securities dealer wishes to insure against declines in the value of an inventory of bonds. Recall from Chapter 5 that this type of risk can be reduced by finding another financial instrument that delivers a high payoff when bond prices fall. That is exactly what happens with the sale of a U.S. Treasury bond futures contract: the seller/short position benefits from price declines. Put differently, the seller of a futures contract—the securities dealer, in this case—can guarantee the price at which the bonds are sold. The other party to this transaction might be a pension fund manager who is planning to purchase bonds in the future and wishes to insure against possible price increases.[5] Buying a futures contract fixes the price that the fund will need to pay. In this example, *both sides use the futures contract as a hedge.* They are both hedgers.[6]

Producers and users of commodities employ futures markets to hedge their risks as well. Farmers, mining companies, oil drillers, and the like are sellers of futures, taking short positions. After all, they own the commodities outright, so they want to stabilize the revenue they receive when they sell. In contrast, millers, jewelers, and oil distributors want to buy futures to take long positions. They require the commodity to do business, so they buy the futures contract to reduce risk arising from fluctuations in the cost of essential inputs. (See Applying the Concept: Who Can Use Commodity Futures Markets? for a detailed example of this process.)

What about speculators? Their objective is simple: They are trying to make a profit. To do so, they bet on price movements. Sellers of futures are betting that prices will fall, while buyers are betting that prices will rise. Futures contracts are popular tools for speculation because they are cheap. An investor needs only a relatively small amount of investment—the margin—to purchase a futures contract that is worth a great deal. Margin requirements of 10 percent or less are common. In the case of a futures contract for the delivery of $100,000 face value worth of 10-year, 6 percent coupon U.S. Treasury bonds, the Chicago Board of Trade (the clearing corporation that guarantees the contract) requires an initial margin of only $2,700 per contract. That is, an investment of only $2,700 gives the investor the same returns as the purchase of $100,000 worth of bonds. It is as if the investor borrowed the remaining $97,300 without having to pay any interest.[7]

---

[5]Recall from chapters 4 and 6 that bond prices and interest rates move in opposite directions. That means the bond dealer who sells the futures contract is insuring against interest rate increases.

[6]Hedgers who buy futures called *long hedgers* and hedgers who sell futures are called *short hedgers*.

[7]It is even possible to arrange a margin account so that the balance earns interest.

APPLYING THE CONCEPT
WHO CAN USE COMMODITY FUTURES MARKETS?

Commodity prices are notoriously volatile, a fact that makes farming a risky business. In the industrialized world, farmers use futures contracts to hedge the risk arising from price fluctuations. For instance, I have a friend who owns a 2,500-acre wheat farm. Wheat farming is risky because the farmer's profits depend on the price of wheat at harvest time. To guarantee the price of the wheat he grows, my friend relies on wheat futures. As he plants, investing heavily in his crop, he simultaneously sells futures contracts. The contracts obligate him to deliver the wheat when it is ripe and fix the price he will receive when he does. They are a hedge against the risk of price fluctuations.

Imagine what would happen without this kind of insurance. If prices collapsed, in the absence of insurance the farmer could go bankrupt. Unable to guarantee the harvest price, the farmer would surely plant a smaller, less risky crop. Thus, the ability of people to buy insurance increases their willingness to take risks.

But who has access to commodity futures markets? Remember that trading in futures markets requires the posting of margin; poor farmers need not apply. This hard fact is particularly unfortunate for people in less-developed countries. Growth is the way out of poverty, and risk taking increases growth. But without insurance, farmers in poor countries, like the coffee growers in Latin America, cannot risk planting large crops. So they will remain poor.

Futures markets, and derivatives in general, allow people to transfer risk to those who are equipped to handle it. They increase the risk-taking capacity of the economy, making everyone better off. In parts of the world where people do not have access to futures markets, the economy suffers.

To see the impact of this kind of leverage on the return to the buyer and seller of a futures contract, recall from our earlier example that a decline of 10/32nds in the price of the Treasury bond futures contract meant that the short position/seller gained $312.50 while the long position/buyer lost $312.50. With a minimum initial investment of $2,700 for each contract, this represents an 11.6 percent gain to the futures contract seller and a 11.6 percent loss to the futures contract buyer. In contrast, the owner of the bond itself would have gained $312.50 on an approximately $100,000 investment, which is a return of just 0.313 percent! *Speculators, then, can use futures to obtain very large amounts of leverage at a very low cost.*

Arbitrage and the Determinants of Futures Prices

To understand how the price of a futures contract is determined, let's start at the settlement date and work backward. On the settlement or delivery date, we know that the price of the futures contract must equal the price of the underlying asset the seller is obligated to deliver. The reason is simple: If, at expiration, the futures price were to deviate from the asset's price, then it would be possible to make a risk-free profit by engaging in offsetting cash and futures transactions. If the current market price of a bond were below the futures contract price, someone could buy a bond at the low price and simultaneously sell a futures contract (take a short position and promise to deliver the bond on a future date). Immediate exercise of the futures contract and delivery of the bond would yield a profit equal to the difference between the market price and the futures price. Thinking about this example carefully, we can see that the investor who engages in these transactions has been able to make a profit without taking on any risk or making any investment.

The practice of simultaneously buying and selling financial instruments in order to benefit from temporary price differences is called arbitrage, and the people who engage in it are called arbitrageurs. Arbitrage means that two financial instruments with the same risk and promised future payments will sell for the same price. If, for example, the price of a specific bond is higher in one market than in another, an arbitrageur can buy at the low price and sell at the high price. The increase in demand in the market where the price is low drives the price up there, while the increase in supply in the market where the price is high drives the price down there, and the process continues until prices are equal in the two markets. As long as there are arbitrageurs, on the day when a futures contract is settled, the price of a bond futures contract will be the same as the market price—what is called the spot price—of the bond.

So we know that on the settlement date, the price of a futures contract must equal the spot price of the underlying asset. But what happens before the settlement date? The principle of arbitrage still applies. The price of the futures contract depends on the fact that someone can buy a bond and sell a futures contract simultaneously. Here's how it's done. First, the arbitrageur borrows at the current market interest rate. With the funds, the arbitrageur buys a bond and sells a bond futures contract. Now the arbitrageur has a loan on which interest must be paid, a bond that pays interest, and a promise to deliver the bond for a fixed price at the expiration of the futures contract. Because the interest owed on the loan and received from the bond will cancel out, this position costs nothing to initiate.[8] As before, if the market price of the bond is below the futures contract price, this strategy will yield a profit. *Thus, the futures price must move in lockstep with the market price of the bond.*

To see how arbitrage works, consider an example in which the spot price of a 6 percent coupon 10-year bond is $100, the current interest rate on a 3-month loan is also 6 percent (quoted at an annual rate), and the futures market price for delivery of a 6 percent 10-year bond is $101. An investor could borrow $100, purchase the 10-year bond, and sell a bond future for $101 promising delivery of the bond in three months. The investor could use the interest payment from the bond to pay the interest on the loan and deliver the bond to the buyer of the futures contract on the delivery date. This transaction is completely riskless and nets the investor a profit of $1—without even putting up any funds. A riskless profit is extremely tempting, so the investor will continue to engage in the transactions needed to generate it. Here that means continuing to buy bonds (driving the price up) and sell futures (forcing the price down) until the prices converge and no further profits are available.[9]

Table 9.2 summarizes the positions of buyers and sellers in the futures market.

---

[8]Unlike you and me, the arbitrageur can borrow at an interest rate that is close to the one received from the bond. There are two reasons for this. First, the arbitrageur is likely to be a large financial intermediary with a very high credit rating; second, the loan is collaterallized by the bond itself.

[9]In a commodity futures contract, the futures price will equal the present value of the expected spot price on the delivery date, discounted at the riskless interest rate.

	Buyer of a Futures Contract	**Seller of a Futures Contract**
Table 9.2 Who's Who in Futures		
This is called the	*Long* position	*Short* position
Obligation of the party	Buy the commodity or asset on the settlement date	Deliver the commodity or asset on the settlement date
What happens to this person's margin account after a *rise* in the market price of the commodity or asset	*Credited*	*Debited*
Who takes this position to *hedge?*	The *user* of the commodity or *buyer* of the asset who needs to insure against the price *rising*	The *producer* of the commodity or *owner* of the asset who needs to insure against the price *falling*
Who takes this position to *speculate?*	Someone who believes that the market price of the commodity or asset will *rise*	Someone who believes that the market price of the commodity or asset will *fall*

Options

Everyone likes to have options. Having the option to go on vacation or buy a new car is nice. The alternative to having options, having our decisions made for us, is surely worse. Because options are valuable, people are willing to pay for them when they can. Financial options are no different; because they are worth having, we can put a price on them.

Calculating the price of an option is incredibly complicated. In fact, no one knew how before Fischer Black and Myron Scholes figured it out in 1973. Traders immediately programmed their famous Black-Scholes formula into the computers available at the time, and the options markets took off. By June 2000, the market value of outstanding options was in the neighborhood of $500 billion. Today, millions of options contracts are outstanding, and millions of them change hands every day.

Before we learn how to price options, we'll need to master the vocabulary used to describe them. Once we have the language, the next step is to move on to how to use options and how to value them.

Calls, Puts, and All That: Definitions

Like futures, options are agreements between two parties. There is a seller, called an *option writer,* and a buyer, called an *option holder.* As we will see, option writers incur obligations, while option holders obtain rights. There are two basic options, *puts* and *calls.*

A **call option** is the right to buy—"call away"—a given quantity of an underlying asset at a predetermined price, called the **strike price** (or *exercise price*), on or before a specific date. For example, a January 2005 call option on 100 shares of IBM stock at a strike price of 90 gives the option holder the right to buy 100 shares of IBM for $90 apiece prior to the third Friday of January 2005. The writer of the call option *must* sell the shares if and when the holder chooses to use the call option. The holder of the call is *not* required to buy the shares; rather, the holder has the option to buy and will do so only if buying is beneficial. When the price of IBM stock exceeds the option strike price of 90, the option holder can either call away the 100 shares from the option writer by *exercising* the option or sell the option to someone else at a profit. If the market price rose to $95, for example, then exercising the call would allow the holder to buy the stock from the option writer for $90 and reap a $5 per share profit. Whenever the price of the stock is above the strike price of the call option, exercising the option is profitable for the holder, and the option is said to be in the money (as in "I'm in the money!"). If the price of the stock exactly equals the strike price, the option is said to be at the money. If the strike price exceeds the market price of the underlying asset, it is termed out of the money.

A put option gives the holder the right but not the obligation to sell the underlying asset at a predetermined price on or before a fixed date. The holder can "put" the asset in the hands of the option writer. Again, the writer of the option is obliged to buy the shares should the holder choose to exercise the option. Returning to the example of IBM stock, consider a put option with a strike price of 90. This is the right to sell 100 shares at $90 per share, which is valuable when the market price of IBM stock falls below $90. If the price of a share of IBM stock were $80, then exercising the put option would yield a profit of $10 per share.

The same terminology that is used to describe calls—in the money, at the money, and out of the money—applies to puts as well, but the circumstances in which it is used are reversed. Since the buyer of a put obtains the right to sell a stock, the put is *in the money* when the option's strike price is *above* the market price of the stock. It is *out of the money* when the strike price is *below* the market price.

While it is possible to customize options in the same way as forward contracts, many are standardized and traded on exchanges, just like futures contracts. The mechanics of trading are the same. A clearing corporation guarantees the obligations embodied in the option—those of the option writer. And the option writer is required to post margin. Because option holders incur no obligation, they are not required to post margin.

There are two types of calls and puts: American and European. American options can be exercised on any date from the time they are written until the day they expire. As a result, prior to the expiration date, the holder of an American option has three choices: (1) continue to hold the option, (2) sell the option to someone else, or (3) exercise the option immediately. European options can be exercised only on the day that they expire. Thus, the holder of a European option has two choices on a date prior to expiration: hold or sell. The vast majority of options traded in the United States are American.

Using Options

Who buys and sells options, and why? To answer this question, we need to understand how options are used. *Options transfer risk* from the buyer to the seller, so they can be used for both hedging and speculation. Let's take hedging first. Remember that a hedger is buying insurance. For someone who wants to purchase an asset such as a bond or a stock in the future, a call option ensures that the cost of buying the asset will not rise. For someone who plans to sell the asset in the future, a put option ensures that the price at which the asset can be sold will not go down.

To understand the close correspondence between options and insurance, think of the arrangement that automobile owners have with their insurance company. The owner pays an insurance premium and obtains the right to file a claim in the event of an accident. If the terms of the policy are met, the insurance company is obligated to pay the claim. If no accident occurs, then there is no claim and the insurance company makes no payment; the insurance premium is lost. In effect, the insurance company has sold an American call option to the car's owner where the underlying asset is a working car and the strike price is zero. This call option can be exercised if and only if the car is damaged in an accident on any day before the policy expires.

Options can be used for speculation as well. Say that you believe that interest rates are going to fall over the next few months. There are three ways to bet on this possibility. The first is to purchase a bond outright, hoping that its price will rise as interest rates fall. This is expensive, since you will need to come up with the resources to buy the bond. A second strategy is to buy a futures contract, taking the long position. If the market price of the bond rises, you will make a profit. As we saw in the last section, this is an attractive approach, since it requires only a small investment. But it is also very risky, because the investment is highly leveraged. Both the bond purchase and the futures contract carry the risk that you will take a loss, and if interest rates rise substantially, your loss will be large.

The third strategy for betting that interest rates will fall is to buy a call option on a U.S. Treasury bond. If you are right and interest rates fall, the value of the call option will rise. But if you are wrong and interest rates rise, the call will expire worthless and your losses will be limited to the price you paid for it. This bet is both highly leveraged and limited in its potential losses.

In the same way that purchasing a call option allows an investor to bet that the price of the underlying asset will rise, purchasing a put option allows the investor to bet that the price will fall. Again, if the investor is wrong, all that is lost is the price paid for the option. In the meantime, the option provides a cheap way to bet on the movement in the price of the underlying asset. The bet is highly leveraged, since a small initial investment creates the opportunity for a large gain. But unlike a futures contract, a put option has a limited potential loss.

So far we have discussed only the purchase of options. For every buyer there must be a seller. Who is it? After all, an option writer can take a large loss. Nevertheless, for a fee, some people are willing to take the risk and bet that prices will not move against them. These people are simply speculators. A second group of people who are willing to write options are insured against any losses that may arise. They are primarily dealers who engage in the regular purchase and sale of the underlying asset. These people are called *market makers* since they are always there to make the market. Because they are in the business of buying and selling, market markers both own the underlying asset so that they can deliver it and are willing to buy the underlying asset so that they have it ready to sell to someone else. If you own the underlying asset, writing a call option that obligates you to sell it at a fixed price is not that risky. These people write options to obtain the fee paid by the buyer.[10]

Writing options can also generate clear benefits. To see how, think about the case of an electricity producer who has a plant that is worth operating only when electricity prices exceed a relatively high minimum level. Such peak-load plants are relatively common. They sit idle most of the time and are fired up only when demand is so

[10]For a discussion of who buys and sells options, see Josef Lakonishok, Inmoo Lee, and Allen M. Poteshman, "Investor Behavior in the Option Market," National Bureau of Economic Research Working Paper No. 10264, January 2004.

Table 9.3   A Guide to Options

	Calls	Puts
Buyer	*Right* to *buy* the underlying asset at the strike price prior to or on the expiration date. "Hey, send it over!"	*Right* to *sell* the underlying asset at a fixed price prior to or on the expiration date. "Here it is; it's yours now!"
Seller	*Obligation* to *sell* the underlying asset at the strike price prior to or on the expiration date.	*Obligation* to *buy* the underlying asset at the strike price prior to or on the expiration date
Option is *in the money* when	Price of underlying asset is *above* the strike price of the call	Price of underlying asset is *below* the strike price of the put
Who *buys* one	Someone who • Wants to *buy* an asset in the future and insure the price paid will not *rise* • Wants to bet that the price of the underlying asset will rise	Someone who • Wants to *sell* an asset in the future and insure the price paid will not fall • Wants to bet that the price of the underlying asset will fall
Who *sells* one to speculate	Someone who • Wants to bet that the market price of the underlying asset will *not* rise • A broker who is always willing to sell the underlying asset and is paid to take the risk	Someone who • Wants to bet that the market price of the underlying asset will *not* fall • A broker who is always willing to buy the underlying asset and is paid to take the risk

high that prices spike. The problem is that when they are not operating—which is the normal state of affairs—the owner must pay maintenance charges. To cover these charges, the producer might choose to write a call option on electricity. Here's how the strategy works. For a fee, the plant owner sells a call option with a strike price that is higher than the price at which the plant will be brought on line. The buyer of the call might be someone who uses electricity and wants insurance against a spike in prices. The option fee will cover the producer's maintenance cost while the plant is shut down. And, since the producer as option writer owns the underlying asset here—electricity—he or she is hedged against the possibility that the call option will pay off. As the price of electricity rises, the plant's revenue goes up with it.

Options are very versatile and can be bought and sold in many combinations. They allow investors to get rid of the risks they do not want and keep the ones they do want. In fact, options can be used to construct synthetic instruments that mimic the payoffs of virtually any other financial instrument. For example, the purchase of an at-the-money call and simultaneous sale of an at-the-money put gives the exact same payoff pattern as the purchase of a futures contract. If the price of the underlying asset rises, the call's value increases just as a futures contract does, while the put remains worthless. If the price falls, the put seller loses, just as a futures contract does, while the call is out of the money. Finally, options allow investors to bet that prices will be volatile. Buy a put and a call at the same strike price, and you have a bet that pays off only if the underlying asset price moves up or down significantly.

In summary, options are extremely useful. Remember the example at the beginning of the chapter, in which the snowmobile manufacturer Bombardier purchased insurance so it could offer its customers a rebate? What it bought were put options with a payoff tied to the amount of snow that fell. The puts promised payments in the event of low snowfall. This hedged the risk the company incurred when it offered rebates to the purchasers of its snowmobiles. The providers of this insurance, the sellers of the snowfall options, may have been betting that snowfall would be low. That is, they may have been speculating—but not necessarily. After all, there are many companies whose sales and profits rise during warm weather and who are well positioned to take such a risk. Insurance companies, for instance, have lower expenses during warm winters, since there are fewer accident claims when there is less snow. If there is little snow, the insurance company has the funds to make the payments, while if there is lots of snow they can use the option premium they were paid to write the put to help pay the cost of the claims they face.[11]

Pricing Options: Intrinsic Value and the Option Premium

An option price has two parts. The first is the value of the option if it is exercised immediately, and the second is the fee paid for the option's potential benefits. We will refer to the first of these, the value of the option if it is exercised immediately, as the *intrinsic value*. The second, the fee paid for the potential benefit from buying the option, we will call the option premium.[12] This means that

$$\text{Option Price} = \text{Intrinsic Value} + \text{Option Premium}$$

As an example, before we launch into a discussion of option valuation in general, let's apply what we know about present value and risk analysis. Consider the example of an at-the-money European call option on the stock of XYZ Corporation that expires in one month. Recall that a European option can be exercised only at expiration and that an at-the-money option is one for which the current price equals the strike price. In this case, both equal $100. So, to start with, the intrinsic value of this call option is zero. To the extent that it has any value at all, that value resides entirely in the option premium. Assume that, over the next month, the price of XYZ Corporation's stock will either rise or fall by $10 with equal probability. That is, there is a probability of $\frac{1}{2}$ the price will go up to $110, and there is a probability of $\frac{1}{2}$ it will fall to $90. What is the value of this call option?

To find the answer, we can compute the expected present value of the payoff. Let's assume that the interest rate is so low that we can ignore it. (If the payoff were postponed sufficiently far into the future or the interest rate were high enough, we could

---

[11]Bombardier purchased its snowfall insurance from Enron (prior to that company's bankruptcy). As it turned out, there was sufficient snowfall so no payments were made either from Bombardier to the buyers of the snowmobiles or from Enron to Bombardier.

[12]The option premium is also known as the *extrinsic value* of the option, as well as the *time* or *volatility value*. We will use the term *option premium* to emphasize its similarity to a risk premium.

not ignore the present-value calculation but would have to divide by one plus the interest rate.) Now notice that the option is worth something only if the price goes up. In the event that XYZ's stock price falls to $90, you will allow the option to expire without exercising it. For a call option, then, we need to concern ourselves with the upside, and the expected value of that payoff is the probability, $\frac{1}{2}$, times the payoff, $10, which is $5. This is the option premium.

Now think about what happens if, instead of rising or falling by $10, XYZ's stock will rise or fall by $20. This change increases the standard deviation of the stock price. In the terminology used in options trading, the stock price *volatility* has increased. Doing the same calculation, we see that the expected payoff is now $10. As the volatility of the stock price rises, the option premium rises with it.

General Considerations In general, calculating the price of an option and how it might change means developing some rules for figuring out its intrinsic value and option premium. We can do that using the framework from Chapter 3. Recall that the value of any financial instrument depends on four attributes: the size of the promised payment, the timing of the payment, the likelihood that the payment will be made, and the circumstances under which the payment will be made.[13] As we consider each of these, remember that the most important thing about an option is that the buyer is not obligated to exercise it. An option gives the buyer a choice! What this means is that someone holding an option will never make any additional payment to exercise it, so its value cannot be less than zero.

Since the option can either be exercised or expire worthless, we can conclude that the intrinsic value depends only on what the holder receives if the option is exercised. The intrinsic value is the difference between the price of the underlying asset and the strike price of the option. This is the *size of the payment* that the option represents, and it must be greater than or equal to zero—the intrinsic value cannot be negative. For an in-the-money call, or the option to buy, the intrinsic value to the holder (the long position) is the market price of the underlying asset minus the strike price. If the call is at the money or out of the money, it has no intrinsic value. Analogously, the intrinsic value of a put, or the option to sell, equals the strike price minus the market price of the underlying asset, or zero, whichever is greater.

At expiration, the value of an option equals its intrinsic value. But what about prior to expiration? To think about this question, consider an at-the-money option—one whose intrinsic value is zero. Prior to expiration, there is always the chance that the price of the underlying asset will move so as to make the option valuable. This potential benefit is represented by the option premium. *The longer the time to expiration*, the bigger the likely payoff when the option does expire and, thus, the more valuable it is. Remember that the option payoff is asymmetric, so what is important is the chance of making profit. In the last example, think about what will happen if the option expires in three months instead of one and the stock price has an equal probability of rising or falling $10 each month. The expected payoff of the call option rises from $5 after one month and to $7.50 after three. (After three months, the stock can either rise by $30 with probability $\frac{1}{8}$, rise by $10 with probability $\frac{3}{8}$, fall by $10 with probability $\frac{3}{8}$, or fall by $30 with probability $\frac{1}{8}$. When the price falls, the call option is not exercised, so the expected value of the three-month call is $(\frac{1}{8} \times \$30 + \frac{3}{8} \times \$10) = \$7.50$.)

The likelihood that an option will pay off depends on the volatility, or standard deviation, of the price of the underlying asset. To see this, consider an option on IBM stock that is

---

[13]Because the pricing of European options is easier to understand, we will talk about options as if they can be exercised only at the expiration date. The principles for pricing American options are the same, however.

Table 9.4   Factors Affecting the Value of Options

Option Value = Intrinsic Value + Option Premium

Increase in one factor, holding all others fixed	Call (the right to buy)	Put (the right to sell)
Increase in the strike price	Decrease (intrinsic value falls)	Increase (intrinsic value rises)
Increase in the market price of the underlying asset	Increase (intrinsic value rises)	Decrease (intrinsic value falls)
Increase in the time to expiration	Increase (option premium rises)	Increase (option premium rises)
Increase in the volatility of the underlying asset price	Increase (option premium rises)	Increase (option premium rises)

RISK

currently at the money—one with a strike price that equals the current price of the stock. The chance of this option being in the money by the time it expires increases with the volatility of IBM's stock price. Think about an option on an asset whose price is simply fixed—that is, whose standard deviation is zero. This option will never pay off, so no one would be willing to pay for it. Add some variability to the price, however, and there is a chance that the price will rise, moving the option into the money. That is something people will pay for. Thus, the option premium increases with the volatility of the price of the underlying asset. Taking this analysis one step further, we know that regardless of how far the price of the underlying asset falls, the holder of a call option cannot lose more. In contrast, whenever the price rises higher, the call option increases in value. Increased volatility has no cost to the option holder, only benefits.

We have emphasized that options provide insurance, allowing investors to hedge particular risks. The bigger the risk being insured, the more valuable the insurance, and the higher the price investors will pay. Thus, *the circumstances under which the payment is made* have an important impact on the option premium. As with futures, however, both writers and holders of options may be hedging risks, so it is impossible to know exactly how risk will affect the option price. Table 9.4 summarizes the factors that affect the value of options.

The Value of Options: Some Examples

To see how options are valued, we can examine a simple example. The daily news reports the prices of options that are traded on organized exchanges. Table 9.5 shows the prices of IBM puts and calls on April 19, 2004, as reported in *The Wall Street Journal*. Panel A shows the prices of options with different strike prices but the same expiration date, July 2004. Panel B shows the prices of options with different expiration dates but the same strike price. From the top of the table we can see that the price of IBM stock, the underlying asset on which these options were written, was $92.28 per share at the close of that day.

Table 9.5 Prices of IBM Puts and Calls

At Close on Friday, April 19, 2004
IBM Stock Price at close = $92.28

A. July Expiration

Strike Price	Calls			Puts		
	Price	Intrinsic Value	Call Premium	Price	Intrinsic Value	Put Premium
$80	$12.70	$12.28	$0.42	$0.60	$0	$0.60
85	8.60	7.28	1.32	1.30	0	1.30
90	5.10	2.28	2.82	2.75	0	2.75
95	2.45	0	2.45	5.20	2.72	2.48
100	1.00	0	1.00	9.00	7.72	1.28
105	0.35	0	0.35	13.40	12.72	0.68

B. Strike Price of 90

Expiration Month	Calls			Puts		
	Price	Intrinsic Value	Call Premium	Price	Intrinsic Value	Put Premium
May	3.40	2.28	1.12	1.25	0	1.25
July	5.10	2.28	2.82	2.75	0	2.75
October	6.50	2.28	4.22	4.40	0	4.40

Intrinsic value of a call = Stock price − Strike price or zero, whichever is larger.

Intrinsic value of a put = Strike price − Stock price or zero, whichever is larger.

Option premium = Option price − Intrinsic value.

By examining the table, we can discover the following:

- At a given price of the underlying asset and time to expiration, the higher the strike price of a call option, the lower its intrinsic value and the less expensive the option. That is, as you read down the column labeled "Strike Price" in Panel A, the intrinsic value under "Calls" (IBM stock price minus the strike price) falls. For example, as the strike price goes from $80 to $90, the intrinsic value falls from $12.28 to $2.28.

- At a given price of the underlying asset and time to expiration, the higher the strike price of a put option, the higher the intrinsic value and the more expen-

YOUR FINANCIAL WORLD
Should You Accept Options as Part of Your Pay?

What if someone offers you a job in return for a salary and stock options? Should you take it? Before you do, ask questions! Let's look at what you need to know. Many firms that offer options on their own stock to employees view the options as a substitute for wages. Employees receive call options that give them the right to purchase the company's stock at a fixed price. The strike price is usually set at the current market price of the stock, so that when employees receive the options, they are at the money. Normally, the expiration date is from one to 10 years in the future. Since the options are long-term, they will have substantial value, as measured by the option premium. But there is a catch. Employees generally are not allowed to sell them and may need to remain with the firm to exercise them.

Nevertheless, the price of the company's stock could skyrocket, so the options may bring a substantial payoff. To take an extreme example, from January 1991 to January 2000, Microsoft's stock price rose from $2 to $116 per share. An employee with 1,000 options to purchase the stock at $2 would have made $114,000 by exercising them. Though Microsoft employees were winners, there are many losers in the options game. Employees holding options to purchase stock in Enron or WorldCom, both of which went bankrupt in 2001, got nothing.

So what should you do? If taking the options means accepting a lower salary, then you are paying for them, and you should think hard before you take the offer. Stock options are almost like lottery tickets, but with a drawing that may not occur for years. They give you a small chance to make a large profit. But investing in the same company that pays your salary is a risky business. If the company goes broke or you lose your job, the options will be worthless to you. So think hard before you trade a high-paying job for a lower-paying job with options.[*]

[*]For a comprehensive discussion of employee stock options, see Chapter 1 of John Martinsen, *Risk Takers: Uses and Abuses of Financial Derivatives* (Boston: Pearson Education, Inc., 2005).

sive the option. (See the "Intrinsic Value" column for puts in Panel A.) As the strike price rises from $95 to $105, the intrinsic value of the IBM put (the strike price minus the IBM stock price) rises from $2.72 to $12.72.

- The closer the strike price is to the current price of the underlying asset, the larger the option premium. (See the two columns in Panel A labeled "Call Premium" and "Put Premium.") For a call option with a strike price of $90 and an intrinsic value of $2.28, the premium is $2.82. As the strike price goes down to $85, the option premium falls to $1.32.

- Deep in-the-money options have small option premiums (see the call premiums in Panel A). Because a deep in-the-money call option is very likely to expire in the money, buying one is much like buying the stock itself. Note that the call with a strike price of $80 and an intrinsic value of $12.28 has a premium of only $0.42, far less than the $2.82 premium of a call with an intrinsic value of $2.28.

- The longer the time to expiration at a given strike price, the higher the option price. As you read down the prices of both puts and calls in Panel B of Table 9.5, you can see that the longer the time to expiration, the more the price goes up. That is because the option premium is going up. A $90 IBM call that expires in May sells for $3.40, while one that expires two months later sells for $5.10. The same rule applies to puts.

TOOLS OF THE TRADE
Options and Investment under Uncertainty

When a firm has an opportunity to build a new plant or enter a new line of business, it has an option. These so-called *real options* are analogous to the financial options we have just discussed. The similarity has important implications for both the way a company makes its own investment decisions and the behavior of investment throughout the economy.

To see what insights we gain from thinking in terms of options, we need to go back to our discussion of present value and internal rate of return in Chapter 4. There we examined a simple investment decision in which a firm was considering whether to purchase a machine up front in exchange for a future revenue stream that would come from the machine's output. Recall that the decision to make the investment depends on whether the present value of the future revenue exceeds the cost of the purchase. As we put it in Chapter 4, the firm should make the investment if the internal rate of return on the project exceeds the cost of financing.

This traditional present-value approach ignores three important characteristics of real-life investment.

- *Uncertainty.* You don't know exactly what the future rewards of the investment will be.
- *Irreversibility.* Once the decision to invest is made, you cannot fully recover the costs.
- *Timing.* You decide when to make the investment and can delay it if you want.

These characteristics have an impact on how investment decisions are made. If uncertainty were the only issue, we could treat real investments the same way we treated bonds and stocks in Chapter 5. That is, risk requires compensation in the form of a risk premium. The higher the risk, the higher the risk premium and the higher the yield investors require to hold an asset. The same is true of a firm making an investment: Uncertainty simply raises the internal rate of return required to undertake the investment.

Irreversibility and timing complicate the decision. Combined, they imply that when a firm makes an investment, it exercises an option to invest. Think of it as a call option to buy the project. Exercising the option means giving up the possibility of obtaining new information that might make the project more or less desirable. The lost value of the new information becomes one of the costs of undertaking the investment, one the firm must account for when it makes the decision.

This extra cost helps to explain the fact that most companies require investment projects to meet internal rates of return much higher than the cost of the funds invested. In fact, these *hurdle rates* can be several times the market yield on a corporate bond. The explanation is that the required return incorporates the value of the option to wait.

Connecting the firm's investment decision to macroeconomic investment is straightforward. The value of an option depends on the volatility of the underlying asset price. When that volatility goes up, the value of the option rises with it. In an investment decision, the present value of the future revenue is the analog to the price of the underlying asset. When uncertainty about the investment's return rises, the value of the option goes up. Put differently, the value of waiting for more information rises, and the firm will delay. Delay means lower investment. Thus, if uncertainty about general economic conditions rises, we would expect investment to fall overall.[*]

[*]Entire books have been written about real options and investment under uncertainty. For a brief discussion, see Chapter 21 in Richard A. Brealey and Stewart Myers, *Principles of Corporate Finance*, 7th ed., (New York: McGraw-Hill/Irwin, 2003); and Chapter 17 of Robert McDonald, *Derivatives Markets* (New York: Addison Wesley, 2002).

Swaps

Government debt managers—the people at the U.S. Treasury who decide when and how to issue U.S. Treasury bonds, notes, and bills—do their best to keep public borrowing costs as low as possible. That means (a) selling bonds at the lowest interest rates possible and (b) ensuring that government revenues will be available when payments must be made. Because of the structure of financial markets, keeping interest costs low usually is not a problem. Demand for long-term government bonds is high. (They are used as collateral in many financial transactions.) Thus, government debt managers can sell them at relatively high prices.

Managing government revenues is more of a challenge. Revenues tend to rise during economic booms and fall during recessions. Even if tax revenues fall, the government must still make its bond payments. Short-term interest rates, like tax revenues, tend to move with the business cycle, rising during booms and falling during recessions. (Improvements in general business conditions raise the corporate bond supply, lowering bond prices and raising interest rates.) Ensuring that future interest expenses match future tax revenues might be easier if government borrowers issued short-term bonds.

This difficulty leaves the public debt manager in a quandary. Which is more important, keeping interest costs down by issuing long-term debt or matching costs with tax revenues by issuing short-term debt? Fortunately, derivatives allow government debt managers to meet both these goals using a tool called an interest-rate swap.

Understanding Interest-Rate Swaps

Interest-rate swaps are agreements between two counterparties to exchange periodic interest-rate payments over some future period, based on an agreed-upon amount of principal—what's called the **notional principal**. The term *notional* is used here because the principal of a **swap** is not borrowed, lent, or exchanged; it just serves as the basis for calculation of the periodic cash flows between the counterparties to the swap. In the simplest type of interest-rate swap, one party agrees to make payments based on a fixed interest rate, and in exchange the counterparty agrees to make payments based on a floating interest rate. The effect of this agreement is to transform fixed-rate payments into floating-rate payments and vice versa.

Figure 9.1 shows a typical interest-rate swap. A bank agrees to make payments to a swap dealer at a fixed interest rate, say 7 percent, in exchange for payments based on

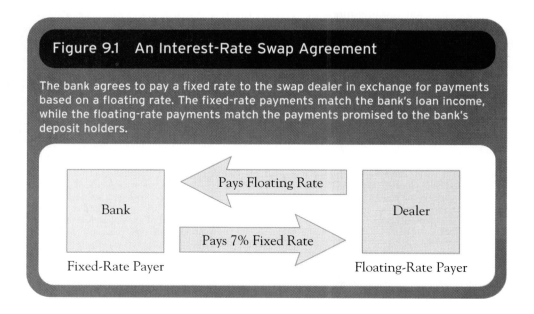

Figure 9.1 An Interest-Rate Swap Agreement

The bank agrees to pay a fixed rate to the swap dealer in exchange for payments based on a floating rate. The fixed-rate payments match the bank's loan income, while the floating-rate payments match the payments promised to the bank's deposit holders.

Bank — Fixed-Rate Payer

Pays Floating Rate

Pays 7% Fixed Rate

Dealer — Floating-Rate Payer

a floating rate determined in the market.[14] Both payments are based on the same agreed-upon principal, say $100 million. That is, the notional principal on the swap is $100 million. The bank is the fixed-rate payer and the swap dealer is the floating-rate payer. Put slightly differently, the two parties enter into a series of forward agreements in which they agree today to exchange interest payments on a series of future dates for the life of the swap. As in a futures contract, no payment is made at the outset.[15]

Now let's return to the government debt manager's problem. Remember that the government can issue long-term debt cheaply but its revenues tend to fluctuate with the short-term interest rate, going up when short-term interest rates rise and down when they fall. The solution is to sell long-term bonds and then enter into an interest-rate swap. The government becomes the floating-rate payer for the term of the bonds.[16]

Pricing and Using Interest-Rate Swaps

RISK

Pricing interest-rate swaps means figuring out the fixed interest rate to be paid. To do so, financial firms begin by noting the market interest rate on a U.S. Treasury bond of the same maturity as the swap, called the *benchmark*. The rate to be paid by the fixed-rate payer, called the *swap rate*, will be the benchmark rate plus a premium. The difference between the benchmark rate and the swap rate, called the swap spread, is a measure of risk. In recent years, the swap spread has attracted substantial attention as a measure of systematic risk, or overall risk in the economy. When it widens, it signals that general economic conditions are deteriorating.

Interest-rate swaps are just one example of the exchange of future payoffs. Investors engage in a wide variety of swaps involving foreign exchange and equities, though interest-rate swaps are the most important. By one estimate, at the end of June 2002, the notional value of interest-rate swaps worldwide exceeded $50 trillion—more than 10 times the total of foreign currency swaps and equity-linked swaps at the time.[17]

Who uses all these interest-rate swaps? Two groups have a comparative advantage in issuing bonds of a particular maturity. The first group is government debt managers, who find long-term fixed-rate bonds cheaper to issue but prefer short-term variable-rate obligations for matching revenues with expenses. The second group uses interest-rate swaps to reduce the risk generated by commercial activities. The prime example is a bank that obtains funds by offering interest-bearing checking accounts but makes mortgage loans at a fixed rate. In essence, the bank is issuing short-term variable-rate bonds (the checking accounts) and buying long-term fixed-rate bonds (the

---

[14]The floating rate is the interest rate at which banks make loans to each other. Specifically, it is the London Interbank Offered Rate (LIBOR), the rate at which banks in London make loans to each other.

[15]Because the principal is never at risk, interest-rate swaps are much safer than loans. Even the risk on the interest payments is low, since if one party stops payments on its side, the other party is no longer obligated to continue paying.

[16]Interest-rate swaps can be much more complex than this example. The two sides of the agreement may be based on different floating rates, or they may be stated in different currencies. In fact, the first swap was invented by an investment banker in 1981 in response to the fact that the World Bank had issued bonds in dollars while IBM had issued bonds in German deutsche marks and Swiss francs, and each preferred to make interest payments in the currency of the other. (The World Bank is one of the world's largest sources of financing for development assistance. Its primary role is to help the poorest countries in the world to improve their living standards.) Though issuing bonds was cheaper in those currencies, IBM's revenues were mainly in dollars and the World Bank's were mainly in other currencies. The solution was to swap payments: The two parties essentially traded liabilities. The World Bank agreed to make the interest and principal payments on the bonds IBM had issued in Germany and Switzerland, and in exchange, IBM agreed to make the interest and principal payments on the World Bank's dollar-denominated loans.

[17]Data on interest-rate swaps are collected and regularly published by the Bank for International Settlements in Basel, Switzerland. For recent information, see its Web site, www.bis.org.

YOUR FINANCIAL WORLD
Should You Believe Corporate Financial Statements?

Corporations work hard to appear as profitable as possible. They employ squadrons of accountants and financial wizards to dress up their financial statements so that reported profits are as high and stable as possible. While financial statements must meet exacting accounting standards, that does not mean they accurately reflect a company's true financial position. The problem is that the standards are so specific they provide a road map for the creation of misleading statements. Remember that derivatives render the names attached to particular risks and payoffs arbitrary and irrelevant. But accounting regulations are all about names. That is the way the system works, and there is nothing illegal about it.

So what are investors supposed to do? First, never trust an accounting statement that doesn't meet the standards set forth by financial regulators. In recent years, especially during the Internet boom of the late 1990s, firms published so-called pro forma financial statements based on their own definitions of revenue and costs. To look profitable, these companies had to make their own accounting rules. Such tinkering implies that a firm has something to hide.

Second, the more open a company is in its financial accounting, the more likely that it is honest. One of the lasting effects of Enron's collapse is that investors now punish companies that publish opaque financial statements. Honesty really is the best policy; the more information a firm makes public, the more credible it will be with investors.

Finally, remember that diversification reduces risk. If you own shares in many different companies, you are better protected against the possibility that some of them will be less than honest in their disclosures.

mortgages) with the borrowed funds. The problem is, changes in the slope of the yield curve create risk. That is, the revenue from the mortgages may fall short of the payments due on the checking accounts. Swaps insure the bank against such a shortfall.

In thinking about the size and importance of particular interest-rate swaps, we need to keep several points in mind. The first is that the primary risk in a swap is the risk that one of the parties will default. That risk is not very high, however, because the other side can always enter into another agreement to replace the one that failed. (The case of Long-Term Capital Management described in Applying the Concept is a rare exception when widespread default became a real possibility.) Second, unlike futures and options, swaps are not traded on organized exchanges; they are bilateral agreements between two financial intermediaries. For various reasons, a bank that enters into a swap agreement with another bank may not want to make the same kind of arrangement with a pension fund. Thus, swaps are very difficult to resell.

APPLYING THE CONCEPT
WHAT WAS LONG-TERM CAPITAL MANAGEMENT DOING?

From mid-August to late September 1998, Long-Term Capital Management (LTCM), an unregulated *hedge fund* based in Greenwich, Connecticut, lost over $2.5 billion, placing itself in danger of default. (For a detailed description of hedge funds, see the *Tools of the Trade* box in Chapter 13.) The prospect of LTCM's failure struck fear into world financial markets, prompting the Federal Reserve Bank of New York to form a group of 14 banks and investment companies to purchase the company. How did so much wealth disappear so fast, and why did so many people care? There has never been a comparable case in which the financial community was so desperate to avoid a bankruptcy.

The answer is that LTCM had engaged in a large number of complex speculative transactions, including interest-rate swaps and options writing, which all failed simultaneously. One of the bets LTCM had made was based on the belief that interest-rate spreads would shrink.* Following the Russian government bond default on August 17, 1998, financial market participants' willingness to take on risk declined dramatically, so the risk premium exploded. (Recall the discussion of this episode in Chapter 6.) As a result, the spread between corporate bonds and U.S. Treasury bonds grew in a way that had never before occurred. By relying on historical data, LTCM lost billions. While the interest-rate spread did eventually shrink, so that the bets LTCM had made paid off in the long run, marking to market drove the fund bankrupt.

The really scary part of this episode was that many of the transactions LTCM had engaged in involved instruments that could not easily be resold. The most amazing discovery was the $1\frac{1}{4}$ trillion (yes, trillion) in interest-rate swaps. Granted, this was a notional principal of all the transactions added together, but the problem is that swaps are individualized, bilateral transactions. The fact that LTCM was willing to make a swap agreement with a particular counterparty was no guarantee that some other party would. Thus, a normal bankruptcy settlement, in which assets are sold off in the marketplace and the proceeds given to the failed company's creditors, was not an option. LTCM's failure would mean it could not honor its side of the agreements, which would mean the counterparties would not be able to honor their own agreements, creating a cascade of failure. Its collapse would jeopardize the entire financial system. Large banks, insurance companies, pension funds, and mutual-fund companies with whom LTCM did business were at risk of being bankrupted themselves.

In short, while one person's derivatives loss is another's gain, the system works only if the winners can collect. In this case, the Federal Reserve had no choice but to step in and ensure that the financial system remained sound. LTCM was essentially sold to its creditors—the banks from which it had borrowed—and then closed down about a year later.

*LTCM had also used options to place a huge bet that European stock-market volatility would fall; it didn't.

IN THE NEWS

Enron Had More Than One Way to Disguise Rapid Rise in Debt

The New York Times

By Daniel Altman

February 17, 2002

Enron hid billions in loans in plain sight.

The company took advantage of accounting rules to count large loans from Wall Street firms as financial hedges instead of debt on its balance sheet, according to accountants and industry analysts. The effect was to mask its weakening financial condition. Records show that Enron received $3.9 billion worth of such loans from 1992 through 2001, including at least $2.5 billion in the three years before the company filed for bankruptcy protection. Those loans were in addition to the $8 billion to $10 billion in long-term and short-term debt that the company disclosed in its financial reports in those last three years.

Partly because of the way the loans were accounted for, the company reported a surge in its hedging activity, accomplished using financial contracts called derivatives, during its last few years. When pressed about the increase by skeptical analysts, Enron officials said the numbers reflected hedges for commodities trades, not new financing.

Enron's accounting treatment conformed to existing recommendations from the Financial Accounting Standards Board, the nation's accounting rule maker, said Timothy S. Lucas, director of research and technical activities at the board [at the time].

To keep growing at a brisk pace in its final years, Enron needed billions in financing. Had the company raised the money by issuing more debt or taking out conventional loans, rating agencies might have become concerned and downgraded its credit, making it harder and more expensive for Enron to borrow in the future.

So instead, Enron engaged in sophisticated transactions with J. P. Morgan Chase, Citigroup and Credit Suisse First Boston. Enron entered into derivative contracts that mimicked loans but could be accounted for in less obvious ways.

From late 1999 through early 2001, Citigroup lent Enron $2.4 billion in a series of transactions known as prepaid swaps, said people close to the deals. In a swap, two parties trade the future returns on investments over a set period of time. For example, one party might pay a small amount to receive a fixed interest rate on a corporate bond in lieu of uncertain gains on the same corporation's stock. The counterparty accepts the payment and swaps the return on the bond for the return on the stock. Neither party actually needs to hold the underlying assets, as long as the payments are made.

Typically, neither party in a swap exchange receives all the agreed payments up front. In these transactions, though, Citigroup paid an estimate of the fair value of its portion of the swaps—hundreds of millions of dollars each time—immediately. Enron was obliged to repay the cash over five years, though its payments might have varied with market conditions. The transactions, though technically derivatives trades known as prepaid swaps, perfectly replicated loans.

Enron's balance sheet told a different story. The company posted the banks' loans as "assets from price risk management." The repayments that Enron owed the banks were listed as "liabilities from price risk management."

Close readers of Enron's financial statements would have seen lines identified as assets and liabilities from price risk management in the assets and liabilities sections. These lines grew far faster than the quantities of commodities traded by the company. From the fourth quarter of 1999 to the first quarter of 2001, price risk management grew to $22 billion from roughly $5 billion in assets and liabilities.

The banks had little reason to worry about the swaps cum loans. In Credit Suisse First Boston's case, the amount was relatively small and time involved was short.

Citigroup went a step further by hedging itself against losses on the entire $2.4 billion in Enron exposure. In effect, it bought insurance by making other derivatives trades.

Citigroup set up trusts to sell securities called "linked Enron obligations" and "credit-linked notes," for which investors paid $2.4 billion in principal. Both types of securities paid a constant return unless Enron missed a payment

continued on next page

to Citigroup or went bankrupt. In that case, Citigroup would take the investors' principal and replace it with a slice of Enron's debt with the same face value. An investor who held $100,000 worth of the notes when Enron filed for bankruptcy would have received the rights to $100,000 in debt issued by Enron.

In the spring of 2001, fuel prices fell. Enron's assets and liabilities in the category labeled "price risk management" dropped sharply [and by the end of the year Enron was bankrupt].

LESSONS OF THE ARTICLE

Derivatives render the actual names of financial instruments irrelevant, since their risks and payments can be divided up arbitrarily. Accounting rules make this practice of relabeling attractive because firms must publicly disclose some of these assets and liabilities but not others. Enron's use of swaps to hide what was essentially debt abused the spirit, if not the letter, of these rules. The legal use of derivatives to conceal future payment obligations from investors, tax authorities, and credit rating agencies is a common practice.

Terms

American option, 210

arbitrage, 208

arbitrageurs, 208

at-the-money option, 210

call option, 209

clearing corporation, 204

derivatives, 202

European option, 210

fixed-rate payer, 220

floating-rate payer, 220

forward contract, 203

futures contract, 204

hedger, 206

interest-rate swap, 219

in-the-money option, 210

long futures position, 204

margin, 205

notional principal, 219

option premium, 213

out-of-the-money option, 210

put option, 210

short futures position, 204

speculator, 206

spot price, 208

strike price, 209

swap, 219

swap spread, 220

Chapter Lessons

1. Derivatives transfer risk from one person or firm to another. They can be used in any combination to unbundle risks and resell them.

2. Futures contracts are standardized contracts for the delivery of a specified quantity of a commodity or financial instrument on a prearranged future date, at an agreed-upon price. They are a bet on the movement in the price of the underlying asset on which they are written, whether it is a commodity or a financial instrument.

   a. Futures contracts are used both to decrease risk, which is called hedging, and to increase risk, which is called speculating.

b. The futures clearing corporation, as the counterparty to all futures contracts, guarantees the performance of both the buyer and the seller.

c. Participants in the futures market must establish a margin account with the clearing corporation and make a deposit that ensures they will meet their obligations.

d. Futures prices are marked to market daily, as if the contracts were sold and repurchased every day.

e. Since no payment is made when a futures contract is initiated, the transaction allows an investor to create a large amount of leverage at a very low cost.

f. The prices of futures contracts are determined by arbitrage within the market for immediate delivery of the underlying asset.

3. Options give the buyer (option holder) a right and the seller (option writer) an obligation to buy or sell an underlying asset at a predetermined price on or before a fixed future date.

a. A call option gives the holder the right to buy the underlying asset.

b. A put option gives the holder the right to sell the underlying asset.

c. Options can be used both to reduce risk through hedging and to speculate.

d. The option price equals the sum of its intrinsic value, which is the value if the option is exercised, plus the option premium.

e. The intrinsic value depends on the strike price of the option and the price of the underlying asset on which the option is written.

f. The option premium depends on the time to expiration and the volatility in price of the underlying asset.

4. Interest-rate swaps are agreements between two parties to exchange a fixed for a variable interest-rate payment over a future period.

a. The fixed-rate payer in a swap pays the U.S. Treasury bond rate plus a risk premium.

b. The flexible-rate payer in a swap normally pays the London Interbank Offered Rate (LIBOR).

c. Interest-rate swaps are useful when a government, firm, or investment company can borrow more cheaply at one maturity but would prefer to borrow at a different maturity.

d. Swaps can be based on an agreed-upon exchange of any two future sequences of payments.

5. Derivatives allow firms to arbitrarily divide up and rename risks and future payments, rendering their actual names irrelevant.

Problems

1. At the end of the movie *Trading Places*, the characters Billy Ray Valentine (played by Eddie Murphy) and Lewis Winthorp (played by Dan Aykroyd) bankrupted Randolph and Mortimer Duke (played by Ralph Bellamy and Don Ameche) while trading in the futures market for orange juice. Winthorp and Valentine convinced the Dukes that the Secretary of Agriculture was about to announce that the crop had been heavily damaged by the cold, when in fact it had not.

    a. Assuming that prices would rise, what futures transaction were the Dukes engaging in, and why?

    b. At the close of the market, the Dukes faced a margin call of $390 million. Why did they need to come up with so much money immediately?

2. An agreement to lease a car can be thought of as a set of derivative contracts. Describe them.

3. In spring 2002, an electronically traded futures contract on the stock index, called an e-mini future, was introduced. The contract was one-fifth the size of the standard futures contract and could be traded on the 24-hour Globex electronic trading system. Why might someone introduce a futures contract with these properties?

4. A hedger has purchased a contract in the wheat futures market. What is the hedger's position? Describe the risk that is hedged in this transaction.

5. Wheat is costly to own. You need a silo to store it in and energy to keep it warm and dry—wet wheat rots. How does the existence of storage costs affect the arbitrage process that determines the price of a wheat futures contract?

6. A futures contract on a payment of $250 times the Standard & Poor's 500 Index is traded on the Chicago Mercantile Exchange. At an index level of $1,000 or more, the contract calls for a payment of over $250,000. It is settled by a cash payment between the buyer and the seller. Who are the hedgers and who are the speculators in the S&P 500 futures market?

7. A large bank can sell three-month commercial paper at a 4 percent interest rate. One of the firm's traders has been studying the spot and futures markets for the 10-year, 6 percent coupon U.S. Treasury bond in order to determine whether it is possible to profit on the futures without taking any risk. Describe the computation the trader will need to do. How is the futures price determined? If the Treasury bond is selling at par, what will the futures price be?

8. When you are thinking of buying a car, you always have the option of waiting. Using the terminology introduced in this chapter, describe how to value such an option.

9. Desperate to cover up hundreds of millions of dollars in losses, John M. Rusnak, a currency trader for a Baltimore bank, sold a series of deep in-the-money calls to generate $200 million in cash. Describe the transaction that generated the income. What do you think happened to Mr. Rusnak when the options expired? Explain how this transaction could be interpreted as something other than the simple sale of call options.

10. What are the risks and rewards of writing and buying options? Are there any circumstances under which you would get involved? Why or why not? (Hint: Think of a case in which you own shares of the stock on which you are considering writing a call.)

11. Consider a three-month at-the-money European call option on the XYZ Corporation. XYZ's stock rises or falls with equal probability by $10 each month, starting where it ended the previous month. When the option is purchased, the stock is priced at $100, so after three months the price could be as high as $130 or as low as $70. Derive the value of this call option.

12. The Federal National Mortgage Association, known as Fannie Mae, is in the business of providing mortgages. Because of the agency's size and credit rating, it has easy access to the commercial paper market and can raise large quantities of

six-month loans. Borrowing commercial paper and lending on home mortgages create risk. What is that risk, and how can Fannie Mae use interest-rate swaps to manage it?

13. Find a recent listing of stock options prices in the financial news or on a financial Web site. Pick a stock for which many options are traded. Using the data you have collected, compute and comment on the following for both puts and calls:

    a. The change in the option premium as the strike price for options of the same expiration date changes.

    b. The change in the option premium as the expiration date for options of the same strike price changes.

14. One concern of investors is that a company's managers will act to protect their jobs at the expense of the company's profitability. That is, managers do not necessarily maximize the value of the company to the shareholders. Stock options are viewed as a mechanism for aligning the interests of managers with those of the firm's owners.

    a. Describe how stock options can accomplish this goal.

    b. If the market price of a firm's stock has fallen dramatically in recent years, and the managers' stock options were issued at a strike price that put them in the money when stock price was high, what has happened to the managers' incentive to maximize the stock price?

    c. Following a stock price decline, the firm's directors announce that in six months they will reprice the managers' options at the market price of the firm's stock. What is the managers' incentive now?

15. Concerned about possible disruptions in the oil stream coming from the Middle East, the chief financial officer (CFO) of American Airlines would like to hedge the risk of an increase in the price of jet fuel. What tools can the CFO use to hedge this risk?

www.mhhe.com/cecchettile

Chapter 10

Foreign Exchange

Every year, moving goods and services around the globe becomes easier. By 2004, the volume of international transactions had grown to one-quarter of world GDP, or about $9 trillion. Today, Americans buy shoes made in China, computers assembled in Singapore, and fruit grown in Chile. But global business deals aren't limited to goods and services. Individuals, companies, and governments also invest abroad, buying and selling stocks and bonds in financial markets around the globe. The magnitude of the international flow of goods, services, and assets is impossible to ignore. To understand the nature of these transactions, we must become familiar with a key tool that makes this trade possible: *exchange rates*.

Whenever you buy something that has been made overseas, whether it is an article of clothing, a car, a stock, or a bond, someone somewhere has exchanged dollars for the currency used where the item was made. The reason is simple: You want to use dollars to pay for an imported shirt that you buy in a local store, but the Malaysian producer wants to be paid in ringgit. All cross-border transactions are like this; the buyer and seller both want to use their own currency. The exchange rate, at its most basic level, is the tool we use to measure the price of one currency in terms of another.

Exchange rates have broad implications both for countries and for individuals. Take the case of South Korea in the winter of 1998. As economic and financial turmoil spread through Asia starting in the summer of 1997, output and employment plunged. In Korea, large industrial companies and financial institutions approached bankruptcy. From October 1997 to January 1998, the number of South Korean *won* needed to purchase one dollar more than doubled, rising from 900 to 1,900 (see Figure 10.1). The consequences were dramatic, both inside and outside the country. When the cost of buying won plummeted, South Korean products became much cheaper for foreigners to buy. As the value of the won dropped, the U.S. prices of Hyundai cars and Samsung televisions fell with it. At the same time, U.S.-made products became extremely expensive for South Koreans to buy. In fact, the crisis became so severe that many Korean students at U.S. colleges and universities had to go home. The price of a U.S. education, measured in won, had doubled, and many Korean students just couldn't afford to continue.

Exchange rates go through long swings as well as sudden spikes. In 1973, the currency used in the United Kingdom, the British pound or "pound sterling," was worth $2.50. Over the next 30 years, the value of the pound declined gradually until by mid-2004 it was worth only $1.85—a fall of 26 percent (see Figure 10.2). Nevertheless, Americans visiting Great Britain during the summer of 2004 did not return thinking that their vacations had been inexpensive. At an exchange rate of $1.85, a low-priced hotel room in London cost about the same as a fairly expensive room in New York, and even a trip to McDonald's was 16 percent more expensive than in the United States.

How are foreign exchange rates determined, and what accounts for their fluctuation over days, months, years, and decades? This chapter provides an introduction to foreign exchange rates and exchange markets.

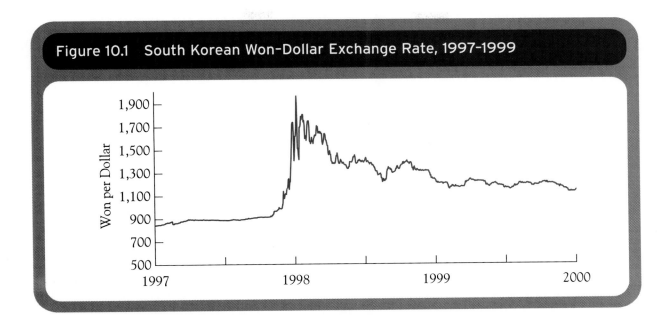

Figure 10.1   South Korean Won-Dollar Exchange Rate, 1997-1999

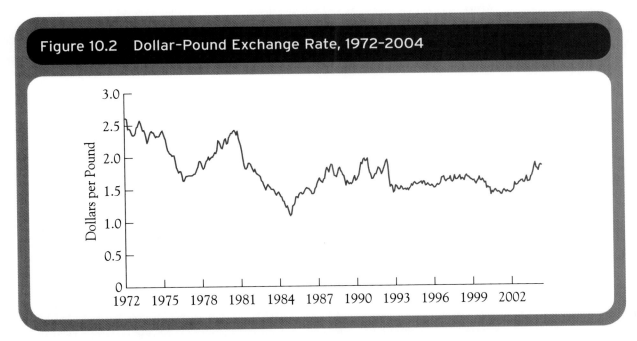

Figure 10.2   Dollar-Pound Exchange Rate, 1972-2004

Foreign Exchange Basics

After graduation, you are planning to travel to Europe. You would like to see the Eiffel Tower in Paris, the Colosseum in Rome, and the Parthenon in Athens. As you pack, you worry a little about paying your hotel bills and the tab for all that great food you expect to eat. The waiters in French, Italian, and Greek restaurants aren't interested in your dollar bills; they want to be paid in their own currency. But you are fortunate, for

"When did your dad first explain foreign-currency exchange rates to you?"

while the French, Italians, and Greeks speak different languages, they all use the same coins and bills. In fact, buying anything in Europe—at least in the countries that are members of the European Monetary Union—means exchanging your dollars for **euros**. So when you get to Europe, you will care about the number of euros you can "buy" for one dollar. The price of euros in dollars is called the dollar–euro exchange rate.

The Nominal Exchange Rate

Exchanging dollars for euros is like any other economic transaction: you are using your money to buy something—in this case, money to spend in another country. The price you pay for this currency is called the nominal exchange rate, or simply the *exchange rate*. Formally defined, the **nominal exchange rate** *is the rate at which one can exchange the currency of one country for the currency of another country*. The dollar–euro exchange rate is the number of dollars you can get for each euro. In summer 2004, one euro (the symbol for the euro is €) would buy $1.24. So an American who went to Europe in the summer of 2004 paid $124 for €100.[1]

Exchange rates change every day. Figure 10.3 shows the dollar–euro exchange rate over the first five and a half years of the euro's circulation, from January 1999 to August 2004. The figure plots the number of dollars per euro, which is the conventional way to quote the dollar–euro exchange rate. When the euro was introduced, it was worth $1.17. But by October 2000, less than two years later, it could be exchanged for only 83 cents. Such a decline in the value of one currency relative to another is called a **depreciation**. During the first 22 months of the euro's existence, it depreciated nearly 30 percent relative to the dollar. Later in this chapter, we will consider the reasons for large movements in exchange rates.

At the same time that the euro was falling in value, the dollar was rising. After all, if you can buy fewer dollars with one euro, you can get more euros for one dollar. The rise in the value of one currency relative to another is called an **appreciation**. During 1999 and 2000, the euro's depreciation was matched by the dollar's appreciation; they

[1]Actually, the price was a bit higher, counting the fee charged by the currency dealer.

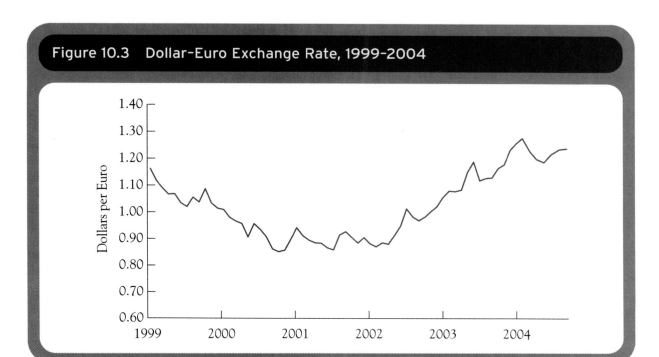

Figure 10.3   Dollar-Euro Exchange Rate, 1999-2004

are really one and the same. When one currency goes up in value *relative to another*, the other currency must go down.

Note that, theoretically, exchange rates can be quoted in units of either currency—for example, as the number of dollars needed to buy one euro or as the number of euros needed to buy one dollar. The two prices are equivalent; one is simply the reciprocal of the other. In practice, however, each currency has its convention. The price of the British pound is quoted in the same way as the euro, so that people talk about the number of dollars that can be exchanged for one pound (£). The price of the Japanese **yen** (¥) is quoted as the number of yen that can be purchased with one dollar.

Unfortunately, there is no simple rule for determining which way a particular exchange rate should be quoted. Most rates tend to be quoted in the way that yields a number larger than one. The fact that €1 equaled $1.17 when the euro was created on January 1, 1999, is the likely explanation for why we talk about the number of euros needed to purchase one dollar. Ever since, people have quoted dollars per euro, even though there have been significant periods of time when the number was less than one. If you need to guess which way to quote an exchange rate, the best guess is that it is the way that yields a number larger than one. But the real solution is always to state the units explicitly, to avoid confusion.

A 20-euro note used in the countries that participate in the European Monetary Union

SOURCE: © *Reuters/CORBIS.*

The Real Exchange Rate

While it may be interesting to know that one euro is worth $1.24, you are interested in more than just the rate at which one country's currency can be exchanged for another. What you really want to know when you travel to Europe is how much you

YOUR FINANCIAL WORLD

Following Exchange Rates in the News

Exchange rates are reported in the business news. *The Wall Street Journal* carries a daily Foreign Exchange column that describes events in the markets, as well as a table reporting the most recent nominal exchange rates between the U.S. dollar and various foreign currencies. (Because the rates quoted are generally for transactions of $1 million or more, they normally are not available to tourists.) The column and the table, one of which is reprinted here, appear in both the print and online versions of the paper. Let's run through Table 10.1 to see how to read it.

Column 1: The name of the country (name of the currency).

Columns 2 and 3: The number of dollars that could be purchased per unit of foreign currency at the close of business the previous day (column 2) and two days before (column 3). From column 2, we can see that on Friday, August 13, 2004, one British pound purchased $1.8427.

Columns 4 and 5: The number of units of foreign currency needed to purchase one dollar at the close of business on the same two days. From column 4, we can see that on Friday, August 13, 2004, you could exchange 110.67 Japanese yen for one dollar.*

For large foreign currency markets, like Britain's and Japan's, the table quotes the forward as well as the spot rates. *Spot rates* are the rates for an immediate exchange (subject to a two-day settlement period). *Forward rates* are the rates at which foreign currency dealers are willing to commit to buying or selling a currency in the future, so they give some indication of whether market participants expect currencies to appreciate or depreciate over time.

In thinking about foreign exchange rates, be sure to keep track of whether you are quoting the number of U.S. dollars that can be exchanged for one unit of foreign currency, as in columns 2 and 3 of the table, or the number of units of foreign currency that can be purchased with one dollar. They are easy to confuse. If you went to Europe and confused $1.2372 per euro with €0.8083 per dollar, you would think everything was less expensive that it really is, and you end up buying something that you really could not afford.

*Note the reciprocal nature of the two sets of rates. If you divide the numbers in columns 2 and 3 into one, you will get the numbers in columns 4 and 5, respectively.

can buy with that euro. When all is said and done, will you return home thinking that your trip was cheap or expensive?

Because nominal exchange rates do not provide an answer to this question, we now turn to the concept of a real exchange rate, *the rate at which one can exchange the goods and services from one country for the goods and services from another country.* It is the cost

continued from previous page

Table 10.1 Foreign Exchange Rates

Friday, August 13, 2004, 4:00 p.m. Eastern Time

(1) Country	U.S. $ equiv.		Currency per U.S. $	
	(2) Friday	(3) Thursday	(4) Friday	(5) Thursday
Argentina (Peso)ʸ	0.3317	0.3320	3.0148	3.0120
Australia (Dollar)	0.7171	0.7150	1.3945	1.3986
Brazil (Real)	0.3312	0.3295	3.0193	3.0349
Canada (Dollar)	0.7641	0.7518	1.3087	1.3301
China (Renminbi)	0.1208	0.1208	8.2781	8.2781
Hong Kong (Dollar)	0.1282	0.1282	7.8003	7.8003
Hungary (Forint)	0.004987	0.004931	200.52	202.80
India (Rupee)	0.02164	0.02166	46.211	46.168
Japan (Yen)	0.009036	0.009020	110.67	110.86
1-month Forward	0.009049	0.009032	110.51	110.72
3-months Forward	0.009076	0.009058	110.18	110.40
6-months Forward	0.009126	0.009107	109.58	109.81
Malaysia (Ringgit)ᵇ	0.2632	0.2632	3.7994	3.7994
Mexico (Peso)ᵃ	0.0878	0.0875	11.3856	11.4273
Russia (Ruble)ᵃ	0.03419	0.03416	29.248	29.274
South Korea (Won)	0.0008651	0.0008639	1155.94	1157.54
Sweden (Krona)	0.1341	0.13311	7.4571	7.5131
Switzerland (Franc)	0.8073	0.7968	1.2387	1.2550
Taiwan (Dollar)	0.02938	0.02933	34.037	34.095
Thailand (Baht)	0.02408	0.02409	41.528	41.511
U.K. (Pound)	1.8427	1.8229	0.5427	0.5486
1 month Forward	1.8376	1.8178	0.5442	0.5501
3 months Forward	1.8281	1.8081	0.5470	0.5531
6 months Forward	1.8148	1.7951	0.5510	0.5571
Euro	1.2372	1.2262	0.8083	0.8155

ᵃRussian Central Bank rate. ᵇGovernment rate. ʸFloating rate.

of a basket of goods in one country *relative* to the cost of the same basket of goods in another country. To grasp this concept, we will start with the real exchange rate between two cups of espresso, one American and the other Italian. The local Starbucks charges $1.45 for an espresso; in Florence, Italy, a cup of espresso costs €0.80. (Yes, the Italian version is better and espresso is a luxury in the United States, but for the sake of the example, let's pretend they're the same.) At a nominal exchange rate of $1.24 per euro, this means that to buy an espresso on your European vacation, you need to spend $0.992. More important, you can exchange one cup of Starbucks espresso for roughly 1.5 cups of Italian espresso. This is the *real* exchange rate. You will return from your European vacation thinking that espresso was very cheap in Italy.

There is a simple relationship between the real exchange rate and the nominal exchange rate, which we can infer from our espresso calculation. To compute the real exchange rate, we took the euro price of an espresso in Italy and multiplied it by the nominal exchange rate, the number of dollars per euro. Then we divided it into the dollar price of a cup of espresso in the United States:

Real coffee exchange rate

$$
\begin{aligned}
&= \frac{\text{Price of an espresso at Starbucks in dollars (\$1.45)}}{\text{Price of an espresso in Italy in euros (€0.80)} \times \text{Dollars per euro (\$1.24 / €)}} \\[2mm]
&= \frac{\text{Dollar price of coffee in the U.S. (\$1.45)}}{\text{Dollar price of coffee in Italy (€0.80)} \times (\$1.24 / €)} \\[2mm]
&= \frac{\$1.45}{\$0.992} \\[2mm]
&= \mathbf{1.46}
\end{aligned}
\tag{1}
$$

At these prices and exchange rate, one cup of Starbucks espresso buys 1.46 cups of Italian espresso. Note in equation (1) that the units of measurement cancel out. In the denominator, we multiplied the price in euros times the nominal exchange rate (measured as dollars per euro) to get an amount stated in dollars. Then we divided that number into the numerator, also expressed in dollars. The real exchange rate has no units of measurement.

In summary, to figure out the real coffee exchange rate in equation (1), we divided the dollar price of coffee in the United States by the dollar price of coffee in Italy. We can use the same procedure to compute the real exchange rate more broadly by comparing the prices of a set of goods and services that are commonly purchased in any country. If we can transform a basket of goods and services produced in the United States into more than one basket produced in Europe, as in the coffee example, then we are likely to return from a trip to Paris, Rome, and Athens thinking that the cost of living there is relatively cheap. Using this idea, we can write the real exchange rate as

$$
\text{Real exchange rate} = \frac{\text{Dollar price of domestic goods}}{\text{Dollar price of foreign goods}}
\tag{2}
$$

From this definition of the real exchange rate, we can see that whenever the ratio in equation (2) is more than one, foreign products will seem cheap.

The real exchange rate, then, is much more important than the nominal exchange rate. It is the rate that measures the relative price of goods and services across countries, telling us where things are cheap and where they are expensive. The real exchange rate is the guiding force behind international transactions. When foreign goods are less expensive than domestic goods, their prices create an incentive for people to buy imports. Competing with foreign imports becomes more difficult for local producers. Think about what would happen if you could ship cups of espresso to the United States from Italy and sell them in an import shop. Starbucks would lose business. Obviously, you can't do that with freshly brewed coffee, but you can do it with clothing, electronics, cars, airplanes, and a wide variety of other goods and services. As a result, the competitiveness of U.S. exports depends on the real exchange rate. *Appreciation* of the real exchange rate makes U.S. exports more expensive to foreigners, reducing their competitiveness, while *depreciation* of the real exchange rate makes U.S. exports seem cheaper to foreigners, improving their competitiveness.

Foreign Exchange Markets

The volume of foreign exchange transactions is enormous. On an average day in 2001, $1.2 trillion in foreign currency was traded in a market that operates 24 hours a day.[2] To get a sense of how huge this number is, compare it to world output and trade. The International Monetary Fund estimates that in 2003, world GDP (at market prices) was roughly $36 trillion, and international trade transactions (measured as exports) accounted for $9.2 trillion of that amount. But these are annual numbers. If there are 260 business days in a normal year, the volume of foreign exchange transactions is over $300 trillion—8 times world GDP and 34 times world trade volume.

Because of its liquidity, the U.S. dollar is one side of roughly 90 percent of these currency transactions.[3] That means that someone who wishes to exchange Thai baht for Japanese yen is likely to make two transactions, the first to convert the baht to dollars and the second to convert the dollars to yen. Most likely these transactions will take place in London, because the United Kingdom is home to 31 percent of foreign exchange trades—about double the volume in New York. Other significant foreign exchange trading takes place in Tokyo (9 percent), Singapore (6 percent), Frankfurt (5 percent), and Zurich (4 percent).[4]

Exchange Rates in the Long Run

How are exchange rates determined? To answer this question, we will divide our discussion into two parts. This section will look at the determination of the long-run exchange rate and the forces that drive its movement over an extended period, such as a year or more. The next section will consider what causes exchange rates to vary over the short term—a few days or months.

The Law of One Price

The starting point for understanding how long-run exchange rates are determined is *the law of one price*. The law of one price is based on the concept of *arbitrage*—the idea that identical products should sell for the same price. Recall from our discussion in Chapter 9 that two financial instruments with the same risk and promised future payments will sell for the same price. We might refer to this phenomenon as financial arbitrage. If we extend the concept of arbitrage from financial instruments to goods and services, we can conclude that identical goods and services should sell for the same price regardless of

---

[2]This estimate comes from a triennial survey by the Bank for International Settlements in Basel, Switzerland. The complete survey is available at www.bis.org.

[3]The liquidity of the market for dollars creates a premium, driving up the dollar's value in the same way that liquidity increases the price of a bond.

[4]The growing importance of the euro means that over time the dollar will become less important, and trading in Frankfurt is likely to increase in volume.

where they are sold. Identical televisions or cars should cost the same whether they are sold in St. Louis or Philadelphia. When they don't, someone can make a profit.

For instance, if a 27-inch Sony television were cheaper in St. Louis than in Philadelphia, someone could buy it in St. Louis, drive to Philadelphia, and sell it at a profit. This opportunity to profit from arbitrage would increase demand for televisions in St. Louis, where the price is low, and increase the supply of televisions in Philadelphia, where the price is high. Higher demand drives prices up, while a larger supply forces them down. The process will continue until the television sells for the same price in both cities. Of course, complete price equalization occurs only in the absence of transportation costs. If it costs $10 to transport the television 900 miles from the Mississippi River to the East Coast, then arbitrage will continue until the price in St. Louis is within $10 of the price in Philadelphia.

We can extend the law of one price from cities in the same country to cities in different countries. Instead of St. Louis and Philadelphia, think of Detroit, Michigan, and Windsor, Ontario—two cities separated by the Detroit River and the Canadian border. The river can be crossed by bridge or tunnel in roughly one minute. Ignoring transportation costs, then, once we have converted a price from U.S. to Canadian dollars, the cost of a television should be the same in both cities. If a TV costs $500 in the United States, at a nominal exchange rate of 1.31 Canadian dollars per U.S. dollar (see Table 10.1), the Canadian price should be (500 × 1.31) = 655 Canadian dollars. That is, the law of one price tells us that

$$\text{Canadian dollar price of a TV in Windsor, Ontario} = \frac{\text{(U.S. dollar price of a TV in Detroit)}}{\times \text{(Canadian dollars per U.S. dollar)}} \quad (3)$$

This example shows once again the importance of using the correct units when working with exchange rates. In converting the U.S. dollar price to Canadian dollars, we multiply by the number of Canadian dollars needed to buy one U.S. dollar. That is, we compute (U.S. dollars) times (Canadian dollars/U.S. dollar) equals Canadian dollars. This is the same calculation we did earlier to figure out the U.S. dollar price of an Italian cup of coffee. There, we multiplied (euros) times (U.S. dollars/euro) to get U.S. dollars.

Returning to the law of one price, we can see immediately that it fails almost all the time. The fact is that the same commodity or service sells for vastly different prices in different countries. Why? Transportation costs can be significant, especially for heavy items like marble or slate. Tariffs—the taxes countries charge at their borders—are high sometimes, especially if a country is trying to protect a domestic industry. And technical specifications can differ. A television bought in Paris will not work in St. Louis because it requires a different input signal. A car sold in Great Britain cannot be used in the United States or continental Europe because its steering wheel is on the right. Moreover, tastes differ across countries, leading to different pricing. Finally, some things simply cannot be traded. A haircut may be cheaper in New Delhi than in Philadelphia, but most Americans simply can't take advantage of that price difference.

Purchasing Power Parity

Since the law of one price fails so often, why do we bother with it? Because even with its obvious flaws, the law of one price is extremely useful in explaining the behavior of exchange rates over long periods, like 10 or 20 years. To see why, we need to extend the law from a single commodity to a basket of goods and services. The result is the theory of purchasing power parity (PPP), which means that one unit of U.S. domestic currency will buy the same basket of goods and services anywhere in the world. This idea may sound absurd, but let's look at its implications.

According to the theory of purchasing power parity, the dollar price of a basket of goods and services in the United States should be the same as the dollar price of a basket of goods and services in Mexico, Japan, or the United Kingdom. In the case of the United Kingdom, this statement means that

Dollar price of basket of goods in U.S. = Dollar price of basket of goods in U.K.   (4)

Rearranging this expression gives us

$$\frac{\text{Dollar price of basket of goods in U.S.}}{\text{Dollar price of basket of goods in U.K.}} = 1 \qquad (5)$$

The left-hand side of equation (5) is familiar: It is the real exchange rate (see equation 2). Thus, *purchasing power parity implies that the real exchange rate is always equal to one*. The implication of this conclusion is straightforward. It is that the purchasing power of a dollar is always the same, regardless of where in the world you go.

This idea must seem doubly absurd. If a dollar doesn't even buy the same number of cups of coffee in Italy and the United States, how can it have the same purchasing power all the time, everywhere in the world? On any given day, it doesn't. But over the long term, exchange rates do tend to move, so this concept helps us to understand changes that happen over years or decades. To see how, remember that the dollar price of a foreign basket of goods is just the foreign currency price of the basket of goods times the number of dollars per unit of foreign currency. This means that if we quote the price of a basket of goods in the United Kingdom in pounds instead of dollars, then

$$\frac{\text{Dollar price of basket of goods in U.S.}}{(\text{Pound price of basket of goods in U.K.}) \times (\text{Dollars per pound})} = 1, \qquad (6)$$

so

$$\frac{\text{Dollar price of basket of goods in U.S.}}{\text{Pound price of basket of goods in U.K.}} = (\text{Dollars per pound}) \qquad (7)$$

That is, purchasing power parity implies that when prices change in one country but not in another, the exchange rate should change as well. When prices rise within a country, the effect is called inflation. If inflation occurs in one country but not in another, the change in prices creates an international inflation differential. So purchasing power parity tells us that changes in exchange rates are tied to differences in inflation from one country to another. Specifically, the currency of a country with high inflation will depreciate.

To see this point, think about what would happen if there were no inflation in the United Kingdom, but prices in the United States doubled. We would not expect the dollar–pound exchange rate to stay the same. Instead, we would predict that one dollar would now buy half as many British pounds as it did before (that is, twice as many dollars would be needed to purchase one pound).[5] There is strong evidence to support this conclusion, but the data must be drawn over fairly long periods, and the relationship is not perfect.

[5] It is possible to show this mathematically. If P represents the domestic (U.S.) currency price of a basket of goods, P^f the foreign currency price of the foreign (British) basket of goods, and e the nominal exchange rate, expressed as the domestic currency price of foreign currency (dollars per pound), then purchasing power parity tells us that $(P/eP^f) = 1$ (eq. 5), so $e = (P/P^f)$ (eq. 7). This expression immediately implies that the change in the exchange rate equals the difference between domestic and foreign inflation.

Take, for instance, the U.S. dollar–British pound exchange rate plotted in Figure 10.2 (page 229). Recall that in 1973, one pound was worth around $2.50. By August of 2004, a pound was worth $1.85—a decline of 26 percent, or an average of nearly $\frac{4}{5}$ percent per year for 31 years. Over the same period, U.S. prices increased an average of 4.92 percent per year, while British prices increased an average of 7.18 percent per year—a difference of 2.26 percent per year.[6] While the relationship between the inflation and exchange rates is not perfect, it surely explains much of the movement in the dollar–pound exchange rate over the 31-year period.

What is true for the United Kingdom is true for the rest of the world. To confirm it, we can look at a plot of (a) the historical difference between inflation in other countries and inflation in the United States against (b) the percentage change in the number of units of other countries' currencies required to purchase one dollar—that is, the average annual depreciation of the exchange rate.

Figure 10.4 presents data for 80 countries drawn from files maintained by the International Monetary Fund. Each point represents a country. The difference between its average annual inflation and that of the U.S. is on the horizontal axis, and the average annual percentage change in the exchange rate between the country's currency and the U.S. dollar is on the vertical axis. Points further to the right represent countries with higher levels of inflation, and points higher up are countries whose dollar-exchange rate experienced more depreciation over the 32-year period of the sample. The solid line is a 45-degree line that is consistent with the theoretical prediction of purchasing power parity. On the 45-degree line, exchange rate movements exactly equal differences in inflation. Granted, the points don't all lie exactly on the line, but the pattern is clearly there. The higher a country's inflation, the greater the depreciation in its exchange rate.

Take the extreme example of Bolivia. From 1974 to 2003, Bolivia's inflation minus U.S. inflation averaged 50.95 percent per year, and the Bolivian currency (originally the Bolivar, now the Boliviano) depreciated at an average annual rate of 53.6 percent. Putting that into perspective, the 2003 Bolivian price level was more than 380,000 times the 1974 Bolivian price level, and the exchange rate depreciated by roughly the same multiple. That means purchasing one dollar in the foreign exchange market required 390,000 times as many Bolivianos in 2003 as in 1974. (Bolivian inflation averaged 53.5 percent per year from 1974 to 2003, so the price level rose by 1.535^{30} over the 30 years.) Importantly, Figure 10.4 shows that there are no countries with high inflation differentials and small exchange rate changes or big exchange rate changes and low inflation differentials. All of the points lie close to the 45-degree line.

The data in Figure 10.4 tell us that purchasing power parity held true over a 30-year period. Even if we look at a decade, the connection between movements in the exchange rate and differences in inflation across countries holds up to scrutiny. But the same exercise applied to periods of a few weeks, months, or even years would be a total failure. We know that from examining the plots of the Korean won–U.S. dollar exchange rate in Figure 10.1 and the dollar–euro exchange rate in Figure 10.3. Recall that the Korean won went through a sudden, steep depreciation, falling from 900 to 1,900 won to the dollar in just a few months, at the end of 1997. The pattern of Korean inflation at the time, a relatively steady $7\frac{1}{2}$ percent versus $1\frac{1}{2}$ percent in the United States, simply cannot explain this sudden change.

---

[6]Data on inflation in the United Kingdom are available from National Statistics at www.statistics.gov.uk. The computation here uses the retail price index, the U.K. equivalent of the U.S. consumer price index.

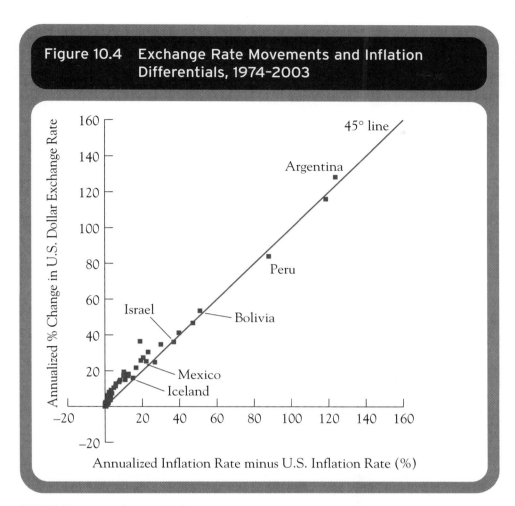

Figure 10.4   Exchange Rate Movements and Inflation Differentials, 1974-2003

SOURCE: *The International Monetary Fund*

Similarly, from the euro's inception in January 1999, the dollar–euro rate fell steadily for two years, dropping more than 25 percent (see Figure 10.3). At the same time, inflation in the euro area ran a full percentage point *below* U.S. inflation. Examples like these are the norm, not the exception. Over weeks, months, and even years, nominal exchange rates can deviate substantially from the levels implied by purchasing power parity. So, while the theory can help us to understand long swings in exchange rates, it provides no explanation for the short-term movements we see all the time. Fortunately, we do have some equipment in our tool kit that we can use to explain short-term movements in exchange rates.

Before continuing, we should note the meaning of two additional terms. We often hear currencies described as **undervalued** or **overvalued**. When people use these terms, they have in mind a current market rate that deviates from what they consider to be purchasing power parity. For example, a person who thinks that one dollar should purchase one euro—that is, that one to one is somehow the "correct" long-run exchange rate—would say that if one dollar purchases only €0.90, it is *undervalued* relative to the euro, or the euro is *overvalued* relative to the dollar.

APPLYING THE CONCEPT
THE BIG MAC INDEX

By the close of the 20th century, the Big Mac was available to consumers in 121 countries. Regardless of where it was sold, a Big Mac was defined as "two all-beef patties, special sauce, lettuce, cheese, pickles, onions on a sesame seed bun." Needless to say, every McDonald's restaurant requires payment in the local currency. In 1986, the staff of *The Economist* magazine realized that this presented an opportunity. Together, the market exchange rate and the price of a Big Mac would allow them to estimate the extent to which a country's currency deviates from the level implied by purchasing power parity.

Twice a year, under headlines like "Big MacCurrencies" and "Burgernomics," *The Economist* publishes a list of Big Mac prices in about 50 countries. A portion of the list from the May 27, 2004, edition is reprinted here. Using Big Mac prices as a basis for comparison, it shows the extent to which each country's currency was undervalued or overvalued relative to the U.S. dollar. As you look at Figure 10.5, you will realize that with the exception of the pound and the euro, all exchange rates are quoted as the number of units of local currency required to purchase one dollar.

To see how the Big Mac index works, take the case of Brazil, in the fourth row. The Brazilian currency is called the *real* (rhymes with *royale*) and in May 2004, the price of a Big Mac in Rio de Janeiro was 5.38 real. At an exchange rate of 3.16 real per dollar (fifth column), that was equivalent to (5.38/3.16) = $1.70 (third column).* To figure out the purchasing power parity value of one dollar in Brazilian real, we can use the relationship in equation (7), which tells us to divide the price of a Big Mac in real by the U.S. price: 5.38 real per Big Mac/$2.90 per Big Mac = 1.86 real per dollar (fourth column).† If the theory of purchasing power parity holds, then 1.86 real should buy one dollar. Instead, the price of one dollar in the currency markets was 3.16 real, which means that the Brazilian real was *undervalued* by 41 percent (sixth column).

The Big Mac index is a clever idea, and it works remarkably well considering that it is based on a single commodity that is not tradable and whose local price surely depends on costs like wages, rent, and taxes.

*Small differences in numbers are due to rounding.

†The Brazilian exchange rate is quoted here in terms of foreign currency per dollar—that is, real per dollar. Equation (7) shows the ratio of prices for an exchange rate quoted as dollars per unit of foreign currency—that is, dollars per pound. Therefore, we inverted the formula for use in this example.

continued on next page

continued from previous page

Figure 10.5 *The Economist's* Big Mac Index

Note that all exchange rates except the pound and the euro are quotes as the number of units of the local currency required to purchase one U.S. dollar.

	Big Mac Prices				
	In local currency	In dollars	Implied PPP* of the dollar	Actual dollar exchange rate (5/27/2004)	Under (–)/ over (+) valuation against the dollar, %
United States	$2.90	2.90			
Argentina	Peso 4.30	1.48	1.50	2.93	–49
Australia	A$3.21	2.27	1.12	1.41	–22
→ Brazil	*Real* 5.38	1.70	1.86	3.16	–41
Britain	£1.86	3.37	1.54	1.81+	16
Canada	C$3.19	2.33	1.10	1.37	–20
Chile	Peso 1363	2.18	483	625.00	–25
China	Yuan 10.42	1.26	3.59	8.27	–57
Czech Republic	Koruna 55.91	2.13	19.5	26.25	–27
Denmark	DKr27.41	4.46	9.57	6.15	54
Euro area	€2.71	3.28	1.06	1.21§	13
Hong Kong	HK$12.00	1.54	4.14	7.79	–47
Hungary	Forint 321	2.52	183	208.33	–13
Indonesia	Rupiah 23,312	1.77	5552	9250.69	–39
Japan	¥198	2.33	90.3	111.89	–20
Malaysia	M$8.85	1.33	1.74	3.80	–54
Mexico	Peso 15.21	2.08	8.28	11.44	–28
New Zealand	NZ$3.35	2.65	1.50	1.61	–8
Peru	New Sol 8.94	2.57	3.10	3.37	–11
Philippines	Peso 137.99	1.23	23.8	55.87	–57
Poland	Zloty 4.71	1.63	2.17	3.83	–44
Russia	Rouble 47.25	1.45	14.5	28.99	–50
Singapore	S$2.48	1.92	1.14	1.71	–34
South Africa	Rand 12.64	1.86	4.28	6.58	–36
South Korea	Won 2,194	2.72	1,103	1179.66	–6
Sweden	SKr20.42	3.94	10.30	7.51	36
Switzerland	SFr5.01	4.90	2.17	1.27	69
Taiwan	NT$164.32	2.24	25.90	33.53	–23
Thailand	Baht 91.28	1.45	20.30	40.75	–50
Turkey	Lira 2,154,532	2.58	1,362,069	1485884.10	–11
Venezuela	Bolivar 4,943	1.48	1,517	1916.08	–49

*Purchasing-power parity: local price divided by price in the United States.
+Dollars per pound
§Dollars per euro

SOURCE: The Economist Newspaper *May 27, 2004. Local currency prices of the Big Mac are estimated using the exchange rate on May 27, 2004 and the dollar currency price as reported by* The Economist. *Copyright © 2004 The Economist Newspaper Ltd. All rights reserved. Reprinted with permission. Further reproduction prohibited. www.economist.com.*

TOOLS OF THE TRADE
Accounting for International Transactions

Cross-border transactions fall into two categories: (1) the buying and selling of goods and services and (2) the purchase and sale of assets, such as stocks and bonds. Trade in furniture, shoes, financial services, and the like makes up what is called the **current account**. The balance in a country's current account represents the net flow of goods and services between that country and the rest of the world—roughly, its exports minus its imports.[*] When the current account has a negative balance, it indicates that the country's residents are buying more from foreigners than they are selling to them, so that imports exceed exports. This is called a **current account deficit**. When exports exceed imports, the current account is said to be in **surplus**.

To grasp the importance of the current account, you need to realize that countries have budgets, just like individuals. If you spend more than your income, you have two options: sell something you own or get a loan. What is true for an individual is also true for a country. Think of the revenue earned from selling exports to foreigners as the country's income and the cost of imports bought from overseas as its spending. When spending exceeds income, the result is a current account deficit. To pay for its overspending, the country must either sell something it owns or borrow.

Take an example in which there is only one international transaction, your purchase of a new television set made in South Korea. When you go to buy your new TV, you want to pay in dollars, but the Samsung dealer wants to be paid in Korean won. Since you have sold nothing to anyone in South Korea, you have no won to pay. There are two ways to get the won you need. You can appeal to a South Korean to purchase some asset you own, like a few shares of IBM stock, or you can try to get a South Korean to give you a loan—in essence, to buy a bond that you issue. Only after you have sold an asset to someone who has won will you be able to pay for and import the television set.

The transfer of assets among people from different countries shows up in the **capital account**, which measures the net trade in financial and nonfinancial assets. (Remember that all the services people buy from foreigners, including financial services, are included in the current account.) When a country is a net seller of assets, its **capital account** is in **surplus**. As the example suggests, there is a tight relationship between the current account and the capital account. In fact, *any country with a current account deficit must have a capital account surplus of equal size*. The sum of the two must always be zero.[†]

As you consider the growing economic links among the countries of the world, remember the implications of this lesson in international accounting. When a country is buying more from foreigners than it is selling abroad, it must be borrowing to pay for the difference. A current account deficit can arise for only two reasons: either domestic residents demand foreign-produced goods, or foreigners find domestic investment attractive.

A country's current account is linked to its exchange rate. The current account cannot remain permanently in surplus or deficit; in the long run, exports and imports must tend toward balance. The exchange rate is the mechanism that adjusts the balance between exports and imports. For a country with a current account deficit, whose imports exceed its exports, we would expect to see a depreciation in its exchange rate. This movement in the exchange rate will make foreign goods more expensive for domestic residents to purchase, thereby reducing imports. It will also make the country's exports cheaper for foreigners to buy.

Conversely, we would expect the currency of a country with a current account surplus to appreciate. The timing and speed of the adjustment will depend on factors such as the relative attractiveness of investing in the country. So long as foreign investors are willing to purchase its assets, a country can run a current account deficit without worrying about a fall in the value of its currency. (We'll see how this works in the next section.)

---

[*]The current account also includes net investment income, foreign aid, and monetary gifts from residents of one country to residents of another. Net outflows are subtracted from the current account.

[†]What is true in theory isn't always true in the real world. Because international transactions are so difficult to account for, government statisticians cannot always compute the current and capital accounts accurately. A country with a current account deficit will not necessarily have a matching capital account surplus—that is, the data may not match. The statistical discrepancy that arises from these measurement difficulties can be quite large. In 1998, it was $130 billion, more than half the size of the U.S. current account deficit, which was $200 billion. But in 2003, when the U.S. current account deficit was nearly $550 billion, the statistical discrepancy was only $35 billion. (All numbers are as of April 2004.)

Exchange Rates in the Short Run

While purchasing power parity helps us to understand movements in nominal exchange rates over decades, it cannot explain the weekly, monthly, or even yearly movements we see. What can? What sorts of phenomena are responsible for the nearly constant movement in exchange rates? To explain short-run changes in nominal exchange rates, we turn to an analysis of the supply of and demand for currencies. Since, in the short run, prices don't move much, these nominal exchange rate movements represent changes in the real exchange rate. That is, a one or two percent change in the *nominal* dollar–euro exchange rate over a day or week creates a roughly equivalent change in the *real* dollar–euro exchange rate.

The Supply of Dollars

As is always the case in discussing foreign exchange, we need to pick a home country and stick to it. The most natural choice for us is the United States, so we'll use the U.S. dollar as the domestic currency. Consistent with this, we will discuss the number of units of foreign currency that it takes to purchase one dollar. For example, we will talk about the number of euros per dollar.

Who supplies dollars to the foreign exchange markets? People who have them, of course—primarily people in the United States.[7] There are two reasons why someone who is holding dollars would want to exchange them for euros or yen: (1) to purchase goods and services produced abroad, like a Japanese television set, dinner in Paris, or tuition at a foreign university; and (2) to invest in foreign assets, such as bonds issued by the German telecommunications company Deutsche Telekom, or shares in Honda, the Japanese manufacturer of cars and motorcycles.

Figure 10.6 shows the supply of dollars in the dollar–euro market. Just like any other supply curve, it slopes upward. The higher the price a dollar commands in the market, the more dollars are supplied. And the more valuable the dollar, the cheaper are foreign-produced goods and foreign assets *relative to domestic ones* in U.S. markets.

To see why, suppose you are planning to buy a car. You have narrowed your options to a German-made Volkswagen Jetta and an American-made Saturn L100. Price is important to you. Since the Volkswagen is manufactured abroad, a change in the value of the dollar will affect your decision. As the dollar increases in value, the price of the Jetta falls and you become more likely to buy the Jetta. If you do, you will be supplying dollars to the foreign exchange market. What is true for your car purchase is true for everything else. The more valuable the dollar, the cheaper foreign goods, services, and assets will be and the higher the supply of dollars in the dollar–euro market. Thus, *the supply curve for dollars slopes upward*, as shown in Figure 10.6.

The Demand for Dollars

Foreigners who want to purchase American-made goods, assets, or services need dollars to do so. Suppose a European student would like to attend college in the United States. The school will accept payment only in dollars, so paying the tuition bill means exchanging euros for dollars. The lower the dollar–euro exchange rate—the fewer euros needed to buy one dollar—the cheaper the tuition bill will be from the viewpoint of a European student. At a given dollar price, the fewer euros needed to purchase one dollar, the cheaper are American-made goods and services. And the cheaper a good or service, the higher the demand for it. The same is true of investments. The

---

[7]The suppliers could also include holders of U.S. currency in Russia or Colombia, as well as foreign owners of U.S. stocks or bonds. But including them would complicate the analysis unnecessarily.

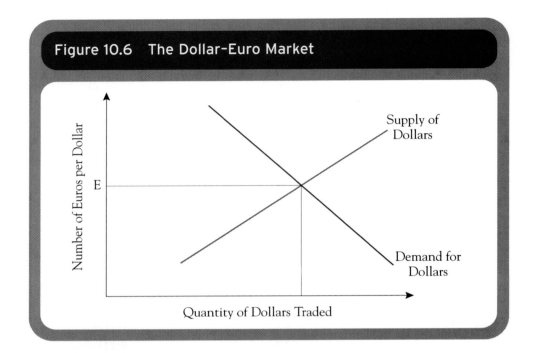

Figure 10.6 The Dollar-Euro Market

cheaper the dollar—the lower the dollar–euro exchange rate—the more attractive are U.S. investments and the higher is the demand for dollars with which to buy them. Thus, *the demand curve for dollars slopes downward* (see Figure 10.6).

Equilibrium in the Market for Dollars

The equilibrium exchange rate, labeled *E* in Figure 10.6, equates the supply of and demand for dollars. Because the values of all the major currencies of the world (including the dollar, the euro, the yen, and the pound) float freely, they are determined by market forces. As a result, fluctuations in their value are the consequence of shifts in supply or demand.

Shifts in the Supply of and Demand for Dollars

Shifts in either the supply of or the demand for dollars will change the *equilibrium exchange rate*. Let's begin with *shifts in the supply of dollars*. Remember that Americans wanting to purchase products from abroad or to buy foreign assets will supply dollars to the foreign exchange market. Anything that increases their desire to import goods and services from abroad, or their preference for foreign stocks and bonds, will increase the supply of dollars, leading to a depreciation of the dollar. Figure 10.7 shows the mechanics of this process.

What causes Americans' preferences for foreign goods, services, and assets to increase, prompting them to supply more dollars to the foreign exchange market? This question has many answers. The list includes the following possibilities:

A rise in the supply of dollars Americans use to purchase foreign goods and services can be caused by

- *An increase in Americans' preference for foreign goods.* For instance, a successful advertising campaign might convince American consumers to buy more

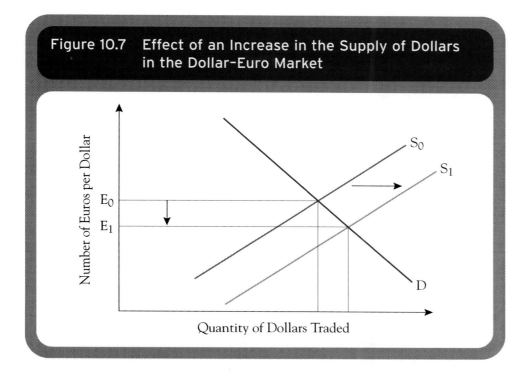

Figure 10.7   Effect of an Increase in the Supply of Dollars in the Dollar-Euro Market

imported olive oil. To fill the new orders, U.S. importers would exchange dollars for euros, shifting the dollar supply curve to the right.

- *An increase in U.S. real GDP and real income.* With an increase in income, consumption of everything, including imports, rises. Again, importers need to exchange dollars to provide the extra goods and services, so the dollar supply curve shifts to the right.

A rise in the supply of dollars Americans use to purchase foreign assets can be caused by

- *An increase in the* real *interest rate on foreign bonds (relative to U.S. bonds).* With U.S. real interest rates holding steady, an increase in the return on foreign bonds would make them a more appealing investment. Since buying German bonds means exchanging dollars for euros, a rise in the desire to purchase foreign bonds shifts the supply curve for dollars to the right. (Remember that the real interest rate is the nominal interest rate minus expected inflation, so real interest rates increase either when the nominal interest rate rises and expected inflation holds steady or when expected inflation falls and the nominal interest rate remains the same.)

TIME

- *An increase in American wealth.* Just as an increase in income raises consumption of everything, an increase in wealth raises investment in everything. The wealthier we are, the more foreign investments we will make, and the more dollars we will exchange for euros, shifting the supply of dollars to the right.

- *A decrease in the riskiness of foreign investments relative to U.S. investments.* Lower-risk bonds are always more desirable than others, regardless of their country of origin. If the risk associated with foreign investments falls, Americans will want more of them. To get them, they will increase the supply of dollars in the foreign exchange market.

RISK

TIME

- An *expected depreciation of the dollar.* If people think the dollar is going to lose value, possibly because of inflation, they will want to exchange it for foreign currency. To see why, assume that the euro is currently worth €1.10 per dollar and that you expect it to move to €1/$1 over the next year. If you exchange $100 for euros today, you will get €110. Reversing the transaction a year later, you will be left with $110: a 10 percent return. The point is simple: if investors think the dollar will decline in value—it will depreciate—they will sell dollars, increasing the supply of dollars in the foreign exchange market.

To understand *shifts in the demand for dollars,* all we need to do is review the list just presented, this time from the point of view of a foreigner. Anything that increases the desire of foreigners to buy American-made goods and services, or to invest in U.S. assets, will increase the demand for dollars. Increases in demand come about when foreigners prefer more American-made goods, when foreign real GDP and real income rise, when the real yield on U.S. bonds rises (relative to the yield on foreign bonds), when foreign wealth increases, when the riskiness of American investments falls, and when the dollar is expected to appreciate. All these events increase demand, shifting the demand curve to the right and causing the dollar to appreciate (see Figure 10.8). Table 10.2 summarizes all the events that increase the supply of and demand for dollars in the foreign exchange market.

Explaining Exchange Rate Movements

The supply and demand model of the determination of exchange rates helps to explain short-run movements in currency values. Let's return to the 30 percent appreciation of the dollar relative to the euro that occurred between January 1999 and

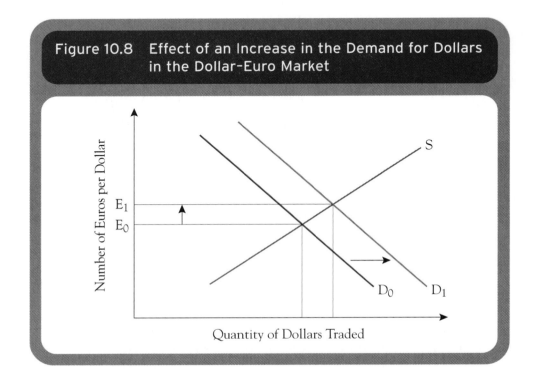

Figure 10.8   Effect of an Increase in the Demand for Dollars in the Dollar-Euro Market

Table 10.2   Causes of an Increase in the Supply of and Demand for Dollars

Increased Supply (Leads to a fall in the value of the dollar)	Increased Demand (Leads to a rise in the value of the dollar)
Increase in American preference for foreign goods	Increase in foreign preference for American goods
Increase in U.S. real GDP	Increase in foreign real GDP
Increase in real interest rate on foreign bonds (relative to U.S. bonds)	Increase in real interest rate on U.S. bonds (relative to foreign bonds)
Increase in American wealth	Increase in foreign wealth
Reduction in riskiness of foreign investment (relative to U.S. investment)	Reduction in riskiness of U.S. investment (relative to foreign investment)
Expected depreciation of the dollar	Expected future dollar appreciation

October 2000 (see Figure 10.3 on page 231). Over this period, the number of euros required to purchase one dollar increased. Our model allows us to conclude that the cause was either a decrease in the dollars supplied by Americans or an increase in the dollars demanded by foreigners. The first would shift the supply curve to the left and the second would shift the demand curve to the right, increasing the equilibrium exchange rate and making dollars more valuable. To figure out which of these is right, we need to look for other evidence.

Looking at the statistics on the supply of dollars, we see that the U.S. current account deficit—exports minus imports—increased from $200 billion at the end of 1998 to $450 billion by the close of 2000. That is, Americans increased their purchases of foreign goods during this period, *raising* the supply of dollars. But at the same time, investment funds were pouring into the United States from abroad (see this chapter's Tools of the Trade). Fall 1998 was a time of extreme financial stress, and during times of crisis, investors tend to shift into the safest place, which they view as the United States. Moreover, 1999 was the peak of the U.S. stock-market bubble. Foreign capital streamed toward the dot-com companies, especially those on the Nasdaq (see the discussion at the end of Chapter 8). As a result, foreigners' demand for dollars skyrocketed, outstripping the increased supply of dollars and driving up the "price"—the exchange rate. In the long run, however, such a move was unsustainable, so the dollar eventually depreciated, returning to a level more consistent with the theory of purchasing power parity.

APPLYING THE CONCEPT
THE FALL OF THE KOREAN WON

The Asian financial crisis began in the summer of 1997 in Thailand and Indonesia. Both countries were devastated. While experts thought some other emerging countries, like Malaysia or even Brazil, could be affected, no one believed that the strong industrial countries were in danger. South Korea, the 11th largest country in the world, with a GDP of $476.6 billion, did not seem to be at risk. But in December 1997, Korea was plunged into crisis as the won collapsed and the Korean economy imploded with it. In just a few months, the number of won per dollar went from 900 to 1,900 (see Figure 10.1, page 229). What had happened?

We can use the supply and demand apparatus to understand this episode in financial history. We know there are two reasons that the Korean won *could* depreciate: a decline in the supply of dollars from people who want to buy won and an increase in the demand for dollars from

Figure 10.9 Effect of an Increase in the Demand for Dollars in the Dollar-Korean Won Market

When investors lost confidence in Korea, they sold Korean assets and refused to buy new ones. They took their won proceeds to the foreign exchange market to buy dollars, shifting the demand for dollars from D_0 to D_1, and reducing the supply of dollars to the won market from S_0 to S_1. The result was a steep increase in the number of won needed to purchase a dollar. The exchange rate rose from E_0 to E_1, and the won *depreciated* while the dollar *appreciated*.

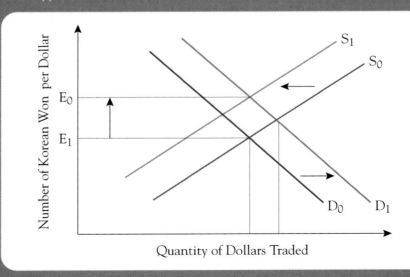

continued on next page

continued from previous page

individuals who want to sell won. Thus, there are two possible explanations for what happened at the end of 1997. Either Koreans suddenly decided to increase their consumption of foreign-produced goods and investment abroad or foreigners decided to stop purchasing Korean products and assets. The first possibility, which would cause an increase in the demand for dollars similar to the one shown in Figure 10.8, is completely implausible. Why would Koreans suddenly buy many more foreign-made goods, services, and assets—enough to halve the value of their currency? And how could they do so at a time when their economy was shrinking by 10 percent? The answer is that they didn't.

To explain what happened, we need to look at the behavior of foreigners who not only removed funds from Korea but refused to send new funds there. Because these investors believed that the Korean government did not have sufficient resources to bail out the country's banks, they became fearful that the country's financial system would collapse.* In the language of supply and demand, this loss of confidence both increased the demand for and decreased the supply of dollars in the dollar-won market. The result is shown in Figure 10.9. The rush to sell Korean assets and exchange the proceeds for dollars drove the value of the won down more than 50 percent.

*We will discuss why a government might engage in a bank bailout in the next section of this book.

Government Policy and Foreign Exchange Intervention

The more a country relies on exports and imports, the more important its exchange rate. Currency appreciation drives up the price foreigners pay for a country's exports as it reduces the price residents of the country pay for imports. This shift in foreign versus domestic prices hurts domestic businesses. Companies with big export businesses suffer the most, along with businesses whose products compete with imported goods. They often respond by pressuring elected officials to reduce the value of the currency. After all, government policymakers control the prices of lots of goods and services. Milk, rent, and electric power are just a few possibilities. Why not exchange rates too?

MARKETS

Government officials can intervene in foreign exchange markets in several ways. Some countries adopt a fixed exchange rate and act to maintain it at a level of their choosing. We will discuss the implications of this approach in Chapter 19. For now, all we need to know is that exchange rates can be controlled if policymakers have the resources available and are willing to take the necessary actions.

Large industrialized countries and common currency zones like the United States, Europe, and Japan generally allow currency markets to determine their exchange rate. Even so, there are occasions when officials in these countries try to influence the currency values. Sometimes they make public statements in the hope of influencing currency traders. But talk is cheap, and such statements rarely have an impact on their own. At other times, policymakers will buy or sell currency in an attempt to affect demand or supply. This approach is called a foreign exchange intervention.

IN THE NEWS

The Muscle-Bound Dollar May Now Be an Achilles' Heel

The New York Times

by Jeff Madrick

May 16, 2002

The dollar has long been the wild card in the economic outlook. Its surprising strength in the 1990s helped keep inflation in check by reducing import prices. A high dollar also attracted hundreds of billions of dollars in investment to compensate for the low savings rate among Americans. And while the dollar rose more than 40 percent since 1995, the gross domestic product kept growing strongly, anyway. The high dollar greatly raised world prices for the nation's manufacturing exports, but record trade deficits only partly offset other fast-growing components of GDP.

This pattern, however, has long been too good to stay true. As the expansion shows signs of weakness, it is time to encourage a modest decline in the dollar to stoke manufacturing sales, which have been hit hard by the high dollar.

It is also time to recognize the serious imbalances the strong dollar has created. The United States owes trillions of dollars of debt it took on to finance current account deficits. As important, the high dollar has done longer-term damage to some industries by discouraging investment in globally competitive goods.

Those most hurt are lining up in Washington to demand relief. Jerry Jasinowski, head of the National Association of Manufacturers, testified before Congress recently that the high dollar cost manufacturers $140 billion and 500,000 jobs the last 18 months.

But although vested interests may be clouding the debate, the arguments for a lower dollar are persuasive. The first is that a high dollar is going to restrain the expansion. America's rapid growth began in the mid-1990s, let us remember, when the dollar was 40 percent lower.

When the dollar took off in the mid-1990s, manufacturing profit rates declined again. Capital investment remained high only because of the inflow of capital from abroad and high stock prices. But now, Mr. Jasinowki's member companies report that their exports are on average 25 percent more expensive than rival products from other nations. Investment is way down.

A second argument in favor of a lower dollar is that its level is unsustainable. As J. Fred Bergsten of the Institute of International Economics points out, the nation must import $4 billion in capital a day to compensate for its current account deficit and capital outflows.

Mr. Bergsten is concerned that if the nation does not act now, a sharper fall is decidedly possible. The trade

Some countries hardly ever attempt to influence their exchange rates in this way, while others intervene in the markets frequently. Between 1997 and 2004, the United States intervened only twice; both times it was pressured to do so by other allies. Among the major industrialized countries, the Japanese are the most frequent participants in foreign exchange markets. The spring of 2002 provides a good example of their approach.

In the latter half of the 1990s, the Japanese economy was stagnant; real GDP grew at a rate of about 1 percent. In 2001, the economic situation worsened and output fell 2 percent. After trying almost every other approach imaginable to resuscitate the economy, Japanese officials decided to see if depreciating the yen would help. The idea was to help Japanese exporters increase their foreign sales by reducing the prices foreigners paid for Japanese products. In late May 2002, Japan's Ministry of Finance sold yen in exchange for dollars, hoping to drive down the price by increasing the supply of yen. While the yen did depreciate very modestly as a

deficit has reached 4 percent of GDP—not merely unprecedented in recent times but a point at which it has almost always become unsustainable in other nations. If the dollar falls too far too fast, it could ignite inflation and influence the Federal Reserve to raise interest rates so high as to weaken the economy.

A third argument, too often ignored, is that over an extended period, a high dollar misallocates capital resources. Some export industries are neglected, while those that import low-price supplies, often services, attract more investment than is optimal. The 1990s boom disguised this impact, but it is harder to reduce a trade deficit when companies do not develop new export products because those products will be chronically overpriced in the world market. Technology-intensive industries have long run a substantial trade surplus, for example, but Mr. Jasinowski calculates they are now importing $20 billion more in goods than they are exporting.

By traditional measures, Mr. Jasinowski and Mr. Bergsten argue that the dollar is overvalued 20 to 25 percent. Mr. Bergsten would like to see the Treasury "lean against the wind" and even buy undervalued currencies, like the euro or yen. [But] such policies usually make economists nervous. Some say intervention usually does not work, in part because it is offset by shifts in the money supply. But Mr. Bergsten notes that intervention [has worked occasionally].

The greater danger is that a change in dollar policy could precipitate the very collapse we fear most. Again, Mr. Bergsten says such routs have been stemmed in the past. In 1987, for example, central banks bought dollars after a two-year slide.

There is no way to avoid risks when it comes to influencing currency levels. The question is whether the risk of dollar neglect is greater than the risk of pushing it down. Given questions about the strength of this expansion, the rapidly growing trade deficit and enormous levels of foreign debt, ignoring the high dollar will only make matters worse in a year or two.

A lower dollar might even help the Europeans. While it would make their exports less competitive, it would enable the European Central Bank to reduce Europe's high interest rates because inflation would be less a threat.

It is time to face forthrightly the imbalances created in the late 1990s rather than resort to outworn shibboleths about how the markets must set currency rates.

LESSONS OF THE ARTICLE

Exchange rates can be overvalued for long periods. When they are, some people are hurt while others benefit. An overvalued dollar hurt U.S. export industries in the late 1990s, forcing them to contract. The drop in exports created pressure on U.S. policymakers to act to reduce the value of the currency. Because an overvalued currency tends to go hand in hand with a current account deficit, the pressure for adjustment is substantial. Yet there is little consensus on how to bring about a depreciation. Good solutions are hard to find.

result of intervention, by the end of the month its price was higher than it had been before the intervention.

Why did the Japanese government's policy fail? Shouldn't an increase in the supply of yen, regardless of where it comes from, lead to a depreciation? The primary reason the intervention didn't work was that, while the Japanese Ministry of Finance was selling yen, the Bank of Japan was buying them. We'll study the details when we get to Chapter 19, but here is a quick version of the story. The Bank of Japan is in charge of monetary policy in Japan, which means controlling a particular short-term interest rate. Operationally, the result was that, within a few days, the Bank of Japan reversed the Ministry's foreign-exchange intervention. If it hadn't, the interest rate it wished to control would have changed. Thus, foreign exchange interventions will be ineffective unless they are accompanied by a change in the interest rate. That is the reason countries like the United States rarely intervene in the foreign exchange markets.

YOUR FINANCIAL WORLD
Investing Overseas

More diversification is always better. Increasing the number of independent risks in a portfolio by spreading investments across a broader set of stocks and bonds can reduce risk without decreasing the expected return. That is the rationale behind investing in mutual funds and the reason for investing abroad as well. In the same way that someone living in Kansas would not hesitate to invest in an Ohio company, there is no reason why someone who lives in the United States should hesitate to invest outside the United States.

For many years, sophisticated financial advisors have been telling their clients in the United States to hold a portion of their equity portfolios in foreign stocks. But you don't need an investment advisor to heed this advice. As soon as you begin to save for your retirement—which should be as soon as you get a steady job—you should diversify your investments internationally. So long as the returns on stocks in other countries do not move in lockstep with the U.S. stock market, holding them will reduce the risk in your investment portfolio. The data indicate that the returns on other countries' stock markets do move independently of the U.S. stock market. And the benefits of diversification are not counteracted by exposure to the risk of exchange rate fluctuations. True, buying British stock means trading dollars for pounds and then changing back to dollars at a later date. In the meantime, the exchange rate could move. But the evidence shows us that holding foreign stocks reduces risk without sacrificing returns, despite the risk of exchange rate fluctuations.

Terms

Chapter Lessons

1. Different areas and countries of the world use different currencies in their transactions.
   a. The nominal exchange rate is the rate at which the currency of one country can be exchanged for the currency of another.
   b. A decline in the value of one currency relative to another is called depreciation.
   c. An increase in the value of one currency relative to another is called appreciation.

   d. When the dollar appreciates relative to the euro, the euro depreciates relative to the dollar.

   e. The real exchange rate is the rate at which the goods and services of one country can be exchanged for the goods and services of another.

   f. Over $1 trillion worth of currency is traded every day in markets run by brokers and foreign exchange dealers.

2. In the long run, the value of a country's currency is tied to the price of goods and services in that country.

   a. The law of one price states that two identical goods should sell for the same price, regardless of location.

   b. The law of one price fails because of transportation costs, differences in taxation and technical specifications, and the fact that some goods cannot be moved.

   c. The theory of purchasing power parity applies the law of one price to international transactions; it states that the real exchange rate always equals one.

   d. Purchasing power parity implies that countries with higher inflation than other countries will experience exchange rate depreciation.

   e. Over decades, exchange rate changes are approximately equal to differences in inflation, implying that purchasing power parity holds.

3. In the short run, the value of a country's currency depends on supply of and demand for the currency in foreign exchange markets.

   a. When people in the United States wish to purchase foreign goods and services or invest in foreign assets, they must supply dollars to the foreign exchange market.

   b. The more foreign currency that can be exchanged for one dollar, the greater will be the supply of dollars. That is, the supply curve for dollars slopes upward.

   c. Foreigners who wish to purchase American-made goods and services or invest in U.S. assets will demand dollars in the foreign exchange market.

   d. The fewer units of foreign currency needed to buy one dollar, the higher the demand for dollars. That is, the demand curve for dollars slopes downward.

   e. Anything that increases the desire of Americans to buy foreign-made goods and services or invest in foreign assets will increase the supply of dollars (shift the supply curve for dollars to the right), causing the dollar to depreciate.

   f. Anything that increases the desire of foreigners to buy American-made goods and services or invest in U.S. assets will increase the demand for dollars (shift the demand curve for dollars to the right), causing the dollar to appreciate.

4. Some governments buy and sell their own currency in an effort to affect the exchange rate. Such foreign exchange interventions are usually ineffective.

Problems

1. If the U.S. dollar–British pound exchange rate is $1.50 per pound, and the U.S. dollar–euro rate is $0.90 per euro:

   a. What is the pound per euro rate?

   b. How could you profit if the pound per euro rate were above the rate you calculated in part a? What if it were lower?

2. If a compact disc costs $15 in the United States and £13 in United Kingdom, what is the real CD exchange rate? Look up the current dollar–pound exchange rate in a newspaper or an online source and compare the two prices. What do you conclude?

3. Suppose the euro–dollar exchange rate moves from $0.90 per euro to $0.92 per euro. At the same time, the prices of European-made goods and services rise 1 percent, while prices of American-made goods and services rise 3 percent. What happens to the real exchange rate between the dollar and the euro? Assuming the same change in the nominal exchange rate, what if inflation were 3 percent in Europe and 1 percent in the United States?

4. The same television set costs $500 in the United States, €450 in France, £300 in United Kingdom, and ¥100,000 in Japan. If the law of one price holds, what are the euro–dollar, pound–dollar, and yen–dollar exchange rates? Why might the law of one price fail?

5. If inflation is 2 percent in the United States and 0 percent in Japan, what does the theory of purchasing power parity imply about long-run changes in the yen–dollar exchange rate?

6. You need to purchase Japanese yen and have called two brokers to get quotes. The first broker offered you a rate of 125 yen per dollar. The second broker, ignoring market convention, quoted a price of 0.0084 dollar per yen. To which broker should you give your business. Why?

7. Suppose you expect the euro to appreciate 5 percent relative to the dollar over the next year.

   a. Find the current value of the euro in the newspaper or on the Internet and compute what your expectation implies about the euro–dollar exchange rate in one year's time.

   b. In the same source, find the interest rate on a one-year U.S. Treasury bond. Using this value, compute the European interest rate that would make the return on a one-year domestic investment equal to the return on a foreign one. Work an example to show your answer is correct.

8. In 1994, BMW built an assembly plant in Spartanburg, South Carolina. Fifteen years earlier, in 1979, Honda did the same in Marysville, Ohio. Why would a European or Japanese car manufacturer choose to build cars in the United States?

9. During the 1990s, the U.S. Secretary of the Treasury often stated that "a strong dollar is in the interest of the United States."

   a. Is this statement true? Explain your answer.

   b. What can the Secretary of the Treasury actually do about the value of the dollar relative to other currencies?

10. On May 23, 2002, a *Wall Street Journal* headline read "Dollar's Drop Could Be Good, Bad or Both for Economy." Several weeks later, another headline read "No Safe Haven: Dollar's Slide Reflects Wariness about the U.S." Explain each of these headlines.

11. As the popularity of American-made films increases worldwide, what should happen to the value of the dollar? Illustrate your answer using a supply and demand graph.

12. During fall 1998, the Federal Reserve reduced U.S. interest rates significantly in response to the world financial crisis. What was the likely impact of the reduc-

tion on the value of the dollar? Looking at Figures 10.1, 10.2, and 10.3, do you see this effect? Why or why not?

13. During the 1990s, growth in the United States exceeded growth in the rest of the world, and the U.S. stock market boomed relative to stock markets in other parts of the world. List the various ways this discrepancy in economic conditions could have affected the value of the dollar. Which of them do you think were more important?

14. In winter 2002, one-year interest rates on Japanese bonds were 0.1 percent; on European bonds, 4 percent; and on U.S. bonds, 2.75 percent. Why wasn't everyone borrowing in the United States and Japan and investing it in Europe?

15. Your investment advisor calls to suggest that you invest in Mexican bonds with a yield of 8.5 percent—3 percent above U.S. Treasury rates. Should you do it? What factors should you consider in making your decision?

Appendix 10

Interest-Rate Parity and Short-Run Exchange Rate Determination

There is another way to think about the determinants of exchange rates in the short run. Rather than focus on the supply of and demand for currency, we can look at exchange rates from an investor's point of view. If the bonds issued in different countries are perfect substitutes for one another, then arbitrage will equalize the returns on domestic and foreign bonds. And since investing abroad means exchanging currencies, the result is a relationship among domestic interest rates, foreign interest rates, and the exchange rate. From this intuition, we can develop an understanding of the short-run movements in exchange rates.

Let's take the example of an American investor with a one-year investment horizon and $1,000 to invest in either a one-year U.S. Treasury bond or a one-year German government bond. Since the investor is from the United States, we will assume that at the end of the year when the bonds mature, she wants to receive dollars. The question is: Which investment is more attractive? To find the answer, we need to compute the dollar return on buying a one-year $1,000 U.S. Treasury bond and compare it to the dollar return on converting $1,000 to euros, buying a German government bond, and converting the proceeds back to dollars after one year. The value of the first investment is easy to find. If the one-year U.S. Treasury interest rate is i, then one year later an initial investment of $1,000 is worth $1,000 \times (1 + i)$. But the currency conversion complicates the calculation of the return to the foreign investment.

Computing the return to investing $1,000 in a one-year German bond requires a series of steps. First, the investor needs to take the $1,000 and convert it to euros. If E is the dollar–euro exchange rate measured as the number of euros per dollar, then $1,000 purchases $E \times 1,000$ euros. Next, the investor purchases the German bond. If the one-year German bond rate is i^f, a $1,000 investment yields $E \times 1,000 \times (1 + i^f)$ euros in one year. Finally, at the end of the year, the investor must exchange the euros for dollars. If we call E^e the expected future exchange rate—the number of euros per dollar in a year's time—then the dollar return to a $1,000 investment in foreign bonds is

$$\text{Value of \$1,000 invested in foreign bonds after one year} = \frac{\$1,000E(1+i^f)}{E^e} \qquad \text{(A1)}$$

Looking at this equation, we can see that for the U.S. investor, the return to holding the German bond has two parts: (1) the interest income and (2) the expected change in the exchange rate. By doing a little algebra and using an approximation, we can rewrite equation (A1) to divide the return into these two parts. The result is

$$\text{Value of \$1,000 invested in foreign bonds after one year} = \$1,000(1+i^f)(1-\frac{\Delta E^e}{E}), \qquad \text{(A2)}$$

where ΔE^e is the expected change in the exchange rate.

This expression tells us that the return on the foreign bond is the foreign interest rate minus the expected percentage change in the dollar–euro exchange rate.

To see why the return depends on the change in the exchange rate, take an example in which the dollar–euro rate is €1/$1 at the start of the year and €1.05/$1 at the end of the year. That is, at the start of the year, you exchange one dollar for one euro, but at the end of the year the dollar is worth 1.05 euros—an appreciation of 5 percent in the value of the dollar. If the German interest rate is 6 percent, then a $1,000 investment will yield $1,000 $\times \frac{1.06}{1.05} =$ $1,010. Because the dollar has appreciated by 5 percent, the return on a 6 percent German bond is only 6 percent – 5 percent = 1 percent.

Returning to our comparison of a domestic and a foreign bond, we know that if the investor is indifferent between the two, their returns must be the same. That must be the case for the two bonds to be perfect substitutes. The implication is that

$$\text{Value of \$1,000 invested in U.S. Treasury bonds for one year} \qquad (\text{A3})$$
$$= \text{Value of \$1,000 invested in foreign bonds after one year.}$$

This means that

$$\$1,000(1+i) = \$1,000(1+i^f)(1 - \frac{\Delta E^e}{E}) \qquad (\text{A4})$$

or

$$i = i^f - \frac{\Delta E^e}{E}.$$

This equation, called the *interest parity condition,* tells us that the U.S. interest rate equals the German interest rate minus the dollar's expected appreciation. (These calculations ignore the risk of exchange rates moving in an unexpected way.)

If the interest parity condition did not hold, people would have an incentive to shift their investments until it did. For instance, if the U.S. interest rate exceeded the German interest rate minus the expected depreciation in the dollar, then foreign and domestic investors would sell German bonds and buy U.S. Treasury bonds. Their action would drive down the price of German bonds and drive up the price of U.S. bonds, raising the foreign interest rate and lowering the domestic rate until the relationship held.

Since we know the current U.S. and German interest rates, the interest parity condition tells us what the current dollar–euro exchange rate should be for a given expected future dollar–euro exchange rate. The interest rate parity condition tells us that the current value of the dollar will be higher

1. the higher U.S. interest rates,
2. the lower German interest rates, and
3. the higher the expected future value of the dollar.

These are the same conclusions we arrived at using supply and demand theory.

Part *III*

Financial Institutions

Chapter 11

The Economics of Financial Intermediation

Economic well-being is inextricably tied to the health of the financial intermediaries that make up the financial system. From Chapter 3, we know that financial intermediaries are the businesses whose assets and liabilities are primarily financial instruments. Various sorts of banks, brokerage firms, investment companies, insurance companies, and pension funds all fall into this category. These are the institutions that pool funds from people and firms who save and lend them to people and firms who need to borrow, as shown in Figure 11.1. They funnel savers' surplus resources into home mortgages, business loans, and investments. As we will see, financial intermediaries are involved in both direct finance—in which borrowers sell securities directly to lenders in the financial markets—and indirect finance, in which a third party stands between those who provide funds and those who use them. Intermediaries investigate the financial condition of the individuals and firms who want financing to figure out which have the best investment opportunities. As providers of indirect finance, banks want to make loans only to the highest-quality borrowers. When they do their job correctly, financial intermediaries increase investment and economic growth at the same time that they reduce investment risk and economic volatility.

Ensuring that the best investment opportunities and highest-quality borrowers are funded is extremely important. As we saw in Chapter 3, there is a strong relationship between financial development and economic development. Any country that wants to grow must ensure that its financial system works. When a country's financial system crumbles, its economy fails with it. That is what happened in the United States in the Great Depression of the 1930s, when a series of bank closings was followed by an increase of over 25 percent in the unemployment rate and a fall of nearly one-third in the level of economic activity (measured by GDP). The Asian crisis of 1997, in which the banking systems of Thailand and Indonesia collapsed, is a more recent example. And the Russian bond default of August 1998, described in Chapter 6, caused a significant deterioration in the Russian economy. Without a stable, smoothly functioning financial system, no country can prosper.

In theory, the market system may seem neat and simple, but the reality is that economic growth is a messy, chaotic thing. The flow of information among parties in a market system is particularly rife with problems—problems that can derail real growth unless they are addressed properly. In this chapter, we will discuss some of these information problems and learn how financial intermediaries attempt to solve them.

The Role of Financial Intermediaries

Markets are great when they work. And financial markets are among the most important markets there are, pricing and allocating economic resources to their most productive uses. But for all the press they get, the startling fact is that markets really aren't all that important as a source of funds for people or businesses. As a general rule, indirect finance through financial intermediaries is much more important than

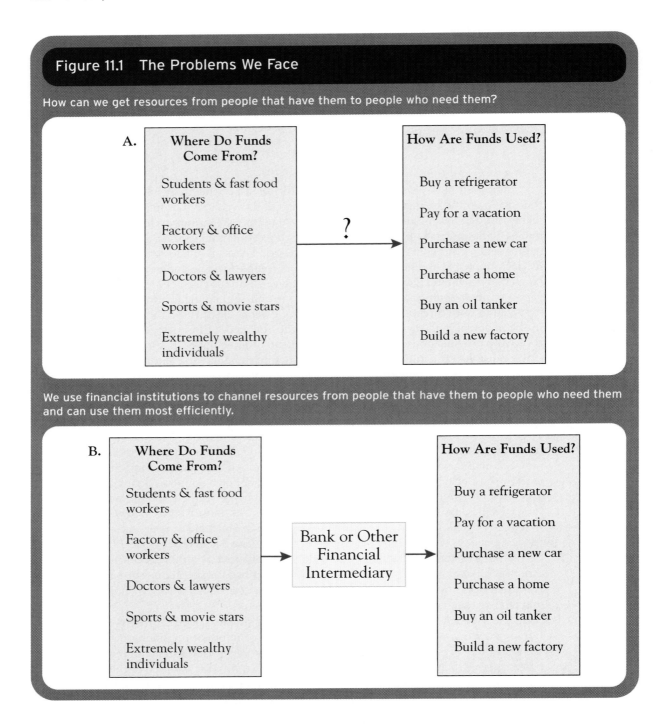

Figure 11.1 The Problems We Face

How can we get resources from people that have them to people who need them?

A.

Where Do Funds Come From?	How Are Funds Used?
Students & fast food workers	Buy a refrigerator
Factory & office workers	Pay for a vacation
Doctors & lawyers	Purchase a new car
Sports & movie stars	Purchase a home
Extremely wealthy individuals	Buy an oil tanker
	Build a new factory

?

We use financial institutions to channel resources from people that have them to people who need them and can use them most efficiently.

B.

Where Do Funds Come From?		How Are Funds Used?
Students & fast food workers		Buy a refrigerator
Factory & office workers	Bank or Other Financial Intermediary	Pay for a vacation
Doctors & lawyers		Purchase a new car
Sports & movie stars		Purchase a home
Extremely wealthy individuals		Buy an oil tanker
		Build a new factory

direct finance through the stock and bond markets. In virtually every country for which we have comprehensive data, credit extended by financial intermediaries is larger (as a percentage of GDP) than stocks and bonds combined.

Table 11.1 illustrates the relative importance of these two types of finance. As you look at the table, note two things. First, to make comparisons across countries of vastly

Table 11.1 The Relative Importance of Direct and Indirect Finance

(Averages for 1980-1995)

Country	Direct Finance		Indirect Finance	
	Stock Market Capitalization as Percent of GDP (A)	Outstanding Domestic Debt Securities as Percent of GDP (B)	Credit Extended by Banks & Other Financial Institutions as Percent of GDP (C)	Ratio of Indirect to Direct Finance C/(A+B) (D)
Industrialized Countries				
France	19.8%	41.2%	90.9%	1.5
Germany	18.6	37.4	92.3	1.6
Greece	8.1	4.3	40.2	3.2
Italy	11.9	28.1	50.5	1.3
Japan	73.0	30.0	169.3	1.6
United Kingdom	76.3	14.4	74.4	0.8
United States	58.2	52.6	130.7	1.2
Emerging Markets Countries				
Argentina	4.8	5.9	15.0	1.4
Brazil	11.9	4.0	24.7	1.6
India	13.2	5.7	26.8	1.4

Note that numbers in columns A, B, and C are as a percentage of GDP. Since these are not components of GDP, there is no reason they should add to 100.

SOURCE: *Data from Demirgüc-Kunt, Asli and Ross Levine, ed.*, Financial Structure and Economic Growth: Data Disk © 2001 Massachusetts Institute of Technology. All Rights Reserved.

different size, we measure everything relative to GDP. Second, there is no reason that the value of a country's stock market, bonds outstanding, or bank loans cannot be bigger than its GDP. In fact, we would expect it to be much larger, as the value of a company to its owners is normally quite a bit more than one year's sales. This means that when you add up all the types of financing, direct and indirect, the numbers will generally sum to more than 100.

To see the lessons from the data in the table, take the example of France (row 1). The value of the French stock market is equivalent to roughly 20 percent of that country's GDP (column A); the value of French debt securities, about 41 percent of its GDP (column B). Adding columns A and B tells us that in France, direct finance equals about 60 percent of GDP. But the credit extended by French banks and other financial intermediaries is equivalent to more than 90 percent of the country's GDP (column C). The final column, D, reports the ratio of indirect to direct finance. For France, the result is 1.5, which means that indirect finance is one and one-half times the size of direct finance. While the table reports the figures for a range of countries, the French case is typical. The difference between emerging markets in the bottom panel of Table 11.1 and industrialized countries in the top panel is in the overall size of their financial markets, not in their composition. Around the world, firms and individuals draw their financing primarily from banks and other financial intermediaries.

What accounts for this pattern of financing? Why are financial intermediaries so important? The answer has to do with information. To understand the importance of information in the role financial intermediaries play in the economy, let's look at the online auction company eBay. This virtual auction house may seem an unlikely place to start, but while eBay deals primarily with physical objects, it faces some of the same information problems as financial firms. As an online intermediary, eBay provides a mechanism through which almost anyone can auction off almost anything. At any time, upwards of 10 million items are for sale at www.ebay.com—everything from $5 dinner plates to $300,000 Italian sports cars.[1] And people buy them! In a single year, eBay reports total transactions valued at over $10 billion, entered into by more than 60 million registered users.

While millions of items are for sale on eBay, if you look carefully you'll notice an absence of financial products. You can purchase collectible coins and paper currency on eBay, but you can't borrow. There are no listings for Samantha's student loan, Chad's car loan, Chloe's credit card balance, or Mort's mortgage—at least, not yet. And though you can buy defaulted bond certificates, like the Reading Railroad bond shown in Chapter 4 (which was purchased on eBay), you can't buy or sell bonds on which the issuer is still making payments. People are selling cars and even real estate on eBay, but no one is auctioning off checking account services.

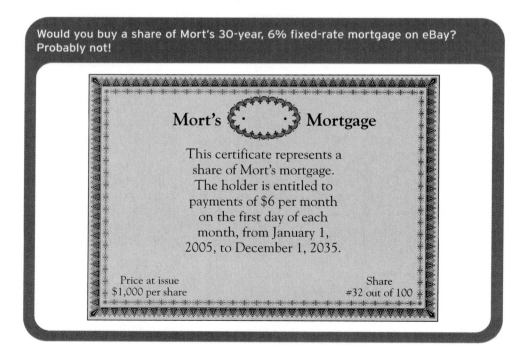

Would you buy a share of Mort's 30-year, 6% fixed-rate mortgage on eBay? Probably not!

Mort's Mortgage

This certificate represents a share of Mort's mortgage. The holder is entitled to payments of $6 per month on the first day of each month, from January 1, 2005, to December 1, 2035.

Price at issue
$1,000 per share

Share
#32 out of 100

---

[1]On August 16, 2004, eBay listed a 1990 Ferrari F40, red, 4600 miles, with a starting bid of $300,000. There were two bids.

Think for a moment about why eBay doesn't auction off mortgages. First, Mort might need a $100,000 mortgage, and not many people can finance a mortgage of that size. The people who run eBay could try to establish a system in which 100 people sign up to lend Mort $1,000 each in return for certificates like the one shown here, but it would be extremely complex and cumbersome. Imagine collecting the payments, figuring out how to repay the lenders, and writing all the legal contracts that go with the transaction. Just as important, before offering to finance Mort's mortgage, lenders would want to know something about Mort and the house he's proposing to buy. Is Mort accurately representing his ability to repay the loan? Does he really intend to buy a house with the loan? The questions are nearly endless, and answering them is both difficult and time consuming.

Financial intermediaries exist so that individual lenders don't have to worry about getting answers to all of these questions. Most people take for granted the ability of the financial system to shift resources from savers to investors, but when you look closely at the details, you're struck by how complicated the task is. It's amazing the enterprise works at all. Lending and borrowing involve both *transactions costs,* like the cost of writing a loan contract, and *information costs,* like the cost of figuring out whether a borrower is trustworthy. Financial institutions exist to reduce these costs.

In their role as financial intermediaries, financial institutions perform five functions: (1) pooling the resources of small savers; (2) providing safekeeping and accounting services, as well as access to the payments system; (3) supplying liquidity, or converting savers' balances directly into a means of payment whenever needed; (4) providing ways to diversify risk; and (5) collecting and processing information in ways that reduce information costs.[2] As we go through these, you'll see that the first four have to do with reducing transactions costs. That is, by specializing and providing these services to large numbers of customers, a financial firm can reduce the cost of providing them to individual customers. As in other fields, experts can do a better job than others, and more cheaply at that. The fifth function on the list, collecting and processing information, is a category all by itself, so we'll consider it in more detail.

While we will not discuss international banks in any depth, it is worth mentioning that they provide an additional set of services that complements those offered by your neighborhood bank. International banks handle transactions that cross international borders. That may mean taking deposits from savers in one country and providing them to investors in another country. It may also mean converting currencies in order to facilitate transactions for customers who do business or travel abroad.

Pooling Savings

The most straightforward economic function of a financial intermediary is to pool the resources of many small savers. By accepting many small deposits, banks empower themselves to make large loans. So, for example, Mort might get his $100,000 mortgage from a bank or finance company with access to a large group of savers, 100 of whom have $1,000 to invest (see Figure 11.2). Similarly, a government or large company that wishes to borrow billions of dollars by issuing bonds will rely on a financial intermediary to find buyers for the bonds.

---

[2]We could add a sixth function, the provision of secrecy. For many years, Swiss banks have charged a very high fee to customers who request anonymous accounts. While in the past people may have had legitimate reasons for depositing their funds anonymously, the view today is that for the most part, this service facilitates criminal behavior. Increased cooperation among governments has made these accounts difficult to get.

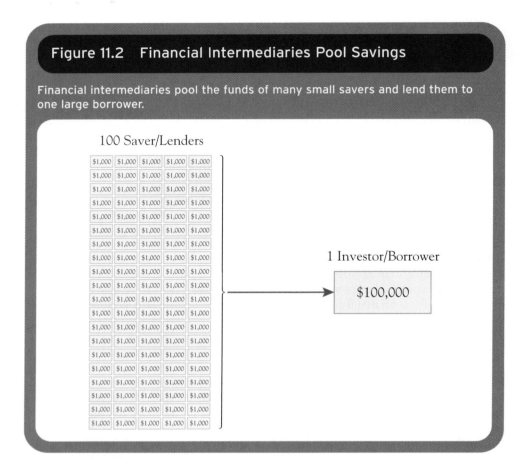

Figure 11.2   Financial Intermediaries Pool Savings

Financial intermediaries pool the funds of many small savers and lend them to one large borrower.

To succeed in this endeavor—pooling people's savings in order to make large loans—the intermediary must attract substantial numbers of savers. This is the essence of indirect finance, and it means convincing potential depositors of the institution's soundness. Banks are particularly adept at making sure customers feel that their funds will be safe. In the past, they did so by installing large safes in imposing bank buildings. Today, they rely on their reputations, as well as on government guarantees like deposit insurance. We'll return to this topic in Chapter 14.

Safekeeping, Payments System Access, and Accounting

Goldsmiths were the original bankers. To keep their gold and jewelry safe, they had to construct vaults. Soon people began asking the goldsmiths to store gold for them in return for a receipt to prove it was there. It didn't take long for someone to realize that trading the goldsmith's receipts was easier than trading the gold itself. The next step came when the goldsmith noticed that there was quite a bit of gold left in the vault at the end of the day, so that some of it could safely be lent to others. The goldsmiths took the resources of those with gold to spare—the savers of the day—and channeled them to individuals who were short—the borrowers. Today, banks are the places where we put things for safekeeping—not just gold and jewelry, but our financial wealth as well. We deposit our paychecks and entrust our savings to a bank or other financial institution because we believe it will keep our resources safe until we need them.

When we think of banks, safekeeping is only one of several services that immediately come to mind. The others are automated teller machines, checkbooks, and monthly bank statements. In providing depositors with access to ATMs, credit and debit cards, checks, and monthly statements, a bank gives them access to the payments system—the network that transfers funds from the account of one person or business to the account of another. The bank gives depositors a way to get cash into their wallets and to finalize payments using credit cards, debit cards, and checks. And since banks specialize in handling payments transactions, they can offer all these services relatively cheaply. Financial intermediaries reduce the costs of financial transactions.

This is not a trivial matter. It would be a disaster if we didn't have a convenient way to pay for things. By giving us one, financial intermediaries facilitate the exchange of goods and services, promoting specialization. Remember that in efficient economies—those that manage to get the most output from a given set of inputs—people and companies concentrate on the activities at which they are best and for which their opportunity cost is lowest. This principle of *comparative advantage* leads to specialization so that each of us ends up doing just one job. But as specialization increases, more and more trading must take place to ensure that each of us ends up with the goods and services we need and want. The more trading, the more financial transactions; and the more financial transactions, the more important it is that those transactions be cheap. If getting hold of money and using it to make payments were costly, that would surely put a damper on people's willingness to specialize. Financial intermediaries, by providing us with a reliable and inexpensive payments system, help our economy to function more efficiently.

Beyond safekeeping and access to the payments system, financial intermediaries provide bookkeeping and accounting services. They help us to manage our finances. Just think about your financial transactions over the past few months. If you work, you were paid, maybe more than once. If you rent an apartment or own a home, you paid the rent or mortgage and probably the electric and gas bills. You paid your phone bill. Then there's transportation. If you have a car, you may have made a loan payment. You surely paid for gasoline and possibly for a repair. You purchased food too, both at the grocery store and in various restaurants. And don't forget the movies and books you bought. As you get older, you may shoulder the expense of having children, along with saving for their education and your retirement. The point is, our financial lives are extraordinarily complex, and we need help keeping track of them. Financial intermediaries do the job: They provide us with bookkeeping and accounting services, noting all our transactions for us and making our lives more tolerable in the process.

Before we continue, we should note that providing safekeeping and accounting services, as well as access to the payments system, forces financial intermediaries to write legal contracts. Writing individualized contracts that ensure that each customer will maintain a checking account balance as required, or repay a loan as promised, would be extremely costly. But a financial intermediary can hire a lawyer to write one very high-quality contract that can be used over and over again, thus reducing the cost of each use. In fact, much of what financial intermediaries do takes advantage of what are known as economies of scale, in which the average cost of producing a good or service falls as the quantity produced increases. As we will see later, information is subject to economies of scale just as other goods and services are.

The door to the largest gold vault in the world at the Federal Reserve Bank of New York. The only entry is through a 10-foot passageway cut into a 9-foot high, 90-ton steel cylinder that rotates 90 degrees to open and close the vault. Many governments keep their gold here.

SOURCE: © *Courtesy of the Federal Reserve Bank of New York.*

MARKETS

YOUR FINANCIAL WORLD
Guard Your Identity

There is a television commercial in which a middle-aged man is sitting in his living room drinking a beer. Out of the man's mouth comes the voice of a woman describing some very expensive clothing she just bought. She didn't care how much the clothes cost because she wasn't paying—she used a credit card that was in the man's name. The ad catches viewers' attention because it is funny. But its primary purpose is to serve as a warning about identity theft, in which one person takes on the identity of another to do things like make credit card purchases.

It is important to realize that someone who has a few pieces of key information about you can get a credit card in your name. To prevent this, you need to protect personal information. Do your best to never tell anyone your birth date and birthplace, your address, or your mother's maiden name. Most importantly, guard your social security number. Since it is unique, it is the key to identity theft. Give out your social security number only when absolutely necessary—on tax forms, for employ-

ment records, and to open bank accounts. If your driver's license has your social security number on it, ask that it be removed. If a business requests it, ask if some alternative number can be used. Importantly, if you get a telephone call or an email from someone you don't know asking for personal data, don't provide it.

Beyond protecting access to personal information, you need to monitor your financial statements closely, looking for things that shouldn't be there. Be on the lookout for unauthorized charges. This means maintaining careful records so that you know what should be on your bank and credit card statements.

Identity theft is a crime, and governments work hard to find and prosecute the offenders. Even so, millions of people are victims each year. Don't be one of them. For more information about identity theft and how to avoid being a victim, see the U.S. Department of Justice's website: www.usdoj.gov/criminal/fraud/idtheft.html.

Providing Liquidity

One function that is related to access to the payments system is the provision of liquidity. Recall from Chapter 2 that *liquidity* is a measure of the ease and cost with which an asset can be turned into a means of payment. When a financial asset can be transformed into money quickly, easily, and at low cost, it is said to be very liquid. Financial intermediaries offer us the ability to transform assets into money at relatively low cost. That's what ATMs are all about—converting deposit balances into money on demand.

Financial intermediaries provide liquidity in a way that is both efficient and beneficial to all of us. To understand the process, think about your bank. Two kinds of customers come through the doors: those with funds, who want to make deposits, and those in need of funds, who want to take out loans. Depositors want easy access to their funds—not just the currency they withdraw every week or so but the larger amounts they may need in an emergency. Borrowers don't want to pay the funds back for a while, and they certainly can't be expected to repay the entire amount on short notice.

In the same way that an insurance company knows that not all its policyholders will have automobile accidents on the same day, a bank knows that not all its depositors will experience an emergency and need to withdraw funds at the same time. The bank can structure its assets accordingly, keeping enough funds in short-term, liquid financial instruments to satisfy the few people who will need them and lending out the rest. And since long-term loans have higher interest rates than short-term money-market instruments—for instance, commercial paper and U.S. Treasury bills—the bank can offer depositors a higher interest rate than they would get otherwise.

Even the bank's short-term investments will do better than an individual depositor's could, because the bank can take advantage of economies of scale to lower its transactions costs. It isn't much more expensive to buy a $1 million U.S. Treasury bill than it is to buy a $1,000 bill. By collecting funds from a large number of small investors, the bank can reduce the cost of their combined investment, offering each individual investor both liquidity and high rates of return. Pooling large numbers of small accounts in this way is very efficient. By doing so, an intermediary offers depositors something they can't get from the financial markets on their own.

The liquidity services financial intermediaries provide go beyond fast and easy access to account balances. Intermediaries offer both individuals and businesses lines of credit, which are similar to overdraft protection for checking accounts. A line of credit is essentially a preapproved loan that can be drawn on whenever a customer needs funds. Home equity lines of credit, credit-card cash advances, and business lines of credit are examples. Like a deposit account, the line of credit provides a customer with access to liquidity, except that in this case withdrawals may exceed deposit balances. To offer this service profitably, a financial intermediary must specialize in liquidity management. That is, it must design its balance sheet so that it can sustain sudden withdrawals.

Diversifying Risk

If you had $1,000 or $10,000 or even $100,000 to invest, would you want to keep it all in one place? Would you be willing to lend it all to a single person or firm? Since by now you have read Chapter 5, you know the answer to this question: Don't put all your eggs in one basket, it's unnecessarily risky. But even without knowing much about diversifying through hedging and spreading risk, you would sense intuitively that lending $1 to each of 1,000 borrowers is better than lending $1,000 to just one borrower, and putting $1 in each of 1,000 different stocks is better than putting $1,000 in one stock. Financial institutions enable us to diversify our investments and reduce risk.

Banks mitigate risk in a straightforward way: They take deposits from thousands or even millions of individuals and make thousands of loans with them. Thus, each depositor has a very small stake in each one of the loans. For example, a bank might collect $1,000 from each of one million depositors and then use the resulting $1 billion to make 10,000 loans of $100,000 each. So each has a 1/1,000,000 share in each of the 10,000 loans.

RISK

To picture this, look back at Figure 11.2 (page 264) and imagine that it shows 10,000 times as many deposits and 10,000 times as many mortgages. Next, picture each of those deposits cut up into 10,000 pieces, each assigned to a different loan. That is, each deposit contributes 10 cents to each loan. That's diversification! And since the bank specializes in taking deposits and making loans, it can minimize the cost of setting up all the necessary legal contracts.

All financial intermediaries provide a low-cost way for individuals to diversify their investments. Mutual-fund companies offer small investors a low-cost way to purchase a diversified portfolio of stocks and eliminate the idiosyncratic risk associated with any single investment. Many of the mutual funds based on the Standard & Poor's 500 index (described in Chapter 8) require a minimum investment of as little as a few thousand dollars. Since the average price of each stock in the index usually runs between $30 and $40, a small investor would need over $15,000 to buy even a single share of stock in each of the 500 companies in the index (not to mention the fees the

Table 11.2 A Summary of the Role of Financial Intermediaries	
1. *Pooling savings.*	Accepting resources from a large number of small savers/lenders in order to provide large loans to borrowers.
2. *Safekeeping and accounting.*	Keeping depositors' savings safe, giving them access to the payments system, and providing them with accounting statements that help them to track their income and expenditures.
3. *Providing liquidity.*	Allowing depositors to transform their financial assets into money quickly, easily, and at low cost.
4. *Diversifying risk.*	Providing investors with the ability to diversify even small investments.
5. *Collecting and processing information services.*	Generating large amounts of standardized financial information.

investor would need to pay to a broker to do it). Thus, the mutual-fund company lets a small investor buy a fraction of a share in each of the 500 companies in the fund. And since mutual fund companies specialize in this activity, the cost remains low.

Collecting and Processing Information

One of the biggest problems individual savers face is figuring out which potential borrowers are trustworthy and which are not. Most of us do not have the time or skill to collect and process information on a wide array of potential borrowers. And we are understandably reluctant to invest in activities about which we have little reliable information. The fact that the borrower knows whether he or she is trustworthy, while the lender faces substantial costs to obtain the same information, results in an *information asymmetry*. Very simply, borrowers have information that lenders don't.

By collecting and processing standardized information, financial intermediaries reduce the problems information asymmetries create. They screen loan applicants to guarantee that they are creditworthy. They monitor loan recipients to ensure that they use the funds as they have claimed they will. To understand how this process works, and the implications it has for the financial system, we need to study information asymmetries in more detail.

Information Asymmetries and Information Costs

Information plays a central role in the structure of financial markets and financial institutions. Markets require sophisticated information to work well; when the cost of obtaining that information is too high, markets cease to function. Information costs make the financial markets, as important as they are, among the worst functioning of all markets. The fact is, the issuers of financial instruments—borrowers who want to

issue bonds and firms that want to issue stock—know much more about their business prospects and their willingness to work than potential lenders or investors—those who would buy their bonds and stocks. This **asymmetric information** is a serious hindrance to the operation of financial markets. Solving this problem is one key to making our financial system work as well as it does.

To understand the nature of the problem and the possible solutions, let's go back to eBay. Why are the people who win online auctions willing to send payments totaling $10 billion a year to the sellers? An amazing amount of trust is involved in these transactions. To bid at all, buyers must believe that an item has been described accurately. And winners must be sure that the seller will send the item in exchange for their payments, because the normal arrangement is for the seller to be paid first.

How can buyers be sure they won't be disappointed by their purchases when they arrive, assuming they arrive at all? The fact that sellers have much more information about the items they are selling and their own reliability creates an information asymmetry. Aware of this problem, the people who started eBay took two steps. First, they offered insurance to protect buyers who don't receive their purchases. Second, they devised a feedback forum to collect and store information about both bidders and sellers. Anyone can read the comments posted in the forum or check an overall rating that summarizes their content. Sellers who develop good reputations in the feedback forum command higher prices than others[3]; buyers who develop bad reputations can be banned from bidding. Without this means of gathering information, eBay probably could not have been successful. Together, the buyers' insurance and the feedback forum make eBay run smoothly.[4]

---

[3] In fact, for a fee, some known sellers with excellent reputations will act as agents for people who don't have an eBay rating.

[4] A low-cost, reliable payments system helps, too. The easier it is for buyers to pay sellers, the more likely both are to use the auction site. Realizing the need for a payments system, eBay users created *PayPal*, which allows buyers and sellers to set up electronic accounts through which to make and receive payments for their eBay transactions. Since many sellers are too small to take credit cards, this innovation greatly facilitated the online exchanges. Initially an independent concern, PayPal became so central to eBay's success that the auction site's owners bought it.

eBay's feedback rating system awards +1 point for each positive comment, 0 points for each neutral comment, and −1 point for each negative comment

SOURCE: *eBay*

APPLYING THE CONCEPT
WHAT'S HAPPENING TO BANK LOANS?

Because information has always been the key element in lending decisions, banks have specialized in determining who is creditworthy and who is not. In the past, the information that was used to certify that a particular borrower was a good credit risk belonged to the bank and could not easily be communicated to others. Thus, the loans had to be held by the bank and were not easily marketable to others.

This has changed in recent years. Large companies no longer go to banks to borrow; instead, they issue bonds and commercial paper. And technological change has brought two important innovations to the lending process: credit scoring and securitization. Today, computers can collect, store, and retrieve huge amounts of information. The financial community has used this digitized information to create statistical models that can predict the likelihood of a borrower defaulting and communicate it in the form of a credit score. Because credit scores are standardized, the loans on which they are based can be resold. But reselling individual loans would be costly and cumbersome, so banks pool them and sell shares in the pool (these are the asset-backed securities mentioned in Chapter 3). Pooling has the added advantage of diversification: individuals who buy shares in the pool are purchasing very small bits of a large number of loans, each with a standard credit score. So while some borrowers will default, no investor has much at stake in any individual loan.

As a result of these improvements in information technology, we would expect banks to decline in importance as a source of credit. Looking at the data in Figure 11.3, we can see that is exactly what has happened. Over the last quarter of the 20th century, the proportion of total credit held by banks fell roughly by half. The number of banks has declined as well, partly because of mergers that created bigger banks. But the importance of banks has declined along with their number. If you look around your community, you can probably find buildings that once housed banks

The two problems eBay faced arise in financial markets, too. In fact, information problems are the key to understanding the structure of our financial system and the central role of financial intermediaries. Asymmetric information poses two important obstacles to the smooth flow of funds from savers to investors. The first, called adverse selection, arises before the transaction occurs. Just as buyers on eBay need to know the relative trustworthiness of sellers, lenders need to know how to distinguish good credit risks from bad. The second problem, called moral hazard, occurs after the transaction. In the same way that buyers on eBay need reassurance that sellers will deliver their purchases after receiving payment, lenders need to find a way to tell whether borrowers will use the proceeds of a loan as they claim they will. The following sections will look at both these problems in detail to see how they affect the structure of the financial system.

continued from previous page

but now are used as restaurants and ice cream parlors. In one well-known store in Cambridge, Massachusetts, you can eat an ice cream sundae at a table inside a renovated bank vault!

Figure 11.3   Credit-Market Debt Held by Banks

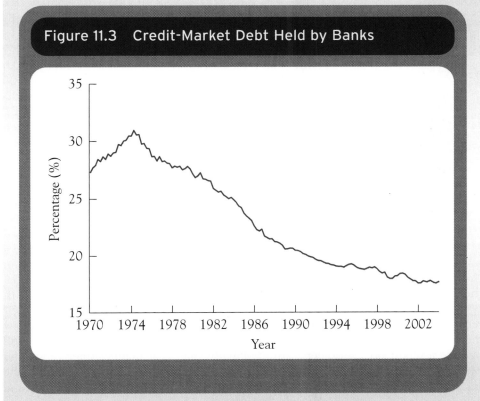

SOURCE: *Ratio of credit-market debt held by commercial banks to total credit-market debt outstanding from the Board of Governors of the Federal Reserve System* Flow of Funds Accounts, *available at www.federalreserve.gov/releases/z1/current/ data.htm.*

Adverse Selection

Used Cars and the Market for Lemons   The 2001 Nobel Prize in Economics was awarded to George A. Akerlof, A. Michael Spence, and Joseph E. Stiglitz "for their analyses of markets with asymmetric information." Professor Akerlof's contribution came first, in a paper published in 1970 titled "The Market for Lemons."[5] Akerlof's paper explained why the market for used cars—some of which may be "lemons"—doesn't function very well. Here's the logic.

[5]See "The Market for 'Lemons': Quality Uncertainty and the Market Mechanism," *Quarterly Journal of Economics* (August 1970). This paper contains very little mathematics and is quite readable. You can find it through your university library using an electronic storage system called JSTOR.

Used Cars: clean, reliable, and priced just right!

SOURCE: © Frank Saragnese/ Getty Images

Suppose the used-car market has only two cars for sale, both 2001 model Honda Accords. One is immaculate, having been driven and maintained by a careful elderly woman who didn't travel much. The second car belonged to a young man who got it from his parents, loved to drive fast, and did not worry about the damage he might cause if he hit a pothole. The owners of these two cars know whether their own cars are in good repair, but used-car shoppers do not.

Let's say that potential buyers are willing to pay $15,000 for a well-maintained car, but only $7,500 for a "lemon"—a car with lots of mechanical problems. The elderly woman knows her car is a "peach." It's in good condition and she won't part with it for less than $12,500. The young man, knowing the poor condition of his car, will take $6,000 for it. But if buyers can't tell the difference between the two cars, without more information they will pay only the average price of $11,250.[6] That is less than the owner of the good car will accept, so she won't sell her car and it disappears from the market. The problem is that if buyers are willing to pay only the average value of all the cars on the market, sellers with cars in above-average condition won't put their cars up for sale. Only the worst cars, the lemons, will be left on the market.

Information asymmetries aside, people like to buy new cars, and when they do, they sell their old cars. People who can't afford new cars, or who would rather not pay for them, are looking to buy good used cars. Together, these potential buyers and sellers of used cars provide a substantial incentive for creative people to solve the problem of adverse selection in the used-car market. Some companies try to help buyers separate the peaches from the lemons. For instance, *Consumer Reports* provides information about the reliability and safety of particular makes and models. Car dealers may try to maintain their reputations by refusing to pass off a clunker as a well-maintained car. For a fee, a mechanic will check out a used car for a potential buyer, and internet services will provide a report on its accident history. Finally, many car manufacturers now offer warranties on the used cars they have certified. We have found ways to overcome the information problems pointed out by Professor Akerlof, and as a result both good and bad used cars sell at prices much closer to their true value.

Adverse Selection in Financial Markets   When it comes to information costs, financial markets are not that different from the used-car market. In the same way that the seller of a used car knows more about the car than the buyer, potential borrowers know more about the projects they wish to finance than prospective lenders. And in the same way that information asymmetries can drive good cars out of the used-car market, they can drive good stocks and bonds out of the financial market. To see why, let's start with stocks.

Think about a simple case in which there are two firms, one with good prospects and one with bad prospects. If you can't tell the difference between the two firms, you will be willing to pay a price based only on their average quality. The stock of the good company will be undervalued. Since the managers know their stock is worth more than the average price, they won't issue it in the first place. That leaves only the firm with bad prospects in the market. And since most investors aren't interested in companies with poor prospects, the market is very unlikely to get started at all.

The same thing happens in the bond market. Remember that risk requires compensation. The higher the risk, the greater the risk premium. In the bond market, this

RISK

---

[6]A risk-averse buyer wouldn't even pay that much.

YOUR FINANCIAL WORLD
Your First Credit Card

Credit card interest rates are outrageous, running to over 30 percent in some cases (really)! In Chapter 4, Your Financial World: Pay Off Your Credit Card discussed how expensive borrowing can be and demonstrated why you should pay off your credit card debt as quickly as possible. The odds are, when you get your first credit card, the interest rate will be extremely high. Why?

Unless your parent signed your credit card papers (or you worked a steady job before starting college), as a student you have no credit history, and the company that issued the card will assume the worst. So you're lumped in with people who have very poor credit, who would rather get lower-interest loans elsewhere but can't. This is adverse selection at its worst. When you get your first credit card,

the assumption is that you are in a group of people who will have a high default rate. No wonder the issuers charge high interest rates. It is compensation for the risk they are taking. And just to prove the point, this is not a very profitable business.*

You need a credit card to build up a credit history, to establish yourself as a person who repays loans promptly. After a while, you'll be able to get a new card at a lower interest rate. But in the meantime, remember that your interest rate is extremely high, so borrowing is very expensive.

*There are a number of studies of the credit card industry. Paul S. Calem and Loretta J. Mester's study "Consumer Behavior and the Stickiness of Credit-Card Interest Rates," *American Economic Review* 85, no. 5 (December 1995), pp. 1327–1336, examines the nature of the credit card industry.

relationship between risk and return affects the cost of borrowing. The more risky the borrower, the higher the cost of borrowing. If a lender can't tell whether a borrower is a good or bad credit risk, the lender will demand a risk premium based on the average risk. Borrowers who know they are good credit risks won't want to borrow at this elevated interest rate, so they will withdraw from the market, leaving only the bad credit risks. The result is the same as for used cars and stocks: Since lenders are not eager to buy bonds issued by bad credit risks, the market will disappear.

Solving the Adverse Selection Problem

From a social perspective, the fact that managers might avoid issuing stock or bonds because they know the market will not value their company correctly is not good. It means that the company will pass up some good investments. And since some of the best investments will not be undertaken, the economy won't grow as rapidly as it could. Thus it is extremely important to find ways for investors and lenders to distinguish well-run firms from poorly run firms. Well-run firms need to highlight their quality so they can obtain financing more cheaply. Investors need to distinguish between high- and low-risk investments so they can adjust their expected rates of return. The question is how to do it.

Recall how buyers and sellers in the used-car market developed ways to address the problem of distinguishing good from bad cars? The answer here is similar. First, since the problem is caused by a lack of information, we can create more information for investors. Second, we can provide guarantees in the form of financial contracts that can be written so a firm's owners suffer together with the people who invested in the company if the firm does poorly. This type of arrangement helps to persuade investors that a firm's stocks and bonds are of high quality. And as we will see later, financial intermediaries can do a great deal to reduce the information costs associated with stock and bond investments.

IN THE NEWS
When Standards Are Unacceptable

The Wall Street Journal

By David Wessel

February 7, 2002

When Lawrence Summers spoke from his U.S. Treasury pulpit,* he preached that no innovation was more important to the success of U.S. capital markets than "generally accepted accounting principles (GAAP)." The transparency and accuracy of corporate reporting, he would say, was part of the intangible infrastructure of the financial system that made American prosperity possible.

That's what makes the Enron scandal so serious. It's more than an isolated case of corporate venality. It highlights that the bookkeeping that is "generally accepted" these days is too often meaningless, if not false.

Enron wasn't the only company to make debt disappear altogether from its books. Global Crossing and Elan weren't the only companies to give money to someone else, take some of it back, and count the income as revenue without counting the outgo as expense. Amazon wasn't the only company to resort to "pro forma" accounting when it was uncomfortable with GAAP.

*Summers was Secretary of the Treasury from July 1999 to January 2001.

Honest bookkeeping is fundamental to a system in which savings are funneled, not through banks, but through stock and bond markets to finance investments that pay off in better living conditions. The decisions of mutual funds, insurers, and pension plans are supposed to direct capital to the most promising uses. If the numbers are bad, the decisions are bad. Savings flow not to the most promising investments but to the ones that paint the prettiest pictures.

This isn't just theory. When companies confess that they didn't make as much as they said they had, their shares suffer. In 2000, investors in companies that restated earnings had losses of $31.2 billion in the three days following the announcements. That's a small slice of the stock market, but it's still a lot of money.

The practice of audited corporate financial statements is a modern one. U.S. Steel Corp. was a lonely pioneer in 1903 when it hired Price, Waterhouse & Co., as it was known then, to certify the accuracy of what's considered the first modern corporate annual report, 40 pages of narrative, numbers and photos. Other companies were slow to follow.

Widespread allegations of fraud and skullduggery after the 1929 stock-market crash changed all that, prompting legislation that forced publicly held companies to submit regular reports that met certain standards. Congress first told the Federal Trade Commission to regulate accounting, then, in 1934, gave the job to the new Securities and Exchange Commission.

Disclosure of Information   One obvious way to solve the problem created by asymmetric information is to generate more information. This can be done in one of two ways, government-required disclosure and the private collection and production of information. In most industrialized countries, *public companies*—those that issue stocks and bonds that are bought and sold in public financial markets—are required to disclose voluminous amounts of information. For example, in the United States the Securities and Exchange Commission requires firms to produce public financial statements that are prepared according to standard accounting practices. Corporations are also required to disclose, on an ongoing basis, information that could have a bearing on the value of their firms. And since August 2000, U.S. companies have been required to release to the public any information they provide to professional stock analysts.[7]

[7]Some people were concerned that Regulation FD, for "fair disclosure," might have the perverse effect of causing firms to make less information public. Fortunately, evidence shows that public corporations are now providing more information to both professional stock analysts and individual investors. Today, virtually all company conference calls—the mechanism used to disseminate information about a firm's financial performance—are open to individual investors.

But over the past decade or two, the truthfulness of the audited reports has deteriorated.

When financial wizards describe some three-card-monte transaction, too many bosses nod rather than risk appearing too dim-witted to understand modern finance—or suggest after the fact that they didn't know what was unfolding.

"It's not good enough for a manager to say, 'The smart guys understand and the MIT guys understand. I don't need to understand. I just manage them,' " warns William McDonough, president of the Federal Reserve Bank of New York.[†] "If the management and the outside directors do not understand the risk transactions that an institution is taking, they are incapable of exercising appropriate oversight. They must either educate themselves or forbid that the risk be taken."

Clever lawyers, investment bankers, chief financial officers, and accountants exploit the gaps in GAAP. The incentives for corporate managers to distort the information they provide investors grew during the 1990s bubble. With compensation more closely tied to stock prices, there are huge rewards from moves that boost shares, even if just temporarily. And there was an urgency to keep stock prices up in order to continue to sell shares to raise capital. "The argument that 'honesty is the best policy' does not work in such markets, since firms would not be around to reap the benefits of their honesty if they cannot raise current finance," says Harvard economist Andrei Shleifer.

[†]In June 2003 William McDonough left the Federal Reserve Bank of New York to become the first chair of the Public Company Accounting Oversight Board, which was created to oversee auditors of public companies in an effort to ensure the accuracy of accounting statements.

So today, too many companies treat accounting rules the way they treat the tax laws: If it isn't expressly forbidden, it's OK. Too few ask: Do our reports give outsiders a reasonable picture of our performance?

The reaction to Enron is heartening, though. The public outrage is unmistakable, which is why Congress is so exercised. The stock market is punishing companies whose reports hide more than they reveal. The result may be the changes in rules, in oversight and—perhaps most important—in attitudes toward corporate honesty that have been so slow in coming.

Reprinted by permission of The Wall Street Journal, Copyright © 2002 Dow Jones & Company, Inc. All Rights Reserved Worldwide.

LESSONS OF THE ARTICLE

The financial system cannot function without information. Unless investors feel secure that they are receiving accurate assessments of firms' financial health, they will not buy stocks and bonds. Thus, adequate accounting rules are crucial to investor confidence: Without satisfactory rules and regulations, financial statements will not convey the information investors require. The accounting scandals of 2001 and 2002 led to a series of changes in accounting rules that were designed to improve investors' confidence in the system. For example, today heads of companies must certify that their firms' financial statements are accurate and sign them.

As we learned in 2001 and 2002, however, these requirements can go only so far in assuring that investors are well informed. Despite government regulations designed to protect investors, Enron, WorldCom, Global Crossing, and numerous other companies managed to distort the profits and debt levels published in their financial statements. With the help of some unethical accountants, company executives found a broad range of ways to manipulate the statements to disguise their firms' true financial condition. As a result, most of us now suspect that public financial statements are virtually meaningless. While accounting practices have changed since then and financial statements may now convey more information than they once did, everyone remains on guard. Information problems persist.

What about the private collection and sale of information? You might think that this would provide investors with what they need to solve the adverse selection problem, but unfortunately it doesn't work. While it is in everyone's interest to produce credible proof of the quality of a company's activities, such information doesn't really exist. In a limited sense there is private information collected and sold to investors. Various research services like Moody's, Value Line, and Dun and Bradstreet collect information directly from firms and produce evaluations.

These reports are not cheap. For example, Value Line charges $600 a year for the print version of its weekly publication. To be credible, the companies examined can't pay for the research themselves, so investors have to. And while some individuals might be willing to pay, in the end they don't have to and so they won't. Private information services face what is called a free-rider problem. A free rider is someone who doesn't pay the cost to get the benefit of a good or service, and free riding on stock-market analysis is easy to do. Even though these publications are expensive, public libraries subscribe to some of them. Reporters for *The Wall Street Journal* and other periodicals read them and write stories publicizing crucial information. And individual investors can simply follow the lead of people they know who subscribe to the publications. Of course, all these practices reduce the ability of the producers of private information to actually profit from their hard work.

Collateral and Net Worth While government-required disclosure and private information collection are crucial, they haven't solved all the information problems that plague investors and the firms they invest in. Fortunately, other solutions exist. One is to make sure that lenders are compensated even if borrowers default. If a loan is insured in some way, then the borrower isn't a bad credit risk.

There are two mechanisms for ensuring that a borrower is likely to repay a lender: collateral and net worth. Recall from Chapter 3 that collateral is something of value pledged by a borrower to the lender in the event of the borrower's default. Collateral is said to *back* or *secure* a loan. Houses serve as collateral for mortgages; cars, as collateral for car loans. If the borrower fails to keep up with the mortgage or car payments, the lender will take possession of the house or car and sell it to recover the borrowed funds. In circumstances like these, adverse selection is not much of a concern; that's why collateral is so prevalent in loan agreements. Loans that are made without collateral—unsecured loans, like credit card debt—generally involve very high interest rates. Adverse selection is the reason. (See Your Financial World: Your First Credit Card.)

Net worth is the owner's stake in a firm, the value of the firm's assets minus the value of its liabilities. Under many circumstances, net worth serves the same purpose as collateral. If a firm defaults on a loan, the lender can make a claim against the firm's net worth. Consider what would happen if a firm with a high net worth borrowed to undertake a project that turned out to be unsuccessful. If the firm had no net worth, the lender would be out of luck. Instead, the firm's owners can use their net worth to repay the lender.

The same is true of a home mortgage. A mortgage is much easier and cheaper to get when a homebuyer makes a substantial down payment. For the lender, the risk is that the price of the home will fall, in which case its value will not be sufficient to fully compensate the lender in the event of a default. But with a large down payment, the homeowner has a substantial stake in the house, so even if the price falls, the mortgage can likely be repaid even if the borrower defaults. From the perspective of the mortgage lender, the homeowner's equity serves exactly the same function as net worth in a business loan.

The importance of net worth in reducing adverse selection is the reason owners of new businesses have so much difficulty borrowing money. If you want to start a bakery, for example, you will need financing to buy equipment and cover the rent and payroll for the first few months. Such seed money is very hard to get. Most small business owners must put up their homes and other property as collateral for their business loans. Only after they have managed to establish a successful business, and have built up some net worth in it can they borrow without pledging their personal property.

APPLYING THE CONCEPT
DEFLATION, NET WORTH, AND INFORMATION COSTS

A casual reader of the business press might get the impression that deflation, when prices are declining on average, is a fate we would rather not contemplate. Deflation is associated with the Great Depression of the 1930s, when consumer prices and output both fell about 30 percent. It is also associated with the Japanese stagnation of the past decade, when output remained virtually unchanged and prices fell for five years running.

Deflation is the opposite of the more familiar inflation. Inflation is when prices are going up, on average. Deflation is when they are going down. A primary reason deflation is so bad is that it aggravates information problems in ways that inflation does not. It does so by reducing a company's net worth. To see why, think about a typical firm's balance sheet. Its assets are buildings, machines, and product inventories. Its liabilities include various kinds of debt, much of it fixed in nominal terms. That is, companies borrow fixed numbers of dollars. Now think about the consequences of a decline in the price level. When prices fall, the dollar value of the firm's liabilities remains the same. The value of the firm's assets, however, tends to fall with the price level. Deflation drives down a firm's net worth, making it less trustworthy as a borrower. Remember, net worth solves the problems of adverse selection and moral hazard, allowing firms to obtain loans. With a low net worth, firms can no longer obtain financing because lenders cannot overcome the difficulty of asymmetric information.

The connection among net worth, information, and the availability of credit to borrowers helps to explain the dynamics of the business cycle. Think about what happens at the start of a recession. The value of a firm (as measured by the present value of its expected future sales) falls, compounding lenders' information problems. Lenders, suddenly more concerned about a borrower's creditworthiness, become more reluctant to make loans. The availability of investment funds falls, pushing the economy further into recession.

Moral Hazard: Problem and Solutions

The phrase *moral hazard* originated when economists who were studying insurance noted that an insurance policy changes the behavior of the person who is insured.[8] Examples are everywhere. A fire insurance policy written for more than the value of the property might induce the owner to arson; a generous automobile insurance policy might encourage reckless driving. Employment arrangements suffer from moral hazard, too. How can your boss be sure you are working as hard as you can if you'll get

[8]The term *moral hazard* has an unfortunate ethical connotation. Actually, it has nothing to do with either morality or hazard as those words are normally understood.

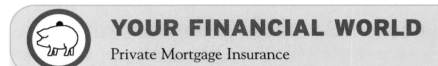

YOUR FINANCIAL WORLD

Private Mortgage Insurance

If you try to buy a house with a down payment of less than 20 percent of the purchase price, the lender may require you to buy private mortgage insurance (PMI). PMI insures the lender in the event that the borrower defaults on the mortgage. This type of insurance can be expensive. For example, if you make a down payment of $10,000, or 10 percent, on a $100,000 home and finance the rest of the purchase price with a 30-year, 6-percent fixed-rate mortgage, the required private mortgage insurance will raise your monthly payment from $530 to $570. But if you want to buy a house and you don't have savings that meet the 20 percent down payment requirement, you will have no choice but to purchase PMI.

Fortunately, you can cancel the insurance when the amount you owe on your mortgage falls to less than 80 percent of the value of your home. This can happen in two ways. The first is that you make your payments, gradually reducing the principal on the loan. (Recall from Chapter 6 that each loan payment is part interest and part repayment of principal.) But paying off the first $10,000 of a $90,000 30-year mortgage will take you at least 10 years. The second way you can cancel your PMI is if the value of your house rises, in which case you can contact the insurance provider and ask to drop the insurance. The law is on your side. So long as you have been making your mortgage payments on time, you have the right to cancel your PMI when your stake in the house—your net worth—rises above 20 percent of its value.

your paycheck at the end of the week whether you do or not? Moral hazard arises when we cannot observe people's actions and so cannot judge whether a poor outcome was intentional or just a result of bad luck.

Thus, a lender's or investor's information problems do not end with adverse selection. A second information asymmetry arises because the borrower knows more than the lender about the way borrowed funds will be used and the effort that will go into a project. Moral hazard plagues both equity and bond financing, making it difficult for all but the biggest, best known companies to issue either stocks or bonds successfully. Let's look at each type of financing and examine the ways people have tried to solve the problem of moral hazard.

Moral Hazard in Equity Financing

If you buy a stock, how do you know the company that issued it will use the funds you have invested in the way that is best for you? The answer is that it almost surely will not. You have given your funds to managers, who will tend to run the company in the way most advantageous to them. The separation of your ownership from their control creates what is called a *principal–agent problem*, which can be more than a little costly to stockholders. Witness the luxurious offices, corporate jets, limousines, and artwork that executives surround themselves with, not to mention the millions of dollars in salary they pay themselves. Managers gain all these personal benefits at the expense of stockholders.

A simple example will illustrate this point. Let's say that your cousin Ina, who is a whiz at writing software, has an idea for a program to speed up wireless Internet access. Together, the two of you estimate she needs $10,000 to write the program and sell it to an interested buyer. But Ina has only $1,000 in savings, so you will have to contribute $9,000. Family etiquette dictates that once you've made the investment, you won't be able to monitor Ina's progress—to tell whether she is working hard or even if she is working at all. If everything goes well, you think you can sell the program to Microsoft for $100,000, which is ten times the initial investment. But Ina had better work quickly or someone else may make it to market first and Ina's program won't be worth nearly as much.

The difficulty in this arrangement is immediately apparent. If Ina works hard and all goes according to plan, she will get 10 percent of the $100,000 (that's $10,000) and you will get the rest, a whopping $90,000. But if Ina runs into programming problems or spends part of the time surfing instead of working, someone else may output the product first, reducing the value of Ina's software to $10,000. The problem is, Ina's decision to go surfing would cost her only $9,000, but it would cost you $81,000! And since you wouldn't be able to tell why the venture failed, you're unlikely to part with your $9,000 in the first place.

"It's been moved and seconded that we fly the company plane to Zurich, split the bank accounts, and go our merry ways."

Solving the Moral Hazard Problem in Equity Financing   Solutions to the moral hazard problem in equity finance are hard to come by. Information on the quality of management can be useful, but only if owners have the power to fire managers—and that can be extremely difficult. Requiring managers to own a significant stake in their own firm is another possibility. If Ina comes up with the entire $10,000, then there is no separation between ownership and control and no question whether Ina will behave in the owner's interest—she is the owner. But people who have good ideas don't always have the resources to pursue them. Ina doesn't have the $10,000 she needs.

During the 1990s, a concerted attempt was made to align managers' interests with those of stockholders. Executives were given stock options that provided lucrative payoffs if a firm's stock price rose above a certain level. This approach worked until managers found ways to misrepresent their companies' profitability, driving up stock prices temporarily so they could cash in their options. Accounting methods have been reformed in an attempt to reduce such abuses, but at this writing, no one has devised a foolproof way of ensuring that managers will behave in the owners' interest instead of their own.

Moral Hazard in Debt Finance   When the managers of a company are the owners, the problem of moral hazard in equity financing disappears. This suggests that investors should prefer debt financing to equity financing. But debt financing has its problems, too. Imagine that instead of buying a 90 percent share in your cousin Ina's software venture, you lend her $9,000 at an 11 percent annual interest rate. The debt contract specifies that she will repay you $9,990 in one year's time. This arrangement dramatically changes Ina's incentives. Now, if she works hard, she gets $90,010, but if she goes surfing, she still has to repay the $9,990, leaving her nothing at the end of the year. Surely this solves your problem.

Moral hazard: How can you be sure that your investment isn't being used to buy one of these vacation homes in Tahiti?

Debt does go a long way toward eliminating the moral hazard problem inherent in equity finance, but it doesn't finish the job. Because debt contracts allow owners to keep all the profits in excess of the loan payments, they encourage risk taking. Suppose Ina decides to use some or all of the $10,000 to buy lottery tickets. That's an extremely risky thing to do. The problem is, if her lottery number comes up, she gets the winnings, but if she loses, you pay the cost. That's not a very desirable outcome for you, the lender. While in the real world the danger isn't quite that extreme, the problem still exists. Lenders need to find ways to make sure borrowers don't take too many risks. Unfortunately, borrowers' limited liability has the same effect that an insurance policy has on the insured. People with risky projects are attracted to debt finance because they get the full benefit of the upside, while the downside is limited to their collateral, if any.

Solving the Moral Hazard Problem in Debt Finance   To some degree, a good legal contract can solve the moral hazard problem that is inherent in debt finance. Bonds and loans often carry *restrictive covenants* that limit the amount of risk a borrower can assume. For example, a covenant may restrict the nature of the goods or services the borrower can purchase. It may require the firm to maintain a certain level of net worth, a minimum balance in a bank account, or a minimum credit rating. Home mortgages often come with restrictive covenants requiring the homeowners to purchase fire insurance or to make monthly deposits toward payment of their property taxes. (Failure to pay property taxes can cause the government to seize the borrower's house, complicating the mortgage company's attempt to recover its principal.)

Table 11.3   The Negative Consequences of Information Costs

1. **Adverse selection.** Lenders can't distinguish good from bad credit risks, which discourages transactions from taking place.
   Solutions include
   - Government-required information disclosure
   - Private collection of information
   - Pledging of collateral to insure lenders against the borrower's default
   - Requiring borrowers to invest substantial resources of their own

2. **Moral hazard.** Lenders can't tell whether borrowers will do what they claim they will do with the borrowed resources; borrowers may take too many risks.
   Solutions include
   - Requiring managers to report to owners
   - Requiring managers to invest substantial resources of their own
   - Covenants that restrict what borrowers can do with borrowed funds

Financial Intermediaries and Information Costs

The problems of adverse selection and moral hazard make direct finance expensive and difficult to get. These drawbacks lead us immediately to indirect finance and the role of financial institutions. Much of the information that financial intermediaries collect is used to reduce information costs and minimize the effects of adverse selection and moral hazard. To reduce the potential costs of adverse selection, intermediaries screen loan applicants. To minimize moral hazard, they monitor borrowers. And when borrowers fail to live up to their contracts with lenders, financial intermediaries penalize them by enforcing the contracts. Let's look more closely at how financial firms screen and monitor borrowers to reduce information costs.

Screening and Certifying to Reduce Adverse Selection

To get a loan, whether from a bank, a mortgage company, or a finance company, you must fill out an application. As part of the process, you will be asked to supply your social security number. The lender uses the number to identify you to a company that collects and analyzes credit information, summarizing it for potential lenders in a credit score.

Your personal credit score (described in Chapter 7 in Your Financial World: Your Credit Rating) tells a lender how likely you are to repay a loan. It is analogous to eBay's feedback forum rating or to an expert appraiser's certification of the authenticity and condition of an original painting. The credit rating company *screens* you and then *certifies* your credit rating. If you are a good credit risk with a high credit score, you are more likely than others to get a loan at a relatively low interest rate. Note that the company that collects your credit information and produces your credit score charges a fee each time someone wants to see it. This overcomes the free-rider problem.

Banks can collect information on a borrower that goes beyond what a loan application or credit report contains. By noting the pattern of deposits and withdrawals from your account, as well as your use of your debit card if you have one, they can learn more about you than you might like. Banks monitor both their individual and their business customers in this way. Again, the information they collect is easy to protect and use. The special information banks have puts them in an almost unique position to *screen* customers and reduce the costs of adverse selection. This expertise helps to explain another phenomenon, the fact that most small and medium-size businesses depend on banks for their financing.

Financial intermediaries' superior ability to screen and certify borrowers extends beyond loan making to the issuance of bonds and equity. Underwriters—large investment banks with solid reputations, like Citigroup, Goldman Sachs, and Merrill Lynch—screen and certify firms seeking to raise funds directly in the financial markets. Without certification by one of these firms, companies would find it difficult to raise funds. Investment banks go to great lengths to market their expertise as underwriters; they want people to recognize their names the world over, just as everyone recognizes Coca-Cola. A can of Coke, the best-selling soft drink in the world, is instantly recognizable, whether the fine print is in English, Chinese, Arabic, or Swedish. Financial institutions have applied this concept, which marketing people call branding, to their certification of financial products. If Goldman Sachs, a

In the financial world, Citigroup, Goldman Sachs, and Merrill Lynch have as much brand recognition as Coke does in the soft drink world.

SOURCE: © *Michael Schwartz / The Image Works*

well-known investment bank, is willing to sell a bond or stock, the brand name suggests it must be a high-quality investment.

Monitoring to Reduce Moral Hazard

If someone weren't watching over your shoulder, you might take the money you borrowed for a business project and fly off to Tahiti. To address the risk that sellers might take the money and run, eBay developed buyers' insurance. In the financial world, intermediaries insure against this type of moral hazard by monitoring both the firms that issue bonds and those that issue stocks.

Car dealers provide an interesting example of how this process works. Dealers have to finance all those shiny new cars that sit on the lot, waiting for buyers to show up. One way to do this is with a bank loan that is collateralized by the cars themselves. But the bank doesn't completely trust the dealer to use the loan proceeds properly. Every so often, the bank manager will send an associate to count the number of cars on the lot. The count tells the manager whether the dealer is using the borrowed funds properly. In monitoring the dealer this way, the bank is enforcing the restrictive covenants contained in the loan contract. Because banks specialize in this type of monitoring, they can do it more cheaply than individual borrowers and lenders.

Many financial intermediaries (other than banks) hold significant numbers of shares in individual firms. When they do, they find ways to monitor the companies' activities. For example, the California Public Employee Retirement System (CalPERS) manages well over $100 billion in assets, the income from which is used to pay retired employees' pensions. About 1.4 million "members" of CalPERS depend on the fund's managers to carefully monitor its investments. Before buying a company's stock, CalPERS' managers do a significant amount of research on the firm; once they have purchased the shares, they monitor the firm's activities very closely. In some cases, they place a representative on the company's board of directors to monitor and protect CalPERS' investment firsthand.

In the case of new companies, a financial intermediary called a venture capital firm does the monitoring. Venture capital firms specialize in investing in risky new *ventures* in return for a stake in the ownership and a share of the profits. To guard against moral hazard and ensure that the new company has the best possible chance of success, the venture capitalist keeps a close watch on the managers' actions.

Finally, the threat of a takeover helps to persuade managers to act in the interest of the stock- and bondholders. If managers don't do a good job of watching out for shareholders' interests, another company can always buy the firm and replace them. In the 1980s, some firms specialized in such tactics. (Michael Milken, whose exploits were summarized in Chapter 7, provided the funds for many takeovers.) When the new owners put their own people in charge of the firm, they eliminate the moral hazard problem.

APPLYING THE CONCEPT
HOW COMPANIES FINANCE INVESTMENT AND GROWTH

A corporation that wants to undertake an investment project can obtain financing in three ways: (1) directly from the financial markets, through the issuance of stocks or bonds; (2) from a financial intermediary, in the form of a loan; and (3) from its own profits. Recall that a company's profits are

continued on next page

continued from previous page

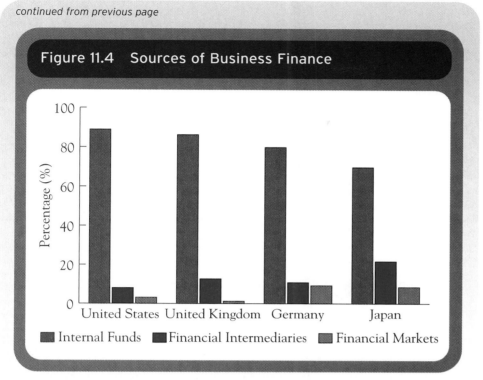

Figure 11.4   Sources of Business Finance

Source: Data are averages for 1970 to 1994, computed from Table 1 of Jenny Corbett and Tim Jenkinson, "How Is Investment Financed?" *The Manchester School Supplement*, 1997, pp. 69–93.

either distributed to shareholders in the form of dividends or retained by the firm. It is the firm's retained earnings that form the third source of investment financing.

Our discussion suggests that information problems make indirect, intermediated finance easier to get than direct finance from the financial markets. The data shown in Figure 11.4 bear that out.* In the United States, for example, financial intermediaries are twice as important as the financial markets as a source of business financing.

What is surprising in Figure 11.4, however, is the vast majority of financing that comes from internal sources. In both the United States and the United Kingdom, over 80 percent of business investment comes from internal sources. The only possible explanation for this fact is that information problems make external financing—obtained either directly from markets or indirectly from financial institutions—prohibitively expensive and difficult to get. It's not just individuals who have to finance their activities without any help. Businesses do, too. The fact that managers have superior information about how their firms are and should be run makes internal finance the rational choice.

*Note that the data used to construct Figure 11.4 are not comparable to those in Table 11.1. Not only do they come from a different source and cover a different period, but they also differ conceptually. Table 11.1 reports the average values of the stock market, marketable debt, and intermediated financing as a percentage of GDP; Figure 11.4 reports the relative percentage of funds raised through each of these mechanisms. As a result, for each country the numbers in Figure 11.4 sum to 100. In Table 11.1, they don't.

Terms

adverse selection, 270	free rider, 276
asymmetric information, 269	moral hazard, 270
collateral, 276	net worth, 276
deflation, 277	unsecured loan, 276
economies of scale, 265	venture capital firm, 282

Chapter Lessons

1. Financial intermediaries specialize in reducing costs by
   a. Pooling the resources of small savers and lending them to large borrowers.
   b. Providing customers with safekeeping and accounting services as well as access to the payments system.
   c. Providing customers with liquidity services.
   d. Allowing for diversification of risk by offering financial instruments in small denominations.
   e. Providing information services.

2. For potential lenders, investigating borrowers' trustworthiness is costly. This problem, known as asymmetric information, occurs both before and after a transaction.
   a. Before a transaction, the least creditworthy borrowers are the ones most likely to apply for funds. This problem, known as adverse selection, is similar to the "lemons" problem in the used-car market.
   b. Lenders and investors can reduce adverse selection by
      i. Collecting and disclosing information on borrowers.
      ii. Requiring borrowers to post collateral and show sufficient net worth.
   c. After a transaction, a borrower may not use the borrowed funds as productively as possible. This problem is known as moral hazard.
      i. In equity markets, moral hazard exists when the managers' interests diverge from the owners' interests.
      ii. Finding solutions to the moral hazard problem in equity financing is difficult.
      iii. In debt markets, moral hazard exists because borrowers have limited liability. They get the benefits when a risky bet pays off, but they don't suffer a loss when it doesn't.
      iv. The fact that debt financing gives managers/borrowers an incentive to take too many risks gives rise to restrictive covenants, which require borrowers to use funds in specific ways.

3. Financial intermediaries can solve the problems of adverse selection and moral hazard.
   a. They can reduce adverse selection by collecting information on borrowers and screening them to check their creditworthiness.
   b. They can reduce moral hazard by monitoring what borrowers are doing with borrowed funds.

Problems

1. Use the concept of adverse selection to explain why the value of a new car drops as soon as you drive it off the dealer's lot.

2. Describe the problem of asymmetric information that an employer faces in hiring a new employee. What solutions can you think of? Does the problem persist after the person has been hired? If so, how? What can be done about it? Is the problem more or less severe for employees on a fixed salary? Why or why not?

3. In some cities, newspapers publish a weekly list of restaurants that have been cited for health code violations by local health inspectors. What information problem is this feature designed to solve? How?

4. In some countries it is very difficult for shareholders to fire managers when they do a poor job. What type of financing would you expect to find in those countries?

5. Define the term *economies of scale* and explain how a financial intermediary can take advantage of such economies.

6. Explain the Internet's impact on asymmetric information problems.

   a. How can the Internet help to solve information problems?

   b. Can the Internet compound some information problems?

   c. On which problem would the Internet have a greater impact, adverse selection or moral hazard?

7. The financial sector is heavily regulated. Explain how government regulations help to solve information problems, increasing the effectiveness of financial markets and institutions.

8. Define deflation and explain how it reduces the value of a borrower's collateral. What is the effect on the information problems a lender faces?

9. How can a sharp rise in interest rates reduce the creditworthiness of potential borrowers?

10. Many insurance companies insist on a physical examination before insuring applicants for life insurance. Why do the companies collect this information? What might happen if they didn't?

11. In 2002 the trustworthiness of corporate financial reporting was called into question when a number of companies corrected their financial statements for past years. What impact did their action have on the financial markets?

12. Firms in some sectors of the economy have more leverage than firms in other parts. Explain how differences in businesses might create such differences in leverage.

13. Would you be happy or unhappy if a company whose stock you owned was bought by a leveraged buyout specialist who financed the purchase with junk bonds? Why?

14. Would you expect the lemons problem to be more or less severe in the emerging-markets countries of Latin America, Eastern Europe, and Asia than in the major industrialized countries? Why or why not? Does your answer depend on the stability of the countries' political regimes?

15. While it is possible to obtain medical insurance as an individual, it is cheaper to get it as part of a large group through your employer. Why?

www.mhhe.com/cecchettie

Chapter 12

Depository Institutions: Banks and Bank Management

Banks are the most visible financial intermediaries in the economy. Most of us use the word *bank* to describe what people in the financial world call depository institutions. These are the financial institutions that accept deposits from savers and make loans to borrowers. What distinguishes depository institutions from nondepository institutions is their primary source of funds—that is, the liability side of their balance sheets. Depository institutions include commercial banks, savings and loans, and credit unions—the financial intermediaries most of us encounter in the course of our day-to-day lives.

Banking is a business. Actually, it's a combination of businesses designed to deliver the services discussed in Chapter 11. One business provides the accounting and record-keeping services that track the balances in your accounts. Another grants you access to the payments system, allowing you to convert your account balances into cash or transfer them to someone else. Yet a third business pools the savings of many small depositors and uses them to make large loans to trustworthy borrowers. A fourth business offers customers diversification services, buying and selling financial instruments in the financial markets in an effort to make a profit. Banks trade in the financial markets not just as a service to their customers but in an effort to earn a profit for their owners as well.

The intent of banks, of course, is to profit from each of these lines of business. Our objective in this chapter is to see how they do it. Surprisingly, not all banks make a profit. While some banks are extremely large, with hundreds of billions of dollars in loans and securities on their balance sheets, their access to funds is no guarantee of profitability. The risk that banks may fail is a problem not just for their owners and managers but for the rest of us, too.

We have emphasized repeatedly that a thriving financial system is a precondition for economic growth. An economy that lacks the institutions to channel resources effectively from savers to investors will perform poorly. This statement applies regardless of whether a country is rich or poor. The United States and Japan provide a striking example. By virtually any standard, both countries are well off. Yet during the 1990s, U.S. banks made substantial profits, while Japanese banks suffered prodigious losses. At the same time, Japan's economy grew at a rate of just over 1 percent, while the U.S. economy grew at a rate well over 3 percent. The financial problems of Japanese banks played an important role in Japan's poor economic performance. Banks are important; when they are poorly managed, we all suffer.

In this chapter, we will examine the business of banking. We will see where depository institutions get their funds and what they do with them. That is, we will study the sources of banks' liabilities and learn how they manage their assets. And because banking is a risky business, we will examine the sources of risk that bankers face, as well as how those risks can be managed.

The Balance Sheet of Commercial Banks

To focus our discussion of depository institutions, we will concentrate on what are called *commercial banks*. These institutions were established to provide banking services to businesses, allowing them to deposit funds safely and borrow them when necessary. Today, many commercial banks offer accounts and loans to individuals as well. To understand the business of commercial banking, we'll start by examining the commercial bank's balance sheet. Recall that a balance sheet is a list of a household or firm's assets and liabilities: the sources of its funds (liabilities) and the uses to which those funds are put (assets). A bank's balance sheet says that

$$\text{Total bank assets} = \text{Total bank liabilities} + \text{Bank capital} \qquad (1)$$

Banks obtain their funds from individual depositors and businesses, as well as by borrowing from other financial institutions and through the financial markets. They use these funds to make loans, purchase marketable securities, and hold cash. The difference between a bank's assets and liabilities is the bank's capital, or *net worth*—the value of the bank to its owners. The bank's profits come both from service fees and from the difference between what the bank pays for its liabilities and the return it receives on its assets (a topic we'll return to later).

Table 12.1 shows a consolidated balance sheet for all the commercial banks in the United States in August of 2004. It reports the sum of all the items on all the balance sheets of the 7800 or so commercial banks that existed in the United States at the time. The government collects these statistics in the course of supervising and regulating the financial system, to ensure bank safety and soundness. The numbers in the table are also related to the measures of money discussed in Chapter 2. Recall that measures such as M1 and M2 include checking account balances, which are liabilities of the banking system.

Assets: Uses of Funds

Let's start with the asset side of the balance sheet—what banks do with the funds they raise. Table 12.1 shows that assets are divided into four broad categories: cash, securities, loans, and all other assets. Roughly 24 percent of assets, or $1.9 trillion, is held in the form of securities; 64 percent ($5 trillion), in the form of loans; and the remaining 12 percent in the form of cash and *"other assets."* The last category includes mostly buildings and equipment, as well as collateral repossessed from borrowers who defaulted. In looking at consolidated figures like the ones in Table 12.1, we can get some sense of their scale by comparing them to *nominal GDP*. In the spring of 2004, U.S. nominal GDP was roughly $11.6 trillion, so total bank assets were equivalent to about two-thirds of one year's GDP.

You should take some comfort in the fact that banks hold the vast majority of their assets in securities and loans. Only a small portion of deposits is held in cash in a bank vault. So if your bank is robbed, the crooks won't get *your* savings. (Even if a robbery did occur, virtually all banks carry insurance against such theft.)

Cash Items Cash assets are of three types. The first and most important is reserves. Banks hold reserves because regulations require it and because prudent business practice dictates it. Reserves include the cash in the bank's vault (and the currency in its ATM machines), called vault cash, as well as the bank's deposits at the Federal Reserve System. Cash is the most liquid of the bank's assets; the bank holds it to meet customers' withdrawal requests.

Table 12.1 Balance Sheet of U.S. Commercial Banks, August 2004

Assets in billions of dollars (numbers in parentheses are percentage of total assets)

Cash items (including reserves)		321.6	(4.1)
Securities		1,893.5	(23.9)
U.S. Government and agency	1,170.7 (14.8)		
State and local government and other	722.8 (9.1)		
Loans		5,044.6	(63.7)
Commercial and industrial	887.1 (11.2)		
Real estate (including mortgage)	2,411.6 (30.5)		
Consumer	672.3 (8.5)		
Interbank	364.7 (4.6)		
Other	708.9 (9.0)		
Other Assets		655.1	(8.3)
Total Commercial Bank Assets		**7,914.8**	

Liabilities in billions of dollars (numbers in parentheses are percentage of total liabilities)

Checkable deposits		645.0	(8.9)
Nontransaction deposits		4,487.7	(62.3)
Savings deposits and time deposits	3,340.9 (46.3)		
Large, negotiable time deposits	1,146.8 (15.9)		
Borrowings		1,589.0	(22.0)
From banks in U.S.	459.1 (6.4)		
From nonbanks in U.S.	1,129.9 (15.7)		
Other liabilities		487.4	(6.8)
Total Commercial Bank Liabilities		**7,209.1**	
Bank Assets – Bank Liabilities = Bank Capital		**705.7**	

SOURCE: *Data are for August 2004, seasonally adjusted, from "Assets and Liabilities of Commercial Banks in the United States," Board of Governors of the Federal Reserve System statistical release H.8, available at www.federalreserve.gov/releases/h8/current.*

Cash items also include what are called cash items in process of collection. When you deposit your paycheck into your checking account, several days may pass before your bank can collect the funds from your employer's bank. In the meantime, the uncollected funds are considered your bank's asset, since the bank is expecting to receive them.

Finally, cash includes the balances of the accounts that banks hold at other banks. In the same way that individuals have checking accounts at the local bank, small banks have deposit accounts at large banks, and those accounts are classified as cash. Over the years, the practice of holding such accounts has declined, so the total quantity of these so-called *correspondent bank* deposits has shrunk.

Banks hold a mere 5 percent of their assets in cash, and it's easy to understand why. Holding cash is expensive; because it earns no interest, cash has a high opportunity cost. That's why banks work hard to minimize the amount of cash they hold, turning as many of their assets as possible into profitable loans and securities.

Securities   The second largest component of bank assets is marketable securities. While banks in many countries can hold stock, U.S. banks cannot, so this category of assets includes only bonds. Banks' bond holdings are split between U.S. Treasury securities, which account for 14.8 percent of their assets, and state and local government bonds, which account for an additional 9.1 percent.[1] Most of these securities are very liquid. They can be sold quickly if the bank needs cash, which makes them a good backup for the bank's cash balances. For this reason securities are sometimes referred to as secondary reserves.

Figure 12.1 shows the trends in the composition of bank assets over the past half century. Focusing on the red line—the one representing securities—we can see that banks once held more than half their assets as securities, twice the proportion they hold today. While securities holdings have fallen, loans have risen in importance.

Loans   Loans are the primary asset of modern commercial banks, accounting for nearly two-thirds of assets. We can divide loans into five broad categories: *business loans, called commercial and industrial (C&I)* loans; real estate loans, including both home and commercial mortgages as well as home equity loans; consumer loans, like auto loans and credit card loans; interbank loans (loans made from one bank to another); and other types, including loans for the purchase of other securities. These types of loan vary considerably in their liquidity. Some, like home mortgages and auto loans, are easily securitized and resold. (We discussed this process in Chapter 3, in connection with asset-backed securities.) Others, like small business loans, can be nearly impossible to resell.

The primary difference among various kinds of depository institutions is in the composition of their loan portfolios. Commercial banks make loans primarily to businesses; savings and loans provide mortgages to individuals; credit unions specialize in consumer loans. See the Tools of the Trade box on page 294 for a more detailed description of the various types of depository institution.

Figure 12.1 shows that over the years, commercial banks have become more involved in the mortgage business. This change happened gradually for a number of reasons. First, the rise of the commercial paper market made direct finance more convenient for large firms, which reduced the quantity of commercial and industrial loans demanded. (Commercial paper is described in detail in Chapter 7.) Second, the creation of mortgage-backed securities meant that banks could sell the mortgage loans they had made. This innovation removed the risk associated with an illiquid asset, encouraging banks to move into the business of home lending. But as we will see later, mortgage lending still has its risks.

Liabilities: Sources of Funds

To finance their operations, banks need funds. They get them from savers and from borrowing in the financial markets. To entice individuals and businesses to place their funds in the bank, institutions offer a range of deposit accounts that provide safekeep-

---

[1]While there is nothing to prevent banks from holding corporate bonds, regulatory rules make the practice expensive. In Chapter 14 we will learn that banks are required to hold capital based on the composition of their balance sheets. The amount of capital required to extend a loan to a corporation is the same as the amount required to purchase a corporate bond. But since interest rates banks can charge on loans are generally higher than interest rates on bonds, there is no reason to purchase a bond.

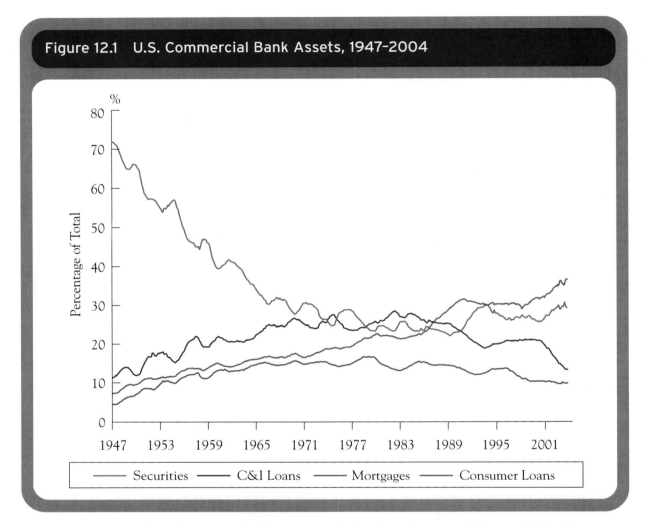

Figure 12.1 U.S. Commercial Bank Assets, 1947–2004

SOURCE: *Monthly data, seasonally adjusted from "Assets and Liabilities of Commercial Banks in the United States," Board of Governors of the Federal Reserve System Statistical Release H.8.*

ing and accounting services, access to the payments system, liquidity, and diversification of risk (see Chapter 11), as well as interest payments on the balance. There are two types of deposit account, transaction and nontransaction accounts. Transaction accounts are known as checkable deposits (which is what they are called in Table 12.1). Looking back at the table, you can see that banks obtain less than 10 percent of their funds from checkable deposits. Most of their funds come from nontransaction deposits, which account for 60 percent of commercial bank liabilities, and from borrowings, which make up an additional 20 percent.

Checkable Deposits   Banks offer customers a variety of options that fall into the category of checking accounts, including NOW, super-NOW, and insured market rate accounts. A typical bank will offer half a dozen or more of these, each with slightly different characteristics. In addition to the names created by banks' marketing departments, economists use various other terms in speaking of checkable deposits.

YOUR FINANCIAL WORLD
Choosing the Right Bank for You

Choosing the right bank takes some work. First, you should decide exactly why you need a bank and whether a particular bank will serve your needs conveniently and cheaply. Shop around for the best deal. Make sure the bank will pay a competitive interest rate on your deposit balance and you won't be paying for services you don't use. You may want to make sure the bank will give you immediate access to your deposits. The ability to reach someone either in person or on the phone during hours that are convenient for you is also important. And be sure the bank has a reputation for courteous, efficient service. Because service isn't cheap, ask what it will cost you. Will you have to pay a fee to see a teller in person? Will you have to pay a fee to cash a check? If you have friends with needs similar to yours, find out where they bank and ask whether they're happy with the cost and service.

The Internet has revolutionized banking. Traditional "bricks and mortar" banks now provide many of their services on the Internet. Using your computer, you can access your account, review and

pay your bills, or transfer funds. In fact, when you decide to open a bank account, you may be tempted to give your business to an Internet bank—one without any local branches. If you do, be careful. Looking at your computer screen, you may not be able to tell where the Web site you are viewing is physically located. While many people think the irrelevance of physical location is a real benefit of the Internet, in making financial transactions, it presents a challenge. Unfortunately, U.S. laws and regulations may not protect transactions with institutions located outside the United States. Instead, the laws and regulations of a foreign bank's home country may apply. So if you choose an Internet bank, make sure that its operations are located in the United States. The easiest way to find out is to verify that the bank is a member of the *Federal Deposit Insurance Corporation (FDIC)*. You can check by going to www.fdic.gov and clicking on "Is My Bank Insured?" If a bank is listed there, it is a legitimate U.S. bank, and your deposits will be insured.

For example, some economists call them "sight deposits," since a depositor can show up to withdraw them when the bank is in sight.

Over the years, financial innovation has reduced the importance of checkable deposits in the day-to-day business of banking. Figure 12.2 shows the dramatic drop in checkable deposits in recent decades, from 40 percent of liabilities in the early 1970s to less than 10 percent in 2004. The reason for their decline is that checking accounts pay little or no interest; they are a low-cost source of funds for banks but a low-return investment for depositors. As interest rates rose through the 1970s and remained high into the 1990s, individuals and businesses realized the benefits of reducing the balances in their checking accounts and began to look for ways to earn higher interest rates. Banks obliged by offering innovative accounts whose balances could be shifted automatically when the customers' checking accounts ran low.[2] Thus, traditional deposit accounts are no longer an important source of bank funds.

Nontransaction Deposits   In 2004, nontransaction deposits, including savings and time deposits, accounted for nearly two-thirds of all commercial bank liabilities. Savings deposits, commonly known as *passbook savings* accounts, were popular for many decades, though they are less so today. Time deposits are *certificates of deposit* (CDs) with a fixed maturity. When you place your savings in a CD at your local bank,

---

[2]This is also related to a practice called *deposit sweeping*, in which banks take checking account balances and put them into savings deposits, thereby reducing the level of reserves they are required to hold. The Tools of the Trade box in Chapter 17 describes this in detail.

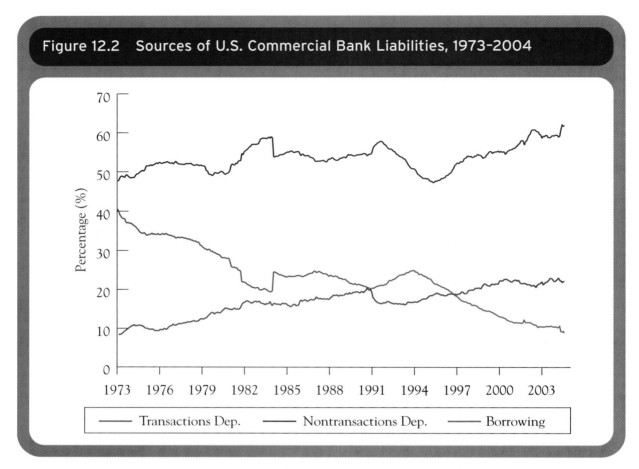

Figure 12.2 Sources of U.S. Commercial Bank Liabilities, 1973–2004

Transactions Dep.   Nontransactions Dep.   Borrowing

SOURCE: *Monthly data, seasonally adjusted from "Assets and Liabilities of Commercial Banks in the United States," Board of Governors of the Federal Reserve System Statistical Release H.8.*

it is as if you are buying a bond issued by that bank. But unlike government or corporate bonds, there isn't much of a resale market for your small CD. So if you want to withdraw your funds before the CD matures, you must get them back from the bank. To discourage early withdrawals, banks charge a significant penalty.

Certificates of deposit come in two varieties: small and large. Small CDs are issued for $100,000 or less; **large certificates of deposit** exceed $100,000 in face value. Large CDs are negotiable, which means that they can be bought and sold in the financial markets, just like bonds and commercial paper. Because large CDs can be resold, they have become an important source of bank financing. When a bank needs funds, it can issue large CDs, in addition to commercial paper and more conventional bonds.

Borrowings   Borrowing is the second most important source of bank funds. Figure 12.2 shows that borrowing has become increasingly important over the past quarter century. Today, borrowings account for over 20 percent of bank liabilities. Banks borrow in a number of ways. First, they can borrow from the Federal Reserve. We'll have much more to say about such **discount loans** in Part IV. For now, think of this source of funds as borrowing from the government. Banks rarely borrow in this way.

Figure 12.3 Mechanics of an Overnight Repurchase Agreement

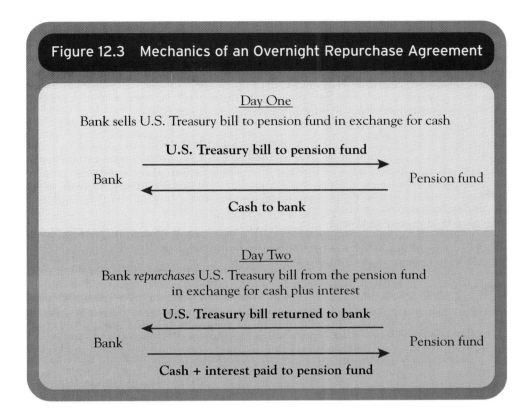

Day One

Bank sells U.S. Treasury bill to pension fund in exchange for cash

U.S. Treasury bill to pension fund

Bank → Pension fund

Cash to bank

Day Two

Bank *repurchases* U.S. Treasury bill from the pension fund
in exchange for cash plus interest

U.S. Treasury bill returned to bank

Bank Pension fund

Cash + interest paid to pension fund

More often, banks borrow from other banks. That is, banks with **excess reserves** will lend their surplus funds to banks that need them through an interbank market called the federal funds market. Loans made in the federal funds market are unsecured—they lack collateral—so the lending bank must trust the borrowing bank. Look back at the balance sheet in Table 12.1; you will see interbank loans listed as an asset and borrowings from banks in the United States listed as a liability.[3] Besides borrowing from U.S. banks in the federal funds market, commercial banks also borrow from foreign banks.

Finally, banks borrow using an instrument called a **repurchase agreement**, or **repo**, a short-term collateralized loan in which a security is exchanged for cash, with the agreement that the parties will reverse the transaction on a specific future date, as soon as the next day. For example, a bank that has a U.S. Treasury bill might need cash, while a pension fund might have cash that it doesn't need overnight. Through a repo, the bank would give the T-bill to the pension fund in exchange for cash, agreeing to buy it back—repurchase it—with interest the next day. In short, the bank gets an overnight loan and the pension fund gets some extra interest. The details are shown in Figure 12.3.

[3]An astute reader will notice that the amount of "Interbank loans" on the asset side of the balance sheet does not match the amount for "Borrowings from Banks in the U.S." on the liability side of the balance sheet. In fact, the two amounts differ by nearly $100 billion. If the data in the table cover the entire banking system, shouldn't loans to banks (assets) equal borrowings from banks (liabilities)? There are two reasons why the amounts do not match. First, the data in the table are constructed from a survey that covers all large banks but only a minority of small banks. Large banks tend to be borrowers, while small banks tend to be lenders. The way in which the data are collected, then, distorts the results. Second, small banks may report their lending to large banks as deposits rather than as interbank loans. For both these reasons, the entry on the liability side of Table 12.1 is larger than the corresponding entry on the asset side.

While the financial landscape is constantly shifting, it is safe to assume that depository institutions will be with us for some time. These are the financial intermediaries for whom deposits are the primary source of funds. There are three basic types of depository institution: commercial banks, savings institutions, and credit unions.

Commercial Banks.

A commercial bank is an institution that accepts deposits and uses the proceeds to make consumer, commercial, and real estate loans. Originally established to meet the needs of businesses, many of these banks now serve individual customers as well. Commercial banks tend to specialize as community, regional and super-regional, or money center banks.

Community Banks.

Community banks are small banks—those with assets of less than $1 billion—that concentrate on serving consumers and small businesses. These are the banks that take deposits from people in the local area and lend them back to local businesses and consumers. Of the more than 7,800 banks in the United States at the end of 2003, nearly 7,300 were community banks.

Regional and Super-Regional Banks.

Regional and super-regional banks are larger than community banks and much less local. Besides consumer and residential loans, these banks also make commercial and industrial loans. Regional banks obtain their funds through borrowing as well as from deposits. These banks can be very large. For example, Bank of America, a super-regional bank with assets of $933 billion, was the second largest bank in the United States in 2004.

Money Center Banks.

A few large banks—only five or six—do not rely primarily on deposit financing. These banks rely instead on borrowing for their funding. They stand at the center of the *money market,* the market for short-term debt. Citigroup and JP Morgan Chase are two examples. (Recall from Chapter 3 that money-market instruments are bonds with a maturity of less than 12 months.)

Savings Institutions.

Savings institutions are financial intermediaries that were established to serve households and individuals. They provide both mortgage and lending services and a place for households to deposit their savings. There are two types of savings institutions, S&Ls and savings banks.

Savings and Loan Institutions.

Savings and loan institutions (S&Ls) were established in the 1800s to help factory workers become homeowners. They accepted workers' savings deposits and used the funds to make loans to homebuyers, most of who were not served by traditional banks. These institutions traditionally specialized in taking short-term deposits and turning them into residential mortgages. The S&Ls that still exist today engage in a much broader range of financial activities.

Savings Banks.

Most savings banks are mutually owned. That is, the depositors are also the legal owners. These institutions specialize in residential mortgages that are funded by deposits. They are permitted to exist only in certain states. Washington Mutual, headquartered in Seattle, is one of the largest.

Credit Unions.

Credit unions are nonprofit depository institutions that are owned by people with a common bond—members of police associations, union members, university students and employees. Credit unions specialize in making small consumer loans. They originated in the 19th century to meet the needs of people who could not borrow from traditional lenders. Before credit unions existed, many ordinary people had nowhere to turn when they faced unexpected home repairs or medical emergencies. The Navy and Pentagon credit unions, as well as those that serve employees of organizations like Boeing, United Airlines, and various state governments, are among the largest.

Not all these depository institutions are likely to survive the financial innovations and economic upheaval of the coming decades. Commercial banks will likely remain with us, but savings institutions have already declined in importance and are at risk of disappearing altogether due to changes in the mortgage business. Whether credit unions remain viable will depend on their continuing ability to exploit their advantage in verifying members' creditworthiness.

Bank Capital and Profitability

Net worth equals assets minus liabilities, whether we are talking about an individual's net worth or a bank's. In the case of banks, however, net worth is referred to as **bank capital**, or *equity capital*. If the bank's owners sold all its assets (without taking a loss) and used the proceeds to repay all the liabilities, capital is what would be left. We can think of capital as the owners' stake in the bank.

Capital is the cushion banks have against a sudden drop in the value of their assets or an unexpected withdrawal of liabilities. It provides some insurance against insolvency (the inability to repay debts when a firm's liabilities exceed its assets). An important component of bank capital is **loan loss reserves**, an amount the bank sets aside to cover potential losses from defaulted loans. At some point a bank gives up hope that a loan will be repaid and the loan is *written off*, or erased from the bank's balance sheet. At that point the loan loss reserve is reduced by the amount of the loan that has defaulted.

Looking once again at the balance sheet in Table 12.1 (page 288), we can see that in August of 2004, bank capital in the U.S. commercial banking system totaled a bit over $700 billion. That $700 billion was combined with $7.2 trillion worth of liabilities to purchase $7.9 trillion in assets. So the ratio of debt to equity in the U.S. banking system was roughly 10 to 1. That's a substantial amount of leverage. (Recall that the term *leverage* refers to the portion of an asset that is purchased using borrowed funds.)

To put this ratio of 10 to 1 into perspective, we can compare it to the debt-to-equity ratio for nonfinancial businesses in the United States, which is only 1 to 1. Household leverage is much lower, less than $\frac{1}{4}$ to 1.[4] Recall from Tools of the Trade in Chapter 5 that leverage increases both risk and the expected return. If you contribute half the purchase price of a house and borrow the other half, both your risk and your expected return double. If you contribute one-fifth of the purchase price and borrow the other four-fifths, your risk and expected return go up by a factor of 5 (see the Tools of the Trade box in Chapter 5). So if a bank borrows $10 for each $1 in capital, its risk and expected return increase a whopping 11 times! Banking, it seems, is a very risky business. As we will see in Chapter 14, one of the explanations for the relatively high degree of leverage in banking is the existence of government guarantees like deposit insurance, which allow banks to capture the benefits of risk taking without subjecting depositors to potential losses.

There are several basic measures of bank profitability. The first is called **return on assets (ROA)**. Return on assets equals a bank's net profit after taxes divided by the bank's total assets:

$$ROA = \frac{\text{Net profit after taxes}}{\text{Total bank assets}} \qquad (2)$$

ROA is an important measure of how efficiently a particular bank uses its assets. By looking at the different units' ROAs, for example, the manager of a large bank can also compare the performance of the bank's various lines of business. But for the bank's owners, return on assets is less important than the return on their own investment, which is leveraged at an average ratio of 11 to 1. The bank's return to its owners is

---

[4]You can arrive at these figures yourself by looking at the *Flow of Funds Accounts of the United States,* which is computed by the Board of Governors of the Federal Reserve (see its Web site). The appropriate tables are B.100 for households and B.102 for nonfarm nonfinancial corporate business; both include assets, liabilities, and net worth for their parts of the U.S. economy.

APPLYING THE CONCEPT

U.S. COMMERCIAL BANK PROFITABILITY IN THE 1990S

To see how profitable U.S. banks are, let's look at some numbers. Table 12.2 reports various measures for the entire commercial banking industry in 1991, 1996, and 2001. Notice first that U.S. banks do very well at their traditional deposit and lending operations. Their net interest margin (fourth line from the bottom) is between $3\frac{1}{4}$ and $3\frac{1}{2}$ percent. Banks turn this margin into a tidy profit. While some years are better than others, return on equity is usually more than 15 percent.

Note too the trend in the composition of bank revenue—how the banking industry makes its profits. The last line of Table 12.2 shows that throughout the early 1990s, net interest income was roughly two-thirds of total income. But by 2001, the proportion had dropped to about 58 percent. Today, fee income rather than interest accounts for nearly half of bank income in the United States. Much of this newly important source comes from off-balance-sheet activities, discussed in the next section.

continued on next page

measured by the **return on equity (ROE)**, which equals the bank's net profit after taxes divided by the bank's capital:

$$ROE = \frac{\text{Net profit after taxes}}{\text{Bank capital}} \tag{3}$$

Not surprisingly, ROA and ROE are related to leverage. One measure of leverage is the ratio of bank assets to bank capital. Multiplying ROA by this ratio yields ROE:

$$\mathbf{ROA} \times \frac{\text{Bank assets}}{\text{Bank capital}} = \frac{\text{Net profit after taxes}}{\text{Total bank assets}} \times \frac{\text{Bank assets}}{\text{Bank capital}}$$

$$= \frac{\text{Net profit after taxes}}{\text{Bank capital}} = \mathbf{ROE} \tag{4}$$

For a typical U.S. bank, the return on assets is 1.2 percent, while the return on equity is 12 to 14 times that high. For large banks, the return on equity tends to be higher than for small banks, which suggests the existence of significant economies of scale in banking.[5] The differential is one possible explanation for the current trend toward bank mergers and ever-larger banks.

Before continuing, it is important to introduce one more measure of bank profitability: net interest income. This measure is related to the fact that banks pay interest on their liabilities, creating interest expenses, and receive interest on their assets, creating interest income. Deposits and bank borrowing create interest expenses; securities and loans generate interest income. The difference between the two is the bank's **net interest income**.

---

[5]Interestingly, while large banks' ROEs exceed those of small banks, their ROAs do not. The implication is that large banks are better than small ones at managing the risks associated with leverage.

continued from previous page

Table 12.2   Profitability of U.S. Commercial Banks

(in millions of dollars, except bottom four rows)

	1991	1996	2001
A. Interest income - Interest expense (Net interest income)	$121,288	$161,172	$210,809
B. Other revenue*	58,482	92,515	153,734
C. Operating costs	124,233	159,241	218,706
D. Gross profit (A + B - C)	55,537	94,446	145,837
E. Loan losses (provisions)	34,128	15,483	41,008
F. Net operating profit (D - E)	21,409	78,963	104,829
G. Realized capital gains from sale of real estate	2,971	530	4,434
H. Net profits before taxes (F + G)	24,380	79,493	109,263
I. Assets	3,420,381	4,554,234	6,454,543
Net interest margin (A/I)	0.0355%	0.0354%	0.0327%
Return on assets (H/I) (ROA)	0.0071	0.0175	0.0169
Return on equity (ROE)	0.1258	0.2147	0.1860
Net interest income/Total income [A/(A + B)]	0.6747	0.6353	0.5782

*Includes fee income and profits from trading on own account but excludes capital gains from real estate sales (G).

SOURCE: Table 1 in Anil K Kashyap, "Sorting Out Japan's Financial Crisis," *Economic Perspectives of the Federal Reserve Bank of Chicago*, 4th Quarter 2002, 42–55. Return on equity is computed using information from Table CB14, "Liabilities and Equity Capital FDIC-Insured Commercial Banks, United States and Other Areas, Balances at End of Year, 1934–2001," on the Federal Deposit Insurance Corporation Web site, www.fdic.gov.

Net interest income can also be expressed as a percentage of total assets to yield a quantity called **net interest margin**. This is the bank's **interest-rate spread**, which is the (weighted) average difference between the interest rate received on assets and the interest rate paid for liabilities. A bank's net interest margin is closely related to its return on assets. Just take the bank's fee income minus its operating costs, divide by total assets, add the result to the net interest margin, and you get its ROA. Roughly equivalent to a manufacturer or retailer's gross profits and gross profit margin, net interest income and net interest margin reveal a great deal about a bank's business.

Well-run banks have high net interest income and a high net interest margin. And since we would expect most of a bank's loans to be repaid, net interest margin tells us not just current profitability but future profitability as well; it is a forward-looking measure. If a bank's net interest margin is currently improving, its profitability is likely to improve in the future.

Off-Balance-Sheet Activities

A financial firm's balance sheet provides only so much information. To generate fees, banks engage in numerous off-balance-sheet activities. Recall that banks exist to reduce transactions costs and information costs as well as to transfer risks. When they perform these services, bankers expect to be compensated. Yet many of these activities do not appear as either assets or liabilities on the bank's balance sheet, even though they may represent an important part of a bank's profits.

For example, banks often provide trusted customers with lines of credit, which are similar to the credit limits on credit cards. The firm pays the bank a fee in return for the ability to borrow whenever necessary. When the agreement is signed, the bank receives the payment and the firm receives a loan commitment. However, not until a loan has actually been made—until the firm has *drawn down* the credit line—does the transaction appear on the bank's balance sheet.

In the meantime, the bank is compensated for reducing both transactions and information costs. Without the loan commitment, the firm would find credit difficult and potentially expensive to obtain on short notice (a transactions cost). And since the bank usually knows the firms to which it grants lines of credit, the cost of establishing their creditworthiness (an information cost) is negligible.

Letters of credit are another important off-balance-sheet item for banks. These letters guarantee that a customer of the bank will be able to make a promised payment. For example, a U.S. importer of television sets may need to reassure a Chinese exporter that the firm will be able to pay for the imported goods when they arrive. This customer might request that the bank send a *commercial letter of credit* to the Chinese exporter guaranteeing payment for the goods on receipt. By issuing the letter of credit, the bank substitutes its own guarantee for the U.S. importer's credit risk, enabling the transaction to go forward. In return for taking this risk, the bank receives a fee.

A related form of the letter of credit is called a *standby letter of credit*. These letters, which are issued to firms and governments that wish to borrow in the financial markets, are a form of insurance. Commercial paper, even when it is issued by a large, well-known firm, must be backed by a standby letter of credit that promises the bank will repay the lender should the issuer default. What is true for large corporations is true for state and local governments as well: in most cases, they need a bank guarantee to issue debt. As with loan commitments, letters of credit expose the bank to risk in a way that is not readily apparent on the bank's balance sheet.

Because off-balance-sheet activities create risk for financial institutions, they have come under increasing scrutiny in recent years. Recall the case of Long-Term Capital Management (LTCM), which we discussed in Chapter 9. While LTCM's balance sheet carried assets worth over $100 billion when the firm got into trouble, the risky instruments that did *not* appear on its balance sheet—the $1.25 trillion in interest-rate swaps—were what scared everyone. By allowing for the transfer of risk, modern financial instruments enable individual institutions to concentrate risk in ways that are very difficult for outsiders to discern.

"What I'd like, basically, is a temporary line of credit just to tide me over the rest of my life."

YOUR FINANCIAL WORLD

The Cost of Payday Loans

If you drive through the streets of most U.S. cities, you will eventually pass a store with a sign saying "Checks Cashed." These financial intermediaries provide loans to people who cannot borrow from mainstream financial institutions such as banks. In addition to their check-cashing business—they charge about 3 percent to cash a payroll or government check, more if the bearer can't produce acceptable identification—these firms offer small loans.

The most common type of loan these stores offer is a *payday loan*. To get one, you just walk into the store with an ID card, a utility or phone bill, a checkbook, and some pay stubs; you come out with cash. Why do you need all these documents? The utility bill proves where you live; the pay stubs establish that you are employed, how much you make, and when you are paid. You need the checkbook so you can write a check that the store will hold until your next payday, when it will send your check to the bank. With just these few requirements, the store will lend you up to $500 for the week or two weeks until you are paid.

The catch is that there is a fee, and it's huge. Payday lenders charge a fee equal to 15 percent of the loan's principal. So if you borrow $500, you will

have to repay a minimum of $575. That's the size of the check you will need to write to get the loan. To understand what this arrangement can mean, suppose that you need to renew the loan on your next payday, so you don't want the lender to cash the check you gave him or her initially. To do this, you will have to pay the fee again. So you keep the loan for a year, paying $75 every two weeks to stay current. At the end of the year you will have paid $1,950 in "interest" (the lender calls it "fees") on a $500 loan. And if you're not careful, you'll still owe the original $500!*

Not surprisingly, at these interest rates, payday loans appeal only to people who can't get credit anywhere else. While data are hard to come by, it appears that well over half of payday borrowers fail to repay their loans, which explains the high fees. These loans, though legal, are for the truly desperate.

*Just in case you think that this can't really happen, several years ago a U.S. Navy Petty Officer took out four payday loans totaling $2,085. After four months, he had paid the lender $7,000 but the amount owed had not decreased. See Rhonda Cook, "Misery at High Interest: Military Wants War on 'Payday Loans,'" *Atlanta Journal-Constitution*, December 4, 2003, p. 1A.

Bank Risk: Where It Comes from and What to Do about It

Banking is risky both because depository institutions are highly leveraged and because of what they do. The bank's goal is to make a profit in each of its lines of business. Some of these are simply fee-for-service activities. For example, a financial institution might act as a broker, buying and selling stocks and bonds on a customer's behalf and charging a fee in return. Banks also transform deposit liabilities into assets such as loans and securities. In the process, they pool savings, provide liquidity services, allow for diversification of risk, and capitalize on the advantages they have in producing information. All along, the goal is to pay less for the deposits the bank receives than for the loans it makes and the securities it buys. That is, the interest rate the bank pays to attract liabilities must be lower than the return it receives on assets.

In the process of all these activities, the bank is exposed to a host of risks. They include the chance that depositors will suddenly withdraw their balances, that borrowers will not repay their loans, that interest rates will change, and that the bank's securities trading operation will do poorly. Each of these risks has a name: *liquidity risk,*

RISK

credit risk, *interest-rate risk*, and *trading risk*. To understand how these risks arise and what can be done about them, we will look at each in detail.

Liquidity Risk

All financial institutions face the risk that their liabilities holders (depositors) will seek to cash in their claims. The holder of a checking account can always walk into the bank and ask for the balance in cash. This risk of a sudden demand for liquid funds is called liquidity risk. Banks face liquidity risk on both sides of their balance sheets. Deposit withdrawal is a liability-side risk, but there is an asset-side risk as well. Recall from our discussion of off-balance-sheet activities that banks provide firms with lines of credit—promises to make loans on demand. When this type of loan commitment is claimed, or *taken down*, the bank must find the liquidity to cover it.

If the bank cannot meet customers' requests for immediate funds, it runs the risk of failure. Even if a bank has a positive net worth, illiquidity can still drive it out of business. Who would put their funds in a bank that can't always provide cash on demand? For this reason, bankers are extremely serious about managing liquidity risk.

To fully understand liquidity risk and how banks manage it, let's look at a simplified balance sheet. Figure 12.4 shows a stripped-down version of the balance sheet of a hypothetical individual bank. Keep in mind that the two sides of a balance sheet must always balance. Any change in the level of assets must be mirrored by an equal change in the level of liabilities.

Figure 12.4 Balance Sheet of a Bank Holding $5 Million in Excess Reserves

Assets		Liabilities	
Reserves	$15 million	Deposits	$100 million
Loans	$100 million	Borrowed funds	$30 million
Securities	$35 million	Bank capital	$20 million

In Figure 12.4 bank liabilities are composed primarily of deposits, along with some borrowing and $20 million of bank capital. Liabilities total $150 million. The bank's assets include $15 million in reserves. Banking regulations require that banks hold a portion of their assets either as vault cash or as noninterest-bearing deposits at the Fed. That portion is stated as a specific percentage of the bank's deposits. If we assume that required reserves are 10 percent of deposits, then the $100 million in deposits shown on the balance sheet means that the bank is required to hold $10 million in reserves. The fact that the bank is holding $15 million in reserves means that it has $5 million in *excess reserves*.

To assess liquidity risk, we need to ask how the bank will handle a customer's demand for funds. What happens if a corporate customer arrives at the bank and requests a withdrawal of $5 million? Since the bank has $5 million in excess reserves, it can honor the customer's request immediately, without difficulty. Similarly, if the bank were forced suddenly to honor a $5 million loan commitment, it could do so by drawing down its reserves. In the past, this was a common way to manage liquidity risk;

banks would simply hold sufficient excess reserves to accommodate customers' withdrawals. This is a passive way to manage liquidity risk.

The problem is, holding excess reserves is expensive, since it means forgoing the interest that could be earned on loans or securities. Banks work hard to find other ways to manage the risk of sudden withdrawals and drawdowns of loan commitments. There are two other ways to manage the risk that customers will require cash: The bank can adjust its assets or its liabilities. To see how it's done, let's look at Figure 12.5. This bank has $10 million in reserves to back its $100 million in deposits, so it has no excess reserves. If a customer makes a $5 million withdrawal, the bank can't simply deduct it from reserves. Instead, the bank will need to adjust another part of its balance sheet.[6]

Figure 12.5   Balance Sheet of a Bank Holding No Excess Reserves

Assets		Liabilities	
Reserves	$10 million	Deposits	$100 million
Loans	$100 million	Borrowed funds	$30 million
Securities	$40 million	Bank capital	$20 million

This bank has two choices in responding to the shortfall created by the $5 million withdrawal: It can adjust either its assets or its liabilities. On the asset side, the bank has several options. The quickest and easiest one is to sell a portion of its securities portfolio. Since some of them are almost surely U.S. Treasury securities, they can be sold quickly and easily at relatively low cost. The result of this action is shown in the top panel of Figure 12.6. Note that assets and liabilities are both $5 million lower than they were prior to the withdrawal (compare Figure 12.5). Banks that are particularly concerned about liquidity risk can structure their securities holdings to facilitate such sales.

A second possibility is for the bank to sell some of its loans to another bank. This option is shown in the bottom panel of Figure 12.6. While not all loans can be sold, some can. Banks generally make sure that a portion of the loans they hold are marketable for just such purposes.

Yet another way to handle the bank's need for liquidity is to refuse to renew a customer loan that has come due. Corporate customers have short-term loans that are periodically renewed, so the bank always has the option of refusing to extend the loan again for another week, month, or year. But this course of action is not very appealing. Failing to renew a loan is guaranteed to alienate the customer and could well drive the customer to another bank. Recall from Chapter 11 that banks specialize in solving information problems by screening to find customers who are creditworthy and then monitoring them to ensure they repay their loans. The idea is to separate good customers from bad ones and develop long-term relationships with the good ones. The last thing a bank wants to do is to refuse a loan to a creditworthy customer it has gone to some trouble and expense to find.

Moreover, bankers do not like to meet their deposit outflows by contracting the asset side of the balance sheet because doing so shrinks the size of the bank. And since

[6]If you're thinking that the bank can finance part of the withdrawal from reserves, since the $5 million withdrawal will reduce required reserves by $500,000, you're right. But that still leaves the bank $4.5 million short.

Figure 12.6 Balance Sheet of a Bank Following a $5 Million Withdrawal and Asset Adjustment

Withdrawal Is Met by Selling Securities

Assets		Liabilities	
Reserves	$10 million	Deposits	$95 million
Loans	$100 million	Borrowed funds	$30 million
Securities	$35 million	Bank capital	$20 million

Withdrawal Is Met by Reducing Loans

Assets		Liabilities	
Reserves	$10 million	Deposits	$95 million
Loans	$95 million	Borrowed funds	$30 million
Securities	$40 million	Bank capital	$20 million

banks make a profit by turning liabilities into assets, the smaller their balance sheets, the lower their profits. For this reason alone, today's bankers prefer to use liability management to address liquidity risk. That is, instead of selling assets in response to a deposit withdrawal, they find other sources of funds.

There are two ways for banks to obtain additional funds. First, they can borrow to meet the shortfall, either from the Federal Reserve or from another bank. The result of such an action is shown in the top panel of Figure 12.7. As you can see, while deposits have fallen by $5 million, borrowing has made up the difference.

A second way to adjust liabilities in response to a deposit outflow is to attract additional deposits. The most common way to do so is to issue large-denomination CDs (with a value over $100,000).[7] In the bottom panel of Figure 12.7, these nontransaction deposits are combined with checking accounts. As we saw earlier, large certificates of deposit have become an increasingly important source of funds for banks. Now we know why: It is because they allow banks to manage their liquidity risk without changing the asset side of their balance sheets.

Credit Risk

Banks profit from the difference between the interest rate they pay to depositors and the interest rate they receive from borrowers. That is, the return on their assets exceeds the cost of their liabilities. At least, that's the idea. But to ensure that this profit-making process works, for the bank to make a profit, borrowers must repay their loans. There is always some risk that they won't. The risk that a bank's loans will not

---

[7]Unlike transactions deposits such as checking accounts, CDs are not subject to a reserve requirement. Thus, a change in the composition of a bank's deposits affects the level of reserves it is required to hold and hence its balance sheet.

Figure 12.7   Balance Sheet of a Bank Following a $5 Million Withdrawal and Liability Adjustment

Withdrawal Is Met by Borrowing

Assets		Liabilities	
Reserves	$10 million	Deposits	$95 million
Loans	$100 million	Borrowed funds	$35 million
Securities	$40 million	Bank capital	$20 million

Withdrawal Is Met by Attracting Deposits

Assets		Liabilities	
Reserves	$10 million	Deposits	$100 million
Loans	$100 million	Borrowed funds	$30 million
Securities	$40 million	Bank capital	$20 million

be repaid is called credit risk. To manage their credit risk, banks use a variety of tools. The most basic are diversification, in which the bank makes a variety of different loans to spread the risk, and credit risk analysis, in which the bank examines the borrower's credit history to determine the appropriate interest rate to charge.

Diversification means spreading risk as widely as possible, which can be difficult for banks, especially those that focus on certain kinds of lending. Since banks specialize in information gathering, it is tempting to try to gain a competitive advantage in a narrow line of business. The problem is, if a bank lends in only one geographic area or only one industry, it exposes itself to economic downturns that are local or industry-specific. It is important that banks find a way to hedge such risks, if they should arise.

INFORMATION

Credit risk analysis produces information that is very similar to the bond rating systems discussed in Chapter 7. There we saw that rating agencies like Moody's and Standard & Poor's produce letter ratings for large corporations wishing to issue bonds. Banks do the same for small firms wishing to borrow, and credit rating agencies perform the service for individual borrowers (see Your Financial World: Your Credit Rating in Chapter 7). Credit risk analysis uses a combination of statistical models and information that is specific to the loan applicant. The result is an assessment of the likelihood that a particular borrower will default. When the bank's loan officers decide to make a loan, they use the customer's credit rating to determine how high an interest rate to charge. To the interest rate they must pay on their liabilities, they add a markup that will allow them to make a profit. The poorer a borrower's credit rating, the higher the interest rate they will charge.[8]

---

[8]Banks can also manage their credit risk by selling *credit derivatives*, a type of option (discussed in Chapter 9) that allows lenders to insure themselves against changes in borrowers' credit ratings. For example, a bank could buy insurance that a particular borrower will not default on a specific loan. For a detailed discussion, see José Lopez, "Financial Instruments for Mitigating Credit Risk," *Federal Reserve Bank of San Francisco Economic Letter*, no. 2001–34, November 23, 2001.

Lending is plagued by the asymmetric information problems discussed in Chapter 11. Because of adverse selection, borrowers with risky projects are more likely than others to apply for loans. And because borrowers have an incentive to take too much risk once they have received the loan, moral hazard is a problem as well. As we saw earlier, financial institutions can mitigate these problems through a combination of methods. They can screen loan applications, monitor borrowers once they receive a loan, and demand that borrowers either put up collateral or demonstrate a high net worth. Moreover, by developing a long-term relationship, banks can reduce the need to collect new information every time the customer needs a new loan.

Interest-Rate Risk

Because banks are in the business of turning deposit liabilities into loan assets, the two sides of their balance sheet do not match up. One important difference between the two sides is that a bank's liabilities tend to be short term, while its assets tend to be long term. This mismatch between the maturities of the two sides of the balance sheet creates **interest-rate risk**.

To understand the problem, think of both the bank's assets and its liabilities as bonds. That is, the bank's deposit liabilities are just like bonds, as are its loan assets. (The bank must be holding some capital as well.) We know that a change in interest rates will affect the value of a bond; when interest rates rise, the price of a bond falls.

APPLYING THE CONCEPT
ENDING DISCRIMINATION IN LENDING

For many years, banks routinely accepted deposits from households in low-income neighborhoods but refused to lend funds to people in those areas. In this practice, known as *redlining*, loan officers would literally draw a line on a map and lend only to those people who lived on one side of the line. The problem was particularly acute in inner cities, where neither businesses nor individuals could obtain financing for normal activities like building and renovation. Redlining contributed to the decline of inner cities, which became increasingly unpleasant and dangerous places.

To understand the reasons for redlining, imagine that a bank's loan officers are considering loan applications from two neighborhoods, each of which offers a wide variety of loan opportunities. These lenders will make loans in both neighborhoods until, holding the interest rate and other relevant factors fixed, the riskiness of the loans in the two neighborhoods is equal. In this way the bank controls its credit risk. But if one of the neighborhoods offers only high-risk opportunities, all the bank's lending will be funneled into the low-risk neighborhood. That is essentially what happened to the inner cities. From the banker's perspective, redlining was just a way to control credit risk. Default rates were so high in some areas, managers said, that responsible lenders simply did not risk lending there.* Unfortunately, given the racial composition of many high-risk neighborhoods, the policy looked discriminatory even though it may have been color-blind.

More important, the longer the term of the bond is, the greater the change in the bond's price at any given change in the interest rate. (Refer back to Chapter 4 to refresh your memory.) Thus, when interest rates rise, banks face the risk that the value of their assets will fall more than the value of their liabilities (reducing the bank's capital). Put another way, if a bank makes long-term loans, it receives payments from borrowers that do not vary with the interest rate. But its short-term liabilities—those with variable interest rates—require the bank to make larger payments when interest rates rise. So rising interest rates reduce revenues relative to expenses, directly reducing the bank's profits.

The best way to see this point is to focus on a bank's revenue and expenses. Let's start by dividing the bank's assets and liabilities into two categories, those that are interest-rate sensitive and those that are not. The term *interest-rate sensitive* means that a change in interest rates will change the revenue produced by an asset. Since newly purchased short-term bonds always reflect a change in interest rates, short-term bonds that are constantly maturing and being replaced with new ones produce interest-rate-sensitive revenue. In contrast, when the bank purchases long-term bonds, it receives a fixed stream of revenue. Purchasing a 5 percent, 10-year bond means getting $5 per $100 of face value for 10 years, regardless of what happens to interest rates in the meantime. So the revenue stream from a long-term bond is not interest-rate sensitive.

Suppose that 20 percent of a bank's assets fall into the first category, those that are sensitive to changes in the interest rate. Another 80 percent fall into the second category,

continued from previous page

Under the assumption that discrimination explained at least part of the observed geographic pattern in lending, in the mid-1970s Congress enacted a series of laws designed to mitigate the problem. In 1975, the Home Mortgage Disclosure Act (HMDA, pronounced "hum dah") required lenders to provide data on their mortgage-lending patterns to ensure there would be no discrimination. And in 1977 the Community Reinvestment Act (CRA) stipulated that depository institutions must lend in the areas where they operate, so that if a bank takes deposits in the inner city, it must make loans there, too.

A quarter century later, these programs have been at least partially successful in encouraging lending in previously redlined areas. Data collected under HMDA are used widely by bank regulators to ensure nondiscriminatory lending. And while bank managers complain bitterly about the paperwork required to establish compliance with the CRA, the regulation appears to have produced many new loans in previously underserved areas.[†]

*The problem of adverse selection, described in Chapter 11, can cause loan markets to fail, giving the appearance of discrimination. Recall that adverse selection arises because a lender can't judge the creditworthiness of a potential borrower. One solution to the problem would be to charge a high interest rate to compensate for the possibility that the loan might be extremely risky. But at a high interest rate, the borrower must be highly successful to pay back the loan—not a likely scenario. So the higher the interest rate is, the lower the chance of repayment, which forces the interest rate even higher. In the end, there is no interest rate at which the lender is both willing to make the loan and secure in the knowledge that the borrower will be able to repay. The result is that risky borrowers cannot obtain loans.

[†]The impact of the CRA on the availability of financing to inner-city residents, especially African Americans, is the subject of substantial disagreement. For a summary of the CRA's impact, past and projected, see William C. Apgar and Mark Duda, "The Twenty-fifth Anniversary of the Community Reinvestment Act: Past Accomplishments," *Economic Policy Review* of the Federal Reserve Bank of New York, 2003.

those that are not sensitive to changes in the interest rate. If the interest rate has been stable at 5 percent for some time, then for each $100 in assets, the bank receives $5 in interest.

The bank's liabilities tend to have a different structure. Let's assume that half the bank's deposits are interest-rate sensitive and half are not. In other words, half the bank's liabilities are deposits that earn variable interest rates, so the costs associated with them move with the market rate. Interest-bearing checking accounts fall into this category. The remainder of the bank's liabilities are time deposits such as certificates of deposit, which have fixed interest rates. The payment a bank makes to the holder of an existing CD does not change with the interest rate.

For the bank to make a profit, the interest rate on its liabilities must be lower than the interest rate on its assets. The difference between the two rates is the bank's net interest margin. Assuming that the interest rate on its liabilities has been 3 percent, the bank has been paying out $3 per $100 in liabilities. Since the bank is receiving 5 percent interest on its assets, its net interest margin is 2 percent (5 minus 3). This margin is the bank's profit.

Now look at what happens if interest rates rise 1 percent for interest-sensitive assets and liabilities. For each $100 in assets, the bank's revenue goes up from $(0.05 \times \$100) = \$5$ to $[(0.05 \times \$80) + (0.06 \times \$20)] = \$5.20$. But the cost of its liabilities goes up too, from $(0.03 \times \$100) = \$3$ to $[(0.03 \times \$50) + (0.04 \times \$50)] = \$3.50$. So a one-percentage point rise in the interest rate reduces the bank's profit from $(\$5 - \$3) = \$2$ per $100 in assets to $(\$5.20 - \$3.50) = \$1.70$, a decline of $0.30, or 15 percent. This example illustrates a general principle: When a bank has more interest-rate-sensitive liabilities than it does interest-rate-sensitive assets, an increase in interest rates will cut into the bank's profits.

The first step in managing interest-rate risk is to determine how sensitive the bank's balance sheet is to a change in interest rates. Managers must compute an estimate of the change in the bank's profit for each one-percentage-point change in the interest rate. This procedure is called *gap analysis*, because it highlights the gap, or difference, between the yield on interest-rate-sensitive assets and the yield on interest-rate-sensitive liabilities. In our example, the gap is (20 percent – 50 percent) = –30. Multiplying this gap times the projected change in the interest rate yields the change in the bank's profit. A gap of –30 tells us that a one-percentage-point increase in the interest rate will reduce the bank's profit by 30 cents per $100 in assets, which is the same answer we got in the last paragraph. Gap analysis can be refined to take account of differences in the maturity of assets and liabilities, but the analysis quickly becomes complicated.[9] Table 12.3 summarizes all of these calculations.

Bank managers can use a number of tools to manage interest-rate risk. The simplest approach is to match the interest-rate sensitivity of assets with the interest-rate sensitivity of liabilities. For instance, if the bank accepts a variable-rate deposit, it then uses the funds to purchase short-term securities. A similar strategy is to make long-term loans at a floating interest rate—as in adjustable-rate mortgages (ARMs)—instead of at the fixed interest rate characteristic of a conventional mortgage. But while this approach reduces interest-rate risk, it increases credit risk. Rising interest rates put additional strain on floating-rate borrowers, increasing the likelihood that they will default on their payments.

---

[9]A more sophisticated examination of interest-rate risk, called *duration analysis*, includes a measure of the interest-rate sensitivity of bond prices. A bond's duration is related to its maturity. The percentage change in the market value = – (duration of the bond) × (percentage-point change in the interest rate). Bankers compute the weighted-average duration of their liabilities and subtract it from the weighted-average duration of their assets to get a duration gap, which can be used to guide the bank's risk management strategy. For a complete treatment, see chapter 9 in Anthony Saunders and Marcia Miller Cornett, *Financial Institutions Management: A Modern Perspective*, 4th ed. (Boston: McGraw-Hill/Irwin, 2003).

Table 12.3   An Example of Interest-Rate Risk

The impact of an interest-rate increase on bank profits (per $100 of assets)

	Assets	**Liabilities**
Interest-rate sensitive	$20	$50
Not interest-rate sensitive	$80	$50
Initial interest rate	5%	3%
New interest rate on interest-rate-sensitive assets and liabilities	6%	4%
	Revenue from Assets	**Cost of Liabilities**
At initial interest rate	(0.05 × $20) + (0.05 × $80) = $5.00	(0.03 × $50) + (0.03 × $50) = $3.00
After interest-rate change	(0.06 × $20) + (0.05 × $80) = $5.20	(0.04 × $50) + (0.03 × $50) = $3.50
Profits at initial interest rate: ($5.00) – ($3.00) = $2.00 per $100 in assets		
Profits after interest-rate change: ($5.20) – ($3.50) = $1.70 per $100 in assets		
Gap Analysis		
Gap between interest-rate-sensitive assets and interest-rate-sensitive liabilities: (Interest-rate-sensitive assets of $20) – (Interest-rate-sensitive liabilities of $50) = (Gap of – $30)		

Besides restructuring their assets in these ways, bankers can use derivatives, specifically interest-rate swaps, to manage interest-rate risk. Recall from Chapter 9 that an interest-rate swap is an agreement in which one party promises to make fixed-interest-rate payments in exchange for floating-interest-rate payments. For a bank that is holding long-term assets and short-term liabilities, an interest-rate swap is exactly the sort of financial instrument that will transfer the risk of rising interest rates to another party.

Trading Risk

There was a time when banks merely took deposits and made loans, holding them until they were completely paid off. Today, banks not only engage in sophisticated asset and liability management but they hire traders to actively buy and sell securities, loans, and derivatives using a portion of the bank's capital, in the hope of making additional profits for the bank's owners. But trading financial instruments is risky. If the price at which an instrument is purchased differs from the price at which it is

IN THE NEWS

Financial Institutions Find It as Hard as Ever to Spot Rogue Traders

Financial Times

by John Gapper

February 07, 2002

It is eerily familiar. The trader in a far-flung operation whose bosses fondly believe he is engaged in risk-free "arbitrage." The dawning realization that he is demanding a suspiciously large amount of cash. The hunt through the trading books and discovery of fake contracts. The confrontation and the hurried flight from justice.

Only the destination of the rogue trader is different. Seven years ago, Nick Leeson chose to relax on a beach in the Malaysian resort of Kota Kinabalu while waiting for the law to catch up with him. The FBI pursued John Rusnak near Gettysburg, where Abraham Lincoln paid tribute to the dead of the Civil War.

This time, the bank will not collapse. Allied Irish Bank (AIB) is only a medium-sized bank by international standards but it can absorb a post-tax £363 million hit to its equity capital. Barings toppled in March 1995 when

presented with the £860 million bill from Mr. Leeson's unauthorized trading in Japanese equity derivatives in Singapore.

But each time it happens, there are painful inquests and earnest resolutions to do better. So why do rogue traders keep popping up? And why do managers of banks take so long to discover long-running frauds at the heart of their financial operations?

The most obvious motive for traders to conceal activities from their employers is to steal money. But there is no direct evidence so far that Mr. Rusnak stole money; and most rogue traders are eventually found to have been deceiving banks for other reasons. One is to foster an illusion that they are making a large trading profit in order to boost annual bonuses, although AIB executives said Mr. Rusnak was "not in any sense a star trader."

Perhaps the overwhelming reason for rogue traders to hide their losses is the belief that they will be able to trade their way out of trouble. Having made an initial loss, they prefer to cover it up with a fake trade rather than confess it to their managers. The longer the deception goes on, the harder it becomes to own up—and the bigger the loss grows.

---

sold, the risk is that the instrument may go down in value rather than up. This type of risk is called **trading risk**, or sometimes **market risk**.[10]

Managing trading risk is a major concern for today's banks. Some of the largest banks in the world have sustained billions of dollars in losses as a result of unsupervised risk taking by employees in their trading operations. The problem is that traders normally share in the profits from good investments, but the bank pays for the losses. Heads, the trader wins; tails, the bank loses. This arrangement creates moral hazard: Traders have an incentive to take more risk than bank managers would like.

The solution to the moral hazard problem in trading is to compute the risk of the portfolios traders generate using measures like standard deviation and value at risk (see Chapter 5). The bank's risk manager then limits the amount of risk any individual trader is allowed to assume and monitors each trader's holdings closely, at least once a day. Moreover, the higher the risk inherent in the bank's portfolio, the more capital the bank will need to hold to make sure the institution remains solvent.

---

[10]Since regulators in the United States won't allow banks to hold stock (equity), the traders employed by the bank can't, either. But since the traders buy and sell derivatives that are based on bonds, commodities, and foreign exchange, the rule against stock ownership doesn't restrict their ability to take risks.

This was certainly a factor in the Barings case, with Mr. Leeson eventually taking huge bets on Japanese equities in a hidden trading account numbered 88888 in a doomed effort to trade his way out of trouble.

The bigger question is why traders such as Mr. Leeson and Mr. Rusnak are not caught sooner. One answer is that many of them are, but the public does not hear about it. Most traders who have hidden losses confess before the losses become too big.

Another reason may be that the bank concerned has relatively weak risk controls or may not even realize it is taking on trading risk. And a third reason why losses remain concealed is because they involve derivative transactions that are poorly understood by senior managers.

But the ultimate safeguard for a bank should be cash. It is relatively easy for a trader to conceal a loss-making trade on paper—as Mr. Rusnak did—by faking the records or making up another position that hedges it. It is much harder to come up with the cash to pay the investor who is the counterparty to the trade.

In other words, no matter what the paper records say, or what is recorded electronically as the *bank's* trading book, *their* treasury should detect from the cash outflow that something is amiss. Mr. Leeson sold options contracts to generate cash but his losses eventually got to the point where he gave himself away by demanding huge sums of cash.

That pattern was repeated at AIB, where Mr. Rusnak managed to keep his trading losses hidden until the end of last year. The treasurer at Allfirst was then alerted by the big cash calls he was making.

Mr. Rusnak appears to have been helped by the steady level of his trading—in contrast to the spiraling growth of Mr. Leeson's losses and the latter's image as a star trader. But the biggest question AIB will face is how it managed to let a trader slowly siphon $750 million without realizing that so much cash was disappearing.

Copyright © 2002 by The Financial Times. Reprinted with permission.

LESSONS OF THE ARTICLE

Trading operations are notoriously difficult to monitor, and they can go dramatically wrong. The problem is analogous to moral hazard in debt finance (discussed in Chapter 11). Traders are gambling with someone else's money, sharing the gains but not the losses from their risk taking. As a result, they are prone to taking too much risk—and in the cases discussed here, to hiding their losses when their trades turn sour. This moral hazard presents a challenge to the bank's owners, who must find ways to rein in traders' tendencies to take too much risk. The tip-off to unbridled risk taking can come when a trader makes too big a profit. Odds are that someone who is making large profits on some days will register big losses on other days. There is no way to make a large profit without taking a big risk.

Other Risks

Beyond liquidity, credit, interest-rate, and trading risk, banks face an assortment of other risks. A bank that operates internationally will face foreign exchange risk and sovereign risk. Foreign exchange risk comes from holding assets denominated in one currency and liabilities denominated in another. For example, a U.S. bank that holds dollar-denominated liabilities might purchase bonds issued by Sony Corporation or make a loan to a Japanese business. Both those assets would be denominated in yen. Thus, when the dollar-yen exchange rate moves, the dollar value of the bank's assets will change. Banks manage their foreign exchange risk in two ways. They work to attract deposits that are denominated in the same currency as their loans, thereby matching their assets with their liabilities, and they use foreign exchange futures and swaps to hedge the risk.

Sovereign risk arises from the fact that some foreign borrowers may not repay their loans, not because they are unwilling to, but because their government prohibits them from doing so. When a foreign country is experiencing a financial crisis, the government may decide to restrict dollar-denominated payments, in which case a U.S. bank would have difficulty collecting payments on its loans in the country. Such circumstances have arisen on numerous occasions. Examples include Asia in 1997, Russia in 1998, and

Argentina in 2002. In all these cases—governments and corporations alike—had difficulty raising enough dollars to repay their dollar-denominated debts. In such crises, a bank has very little recourse in the courts and little hope of recovering the loans.

Managing sovereign risk is difficult. Banks have three options. The first is diversification, which means distributing the bank's loans and securities holdings throughout the world, carefully avoiding too much exposure in any country where a crisis might arise. Second, the bank can simply refuse to do business in a particular country or set of countries. And third, the bank can use derivatives to hedge sovereign risk.

The final risk that banks face is the risk that their computer systems may fail or their buildings burn down (or blow up), what's called operational risk. When terrorists destroyed the World Trade Center towers on September 11, 2001, power and communications were disrupted in a large and important part of lower Manhattan. Many financial firms located in or near the World Trade Center quickly switched to backup sites, but others couldn't. The Bank of New York, a large commercial bank, was one of those that fell victim to operational risk. The Bank of New York plays an extremely important role in the U.S. financial system, handling hundreds of billions of dollars worth of transactions each day in the U.S. Treasury securities market. Prior to September 11, the bank maintained both its primary and backup operations within blocks of the World Trade Center (see Figure 12.8). Not only were power and communications to these buildings knocked out by the terrorist attack, but no one

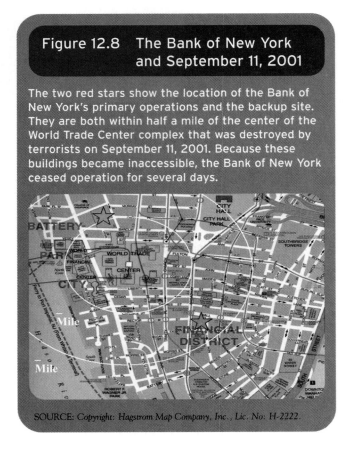

Figure 12.8 The Bank of New York and September 11, 2001

The two red stars show the location of the Bank of New York's primary operations and the backup site. They are both within half a mile of the center of the World Trade Center complex that was destroyed by terrorists on September 11, 2001. Because these buildings became inaccessible, the Bank of New York ceased operation for several days.

SOURCE: Copyright: Hagstrom Map Company, Inc., Lic. No: H-2222.

could even get to them. The bank practically shut down for several days and recovered only slowly. In placing the backup site so close to the bank's primary operations, managers had made an enormous mistake: They had failed to take account of a significant operational risk.[11]

In principle, managing operational risk is straightforward, but in practice it can be difficult. The bank must make sure that its computer systems and buildings are sufficiently robust to withstand potential disasters. That means both anticipating what might happen and testing to ensure the system's readiness. Forecasting the possibilities can be daunting. Who could have predicted what happened on September 11?

Table 12.4 summarizes the four major risks banks face and the recommended risk-management strategies.

Table 12.4   Risks Banks Face and How They Manage Them

Type of Risk	Source of Risk	Recommended Responses
Liquidity Risk	Sudden withdrawals by depositors	1. Hold sufficient cash reserves to meet customer demand. 2. Manage assets–sell securities or loans (contracts the balance sheet) 3. Manage liabilities–attract more deposits (maintains the size of the balance sheet)
Credit Risk	Default by borrowers on their loans	1. Diversify to spread risk. 2. Use statistical models to screen for creditworthy borrowers. 3. Monitor to reduce moral hazard.
Interest-Rate Risk	Mismatch in maturity of assets and liabilities coupled with a change in interest rates	1. Closely match the maturity of both sides of the balance sheet. 2. Use derivatives such as interest-rate swaps.
Trading (Market) Risk	Trading losses in the bank's own account	Closely monitor traders using risk management tools, including value at risk.

[11]For a discussion of the problems that occurred in the U.S. financial system following the destruction of the World Trade Center towers, see the Federal Reserve Bank of New York's *Economic Policy Review*, November 2002, special issue on the economic effects of September 11. Of particular note are Michael J. Fleming and Kenneth D. Garbade, "When the Back Office Moved to the Front Burner: Settlement Fails in the Treasury Market after September 11," and James J. McAndrews and Simon Potter, "Liquidity Effects of the Event of September 11, 2001."

APPLYING THE CONCEPT
THE COLLAPSE OF JAPANESE BANKS

In 1990, of the top 15 financial firms in the world (measured by their stock market value), thirteen were Japanese. By 2001, none were. In a single decade, the assets of Japanese commercial banks had fallen nearly 15 percent, while those of U.S. banks had risen 80 percent. From 1993 through 2001, Japanese banks produced a negative return, reporting cumulative losses of roughly 16.5 percent of Japan's one-year GDP.

Table 12.5 provides the same information for Japanese banks that Table 12.2 (page 297) did for U.S. banks. There are some striking differences between the two tables. First, net interest margins are around 1 percent for Japanese banks (one-third what they are for U.S. banks). Second, net interest income accounted for roughly 80 percent of total bank income in Japan in 1991 and has not fallen much since then. (In U.S. banks, the equivalent ratio was less than 60 percent in 2001.) Third, over the decade, Japanese banks' profits dropped steadily, eventually turning negative. Since Japanese banks are much more highly leveraged than U.S. banks (their assets-to-equity ratio is about 30) their negative profits resulted in enormously negative returns. In 2001, the ROE for Japanese banks was –18 percent.*

Looking closely at Table 12.5, we can see that the poor performance of Japanese banks had two sources. The first was loan losses. In 2001, Japan's banks reported losses of 9.4 trillion yen—over 2 percent of their outstanding loans and more than 1 percent of their assets. Both ratios are more than twice the level in U.S. banks. Added to these loan losses were capital losses of 2.4 trillion yen on the sale of stocks and real estate. Though U.S. banks are not allowed to own stock, Japanese banks are; they hold roughly 5 percent of their assets in the form of equities. From its peak in the late 1980s through 2001, the Japanese stock market fell roughly two-thirds in value, causing significant losses for banks. The real estate market collapsed with the stock market, adding to the problem.

As bad as the numbers in Table 12.5 are, they don't tell the whole story. The reason is that Japanese banks are allowed to compute their financial statements using the values they paid for their assets. Given the collapse of stock and real estate values, current market prices are well below these *book values,* so the value of the assets and bank capital are overstated. Added to these overstated asset values is the manner in which Japanese banks have treated borrowers who cannot pay off their loans. Instead of simply taking the losses, the banks increased the size of the loans, including the interest the borrowers couldn't pay as part of the principal in their new loans. This approach inflates the size of the bank's balance sheet, putting off the day of reckoning when the borrower must finally default. A proper accounting would likely show that most Japanese banks today have negative capital. That is, they are bankrupt.

*For a more detailed account, see Chapter 8 of Takeo Hoshi and Anil K Kashyap, *Corporate Financing and Governance in Japan: The Road to the Future* (Cambridge MA: MIT Press, 2001).

continued from previous page

Table 12.5   Profitability of Japanese Banks

(in trillions of yen, except bottom four rows)

	1991	1996	2001
A. Interest Income – Interest expense (Net interest Income)	¥8.9	¥10.7	¥9.8
B. Other revenue*	2.2	3.7	3.1
C. Operating costs	7.5	8.0	7.0
D. Gross profit (A + B – C)	3.5	6.4	5.9
E. Loan losses (provisions)	1.0	7.3	9.4
F. Net operating profit (D – E)	2.5	–1.0	–3.5
G. Realized capital gains from sale of equities and real estate	0.7	1.2	–2.4
H. Net profits before taxes (F + G)	3.3	0.2	–5.9
I. Assets	914.4	856.0	772.0
Net interest margin (A/I)	0.0097%	0.0125%	0.0127%
Return on assets (H/I) (ROA)	0.0036	0.0002	–0.0076
Return on equity (ROE)	0.1052	0.0060	–0.1796
Net interest income/total income [A/(A + B)]	0.8018	0.7506	0.7597

*Includes fee income and profits from trading for own account but excludes capital gains from real estate sales in G. (Numbers may not add up exactly due to rounding in the original.)

SOURCE: Table 1 in Anil K Kashyap, "Sorting Out Japan's Financial Crisis," *Economic Perspectives of the Federal Reserve Bank of Chicago*, 4th quarter 2002, pp. 42–55. Return on Equity is computed using information from the Bank of Japan's "Financial Statements of Japanese Banks" available at http://www.boj.or.jp/en/siryo/siryo_f.htm.

The impact of these problems has been nothing short of catastrophic for the Japanese economy. Since the banks need to hold capital as a buffer against unpredictable losses on their loans, they can't make new loans. Without new lending, firms cannot grow, and neither can the economy.

Terms

bank capital, 295

cash items in process of collection, 288

credit risk, 303

depository institution, 286

discount loans, 292

excess reserves, 293

federal funds market, 293

foreign exchange risk, 309

interest-rate spread, 297

interest-rate risk, 304

large certificates of deposit, 292

letters of credit, 298

liquidity risk, 300

loan commitment, 298

loan loss reserves, 295

market risk, 308

net interest income, 296

net interest margin, 297

nondepository institution, 286

off-balance-sheet activities, 298

operational risk, 310

repurchase agreement (repo), 293

required reserves, 300

reserves, 287

return on assets (ROA), 295

return on equity (ROE), 296

secondary reserves, 289

sovereign risk, 309

trading risk, 308

vault cash, 287

Chapter Lessons

1. Bank assets equal bank liabilities plus bank capital.

   a. Bank assets are the uses for bank funds.

      i. They include reserves, securities, and loans.

      ii. Over the years, securities have become less important and mortgages more important as a use for bank funds.

   b. Bank liabilities are the sources of bank funds.

      i. They include transaction and nontransaction deposits as well as borrowings from other banks.

      ii. Over the years, transaction deposits have become increasingly less important as a source of bank funds.

   c. Bank capital is the contribution of the bank's owners; it acts as a cushion against a fall in the value of the bank's assets or a withdrawal of its liabilities.

   d. Banks make a profit for their owners. Measures of a bank's profitability include return on assets (ROA), return on equity (ROE), net interest income, and net interest margin.

   e. Banks' off-balance-sheet activities have become increasingly important in recent years. They include

      i. Loan commitments, which are lines of credit firms can use whenever necessary.

      ii. Letters of credit, which are guarantees that a customer will make a promised payment.

2. Banks face several types of risk in day-to-day business. They include

   a. Liquidity risk—the risk that customers will demand cash immediately.

      i. Liability-side liquidity risk arises from deposit withdrawals.

      ii. Asset-side liquidity risk arises from the use of loan commitments to borrow.

      iii. Banks can manage liquidity risk by adjusting either their assets or their liabilities.

   b. Credit risk—the risk that customers will not repay their loans. Banks can manage credit risk by

      i. Diversifying their loan portfolios.

      ii. Using statistical models to analyze borrowers' creditworthiness.

      iii. Monitoring borrowers to ensure that they use borrowed funds properly.

   c. Interest-rate risk—the risk that a movement in interest rates will change the value of the bank's assets more than the value of its liabilities.

      i. When a bank lends long and borrows short, increases in interest rates will drive down the bank's profits.

      ii. Banks use a variety of tools, such as gap analysis, to assess the sensitivity of their balance sheets to a change in interest rates.

      iii. Banks manage interest-rate risk by matching the maturity of their assets and liabilities and using derivatives like interest-rate swaps.

   d. Trading risk—the risk that traders who work for the bank will create losses on the bank's own account. Banks can manage this risk using complex statistical models.

   e. Other risks banks face include foreign exchange risk, sovereign risk, and operational risk.

Problems

1. Explain why one bank might want to borrow from another bank.

2. Why are checking accounts no longer an important source of funds for commercial banks in the United States?

3. Would bankers be pleased with a reduction in the reserve requirement?

4. Suppose you have decided to invest in a bank and are trying to choose which one would make the best investment. You have asked your investment adviser for information on each bank you are considering, including its return on equity. Should you invest in the bank with the highest ROE? Why or why not?

5. Banks hold more liquid assets than most businesses do. Explain why.

6. The volume of commercial and industrial loans made by banks has declined over the past few decades. Explain why. What item has counterbalanced the decline in the value of loans on banks' balance sheets?

7. Explain how a bank uses liability management to respond to a deposit outflow. Why do banks prefer liability management to asset management?

8. Banks carefully consider the maturity structure of both their assets and their liabilities. What is the significance of the maturity structure? What risks are banks trying to manage when they adjust their maturity structure?

9. Define ROA, ROE, and leverage and show how the three are related. Using these concepts, together with the information in Tables 12.2 (page 297) and 12.5 (page 313), determine the amount of equity capital in the U.S. and Japanese banking systems in 2001. Comment on the difference.

10. Define credit risk. Banks face both firm-specific and economy-wide credit risk. How do they manage each?

11. A bank has issued a one-year certificate of deposit for $50 million at an interest rate of 2 percent. With the proceeds, the bank has purchased a two-year Treasury note that pays 4 percent interest. What risk does the bank face in entering into these transactions? What would happen if all interest rates rose by 1 percent?

12. You live in a small town and are having coffee with the owner of the local bank. The bank, which has only a single branch, has been accepting deposits from you and your neighbors for decades. In the course of your conversation, the banker states, "We are an integral part of this community, so we lend only to the people who live here." Is this strategy a sound one? What advice would you give the banker?

13. You are managing a bank with $1 billion in assets, 3 percent of which are reserves; 15 percent securities; 74 percent loans; and 8 percent required bank capital. Twenty percent of the bank's liabilities are transaction deposits; 70 percent nontransaction deposits; and 10 percent borrowings.

    a. Construct the bank's balance sheet.

    b. If the reserve requirement on transactions assets is 10 percent, what are the bank's reserves? Its excess reserves?

    c. In the event of a $20 million withdrawal, what options are available to you to meet the demand for funds? List them in preferential order and explain your preferences.

14. Define operational risk and explain how a bank manages it.

15. On the Federal Reserve Board's Web site, http://www.federalreserve.gov/releases/, under statistical releases, you will find a weekly release called H.8, "Assets and Liabilities of Commercial Banks in the United States." Download the most recent release and construct a table that matches Table 12.1 using the data in the release.

    a. Compare your table to Table 12.1. What are the differences in the data. How can you explain them?

    b. Find the current level of nominal GDP in the United States and use it as a scale for the numbers in your table. Describe what you find.

Chapter 13

Financial Industry Structure

Canada, a nation of 36 million people, has 19 banks.[1] If the United States had the same ratio of banks to population, there would be 158 banks in this country. In fact, more than 7,500 commercial banks and roughly 20,000 depository institutions exist within U.S. borders, all vying to serve some 300 million Americans. While the United States and Canada are extremes, most countries' banking systems more closely resemble the Canadian structure. In Japan, for example, 125 million people depend on about 100 banks; in the United Kingdom, 60 million people are served by fewer than 500 banks.

Amazingly, the United States once had even more banks than it does today. As Figure 13.1 shows, the number peaked at 15,000 in 1984 and has been falling ever since. The figure also shows an odd pattern in the structure of banks. For decades, most U.S. banks were unit banks, or banks without branches. Throughout the 1950s and 1960s, more than two-thirds of banks were unit banks confined to a single building. Over the last quarter of the 20th century, however, the pattern changed. Today, only one-third of banks in the United States are unit banks. What explains this change in structure?

The decline in the total number of banks and the increase in the number of banks with branches are not the only changes the U.S. banking industry has seen in recent years. In April 1998, the Traveler's Insurance Company, together with its investment banking and brokerage subsidiary Salomon Smith Barney, merged with Citibank, then the second largest commercial bank in the country, to become Citigroup. At the time of its creation, Citigroup had $700 billion in assets and over 100 million customers in 100 different countries. It was also illegal. But by the end of 1999, the law that forbid such combinations had been repealed, and Citigroup began buying up even more financial firms. Today, Citigroup not only offers the deposits and loans people expect of a commercial bank; it provides the same assortment of products offered by almost all other financial institutions. Citigroup is an insurance company, a pension fund, a securities broker, a collection of mutual funds, and a finance company, all rolled into one.

The U.S. financial system is composed of both depository and nondepository institutions. Together, they provide a broad menu of services: buying and selling securities, offering loans, insurance, and pensions, and providing checking accounts, credit cards, and debit cards. Most financial institutions perform at least a few of these functions. Visit the Web site of any large bank, for instance, and you will discover that you can get not only checking and savings accounts, loans and credit cards, but insurance and stockbrokerage services. To understand the structure of the financial industry, then, we need to put these services into a broader perspective. The first half of this chapter will consider current trends in the banking industry, including the

---

[1]This is the number of domestic Canadian banks as of May 2004. For a list of Canadian banks, see the Web site of the Office of the Superintendent of Financial Institutions at www.osfi-bsif.gc.ca.

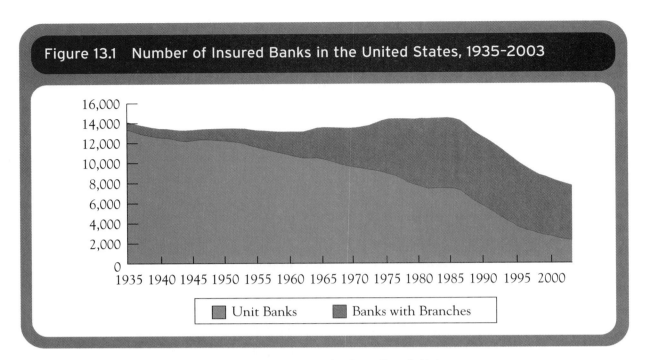

Figure 13.1 Number of Insured Banks in the United States, 1935-2003

Unit Banks   Banks with Branches

SOURCE: *Federal Deposit Insurance Corporation*, Historical Statistics of Banking, *http://www2.fdic.gov/hsob/index.asp*.

tendency toward consolidation with nondepository institutions. The second half of the chapter will study the functions and characteristics of nondepository institutions.

Banking Industry Structure

Today's banking system bears little resemblance to the one Americans knew in 1960 or 1970. Then people used their neighborhood banks. Not only did customers walk into the bank to conduct their business, but they knew the tellers and bank managers they saw there. Today most of us don't go beyond the ATM in the lobby, and if we do, we probably don't recognize the employees inside. Banks have been transformed so that location doesn't matter the way it once did. This change has occurred on both the national and the international level.

The best way to understand the structure of today's banking industry is to trace it back to its roots. That means looking at the legal history of banking. In this section we'll learn that banking legislation is the reason we have so many banks in the United States. We'll look at the trend toward consolidation that has been steadily reducing the number of banks since the mid-1980s. And we'll briefly consider the effects of globalization.

A Short History of U.S. Banking

If you want to start a bank, you can't just rent a space, put up a sign, and open the door. You need permission in the form of a bank charter. Until the Civil War, all bank charters were issued by state banking authorities. Because the authors of the U.S. Constitution feared a strong central government, in the early years of the Republic the federal government was weak and ineffectual. State governments were much more powerful. Until 1863, in fact, there was no national currency. Instead, state banks issued banknotes that circulated in much the way dollar bills do today. But while the state-chartered banks usually promised to redeem their banknotes in gold, they did so only if the bearer presented them at the bank. As the bearer traveled farther and farther from the bank, the value of the notes fell. So a note issued by a New York bank was worth considerably less in Philadelphia than it was in New York.

A $10 banknote issued by the Central Bank of Tennessee in 1853.

Besides currency that did not hold its value from one place to another, the early American financial system was plagued by insufficient capital and fraud. Banks regularly failed, and when they did, their banknotes became worthless. As we saw in Chapter 2, given the license to print money, most people will print too much. With so many different banknotes circulating, telling the sound money from the unsound became inordinately confusing and inefficient. The whole point of printing money is to reduce information costs and facilitate trade. Still, reasonable people hesitated to accept banknotes issued by banks they weren't familiar with, so money was not widely accepted. In the end, the system just didn't work.

Radical change came during the Civil War, when Congress passed the National Banking Act of 1863. While the new law didn't eliminate state-chartered banks, it did impose a 10 percent tax on their issue of banknotes. At the same time, the act created a system of federally chartered banks, or *national banks*, which would be supervised by the Office of the Comptroller of the Currency, inside the U.S. Department of the Treasury. These new national banks could issue banknotes tax-free. Congress's intent was to put the state banks out of business by taking away their source of funds.

While the act did get rid of state-issued banknotes, state banks devised another way to raise funds, by creating demand deposits. This explains the origin of the dual banking system we have today, in which banks can choose whether to get their charters from the Comptroller of the Currency at the U.S. Treasury or from state officials. Roughly two-thirds of U.S. banks now have a state charter and the rest have a federal charter. The decision is related to a bank's profitability. State banking authorities have been more permissive than federal authorities in the types of operations they allow. Because greater flexibility in a bank's operations means a better chance of making a profit, state charters have been the overwhelming choice.[2]

The first national banknote issued in 1863.

[2]There are a number of differences between state- and nationally chartered banks. For example, since the advent of the Federal Reserve in 1914, nationally chartered banks have been required to belong to the Federal Reserve System. Their membership obligated them to hold noninterest-bearing deposits at the Federal Reserve, whose reserve requirements were often higher than those of state banking authorities. And when the FDIC was created in 1933, nationally chartered banks had to subscribe. State-chartered banks could subscribe to state deposit insurance systems, which were often cheaper. These differences led to a general preference for state charters. Over the years, however, the differences between the two have narrowed sharply—for example, all banks are subject to reserve requirements and must purchase deposit insurance from the FDIC—so the preference for state charters is not as pronounced as it was several decades ago.

Furthermore, if the Comptroller of the Currency won't allow a bank to engage in a particular practice, the bank can always change its charter. This ability to switch back and forth between state and federal charters created what amounts to regulatory competition, which has hastened innovation in the financial industry. In the 1990s, changes in banking law required federal and state agencies to coordinate their oversight of financial intermediaries. But the globalization of the financial system, together with banks' ability to move funds easily across international boundaries, means that today regulatory competition exists not so much between state and federal government regulators but between national government regulators.

The next major event in U.S. banking history occurred in 1933, in the midst of the Great Depression. From 1929 to 1933, more than a third of all U.S. banks failed; individual depositors lost $1.5 billion, or about 3 percent of total bank deposits. At the time, total personal income was less than $50 billion, or about $1 billion a week. So on average, the bank failures of the Great Depression cost depositors one and a half weeks' pay. (Today, total personal income in the United States is over $10 trillion, or roughly $200 billion a week, so the equivalent loss would be about $300 billion.) But since failures were concentrated in small banks, small depositors bore the brunt of the collapse. Millions of small savers lost their life savings.

Congress responded to the crisis with the Glass-Steagall Act of 1933, which created the Federal Deposit Insurance Corporation and severely limited the activities of commercial banks. The FDIC provided insurance to individual depositors so they would not lose their savings if a bank failed. The act also restricted bank assets to certain approved forms of debt and separated banking from the securities industry. Depository institutions were forbidden from dealing in securities, providing insurance, or engaging in any of the other activities undertaken by nondepository institutions. As a result, commercial banks were forced to sell off their investment banking operations. This restriction on their activities remained in place until 1999, when the Gramm-Leach-Bliley Financial Services Modernization Act repealed it. We will return to this topic shortly.

Competition and Consolidation

None of the historical events we have discussed explains why there are nearly 8,000 banks in the United States today or why that number has been shrinking since the mid-1980s. To unravel the mystery, let's return to Figure 13.1. Notice the division between banks with branches and banks that don't have branches. As we mentioned in the introduction, banks that do not have branches are called *unit banks*. The alternative, which is familiar to most of us today, is a bank with many branches spread out over a wide geographic area. Large banks like Bank of America and Citibank maintain branches in many cities across many states. We'll return to these banks in a moment. For now, notice from the figure that in 1935, the vast majority of banks had no branches; today, nearly two-thirds of them do. In fact, in 1935 there were 14,125 banks in the United States with a total of 17,237 offices; by 2003 there were 7,769 banks with a whopping 75,159 offices.[3] Today's banks not only have branches, they have lots of them.

---

[3] We can get some idea of where the consolidation process may stop by looking at the structure of the banking industry in California, which represents about 10 percent of the U.S. economy. California has never had branching restrictions; it is home to roughly 300 banks. On that basis, some observers predict that the number of banks in the United States as a whole will eventually decline to about 3,000.

The number of banks and bank branches in the United States tells only part of the story; we also need to look at bank size. Table 13.1 shows that the U.S. banking system is composed of a large number of very small banks and a small number of very large ones. Roughly 1 percent of the banks hold nearly 70 percent of all bank assets. In fact, Bank of America alone accounts for around 10 percent of both assets and deposits in the U.S. banking system.

The primary reason for this structure is the McFadden Act of 1927, which required that nationally chartered banks meet the branching restrictions of the states in which they were located. Since some states had laws that forbade branch banking, the result was a large number of very small banks.[4] Advocates of legal limits on branching argued that they prevented concentration and monopoly in banking in the same way that antitrust laws prevented concentration in manufacturing. They feared that without such limits, a few large banks could drive small ones out of business, reducing the quality of financial services available in small communities.

The McFadden Act produced a fragmented banking system that was almost devoid of large institutions. The result was a network of small, geographically dispersed banks that faced virtually no competition—the opposite of what the act's advocates had intended. Not only that, but the system was prone to failure. In many states, more efficient and modern banks were legally precluded from opening branches to compete with the small, inefficient ones that were already there. In these states, the result was a network of small community banks that faced no competitive pressures to innovate. And since the only loan applications these banks received were from residents of their own communities, their loan portfolios were insufficiently diversified. In a farming town, the bank's fortunes depended on the weather, since its loan portfolio was composed almost

Table 13.1 Number and Assets of Depository Institutions, 2003

(includes commercial banks, savings and loans, and savings banks)

Size of Institution (Assets)	Number	Percent of Total Assets
Less than $100 million	4,390	2.5%
$100 million to $1 billion	4,211	12.8%
$1 billion to $10 billion	471	14.5%
$10 billion or more	110	70.3%
Total	9,182	$9.1 trillion

SOURCE: *FDIC statistics on banking are for the year 2003. The information here differs from that in Figure 13.1 because it includes all depository institutions, not just commercial banks.*

[4]In the nation's early years, the states were starved for revenue; they could neither issue their own currency nor tax interstate trade. The fees the states earned for granting bank charters and the taxes they levied on bank profits became important sources of revenue for state government. The fees gave the state governments an incentive to create many small banks, while the taxes gave them an interest in protecting banks and ensuring they would be profitable. The result was a fragmented banking system with little competition. See R. Krozner and P. Strahan, "What Drives Deregulation? Economics and Politics of the Relaxation of Bank Branching Restrictions," *Quarterly Journal of Economics* 114 (November 1999), pp. 1437–1467.

"Of course, you could try another bank, if there _were_ any other banks."

entirely of agricultural loans. Aware of the problem, the bank manager would eventually stop making loans because the risk was simply too great. When credit ceased to flow into the community, farmers curtailed their operations. In the end, the bank's owners made a healthy profit since the bank was protected from competition—but everyone else in town suffered.

Some banks reacted to branching restrictions by creating bank holding companies. A holding company is a corporation that owns a group of other firms. In some contexts, it may be thought of as the _parent firm_ for a group of subsidiaries. Bank holding companies have been around since the early 1900s. Initially, they were created not just as a way to evade branching restrictions but as a way to provide nonbank financial services in more than one state. In 1956, the U.S. Congress passed the Bank Holding Company Act, which broadened the scope of what bank holding companies could do, allowing them to provide various nonbank financial services. Over the years, changes in laws and regulations have added asset management, investment advice, insurance, leasing, collections, and real estate services to the list of allowable activities.

Beginning in the early 1970s, technology enabled banks to borrow and lend at a distance. The combination of the U.S. mail, telephone service, and finally the Internet dramatically reduced the importance of physical location in banking. Without the need to personally visit the bank to conduct their business, people ceased to care whether a bank was chartered in the state where they lived. Today, ATMs and debit and credit cards allow depositors access to means of payment even when they are far from home. Credit companies can evaluate any individual or firm's creditworthiness, so a bank can make a loan regardless of the borrower's location. In 1976, small businesses were located an average of 16 miles from their banks. By 1992, the average distance was 64 miles.

In changing the way people use the financial system, technology has eroded the value of the local banking monopoly. In the 1970s and 1980s, states responded by loosening their branching restrictions.[5] Then in 1994, Congress passed the Reigle-Neal Interstate Banking and Branching Efficiency Act. This legislation reversed the restrictions put in place almost 70 years earlier by the McFadden Act. Since 1997, banks have been able to acquire an unlimited number of branches nationwide, and the number of commercial banks has fallen nearly in half. What is more, the number of savings institutions—savings and loans plus savings banks—has fallen even more. While some banks couldn't handle the new competition and went out of business, the vast majority disappeared through mergers with other banks. Figure 13.2 shows the pattern of bank failures and mergers from 1970 to 2002.

---

[5]A number of other changes took place as well. For example, until 1980, federal law restricted the interest rate banks could pay on deposits. Under Regulation Q, they were prohibited from paying interest on checking accounts, and were limited to a maximum rate of just over 5 percent on savings deposits. As inflation and interest rates rose in the late 1970s, these restrictions became prohibitive. Many depositors withdrew their funds from banks and placed them in money-market mutual funds, whose interest rates were not restricted by law.

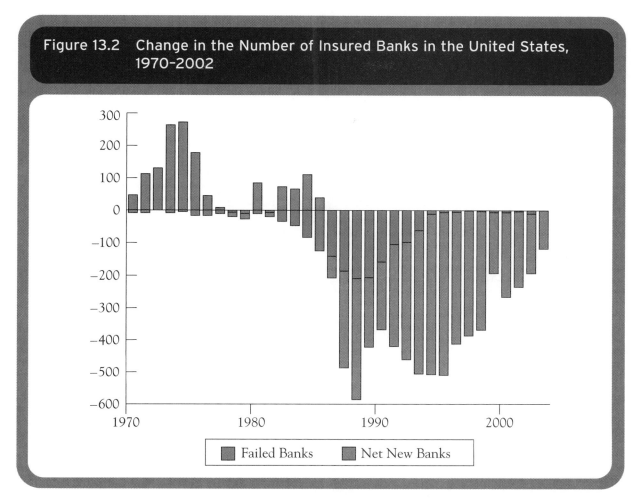

Figure 13.2   Change in the Number of Insured Banks in the United States, 1970–2002

SOURCE: *Federal Deposit Insurance Corporation. Failed banks include both insolvent banks that failed and were merged and insolvent banks that were liquidated. Net new banks equals newly chartered banks minus solvent banks that were involved in unassisted mergers.*

The Reigle-Neal Act allowed banks to diversify geographically. Today a bank that wants to establish operations in a new state can purchase a bank already located in that state. In doing so, it acquires the bank's customers, as well as its employees and their knowledge of the state's business and legal environment. The results have been dramatic. Banks became more profitable: their operating costs and loan losses fell; the interest rates paid to depositors rose while the interest rates charged to borrowers fell. The only people who suffered were the employees of inefficient banks, who had to work harder and were paid less as a result of the new competition. So overall, the deregulation of banks was good for the economy.[6]

[6]One way to tell that deregulation improved growth is to look at what happened in different states. Separating the impact of deregulation from that of a variety of other effects on growth can be tricky. The fact that states deregulated at different times allows economists to disentangle the effects. See J. Jayaranthe and P. Strahan, "The Finance-Growth Nexus: Evidence from Bank Branch Deregulation," *Quarterly Journal of Economics* 111 (1996), pp. 639–670.

Table 13.2 Key Legislation Affecting the U.S. Banking Industry

1927 McFadden Act.	Outlawed interstate branching and required national banks to abide by the laws of the states in which they operated.
1933 Glass-Steagall Act.	Established federal deposit insurance and prohibited commercial banks from engaging in the insurance and securities businesses.
1994 Reigle-Neal Act.	Repealed the McFadden Act's prohibition of interstate branching.
1999 Gramm-Leach-Bliley Act.	Repealed the Glass-Steagall Act's prohibition of mergers between commercial banks and insurance companies or securities firms.

Table 13.2 summarizes the key events in the evolution of the U.S. banking industry over the last century.

The Globalization of Banking

Toward the end of the 20th century, U.S. banking underwent not just a national but an international transformation. An explosion in international trade had increased the need for international financial services. Very simply, every time a Japanese company purchased software produced in the United States or an American bought a television set manufactured in China, payments had to be made across national boundaries. Today, the international banking system has adjusted to the needs of an interdependent, globalized world. Large U.S. banks like JPMorgan Chase and Citibank have stationed ATMs on the streets of Frankfurt, Buenos Aires, and other major capitals. In New York, keen observers can spot the foreign offices of Deutsche Bank, National Westminster Bank, and Tokyo-Mitsubishi. All told, by the end of 2003, 74 U.S. banks had established foreign operations of one type or another, with foreign assets totaling $750 billion. And more than 300 foreign banks with assets totaling more than $1.5 trillion had established a presence in the United States.[7]

There are a number of ways banks can operate in foreign countries, depending on such factors as the legal environment. The most straightforward approach is to open a foreign branch that offers the same services as those in the home country. Certain legal structures also allow U.S. banks to engage in operations outside of the country, opening what looks to the casual observer like a branch (but may have a different legal status). For example, a bank can create an international banking facility (IBF), which allows it to accept deposits from and make loans to foreigners outside the country. Or the bank can create a subsidiary called an Edge Act corporation, which is established specifically to engage in international banking transactions.

---

[7]At the beginning of 2004 the Federal Reserve listed 49 foreign bank agencies with assets of $33.3 billion; 235 branches of foreign banks with assets of $1.11 trillion; 67 U.S. commercial banks that were majority owned by foreign banks with assets of $346.3 billion; and 139 U.S. offices of foreign banks without domestic assets. The list, which is compiled quarterly, is available at http://www.federalreserve.gov/releases/iba/default.htm.

Alternatively, a bank holding company can purchase a controlling interest in a foreign bank. From our point of view, the classification of the particular enterprise is less important than the fact that U.S. banks take advantage of various methods to operate outside the country.

Foreign banks, of course, can take advantage of similar options. They can purchase an interest in a U.S. bank, open branches on U.S. soil, create a U.S. subsidiary, or open what is called an *agency office*. These alternatives differ in the spectrum of financial services they can provide.

MARKETS

The growth of international banking has had an economic impact similar to that of deregulation in the United States. Today, a borrower in France, Brazil, or Singapore can shop for a loan virtually anywhere in the world, and a depositor seeking the highest return can do the same. All this competition has surely made banking a tougher business. Profits are harder for bankers to come by today than they were in 1970, when depositors and borrowers were captive to small local banks. But while bankers' lives may be more difficult, on balance the improved efficiency of the financial system has enhanced growth everywhere.

One of the most important aspects of international banking is the eurodollar market. We first encountered eurodollars in Chapter 2, in our discussion of how to measure the quantity of money. Eurodollars are dollar-denominated deposits in foreign banks. For reasons we will explain shortly, a bank in London, Zurich, or the Cayman Islands might offer its best customers the ability to make their deposits in dollars. In response, Ford Motor Corporation might convert a $1 million deposit in its New York bank to a eurodollar deposit in the bank's Cayman Islands subsidiary. After the $1 million has been deposited in Ford's Cayman Islands account, it is lent back to the New York bank. This series of transactions transforms a deposit liability into a nondeposit liability.

Both Ford and the New York bank have an incentive to do this. For the bank, the Cayman Islands deposit is cheaper. It is not subject to U.S. reserve requirements, nor is the bank required to pay a deposit insurance premium on the balance. Moreover, regulatory supervision is more lax in the middle of the Gulf of Mexico than it is in the United States, which reduces the cost of compliance. Finally, profits from the offshore bank may be subject to a lower corporate income tax rate than profits originating inside the United States. These advantages allow the bank to pay Ford a higher interest rate on the deposit, and they increase the bank's net interest margin.

A number of forces conspired to create the euromarket. Originally, it was a response to restrictions on the movement of international capital that were instituted at the end of World War II with the creation of the Bretton Woods system. (We will learn more about the international monetary system and capital controls in Chapter 19.) To ensure that the pound would retain its value, the British government imposed restrictions on the ability of British banks to finance international transactions. In an attempt to evade these restrictions, London banks began to offer dollar deposits and dollar-denominated loans to foreigners. The result was what we know today as the eurodollar market. The Cold War accelerated the market's development when the Soviet government, fearful that the U.S. government might freeze or confiscate its dollar deposits, shifted them from New York to London.[8] In the United States, a combination of factors propelled the eurodollar market forward. In the 1960s, U.S. authorities tried to prevent dollars from leaving the country and made it costly for foreigners to borrow dollars in the United States for use elsewhere in the

---

[8]These deposits had an added advantage: They were not subject to the interest-rate ceiling in place in U.S. banks at the time. Over the years, oil-producing countries have deposited their dollar revenues in the same London banks. Today, hundreds of banks around the world accept deposits in currencies other than their home currency. They do so to facilitate their customers' international business transactions.

world. Then in the early 1970s, a combination of domestic interest-rate controls and high inflation made domestic deposits much less attractive than eurodollar deposits, which paid comparatively high interest rates.

Today, the eurodollar market in London is one of the biggest and most important financial markets in the world. And the interest rate at which banks lend each other eurodollars, called the London Interbank Offered Rate (LIBOR), is the standard against which many private loan rates are measured. For example, some adjustable-rate home mortgages in the United States carry an interest rate that is pegged to LIBOR.

The Future of Banks

Today's banks are bigger, fewer in number, and more international in reach than the banks of yesteryear; they also have more to offer in the way of services. A typical large commercial bank now offers investment and insurance products as well as the more

YOUR FINANCIAL WORLD

Making Payments on Your Foreign Vacation

You're planning a trip to Paris and are trying to decide how to pay for your purchases and expenses. You have a number of options. You can simply take cash, in $20 or $100 bills, and exchange it for euros when you arrive. Or you can get travelers' checks from the bank. Finally, you can take your ATM and credit cards with you and use them when you need to. Let's consider the pros and cons of each of these choices, assuming that you'll need €200 and the current market exchange rate is $1 = €1.

Cash is the worst option. Whether you take dollars and exchange them in Paris or buy euros at the bank before you leave, you will pay a premium to exchange your dollars into foreign currency. Buying €200 before you leave is likely to cost you between $212 and $220; exchanging your dollars for €200 in Paris will cost you at least $210. In addition, you run the risk that your cash might be stolen. Both expensive and risky, it's a terrible choice.

Travelers' checks are safer than cash, but they tend to be expensive. You will need to buy them before you leave—the fee is usually 1 to 1½ percent of the amount you purchase—and then you will need to exchange them in Paris, again at a fee. While your local bank will sell you travelers' checks denominated in foreign currencies, those tend to be expensive as well, since the exchange rate the bank uses is about 5 percent below the market rate. If the newspaper quotes a rate of one dollar to one euro, you will pay at least $210 for €200 worth

of travelers' checks. And if you pay an additional fee of 1 to 1½ percent, you could end up paying closer to $215.

For most people, an ATM card is the best way to get cash for a foreign vacation. On the back of your ATM card you'll see several symbols for electronic banking networks, such as Plus and Cirrus. Any ATM bearing one of these symbols will give you cash. Since you will get the current market exchange rate, at $2 to $5 per withdrawal, this is usually the cheapest way to get foreign currency. If you withdraw €200 all at once, it will cost you only $202 to $205. Since the fee is charged each time you make a withdrawal, you should get enough cash to last for a while.

Unless you're desperate, don't use a credit card to get a cash advance. Banks charge an additional fee of up to 4 percent for such advances! But when you go shopping in a foreign country, paying with a credit card is smart. Your bank, the issuer of your VISA or MasterCard, charges a small percentage of the purchase price (usually between 1 and 4 percent) but then gives you the interbank exchange rate you see in the newspaper. At a market exchange rate of $1 = €1, a €200 purchase will cost you only $202 to $208.

All these options can be confusing, and none is best for everyone. So when you're planning your trip, take a few minutes to speak to someone in your local bank and figure out what's best for you.

conventional deposit accounts and loans. This trend began in 1998 with Citigroup's creation (see the chapter introduction). At the time Citigroup was established, insurance companies were permitted to own investment banks, so Traveler's Insurance could merge, unchallenged, with the brokerage and investment banking businesses known as Salomon Smith Barney. But the two together could not legally purchase Citibank. They did it anyway and were given five years to sell off those businesses the law prohibited them from keeping. Instead of divesting Citibank, however, Citigroup did the opposite. Managers set to work integrating all the businesses, betting that Congress would amend the law to legalize Citigroup's innovative combination.

In November 1999, the Gramm-Leach-Bliley Financial Services Modernization Act went into effect. The new law effectively repealed the Glass-Steagall Act of 1933, allowing a commercial bank, investment bank, and insurance company to merge and form a financial holding company. Citigroup, with more than 100 million customers in over 100 countries and assets in excess of $1 trillion, became legal. Since then, firms like Merrill Lynch and JPMorgan, which once dealt only in securities,

Table 13.3   Making Payments on Your Foreign Vacation

The Options	Approximate Cost of €200 at a market exchange rate of $1 = €1	Comment
Dollars exchanged for euros in europe	$210 to $215	Risky and expensive
Euros obtained before you leave	$212 to $220	Risky and expensive
Dollar-denominated travelers' checks	$210 to $215	Major brands can be replaced if stolen Nearly as expensive as cash
Euro-denominated travelers' checks	$210 to $215	Must be ordered in advance Can be very expensive
ATM (debit) card	$202 to $205	For most people, the cheapest way to get cash To minimize fees, withdraw large amounts
Credit card	$202 to $208	Economical way to pay for purchases Expensive way to get cash

have purchased commercial banks. To serve all their customers' financial needs, bank holding companies are converting to financial holding companies.

Financial holding companies are a limited form of universal banks, firms that engage in nonfinancial as well as financial activities. Depending on the country, such an arrangement provides more or less separation among the banking, insurance, and securities industries. The most extreme example is Germany, where universal banks do everything under one roof, including direct investment in the shares of nonfinancial firms. In the United States, different financial activities must be undertaken in separate subsidiaries, and financial holding companies are still prohibited from making equity investments in nonfinancial companies.

The owners and managers of these large financial firms cite three reasons to create them. First, they are well diversified, so their profitability does not rely on one particular line of business. This reduced risk should increase the value of the firm.[9] Second,

[9]Financial economists disagree on whether the reduced risk would actually increase the firm's value. Some people argue that firms should not diversify themselves but leave the choice to their stockholders. An investor can always purchase shares in two companies that would otherwise merge, in proportion to whatever risk exposure the investor desires.

IN THE NEWS
Bringing Universal Banks Down to Earth

Financial Times

by Jordi Canals

November 3, 2002

A decade ago, as a financial crisis hit western economies and the influence of capital markets spread, many experts predicted the irreversible decline of traditional commercial banks. As a result, many such institutions reinvented themselves during the 1990s and became big participants in financial markets, along with traditional investment banks.

With Bank America, Citigroup, JP Morgan, ABN Amro, Credit Suisse, and HSBC, a new class of powerful universal banks was born, arranging a formidable combination of different business units under the same corporate umbrella. Unfortunately, the ethical standards of behavior in some universal banks during the past few years have deteriorated so much that public trust in them has fallen.

In the light of recent events, the question now is whether this model of banking is sustainable. The current crisis afflicting these banks underlines the existence of conflicts of interest between their research and corporate finance units. As a result, US regulators are considering setting up an independent stock research organization

funded by investment banks to provide an alternative to Wall Street.

But that would not solve the main problem for universal banks: risk management. In the past decade, they have used their capital muscle to enter the traditional business of investment banks: providing advice to large corporations. They must decide how much lending risk to take up with a customer in order to gain lucrative advisory work. The temptation is to take on too much credit risk; and the failure of a large universal bank can wreak havoc across an economy.

Faced with this danger, would it therefore not be a better solution if regulators unbundled universal banks? The answer is no. The recently repealed Glass-Steagall Act that broke down universal banks in the United States in the 1930s was a good law neither for banks nor for the economy. Too many particular interests became embroiled and eventually distorted its original purpose. A much better solution today would be a combination of strict rules of corporate governance for banks, disclosure and self-regulation. Regulators could thus avoid meddling in an area where the potential for political interference and inefficiency is huge.

But regulators must win from universal banks a clear commitment in three areas. First, the reorganization of universal banks and their transformation into holding companies. Universal banks could break down the con-

these firms are large enough to take advantage of economies of scale. A financial holding company needs only one CEO and one board of directors regardless of its size. Only one accounting system is required to run the company. Third, these companies hope to benefit from economies of scope. In the same way that a supermarket offers all sorts of food and nonfood items under one roof, financial holding companies offer customers a wide variety of services, all under the same brand name. This, too, should reduce costs—or maybe the people who run these firms are just trying to build empires.

While Citigroup was creating the first of these full-service financial firms in the United States, the rest of the financial world was not standing still. Individual firms were working to provide customers with the same services they could obtain from more traditional financial intermediaries. Money-market mutual funds began to compete with banks in providing liquidity services to customers. Mortgage brokers gave consumers a choice in how to borrow for the purchase of a home and then sold the mortgages in the financial marketplace. Today, people who need an auto loan or any kind of insurance can get dozens of price quotes in a few hours just by logging onto the Internet. The screening of loan applicants, which was once the job of the neighborhood banker, has been standardized and now can be done by virtually anyone.

glomerate into retail banking, corporate lending and advisory, brokerage, and research activities. They could give business units legal independence and offer full information on their profitability and financial health. Doing so would not only help regulators and investors but also improve management practices.

Second, improvements in transparency. Regulators should set limits on risk taking and require universal banks to disclose the total risk that they hold with—and the income they generate from—each customer to whom they also provide advisory services. Stock-market regulators would also monitor the recommendations that the bank's research unit applies to the stock of its customers. There is no need to force universal banks to shut down their research units. But if they want to keep them within the corporate group, they should have to set up a formal subsidiary for the purpose. In the end, it is for investors to decide whether they want research from universal banks or from elsewhere.

The third area concerns disclosure of potential conflicts of interest. Universal banks may well end up generating so many conflicts that it would be neither feasible nor efficient to regulate them individually. But regulators and investors do have a right to expect full disclosure from universal banks of potential conflicts of interest. There must be strict sanctions in cases where banks cross the line.

The repeal of the Glass-Steagall Act in the United States was the right decision, even if current events suggest otherwise. Recent misbehavior by some banks is the outcome not of more flexible legislation but of a combination of bad governance, imprudent risk management, unethical behavior, and greed. A clear reorganization of

the business units, better corporate governance, disclosure and strong ethical standards are the right way forward.

But banks should not wait too long before proposing their own reforms, or they may have to accept what regulators foist on them.

The writer is dean of the IESE Business School at the University of Navarra in Barcelona, Spain.

Reprinted from The Financial Times *2002 © Jordi Canals.*

LESSONS OF THE ARTICLE

The Glass-Steagall Act was passed in an effort to eliminate potential conflicts of interest that arise when a firm underwrites securities for one set of customers and manages assets for another set. But by separating investment banking from commercial banking, the law limited the ability of financial institutions to take advantage of economies of scale and scope that might exist in various lines of business. The repeal of the Glass-Steagall Act in 1999 eliminated that problem but renewed concerns about potential mismanagement of large financial holding companies. The solution to that problem is not to turn back but to institute regulations that require public disclosure of potential conflicts of interest.

Then there are discount brokerage firms like Charles Schwab and E-Trade, which provide low-cost access to the financial markets. Unlike the banks of the past, these alternative financial intermediaries don't have balance sheets of their own. Instead, for a fee they provide their customers with access to financial markets.

In fact, thanks to recent technological advances, almost every service traditionally provided by financial intermediaries can now be produced independently, without the help of a large organization. Loan brokers can give large borrowers access to the pooled funds of many small savers. A variety of financial firms, including brokerage firms and mutual-fund companies, provides connections to the payments system, as well as the ability to transform assets into money quickly and at low cost. One of these days, even the electric company may get into the act. And many intermediaries, including mutual-fund companies and pension funds, help customers to spread, share, and transfer risk. Finally, the production of information to mitigate the problems of adverse selection and moral hazard has become a business in and of itself.

As we survey the financial industry, then, we see two trends running in opposite directions. On the one hand, large firms are working hard to provide one-stop shopping for financial services. On the other hand, the industry is splintering into a host of small firms, each of which serves a very specific purpose. Will the future be one of generalists, specialists, or both? We will have to wait and see. In the meantime, let's look more closely at the role of nondepository financial institutions. And as we do, let's think about whether their products can be provided more easily and cheaply alone or together with other financial services.

Nondepository Institutions

A survey of the financial industry reveals a broad array of intermediaries. Besides depository institutions, there are five categories of nondepository institution: insurance companies; pension funds; securities firms, including brokers, mutual-fund companies, and investment banks; finance companies; and government-sponsored enterprises. This classification is neither exhaustive nor meant to imply that an institution's activities are restricted to a particular category. Nondepository institutions also include an assortment of alternative intermediaries, such as pawnshops (see Your Financial World, page 343), payday loan centers (see Your Financial World, page 299), rent-to-own centers, and even loan sharks.

Table 13.4 shows that depository institutions accounted for just under one-third of the $34 trillion in assets held by financial intermediaries in 2004. Over the last three decades of the 20th century, the share of intermediation handled by banks fell steadily. Insurance companies suffered a similar fate as their share of intermediation fell from 18.5 percent in 1970 to 14.5 percent in 2004. Meanwhile, mutual funds have been the big winners, growing from a 3.5 percent share in 1970 to over 20 percent in 2004. Pension funds increased in importance as well, rising from 12.5 percent of all assets in 1970 to 22 percent over the 33-year period.

Our goal in this section is to understand the role of each of these types of nondepository institution in our financial system. We will do so by focusing on the functions of each. Recall from Chapter 11 that the functions of financial institutions can be divided into five categories: (1) pooling the resources of small savers; (2) providing safekeeping and accounting services, which allow people to make payments and track their assets; (3) supplying liquidity by converting resources into means of payment whenever needed; (4) providing diversification services; and (5) collecting and processing information in order to reduce information costs. We will use the same system to classify nondepository institutions.

Table 13.4   Relative Size of U.S. Financial Intermediaries, 1960–2004

	Approx. Number 2000	Assets ($ billion) 2004	Percentage of all Intermediary Assets				
			1960	1970	1980	1990	2004
Depository Institutions							
Commercial banks[a]	8,000	8,043.9	38.2%	37.2%	35.7%	29.3%	23.8%
Savings institutions	1,500	1,556.5	18.8	18.8	18.8	12.1	4.6
Credit unions	10,000	634.5	1.1	1.3	1.5	1.9	1.9
Insurance Companies							
Life insurance	1,500	3,848.8	19.4	14.8	11.0	12.1	11.4
Property and casualty	3,200	1,068.5	4.4	3.7	4.3	4.7	3.2
Pension Funds							
Private pension funds	32,500	4,259.2	6.3	8.1	12.0	14.4	12.6
Government pension funds	1,150	3,255.5	3.3	4.4	4.7	6.5	9.6
Mutual Funds							
Money-market funds	1,300	1,971.9	0.0	0.0	1.8	4.4	5.8
Stock and bond funds	11,000	4,890.4	2.9	3.5	1.6	5.7	14.5
Finance Companies	**2,000**	**1,401.4**	**4.7**	**4.7**	**4.9**	**5.4**	**4.2**
Government-Sponsored Enterprises[b]	**7**	**2,824.9**	**1.0**	**3.4**	**4.2**	**3.7**	**8.4**

Total Assets of All U.S. Financial Institutions in 2004 = $34 trillion

[a]Data of commercial banks includes U.S.-chartered banks, foreign bank offices in the United States, bank holding companies, and banks in U.S.-affiliated areas.

[b]Includes the Federal Home Loan Banks, Federal National Mortgage Association, Federal Home Loan Mortgage Corporation, Farm Credit System, Financing Corporation, Resolution Trust Corporation, and Student Loan Marketing Association.

Source: Board of Governors of the Federal Reserve, Flow of Funds of the United States, June 10, 2004, Tables L.109 to L.128.

Insurance Companies

Insurance companies began with long sea voyages. Centuries ago, transoceanic trade and exploration were fraught with risk, and that risk generated a demand for insurance. Over time, as long, risky voyages of discovery became the norm and the nature of sea travel changed, insurance changed with it. Modern forms of insurance can be traced back to around 1400, when wool merchants insured their overland shipments from London to Italy for 12 to 15 percent of their value. (Overseas shipments were even more expensive to insure.) The first insurance codes were developed in Florence in 1523. They specified the standard provisions for a general insurance policy, such as the beginning and end of the coverage period and the time frame for receipt of payment following a loss. They also stipulated procedures for handling fraudulent claims in an attempt to reduce the moral hazard problem.

In 1688, Lloyd's of London was established. Today, Lloyd's is famous for insuring singers' voices, dancers' legs, even food critics' taste buds, as well as more traditional assets like airplanes and ships.[10] The best-known insurance company in the world, Lloyd's began in a small London coffeehouse whose proprietor, Edward Lloyd, catered to retired sea captains who had prospered in the East Indies spice trade. Having sailed many of the trade routes themselves, these captains possessed special knowledge of the hazards of sea voyages. They used their knowledge to assess the risks associated with particular routes and to dabble in marine insurance. The risks were not inconsequential. In the 17th century, a typical voyage to the Spice Islands (part of Indonesia) and back lasted three years. Only one in three ships returned with their cargo, and as few as one in eight sailors lived to tell of the adventure. The rewards of a successful voyage were coveted spices like nutmeg, a single sack of which could make a sea captain wealthy for the rest of his life.

To obtain insurance, a ship's owner would write the details of the proposed voyage on a piece of paper, together with the amount he was willing to pay for the service, and then circulate the paper among the patrons at Edward Lloyd's coffeehouse. Interested individuals would decide how much of the risk to accept and then sign their names under the description of the voyage. This customary way of doing business became the source of the term *underwriter*. Underwriting was open to anyone who wished to assume the risk associated with sea voyages. Because Lloyd's predated by several centuries the concept of limited liability, in which investors' losses were confined to the amount of their investment, underwriting implied unlimited liability. The saying was that an underwriter was liable down to his last cufflink.

Today, Lloyd's operates in much the same way that it did three centuries ago. It is better thought of as an insurance market than as an insurance company. To participate in the market, individuals known as *names* join together in groups called syndicates. When a new insurance contract is offered, several syndicates sign up for a portion of the risk in return for a portion of the premiums.

Historically, becoming a name with Lloyd's has brought both reputation and risk. The risks were never more apparent than in the early 1990s, when Lloyd's racked up losses in excess of $10 billion as a result of claims on policies that protected firms against the legal damages associated with asbestos. The huge amount exceeded the estimated combined assets of all 34,000 Lloyd's names. Because of their unlimited liability, nearly 2,000 individuals were driven into personal bankruptcy; many of them filed lawsuits claiming that Lloyd's management had misled them. As a result, Lloyd's was reorganized. Today the firm continues to provide insurance through the more conventional structure of a limited liability company. The losses of individual

---

[10]The list of insurance contracts written by Lloyd's is legendary. Through its syndicate structure, it has insured individuals against death or injury caused by a piece of disintegrated satellite falling from the sky; it has also insured Russian cosmonauts traveling to the Mir space station on a U.S. space shuttle. Lloyd's has insured employers against the possibility of two or more of their staff members winning the lottery and failing to return to work. And it has insured Cutty Sark Whisky against the possibility of someone capturing the Loch Ness monster alive and claiming the £1 million prize the company offered. Lloyd's has insured the Olympic Games, the British and Commonwealth Games, the World Athletics Championships, and the World and European Soccer Championships. Lloyd's even insured a 20-year-old who planned to cross the English Channel in a seagoing bathtub, on the condition that he keep the drain plugged.

investors in a syndicate are limited to the amount of their initial investment, and no person is exposed to the possibility of financial ruin.

Two Types of Insurance   At their most basic level, all insurance companies operate like Lloyd's of London. They accept premiums from policyholders in exchange for the promise of compensation if certain events occur. A homeowner pays a premium in return for the promise that if the house burns down, the insurance company will pay to rebuild it. For the individual policyholder, then, insurance is a way to transfer risk. In terms of the financial system as a whole, insurance companies specialize in three of the five functions performed by intermediaries: They pool small premiums and make large investments with them; they diversify risks across a large population; and they screen and monitor policyholders to mitigate the problem of asymmetric information.

Insurance companies offer two types of insurance: life insurance and property and casualty insurance. Life insurers—companies like Prudential of America, Metropolitan Life, and John Hancock Mutual Life—sell policies that protect the insured against the loss of earnings from disability, retirement, or death. Roughly 1,500 companies offer life insurance in the United States. Property and casualty companies sell policies that protect households and businesses from losses arising from accident, fire, and natural disaster. There are 3,200 of these companies in the United States, including well-known firms like State Farm Group, Allstate, and Traveler's. Both types of intermediary allow individuals to transfer their risk to a group. While a single company may provide both kinds of insurance, the two businesses operate very differently.

Life insurance comes in two basic forms, called term and whole life insurance, as well as a variety of hybrids. Term life insurance provides a payment to the policyholder's beneficiaries in the event of the insured's death at any time during the policy's term. The premium depends on the very predictable probability of someone dying. Term policies are generally renewable every year so long as the policyholder is less than 65 years old. Many people obtain term life insurance through their employers, an arrangement called group life insurance.

Whole life insurance is a combination of term life insurance and a savings account. The policyholder pays a fixed premium over his or her lifetime in return for a fixed benefit when the policyholder dies. Should the policyholder decide to discontinue the policy, its cash value will be refunded. As time passes and the policyholder ages, the emphasis of the whole life policy shifts from insurance to savings. Someone who lives to a ripe old age will have accumulated substantial savings in a whole life policy, which can be cashed in if the policyholder chooses. In fact, most whole life policies can be cashed in at any time. Whole life insurance tends to be an expensive way to save, though, so its use as a savings vehicle has declined markedly as people have discovered cheaper alternatives (see Table 13.4).

Most adults have experience with property and casualty insurance because driving a car without it is illegal. Auto insurance is a combination of property insurance on the car itself and casualty insurance on the driver, who is protected against liability for harm or injury to other people or their property. Holders of property and casualty insurance pay premiums in exchange for protection during the term of the policy.

On the balance sheets of insurance companies, these promises to policyholders show up as liabilities. While some claims may already be in process, most of them are future claims. On the asset side, insurance companies hold a combination of stocks and bonds. Property and casualty companies profit from the fees they charge for administering the policies they write; the claims are covered by the premiums. Because the assets are essentially reserves against sudden claims, they have to be liquid. A look at the balance sheet of a property and casualty insurer will show a preponderance of very short-term money-market instruments.

Life insurance companies hold assets of longer maturity than property and casualty insurers, since most of their payments will be made well into the future. While stocks may carry a relatively low risk when held for periods of 25 years or more (recall the discussion in Chapter 8), insurance companies cannot risk the possibility that they may be forced to sell stocks when prices are low in order to pay policyholders' claims. As a result, life insurance companies hold mostly bonds.

The Role of Insurance Companies Like life insurers, property and casualty insurers pool risks to generate predictable payouts. That is, they reduce risk by spreading it across many policies. Recall from Chapter 5 that a group of investments with uncorrelated returns is less risky than any individual investment. The same is true of insurance contracts. While there is no way to know exactly which policies will require payment—who will have an automobile accident, lose a house to fire, or die— the insurance company can estimate precisely the percentage of policyholders who

YOUR FINANCIAL WORLD

How Much Life Insurance Do You Need?

We discussed disability insurance in Chapter 3 and automobile insurance in Chapter 5. What about life insurance? How much should you buy? The first question is whether you should buy any at all. The purpose of life insurance is to take care of the people you are supporting should something unpleasant happen to you. Think of it as replacement income that will be there when you're not. People with young children are the ones who need life insurance the most. If a parent dies, someone will have to raise those children and put them through school, and a life insurance policy will pay the bills. Life insurance is *not* for a single college student with no obligations, so don't let anyone sell it to you if you don't need it.

If you think you need life insurance, the next step is to decide what kind. The best approach is to buy *term life insurance,* which will pay off only if you die. Because other kinds of life insurance include investment components, they are more costly. And since the people who need life insurance most are young families with limited incomes and big expenses, the more affordable the policy, the better. Making your insurance and investment decisions separately is also easier than trying to achieve all your goals with a single vehicle.[*]

Finally, how much life insurance should you buy? If you are married with two small children, most advisors recommend that you buy a term policy worth six to eight times your annual income. While that might cover your family's living expenses until the children are grown, consider carefully whether it will be enough to send them to college. If you and your spouse each earn $35,000 a year, each of you might need $400,000 worth of life insurance. For someone who is between 30 and 40 years old, a $400,000 policy costs about $500 a year, so out of your joint annual income of $70,000, you and your spouse would be spending $1,000 on term life insurance. That's expensive, so don't buy more than you need.

[*]Your parents and grandparents may have purchased whole life insurance policies for two reasons. First, in the past, individuals did not have access to all the investment choices that are available today. Second, tax laws were different; for some people, saving through a whole life insurance policy had tax advantages. But with the creation of tax-deferred savings vehicles like individual retirement accounts (IRAs), those benefits disappeared. Today, you would likely pay a life insurance company much more than the value of any tax benefits to you to administer a whole life insurance policy.

will file claims. Doing so allows managers to compute accurately, with little uncertainty, how much the firm will need to pay out in any given year. From the point of view of policyholders, property and casualty insurance allows them to spread the risk of accident and damage across a large group of individuals.

In Chapter 11, we discussed the problem of asymmetric information in stock and bond finance. Recall that when a lender or investor cannot tell a good borrower or investment from a bad one, the tendency is for only the worst opportunities to present themselves. This phenomenon is adverse selection. Furthermore, once borrowers or entrepreneurs have received financing, they have less incentive to avoid risk than the lender or investor. That problem is called moral hazard.

While adverse selection and moral hazard create significant problems in the stock and bond markets, they create worse problems in the insurance market. A person who has terminal cancer surely has an incentive to buy life insurance for the largest amount possible—that's adverse selection. And without fire insurance, people would have more fire extinguishers in their houses. Fire insurance creates moral hazard, encouraging homeowners to be less careful in protecting their homes than they would otherwise. Insurance companies work hard to reduce both these problems. By screening applicants, they can reduce adverse selection. A person who wants to buy a life insurance policy must undergo a physical evaluation: weight, blood pressure, blood tests, and health history. Only those who pass the exam are allowed to purchase policies. And people who want automobile insurance must provide their driving records, including traffic citations and accident histories. While bad drivers may be allowed to buy car insurance, they will need to pay more for it. By screening drivers and adjusting their premiums accordingly, then, insurance companies can reduce their losses due to adverse selection.

Insurance companies have ways to reduce moral hazard as well. Policies usually include restrictive covenants that require the insured to engage or not to engage in certain activities. To qualify for fire insurance, a restaurant owner might be required to have the sprinkler system examined periodically; to obtain insurance against physical injury, a baseball or basketball player might be precluded from riding a motorcycle. Beyond such covenants, insurance policies often include *deductibles*, which require the insured to pay the initial cost of repairing accidental damage, up to some maximum amount. Or they may require *coinsurance*, in which the insurance company shoulders a percentage of the claim, perhaps 80 or 90 percent, and the insured assumes the rest of the cost.

It is interesting to speculate about the future of insurance in an age in which firms can collect more and more information at lower and lower cost. Remember that insurance is meant to shift risk from individuals to groups, not to shift the responsibility for events that are certain to happen. For example, no one expects an insurance company to

"We cannot write a life policy for your husband, Mrs. Blaine, because he is already dead. In insurance terms, that is considered a preëxisting condition."

APPLYING THE CONCEPT
REINSURANCE AND "CAT BONDS"

To get a mortgage on a home, you'll need insurance. Regardless of where you live, your lender will require you to have fire insurance, and in some places you may also need insurance against natural disasters like floods, earthquakes, or hurricanes. Without such insurance you won't get a mortgage, and without a mortgage you won't buy a house. Clearly, it's in everyone's interest for insurance companies to provide such insurance and spread the risk. But sometimes this kind of insurance isn't easy to obtain.

Imagine that an insurer is thinking of offering earthquake insurance in California. Unlike automobile accidents, when an earthquake hits, a large number of policyholders will all file claims at the same time. The result for the insurance company is a large, undiversified risk. To offer earthquake insurance and stay in business, a property and casualty insurance company must find some way to insure itself against catastrophic risks—large natural disasters that generate a significant number of payouts simultaneously.

Reinsurance companies offer a solution to this problem by providing insurance to insurance companies. Say the California insurer estimates that an earthquake would generate payments of $15 billion (the approximate loss in the 1994 earthquake in Northridge, Los Angeles). The company may have the resources to cover only the first $1 billion of policyholders' claims. To write the full $15 billion worth of insurance, the company will need to buy $14 billion of reinsurance.

Reinsurance companies are enormous; they operate all over the world. Their geographic spread allows them to diversify their risk, since earthquakes don't happen at the same time in both California and Japan. The

sell life insurance to a person with a terminal disease. Herein lies a problem. With the decoding of the human genome, a battery of tests will soon be available to determine each person's probability of developing a terminal disease. Using this information, each of us will have a fairly good idea of our life expectancy and the relative cost of our health care. If applicants withhold this kind of information from insurance companies, the adverse selection problem will become so severe that the industry could collapse. But if applicants reveal the information, those who are unfortunate enough to carry undesirable genes will not be able to obtain insurance. Someone who has a high probability of getting heart disease at a young age will still be able to get automobile insurance, but getting life or health insurance will be very difficult.

The solution to this problem is not obvious, but it seems likely that any answer will involve government intervention. The government could either require insurance companies to provide coverage to everyone or act as an insurer of last resort.

Pension Funds

Like an insurance company, a pension fund offers people the ability to make premium payments today in exchange for promised payments under certain future circum-

continued from previous page

fact that reinsurance companies can spread their risk globally gives them the ability to withstand individual losses, even if they are catastrophic. For this to work, reinsurers have to be big. So big, in fact, that they have become near monopolies, driving up the price of reinsurance in the process.

The rising cost of reinsurance has spurred the creation of a second solution to the problem of insuring catastrophic risk. Financial experts have designed catastrophic bonds, or *cat bonds,* which allow individual investors to share a very small portion of the reinsurance risk. It works like this. Through an investment bank, an insurance company will sell a substantial quantity of cat bonds, immediately investing proceeds in low-risk financial instruments like U.S. Treasury bonds. If a catastrophe occurs, the U.S. Treasury bonds are sold and the resulting funds used to pay the claims the insurance company faces. But if no earthquake, fire, or hurricane hits during the policy period, the cat bond owners receive a substantial return that can be as high as 10 percentage points above the yield on U.S. Treasury bonds of equal maturity.* This high level of compensation, coupled with a very low correlation to the return on most other investments, means that cat bonds can both improve the expected return and lower the risk of a typical investor's portfolio.

The existence of reinsurance and cat bonds benefits everyone. These mechanisms for transferring and spreading the risk of catastrophic disaster improve the risk-return trade-off for individual investors, enable insurance companies to offer more insurance than they could otherwise, and allow prospective homeowners to get the insurance they need—and the mortgage financing they want—to purchase a home.

*One of the first cat bonds to be issued was a $400 million offering in 1997 by the United Service Automobile Association (USAA), an insurer of current and past military personnel and their families. The bond agreement provided that if USAA's losses from a hurricane rated category 3, 4, or 5 exceeded $1 billion over the next year, bondholders would pay 80 percent of the next $500 million in claims.

stances. Also like an insurance company, pension funds do not accept deposits. They do help people to develop the discipline of saving regularly, getting them started early and helping them to stick with it. As we saw in Chapter 4, the earlier a person begins saving and the more disciplined he or she is, the better off that person will be later in life. Saving from an early age means enjoying a higher income at retirement. Pension plans not only provide an easy way to make sure that a worker saves and has sufficient resources in old age; they help savers to diversify their risk. By pooling the savings of many small investors, pension funds spread the risk, ensuring that funds will be available to investors in their old age.

People can use a variety of methods to save for retirement, including employer-sponsored plans and individual savings plans, both of which allow workers to defer income tax on their savings until they retire. Nearly everyone who works for a large corporation in the United States has an employer-administered pension plan. There are two basic types: defined-benefit (DB) pension plans and defined-contribution (DC) pension plans. Regardless of the type, many employer-sponsored plans require a person to work for a certain number of years before qualifying for benefits. This qualifying process is called **vesting**. Think of vesting as the point at which the contributions

TIME

your employer has made to the pension plan on your behalf belong to you. Changing jobs before your pension contributions have been vested can be very costly.

Let's take a look at how the two types of pension plan work. Defined-benefit plans were once more common than they are today. Participants in DB plans receive a lifetime retirement income based on the number of years they worked at the company and their final salary. For example, someone who worked for the same company for 30 years and retired at a salary of $100,000 might receive 2 percent of that salary for each year of service, or $60,000 per year. That may seem good, but to reap such benefits, most people would need to work a very long time for the same firm.

Defined-contribution plans have become more common than defined-benefit plans, and they are very different. These plans are sometimes referred to as "401(k)"

APPLYING THE CONCEPT
PUBLIC PENSIONS AND THE SOCIAL SECURITY SYSTEM

Providing for the elderly is a tremendous challenge for any society. Traditionally, children cared for their parents when they became old. But with the advent of modern industrial societies and an associated increase in geographic mobility, many elderly parents no longer live with their children. Today the expectation is that people will save enough while they are working to pay their own way when they retire. Failing that, the general view is that in a civilized society, government should care for the poor.

During the 20th century, the governments of many countries created pension systems that provided a guaranteed income to the elderly. These programs were financed by tax revenues paid by the young. As long as workers' incomes were growing quickly enough and the population itself was growing, the arrangement worked well. Around 1970, however, both economic growth and population growth began to slow in industrialized countries. At the same time, medical care was improving, raising the prospect of a longer life for everyone. Gradually the ratio of workers to retirees began to fall, so fewer and fewer working people were supporting more and more retirees.

Today, to remain financially viable, these systems must change. The solution—to raise the retirement age to 70 instead of 65 or even 60—has so far been politically unpalatable. Failure to deal with the problem has set the stage for a crisis. In the United States, the Social Security system will soon be unable to meet the obligations currently on its books.

Social Security is not a pension system in the traditional sense of the term. All U.S. workers pay Social Security tax (see the line labeled "FICA" on your pay stub); in return, the government promises to make payments to them when they retire. But with the Social Security taxes it collects from workers, the govern-

SOURCE: *Courtesy of the Social Security Administration*

or "403(b)" accounts after their designations in the Internal Revenue Service code.[11] In a defined-contribution plan, the employee and employer both make contributions into an investment account that belongs to the employee. Unlike a defined-benefit plan, in a DC plan the employer takes no responsibility for the size of the employee's retirement income. Instead, at retirement the employee receives the accumulated funds in the account and must decide what to do with them. The options include accepting a lump sum, removing small amounts at a time, or converting the balance to a fixed monthly payment for life by purchasing an annuity.

---

[11] The 401(k) and 403(b) plans are the same except for that the first is offered by private for-profit corporations and the second by public-sector and nonprofit employers.

continued from previous page

ment can do only one of two things: it can give it to current retirees or spend it on general programs. As such, Social Security is a "pay-as-you-go" system that transfers revenues directly from current workers to current retirees.

This is a very different arrangement from a private pension fund, in which contributions accumulate and are invested for the long term and only after many years are paid out to retirees. Not only is the source of funds different but the allocation of risk differs too. In the current Social Security system, the responsibility to pay retirees belongs to younger generations. They foot the bill; they face the risk. If the economy does poorly, for example, wages of the young who are working fall, making it more burdensome to pay the taxes required to honor promises to retirees. In contrast, in a private pension system, individuals' own savings provide their retirement incomes and they themselves face the risk that the return on their investments may be low.

The Social Security system's finances are in bad shape. In 2003 the government estimated that the present value of its future obligations exceeded the present value of the expected payments into the system by about one year's GDP—more than $10 trillion at the time. (In countries like France, Germany, Italy, and Japan, matters were much worse.) Something must be done to keep the system solvent, and there are only a few options. The government can reduce the benefits promised to future retirees, raise the tax rate that future workers pay, or convert the system into one that mirrors a private pension plan, with individual accounts. Most proposals to fix the system involve some combination of all three of these approaches. For example, suggestions to *privatize* the system involve reducing benefits to those who are currently working, raising their Social Security taxes, and placing new revenues into individual accounts similar to defined-contribution pension funds. In such a system, the government would continue to guarantee that the poor do not starve, but those who are well enough to take care of themselves would have to do so.

At this point, all anyone knows is that the Social Security system will have to change and the faster the better. Many proposals have been offered to fix the looming crisis. In evaluating them, keep in mind these two key questions: Who will pay the bills and who will shoulder the risks?

You can think of a pension plan as the opposite of life insurance. One pays off if you live, the other if you don't.[12] The two vehicles are similar enough that the same institution often offers both. And not surprisingly, the balance sheets of pension funds look a lot like those of life insurance companies; both hold long-term assets like corporate bonds and stocks. The only difference is that life insurance companies hold only half the equities that pension funds do.[13]

While pension plans are required to meet certain management and investment criteria, they can still encounter financial difficulties. Corporations are required to contribute to their pension plans up to the point at which there is only a very small probability that the funds will be unable to meet their obligations. But during years when the plans' investments do well, firms are allowed to withdraw monies from the fund. When the stock market boomed in the years from 1996 to 2000, many corporate pension funds became overfunded, and company managers took withdrawals. They had every incentive to do so, since the withdrawals increased their companies' reported profits. But when the stock market collapsed in 2001–2003, pension funds lost value along with all other investments, and suddenly many of them were underfunded. According to some estimates, in 2002 the underfunding of private pensions in the United States reached several hundred billion dollars. The financial shortfall in defined-benefit plans further strained businesses' ability to remain afloat at a time when they were already doing badly.

Finally, it is worth noting that the U.S. government does provide insurance for private, defined-benefit pension systems. If a company goes bankrupt, the Pension Benefit Guaranty Corporation (PBGC) will take over the fund's liabilities. The PBGC currently guarantees some 32,000 pension funds covering nearly 50 million workers and retirees. But like all insurance, pension insurance creates the moral hazard that a firm's managers will engage in risky behavior. To guard against this possibility, regulators monitor pension funds closely.

Securities Firms: Brokers, Mutual Funds, and Investment Banks

The broad class of securities firms includes brokerages, investment banks, and mutual fund companies. In one way or another, these are all financial intermediaries. The primary services of brokerage firms are accounting (to keep track of customers' investment balances), custody services (to make sure valuable records such as stock certificates are safe), and access to secondary markets (in which customers can buy and sell financial instruments). Brokers also provide loans to customers who wish to purchase stock on margin. And they provide liquidity, both by offering check-writing privileges with their investment accounts and by allowing investors to sell assets quickly. Mutual-fund companies like Vanguard, Fidelity, and Dreyfus offer liquidity services as well; their money-market mutual funds are a key example. But the primary function of mutual funds is to pool the small savings of individuals in diversified portfolios that are composed of a wide variety of financial instruments.

[12]Pensions can be structured to make payments to survivors as well, although the arrangement usually reduces the amount of the payments. This practice is equivalent to extending the term of the benefit to include the life of a spouse or other beneficiary. Since defined-contribution pensions are normally converted to annuities at retirement, the same analysis applies to them. Nevertheless, the structure of such a pension remains complementary to that of a life insurance policy.

[13]The heavier emphasis on equities makes pension funds more risky. This is a risk that is potentially borne by the plans' participants. But as mentioned later in this section, defined-benefit pension plans are insured by the U.S. government, so in reality this is a risk borne broadly by everyone.

All securities firms are very much in the business of producing information. But while brokers and mutual funds provide some investment advice to their retail customers, information is at the heart of the investment banking business. Investment banks like Goldman Sachs, Merrill Lynch, and JP Morgan are the conduits through which firms raise funds in the capital markets. Through their underwriting services, these investment banks issue new stocks and a variety of other debt instruments. Most commonly, the underwriter guarantees the price of a new issue and then sells it to investors at a higher price, a practice called *placing the issue*. The underwriter profits from the difference between the price guaranteed to the firm that issues the security and the price at which the bond or stock is sold to investors. But since the price at which the investment bank sells the bonds or stocks in financial markets can turn out to be lower than the price guaranteed to the issuing company, there is some risk to underwriting. For most large issues, a group of investment banks will band together and spread the risk among themselves rather than one of them taking the risk alone.

Information and reputation are central to the underwriting business. Underwriters collect information to determine the price of the new securities and then put their reputations on the line when they go out to sell the issues. A large, well-established investment bank will not underwrite issues indiscriminately. To do so would reduce the value of the bank's brand, along with the fees the bank can charge.

In addition to underwriting, investment banks provide advice to firms that want to merge with or acquire other firms. Investment bankers do the research to identify potential *mergers and acquisitions* and estimate the value of the new, combined company. The information they collect and the advice they give must be valuable because they are paid handsomely for them. In facilitating these combinations, investment banks perform a service to the economy. Mergers and acquisitions help to ensure that the people who manage firms do the best job possible. Managers who don't get the most out of the resources entrusted to them risk having their company purchased by executives who can do a better job. This threat of a takeover provides discipline in the management of individual companies and improves the allocation of resources across the economy.

Finance Companies

Finance companies are in the lending business. They raise funds directly in the financial markets by issuing commercial paper and securities and then use them to make loans to individuals and corporations. Since these companies specialize in making loans, they are concerned largely with reducing the transactions and information costs that are associated with intermediated finance. Finance companies are particularly good at screening potential borrowers' creditworthiness, monitoring their performance during the term of the loan, and seizing collateral in the event of a default.

Most finance companies specialize in one of three loan types: consumer loans, business loans, and what are called sales loans. Some also provide commercial and home mortgages. *Consumer finance* firms provide small installment loans to individual consumers. If you visit an appliance store to purchase a new refrigerator, you may be offered a deal that includes "no money down and no payments for six months." If you accept this loan offer, you'll be asked to fill out an application and to wait a few minutes while someone checks your credit. The credit is usually supplied not by the store but by a finance company like Household Finance Corporation or Wells Fargo. This kind of consumer credit allows people without sufficient savings to purchase appliances such as television sets, washing machines, and microwave ovens.

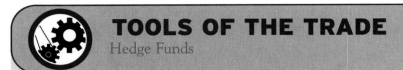

TOOLS OF THE TRADE
Hedge Funds

Hedge funds are strictly for millionaires. These investment partnerships (sometimes referred to as *nontraditional investment funds*) bring together small groups of people who meet certain wealth requirements. To avoid various legal regulations, hedge funds come in two basic sizes: they can have a maximum of either 99 investors, each of whom has at least $1 million in net worth, or 499 investors, each of whom has at least $5 million in net worth. The larger hedge funds can also accept funds from institutional investors like pension funds, mutual funds, and insurance companies so long as their net worth is at least $25 million. The minimum investment in a hedge fund is usually $100,000. These really are millionaires' investment clubs.

Hedge funds are run by a general partner, or manager, who is in charge of day-to-day decisions. Managers are very well paid, receiving an annual fee of at least 2 percent of assets plus 20 percent of profits. In a year in which the fund's return on investment is 10 percent, the manager of an average-size fund of $500 million will receive $20 million in fees.

Because these funds are unregulated, finding out what their portfolios contain can be a challenge even for the fund's investors: the manager simply doesn't tell anyone. This secrecy creates the very real possibility of moral hazard. If a fund starts to incur losses, determining the reason for the fall in value is often impossible. To ensure that the manager's incentives match those of the investors, the manager is required to keep a large fraction of his or her own wealth in the fund. By and large, this requirement solves the problem of moral hazard; fraudulent behavior is extremely rare.

The name *hedge fund* may suggest that these funds employ the diversification techniques discussed in Chapter 5, but they do not. Hedging reduces risk by grouping together individual investments whose returns tend to move in opposite directions, but hedge funds are not low-risk enterprises. Because they are organized as private partnerships, hedge funds are not constrained in their investment strategies; they can trade in derivatives and borrow to create leverage.

A. W. Jones founded the first hedge fund in 1949. His fund combined leverage with short selling (the practice of borrowing a stock or bond whose price you believe will fall, selling it, and then buying it back at a lower price before repaying the lender). Jones divided the fund's equities into two groups: companies whose stock prices he thought would fall and companies whose stock prices he thought would rise. He sold the first group short and used the proceeds to buy shares in the second group. The term *hedge* in the name *hedge fund* comes from the fact that when the market in general went up or down, moving all stocks in the same direction, the fund would take losses on one group of stock but turn a profit on the second. It was hedged against movements in the market as a whole. Instead, Jones turned a profit when the stocks he sold short went down relative to the stocks he purchased. And those profits were substantial.

Today we would refer to Jones's fund as a "long-short hedge fund," since he was long on some stocks and short on others. Roughly 6,000 hedge funds are in existence today, and the long-short approach is only one of the strategies their managers follow. *Macro fund* managers take unhedged positions in the hope of benefiting from shifts in interest rates or national market conditions. *Global fund* managers engage in international stock picking. And the managers of *relative value funds* try to exploit small, transitory differences in the prices of related securities, such as U.S. Treasury bills and bonds. Long-Term Capital Management, the hedge fund that collapsed in September 1998 (see Chapter 9), was following this last strategy, trying to take advantage of price differences between U.S. Treasury bonds of slightly different maturities. Playing games with interest rates is what led the firm to amass $1.25 trillion in interest-rate swaps.

Regardless of the strategies they use, all hedge fund managers strive to create returns that roughly equal those of the stock market (as measured by a comprehensive index like the S&P 500) but are uncorrelated with it. So while individual hedge funds are very risky—something like 10 percent of them close down every year—a portfolio that invests in a large number of these funds can expect returns equal to the stock market average with very little risk at all. That is why people like hedge funds and why successful hedge fund managers are so well paid.

Business finance companies provide loans to businesses. If you want to start your own airline, for example, you will need to acquire some airplanes. That isn't as difficult as it may sound, because you don't need to shell out the entire $100 million price of a new plane. Airplanes, like automobiles, can be leased. That is, a business finance company buys the plane and then leases it back to you, an approach that significantly reduces the cost of starting your new enterprise. While this example is extreme, finance companies will purchase many types of equipment and lease them back to firms.

In addition to equipment leasing, business finance companies provide both inventory loans and accounts receivable loans. Inventory loans enable firms to keep their shelves stocked so that when a customer asks for a product, the firm can fill the order. Accounts receivable loans provide firms with immediate resources in anticipation of receipt of customers' payments. The purpose of both these loan types is to provide short-term liquidity to firms.

Sales finance companies specialize in larger loans for major purchases, such as automobiles. Car dealers customarily offer financing to people who are shopping for a new car. When you purchase a car, at a certain point in the negotiations the salesperson will ask how you intend to pay for it. Unless you have sizable savings or are buying a very cheap car, you will need to borrow. The car business is organized so that you don't need

YOUR FINANCIAL WORLD
Pawnshops

Contrary to their portrayal in the movies and on TV, pawnshops are not disreputable establishments frequented by criminals who are selling stolen goods. They are legitimate businesses that provide a useful service. Think of a pawnshop as a neighborhood nondepository institution that makes collateralized loans and sells a wide variety of merchandise on the side. The pawnshop's main business is to provide very small loans—smaller than a bank would consider—to people who lack access to the conventional financial system.

Say you have something valuable, like a piece of jewelry, a bicycle, or a camera. You need cash, so you take the valuable item to a pawnshop. The pawnbroker will offer you a loan on the condition that you leave the item there as collateral. When you repay the loan along with interest and fees, the pawnbroker will return your collateral. But if you don't repay the loan on time, the pawnbroker takes the collateral and sells it. The merchandise that's for sale in the pawnshop was collateral for defaulted loans.

Needless to say, the terms of the loan are favorable to the pawnbroker, not to you. The loan amount is usually less than half the value of the collateral, and the interest rate is high: 3 to 5 per-cent *per month* is standard. There is also a fee that can drive up the interest rate to several hundred percent per year. While such an arrangement may seem outrageous, it is better than the payday loan described in Chapter 12. Because pawnbrokers' loans are collateralized, the interest rates charged are more reasonable than the ones on payday loans. So if you ever find yourself in dire straits, with no other source of credit, by all means go to a pawnshop.

SOURCE: © *Ralf-Finn Hestoft/CORBIS*

to leave the dealership to get your loan; someone there will take care of it for you. The financing is arranged through a finance company that specializes in making car loans. Every major auto manufacturer owns a finance company, as do large retailers like Sears.

Government-Sponsored Enterprises

You will not be surprised to learn that the U.S. government is directly involved in the financial intermediation system. In some cases the government provides loan guarantees; in others, it charters financial institutions to provide specific types of financing, such as home, farm, and student loans. When Congress wanted to make sure that low- and moderate-income families could get mortgages, it created the Federal National Mortgage Association (Fannie Mae), a private corporation, and the Government National Mortgage Corporation (*Ginnie Mae*), a corporation that is wholly owned by the federal government. Later, Congress chartered the Federal Home Loan Mortgage Corporation (*Freddie Mac*). To encourage farm loans, Congress created the Farm Credit System. And to provide student loans, Congress chartered the Student Loan Marketing Association (*Sallie Mae*).[14]

All these government-sponsored enterprises have the same basic structure. They issue short-term bonds and use the proceeds to provide loans of one form or another. Because of their relationship to the government, these associations and corporations can obtain lower than average interest rates on their liabilities, which they then pass on to homeowners, farmers, and students in the form of subsidized mortgages and loans.

Housing intermediation is by far the largest of these government-sponsored activities, enabling people with low incomes to become homeowners. Because Fannie Mae and Freddie Mac, the two largest of these institutions, are private corporations rather than government agencies, their solvency is not explicitly guaranteed by the government. Instead, both benefit from an implicit guarantee and a line of credit from the U.S. Treasury. The general belief is that because of these corporations' size and their importance to the economy, the federal government will not allow them to fail. This perception allows Fannie Mae and Freddie Mac to borrow at rates lower than those available to private competitors.

In recent years, Fannie Mae and Freddie Mac have been heavily criticized. Federal Reserve officials have been particularly vocal about the problems they see in the structure of the two corporations, suggesting that it could precipitate a financial crisis. During the 1990s, the two companies grew rapidly; by 2003 they either owned or guaranteed nearly half of all residential mortgages in the nation. They did so by borrowing more cheaply than institutions without Treasury connections. As a result, they are now very highly leveraged, much more so than any commercial bank is permitted to be. Recall from Chapter 12 that the average U.S. bank has a leverage ratio (assets divided by capital) of about 11 to 1. Fannie Mae and Freddie Mac have debt-to-equity ratios more than twice as high. Their financial statements for the end of 2003 revealed that both had a leverage ratio of about 30 to 1. With such low levels of capital, Fannie Mae and Freddie Mac cannot withstand significant numbers of defaults. Government officials worry that a dramatic decline in home prices could create enough mortgage defaults to cause these institutions to fail.

In a sense, Fannie Mae and Freddie Mac are victims of their own success. Managers took the government's guarantees, borrowed cheaply, and created an enormous mortgage market that has encouraged home ownership. In other words, they achieved Congress's goal. The question we need to ask today is whether these corporations

---

[14]For details on these programs, see the Web site of the Department of Housing and Urban Development, www.hud.gov/gse.

Table 13.5   Summary of Financial Industry Structure

Financial Intermediary	Primary Sources of Funds (Liabilities)	Primary Uses of Funds (Assets)	Services Provided
Depository Institution (Bank)	Checkable deposits Savings and time deposits Borrowing from other banks	Cash Loans Securities	• Pooling of small savings to provide large loans • Diversified, liquid deposit accounts • Access to payments system • Screening and monitoring of borrowers
Insurance Company	Expected claims	Corporate bonds Government bonds Stocks Mortgages	• Pooling of risk • Screening and monitoring of policy-holders
Securities Firm	Short-term loans	Commercial paper Bonds	• Management of asset pools • Clearing and settling trades
Investment Bank			• Immediate sale of assets • Access to spectrum of assets, allowing diversification • Evaluation of firms wishing to issue securities • Research and advice for investors
Mutual-Fund Company	Shares sold to customers	Commercial paper Bonds Mortgages Stocks Real estate	• Pooling of small savings to provide access to large, diversified portfolios, which can be liquid
Finance Company	Bonds Bank loans Commercial paper	Mortgages Consumer loans Business loans	• Screening and monitoring of borrowers
Pension Fund	Policy benefits to be paid out to future retirees	Stocks Government bonds Corporate bonds Commercial paper	• Pooling of employees' and employers' contributions • Diversification of long-term investments to ensure future income for retirees
Government-Sponsored Enterprise	Commercial paper Bonds Loan guarantees	Mortgages Farm loans Student loans	• Access to financing for borrowers who cannot obtain it elsewhere

have grown so large that they threaten the stability of the financial system. Many people have argued that these government-chartered institutions should be required to hold capital in the same proportion as a commercial bank and that the U.S. government should explicitly distance itself from them. Whether either of these recommendations is implemented will depend more on politics than on economics.

Table 13.5 summarizes the characteristics and roles of financial intermediaries.

Terms

bank charter, 318
bank holding company, 322
defined-benefit pension plan, 338
defined-contribution pension plan, 338
dual banking system, 319
economies of scale, 329
economies of scope, 329
eurodollars, 325
Fannie Mae, 344
financial holding company, 327
hedge fund, 342

London Interbank Offered Rate (LIBOR), 326
property and casualty insurance, 333
reinsurance company, 336
term life insurance, 333
underwriting, 341
unit bank, 317
universal bank, 328
vesting, 337
whole life insurance, 333

Chapter Lessons

1. The United States has a comparatively large but declining number of banks.

   a. The large number of banks in the United States is explained by restrictions on branching, both within and across state lines, that were imposed by the federal government in 1927.

   b. The large number of banks in the United States is a sign of an anticompetitive legal environment.

   c. Since 1997, banks have been permitted to operate in more than one state. This change has increased competition and driven many small, inefficient banks out of business.

   d. Between 1933 and 1999, banks were prohibited from engaging in the securities and insurance businesses.

   e. Banking has been expanding not just across state boundaries but across international boundaries.

      i. Many U.S. banks operate abroad, and a large number of foreign banks do business in the United States.

      ii. Eurodollars—dollar deposits in foreign banks—play an important part in the international financial system.

   f. The financial industry is constantly evolving. With changes in regulations, financial services can now be provided in two ways:

      i. through a large universal bank, which provides all the services anyone could possibly need.

ii. through small specialized firms, which supply a limited number of services at a low price.

2. Nondepository institutions are playing an increasingly important role in the financial system. Five types of financial intermediary may be classified as nondepository institutions.

a. Insurance companies.

i. Life insurance companies insure policyholders against death through term life insurance and provide a vehicle for saving through whole life insurance.

ii. Property and casualty companies insure individuals and businesses against losses arising from specific events, like accidents and fires.

iii. The two primary functions of insurance companies are to:

• allow policyholders to transfer risk.

• screen and monitor policyholders to reduce adverse selection and moral hazard.

b. Pension funds perform two basic services.

i. They allow employees and employers to make payments today so that employees will receive an income after retirement.

ii. They spread risk by ensuring that those employees who live longer than others will continue to receive an income. For this reason, pension funds may be thought of as the opposite of life insurance.

c. Securities firms include three basic types of financial intermediary: brokers, mutual-fund companies, and investment banks.

i. Brokers give customers access to the financial markets, allowing them to buy and sell securities.

ii. Mutual-fund companies provide savers with small-denomination shares in large, diversified investment pools.

iii. Investment banks screen and monitor firms before issuing their securities.

d. Finance companies specialize in making loans to consumers and businesses for the purchase or lease of specific products, such as cars and business equipment.

e. Government-sponsored enterprises supply direct financing and provide loan guarantees for low-interest mortgages, student loans, and agricultural loans.

Problems

1. For many years, you have been using your local small-town bank. One day you hear that the bank is about to be purchased by Bank of America. From your vantage point as a retail bank customer, what are the costs and benefits of such a merger?

2. Consider the impact of the merger in Question 1 from the point of view of a small business owner. Is the purchase of your small community bank good or bad? Explain your answer.

3. Why have technological advances hindered the enforcement of legal restrictions on bank branching?

4. Banks have been losing their advantage over other financial intermediaries in attracting customers' funds. Why?

5. What has been the impact of the Internet on the structure of the banking industry?

6. Describe the economies of scope that large financial holding companies hope to realize. Do you believe they will be successful?

7. Discuss the problems life insurance companies will face as genetic information becomes more widely available.

8. How can the favorable tax treatment of pension funds encourage saving?

9. Why would property and casualty insurers have balance sheets that differ from those of life insurance companies?

10. Insurance companies will not provide fire insurance for the full value of your house and its contents. Why not?

11. What are the benefits of collaboration between a large appliance retailer and a finance company?

12. Why might a person who changes jobs frequently have a lower retirement income than someone who stays with the same employer for a long time?

13. How do insurance companies address the problem of adverse selection?

14. Earnings on the savings accumulated under a whole life insurance policy are not taxed. Such a policy provides insurance that pays benefits when the policyholder dies, plus savings the policyholder can cash in before death. What would happen to the relative demand for whole life insurance if Congress passed a law making the earnings on all savings exempt from taxes? Would insurance companies be for or against such a law? Why?

15. California experiences periodic wildfires that destroy significant numbers of homes. What would happen to the insurance market if the government passed a law requiring that any insurance company operating in the state must provide fire insurance to all those homeowners who ask for it?

16. Could the financial system operate without securities firms? Why or why not?

17. An industry with a large number of small firms is usually thought to be highly competitive. Is that supposition true of the banking industry? What are the costs and benefits to consumers of the current structure of the U.S. banking industry?

18. Explain the following quotation:

    "For the farmers who needed credit in the rural South in the early years of the 20th century, the alternatives were dismal. Few banks would even consider making agricultural loans, and those who did charged extremely high interest rates. Rural credit was fertile ground for loan sharks, and year after year, farmers turned over their crops to help pay exorbitant interest charges on loans made to keep their farms operating. Should a crop fail, the chances of a farmer extricating himself and his family from a loan shark's clutches were virtually non-existent." Raghuram G. Rajan and Luigi Zingales, *Saving Capitalism from the Capitalists* (New York: Crown Business, 2003), p. 13.

19. When the values of stocks and bonds fluctuate, they have an impact on the balance sheet of insurance companies. Why is that impact more likely to be a problem for life insurance companies than for property and casualty companies?

20. Explain how assumptions about the rate of return on a firm's pension fund portfolio can affect the firm's profitability. Why might government regulators want to monitor those assumptions?

Chapter 14

Regulating the Financial System

If every day seems to bring news of a new or continuing financial crisis, that is because such events are quite common. In the past quarter century, 93 countries have experienced a total of 117 systemwide and 51 smaller disruptions in their financial systems.[1] Virtually no part of the world has been spared; large industrialized countries have suffered along with smaller, less developed ones.

When financial crises occur, governments step in and put financial intermediaries back on track. They often do so by assuming responsibility for the banking system's liabilities so that depositors won't lose their savings. But the cleanup can also require the injection of capital into failed institutions. All of this can be very expensive. Table 14.1 lists the top 15 banking crises between 1980 and 2003, along with estimates of the cost to resolve them. In countries like Argentina and Indonesia, the government had to contribute more than half of one year's GDP to get the financial system working again.

These crises not only were expensive to clean up but also had a dramatic impact on growth in the countries where they occurred. Figure 14.1 shows their impact on growth. On the horizontal axis is the cost of the cleanup (the numbers in Table 14.1) and on the vertical axis is the change in economic growth after the crisis. The data show what one would expect: Bigger crises are worse for growth.

Some degree of default is normal at every bank, including well-run ones. But in 1998, when 35 percent of all loans made by Korean banks defaulted at a cost of more than one-fifth the country's annual output, it was more than just bad luck. To put this percentage into perspective, in a normal year a country will invest 10 to 20 percent of its GDP, so the crisis cost Korea between one and two years' worth of business investment. Clearly, the Korean financial system was failing to perform one of its primary functions, the efficient channeling of resources from savers to borrowers so that credit goes to firms based on the merit of their proposed investments. Instead, borrowers who shouldn't have received loans got them, and projects that shouldn't have been funded went ahead. Because resources were wasted, Korea's growth and income were lower than they could have been.[2]

Banking crises are not a recent phenomenon; the history of commercial banking over the last two centuries is replete with periods of turmoil and failure. By their very nature, financial systems are fragile and vulnerable to crisis. Unfortunately, when a country's financial system collapses, its economy goes with it, and with economic crisis comes the risk of violence and revolution. Keeping banks open and operating,

---

[1]Data drawn from Gerald Caprio and Daniela Klingebiel, "Episodes of Systemic and Borderline Financial Crises," unpublished manuscript, The World Bank, January 2003; available at http://econ.worldbank.org/programs/finance/datasets/data?id=23456.

[2]A comprehensive study shows that on average, a banking crisis reduces annual growth in GDP by $2\frac{1}{2}$ percent during the crisis and roughly $\frac{1}{2}$ percent for several years afterward. See John H. Boyd, Pedro Gomis, Sungkyu Kwak, and Bruce D. Smith, "A User's Guide to Banking Crises," unpublished manuscript, The World Bank, April 2000. Available at http://econ.worldbank.org/files/16156_Deposit_Insurance_Design_and_Bailout_Costs.pdf.

Table 14.1 Worst Banking Crises since 1980

Country	Crisis Dates	Estimated Cost of Resolution (as % of GDP)
Argentina*	1980–1982	55%
Indonesia*	1997–1998	55%
China	1990s	47%
Jamaica*	1994	44%
Chile*	1981–1983	42%
Thailand*	1997	35%
Macedonia	1993–1994	32%
Israel	1977–1983	30%
Turkey*	2000	30%
Uruguay	1981–1984	29%
Korea	1998	28%
Côte d'Ivoire	1988–1991	25%
Japan	1990s	24%
Uruguay	1981–1984	24%
Malaysia*	1997–1998	20%

*Indicates a country with more than one banking crisis since 1980. The reported crisis is the largest.

SOURCE: *"Episodes of Systemic and Borderline Financial Crises," by Gerald Caprio Jr. and Daniela Klingebiel © 2003 The World Bank. Reprinted with permission from the International Bank for Reconstruction and Development.*

then, is as essential to maintaining our way of life as a ready military defense. Because a healthy financial system benefits everyone, governments are deeply involved in the way banks and other intermediaries function. As a result, the financial sector is subject to voluminous rules and regulations, and financial institutions must withstand constant scrutiny by official examiners. The importance of this government oversight in ensuring financial stability is hard to exaggerate.

The purpose of this chapter is threefold. First, we will look at the sources and consequences of financial fragility. By and large, financial crises are banking crises, so we will focus on that sector. Next, we will look at the institutional safeguards—for instance, deposit insurance—the government has built into the system in an attempt to avert financial crises. Finally, we'll study the regulatory and supervisory environment of the banking industry.

The Sources and Consequences of Runs, Panics, and Crises

In a market-based economy, the opportunity to succeed is also an opportunity to fail. New restaurants open and others go out of business. Only one in 10 restaurants survives as long as three years. In principle, banks should be no different from restaurants: new

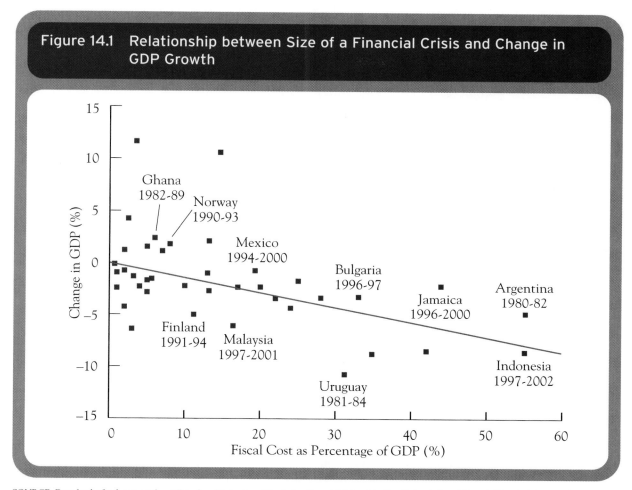

Figure 14.1   Relationship between Size of a Financial Crisis and Change in GDP Growth

SOURCE: *Data for the fiscal costs are from "Episodes of Systemic and Borderline Financial Crises," by Gerald Caprio Jr. and Daniela Klingebiel © 2003 The World Bank. Reprinted with permission from the International Bank for Reconstruction and Development.*

ones should open and unpopular ones close. But few of us would want to live in a world where banks fail at the same rate as restaurants. Banks serve some essential functions in our economy: they provide access to the payments system, and they screen and monitor borrowers to reduce information problems. If your favorite restaurant closes suddenly, you can still eat, but if your bank closes, you lose your ability to make purchases and pay your rent. So while no one suggests that the government appoint officials to minimize restaurant closings, everyone expects the government to safeguard banks.

Banks' fragility arises from the fact that they provide liquidity to depositors. That is, they allow depositors to withdraw their balances on demand. If you want the entire amount in your checking account converted into cash, all you need to do is go to your bank and ask for it; the teller is obligated to give it to you. If a bank cannot meet this promise of withdrawal on demand because of insufficient liquid assets, it will fail.[3]

[3]There is a trade-off between a bank's safety and its profitability. Higher-return assets like loans tend to be less liquid than lower-return assets. The more illiquid a bank's assets, the more likely it is to fail.

Crowds trying get in to the Abacus Federal Savings Bank in New York on April 22, 2003.

SOURCE: *Marilyn K. Yee/The New York Times.*

Banks not only guarantee their depositors immediate cash on demand; they promise to satisfy depositors' withdrawal requests on a first-come, first-served basis.[4] This commitment has some important implications. Suppose depositors begin to lose confidence in a bank's ability to meet their withdrawal requests. They have heard a rumor that one of the bank's largest loans has defaulted, so that the bank's assets may no longer cover its liabilities. True or not, reports that a bank has become insolvent can spread fear that it will run out of cash and close its doors. Mindful of the bank's first-come, first-served policy, frenzied depositors may rush to the bank to convert their balances to cash before other customers arrive. Such a bank run can cause a bank to fail.

A bank run can be the result of either real or imagined problems. No bank is immune to the loss of depositors' confidence just because it is profitable and sound. A recent example is the Abacus Savings Bank, which serves large numbers of immigrants in New York City's Chinatown. In April 2003 news spread through the Chinese-language media that one of the bank's managers had embezzled more than $1 million. Frightened depositors, unfamiliar with the safeguards in place at U.S. banks, converged on three of the institution's branches to withdraw their balances. Because Abacus Savings was financially sound, it was able to meet all requested withdrawals during the course of the day. In the end, as one government official observed, the real danger was that depositors might be robbed carrying large quantities of cash away from the bank. Leaving their funds in the bank would have been safer, but rumor and a lack of familiarity with government-sponsored deposit insurance caused depositors to panic.[5]

What matters during a bank run is not whether a bank is solvent, but whether it is liquid. Solvency means that the value of the bank's assets exceeds the value of its liabilities—that is, the bank has a positive net worth. Liquidity means that the bank has sufficient reserves and immediately marketable assets to meet depositors' demand for withdrawals. False rumors that a bank is *insolvent* can lead to a run that renders a bank illiquid. If people believe that a bank is in trouble, that belief alone can make it so.

When a bank fails, depositors may lose some or all of their deposits, and information about borrowers' creditworthiness may disappear. For these reasons alone, government officials work to ensure that all banks are operated in a way that minimizes their chance of failure. But that is not their main worry. The primary concern is that a single bank's failure might cause a small-scale bank run that could turn into a systemwide bank panic. This phenomenon of spreading panic on the part of depositors is called contagion.

Information asymmetries are the reason that a run on a single bank can turn into a bank panic that threatens the entire financial system. Recall from Chapter 11 that if there is no way to tell a good used car from a bad one, the only used cars on the market will be lemons. What is true for cars is even truer for banks. Most of us are not in a position to assess the quality of a bank's balance sheet. In fact, since banks often make loans based on sophisticated statistical models, only an expert can estimate the worth of a bank's assets. Depositors, then, are in the same position as uninformed buyers in the used car market: They can't tell the difference between a good bank and a bad bank. And who wants to make a deposit in a bank if there is even a small chance that it could be insolvent? So when rumors spread that a certain bank is in trouble,

INFORMATION

---

[4]Economists refer to this commitment to serve customers in sequence as a *sequential service constraint.*

[5]See James Barron, "Chinatown Bank Endures Run as Fear Trumps Reassurances," *The New York Times,* April 23, 2003.

depositors everywhere begin to worry about their own banks' financial condition. Concern about even one bank can create a panic that causes profitable banks throughout the nation to fail, leading to a complete collapse of the banking system.

While banking panics and financial crises can easily result from false rumors, they can also occur for more concrete reasons. Since a bank's assets are a combination of loans and securities, anything that affects borrowers' ability to make their loan payments or drives down the market value of securities has the potential to imperil the bank's finances. Recessions—widespread downturns in business activity—have a clear negative impact on a bank's balance sheet. When business slows, firms have a harder time paying their debts. People lose their jobs and suddenly can't make their loan payments. As default rates rise, bank assets lose value, and bank capital drops. With less capital, banks are forced to contract their balance sheets, making fewer loans. This decline in loans, in turn, means less business investment, which amplifies the downturn. If a recession gets really bad, banks can begin to fail.

The history of banking in the United States shows that downturns in the business cycle put pressure on banks, substantially increasing the risk of panics. Figure 14.2 plots all the recessions from 1871 to 1914 (what is available for the period prior to creation

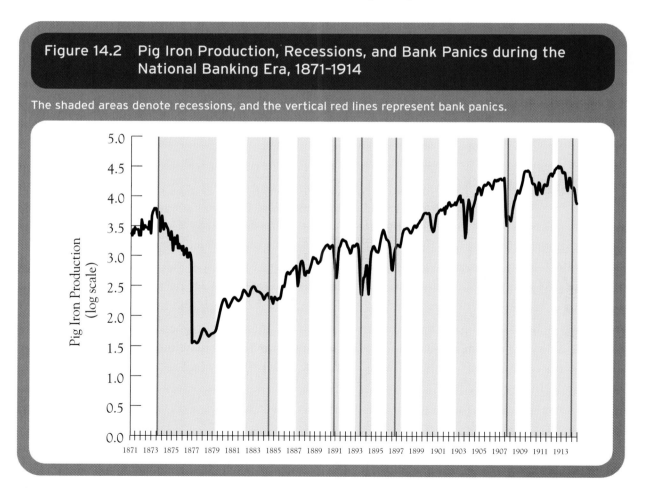

Figure 14.2   Pig Iron Production, Recessions, and Bank Panics during the National Banking Era, 1871–1914

The shaded areas denote recessions, and the vertical red lines represent bank panics.

SOURCE: *Pig iron data are from Frederick Macaulay,* The Movement of Interest Rates, Bond Yields, and Stock Prices in the United States since 1956 *(New York: National Bureau of Economic Research, 1938). The recession dates are from the NBER at www.nber.org and the bank panic dates are from Gary Gorton,* "Banking Panics and Business Cycles," Oxford Economic Papers *40 (1988), pp. 751–788.*

of the Federal Reserve System in 1913). The data make for a striking picture. Eleven business cycles—booms followed by recessions—occurred during this period. Bank panics occurred during seven of them. The next series of severe bank panics occurred during the Great Depression of the 1930s, when output fell by roughly one-third. The conclusion is that bank panics seem to start with real economic events, not just rumors.[6]

Financial disruptions can also occur whenever borrowers' net worth falls, as it does during a deflation (see Applying the Concept: Deflation, Net Worth, and Information Costs in Chapter 11). Companies borrow a fixed number of dollars to invest in real assets like buildings and machines, whose values fall with deflation. So a drop in prices reduces companies' net worth (but not their loan payments). This decline in firms' net worth aggravates the adverse selection and moral hazard problems caused by information asymmetries, making loans more difficult to obtain. If these firms cannot get new financing, business investment will fall, reducing overall economic activity and raising the number of defaults on loans. As more and more borrowers default, banks' balance sheets deteriorate, compounding information problems and creating a full-blown crisis.

The Government Safety Net

There are three reasons for the government to get involved in the financial system:

1. To protect investors.
2. To protect bank customers from monopolistic exploitation.
3. To ensure the stability of the financial system.

First, the government is obligated to protect small investors, many of whom are unable to judge the soundness of their financial institutions. While competition is supposed to discipline all the institutions in the industry, in practice only the force of law can ensure a bank's integrity. As small investors, we rely on the government to protect us from mismanagement and malfeasance.

Second, the growing tendency for small firms to merge into large ones reduces competition, ultimately ending in monopolies. In general, monopolies exploit their customers, raising prices to earn unwarranted profits. Because monopolies are inefficient, the government intervenes to prevent the firms in an industry from becoming too large. In the financial system, that means ensuring that even large banks face competition.

STABILITY

Third, the combustible mix of liquidity risk and information asymmetries means that the financial system is inherently unstable. A financial firm can collapse much more quickly than an industrial company. For a steel corporation, an electronics manufacturer, or an automobile maker, failure occurs slowly as customers disappear one by one. But a financial institution can create and destroy the value of its assets in an astonishingly short period, and a single firm's failure can bring down the entire system.[7]

Government officials employ a combination of strategies to protect investors and ensure the stability of the financial system. First, they provide the safety net to insure

---

[6] A comprehensive study of recent bank crises came to a less definitive conclusion. Boyd, Gomis, Kwak, and Smith suggest that psychological, or irrational, phenomena may have played an important role in crises of the past several decades. See John H. Boyd, Pedro Gomis, Sungkyu Kwak, and Bruce D. Smith, "A User's Guide to Banking Crises," The World Bank, April 2000.

[7] The real culprit in creating this high degree of risk is derivatives. Like dynamite, when used properly derivatives are extremely beneficial, allowing the transfer of risk to those who can best bear it. But in the wrong hands, derivatives can bring down even the largest, most respected institutions. The failure of Barings Bank in 1995 is an example. One of the oldest and best-known banks in England, Barings collapsed in just two months after a single trader wiped out the bank's capital with losses of more than $1 billion on futures positions worth over $17 billion. Bets like that can be made only using derivatives.

small depositors. Authorities both operate as the *lender of last resort,* making loans to banks that face sudden deposit outflows, and provide *deposit insurance,* guaranteeing that depositors receive the full value of their accounts should an institution fail. But this safety net causes bank managers to take on too much risk, leading to the regulation and supervision that we will discuss later in the chapter.

This section will examine the unique role of depository institutions in our financial system. The point is that we need banks. While they are essential, they are also fragile. This leads to a discussion of the components of the safety net and the problems it creates. The next section will look at the government's responses to these problems.

The Unique Role of Depository Institutions

Depository institutions receive a disproportionate amount of attention from government regulators, both because they play a central role in the economy and because they face a unique set of problems. We all rely heavily on banks for access to the payments system. If banks suddenly disappeared, no alternative method of transferring funds would be available to us. Nondepository institutions—insurance companies, pension funds, and the like—do not play the same role as banks in facilitating payments.

Furthermore, banks are prone to runs, a risk nondepository institutions do not face. Banks hold illiquid assets to back their liquid liabilities, promising full and constant value to depositors based on assets of uncertain value. Securities firms, in contrast, hold liquid assets that can be traded rapidly in the secondary markets if customers call to redeem their liabilities. Pension funds and insurance companies may hold illiquid assets, but their liability holders cannot withdraw funds whenever they want.

Moreover, banks are linked to one another both on their balance sheets and in their customers' minds. Interbank loans make up roughly $4\frac{1}{2}$ percent of U.S. bank assets—an amount that represents almost half of all bank capital.[8] If a bank begins to fail, it will default on its loan payments to other banks, creating real financial distress. This interconnectedness of banks is almost unique to the financial industry; nondepository institutions' balance sheets are not nearly so interdependent. While bank failures are contagious, nondepository institutions' problems are not.

While the ramifications of a crisis among nondepository institutions are more limited, they are still damaging both to individuals and to the financial system. As a result, the government also protects individuals who do business with finance companies, pension funds, insurance companies, and securities brokers. For example, government regulations require insurance companies to provide proper information to policyholders and restrict the ways the companies manage their assets. The same is true for securities firms and pension funds, whose assets must be structured to ensure that they will be able to meet their obligations many years into the future.[9]

"Yes, we do have the authority to regulate you."

[8] Take a quick look at Table 12.1 (page 288) and notice that interbank loans and bank capital represent 4.6 and 8.9 percent of total bank assets, respectively.

[9] All nondepository institutions are subject to some form of regulation. State regulators oversee insurance companies; the Pension Benefits Guaranty Corporation regulates private pension funds. Securities firms are overseen by a combination of the Securities and Exchange Commission, the New York Stock Exchange, and the National Association of Securities Dealers, only the first of which is a government agency. Finance companies are regulated by state agencies, as well as by the Federal Reserve if they are subsidiaries of bank holding companies.

The Government as Lender of Last Resort

The best way to stop a bank failure from turning into a bank panic is to make sure solvent institutions can meet their depositors' withdrawal demands. In 1873 the British economist Walter Bagehot suggested the need for a *lender of last resort* to perform this function. Such an institution could make loans to prevent the failure of solvent banks and could provide liquidity in sufficient quantities to prevent or end a financial panic. Specifically, Bagehot proposed that Britain's central bank should lend freely on good collateral at a high rate of interest. By lending freely he meant providing liquidity on demand to any bank that asked for it. Good collateral would ensure the bank's solvency, and the high interest rate would penalize the borrowing bank for failing to hold enough reserves or easily salable assets to meet deposit outflows.

We will discuss the mechanics of central bank lending in Chapter 18. For now, it will suffice to say that the existence of a lender of last resort significantly reduces, but does not eliminate, contagion. The series of three bank panics that occurred during the Great Depression of the 1930s is one example of the failure of a lender of last resort. While the Federal Reserve had the capacity to operate as a lender of last resort in the 1930s, Figure 14.3 shows that banks did not take advantage of the opportunity to borrow when they

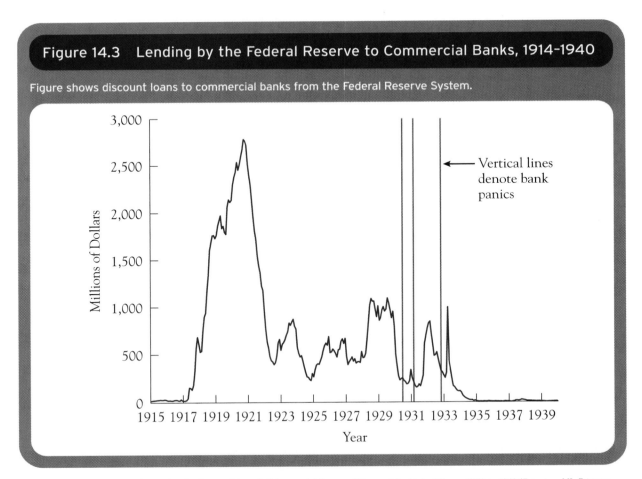

Figure 14.3 Lending by the Federal Reserve to Commercial Banks, 1914–1940

Figure shows discount loans to commercial banks from the Federal Reserve System.

Vertical lines denote bank panics

SOURCE: *Bank panic dates are from Milton Friedman and Anna J. Schwartz,* A Monetary History of the United States: 1863 to 1960 *(Princeton, NJ: Princeton University Press, 1963).*

YOUR FINANCIAL WORLD
Your Investments Are Your Responsibility

If a bank accepts your deposits and makes bad loans with them, your funds are protected in many ways. But if you open a brokerage account and take the broker's advice on how to invest, you don't have the same protection. A broker is liable for outright theft, as well as for questionable practices such as trading your investments simply to generate fees or pursuing an investment strategy that is too risky for your financial condition. But winning compensation requires that you prove the broker's behavior was illegal, not just inadvisable.

If you suspect you have been cheated by your broker or would simply like to know your rights,

visit the Web site of the National Association of Securities Dealers (NASD) at www.nasd.com. The NASD site contains lots of useful investor information. It lists some warning signals to watch for and explains how to pursue a complaint. The Web site also allows you to check your investment advisor's background.

The best investment strategy is to invest only in businesses that you understand. Don't simply follow someone else's advice, even a financial professional's. And don't assume that the government will bail you out if something goes wrong. Your investments are your responsibility.

needed to. In fact, their borrowing fell during panics, reaching levels well below normal compared to the boom years of the 1920s. So as banks became illiquid, the Federal Reserve's lending declined. The mere existence of a lender of last resort, then, will not keep the financial system from collapsing.

There is another flaw in the concept of a lender of last resort. For the system to work, central bank officials who approve the loan applications must be able to distinguish an illiquid from an insolvent institution. But during a crisis, computing the market value of a bank's assets is almost impossible, since there are no market prices. (If a bank could sell its marketable assets in the financial markets, it wouldn't need a loan from the central bank.) Because a bank will go to the central bank for a direct loan only after having exhausted all opportunities to sell its assets and borrow from other banks without collateral, its illiquidity and its need to seek a loan from the government raise the question of its solvency. Officials, anxious to keep the crisis from deepening, are likely to be generous in evaluating the bank's assets and to grant a loan even if they suspect the bank may be insolvent. Knowing this, bank managers will tend to take too many risks.

In other words, the central bank's difficulty in distinguishing a bank's insolvency from its illiquidity creates moral hazard for bank managers. It is important for a lender of last resort to operate in a manner that minimizes the tendency for bankers to take too much risk in their operations.

Government Deposit Insurance

Congress's response to the Federal Reserve's inability to stem the bank panics of the 1930s was deposit insurance. The Federal Deposit Insurance Corporation guarantees that a depositor will receive the full account balance up to some maximum amount even if a bank fails. Bank failures, in effect, become the problem of the insurer; bank customers need not concern themselves with their bank's risk taking. So long as a bank has deposit insurance, customers' deposits are safe, even in the event of a run or bank failure.

Here's how the system works. When a bank fails, the FDIC resolves the insolvency either by closing the institution or by finding a buyer. The first approach, closing the bank, is called the payoff method. The FDIC pays off all the bank's depositors, then

APPLYING THE CONCEPT

THE DAY THE BANK OF NEW YORK BORROWED $23 BILLION

While the existence of a lender of last resort may encourage bank managers to take too many risks, very few people would argue for abolishing the safeguard outright. There have been days when the system worked exactly as it should. November 20, 1985, was one of them. On that day the Bank of New York's computer system went haywire. BONY, as it is known, plays a central role in the U.S. Treasury securities market. The bank acts as a clearinghouse, buying bonds from sellers and then reselling them to buyers.

On November 20, a software error prevented BONY from keeping track of its Treasury bond trades.* For 90 minutes transactions poured in, and the bank accumulated and paid for U.S. Treasury bonds, notes, and bills. Importantly, BONY promised to make payments without actually having the funds. But when the time came to deliver the securities and collect from the buyers, BONY employees could not tell who the buyers and sellers were or what quantities and prices they had agreed to. The information had been erased. By the end of the day, the Bank of New York had bought and failed to deliver so many securities that it was committed to paying out $23 billion that it did not have.

Without a way to come up with $23 billion, BONY wasn't able to make payments to sellers who had delivered their securities. These sellers had made additional transactions in the expectation that they would be paid. Unless BONY found a way to make the promised payments, the problem would spread to other institutions. The Federal Reserve, as lender of last resort, stepped in and made a loan of $23 billion, preventing a computer problem at one very important bank from becoming a full-blown financial crisis.

*BONY's computers could store only 32,000 transactions at a time. When more transactions arrived than the computer could handle, the software's counter restarted at zero. Since the counter number was the key to where the trading information was stored, the information was effectively erased. (Had all the original transactions been processed before the counter restarted, there would have been no problem.)

sells all the bank's assets in an attempt to recover the amount paid out. Under the payoff method, depositors whose balances exceed the insurance limit, currently $100,000, suffer some losses.

In the second approach, called the **purchase-and-assumption method**, the FDIC finds a firm that is willing to take over the failed bank. Since the failed institution is insolvent—on the balance sheet, its liabilities exceed its assets—no purchaser will do so for free. In fact, the FDIC has to pay banks to purchase failed institutions. That is, the FDIC sells the failed bank at a negative price. Depositors prefer the purchase-and-assumption method to the payoff method because the transition is typically seamless, with the bank closing as usual at the end of the week and reopening on Monday morning under new ownership. In a purchase and assumption, no depositors, even those whose account balances exceed the deposit insurance limit, suffer a loss.

Deposit insurance has been extraordinarily successful in eliminating bank runs and financial crises. Even so, the most notorious bank run in recent decades can be traced to problems with deposit insurance. Until the mid-1980s, some states had their own deposit insurance funds for banks in their states. In 1985 the failure of a large Ohio bank jeopardized that state's deposit insurance fund. People whose deposits were insured by the Ohio fund rather than the FDIC became nervous, precipitating a run on the bank. In the end, Ohio's insurance fund failed, and all the institutions it had insured shifted to the FDIC.

No private insurance fund is big enough to withstand a run on all the banks it insures—that is, no insurance fund except the FDIC. Because the U.S. Treasury backs the FDIC, it can withstand virtually any crisis.

Problems Created by the Government Safety Net

We know that insurance changes people's behavior. Protected depositors have no incentive to monitor their bankers' behavior. Knowing this, bankers take on more risk than they would normally, since they get the benefits while the government assumes the costs. In protecting depositors, then, the government creates moral hazard.[10] This is not just a theory. We can find evidence for this assertion by comparing bank balance sheets before and after the implementation of deposit insurance. Recall from Chapter 12 that commercial banks in the United States have significant leverage; their assets are 11 times the size of their capital. In the 1920s, before the deposit insurance system was created, banks' ratio of assets to capital was about 4 to 1. Most economic and financial historians believe that government insurance led directly to the rise in risk.

And that is not the only problem. Because government officials are obsessed with avoiding financial crises, they pay close attention to the largest institutions. While the failure of a small community bank is unfortunate, the prospect of a large financial conglomerate going under is a regulator's worst nightmare. The disruption caused by the collapse of an institution that holds hundreds of billions of dollars in assets is too much for most people even to contemplate. In effect, some banks are just too big to fail. The managers of these banks know that if their institutions begin to founder, the government will find a way to bail them out. The deposit insurer will quickly find a buyer or the government, as lender of last resort, will make a loan. Depositors will be made whole, and the managers of the bank may even keep their jobs.

The government's too-big-to-fail policy limits the extent of the market discipline depositors can impose on banks. Normally, a corporation with millions of dollars to deposit is concerned about the riskiness of its bank's assets, given the limits of government deposit insurance. If the bank fails, the corporation could face significant losses. Thus, the threat of withdrawal of these large balances restrains the bank from taking on too much risk.[11] But for very large banks, the deposit insurance ceiling is meaningless, because everyone knows that authorities will not permit the bank to fail. With virtually no monitoring by depositors and no threat that their balances will be withdrawn, bank managers can do whatever they like. The too-big-to-fail policy compounds the problem of moral hazard, encouraging managers of large banks to engage in extremely risky behavior (and putting small banks at a competitive disadvantage).

---

[10]Before 1991, the problem was even worse than it is today. The FDIC once charged the same insurance premium to all banks, regardless of the riskiness of their assets. Today premiums are risk based (if not perfectly so).

[11]Today, large depositors can engage in what is known as a *silent run* on a bank. Rumors that a bank is in trouble can lead to the electronic withdrawal of deposits that exceed the insurance ceiling. Since the withdrawals are made by wire transfer, no customers can be seen lining up at the bank; these runs are silent and invisible.

APPLYING THE CONCEPT
THE IMPACT OF CHANGING DEPOSIT INSURANCE LIMITS

When the Federal Deposit Insurance Corporation began on January 1, 1934, it insured deposits up to $2,500. That limit was quickly raised to $5,000 and over the next 45 years reached $100,000. In 2002 Congress heard calls to raise the limit again, to $130,000.

Is raising the deposit insurance limit a good idea? To evaluate this proposal, we can study the history of the limit. Figure 14.4 compares the nominal insurance limit from 1934 to 2004 to the same limit adjusted for inflation. A deposit insurance limit of $5,000 in mid-1934 was equivalent to a deposit insurance limit of $71,000 in 2004. The comparison shows how large the last increase, which occurred in 1980, really was. The rise to a $100,000 limit increased the inflation-adjusted ceiling to four times its early level.

The consensus is that the last increase was a disaster because it gave shaky institutions an opportunity to use high interest rates to attract more insured deposits. Remember that the existence of insurance causes depositors to care less than they would otherwise about what banks do with their funds. And when a bank is doing poorly, managers have nothing to lose by using the new deposits to make risky loans. In the 10 years after the insurance limit was raised, several thousand banks and savings and loans failed—more than four times the number in the FDIC's first 46 years. While a vast majority of the institutions that failed in the 1980s were small, the cost of reimbursing depositors exceeded $180 billion. The bill was ultimately paid by U.S. taxpayers.

Moral hazard is a very real problem, then. The higher the deposit insurance limit, the more likely that insured banks will make risky loans. Beyond that, only 2 percent of U.S. households have bank accounts whose deposits are not fully insured, so the proposed increase in deposit insurance would help only a relatively small group of people at a potentially high cost. If we think of the primary goal of deposit insurance as protecting the average consumer, then surely we needn't worry about people whose cash levels exceed $100,000. Chances are those people are

Regulation and Supervision of the Financial System

Government officials employ three strategies to ensure that the risks created by the safety net are contained. Government *regulation* establishes a set of specific rules for bank managers to follow. Government *supervision* provides general oversight of financial institutions. And formal *examination* of banks' books by specialists provides detailed information on the firms' operation. As we look at each of these, keep in mind that the goal of government regulation is not to remove all the risk that investors face. Financial intermediaries themselves facilitate the transfer and allocation of risk, improving economic efficiency in the process. Regulating risk out of existence would eliminate one of the purposes of financial institutions.

continued from previous page

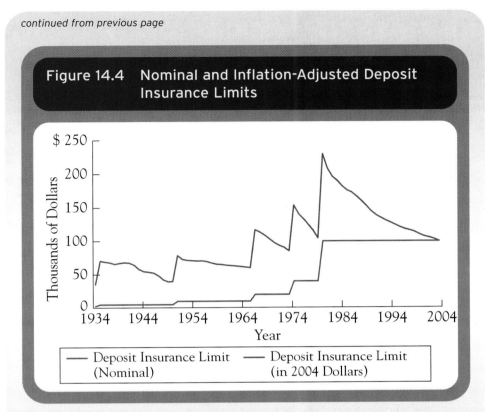

Figure 14.4   Nominal and Inflation-Adjusted Deposit Insurance Limits

— Deposit Insurance Limit (Nominal)   — Deposit Insurance Limit (in 2004 Dollars)

SOURCE: *Nominal insurance limit is from the FDIC and the insurance limit in 2004 dollars is computed using the consumer price index (CPI) from the Bureau of Labor Statistics.*

capable of monitoring the risks their bankers take. The true beneficiaries of a higher insurance limit would be small banks that rely heavily on large deposits. Deposit insurance would lower their cost of funds because an insured deposit commands a lower interest rate than an uninsured one.

Maybe Congress should consider lowering the deposit insurance limit, not raising it?

Wary of asking taxpayers to pick up the bill for bank insolvencies, officials created regulatory requirements that are designed to minimize the cost of such failures to the public. The first screen, put in place to make sure the people who own and run banks are not criminals, is for a new bank to obtain a charter. Once a bank has been chartered and has opened for business, a complex web of detailed regulations restricts competition, specifies what assets the bank can and cannot hold, requires the bank to hold a minimum level of capital, and makes public information about the bank's balance sheet.

As we all know, rules are one thing; enforcement is another. Posting a speed limit on an interstate highway is only the first step in preventing people from driving too fast. Unless the police patrol the highways and penalize speeding drivers, such laws are worthless. The same is true of banking regulations. The best-designed regulatory structure in the world won't be worth the paper it's written on unless someone mon-

YOUR FINANCIAL WORLD

Are Your Deposits Insured?

The sign says "Each depositor insured to $100,000." But what does it really mean? Are your deposits fully insured? The answer to this question can be complicated. Here are a few things to keep in mind.

First, deposit insurance covers individuals, not accounts. It insures depositors. This means that if you hold your accounts jointly with a spouse, parent, sibling, friend, or business partner, the FDIC will insure each of you up to $100,000, assuming that each person has an equal share in the account. For instance, if you hold a savings account jointly with your spouse or partner, deposit insurance will cover a total balance of $200,000, or $100,000 for each of you.

Second, because deposit insurance covers individuals rather than accounts, if you have more than one account at the same bank, all in your own name, they will be insured together up to the insurance limit. For example, if you have a checking account, a savings account, and a personal business account (an account for what is known legally as a sole proprietorship), they will be added together and insured up to the $100,000 maximum.

Finally, if you have accounts at more than one bank, they will be insured separately, up to a total of $100,000 at each bank. But if the two banks should decide to merge, your accounts will be covered as if they had been opened at the same bank.

The average college student's reaction to this news is "I wish I were rich enough to worry about whether my combined checking and savings account balance is more than $100,000!" But bear in mind that deposit insurance covers retirement accounts, too, and you may hit that limit sooner than you think. If you deposit $200 per month into an individual retirement account (IRA), for example, at 6 percent annual interest you will hit the $100,000 ceiling in just over 20 years. As you may recall from Chapter 4, a $100,000 retirement account won't get you very far. So insuring your retirement savings is something you will need to worry about.

Finally, like all government regulations, the rules for government deposit insurance can change. If you really need to know whether you are insured or just want the peace of mind of knowing that your information is current, you can check the FDIC's Web site, www.fdic.gov.

itors banks' compliance. Government supervisors are the highway patrol of the banking world. They monitor, inspect, and examine banks to make sure their business practices conform to regulatory requirements.

Banks are regulated and supervised by a combination of the U.S. Treasury, the Federal Reserve, the FDIC, and state banking authorities (see Table 14.2). The overlapping nature of this regulatory structure means that more than one agency works to ensure the soundness of each bank. A bank can effectively choose its regulators by choosing whether to be a state or national bank and whether or not to belong to the Federal Reserve System. If one regulator allows an activity that another prohibits, a bank's managers can threaten to switch, or argue that a competitor who answers to a more permissive regulator has an unfair advantage.

The consequences of such regulatory competition are twofold. First, regulators force each other to innovate, improving the quality of the regulations they write. Because this outcome ensures that regulators and banks follow current best practice, it is unambiguously positive.[12] But regulatory competition has a less desirable outcome: It allows bank managers to look for the most lenient regulator—the one whose

---

[12]Regulatory competition bears some similarity to federalism in its sensitivity to local differences. In the words of the late Supreme Court Justice Louis Brandeis, federalism means "that a single courageous state may, if its citizens choose, serve as a laboratory; and try novel social and economic experiments without risk to the rest of the country." The same is true, to a lesser extent, of bank regulators and supervisors.

Table 14.2 Regulators of Depository Institutions

Type of Intermediary	Regulators
Commercial Banks	1. Federal Deposit Insurance Corporation 2. Office of the Comptroller of the Currency (Nationally chartered banks) 3. Federal Reserve System (State-chartered banks that are Federal Reserve members) 4. State authorities (All state-chartered banks)
Savings Banks Savings and Loans	1. Office of Thrift Supervision 2. Federal Deposit Insurance Corporation 3. State authorities
Credit Unions	1. National Credit Union Administration 2. State authorities

rules and enforcement are the least stringent. Especially since the repeal of the ban on interstate branching, regulatory agencies have tried to prevent this outcome. Today state authorities usually defer to the Federal Reserve, whose supervisors impose uniform regulations on all state-chartered banks. The Comptroller of the Currency cooperates with the Fed to ensure that national banks receive similar treatment.

Restrictions on Competition

One long-standing goal of financial regulators has been to prevent banks from growing too big and powerful, both because their failure might threaten the financial system and because banks that have no real competition exploit their customers. As we saw in Chapter 13, throughout most of the 20th century banks faced numerous restrictions that kept them small. And until 1999, banks could not own securities firms or insurance companies.

While recent legislation has changed the banking industry, restrictions on bank size remain. Bank mergers still require government approval. Before granting it, officials must be convinced on two points. First, the new bank must not constitute a monopoly in any geographic region. Second, if a small community bank is to be taken over by a large regional bank, the small bank's customers must be well served by the merger.

But government officials also worry that the greater the competition among banks, the more difficulty banks will have making a profit. Competition reduces the prices customers must pay and forces companies to innovate in order to survive. These effects are as true of the market for deposits and loans as they are of the markets for cars and computers. Competition raises the interest rate bankers pay on deposits and lowers the interest rate they receive on loans; it spurs them to improve the quality of the services they provide. Normally we think of these effects of competition as being positive, but there is a negative side as well. Lower interest margins and reduced fee income cause bankers to look for other ways to turn a profit. Some may be tempted to assume more risk—that is, to make loans and purchase securities that are riskier than advisable.

There are two ways to avoid this type of moral hazard. First, government officials can explicitly restrict competition. That is the solution regulators have chosen in a number of countries; it was also one of the purposes of branching restrictions.[13] (Branching restrictions create networks of small, geographically separated independent banks that face very little competition in their regions.) A second way to combat bankers' tendency to take on too much risk is to prohibit them from making certain types of loans and from purchasing particular securities.

Asset Holding Restrictions and Minimum Capital Requirements

The simplest way to prevent bankers from exploiting their safety net is to restrict banks' balance sheets. Such regulations take two forms: restrictions on the types of asset banks can hold and requirements that they maintain minimum levels of capital. While banks are allowed to build big office buildings and buy corporate jets for top executives, their financial assets are heavily restricted. U.S. banks cannot hold common stock.[14] Regulations also restrict both the grade and quantity of bonds a bank can hold. For example, banks are generally prohibited from purchasing bonds that are below investment grade, and their holdings from any single private issuer cannot exceed 25 percent of their capital. The size of the loans they can make to particular borrowers is also limited. For example, the Federal Reserve requires that one bank's exposure to another not exceed 25 percent of the bank's capital. While these restrictions on asset holdings are quite detailed, they are really just a matter of common sense and sound risk management. In effect, regulators are telling bankers to do what they should be doing already: holding a well-diversified portfolio of liquid, high-grade bonds and loans.[15]

Minimum capital requirements complement these limitations on bank assets. Recall that bank capital represents the net worth of the bank to its owners. Capital serves as both a cushion against declines in the value of the bank's assets, lowering the likelihood of the bank's failure, and a way to reduce the problem of moral hazard. Capital requirements take two basic forms. The first requires most banks to keep their ratio of capital to assets above some minimum level, regardless of the structure of their balance sheets.[16] The second requires banks to hold capital in proportion to the riskiness of their operations. The computation is extremely complicated and the rules change frequently, but basically a bank must first compute the risk-adjusted level of its assets given the likelihood of a loan or bond default. Then a capital charge is assessed against that level. Of course, banks face a multitude of other risks, including trading risk, operational risk, and the risk associated with their off-balance-sheet

---

[13]Until the early 1970s, regulation restricted the interest rates U.S. banks could pay on deposits. Regulation Q prohibited interest payments on demand deposits and placed a ceiling on interest payments on time and savings deposits. Its purpose was to restrict competition in order to improve banks' profitability.

[14]Common stock holdings were one of the sources of the problems Japanese banks faced in the 1990s. As the Japanese stock market collapsed, the value of Japanese bank assets declined precipitously, to the point where many banks became insolvent.

[15]One could also argue that such regulations give conservative bank managers a ready defense against shareholder pressure to improve profits by taking additional risks.

[16]The minimum ratio of capital to assets depends on the supervisor's views of the bank's health. A bank with a poor rating will be required to keep capital at 4 percent of assets.

operations. Regulators require banks to hold capital based on assessments of those risks as well. (See Tools of the Trade for a description of recent changes in capital requirements.)

Disclosure Requirements

Banks are required to provide information, both to their customers about the cost of their products and to the financial markets about their balance sheets. Regulations regarding disclosures to customers are responsible for the small print on loan applications and deposit account agreements; their purpose is to protect consumers. A bank must tell you the interest rate charged on a loan and must do so in a standardized way that allows you to compare interest rates at competing banks. (This regulation is similar to the one that requires grocery stores to show the price of cheese, peanut butter, or popcorn per ounce, allowing customers to tell which brand or size is cheapest.) The bank must also tell you the fees it charges to maintain a checking account—the cost of check clearing, the monthly service charge, the fee for overdrafts, and the interest rate paid on the balance, if any.

Disclosure of accounting information to the financial markets protects depositors in a different way. It allows both regulators and the financial markets to assess the quality of a bank's balance sheet. Since the information is published in a standardized format according to clearly specified accounting rules, government officials can easily tell whether a bank is obeying the regulatory rules, and financial analysts can compare one bank to another. With this information, both regulators and the financial markets can penalize banks that are taking too much risk.[17]

Supervision and Examination

The government enforces banking rules and regulations through an elaborate oversight process called **supervision**, which relies on a combination of monitoring and inspection. Supervision is done both remotely, using the detailed reports banks are required to file, and through on-site **examination**. All chartered banks must file quarterly reports known as **call reports**,[18] which detail the level and sources of their earnings, asset holdings, and liabilities. Supervisors process the reports using a statistical model that allows them to identify institutions whose solvency is deteriorating and to spot industry trends.

Examiners also visit banks in person. Every depository institution that is insured by the FDIC is examined at least once a year. Examiners arrive at a bank unannounced and look into virtually every aspect of its operation. They once counted the cash in each teller's drawer. While they no longer do that, they do call borrowers randomly to confirm that they actually have a loan and that the balance on the bank's books is correct. Examiners also verify that the loan collateral really exists, even visiting farms to make sure the grain that backs a farm loan is actually in the silo. At the largest institutions, examiners are on site all the time. They follow a process known as *continuous examination*, which is a bit like bridge painting—once they get to the end of the process, they go back to the beginning and start over.

---

[17]Writing disclosure rules turns out to be extremely difficult, especially for off-balance-sheet activities. For example, regulators need to know whether a bank that buys or sells interest-rate swaps is hedging risk on its balance sheet or taking on more risk. Since positions can change very quickly, sometimes minute by minute, regulators are challenged to figure out exactly what should be reported and when.

[18]The official name is the *Consolidated Reports of Conditions and Income*.

TOOLS OF THE TRADE
The Basel Accords, Old and New

Global financing took off in the 1980s as bankers realized they could expand their operations across national boundaries and turn a profit international-ly. While this was a welcome development for most bank customers, not everyone appreciated the competition from abroad. In some countries, bankers complained that the foreign banks that were invading their turf held an unfair competitive advantage.

Because no one likes competition, we should always be suspicious of this sort of complaint. But in this case, the bankers did have a point. Since for-eign banks operate under different regulatory rules, competing with a bank whose home country allows it to hold a lower level of capital is impossi-ble. Holding extra capital is costly. Banks that hold less capital than others, and therefore take on more leverage, have lower costs and can offer bor-rowers lower interest rates.

This legitimate complaint led to a movement to create international regulations that would pro-mote financial stability within countries and ensure a competitive balance with banks that operate globally. The result was the 1988 Basel Accord, named after the Swiss town where the world's bank regulators meet. The accord estab-lished a requirement that internationally active banks must hold capital equal to or greater than 8

Table 14.3 1988 Basel Accord Risk Weights	
Borrower	**Risk Weight**
Bonds issued by industrialized countries*	Zero
Claims on industrialized countries' banks	20%
Residential mortgages	50%
Consumer and corporate loans	100%

*Industrialized countries are defined as members of the Organization for Economic Cooperation and Development (OECD). Currently, 30 coun-tries belong to the OECD, including Mexico, Turkey, and Korea as well the United States, Germany, Japan, and Great Britain.

percent of their risk-adjusted assets. Assets would be placed in one of four different categories based on their risk of default. The associated risk weights would range from zero to 100 percent (see Table 14.3).

The most important part of a bank examination is the evaluation of past-due loans. Bank managers are understandably reluctant to write off a loan, wanting to keep it on the books as long as possible after the borrower has begun to miss pay-ments. Loan officers exercise substantial discretion in deciding when to declare a loan in default. For example, they can choose to increase the size of the loan by the missed interest payments. The examiner's job is to make sure that when borrowers stop making payments, loans are written off and the bank's balance sheet properly reflects the losses.

Supervisors use what are called the CAMELS criteria to evaluate the health of the banks they monitor. This acronym stands for Capital adequacy, Asset quality, Management, Earnings, Liquidity, and Sensitivity to risk. Examiners give the bank a rating from one to five in each of these categories, one being the best, and then com-bine the scores to determine the overall rating. The CAMELS ratings are *not* made public. Instead, they are used to make decisions about whether to take formal action against a bank or even to close it. Current practice is for supervisors to act as consult-ants, advising banks how to get the highest return possible while keeping risk at an acceptable level that ensures they will stay in business.

continued from previous page

The Basel Accord had several positive effects. First, by linking minimum capital requirements to the risk a bank takes on, it forced regulators to change the way they thought about bank capital. Second, it created a uniform international system. Finally, the accord provided a framework that less developed countries could use to improve the regulation of their banks.

While the Basel Accord was constructive, it did have some severe limitations. In adjusting for asset risk, the accord failed to differentiate between bonds issued by the U.S. government and those issued by emerging-market countries like Turkey: both received a weight of zero. And a corporate bond received a weight of 100 percent regardless of whether it was AAA rated or junk. Not only that, but a bank got no credit for reducing risk through diversification. Making one loan of $100 million received the same risk weight as making 1,000 loans of $100,000 each. These shortcomings encouraged banks to shift their holdings toward riskier assets in ways that did not increase their required bank capital.

By the mid-1990s, bank regulators and supervisors had concluded that the Basel Accord needed revision. From 1998 to 2003, the Basel Committee on Banking Supervision, which wrote the original accord, negotiated a revised framework for determining whether banks have sufficient capital. The new Basel Accord is based on three pillars: a revised set of minimum capital requirements; supervisory review of bank balance sheets; and increased reliance on market discipline to encourage sound risk management practices. The first measure refines the estimation of risk-adjusted assets to reflect more accurately the risk banks actually take. For example, bonds issued by highly rated corporations receive a 20 percent weight; junk bonds, a 150 percent weight. The second measure requires supervisors to attest to the soundness of bank managers' risk estimation and control methods. Supervisors now review the way banks assess their risk and decide how much capital they should hold. The third measure requires banks to make public their risk exposure and the level of capital they hold. Banks that can show they are behaving responsibly will be rewarded in the market with better credit ratings and higher stock prices.[*]

The Basel Accord is not a law but a set of recommendations for banking regulation and supervision. The Committee that writes and amends the accord has no direct authority over the banks in any country. Instead, its members work to develop a code of best practice that will help government officials around the world to ensure the safety and soundness of their banking systems.

[*]The Basel Committee on Banking Supervision constantly revises its recommendations to bank regulators. For information about the committee's activities and the Basel Accords in general, see its Web site at www.bis.org/bcbs/aboutbcbs.htm.

The Challenge to Regulators and Supervisors

Thus far, our discussion has focused on the regulation and supervision of depository institutions. But recent changes in the law, together with technological innovation, have challenged the traditional structure of regulation and supervision. Today, we bank in a bazaar where a wide range of intermediaries offers a broad array of financial services. We no longer know or care whether the product or service we buy is supplied by someone in town or on the other side of the country. In fact, when you call the bank, the person who answers the phone may live in India, for all you know. Telecommunications has made the location of financial service providers irrelevant.

Besides the globalization of financial services, other changes have challenged regulators and supervisors. First, today's marketplace offers financial instruments that allow individuals and institutions to price and trade almost any risk imaginable. Moreover, because derivatives allow the transfer of risk without a shift in the ownership of assets, a financial institution's balance sheet need not say much about its health. To understand the meaning of this change, consider the traditional rules for computing the minimum required level of bank capital. Historically, the minimum

APPLYING THE CONCEPT
THE HORROR OF THE ZOMBIE S&LS

We all trust that zombies—the walking dead—are confined to horror movies. But in the banking world, clever managers can find ways to keep a dead bank liquid, even though any sensible accounting would show that it is insolvent. Unless bank supervisors find these insolvent financial institutions and shut them down, they can continue operating in the world of the living.

Such was the case in the 1980s savings and loan crisis. In the late 1970s, as inflation and interest rates rose, traditional depository institutions—both banks and savings and loan institutions—faced a problem. The law set a ceiling on the interest rate they could offer that was well below the market rate. Depositors reacted by withdrawing their funds and placing them in money-market mutual funds, which offered interest rates far above the ceiling in the banking industry. The problem was especially acute at savings and loans (S&Ls), the institutions that used the deposits in interest-bearing savings accounts to fund home mortgages. At the same time, banks were losing their business customers to the growing commercial paper market.

Congress recognized that without a change in the regulations, high market interest rates, together with the financial innovation occurring at the time, would kill these institutions. New legislation removed the cap on deposit interest rates, eliminated restrictions on the interest rates charged on loans, expanded the assets banks and S&Ls could hold, and raised the deposit insurance ceiling from $40,000 to $100,000.

The newly competitive environment Congress established was a mixed blessing, however, especially for S&Ls. Once sheltered from competition, they were poorly equipped to manage the new risks they faced. Nevertheless, they expanded rapidly, offering high interest rates to attract new deposits and using the funds to make high-risk commercial real estate loans. Unfortunately, regulators and supervisors lacked the resources to monitor what was going on. No one really knew how to evaluate the new balance sheets S&L managers were constructing.

capital level was based on measures such as the default risk of a bank's assets. But in a world where banks can buy and sell derivatives that promise payment in the event of default—so-called *credit derivatives*—such measures become almost meaningless. Regulators and supervisors need to adapt. (See Tools of the Trade for a discussion of recent attempts at modernizing financial regulations.)

Added to the challenge of globalization and financial innovation is the fact that during the 1990s, Congress removed the functional and geographic barriers that once separated commercial banking from other forms of intermediation and outlawed interstate banking. Regulators and supervisors have not yet adapted to these legislative reforms. Institutions like Citigroup now are not just commercial banks but investment banks, insurance companies, and securities firms all rolled into one. Each part of these large organizations is regulated and supervised by different agencies, both functionally and geographically. Surely it would serve the public interest more to

continued from previous page

The result was disaster. By 1982, roughly half of all savings and loans were insolvent, and regulators knew it. But instead of closing them down, regulators came under political pressure to be more tolerant in their interpretation of the rules, exercising what is called forbearance. For example, examiners would allow an S&L to ignore a decline in the value of the bonds it owned as the result of interest-rate increases. There were two reasons for this policy. First, regulators were human, and they wanted to hide their mistakes. Closing insolvent institutions would have meant publicly admitting that a problem existed. Second, the massive closings would have bankrupted the deposit insurance fund. At the time, S&Ls had their own deposit insurance fund, and its assets were clearly insufficient to cover their losses. The result: thousands of zombie S&Ls.

Knowing their institutions were insolvent, some S&L managers offered higher and higher interest rates to attract deposits and then made riskier and riskier loans. A moral hazard problem that had been bad to begin with suddenly got worse. By offering high deposit rates, bankrupt S&Ls sucked the funds out of healthy institutions, becoming vampires instead of zombies.

In the end, regulatory forbearance cost the government $150 billion, the amount needed to fund the deposit insurance guarantees when the zombie S&Ls finally closed. Having learned from this mistake, Congress passed a series of laws that improved the process of bank regulation. Today, assets must be accounted for at their market value. Also, the FDIC is required to charge risk-based premiums for deposit insurance, a policy that began in 1993. Just as a high-risk driver pays more for auto insurance than a careful driver, a bank with a risky balance sheet pays more to insure its deposits than a more cautious institution.

Most important, regulators are now obligated to immediately close institutions whose capital falls below 2 percent of their assets, a policy known as prompt corrective action. The purposes of this policy are to limit claims on the deposit insurance fund and to eliminate regulators' discretion in allowing insolvent institutions to continue operating. The zombies have been sent back to the movies—at least for now.

RISK

minimize the likelihood that such an institution as a whole might fail rather than examine each business line separately. One of the benefits of a large, well-diversified institution is that some parts can do badly without bankrupting the entire enterprise. In spreading the risk, these corporations stabilize their profits.

Realizing this truth, regulators and supervisors have begun to think about their jobs in a different way. In the future they will have no choice but to combine forces along both geographic and functional lines. State and federal agencies must either learn to cooperate or merge, as must regulators of banks, insurance companies, and securities firms. A compelling case can be made for a super-regulator that would make the entire process more uniform and coherent. Finally, as the international financial system becomes more and more integrated, the need for cooperation across national borders will increase. The day may come when the world needs an international super-regulator to write the rules for the global financial system.

IN THE NEWS
Judging the Effects of New Rules on Bank Capital

The Economist

May 8th, 2003

A change in international rules on bank capital looks inevitable. Most banks, at least in Europe, seem resigned to this, even though for some it will mean big increases in capital requirements. Admittedly change will not come until January 2007, when the new rules known as Basel 2 are scheduled to take effect. A recent paper from the Basel committee on banking supervision is meant to be almost the last word. Its numbers stem from a third quantitative impact study of the effect of Basel 2 on the capital charges of 365 banks.

The average impact seems acceptable: a decrease in charges for many classes of credit risk, offset by a totally new charge for operational risk—the risk of all manner of mishaps and foul-ups, from a lost document to a bomb blast. That leaves the overall minimum regulatory capital in the banking system about the same as now, as the Basel supervisors had promised. National regulators will be expected to add more charges, at their discretion, to keep their banks well above the minimum.

But the devil is in the detail. Hardly any bank represents the average. Many banks specialising in such areas as securities custody and asset management are [very upset]. Thanks to the new operational risk element, these products attract a capital charge for the first time. On the other hand, banks that focus on retail and small business lending have reason to celebrate. Their capital charges may fall by up to 20 percent (see Figure 14.5).

Does Basel 2 align capital charges and the risks in the financial system more accurately than the present regime,

Basel 1, which has been in force since 1988? Almost everyone agrees that Basel 2 is taking banks' regulatory capital closer to *economic capital*, the theoretically ideal cushion against unexpected losses. But opinion is divided over whether this is a good thing. Some critics claim the process does not go far enough: it does not yet allow banks to use evolving techniques, such as portfolio models of credit risk, to get ever closer to economic capital. Others fear that the Basel 2 calculations are too finicky and costly to make economic sense for all but the biggest banks.

One or two European banks believe that Basel 2 could, at worst, blow up one or two European banking systems. The more sensitive the capital calculation is to risk, the more volatile the capital requirement is likely to be. If too many banks require extra capital at the same time, that alone could cause a capital crisis in the banking sector of a country or an entire continent.

Alarmist? Perhaps. In Germany, after all, the banks are already undergoing a capital crisis of sorts without any help from Basel 2. And because regulators have been fine-tuning their calculations at the bottom of the business cycle, there may be less danger that Basel 2 will spur reckless lending when conditions improve. Moreover, because national regulators will be expected to add charges according to the quality of the banks' management and their mix of business, there is some scope for flexibility.

However, the danger of giving discretion to regulators is that practice will vary from country to country. For this reason the Basel committee is spending almost as much time on coordinating supervisors as it is with banks. But there are two big potential sources of discrepancy. The first is between America and Europe. American supervisors have said that Basel 2 will be mandatory for only 10

At the ground level supervisors are likely to remain specialized, divided among different agencies and focused on distinct financial activities. One group will supervise banks, while another supervises insurance companies, even if they belong to larger conglomerates. Still, the supervisor's role is changing. In the past, a supervisor would look carefully at individual transactions, such as loans. Today, supervisors test the risk management systems banks have put in place to minimize the likelihood of catastrophe. When supervisors find that one of these systems is deficient, they help to fix it. Thus, government officials are spreading knowledge and expertise, helping managers to run their organizations safely and profitably. In the future, supervisors will be more like management consultants who come into an organization to solve problems and teach best practice.

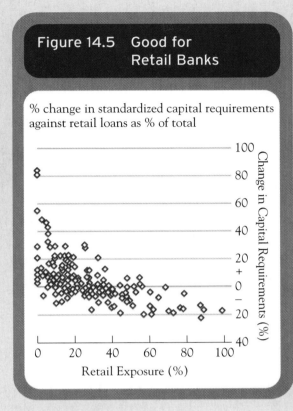

Figure 14.5 Good for Retail Banks

% change in standardized capital requirements against retail loans as % of total

Change in Capital Requirements (%)

Retail Exposure (%)

Source: Bank for International Settlements

internationally active American banks, while 10 more may adopt the regime voluntarily. Other American banks will be supervised according to the cruder Basel 1, with a few local enhancements. Across the Atlantic, the European Union is committed to writing Basel 2 into EU law, to be applied to all banks and investment firms regardless of size and scope.

Second, there may be inconsistency within Europe. Even when Basel 2 becomes law across the EU, its implementation will rely on rule making in member states, and thereafter on the discretion of national regulators. This will give supervisors plenty of scope to favor their national champions.

Some critics of Basel 2 would say that bank supervisors have been too selective already, by tweaking their calculations so that lending to retail and small business customers will not be jeopardized. If lending to those sectors later proves to have been reckless, then these very clients—either as consumers or as taxpayers—will in any case end up bearing a large share of the cost.

LESSONS OF THE ARTICLE

The continuous process of financial innovation means that bank regulators and supervisors are constantly adjusting the rules. After 15 years, the original Basel Accord needs revision to accommodate changes in the way financial intermediaries do business. Old ideas about risk no longer apply, so the rules must be rewritten. Rewriting the accord has required substantial international cooperation. Without that cooperation, banks could simply move to those countries with the most permissive regulations, jeopardizing the integrity of the system. But as the article notes, while cooperation is essential, it is difficult to achieve, since the details of the regulations have different effects on different types of bank.

Just as important, regulators must recognize that the goal of financial stability does not mean the stability of individual financial institutions. Too often supervisors have viewed their role as ensuring that no firm fails. The government official's job is not to stabilize the profits of an individual bank or insurance company. To do so would be to defeat the purpose of competition, rendering the entire system less efficient than it could be. Rather, the regulator's goal should be to prevent large-scale catastrophes.

STABILITY

Terms

bank panic, 352
bank run, 352
Basel Accord, 366
call reports, 365
CAMELS, 366
contagion, 352
deposit insurance, 357
examination, 365
forbearance, 369
illiquid, 352

insolvent, 352
lender of last resort, 356
payoff method, 357
prompt corrective action, 369
purchase-and-assumption method, 358
regulation, 361
regulatory competition, 362
supervision, 365
too-big-to-fail policy, 359

Chapter Lessons

1. The collapse of banks and the banking system disrupts both the payments system and the screening and monitoring of borrowers.

    a. Banks fail when their liabilities exceed their assets.

    b. Because banks guarantee their depositors cash on demand on a first-come, first-served basis, they are subject to runs.

    c. A bank run can occur simply because depositors have become worried about a bank's soundness.

    d. The inability of unsophisticated depositors to tell a sound from an unsound bank can turn a single bank's failure into a bank panic, causing even sound banks to fail through a process called contagion.

    e. A financial crisis in which the entire banking system ceases to function can be caused by

        i. False rumors.

        ii. The actual deterioration of bank balance sheets for economic reasons.

2. The government is involved in every part of the financial system.

    a. Government officials may intervene in the financial system in order to

        i. Protect small depositors.

        ii. Protect bank customers from exploitation.

        iii. Ensure the stability of the financial system.

    b. Most financial regulations apply to depository institutions.

    c. Nondepository institutions are also heavily regulated, but because they are not prone to runs, government oversight of these institutions is less intrusive than in the banking industry.

    d. The U.S. government has established a two-part safety net to protect the nation's financial system.

        i. The Federal Reserve acts as the lender of last resort, providing liquidity to solvent institutions in order to prevent the failure of a single bank from becoming a systemwide panic.

ii. The Federal Deposit Insurance Corporation (FDIC) insures individual depositors, preventing them from withdrawing their deposits at the first whiff of trouble, thus eliminating bank runs.

e. The government's safety net encourages bank managers to take more risk than they would otherwise, increasing the problem of moral hazard.

3. Through regulation and supervision, government officials reduce the amount of risk banks can take, lowering their chances of failure. Regulators and supervisors

a. Restrict competition.

b. Restrict the types of assets banks can hold.

c. Require banks to hold minimum levels of capital.

d. Require banks to disclose their fees to customers and their financial indicators to investors.

e. Monitor banks' compliance with government regulations.

Problems

1. Explain how a bank run can turn into a bank panic.

2. In analyzing data from around the world, a researcher observes that countries whose governments offer deposit insurance are more likely to have financial crises than other countries. Why?

3. Will knowing about the too-big-to-fail policy affect your choice of where to open a bank account? Why or why not?

4. Discuss the regulations that are designed to reduce the moral hazard created by deposit insurance.

5. How does the existence of a lender of last resort create moral hazard?

6. Distinguish between illiquidity and insolvency. Why is it difficult for a lender of last resort to tell insolvency from illiquidity? Does the distinction matter?

7. A government is considering changing its deposit insurance system from one in which deposits are implicitly guaranteed (that is, if a bank fails, people trust the government to put enough resources into the bank so that depositors will lose nothing) to one with an explicit ceiling. What would be the impact of such a change on depositors? On bankers?

8. Why do regulators insist that banks hold a minimum level of capital?

9. Many of the people the government employs to supervise and monitor banks eventually leave the government to work for the banks. Is this revolving door a problem? Why or why not?

10. Before the Federal Reserve's creation, banks tried banding together against the threat of bank runs. Under what circumstances would such an approach work? When would it not work?

11. Given the increasing complexity of the banking system, some people have proposed that banks be required to issue uncollateralized bonds, whose market prices could provide valuable information about banks' financial health. What is the logic behind such a proposal? Do you think it would work?

www.mhhe.com/cecchetti1e

12. Could an insurance company or a pension fund be subject to a run? Why or why not? Does the government need to guarantee deposits in these institutions?

13. Current technology allows large bank depositors to withdraw their funds electronically at a moment's notice. They can do so all at the same time, without anyone's knowledge, in what is called a silent run. When might a silent run happen, and why?

14. If you ran a large international bank headquartered in the United States, would you be for or against uniform regulations for all international banks, regardless of where they are based? What difference would it make if each country regulated its own banks, even those that have operations abroad?

15. Using the example of the Great Depression, explain why the existence of a lender of last resort is no guarantee of financial stability.

Part *IV*

Central Banks, Monetary Policy, and Financial Stability

Chapter 15

Central Banks in the World Today

In 1998, a financial meltdown in Russia and the multibillion-dollar collapse of Long Term Capital Management in the United States shook financial markets around the world. In the largest of the world's securities markets, trading nearly ground to a halt as dealers who normally offered to buy and sell reduced the extent of their participation. Investors verged on panic, fleeing real or imagined risks and rushing to the safest, most liquid assets they could find.[1] On Thursday, October 15, at 3:04 p.m., following an unscheduled conference call, the Federal Reserve's Federal Open Market Committee announced a quarter-percentage-point cut in interest rates and issued this statement:

"Growing caution by lenders and unsettled conditions in financial markets more generally are likely to be restraining aggregate demand in the future. Against this backdrop, further easing of the stance of monetary policy was judged to be warranted to sustain economic growth in the context of contained inflation."

—(Federal Reserve Press Release, October 15, 1998)

Almost immediately, financial markets began to calm down. A second interest rate cut of the same size came during the Fed's regular meeting a month later, providing more balm for the markets. Over the next few months, things slowly returned to normal. Government officials had done what they were supposed to do: They had fixed a financial problem before it became serious enough for most of us to notice it.

The Federal Reserve (the Fed for short) is the United States' **central bank**. The people who work there are responsible for making sure that our financial system functions smoothly, so that the average citizen can carry on without worrying about it. During the treacherous fall of 1998, the Fed clearly did its job. But central banks don't act only during times of crisis. Their work is vital to the day-to-day operation of any modern economy. Today there are over 170 central banks in the world; virtually every country has one. The 15 republics that constituted the Soviet Union became independent in 1990. Within a year, 12 of them had established or reestablished a central bank; by 1993, they all had.[2]

Despite the constant presence of central banks in the news and their unprecedented power, most people have only a vague idea of what they are and what they do. This chapter explains the role of modern central banks in our economic and financial system and examines the complexities policymakers face in meeting their responsibilities.

---

[1] Federal Reserve Bank of New York President William McDonough called this episode "the worst financial crisis since World War II." It followed the collapse of Thailand and Indonesia in the summer of 1997 and the financial crisis in Korea in January 1998. For further detail, see Chapters 7, 9 and 10.

[2] Most central banks maintain a Web site, which you can access from www.bis.org/cbanks.htm.

The Basics: How Central Banks Originated and Their Role Today

The central bank started out as the government's bank and over the years added various other functions. A modern central bank not only manages the government's finances but provides an array of services to commercial banks. It is the bankers' bank. Let's see how this arrangement came about.

The Government's Bank

Governments have financial needs of their own. Some rulers, like King William of Orange, created the central bank to finance wars. Others, like Napoléon Bonaparte, did it in an effort to stabilize their country's economic and financial system.[3]

While central banks have been around since the late 1600s, these early examples are really the exceptions, as central banking is largely a 20th-century phenomenon. In 1900, only 18 countries had central banks. Even the U.S. Federal Reserve did not begin operating until 1914.[4] As the importance of the government and the financial system grew, the need for a central bank grew along with it. Today it is hard to imagine not having one.

As the government's bank, the central bank occupies a privileged position: It has a monopoly on the issuance of currency. *The central bank creates money.* Historically, central bank money has been seen as more trustworthy than that issued by kings, queens, or emperors. Rulers have had a tendency to default on their debts, rendering their currencies worthless. By contrast, early central banks kept sufficient reserves to redeem their notes in gold. People must have faith in money if they are to use it, and experience tells us that this type of institutional arrangement creates that faith. Today the Federal Reserve has the sole legal authority to issue U.S. dollar bills.[5]

The ability to print currency means that the central bank can control the availability of money and credit in a country's economy. As we'll see in later chapters, most central banks go about this by adjusting short-term interest rates. This activity is what we refer to as **monetary policy**. In today's world, central banks use monetary policy to stabilize economic growth and inflation. An expansionary or accommodative policy, through lower interest rates, raises both growth and inflation over the short run, while tighter or restrictive policy reduces them.[6] We will discuss the mechanics of monetary policy in more detail in Chapter 17.

---

[3]The Bank of England was chartered in 1694 for the express purpose of raising taxes and borrowing to finance a war between Austria, England, and the Netherlands on one side and Louis XIV's France on the other. The Banque de France was created in 1800 in the aftermath of the deep recession and hyperinflation of the French Revolutionary period. For a more detailed discussion, see Glyn Davies' *The History of Money from Ancient Times to the Present Day* (Cardiff: University of Wales Press), 1994.

[4] For two short periods in the 19th century, the United States did have a national bank that served many of the functions of a central bank. Early American dislike for the centralization of power doomed these institutions, the First Bank of the United States (1791–1811) and the Second Bank of the United States (1816–1836). In the next chapter, we will see how industrial and financial development after the Civil War convinced people that they simply could not live without a central bank. See Michael F. Bryan and Bruce Champ's "Fear and Loathing of Central Banks in America," *Economic Commentary* of the Federal Reserve Bank of Cleveland, June 2002, for a brief description of this history.

[5]While once upon a time you could redeem dollar bills for gold, today all the Federal Reserve promises is that it will give you a crisp new dollar bill for a worn old one—and that is enough for the average person, given the public's faith in the Federal Reserve.

[6]To fully appreciate why expansionary monetary policy raises growth and inflation over the short run, we need to develop a macroeconomic model of what determines output and inflation. In the long run, however, monetary policy does not affect growth. This relationship is the subject of Chapters 20, 21, and 22.

Understanding why a country would want to have its own monetary policy is important. At its most basic level, printing money is a very profitable business. A $100 bill costs only a few cents to print, but it can be exchanged for $100 worth of goods and services. It is logical that governments would want to maintain a monopoly on printing money and to use the revenue it generates to benefit the general public.[7]

Government officials also know that losing control of the printing presses means losing control of inflation. A high rate of money growth creates high inflation. That is the real reason the republics of the former Soviet Union needed to establish their own central banks. After the collapse of the Soviet Union, the Russian ruble circulated throughout the area, and the central bank of the Russian Republic controlled how fast the quantity of rubles increased. This arrangement did not work well; by 1992, inflation throughout the *ruble zone* exceeded 1,000 percent per year. Not surprisingly, the monetary system soon collapsed. By late 1993, countries were issuing their own currencies in an attempt to control inflation locally. Moldova, one of the more successful, was able to reduce its inflation to 30 percent by 1995.

The primary reason for a country to create its own central bank, then, is to ensure control over its currency. Giving the money-printing monopoly to someone else can be disastrous. Nevertheless, some countries have done it; the European Monetary Union comes to mind immediately. A dozen European countries recently ceded their right to conduct independent monetary policy to the European Central Bank, as part of a broader move toward economic integration. But they did it after instituting strict controls that ensured inflation would remain low. There is very little risk that European monetary policy will be misused.

The Bankers' Bank

The political backing of the government, together with their sizable gold reserves, made early central banks the biggest and most reliable banks around. The notes issued by the central bank were viewed as safer than those of smaller banks, making it easier for holders to convert their deposits into cash. This safety and convenience quickly persuaded most other banks to hold deposits at the central bank as well.

As the bankers' bank, the central bank took on the roles it plays today. The important day-to-day jobs of the central bank are to (1) provide loans during times of financial stress, (2) manage the payments system, and (3) oversee commercial banks and the financial system. The central bank's ability to print money means that it can make loans even when no one else can, including during a crisis. We discussed financial panics in Chapter 14, where we learned that a bank will collapse if all its depositors try to withdraw their account balances at the same time. No bank, no matter how well managed, can withstand a run. To stave off such a crisis, the central bank can lend cash to sound banks. We will take up this "lender of last resort" function in Chapter 18. For now, all we need to say is that by ensuring that sound banks and financial institutions can continue to operate, the central bank makes the whole financial system more stable. Many people believe this is the most important function of any modern central bank.

Second, every country has to have a secure and efficient payments system. People need ways to pay each other, and financial institutions need a cheap and reliable way

[7]When we list the objectives of the central bank later in the chapter, however, we will explicitly exclude profit maximization.

to transfer funds to one another.[8] The fact that all banks have accounts there makes the central bank the natural place for these *interbank* payments to be settled. In today's world, interbank payments are extremely important. Look at the daily volume on the Federal Reserve's *Fedwire* system. In 2003, an average of almost $3 trillion per day was transferred over the Fedwire—nearly one-quarter of the annual U.S. gross domestic product.

Finally, as we saw in our discussion of banking regulation, someone has to watch over private banks and nonbank financial institutions so that savers and investors can be confident they are sound. Those who monitor the financial system must have sensitive information. For example, they need to know the exact methods institutions use to make lending and credit decisions. Needless to say, such knowledge would be very useful to the institutions' competitors. Government examiners and supervisors are the only ones who can handle such information without conflict of interest. In some countries they are housed in the central bank, while in others they work in separate agencies. In the United States, as we saw in Chapter 14, the examiners work in various places, including the Federal Reserve.

As the government's bank and the bankers' bank, central banks are the biggest, most powerful players in a country's financial and economic system. Central bankers are supposed to use this power to stabilize the economy, making us all better off. And for the most part, that is what they do. But any institution with the power to ensure that the economic and financial systems run smoothly also has the power to create problems. Central bankers that are under extreme political pressure, or are simply incompetent, can wreak havoc on the economic and financial systems. By lending to weak financial institutions that should have been closed, the Bank of Thailand helped to create the Asian financial crisis of 1997. And the failure of the Bank of Russia to exert any control over the expansion of money and credit led to very high inflation, contributing to the fact that the Russian economy shrank by nearly 50 percent during the 1990s.

Before we go on to examine the goals and objectives of central bankers in detail, it is essential that we understand what a modern central bank is *not*. First, a central bank does not control securities markets, though it may monitor and participate in bond and stock markets. Second, the central bank does not control the government's budget. In the United States, the budget is determined by Congress and the president through fiscal policy. The U.S. Treasury then administers the government, managing the collection of funds through the tax system and writing checks to pay for the government's expenditures. The Fed acts only as the Treasury's bank, providing a place for money paid to the government to be deposited, making good on the government's checks, and helping to borrow funds when they are needed. Not just in the United States but throughout the world, the common arrangement today is for the central bank to serve the government in the same way that a commercial bank serves a business or an individual. The treasury or finance ministry manages fiscal policy, and the central bank offers a set of services that make such management possible.

Table 15.1 lists the functions of a modern central bank.

---

[8]Prior to the creation of the Federal Reserve's payment system, banks were not always willing to honor the obligations of other banks at par. Thus, a $100 bank note from a particular Philadelphia bank might be worth only $95 in New York. And the discount would vary depending on the perceived creditworthiness of the Philadelphia bank. This system was very cumbersome and expensive. One of the jobs of the Federal Reserve is to act as an intermediary, insuring that all banks' commitments are valued at par so that the rest of us don't have to worry.

> ### Table 15.1 The Functions of a Modern Central Bank
>
> 1. *The Government's Bank*
>   - a. Manages the finances of the government.
>   - b. Through interest rates, controls the availability of money and credit.
> 2. *The Bankers' Bank*
>   - a. Guarantees that sound banks can do business by *lending* to them, even during crises.
>   - b. Operates a *payments system* for interbank payments.
>   - c. *Oversees* financial institutions to ensure confidence in their soundness.

Stability: The Primary Objective of All Central Banks

The central bank is part of the government. Whenever we see an agency of the government involving itself in the economy, we need to ask why. What makes individuals incapable of doing what we have entrusted to the government? In the case of national defense and pollution regulation, the reasons are obvious. Most people will not voluntarily contribute their resources to the army. Nor will they spontaneously clean up their own air. To put it slightly differently, government involvement is justified by the presence of externalities or public goods; that is, when individuals do not pay the full costs or capture the complete benefits from their actions.

The rationale for the existence of a central bank is equally clear. While economic and financial systems may be fairly stable most of the time, when left on their own they are prone to episodes of extreme volatility. Prior to the advent of the Fed, the U.S. financial system was extremely unstable. It was plagued by numerous panics. Even with a central bank, these systems don't necessarily work well. The historical record is filled with examples of failure, like the Great Depression of the 1930s, when the banking system collapsed, economic activity plunged by one-third, and one-quarter of Americans were unemployed for nearly a decade. Economic historians blame the Federal Reserve for the severity of that episode. The claim is that monetary policymakers failed to provide adequate money and credit, with the result that of the country's 25,000 banks, nearly 10,000 were closed.[9] Monetary policy failed in the 1930s, but since then the Fed's performance has been much better.

Central bankers work to reduce the volatility of the economic and financial systems by pursuing five specific objectives:

STABILITY

1. Low and stable inflation.
2. High and stable real growth, together with high employment.
3. Stable financial markets.
4. Stable interest rates.
5. A stable exchange rate.

[9]Although numerous, fortunately the failed banks were small, accounting for roughly 13 percent of the deposits in the banking system.

It is important to realize that instability in any of these—inflation, growth, financial markets, interest rates, or exchange rates—poses an economywide risk that individuals can't diversify away. Recall from Chapter 5 that systematic risk, where everyone is affected, differs from idiosyncratic risk, which affects only a particular organization or individual. The job of the central bank is to improve general economic welfare by managing and reducing systematic risk.[10] Keep in mind that it is probably impossible to achieve all five of the central bank's objectives simultaneously. Trade-offs must be made. As we will see, stabilizing inflation may result in less stable growth, and stable interest rates may be inconsistent with all the other objectives.

Low, Stable Inflation

In 2002, the director of research of the International Monetary Fund (the closest thing there is to a world central bank) summarized virtually every economist's view when he said, "Uncontrolled inflation strangles growth, hurting the entire populace, especially the indigent."[11] That is why many central banks take as their primary job the maintenance of price stability. That is, they strive to eliminate inflation. The consensus is that when inflation rises, the central bank is at fault. Price stability is the primary objective of the central bank.

The rationale for keeping the economy inflation free is straightforward. Standards, everyone agrees, should be standard. A pound should always weigh a pound, a cup should always hold a cup, and a yard should always measure a yard. Similarly, a dollar should always be worth a dollar. What is true for physical weights and measures should be true for the unit of account as well. The purchasing power of one dollar, one yen, or one euro should remain stable over long periods. Maintaining price stability enhances money's usefulness both as a unit of account and as a store of value.

Prices are central to everything that happens in a market-based economy. They provide the information individuals and firms need to ensure that resources are allocated to their best uses. When a seller can raise the price of a product, for example, that is supposed to signal that demand has increased, so producing more is worthwhile. But inflation degrades the information content of prices. When all prices are rising together, understanding the reasons becomes difficult. Did consumers decide they liked an item, shifting demand? Did the cost of producing the item rise, shifting supply? Or was inflation responsible for the jump in price? If the economy is to run efficiently, we need to be able to tell the difference.

If inflation were predictable—say, 10 percent year in and year out—we might be able to adjust, eventually. But unfortunately, as inflation rises, it becomes less stable. If our best guess is that inflation will be 2 percent over the coming year, we can be fairly certain that the result will be a price level increase of between 1 and 3 percent. But experience tells us that when we expect inflation to be around 10 percent, we shouldn't be surprised if it ends up anywhere between 8 and 12 percent. The higher inflation is, the less predictable it is, and the more systematic risk it creates.[12]

Moreover, the fact is high inflation is bad for growth.[13] This fact is obvious in extreme cases, such as in 1985, when inflation reached 11,000 percent in Bolivia, or in 1983,

RISK

---

[10]Some people like volatility. Traders in the financial markets will say that volatility creates risk, and risk creates opportunity. Without volatility, traders can't profit. But what is true for traders is not true for the rest of us. We want our economy to be calm and under control, so our jobs will be secure and our paychecks predictable.

[11]Kenneth S. Rogoff, "An Open Letter to Joseph Stiglitz," International Monetary Fund, July 2, 2002.

[12]Inflation is costly for other reasons as well. They include the cost of going to the bank more often, the cost of changing prices more often, and distortions created by the way the tax system is written.

[13]For evidence on this point, see Michael Bruno and William Easterly, "Inflation Crises and Long-Run Growth," *Journal of Monetary Economics* 41 (February 1998), pp. 3–26.

YOUR FINANCIAL WORLD
Why Inflation Is Bad for You

If you ask most people why inflation is bad, they will say it is responsible for a decline in what they can purchase with their incomes. For them, inflation causes a drop in their standard of living: Prices have gone up, but their incomes, including their wages, haven't. Economists view inflation differently. To them, inflation is when everything that is denominated in dollars goes up proportionally—prices, incomes, savings account balances, everything. It is as if everything is suddenly measured in cents instead of dollars. How could this possibly make anyone worse off?

The answer is that inflation creates risk. The higher it is, the greater the risk. When inflation is averaging 2 percent per year, chances are slim that it will suddenly rise to 5 percent. But if inflation is averaging 15 percent, there is a good chance it will end up at 18 percent next year.

To see how this affects virtually everyone, recall from Chapter 6 that unpredictable inflation makes bonds risky. Higher-than-expected inflation reduces the real return a bondholder receives. Since the real return is the nominal return minus expected inflation, if the nominal interest rate is 5 percent and inflation turns out to be 2 percent, then the real return drops to 3 percent. If inflation ends up at 5 percent, the real return is zero. That's a risk. Since risk requires compensation, inflation risk drives up the interest rate required to entice investors to hold bonds.

Now think about two common financial transactions: getting a home mortgage and saving for retirement. When you buy a house, your goal is to get the lowest mortgage interest rate you can find. Inflation risk drives up mortgage interest rates, increasing your monthly payments and forcing you to purchase a less expensive house. Turning to your retirement savings, inflation risk makes it more difficult to know how much to save, because you are unsure what the purchasing power of your savings will be 40 or 50 years from now. Long-term planning is hard enough without the added burden of inflation risk.

---

when it reached nearly 5,000 percent in Ukraine. In such cases of hyperinflation—when prices double every 2 to 3 months—prices contain virtually no information, and people use all their energy just coping with the crisis, so growth plummets. In Bolivia, growth went from more than plus 6 percent in the late 1970s to minus 5 percent during the hyperinflation. The Ukrainian economy shrank by more than 20 percent the year inflation peaked. Only when inflation was brought under control did these economies begin to grow again.

Because low inflation is the basis for general economic prosperity, most people agree that it should be the primary objective of monetary policy. But how low should inflation be? As the In the News article toward the end of this chapter explains, zero is probably too low. There are a couple of reasons for this. First, if the central bank tries to keep inflation at zero, there is a risk of deflation—a drop in prices. Deflation makes debts more difficult to repay, which increases the default rate on loans, affecting the health of banks. Recall from Chapter 11 that deflation increases the information problems lenders face, and may prevent some borrowers from obtaining loans. We'll come back to this topic in Chapter 23. Second, if inflation were zero, an employer wishing to cut labor costs would need to cut nominal wages, which is difficult to do. With a small amount of inflation, the employer can simply leave wages as they are, and workers' real wages will fall. So a small amount of inflation makes labor markets work better, at least from the employer's point of view.[14]

---

[14]Added to all of this is the fact that measured inflation tends to overstate true inflation. That is, inflation statistics are biased upward. Most economists believe the bias to be about 1 percentage point. And the objective of central bankers should be to keep measured inflation somewhat above 1 percent so that there is virtually no true inflation. Your Financial World in Chapter 20 discusses the issue of inflation measurement in more detail.

High, Stable Real Growth

In January 2000, near the end of the longest economic expansion in U.S. history, Governor of the Federal Reserve Board Laurence H. Meyer observed, "Supporting maximum sustainable growth is very much the business of monetary policy."[15] Central bankers make this sort of statement all the time. What they mean is that they are working to dampen the fluctuations of the business cycle. Booms are popular, but recessions are not. In recessions, people get laid off and businesses fail. Without a steady income, individuals struggle to make their auto, credit card, and mortgage payments. Consumers pull back, hurting businesses that rely on them to buy products. Reduced sales lead to more layoffs, and so on. The longer the downturn goes on, the worse it gets.

By adjusting interest rates, central bankers work to moderate these cycles and stabilize growth and employment. The idea is that there is some long-run *sustainable* level of production called **potential output** that depends on things like technology, the size of the capital stock, and the number of people who can work.[16] Growth in these *inputs* leads to growth in *potential output—***sustainable growth**. In the United States, growth usually runs around 3 percent per year. Over the short run, output may deviate from this potential level, and growth may deviate from its long-run sustainable rate. In recessions, the economy stalls, incomes stagnate, and unemployment rises. By lowering interest rates, monetary policy makers can moderate such declines.

Similarly, there are times when growth rises above sustainable rates, and the economy overheats. These periods may seem to bring increased prosperity, but since they don't last forever, they are followed by reduced spending, lower business investment, and layoffs. A period of above-average growth has to be followed by a period of below-average growth. The job of the central bank during such periods is to raise interest rates and keep the economy from operating at unsustainable levels. In the long run, lower volatility produces higher average growth (see Applying the Concept: Stable Countries Grow Faster).

The importance of keeping sustainable growth as high as possible is hard to overstate. The difference between an economy that grows at 4 percent per year and one that grows at 2 percent per year is the difference between an economy that doubles in size over 18 years and one that grows by less than 50 percent in the same period. (This calculation uses the rule of 72 described in Your Financial World in Chapter 4.) Keeping employment high is equally important. It is impossible to recover later what unemployed people would have produced had they been working during a downturn. You can't get the lost time back. Our hope is that policymakers can manage the country's affairs so that we will stay on a high and sustainable growth path.

The levels of growth and employment aren't the only things of importance, though. Stability matters too. Fluctuations in general business conditions are the primary source of systematic risk, a kind of risk that can't be diversified away. As we have said a number of times, uncertainty about the future makes planning more difficult, so getting rid of uncertainty makes everyone better off.

Financial System Stability

The Federal Reserve was founded to stop the financial panics that plagued the United States during the late 19th and early 20th centuries. It took a while to work out the kinks in the system. As we have seen, the U.S. financial system collapsed again in the early 1930s, as policymakers at the Federal Reserve watched. Since then, officials

[15]Laurence H. Meyer, "Sustainability and Monetary Policy," remarks before the National Economists Club and the Society of Government Economists, Washington, D.C., January 20, 2000.

[16]We will discuss the concept of potential output in more detail in Chapter 21.

APPLYING THE CONCEPT
STABLE COUNTRIES GROW FASTER

For most countries, stable growth means faster growth. Figure 15.1 plots average annual growth in a sample of countries both large and small on the vertical axis and the standard deviation, or volatility, of growth in those countries on the horizontal axis. Remember from Chapter 5 that the standard deviation is a measure of risk. The figure shows a clear negative correlation: Points range from the top left to the lower right. High growth is less volatile than low growth.

It is plausible that stability actually causes higher growth.* To see how such a relationship might arise, we need to remember some key facts:

- Unstable growth creates risk for investors.
- Investors require compensation for risk, so interest rates will be higher.
- Higher interest rates mean lower levels of borrowing by businesses.
- Lower levels of borrowing by business mean fewer resources for companies to invest.
- Fewer resources for companies to invest mean less growth.

To understand how this process works, think about getting a loan to buy a car. The more certain you are that you will have a good, steady job over the next few years, the larger the loan you will feel comfortable taking on. If you are nervous that you might lose your job, you will be cautious. What is true for you and your car loan is true for every person and every company. The greater the uncertainty about future business conditions, the more cautious people are in making investments of all kinds.

*Figure 15.1 establishes a correlation between the level and volatility of growth, not a causal relationship. While high growth leads to stability, theoretical explanations focus on the reverse relationship. For a more detailed discussion of the relationship between correlation and causality, see Tools of the Trade in Chapter 23.

continued on next page

have figured out how to avert most crises. The Fed's actions in 1998, described in the introduction to this chapter, show that today's central banks can move quickly to quell investors' anxieties. Financial system stability is an integral part of every modern central banker's job. It is essential for policymakers to ensure that the markets for stocks, bonds, and the like continue to operate smoothly and efficiently.

The financial system is like plumbing: When it works, we take it for granted, but when it doesn't work, watch out. If people lose faith in banks and financial markets, they will rush to low-risk alternatives, and intermediation will stop. Savers will not lend and borrowers will not be able to borrow. Getting a car loan or a home mortgage becomes impossible, as does selling a bond to maintain or expand a business. When the financial system collapses, economic activity does, too.

The possibility of a severe disruption in the financial markets is a type of systematic risk. Nothing that a single individual does can eliminate it. Central banks must control this systematic risk, making sure that the financial system remains in good work-

continued from previous page

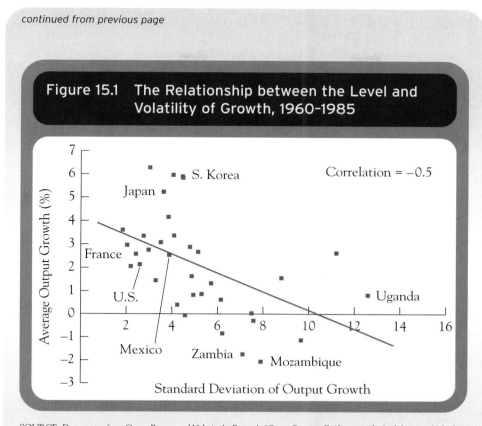

Figure 15.1   The Relationship between the Level and Volatility of Growth, 1960-1985

SOURCE: *Data comes from Garey Ramey and Valerie A. Ramey's "Cross-Country Evidence on the Link between Volatility and Growth,"* American Economic Review 85 (December 1995), pp. 1138–1151.

ing order. The *value at risk*, not the standard deviation, is the important measure here. Recall from Chapter 5 that value at risk measures the risk of the maximum potential loss. When thinking about financial stability, central bankers want to minimize the risk of a disaster and keep the chance of this maximum loss as small as possible.

"Personally, I liked this roller coaster a lot better before the Federal Reserve Board got hold of it."

SOURCE: © *The New Yorker Collection 1997. Robert Mankoff from cartoonbank.com. All Rights Reserved.*

Interest-Rate and Exchange-Rate Stability

If you ask them, most central bankers will tell you that they do their best to keep interest rates and exchange rates from fluctuating too much. They want to eliminate abrupt changes. But if you press them further, they will tell you that these goals are secondary to those of low inflation, stable growth, and financial stability. The reason for this hierarchy is that interest-rate stability and exchange-rate stability are means for achieving the ultimate goal of stabilizing the economy; they are not ends unto themselves.

It is easy to see why interest-rate volatility is a problem. First, most people respond to low interest rates by borrowing and spending more. Individuals take out loans to purchase cars, new appliances and the like, while corporations issue more bonds and use the proceeds to enlarge their operations. Conversely, when interest rates rise, people borrow and spend less. So, by raising expenditure when interest rates are low and reducing expenditure when interest rates are high, interest-rate volatility makes output unstable. Second, interest-rate volatility means higher risk—and a higher risk premium—on long-term bonds. (Remember from Chapter 7 that the long-term interest rate is the average of expected future short-term interest rates plus a risk premium that compensates for the volatility of short-term interest rates.) Risk makes financial decisions more difficult, lowering productivity and making the economy less efficient. Since central bankers control short-term interest rates, they are in a position to control this risk and stabilize the economy.

Stabilizing exchange rates is the last item on the list of central bank objectives.[17] The value of a country's currency affects the cost of imports to domestic consumers and the cost of exports to foreign buyers. When the exchange rate is stable, the dollar price of a car produced in Germany is predictable, making life easier for the foreign automobile manufacturer, the domestic retailer, and the American car buyer. Planning ahead is easier for everyone.

Different countries have different priorities. While the Federal Reserve and the European Central Bank may not care much about exchange-rate stability, the heads of central banks in small, less developed countries do. In *emerging-markets countries* where exports and imports are central to the structure of the economy, officials might reasonably argue that good overall macroeconomic performance follows from a stable exchange rate.

Table 15.2 summarizes the five objectives of a modern central bank.

Meeting the Challenge: Creating a Successful Central Bank

The 1990s were amazing in many ways. The Internet and cell phones came into widespread use. Overall economic conditions improved nearly everywhere. Growth was higher, inflation lower, and both more stable than in the 1980s. In the United States, inflation fell from 6 percent at the start of the decade to less than 2 percent at the end. Meanwhile, real growth rose from less than 3 percent to more than 4 percent.

---

[17]As we will see in Chapter 19, the Federal Reserve is not officially in charge of exchange-rate policy in the United States; the Secretary of the Treasury is. But, because of the way in which exchange rates are determined, they cannot be independent of interest-rate policy. Since the Fed controls interest rates, it effectively controls exchange rates as well.

STABILITY

Table 15.2 The Objectives of a Modern Central Bank	
1. *Low, stable inflation.*	Inflation creates confusion and makes planning difficult. When inflation is high, growth is low.
2. *High, stable growth.*	Stable, predictable growth is higher than unstable, unpredictable growth.
3. *Financial system stability.*	A stable financial system is a necessity for an economy to operate efficiently.
4. *Stable interest rates.*	Interest-rate volatility creates risk for both lenders and borrowers.
5. *Stable exchange rates.*	Variable exchange rates make the revenues from foreign sales and the cost of purchasing imported goods hard to predict.

Volatility declined, too. But the United States wasn't the only country where economic conditions improved; the same thing happened around the globe.[18]

What explains this phenomenon? A prime candidate is that technology sparked a boom just as central banks became better at their jobs. First, monetary policymakers realized that sustainable growth had gone up, so they could keep interest rates low without worrying about inflation. Second, central banks were redesigned. It wasn't just that new central banks were established, like the ones set up in the 15 republics of the former Soviet Union. The structure of existing central banks changed significantly. The Bank of England is over 300 years old (its building in London has stood for nearly 200 years) but its operating charter was completely rewritten in 1998. The same year brought major changes in the organizational structure of the Bank of Japan. Federal Reserve operations have changed, too. The first public announcement of a move in the federal funds rate was made on February 4, 1994. On January 19, 2002, the regular issuance of a statement explaining interest-rate decisions became an official part of Federal Reserve procedures.[19]

Many people believe that improvements in economic performance during the 1990s were related at least in part to the policy followed by these restructured central banks. Improving monetary policy is not just a matter of finding the right person for the job. There is an ample supply of highly qualified people. In fact, in many countries there is a long history of central bankers who have tried but failed because they weren't free to pursue effective policies. Successful policymaking is as much a consequence of the institutional environment as of the people who work in the institutions. Nowhere is that more true than in central banking.

Today there is a clear consensus about the best way to design a central bank and what to tell monetary policy makers to do. To be successful, a central bank must (1) be inde-

[18]Stephen G. Cecchetti and Michael Ehrmann compared 1985–1989 to 1993–1997 in a set of 23 industrialized and emerging-markets countries and found that annual inflation fell an average of five percentage points, annual growth rose an average of one percentage point, and both were significantly more stable. See "Does Inflation Targeting Increase Output Volatility? An International Comparison of Policymakers' Preferences and Outcomes" in Norman Loayza and Klaus Schmidt-Hebbel (eds.), *Monetary Policy: Rules and Transmission Mechanisms,* Proceedings of the Fourth Annual Conference of the Central Bank of Chile, Santiago, Chile: Central Bank of Chile, 2002, pp. 247–274.

[19]See Chapter 16 for a discussion of the most important changes in the Federal Reserve's structure and operations.

YOUR FINANCIAL WORLD

Does News about the Fed Affect Your Daily Life?

On an average day the *The Wall Street Journal* mentions the Federal Reserve in about five stories. Reporters and editors obviously think people should care what the central bank is doing. Do we really need to follow news about the Fed every day?

The preoccupation with the central bank comes from the fact that it adjusts interest rates. News reports invariably predict the timing and direction of the next move in interest rates. While we all care about interest rates—they measure the cost of a car loan or mortgage, and the return we get on investments—on a normal day, the interest rate on a loan doesn't change.

Sometimes Federal Reserve actions do have an effect on everyone, however. On July 15, 2003, Federal Reserve chairman Alan Greenspan suggested that interest rates might not fall as much as people in the financial markets thought they would. As a result, the yield on a $4\frac{1}{4}$% coupon 10-year U.S. Treasury bond rose 0.21 percentage point, from 3.72 percent to 3.93 percent. That may not seem like much, but it meant that the owner of a $1,000 10-year Treasury bond lost $17.40 in one day—that's

how much the price of the bond fell. And the increase translated directly into a rise in the interest rates everyone pays to borrow. Because of Chairman Greenspan's comments, mortgage rates rose nearly one-quarter of a percentage point in a single day, with a 30-year fixed-rate mortgage rising from roughly $5\frac{1}{2}$ to $5\frac{3}{4}$ percent.* This alone drove the monthly payment on a $100,000 mortgage up from $559 to $574.

Events like this one don't happen often. Understanding when and how they might occur requires knowing how the Fed operates and what sort of news is likely to precipitate changes in interest rates. That means following long-term economic trends to gain some sense of what the Fed is likely to do, and when.

*Chapter 18 will discuss the exact mechanism that causes this. Briefly, Chairman Greenspan's comments led people to think the Federal Reserve was going to raise the interest rate that it controls—the overnight interbank lending rate. This raised long-term interest rates because, according to the expectations hypothesis of the term structure described in Chapter 7, they are an average of expected short-term interest rates.

pendent of political pressure, (2) make decisions by committee, (3) be accountable to the public and transparent in communicating its policy actions, and (4) operate within an explicit framework that clearly states its goals and the tradeoffs among them.

The Need for Independence

The idea of central bank independence—that central banks should be independent of political pressure—is a new one. After all, the central bank originated as the government's bank. It did the bidding first of the king or emperor and then of the democratically elected congress or parliament. Politicians rarely give up control over anything, much less something as important as monetary policy. But in the 1990s, nearly every government that hadn't already done so made the central bank independent of the finance ministry. The Banque de France became independent in 1993. Political control of the Bank of England and the Bank of Japan ended in 1998. And the new European Central Bank was independent from the day it opened on July 1, 1998.

Independence has two operational components. First, monetary policymakers must be free to control their own budgets. If politicians can starve the central bank of funding, then they can control the bank's decisions. Second, the bank's policies must not be reversible by people outside the central bank. Prior to 1998, policymakers at the Bank of England merely recommended interest-rate changes to the Chancellor of the Exchequer, a political official. That is, interest rate policy was ultimately decided by the British equivalent of the U.S. Secretary of the Treasury. Since 1998, the Bank of England's Monetary Policy Committee has made those decisions autonomously. The same is true in the United States, where the Federal Open Market Committee's decisions on when to raise or lower interest rates cannot be overridden by the President, Congress, or the Supreme Court.

Successful monetary policy requires a long time horizon. The impact of today's decisions won't be felt for a while—several years, in many instances. Democratically elected politicians are not a particularly patient bunch; their time horizon extends only to the next election. The political system encourages members of Parliament and members of Congress to do everything they can for their constituents before the next election—including manipulating interest rates to bring short-term prosperity at the expense of long-term stability. The temptation to forsake long-term goals for short-term gains is simply impossible for most politicians to resist. Given the ability to choose, politicians will select monetary policies that are overly accommodative. They will keep interest rates too low and money growth rates too high. This raises output and employment quickly (before the election), but causes inflation to go up later (after the election). Low interest rates are very popular because there are more borrowers than lenders.

Knowing these tendencies, governments have moved responsibility for monetary policy into a separate, largely apolitical, institution. To insulate policymakers from the daily pressures faced by politicians, governments must give central bankers control of their budgets and authority to make irreversible decisions and must appoint them to long terms.

Decision Making by Committee

Should important decisions be made by an individual or by a committee? Military planners know they can't have groups making decisions in the heat of a battle; someone has to be in charge. But monetary policy isn't war. Monetary policy decisions are made deliberately, after significant amounts of information are collected and examined. Occasionally a crisis does occur, and in those times someone does need to be in charge. But in the course of normal operations, it is better to rely on a committee than an individual. Though extraordinary individuals can be trusted to make policy as well as a committee, building an institution on the assumption that someone of exemplary ability will always be available to run it is unwise. And given the difficulty of removing a central bank governor—a feature that is built into the central bank system—the cost of putting the wrong person in charge can be very high.

The solution, then, is to make policy by committee. Pooling the knowledge, experience, and opinions of a group of people reduces the risk that policy will be dictated by an individual's quirks. Besides, in a democracy, vesting so much power in one individual poses a legitimacy problem. For these reasons, monetary policy decisions are made by committee in all major central banks in the world. The Federal Reserve has its Federal Open Market Committee, the European Central Bank its Governing Council, and the Bank of Japan its Monetary Policy Committee. The number of members varies from 9 in Japan to (currently) 18 at the ECB—but, crucially, it is always bigger than one.

The Need for Accountability and Transparency

There is a big problem with central bank independence: It is inconsistent with representative democracy. The idea of putting appointed technocrats in charge of one of the most important government functions is inherently undemocratic. Politicians answer to the voters; by design, independent central bankers don't. How can we have faith in our financial system if there are no checks on what the central bankers are doing? The economy will not operate efficiently unless we trust our policymakers to do the right thing.

APPLYING THE CONCEPT
INDEPENDENT CENTRAL BANKS DELIVER LOWER INFLATION

What finally drove politicians to give up control over monetary policy? It was the realization that independent central bankers would deliver lower inflation than they themselves could. Researchers noticed that the degree of control politicians can exert over central banks varies greatly across countries, and is related to inflation outcomes. Figure 15.2 shows an index of central bank independence on the horizontal axis and average inflation from 1973 to 1988 on the vertical axis. Note that Germany and Switzerland, the two countries with the most independent central banks, had the lowest inflation, averaging around 3 percent per year over the 15-year period. Conversely, New Zealand and Spain, the two countries with the least independent central banks, had the highest inflation—between 7 and 9 percent. Even the politicians were convinced. They knew that the more control they had over the central bank, the more money they were likely to create. While printing more money relieves short-term fiscal problems, it eventually drives inflation higher. Politicians voluntarily tied their own hands, handing over control of monetary policy to an independent central bank.

The design of the European Central Bank (ECB) is a clear example of the logic that independence leads to lower inflation. Politicians in Spain, Italy, and France, where inflation had been running over 6 percent per year for several decades, wanted their economies to be more like Germany's. In hopes that the new institution would deliver low inflation, they chose the German central bank, the Deutsche Bundesbank, as a model. By most accounts, the ECB is the most independent central bank in the world. And, as one would expect, inflation has been consistently low in the Europe.

Proponents of central bank independence realized they would need to solve this problem if their proposals were going to be accepted. Their solution was twofold. First, politicians would establish a set of goals; second, the policymakers would publicly report their progress in pursuing those goals. Explicit goals foster accountability and disclosure requirements create transparency. While central bankers are powerful, our elected representatives tell them what to do and then monitor their progress. That means requiring plausible explanations for their decisions, along with supporting data.

The institutional means for assuring accountability and transparency differ from one country to the next. In some cases, the government establishes an explicit numerical target for inflation, while in others the central bank defines the target. In the United Kingdom, the government sets a specific target each year; in the European Union, the central bank is asked only to pursue "price stability" as its primary objective; in the United States, the Federal Reserve is asked to deliver price stability as one of a number of objectives. Similar differences exist in the timing and content of information made public by central banks. Today every central bank announces its policy actions almost immediately, but the extent of the statements that accompany the

continued from previous page

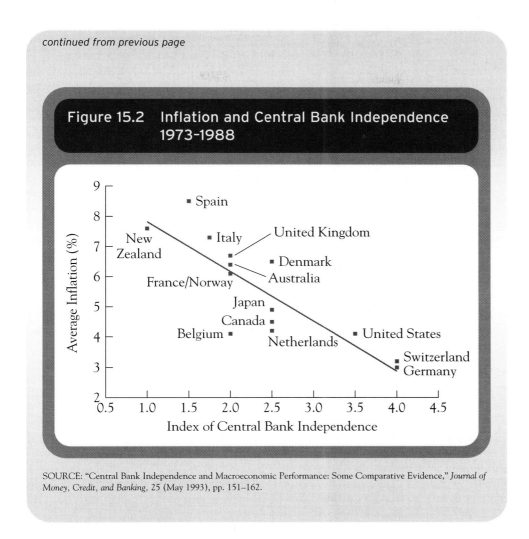

Figure 15.2   Inflation and Central Bank Independence 1973–1988

SOURCE: "Central Bank Independence and Macroeconomic Performance: Some Comparative Evidence," *Journal of Money, Credit, and Banking*, 25 (May 1993), pp. 151–162.

announcement and the willingness to answer questions vary. The Federal Reserve's statements tend to be only a few sentences long, and no one answers questions. In contrast, the president and vice president of the European Central Bank hold a press conference to answer questions on a statement several pages in length.[20]

It is difficult to know how important these differences in communications strategy are. Central bank statements are very different today than they were in the early 1990s. Until 1994, for example, the Federal Reserve didn't announce its policy decisions publicly. Secrecy, once the hallmark of central banking, is now understood to damage both the policymakers and the economies they are trying to manage. For monetary policy to be a stabilizing force, central bankers need to explain their actions in periodic public statements, like the ones that follow every Federal Open Market Committee meeting. In essence, the economy and financial markets should respond to information that everyone receives, not to speculation about what poli-

INFORMATION

[20]We will come back to the issue of how central banks formulate and communicate their objectives as part of our discussion of central bank structure in Chapter 16.

cymakers are doing. Thus, policymakers need to be as clear as possible about what they are trying to achieve and how they intend to achieve it. There really shouldn't be any surprises.

The Policy Framework, Policy Trade-offs, and Credibility

We've seen that a modern central bank has a long list of objectives—low, stable inflation; high, stable growth; a stable financial system; and stable interest and exchange rates. To meet these objectives, central bankers must be independent, accountable, and good communicators. Together these qualities make up what we will call the monetary policy framework. The framework exists to resolve ambiguities that arise in the course of the central bank's work. Looking at the bank's objectives, we can see the problem. Setting a goal of low inflation is easy, but there are many ways to measure inflation. (See the discussion of inflation statistics in Your Financial World, Chapter 20.) The central bank needs to decide which measure to use and then stick with it. Thus, the European Central Bank is explicit about the measure of inflation it uses in evaluating the success or failure of its policy. It is called the harmonized index of consumer prices, or HICP. More important than the details, though, is the fact that officials have told us what they are trying to do. Their statement helps people to plan at the same time that it holds officials accountable to the public.

The monetary policy framework also clarifies the likely responses when goals conflict with one another. There is simply no way that policymakers can meet all their objectives at the same time. They have only one instrument—the interest rate—with which to work, and it is impossible to use a single instrument to achieve a long list of objectives. To take a recent example, by the end of 2000, a recession appeared to be looming in the United States. Businesses were reducing their production levels and starting to lay off workers. When the economy is slowing, the standard solution is to ease policy by lowering interest rates. Starting on January 3, 2001, and almost once a month for the rest of the year, the Federal Reserve's Federal Open Market Committee did just that. Eleven times in just over 11 months it lowered the target interest rate. As a result, the recession that began in March 2001 was extremely mild. But there was a cost. Obviously, if interest rates are changing every month, they are not stable. More important, lowering the interest rate means increasing the availability of money and credit at the risk of raising inflation. The goal of keeping inflation low and stable, then, can be inconsistent with the goal of avoiding a recession. By the end of 2001, inflation had gone up slightly, but most people thought the Fed had done a good job of moderating the recession.

Central bankers face the trade-off between inflation and growth on a daily basis. In October 1998, in announcing that "further easing of the stance monetary policy was judged to be warranted to sustain economic growth in the context of contained inflation" (that's the quote at the beginning of this chapter), the Federal Open Market Committee was trying to calm fears that its members had lost sight of the long-term goal of price stability. The Fed had chosen to reduce interest rates to head off a financial crisis and stabilize real economic activity. Its members had decided that inflation was a problem for another day. As is often the case, policymakers were forced to choose among competing objectives.

Since policy goals often conflict, central bankers must make their priorities clear. The public needs to know whether policymakers are focusing primarily on price stability, as is the case in many countries, or whether they are willing to allow a modest rise in inflation to avoid a slowdown in economic activity. The public also needs to know the role that interest-rate and exchange-rate stability plays in policy delibera-

Table 15.3   The Principles of Central Bank Design

1. *Independence.*	To keep inflation low, monetary decisions must be made free of political influence.
2. *Decision making by committee.*	Pooling the knowledge of a number of people yields better decisions than decision making by an individual.
3. *Accountability and transparency.*	Policymakers must be held accountable to the public they serve and clearly communicate their objectives, decisions, and methods.
4. *Policy framework.*	Policymakers must clearly state their policy goals and the tradeoffs among them.

tions. This important part of the policy framework limits the discretionary authority of the central bankers, ensuring that they will do the job they have been entrusted with. Thus, it is an essential part of the bank's communication responsibilities.

Finally, a well-designed policy framework helps policymakers establish **credibility**. For central bankers to achieve their objectives, everyone must trust them to do what they say they are going to do. This is particularly important when it comes to keeping inflation low. The reason is that most economic decisions are based on expectations about future inflation. We saw this relationship when we studied the determination of interest rates: The nominal interest rate equals the real interest rate plus expected inflation. The same is true for wage and price decisions. Firms set prices based partly on what they believe inflation will be in the future. They make wage agreements with workers based on expected future inflation. The higher their expectations for future inflation, the higher prices, wages, and interest rates will be. Expected inflation creates inflation.[21] Successful monetary policy, then, requires that inflation expectations be kept under control. The most straightforward way for the central bank to do so is to announce its objectives, show resolve in meeting them, and explain its actions clearly along the way.

Table 15.3 summarizes the principles of central bank design and can serve as a check list for evaluating the operation of any central bank we come across.

Fitting Everything Together: Central Banks and Fiscal Policy

Before a European country can join the common currency area and adopt the euro, it must meet a number of conditions. Two of the most important are that the country's annual budget deficit—the excess of government spending over revenues each year—cannot exceed 3 percent of GDP and the government's total debt—its accumulated level of outstanding bonds and other borrowings—cannot exceed 60 percent of GDP.[22] Once a country gains membership in the monetary union, failure to maintain these standards triggers substantial penalties.[23]

---

[21]We will come back to this when we discuss business cycles in Chapter 22.

[22]In practice, these limits were open to political interpretation, so countries that failed to meet them were allowed to join anyway. For example, in fall of 1998, Belgium's debt was 122 percent of its GDP—more than double the stated limit. But because the debt was forecasted to decline in the future, the requirement was waived.

[23]The "Stability and Growth Pact of 1997" dictates that "medium-term budgets" must be "close to balance or in surplus." The exact mechanism came under significant strain in 2003. The previously agreed upon penalties that would be triggered by budget deficits in excess of 3 percent of GDP were not levied on the offending countries. Nevertheless, we can expect some form of fiscal discipline based on the pact to be enforced within the euro area.

IN THE NEWS

A Little Bit of Inflation Could Go a Long Way

The New York Times

by Tom Redburn

June 2, 2002

Everybody knows it's possible to have too much of a good thing. Too much rich food leads to indigestion; too many e-mail messages can drive you to the delete button.

The same is true of the Federal Reserve's long crusade to eliminate inflation from the American economy. That campaign, begun courageously by [then Federal Reserve Board chairman] Paul Volcker in 1979 when prices were spiraling higher at double-digit rates and carried on brilliantly by [his successor] Alan Greenspan over the last 15 years, is one of the great success stories of economic policy, helping to lay the foundation for much of the prosperity of recent years.

But enough is enough.

The danger is not just that the economy could fall into a deep deflationary pit, as it did in the Depression or as Japan's economy is doing today. The Fed will do every-

Alan Greenspan
SOURCE: © Brooks Kraft/Corbis

Paul Volcker
SOURCE: © Lisa Quinones/Black Star

thing in its power to prevent that. The more subtle risk is from the conventional view—particularly among bond market vigilantes—that zero inflation is the ideal and should be pursued without question. That stern attitude blocks the modest upward creep in the overall price level that is needed to properly grease the wheels of commerce.

Some Fed officials, even those long identified with a hawkish anti-inflationary stance, have begun to recognize this danger.

Remember that the central bank does not control the government's budget. Fiscal policy, the decisions about taxes and spending, are the responsibility of elected officials. But by specifying a range of "acceptable" levels of borrowing, Europeans are trying to restrict the fiscal policies that member countries enact. For the European Central Bank to do its job effectively, all the member countries' governments must behave responsibly.[24]

While fiscal and monetary policymakers share the same ultimate goal—to improve the well-being of the population—conflicts can arise between them. Fiscal policymakers are responsible for providing national defense, educating children, building

[24]While at this writing the U.S. has no explicit government budget restrictions, it has in the past. Following the large deficits of the 1980s, the U.S. Congress put restrictions on the size of the federal deficit. These expired in the late 1990s, and during the first few years of the 21st century, deficits began to rise again. One has to suspect that Congress will eventually be forced to address these problems and the likely outcome will be budget restrictions of the type that are in place in Europe.

"I always think of myself as pretty resolute when it comes to inflation," Robert Parry, president of the Federal Reserve Bank of San Francisco, said in a mid-May talk. "But perhaps a little bit of inflation is a little bit safer than zero."

William McDonough, the president of the Federal Reserve Bank of New York, was explicit about his willingness to tolerate a small amount of inflation. Not long ago, when consumer price inflation was running at 1.4 percent, he said, "If that's not price stability, what is?"

This unusually candid talk, coming from central bankers inculcated by their own code of silence never to say a kind word about inflation, is a positive sign. But even an inflation rate somewhat higher than today's would be nothing to fear. Indeed, it would be welcome.

Already, inflation, by just about every important indicator, is low and headed lower.

"One is a lovely number," James Glassman, senior economist at J. P. Morgan Securities, wrote in a recent report. "Most measures of inflation have eased into a range that brackets 1 percent annually."

With inflation so low, however, prices for most goods are still falling. The only signs of price increases are in housing and in services, particularly for medical services where past gains from managed care are beginning to erode. As a result, corporate profits in many sectors remain depressed, retarding the revival of investment needed to sustain a healthy economic recovery.

It is important to remember that a market economy works through price fluctuations that respond to changes in supply and demand. In the absence of inflation, the only way to signal relative differences across the full range of goods and services is for some prices to fall in absolute terms even as others are rising.

A modicum of inflation allows this price signaling to occur without squeezing so many producers to cut prices. As long as the central bank does not allow it to get out of control, this kind of modest upward price movement creates an environment more conducive to economic growth than a determination to squelch inflation at all cost.

Fortunately for the economy, Fed officials are recognizing that overall price stability is not an unalloyed virtue. And with inflation tame, Mr. Glassman said, "The Fed will have little fear of allowing the economy to regain its stride."

Copyright © 2002 by The New York Times Co. Reprinted by permission.

LESSONS OF THE ARTICLE

Federal Reserve officials make their views known to the public so that financial markets will not be surprised. While their objective is to keep inflation low and stable, they are clearly willing to tolerate small amounts of inflation, which they believe help the economy to function more smoothly. When inflation is low, policymakers can focus their efforts on ensuring that growth remains high. Importantly, a little steady inflation is unlikely to cause problems of the sort mentioned in Your Financial World: Why Inflation Is Bad for You in this chapter.

and maintaining transportation systems, and aiding the sick and poor. They need resources to pay for these services. Thus, funding needs create a natural conflict between monetary and fiscal policymakers. Central bankers, in their effort to stabilize prices and provide the foundation for high sustainable growth, take the long view, imposing limits on how fast the quantity of money and credit can grow. In contrast, fiscal policymakers tend to ignore the long-term inflationary effects of their actions and look for ways to spend resources today at the expense of prosperity tomorrow. For better or worse, their time horizon extends only until the next election. Some fiscal policymakers resort to actions intended to get around restrictions imposed by the central bank, eroding what is otherwise an effective and responsible monetary policy.

In the earliest days of central banks, a government that needed money would simply order the bank to print some. Of course, the result was inflation and occasionally hyperinflation. That is what led to the evolution of the independent central banks. Today the central bank's autonomy leaves fiscal policymakers with two options for financing government spending. They can take a share of income and wealth from the country's citizens through taxes, or they can borrow by issuing bonds in the financial markets.[25]

Because no one likes taxes, and officials fear angering the electorate, politicians often turn to borrowing in order to finance some portion of their spending. But a country can issue only so much debt. Beyond some limit, future tax revenues will not cover the payments that are due to lenders. At that point, the only solution is to turn to the central bank for the means to finance spending. As a technical matter, the government will "sell" new bonds directly to the central bank—bonds that no one else wants to buy. But doing so creates a monetary expansion, which leads to inflation. In fact, if officials can't raise taxes and are having trouble borrowing, inflation is the only way out.

While central bankers hate it, inflation is a real temptation to shortsighted fiscal policymakers. It is a way to get money in their hands. The mechanism is straightforward. The government forces the central bank to buy its bonds and then uses the proceeds to finance spending. But doing so increases the quantity of money in circulation, sparking inflation. While the rise in inflation may ultimately do great damage to the country's well-being, it also benefits fiscal policymakers: It reduces the value of the bonds the government has already sold, making them easier to repay.

To see why, let's assume the government sells $100 billion worth of 10 percent, 10-year bonds. The result is an obligation to pay $10 billion in interest annually and a lump sum of $100 billion in 10 years. The plan is to make the interest payments using income tax revenue and worry about repaying the principal later. (Ten years is an eternity to the politicians who make these decisions. They generally try to avoid committing to specific, long-term payment plans lest the information hurt their chances for re-election.) Say the government gets its revenue from a 20 percent income tax on income of $100 billion. That means 50 percent of the $20 billion per year in tax collections will go to pay the interest on the debt.

Now look at the impact of inflation. To simplify the calculations, let's assume that the price level suddenly doubles, increasing income from $100 billion to $200 billion. This doubles tax collections from $20 billion to $40 billion. But since the interest payments stay the same, they now account for only 25 percent of revenue. So the politicians get a bonus. And when the time finally comes to repay the $100 billion, it is worth only half as much. Inflation is a way for governments to default on a portion of the debt they owe.

While many politicians do act in their countries' long-term interests, there are plenty of examples of poor fiscal policymaking. Following the collapse of the Soviet Union, Russia had very few sources of revenue. Taxes were hard to collect and lenders were skeptical of the new government's ability to repay its loans, so interest rates were extremely high. Then there was the fact that almost everyone worked for the government. In short, expenses were high and revenue was low. Russian politicians turned to the Central Bank of Russia. The result was inflation of more than 14 percent per *month* for five consecutive years.

In early 2002, Argentina's economy collapsed when banks refused to honor their depositors' withdrawal requests. Unemployment skyrocketed, output plummeted, and the president was forced to resign. The full story is complicated, but we can understand one aspect of it without much trouble. During 2001, Argentina's provincial governments (the equivalent of the state governments in the United States) began to

---

[25]The fiscal policymakers can also sell some government assets, but that approach can't be sustained for long, so we will not pursue its implications.

experience significant budget problems. Their response was to start paying their employees with government bonds. But unlike the bonds we normally see, these were in small denominations—1, 2, 5, 10, 20 pesos, and so on. Not surprisingly, these small-denomination bonds were immediately used as means of payment, becoming money in effect. By mid-2002, this new form of money accounted for roughly 40 percent of the currency circulating in Argentina and the Central Bank of Argentina lost control over the amount of money circulating in the economy.

So, we see that the actions of fiscal policymakers can subvert the best efforts of central bankers. The Central Bank of Argentina was independent and its policymakers were well regarded. But if the government can shut down the banking system and issue its own money, then the central bank's independence is irrelevant. The Federal Reserve, the European Central Bank, the Bank of Japan, and 170 other central banks around the world are independent at the pleasure of their governments. When faced with a fiscal crisis, politicians often look for the easiest way out. If that way is inflating the value of the currency today, they will worry about the consequences tomorrow.

This brings us back to the criteria for inclusion in the European Monetary Union. The founders of the system wanted to ensure that participating governments kept their fiscal houses in order so that none of them would be tempted to pressure the European Central Bank to create inflation and bail them out. Monetary policy can meet its objective of price stability only if the government lives within its budget and never forces the central bank to finance a fiscal deficit.

In summary, responsible fiscal policy is essential to the success of monetary policy. But that is just the final point. Our discussions earlier in the chapter allowed us to conclude that there is no way for a poorly designed central bank to stabilize prices, output, the financial system, and interest and exchange rates, regardless of the government's behavior. To be successful, a central bank must operate in a particular way. It must be independent, accountable, and clear about its goals. It must have a well-articulated communications strategy and a sound decision-making mechanism. We turn in Chapter 16 to a detailed discussion of the structure of major central banks to see what makes them successful.

Terms

accountability, 390

central bank, 376

central bank independence, 388

credibility, 393

exchange-rate stability, 386

financial system stability, 384

fiscal policy, 379

hyperinflation, 382

interest-rate stability, 386

monetary policy, 377

monetary policy framework, 392

potential output, 383

price stability, 381

sustainable growth, 383

transparency, 390

Chapter Lessons

1. The functions of a modern central bank are to
   a. Adjust interest rates to control the quantity of money and credit in the economy.
   b. Operate a payments system.
   c. Lend to sound banks during times of stress.
   d. Oversee the financial system.

2. The objective of a central bank is to reduce systematic risk in the economic and financial system. Specific objectives include
   a. Low and stable inflation.
   b. High and stable growth and employment.
   c. Stable financial markets and institutions.
   d. Stable interest rates.
   e. Stable exchange rates.
   Because these objectives often conflict, policymakers must have clear priorities.

3. The best central banks
   a. Are independent of political pressure.
   b. Make decisions by committee rather than by an individual.
   c. Are accountable to elected representatives and the public.
   d. Communicate their objectives, actions, and policy deliberations clearly to the public.
   e. Articulate clearly how they will act when their goals conflict.
   f. Are credible in their efforts to meet their objectives.

4. Fiscal policy can make the central bank's job impossible because
   a. Politicians take a short-term view, ignoring the inflationary impact of their actions over the long term.
   b. Politicians are predisposed toward financing techniques that will create inflation.
   c. Inflation provides immediate revenue and reduces the value of the government's outstanding debt.
   d. Responsible fiscal policy is a precondition for successful monetary policy.
   e. Central banks remain independent at the pleasure of politicians.

Problems

1. For many central banks, the primary goal is to control inflation.
   a. What are the costs of inflation?
   b. Does anyone benefit from inflation? If so, who benefits and how?

2. Provide arguments for and against the proposition that a central bank should be allowed to set its own objectives.

3. Explain how transparency helps eliminate the problems that are created by central bank independence.

4. In 1998, Brazil was on the verge of a financial crisis. Foreign investors did not believe the government would be able to repay the bonds it had issued, so the interest rate began to rise. That made investors even less confident of Brazil's ability to make the required payments, so the interest rate rose even higher. The solution to the problem involved both monetary and fiscal policy. At the central bank, the governor was replaced and a new policy framework was put into place. Meanwhile, fiscal policymakers promised they would restrain their profligate spending and cut the budget deficit. Explain why these events helped to avert a crisis.

5. The Maastricht Treaty, which established the European Central Bank, states that the governments of the countries in the European Monetary Union must not seek to influence the members of the central bank's decision-making bodies. Why is freedom from political influence crucial to the ECB's ability to maintain price stability?

6. Most central banks publish volumes of material to inform the public about what they do and how they do it. In many cases, they are responding to reporting obligations mandated by the legislation that established the bank. Is such reporting important, or is it a waste of paper?

7. In 1900, there were 18 central banks in the world; 100 years later, there were 174. Why does nearly every country in the world now have a central bank?

8. The power of a central bank is based on its monopoly over the issuance of currency. Economics teaches us that monopolies are bad and competition is good. Would competition among several central banks be better? Provide arguments both for and against.

9. In the 1970s and 1980s, Argentina experienced a series of hyperinflationary episodes, during which inflation averaged about 300 percent per year. Finally, after two decades, authorities decided to create a system in which the Argentinean peso could be converted to U.S. dollars on a one-to-one basis. If the central bank wanted to print more pesos, it would need to obtain dollars to back them. Discuss the possible sources of Argentina's high inflation and explain why the change in policy was expected to eliminate it. (For 10 years, the system worked with virtually no inflation. But in January 2002, the monetary system collapsed, along with the Argentinean economy.)

10. During the 19th century, a $100 bank note (or check) issued in Philadelphia would not necessarily be worth $100 in New York. Why? How could the creation of a central bank solve this problem?

11. As chairman of the Federal Reserve, Alan Greenspan has never been willing to clarify what he means by the objective of "price stability." The European Central Bank defines the objective explicitly in terms of the rate of change in a particular price index. Why would Greenspan shy away from an explicit definition? What are the pros and cons of the two strategies?

12. Inflation hit 5,000 percent in Ukraine in 1993. The government had promised to provide many companies with subsidies, essentially giving them money. How was this promise connected to the inflation? What was the solution?

13. Since 1993, the Bank of England has published a quarterly *Inflation Report*. Find a copy of the report on the bank's Web site, www.bankofengland.co.uk. Describe its contents and explain why the bank might publish such a document.

www.mhhe.com/cecchetti1e

14. After the end of the First World War in 1919, the Treaty of Versailles required the loser, Germany, to make large payments called reparations to the winners, the United States, the United Kingdom, and their allies. To make the payments, the German government had to find a source of revenue. With the country in ruins, there were very few options. Over the next four years, Germany experienced severe hyperinflation. Things got progressively worse, and from January 1922 to November 1923, prices rose by a factor of nearly 22 billion. Discuss the connection between the reparations payments and the hyperinflation.

15. Explain the costs of each of the following conditions and explain who bears them.

    a. Interest-rate instability

    b. Exchange-rate instability

    c. Inflation

    d. Unstable growth

Chapter 16

The Structure of Central Banks: The Federal Reserve and the European Central Bank

The instability and chaos that accompany financial panics damage more than just the banks that are directly involved. Fear of losing one's savings is a great disincentive to making bank deposits, and fewer deposits means smaller banks and fewer loans. Everyone is slow to regain confidence in the financial system after a panic, making it hard for anyone to get financing. New businesses can't get the resources they need to get started; established companies can't find the financing they need to expand. The more frequent the panics, the worse the situation gets, and the slower the economy grows.

This was the position the United States found itself in during the late 19th and early 20th centuries. Between 1870 and 1907, the nation experienced 21 financial panics of varying severity. In the mostly agrarian economy of the time, a typical crisis began with either a crop failure that left farmers with nothing to sell or a bumper crop that drove prices down below costs. Either way, farmers defaulted on their loans. The losses damaged the balance sheets of rural banks, leading them to withdraw funds from larger banks in New York or Chicago, where they held deposits. If the rural banks' withdrawals were large enough, the urban banks would be forced to call in their own loans or to refuse renewal of loans that were coming due. As word of the financial difficulties spread, other banks would become concerned and begin to call in their loans as well. Finally, when average people (small depositors) heard of the problem, they would flock to their local banks, demanding to receive their balances in the form of currency or gold.[1]

Unless confidence in the system was restored quickly, such runs left bankers with no choice but to close their doors. During the Panic of 1907, an astonishing two-thirds of banks found themselves temporarily unable to redeem deposits in cash. The situation led one prominent German banker to observe that the U.S. banking system was at the same point in the early 1900s that Europe's had been in the 1400s. In the intervening centuries, Europeans had developed a system of central banks; Americans hadn't.

The prevailing philosophy of many 19th-century Americans was that centralized government of any form should be kept to a minimum. But the punishing effects of frequent financial panics led people to reconsider the merits of a powerful central bank. In 1913, Congress passed the Federal Reserve Act, which created the U.S. Federal Reserve System. As the central bank's knowledge of how policy mechanisms worked grew, its governance improved. By the 1990s, the Fed was widely recognized as a key promoter of low inflation and high sustainable growth.

While central banking had stabilized European financial systems before 1900, the 20th century was another story. In that century, Europe experienced high inflation, low growth, high and volatile interest rates, and unstable exchange rates. After two

---

[1]The process could also go the other way, from the big banks to the small ones. A large loan default in New York, for example, would force the large city bank to try to acquire reserves from the small country banks. The small banks would then be forced to start calling in loans, and the process would go on from there.

"I don't know a damn thing about monetary policy, but I know what I like."

world wars, governments' free spending led to unrelenting fiscal deficits. When European economies stagnated in the 1970s and 1980s, a consensus built that inflation was the fundamental problem and poor monetary policy was to blame. Leaders came to believe that the only way to ensure both political and economic stability was to forge closer ties among the continent's countries. They decided the best solution was a common currency and a single central bank.[2] The result was the European monetary union, with its common currency, the euro, and its central bank, the *European Central Bank (ECB)*.

Europe's monetary union was the natural outgrowth of a decades-long process that established the free movement of goods, services, and capital throughout the continent of 450 million people. Like the Fed, the ECB is based on principles that support the goal of price stability (principles we learned about in Chapter 15). We turn now to an examination of these two central banks to see how their structure helps them to meet their objectives.

The Structure of the Federal Reserve System

The Federal Reserve Act, passed in 1913 and amended several times since then, establishes a system that is composed of three branches with overlapping responsibilities. There are a central governmental agency, called the *Board of Governors of the Federal Reserve System*, located in Washington D.C.; the 12 regional *Federal Reserve Banks*, distributed throughout the country; and the *Federal Open Market Committee*. In addition, a series of advisory committees makes recommendations to the board and the regional Federal Reserve Banks. Finally, there are the private banks that are members of the system. This complex structure diffuses power in a way that is typical of the U.S. government, creating a system of checks and balances that reduces the tendency for power to concentrate at the center.

All national banks (those chartered by the federal government) are required to belong to the Federal Reserve System. State banks that receive their charters from individual state banking authorities have the option of joining, but fewer than 20 percent take it due to its cost. Prior to a change in the law in 1980, member banks were required to hold noninterest-bearing reserve deposits at the Fed, while nonmember banks could hold reserves in interest-bearing securities, such as U.S. Treasury bills. Today, members and nonmembers alike must hold noninterest-bearing reserve deposits at the Fed, so there is no real distinction between them.

---

[2]German Chancellor Helmut Kohl was one of the most vocal champions of European integration, especially the monetary union. Kohl has said that achieving monetary union was "the difference between war and peace in the 21st century." This statement may seem an exaggeration, but the Germans had spent the first half of the 20th century trying to dominate Europe by force. After the Second World War, many people felt that economic integration was the best way to prevent another war. See Matt Marshall, *The Bank: The Birth of Europe's Central Bank and the Rebirth of Europe's Power*, (London, UK): Random House Business Books, 1999).

The Federal Reserve Banks

In the heart of Wall Street, two blocks from the site where the World Trade Center towers once stood, sits a large, fortresslike building that is the home of the Federal Reserve Bank of New York. Deep in the fourth subbasement is the largest gold vault in the world, stocked with many more bars than Fort Knox. All of this gold belongs to foreign countries and international organizations like the International Monetary Fund. It is stored there for free. You can take a tour to see the gold vault if you call ahead, but you won't get into the rest of the building without an invitation. When the bank was built, one of the vaults held cash, but today that vault is filled with excess furniture. Cash is stored across the Hudson River in New Jersey, in a three-story vault the size of a football field. People rarely enter the vault, and there are no tours—just thick walls, fences, security cameras, and guards with guns. (The cash is stored on pallets of about 160 shrink-wrapped blocks of 4,000 notes each. It is moved around entirely by small robotic forklifts.)

The Federal Reserve Bank of New York is the largest of the 12 regional Federal Reserve Banks, which, together with their branches, form the heart of the Federal Reserve System. (All twelve have cash vaults, but only New York has gold.) Figure 16.1 shows the location of the banks and the region each one serves. From a modern vantage point, this map looks very odd. Why is nearly one-third of the continental United States served by a single bank in San Francisco while the Philadelphia district is so small? And why are two of the 12 banks in Missouri?

One explanation is that the lines were drawn in 1914, so they represent the population density at the time. Then there was politics. Senator Carter Glass, one of the authors of the Federal Reserve Act, was from Richmond, Virginia, the headquarters of the fifth district; Speaker of the House Champ Clark came from Missouri, the state with two Reserve Banks. But more important, politicians decided that no district should coincide with a single state. The Federal Reserve Bank of New York, for example, serves all of New York State as well as northern New Jersey (where the cash vault is), a small slice of southwestern Connecticut, Puerto Rico, and the Virgin Islands. The purpose of this arrangement is twofold: to ensure that every district contains as broad a mixture of economic interests as possible and that no person or group can obtain preferential treatment from the Reserve Bank.[3]

Reserve Banks are strange creations, part public and part private. They are federally chartered banks and private, nonprofit organizations, owned by the commercial banks in their districts. As such, they are overseen by both their own boards of directors and the Board of Governors, an arm of the federal government. The method for choosing the nine members of the boards of directors ensures the inclusion of not only bankers but other business leaders and people who represent the public interest. Some directors are chosen by the banks, others by the Board of Governors. Though the range of views represented is wide, everyone has an interest in ensuring economic and financial stability.

Each Reserve Bank has a president who is appointed for a five-year term by the bank's board of directors with the approval of the Board of Governors. (All 12 presidents' terms run concurrently, starting and ending at exactly the same time.) Presidents tend to come from one of three groups. Some have worked their way up

The gold vault at the Federal Reserve Bank of New York. It contains about 10 percent of all the gold that has ever been taken out of the ground: 250 million ounces worth over $95 billion at 2004 market prices. A single gold bar in this picture weighs 400 ounces and is worth about $150,000.

Source: © Courtesy of the Federal Reserve Bank of New York.

STABILITY

---

[3]The location of major rail lines also played a role in the cities chosen. Since the Federal Reserve was going to be involved in the payments system, it was important that there be a way to transport paper checks quickly from virtually anywhere in the country to one of the 12 reserve banks.

Figure 16.1 The Federal Reserve System

The 12 Federal Reserve Banks and the geographic regions they service.

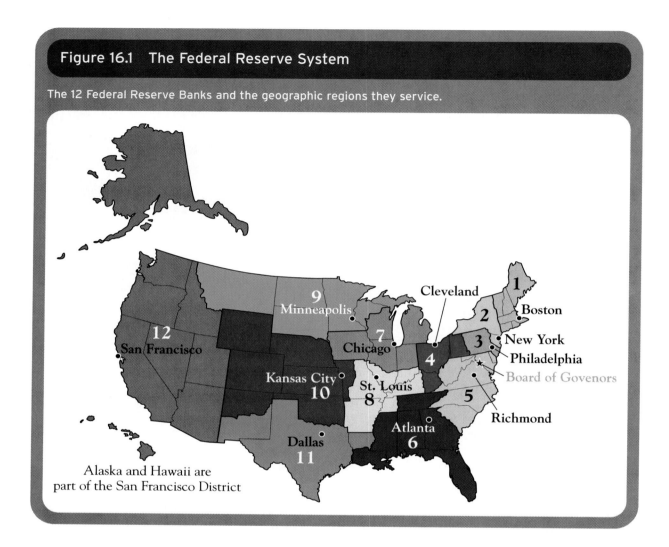

Alaska and Hawaii are
part of the San Francisco District

inside the Federal Reserve System and are experts on the business of the regional banks. Others are academic economists who have studied the financial system. Then there are former bankers, people who were once customers of the Federal Reserve. Since the presidents work together, the fact that they come from diverse backgrounds means that collectively they have the experience to manage the wide-ranging responsibilities of the Federal Reserve Banks.

The Reserve Banks conduct the day-to-day business of the central bank, serving as both the government's bank and the bankers' bank. Here is a brief list of the functions they perform:

1. As the bank for the U.S. government, they
   a. Issue new currency (Federal Reserve notes) and destroy old, worn currency.
   b. Maintain the U.S. Treasury's bank account, paying checks, and processing electronic payments.
   c. Manage the U.S. Treasury's borrowings. That means issuing, transferring, and redeeming U.S. Treasury bonds, notes, and bills. But like you and your bank, the Treasury decides what it wants, and the Federal Reserve Banks just do it.

2. As the bankers' bank, they
   a. Hold deposits (on which they pay no interest) for the banks in their districts;
   b. Operate and ensure the integrity of a payments network for clearing paper checks and transferring funds electronically.
   c. Make funds available to commercial banks within the district through *discount loans* on which they charge interest at the *discount rate*.
   d. Supervise and regulate financial institutions in the district to ensure their safety and soundness, as well as evaluate proposed bank mergers and new operations.
   e. Collect and make available data on business conditions.

In addition to these duties, the Federal Reserve Bank of New York provides services to foreign central banks and to certain international organizations that hold accounts there. The Federal Reserve Bank of New York is also the system's point of contact with financial markets. It is where Treasury securities are auctioned, foreign currency is bought and sold, and the Federal Reserve's own portfolio is managed through what are called *open market operations*.[4]

Finally, the Reserve Banks play an important part in formulating monetary policy. They do it both through their representation on the Federal Open Market Committee (FOMC), which makes interest-rate decisions, and through their participation in setting the discount rate, the interest rate charged on loans to commercial banks. The Federal Reserve Act specifies that the discount rate is to be set by each of the Reserve Bank's board of directors, with the approval of the Board of Governors,[5] and strictly speaking, it is. But the directors have virtually no say over the discount rate, because it is set automatically at a premium above the overnight interest rate that the FOMC controls. Once the FOMC makes its decision, there is nothing left for anyone else to do. (We will learn more about this topic in Chapter 18.)

The Board of Governors

The headquarters of the Federal Reserve System sits at the corner of 20th and C Streets in northwest Washington, D.C., a short walk from the White House in one direction and the State Department in the other. The seven members of the board, who are called governors, are appointed by the president and confirmed by the U.S. Senate for 14-year terms. The long terms are intended to protect the board from political pressure. The fact that the terms are staggered—one beginning every two years—limits any individual president's influence over the membership.[6] The board has a chairman and a vice chairman, appointed by the president from among the seven governors for four-year renewable terms. The board's membership usually includes academic economists, economic forecasters, and bankers. To ensure adequate regional representation on the board, no two governors can come from the same Federal

---

[4]When the Fed was founded, all the Reserve Banks could engage in open market operations. But over time officials realized that such an arrangement was inefficient, so operations were centralized in New York, where the financial markets were located. Today operations could be done virtually anywhere in the country, but the people with the knowledge to do them are currently located in New York.

[5]The board of directors of every Reserve Bank must meet every two weeks, either in person or by conference call, to make a discount rate recommendation to the Board of Governors.

[6]In recent years, four out of every five governors have resigned prior to the end of their terms. Someone has been appointed to fill the remaining portion of the term. A person who has been appointed under those circumstances can be reappointed for a full term. (That is why Alan Greenspan has been able to remain chair for nearly 20 years.) A board member who serves a full term may not be reappointed, however.

YOUR FINANCIAL WORLD
Treasury Direct

The Federal Reserve takes care of the U.S. Treasury's banking needs. It is the government's banker, issuing U.S. Treasury bonds when the government needs to borrow, keeping track of who owns the Treasury bonds, making interest payments on them every six months, and paying the principal when they mature. Although much of the Treasury's debt is bought and held by large financial institutions like banks, pension funds, and insurance companies, you can buy it yourself, without anyone's help, through Treasury Direct.

Treasury Direct lets you purchase as little as $1,000 worth of Treasury securities without paying any broker fees. All you need to do is fill out a few forms, write a check, and send them in. (You will have to use paper the first time, but after that you can do it electronically.) Everything you need to get started is available at the Bureau of Public Debt's Web site, http://www.publicdebt.treas.gov/sec/sectrdir.htm.

As a technical matter, buying a government bond means bidding at an auction that is held two or three times a week. How do you know what price to bid? Individuals aren't experts on bond pricing,

so if they had to figure out how much to bid, Treasury Direct would never work. The solution is to place what is called a *noncompetitive bid*. This guarantees you will receive the bond you want at the average auction price, which is based on the bids of people who know what they are doing. Individuals send in checks to cover the face value of the bonds they want, and since the auction is normally designed so that the purchase price is less than face value, you get a small refund in the mail a few weeks later. The only complicated part of this is deciding exactly which bonds you want to buy.

Once you have bought the bonds, you will receive a notice of the interest payments, as well as periodic statements listing what you own. If you decide you want to sell the bonds, the Fed will do it for you at the highest market price. Treasury Direct is by far the cheapest way to buy U.S. Treasury securities, especially in small amounts and for issues like Treasury Inflation Protection Securities (see the discussion of TIPS in *Your Financial World*, Chapter 6), which are difficult to purchase on the open market but easy to buy at auction.

Reserve district. The Federal Reserve Act explicitly requires "a fair representation of the financial, agricultural, industrial, and commercial interests."

Together with a staff of several thousand, the Board of Governors of the Federal Reserve System performs the following duties:

- Analyzes financial and economic conditions, both domestic and international.
- Administers consumer credit protection laws.
- Supervises and regulates the regional Reserve Banks, including their budgets and their presidents' salaries.
- Sets the reserve requirement, which determines the level of reserves banks are required to hold.
- Approves bank merger applications.
- Along with the Reserve Banks, regulates and supervises the banking system, examining individual banks for safety and soundness and for compliance with the law.[7]
- Collects and publishes detailed statistics about the system's activities and the economy at large. On the board's Web site, you can find information about the

[7]As we learned in Chapter 14, this responsibility is shared with a number of other government agencies. The Fed has primary responsibility for regulating and supervising bank holding companies and state-chartered banks that belong to the Federal Reserve System, as well as some other financial institutions that do business abroad.

amount of money in the economy (M1, M2, and so on), interest rates, exchange rates, the banking system's assets and liabilities, the level of production in U.S. industry, and the level of household wealth.

The seven governors do not have their own support staff. Instead, they request help and information from the managers of various departments, who assign individuals to specific tasks. The managers answer to the chair of the Board of Governors.

The Board Room at the Federal Reserve Building in Washington, D.C., with its oblong table. This is the meeting place of the Federal Open Market Committee and Board of Governors of the Federal Reserve System.

SOURCE: *Dennis Brack/Black Star*

The Federal Open Market Committee

When most people think about the Federal Reserve, what comes to mind is not the payments systems or bank supervision but interest-rate setting. And when the business press discusses the Fed, its attention is really on the **Federal Open Market Committee (FOMC)**. This is the group that sets interest rates to control the availability of money and credit to the economy. The FOMC has been around since 1936 and has 12 voting members. These are the seven governors, the president of the Federal Reserve Bank of New York, and four Reserve Bank presidents. The chair of the Board of Governors chairs the FOMC as well, and the committee's vice chair is the president of the Federal Reserve Bank of New York. While only five of the 12 Reserve Bank presidents vote at any one time, all of them participate in the meeting.

The FOMC could control any interest rate, but the rate it chooses to control is the **federal funds rate**, the rate banks charge each other for overnight loans on their excess deposits at the Fed. We will discuss the details of this arrangement in the next two chapters. For now, keep in mind that the rate the FOMC controls is a nominal interest rate. Since inflation doesn't change quickly, however, the FOMC in effect controls the *real* interest rate. (Recall that the real interest rate equals the nominal interest rate minus expected inflation.) The real interest rate plays a central role in economic decisions. The higher the real interest rate, the more expensive borrowing is, and the less likely a company is to build a new factory or an individual is to purchase a new car. Furthermore, the lower the level of purchases by firms and households, the lower the level of growth will be. So by controlling the federal funds rate, the FOMC influences real growth. (The macroeconomic model that explains this mechanism is presented in Part V.)

The FOMC currently meets eight times a year, or roughly once every six weeks, in the Board Room at the Federal Reserve Building in Washington, D.C.[8] During times of crisis, the committee can confer and change policy over the telephone. Because these "inter-meeting" policy shifts signal the financial markets that the FOMC believes conditions are dire, they are reserved for extraordinary times, like the financial crisis of October 1998 (described in the last chapter) and the aftermath of the terrorist attacks on the World Trade Center of September 2001.

A normal FOMC meeting runs from 9:00 a.m. until 1:00 p.m. on a Tuesday.[9] In addition to the seven governors and 12 Reserve Bank presidents, numerous board staff members attend, along with at least one senior staff member from each Reserve Bank.

---

[8]The committee is required to meet at least four times a year and has met as many as 19 times in one year.

[9]Twice a year, the meeting takes place over a two-day period, starting on Tuesday afternoon around 2:00 p.m. and finishing on Wednesday at 1:00 p.m. These meetings take place in February and June, just before the issuance of the biannual Monetary Policy Report to Congress.

In all, between 50 and 60 people are there. The primary purpose of the meeting is to decide on the target interest rate and produce a policy directive. The FOMC itself does not engage in the financial market transactions that are required to accomplish its short-term objectives. That job falls to the system open market account manager, who, together with his or her staff, works for the Federal Reserve Bank of New York. The policy directive simply instructs the New York Fed's staff to buy and sell U.S. Treasury securities so as to maintain the market federal funds rate at the target.

To figure out who really controls interest-rate decisions, we need to look closely at how the FOMC works, focusing on the information that is distributed in advance and the mechanics of the meeting.[10] Three important documents are distributed to all attendees prior to each meeting. Named for the colors of their covers, they are the *beige book*, the *green book*, and the *blue book*. The beige book is a compilation of anecdotal information about current business activity, collected by the staffs of the Reserve Banks and published about two weeks before the meeting itself. This is the only FOMC document that is released to the public before the meeting. The green book is the Board staff's economic forecast for the next few years; it is distributed the Thursday before the meeting. On Saturday, three days before the meeting, each participant receives the blue book, with its discussion of financial markets and current policy options. The green and blue books are treated as secret documents and are not released to the public until five years after the meeting.

An FOMC meeting is a formal proceeding that can be divided into three parts: reports by the staff, statements of the members (except for the chair but including the seven nonvoting Reserve Bank presidents), and comments by the chair. Here's the order in which people speak:

1. The system open market account manager reports on financial market conditions and actions taken to maintain the target interest rate since the last meeting.

2. The director of the Division of Research and Statistics at the Federal Reserve Board presents the staff's forecast (from the green book).

3. One at a time, committee members (including Reserve Bank presidents who are not currently voting) discuss the economic outlook, including specific regional information. People speak for about five minutes each in an order that changes from meeting to meeting. The chair typically does not participate in this round of comments.

4. The director of monetary affairs, who doubles as the secretary of the FOMC, describes the two or three policy options (from the Blue book). One option is always to maintain the target interest rate at its current level.

5. Again, one at a time, the committee members discuss the policy options. The chair speaks first, often at length, and ends by recommending what action should be taken. The remaining 18 members (both voting and nonvoting) then state whether they agree or disagree with the recommendation.

6. A vote is taken, with the chair voting first.

There is virtually no give and take among the committee members during the meeting, and most of participants read prepared statements. The meeting adjourns around 1:00 p.m. and at 2:15 p.m. Eastern Standard Time, the committee's directive is made public, along with a brief explanatory statement.

---

[10]For a detailed description of an FOMC meeting, see Laurence H. Meyer, "Come with Me to the FOMC," *The Region*, Federal Reserve Bank of Minneapolis, June 1998.

Table 16.1   A User's Guide to the Fed

The Federal Reserve System is complicated, so here is a list of the key players:

Chair of the Board of Governors. Most powerful person in the Federal Reserve System. Also Chair of the FOMC. Effectively controls FOMC meetings and interest-rate policy. Appointed by the president to a four-year term; must be one of the governors.

Governors of the Board. Supervise and regulate much of the financial industry. All are voting members of the FOMC. Appointed by the president to 14-year terms.

President of the Federal Reserve Bank of New York. Runs the biggest and most important of the Reserve Banks, where monetary policy operations are carried out and much of the Fed's work for the Treasury is done. Appointed by the Bank's board of directors, with the approval of the Board of Governors, for a five-year term. Also vice chair of the FOMC.

Presidents of the other Federal Reserve Banks. Provide services to commercial banks in their districts. Also attend FOMC meetings and vote every two or three years.

The board and all the Reserve Banks maintain Web sites that publish data, economic research, speeches, and information about customer services. In addition, the FOMC maintains a Web site that lists meeting times and links to the transcripts, minutes, and statements of the committee. The place to start is www.federalreserve.gov.

To see where the committee's power lies and who controls interest-rate decisions, notice a few things. To begin with, the governors make up a majority of the committee, and they work together daily. Second, beyond the beige book, which is made available to the public, the only information distributed to all committee members before a meeting is the green book forecast and the blue book of policy options. These are both prepared by the Federal Reserve Board staff, which is controlled by the chair. While the Reserve Bank presidents may have asked their staffs to analyze other policy options, the governors do not have access to any alternative information. Third, the chair waits for everyone to speak before making a policy recommendation, with which other committee members can then agree or disagree. Fourth, when the committee votes, the chair votes first. Finally, though the votes are made public immediately after the meeting, committee members observe a blackout period; from the Tuesday preceding an FOMC meeting to the Friday following the meeting, they do not speak publicly about the economic outlook or current monetary policy. Dissenters, who are identified immediately in the press release that comes the afternoon of the meeting, must wait until the following week to explain their views in public. And remember, the Board of Governors controls the Reserve Banks' budgets, as well as the salaries of their presidents.

Press reports, then, do give a good sense of where the FOMC's power lies. The chair really does control monetary policy, so if you want to know whether interest rates are likely to go up, go down, or stay the same, that is the person you should watch. To have an impact on policy, governors or Reserve Bank presidents must build support for their positions through their statements at the meeting and in public speeches until finally the chair has no choice but to acquiesce. While the chair is very powerful, the committee structure provides an important check on his or her power.

TOOLS OF THE TRADE
Decoding the FOMC's Statement

Following every meeting, the FOMC issues a press release announcing its policy decision. This is the **FOMC statement** that is the basis for the news stories and analysis that follow, so it is worth taking the time to examine its structure and content. The press release from January 26, 2003, is representative. Let's take a look at it.

> The Federal Open Market Committee decided today to keep its target for the federal funds rate unchanged at $1\frac{3}{4}$ percent.
>
> The information that has become available since the last meeting of the Committee confirms that economic activity is continuing to increase. However, both the upward impetus from the swing in inventory investment and the growth in final demand appear to have moderated. The Committee expects the rate of increase of final demand to pick up over coming quarters, supported in part by robust underlying growth in productivity, but the degree of strength remains uncertain.
>
> In these circumstances, although the stance of monetary policy is currently accommodative, the Committee believes that, for the foreseeable future, against the background of its long-run goals of price stability and sustainable economic growth and of the information currently available, the risks are balanced with respect to the prospects for both goals.
>
> Voting for the FOMC monetary policy action were: Alan Greenspan, Chairman; William J. McDonough, Vice Chairman; Susan S. Bies; Roger W. Ferguson, Jr.; Edward M. Gramlich; Jerry L. Jordan; Robert D. McTeer, Jr.; Mark W. Olson; Anthony M. Santomero; and Gary H. Stern.

This statement has four paragraphs. Let's examine each of them.

Paragraph 1: States the current target for the interest rate the FOMC controls (the federal funds rate) and whether it has changed.

Paragraph 2: Provides a brief synopsis of the committee's view of current economic conditions. This paragraph is informative both in what it says and in what it leaves out, but to understand its implications, you need to be following the economy very closely.

Paragraph 3: Begins by noting that the committee believes its policy is "accommodative." This term means that the current federal funds rate target is relatively low and should encourage the economy to expand quickly. (The term *restrictive* is the opposite of *accommodative* and suggests that the FOMC has set the interest-rate target relatively high in order to slow the economy down.) The phrase "the risks are balanced" in the last sentence is important. Use of the term balanced means that the next interest rate move is equally likely to be up or down. There are only two other choices for the wording of this sentence. It can say that "the risks are toward higher inflation," suggesting that the next move for the interest rate is likely to be up, or that it can say "the risks are toward lower growth," suggesting that the next move is likely to be down.*

Paragraph 4: Reports the vote. At the time of this vote there were two vacancies on the Board of Governors, so there were only 10 voting members on the committee.

To the practiced eye, this statement paints a clear picture. To see it, start by noticing that the interest-rate target was already very low at the time of the statement: $1\frac{3}{4}$ percent. Remember that it is a nominal interest rate, so it can't drop below zero. Now look at the second paragraph. The committee was clearly concerned that growth might remain sluggish. Finally, the third paragraph states that the risks are balanced. With the interest rates very low and the risks balanced, a decrease in the interest rate is unlikely; and with the economy growing slowly, an increase is equally unlikely. So the message is "We aren't going to change interest rates until we see clear signs that the economy has changed."

In short, this formal statement tells us about the current state of the economy and what the FOMC's next policy action will likely be. Often it goes even further, indicating what will trigger the next move.

*In the last few years, the exact wording of this sentence has been changing. You can check more recent statements on the FOMC Web site at www.federalreserve.gov/fomc/.

Assessing the Federal Reserve System's Structure

In the last chapter, we developed a checklist for assessing a central bank's structure. We said that an effective central bank is one in which policymakers are independent of political influence, make decisions by committee, are accountable and transparent, and state their objectives clearly.[11] Let's evaluate the Federal Reserve System using these criteria.

Independence from Political Influence

We set out three criteria for judging a central bank's independence: budgetary independence, irreversible decisions, and long terms. The Fed meets each of these. It controls its own budget. The Fed's substantial revenue is a combination of interest on the government securities it holds and fees charged to banks for payments system services, including check clearing, electronic funds transfers, and the like. In fact, the Fed's income is so large that, in a typical year, 95 percent of it is returned to the U.S. Treasury.[12] Interest-rate changes are implemented immediately and can be changed only by the FOMC—no one else can reverse or change them. The terms of the governors are 14 years; the chair's term runs for four years; and the Reserve Bank presidents serve for five years (and they aren't even appointed by politicians).

Even though the structural elements required to maintain an independent monetary policy are in place, the Fed does occasionally come under political attack. As we have said, raising interest rates is never popular. But so long as policymakers are successful in stabilizing inflation, growth, and the financial system, political problems can be minimized.

Decision Making by Committee

The Fed clearly makes decisions by committee, because the FOMC *is* a committee. While the chair of the Board of Governors may dominate policy decisions, the fact that there are 12 voting members provides an important safeguard against arbitrary action by a single individual. In the Federal Reserve, no one person can become a dictator.

Accountability and Transparency

The FOMC releases huge amounts of information to the public. Prior to each meeting, the committee publishes the beige book and makes it publicly available. Immediately after the meeting comes the announcement of the policy decision, together with the explanatory statement. About six weeks later, two days following the next FOMC meeting, a detailed anonymous summary—the minutes—is published. After a five-year waiting period, the FOMC publishes the word-for-word transcript of a meeting. Added to these documents is the twice-yearly "Monetary Policy Report to Congress," which includes the members' forecasts for inflation and growth over the next two years. This report is accompanied by the chair's appearance before Congress to discuss the state of the nation's economy. Members of the FOMC also

INFORMATION

---

[11]We also noted the need for fiscal policy cooperation.

[12]You can approximate the Fed's interest income by multiplying the value of its securities holdings—about $748 billion in 2004—by the U.S. Treasury's one-year interest rate, roughly 2.1 percent in 2004. You'll get a number around $16 billion.

APPLYING THE CONCEPT
THE EVOLUTION OF FEDERAL RESERVE INDEPENDENCE

Like most large bureaucracies, the Federal Reserve moves very slowly and deliberately. Nevertheless, there have been some defining moments when the Fed's structure changed suddenly and significantly. The first one came in 1935, after the economywide financial failures that led to the Great Depression of the 1930s. To remove monetary policy from the political arena, the Secretary of the Treasury and the Comptroller of the Currency, two political appointees who served at the pleasure of the president, were kicked off the Federal Reserve Board, and the FOMC was created.

But independence in name is not independence in fact. During World War II, the Federal Reserve became part of the war effort, which meant ensuring a cheap source of funds for the Treasury. The Fed worked to keep interest rates low by making sure that bond prices remained high. Importantly, when the Treasury went to issue securities, to keep prices high the Fed would buy what the public refused to purchase. Early in 1951, the Secretary of the Treasury, who was under pressure to finance the new Korean War, tried to force the Fed to purchase significant quantities of bonds directly from the Treasury. Faced with rising inflation, the FOMC had announced its desire to *curtail* credit growth by reducing the rate at which it purchased government debt. President Truman was forced to step in and resolve the standoff. On March 4, 1951, the president, the secretary of the Treasury, and the Federal Reserve chair reached an "accord" and issued a joint announcement establishing the FOMC's independence in setting interest rates and controlling the rate of monetary expansion.*

These two events provided the foundation for the Federal Reserve's independence in forming monetary policy. Of course, the FOMC's ability to do its job still depends on the willingness of politicians to refrain from interference. The president and the secretary of the Treasury can make comments criticizing the FOMC's monetary policy decisions, and Congress does have the ability to revoke the Fed's independence. Fortunately, in recent years, politicians have been supportive of both its day-to-day policies and its institutional structure.

*For a brief summary of this history, see Carl E. Walsh, "Federal Reserve Independence and the Accord of 1951," *Federal Reserve Bank of San Francisco Weekly Letter*, No. 93-21, May 28, 1993.

give frequent public speeches, and occasionally they testify before Congress. In an average year, the chair gives 15 to 20 speeches, and other governors and Reserve Bank presidents speak 5 to 10 times each. All of these communications—the beige book, the statement, the minutes, the transcripts, the biannual report, the testimony, and the speeches—can be found on various Fed Web sites.

This avalanche of information certainly seems enough to give everyone a sense of what the FOMC is doing and why. But lots of information isn't always the right information. A few things are missing from the Fed's communications. First and foremost, there is no regular press conference, nor any real questioning of the chair on the FOMC's current policy stance. And there is the short period before and after the FOMC's meeting when no member will comment publicly on monetary policy. Second, the inputs into the decision-making process—documents like the staff forecast in the green book and the policy options in the blue book—and the meeting transcript are not made public until five years after the fact. Finally, as we will discuss in a moment, the committee's refusal to state its objectives clearly and concisely hampers communication.

Policy Framework

The Congress of the United States has set the Federal Reserve's objectives: "The Board of Governors of the Federal Reserve System and the Federal Open Market Committee shall maintain long run growth of the monetary and credit aggregates commensurate with the economy's long run potential to increase production, so as to promote effectively the goals of maximum employment, stable prices, and moderate long-term interest rates."

"I've called the family together to announce that, because of inflation, I'm going to have to let two of you go."

What should we make of this vague statement? Some people see ambiguity as advantageous. Because laws are difficult to change, they argue, we wouldn't want the Fed's objectives to be extremely specific; the imprecision of the language means the Fed can essentially set its own goals. That would be fine if the FOMC were willing to tell us exactly how it interprets this broad mandate, providing us with technical definitions for the phrases "maximum employment" and "stable prices," along with some sense of their relative priority. But the only thing that Fed officials are willing to say is that they strive to attain "price stability and maximum sustainable economic growth." Many people have argued that this system should be replaced by one in which the FOMC's objectives are made clear and the committee announces a specific numerical objective for consumer price inflation over some horizon. So, for example, members might agree and then publish that they are working to keep CPI inflation between 2 and 3 percent over the coming five years.

STABILITY

The European Central Bank

In 1995, Romans shopped with *lire*, Berliners with *deutsche marks*, and Parisians with *francs*. The Banca d'Italia, Italy's central bank, controlled the number of lire that circulated, while the Bundesbank managed the quantity of deutsche marks and the Banque de France, the volume of francs. But on January 1, 1999, the majority of Western European countries adopted a common currency. Today, residents of Rome, Berlin, and Paris all make their purchases in euros, and monetary policy is the job of the European Central Bank (ECB). In the same way that a dollar bill is worth a dollar everywhere in the United States, a euro note is worth a euro everywhere in the euro area. By 2004, the euro had become the currency of 12 countries (see the map in Figure 16.2).

The agreement to form a European monetary union was formalized in the Treaty of Maastricht, named for the Dutch city in which it was signed in 1991. The treaty initiated a lengthy process that led ultimately to the creation of the European System of

YOUR FINANCIAL WORLD
The Fed Can't Save You from a Stock-Market Crash

Will the Federal Reserve keep the stock market from crashing, helping us all to sleep better at night? We have already said that the central bank's job is to reduce systematic risk by stabilizing prices, output growth, and the financial system. But there is only so much that a central bank can, should, or will do. In the end, no one can save us from all the risks we face.

The history of the stock market in the late 1990s and early 2000s provides a stark illustration of the pressures central bankers face and the limits of their actions. As equity prices rose in 1998 and 1999, many investors came to believe that Federal Reserve Board chair Alan Greenspan would not let the stock market decline significantly. He and his colleagues on the FOMC would bail everyone out. Their reasoning went like this: Changes in wealth change consumption patterns. That is, the richer we all become, the more we spend; conversely, the poorer we are, the less we spend. A stock-market crash would reduce spending, sending the economy into a severe recession—something the "Greenspan Fed" would not allow. For investors, this assumption meant that they could buy stocks without worrying about the downside; they need not fear a crash.* While owning stock used to be risky, it wasn't any-

more. Or so many people believed in 1999. And the lower the perceived risk, the smaller the risk premium became. This drove prices up even further. (Remember that the lower the risk, the more you will pay for a financial instrument.)

What happened? The answer is that the Fed doesn't control the stock market; it merely sets interest rates and ensures that banks have funds to honor their commitments. As the stock market declined through 2001 and 2002, the FOMC lowered its interest-rate target from 6 percent to 1 percent to avert a recession. Growth was sluggish for a few years, and inflation rose only slightly. But keeping stocks from falling from their unsustainable heights was beyond the Fed's control, even if members had wanted to do it. No one can eliminate the risk that is inherent in an investment—not even the most powerful central bank in the world.

*This expectation came to be known as the "Greenspan put." Recall from Chapter 10 that a put option on a stock is the right to sell your shares at a fixed price, regardless of their market value. The idea was that the Fed had, in effect, sold investors a put option on their stocks. If the market started to go down, they could simply sell their shares to Greenspan. See James Grant and Jeremy Grant, "Supreme Confidence in an Inexact Science," *Financial Times*, February 7, 2000.

Central Banks (ESCB), which is composed of the European Central Bank (ECB) in Frankfurt, Germany, and the National Central Banks (NCBs) in the 25 countries in the European Union. The ECB and the NCBs of the 12 countries that participate in the monetary union make up what is known as the Eurosystem, which shares a common currency and common monetary policy. At this writing, Denmark, Sweden, and the United Kingdom, as well as the 10 countries that joined the European Union on May 1, 2004, remained outside the Eurosystem and retained control over their monetary policy.

A myriad of names and abbreviations are associated with central banking in Europe. To avoid confusion, we will refer to the institution that is responsible for monetary policy in the euro area as the European Central Bank. Our goal is to understand its basic organizational structure.[13] As we examine the ECB, keep in mind that, in economic terms, Europe is larger than the United States.

[13]Two publications are helpful in understanding European monetary policy. *The Monetary Policy of the ECB* published by the ECB in 2004, provides a technical description of how things work. For a more academic discussion of monetary policy strategy, written by the top economists at the ECB, see Otmar Issing, Vitor Gaspar, Ignazio Angeloni, and Oreste Tristani, *Monetary Policy in the Euro Area*, (Cambridge, UK: Cambridge University Press, 2001).

Figure 16.2   The European System of Central Banks

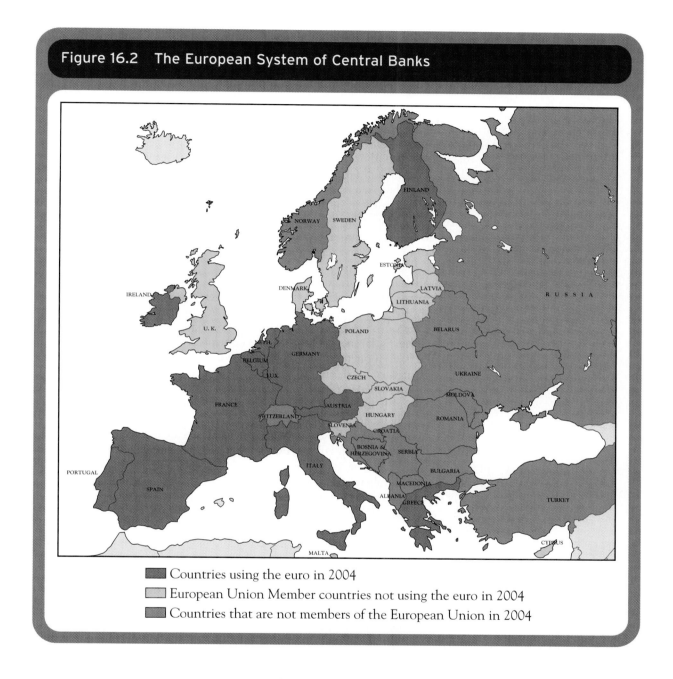

- Countries using the euro in 2004
- European Union Member countries not using the euro in 2004
- Countries that are not members of the European Union in 2004

Organizational Structure

The Eurosystem mirrors the structure of the Federal Reserve System in several ways. There is the six-member **Executive Board of the ECB**, which is similar to the Board of Governors; the **National Central Banks**, which play many of the same roles as the Federal Reserve Banks; and the **Governing Council**, which formulates monetary policy, just as the FOMC does.[14] The Executive Board has a president (currently Jean Claude Trichet of France) and a vice president (Lucas Papademos of Greece), who play the same role as the Fed's chair and vice chair. Executive Board members are appointed by a committee composed of the heads of state of the countries that participate in the monetary union.

The ECB and the NCBs together perform the traditional operational functions of a central bank, which we learned about in the last chapter. In addition to using interest rates to control the availability of money and credit in the economy, they are responsible for the smooth operation of the payments system and the issuance of currency. While the details differ from country to country, the National Central Banks continue to serve as bankers to the banks and governments in their countries, just as the Federal Reserve Banks do in the United States.

There are several important differences between the Fed and the ECB, however. Some exist by design and others as a result of the way the system came into being. First, the ECB does not supervise and regulate financial institutions. Second, the implementation of monetary policy—the ECB's day-to-day interaction with the financial markets—is accomplished at all the national central banks, rather than being centralized as it is in the United States.[15] Third, the ECB's budget is controlled by the National Central Banks, not the other way around. This arrangement means that the NCBs control the finances of the Executive Board and its headquarters in Frankfurt.[16]

The focus of the ECB's activity is on the control of money and credit in the Eurosystem—that is, on monetary policy. The Governing Council, the equivalent of the Fed's FOMC, is composed of the six Executive Board members and the governors of the 12 (as of 2004) central banks in the Euro area. Meetings to consider monetary policy actions are held monthly in Frankfurt, at the ECB's headquarters, and are attended solely by the 18 council members and someone charged with taking notes. No staff members are present. Decisions are made by consensus; no formal votes are taken. The issue of voting has been a contentious one, but the ECB is adamant in its refusal to take votes (or to publicly admit to it). The rationale for this position seems very reasonable. The Governing Council members are charged with setting policy for the euro area as a whole, regardless of economic conditions in the individual countries they come from. If votes were taken, they would ultimately become public. For the Governor of the Banque de France to vote to raise interest rates at a time when the French economy is on its way into a recession would be difficult, even if it is the right thing to do for Europe as a whole. Formal voting, as it is done at the FOMC, would get in the way of good policy.[17]

A number of important safeguards were included in the Treaty of Maastricht to ensure the central bank's independence. First, there are the terms of office: Executive

[14]While the ECB may appear to be modeled after the Federal Reserve System, its structure is actually based on that of the Deutsche Bundesbank, the German central bank. While Europeans uniformly viewed the Bundesbank as being successful in stabilizing the post-World War II German economy, so it was a natural model, the real reason for the new structure was politics. The designers of the ECB had to find a way to create a common central bank that incorporated all of the existing national central banks. This meant adding a new central administration while retaining what was already there.

[15]There are two reasons to question the long-run sustainability of this structure. First, there is the inefficiency of maintaining operations in 12 countries at once. Over time, we would expect a single pan-European financial system to develop, and as it does there will be less justification for maintaining market interactions in more than one place. Second, the ECB itself is a bank; unlike the Board of Governors, it has an operational capacity. This fact suggests that, inevitably, the day-to-day business of financial management will gravitate toward the ECB in Frankfurt.

[16]Another difference is that the ECB pays interest on reserves. We will discuss this matter in more detail in Chapter 18.

[17]An important difference between the ECB's Governing Council and the FOMC is that the Governors of the Federal Reserve Board always hold the majority of the seats on the FOMC (7 out of 12) while the Executive Board members are always a minority on the Governing Council (6 out of a current 18). In the Eurosystem, power is less centralized than it is at the Fed.

Table 16.2 Key Players in the European Central Bank

European Central Bank (ECB)	The central authority in Frankfurt, Germany, that oversees monetary policy in the common currency area. (Established July 1, 1998.)
National Central Banks (NCBs)	The central banks of the countries that belonged to the European Union prior to the monetary union.
European System of Central Banks (ESCB)	The ECB plus the NCBs of all the countries in the European Union, including those that do not participate in the monetary union.
Eurosystem	The ECB plus the NCBs of participating countries; together, they carry out the tasks of central banking in the euro area.
ECB Executive Board	The six-member body in Frankfurt that oversees the operation of the ECB and the Eurosystem.
Governing Council	The (currently) 18-member committee that makes monetary policy in the common currency area.
Euro	The currency used in the countries of the European Monetary Union.
Euro area	The countries that use the euro as their currency.

Board members serve eight-year terms (without the possibility of reappointment), and member nations must appoint their central bank governors for a minimum of five years. Second, the ECB's financial interests must remain separate from any political organization. Third, the treaty states explicitly that the Governing Council cannot take instructions from any government, so its policy decisions are irreversible. The fact that the ECB is the product of a treaty agreed to by all of the countries of the European Union makes it extraordinarily difficult to change any of the terms under which it operates. People who study central banks generally agree that these provisions make the ECB the most independent central bank in the world.

Before we move on, it is worth noting that 10 eastern European countries—Cyprus, the Czech Republic, Estonia, Hungary, Latvia, Lithuania, Malta, Poland, Slovakia, and Slovenia—joined the European Community on May 1, 2004, and are likely to enter the monetary union in the coming years. As they do, some difficult decisions must be made. When it began in 1999, people already wondered how the ECB's 18-member Governing Council managed to make decisions. Imagine what could happen if membership were enlarged to 28! In anticipation of this problem, the Governing Council has adopted a complex system of rotation that bears a passing resemblance to the system used by the FOMC. The Executive Board members have permanent places on the Governing Council, just as the Board of Governors does, while the remaining central bank governors rotate.[18]

Accountability and Transparency

Like the Federal Reserve, the ECB distributes large volumes of information both on paper and on its Web site, in all of the ECB's official languages. Included are a weekly balance sheet; a monthly statistical bulletin; an analysis of current economic conditions; biannual forecasts of inflation and growth; research reports relevant to current

INFORMATION

---

[18]For a complete discussion, see "Governing Council Formally Recommends New Voting System," Press Release of February 4, 2003, and the referenced document, both available at www.ecb.int.

policy; and an annual report. In addition, the president of the ECB appears before the European Parliament every quarter to report on monetary policy and answer questions, and Governing Council members speak regularly in public. But the most important aspect of the ECB's communication strategy concerns statements about the Governing Council's policy deliberations. (Like the FOMC, the Governing Council of the ECB targets a short-term interest rate on interbank loans.)

Following each of the Governing Council's monthly meetings on monetary policy, the president and vice president of the ECB hold a news conference in Frankfurt. The proceedings begin with the president reading a several-page statement announcing the council's interest-rate decision, together with a brief report on current economic and financial conditions in the euro area. The president and vice president then answer questions. A transcript of all their remarks is posted on the ECB's Web site (www.ecb.int) soon afterward. This procedure contrasts starkly with the FOMC's practice of issuing a terse statement and refusing to answer questions immediately after its meetings. On the other hand, the FOMC issues minutes of its meetings within six weeks, while the ECB does not make its minutes public for 20 years. Minutes of the ECB's very first Governing Council meeting, which do not identify who said what, are not scheduled to be released until 2019. Furthermore, the Governing Council does not keep verbatim transcripts of meetings. While observers generally sympathize with the view that transcripts eliminate spontaneity from a meeting, the same cannot be said of minutes. It is hard to justify such a long lag in making public an anonymous summary of the Governing Council's deliberations.

In assessing whether the ECB's communications strategy is sufficient, we need to ask two questions. First, does the information that is released minimize the extent to which people will be surprised by future policy actions? Second, does it hold policymakers accountable for their decisions? On the first issue, the primary problem turns out to be that often a number of conflicting opinions are expressed. While confusion in communication was a problem when the ECB first got started, the Governing Council now knows the importance of providing a unified public front, and its members' public statements are more consistent. On the second issue, indications are that the system is working and that there is accountability. The ECB is forced to justify its actions to the European public, explaining its policies and responding to criticisms.

The Price Stability Objective and Monetary Policy Strategy

The Treaty of Maastricht states, "The primary objective of the European System of Central Banks [ESCB] shall be to maintain price stability. Without prejudice to the objective of price stability, the ESCB shall support the general economic policies in the [European] Community," including the objective of sustainable and noninflationary growth. Like the Fed's legislatively dictated objectives, this statement is quite vague. The Governing Council's response has been to explain its interpretation of the statement and describe the factors that guide its policy decisions. Before assuming operational responsibility on January 1, 1999, the Council prepared a press release entitled "A Stability-Oriented Monetary Policy Strategy."[19] The strategy has two

---

[19]On May 8, 2004, the Governing Council published an evaluation of its policy strategy. A summary, together with background research documents, is available on the ECB's Web site at www.ecb.int.

parts. First, there is a numerical definition of price stability. Second, the Governing Council announces its intention to focus on a broad-based assessment of the outlook for future prices, with money playing a prominent role.[20]

The ECB's Governing Council defines price stability as inflation of close to 2 percent, based on a euro-area-wide measure of consumer prices. The index, called the harmonized index of consumer prices (HICP), is similar to the American consumer price index (CPI). The HICP is an average of retail price inflation in all the countries of the monetary union, weighted by the size of their gross domestic products. So inflation in Germany, where roughly one-third of the total economic activity in the euro area occurs, is much more important to policy decisions than inflation in Ireland, whose economy is about one-thirtieth the size of Germany's. This arrangement has important implications for monetary policy operations, because there will surely be times when the proper policy for Ireland is to raise interest rates but the proper policy for Germany is to lower them. Given Ireland's relative size, a change in inflation or growth there has little impact on the euro area as a whole. The same is true for a number of other small countries in the union.

The fact that the economically large countries matter much more than the small ones can affect the dynamics of the Governing Council's policymaking. Remember that a group including the heads of all the euro-area national central banks, as well as the members of the Executive Board, makes interest-rate decisions. While the Governing Council's job is to stabilize prices in the euro area as a whole, one wonders whether activities in the smaller countries will have undue influence on its policy decisions. To understand this concern, imagine what would happen if all the Governing Council's members pressed for actions appropriate to their own countries. The result would be a policy appropriate to the median country. And since there are only three large countries in the ECB—Germany, France, and Italy—the median country is likely to be fairly small. The custom of drawing half the Executive Board members from the large countries and half from the small ones is not a foolproof counterweight to this tendency. (See *In the News* for a comparison of regional voting biases in the Fed and the ECB.)

These potential shortcomings notwithstanding, evidence strongly suggests that the ECB is doing the job it is supposed to do. That is, the Governing Council's policy has been appropriate to the euro area; it has not been skewed toward smaller countries' concerns. The specificity of the price stability objective set forth in the Treaty of Maastricht holds policymakers accountable, giving them very little discretion in their decision making.

---

[20]The ECB refers to this statement as its "two-pillar" strategy. Observers have been critical of the way money is included in the policy framework. If the goal is to stabilize prices, why isn't money growth just one of a wide range of indicators that are factored into policy decisions?

Table 16.3 Comparing the FOMC to the ECB's Governing Council

	FOMC	Governing Council
Independence		
Budgetary control	Controlled by the Board of Governors.	Controlled by the NCBs.
Decisions irreversible	Yes.	Yes.
Terms of appointment	Governors 14 years, Reserve Bank Presidents 5 years.	Executive Board members 8 years; heads of NCBs minimum of 5 years.
Threat of legislative change	Requires an act of Congress.	Requires agreement of all signatories to Treaty of Maastricht.
Decision making		
	Committee of 19 members, 12 voting at one time.	Committee of 18 members, all participating equally.
Accountability and Transparency		
Policy deliberations	Immediate release of target interest rate with a brief statement and the votes of the committee members.	Immediate release of target interest rate with an explanatory statement; the president and vice president answer questions.
	Minutes of the meeting released two days after the next meeting (six to eight weeks later).	Minutes of the meeting released after 20 years.
	Transcripts released after 5 years.	No transcripts.
Other information	Twice-yearly reports to Congress.	Quarterly report to the European Parliament.
	Public speeches of members.	Public speeches of members.
	Data collection and dissemination.	Data collection and dissemination.
	Publication of research reports, along with forecasts of inflation and growth	Publication of research reports, along with twice-yearly forecasts of inflation and growth.
Policy framework		
	Dual mandate of price stability and sustainable economic growth. No clear definition or statement of trade-offs between the two goals.	Price stability is paramount and defined numerically. All else is secondary goals.
Cooperation with Fiscal Policymakers	No explicit mechanism.	Rigid requirements for member countries' deficits and debt levels.

APPLYING THE CONCEPT
THE NEW BANK OF JAPAN

The 1990s were difficult for Japan. After two decades of real growth averaging $4\frac{1}{2}$ percent per year, the growth rate fell to about $1\frac{1}{2}$ percent a year. At the same time, the Japanese stock market fell by two-thirds, and the banking system practically stopped functioning.

The Japanese Ministry of Finance (commonly known as the "MoF") has been blamed for the mess. Until 1998, the MoF controlled virtually every aspect of the financial system, including monetary policy. It could tell the Bank of Japan (BoJ) where to set its interest-rate target, whom to hire and fire, and what its budget should be. When times were good, the fact that the BoJ worked for the politicians didn't really matter. With high growth rates, resources were abundant, and there was little to fight over. But a decade of stagnation coupled with the meltdown of the country's banking system created strains that the system simply couldn't withstand.

Since 1998, Japanese interest-rate decisions have been made by a nine-member board at the Bank of Japan that is independent of the MoF. The board includes the governor, two deputy governors, and six "outside" experts appointed by the prime minister and approved by the Japanese Parliament (called the Diet). The Bank of Japan Law, which established this structure, states that the policy board's primary goal is the "pursuit of price stability, contributing to the sound development of the national economy." The wording and implications of this statement of BoJ's objective closely resemble the ECB's, with its primary goal of price stability.

The Bank of Japan's policy board meets twice a month, announces its decisions at a press conference following each meeting, and publishes detailed minutes about a month later. These actions, together with frequent public speeches by the nine board members and numerous publications posted on the BoJ Web site, ensure that the financial markets and the public are well informed about the way monetary policy is made in Japan. Furthermore, important BoJ documents are translated into English.

All in all, the BoJ's system of independence, accountability, transparent communication, and monetary policy framework meets most of the requirements we have listed for success. Even so, the Japanese economy continued to struggle for years after the current structure was put into place. There are several possible explanations for its failure to thrive. One is Japan's continuing financial crisis. By most accounts, the Japanese banking system is insolvent, so banks are not playing their essential role as financial intermediaries. That is, resources are not being transferred from savers to investors, regardless of what the central bank does. Another possibility is that the BoJ has not been sufficiently aggressive in expanding money and credit. But since overnight interest rates—the Board's policy target—were held at zero for some time, lowering interest rates further was impossible. Economic expansion, then, will need to take place by less conventional means. We will explore the possibilities in Chapter 23.

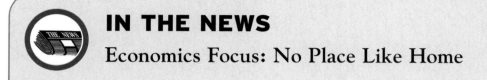

IN THE NEWS

Economics Focus: No Place Like Home

The Economist

March 21, 2002

Why voting patterns at the Fed might have implications for the European Central Bank

IS THE Fed biased? Even asking the question is enough to ruffle feathers at that august institution. Yet new research suggests that the voting behavior of the Fed's key policymakers may be surprisingly biased—and, more importantly, in a way that has implications for the European Central Bank.

The Fed's founders were anxious to eliminate the possibility of bias, either in favor of one region against another, or of large banks against small. Indeed, fear of bias had scuppered two earlier attempts to create an American central bank. The complex voting system of the Fed's main policy body, the Federal Open Market Committee (FOMC), is intended to ensure the broadest range of views.

Research into possible bias has tended to concentrate on the voting behavior of the 12 Federal Reserve Bank presidents, who represent each of the Fed's districts. Only five have voting rights: the president of the New York Fed, and four others on a rotating basis. The votes of this group show the influence of regional as well as national economic developments. As a guard against this, the seven members of the Washington-based Board of Governors, who have permanent voting rights, outnumber them.

But might the governors also be biased? Research by Ellen Meade and Nathan Sheets suggests that they are.* It turns out that governors tend to vote against the majority when there is a significant gap between the unemployment rate in their "home" region and the national rate. When the regional rate was, on average, 0.7 percent higher than the national, a governor would vote against the majority view and in favor of easier monetary policy; when it was, on average, 1.1 percent lower than the national rate, he or she would vote in favor of tighter policy. Perhaps surprisingly, governors are more sensitive to regional developments than are the district bank presidents.

Meanwhile in Europe

Is this regional bias among FOMC members something found in other central banks? What about the supra-

national European Central Bank (ECB), whose structure bears a superficial resemblance to the Fed's? Hard facts are difficult to come by because of the European bank's secretive working methods: it does not publish records of meetings.

The ECB's Governing Council, like the FOMC, comprises two groups: six policymakers based in Frankfurt [the Executive Board], plus the heads of the 12 national central banks in the euro area. But at the ECB, voting does not rotate—all 18 members have an equal say. That immediately builds in the possibility of national bias, since six countries have two representatives on the governing council.

Ms. Meade and Mr. Sheets were not deterred by the absence of voting records. They devised an experiment to test whether ECB policy decisions might be affected by national loyalties. Since (unlike the Fed) inflation is the ECB's sole policy objective, they made a working assumption that each council member would cast his vote according to the difference between national and euro-area inflation rates, and that he would vote in a certain way if that difference were above a certain threshold. With one exception, it seems that all the interest rate changes made since the ECB started in 1999 were those which would have resulted if all council members had voted simply on the basis of differences in their national and euro-area inflation rates.

There has long been a suspicion that policymakers—not just in the ECB but in a variety of European institutions—retain at least some loyalty to their home country. That, after all, must be one reason why member governments expend so much effort and political capital in trying to secure posts for their own nationals.

LESSONS OF THE ARTICLE

FOMC members are supposed to make policy for the country as a whole. The same is true of the ECB's Governing Council: its objective is to stabilize prices in the euro area. Neither group is supposed to give special consideration to economic conditions in members' home areas. The two central banks are designed to minimize the potential importance of regional influences. While safeguards may reduce these effects, they may be nearly impossible to eliminate completely.

*Ellen Meade and Nathan Sheets, "Regional Influences on U.S. Monetary Policy: Some Implications for Europe," Discussion Paper Number 523. Centre for Economic Performance.

Terms

Chapter Lessons

1. The Federal Reserve System is the central bank of the United States. Its decentralized structure comprises three primary elements:

   a. Twelve Federal Reserve Banks, each with its own board of directors, that

      i. Serve as the government's bank, issuing currency, maintaining the U.S. Treasury's bank account, and handling the Treasury's securities.

      ii. Serve as the bankers' bank, holding deposits, operating a payments system, making loans, and evaluating the safety and soundness of financial institutions in their regions.

   b. The seven-member Board of Governors in Washington, D.C., including the chair

      i. Regulates and supervises the financial system.

      ii. Oversees the Federal Reserve Banks.

      iii. Publishes economic data.

   c. The Federal Open Market Committee

      i. Makes monetary policy by setting interest rates.

      ii. Has 12 voting members, including the seven governors and five of the 12 Reserve Bank presidents.

      iii. Meets eight times a year.

      iv. Is controlled largely by the chair.

2. The FOMC's success in meeting its objectives is enhanced by

   a. Its independence, which comes from its members' long terms, budgetary autonomy, and the irreversibility of its policy decisions.

   b. Clear communication of its policy decisions through an explanatory statement that is distributed immediately and minutes that are published following the next meeting.

   c. Regular public appearances of the committee's members.

   It is impaired by

   a. Its unwillingness to define exactly what it means by the stated goals of price stability and sustainable economic growth.

www.mhhe.com/cecchettile

b. Its unwillingness to respond to questions about its policy stance in a timely manner.

3. The European Central Bank (ECB) is the central bank for the countries that participate in the European monetary union.

   a. The ECB is composed of three distinct parts:

      i. The National Central Banks (NCBs) provide services to the banks and governments in their countries.

      ii. The European Central Bank in Frankfurt, with its six-member Executive Board, oversees the monetary system.

      iii. The Governing Council makes monetary policy decisions.

   b. The ECB's primary objective is to stabilize prices in the common currency area.

   c. The ECB's success in meeting its policy objectives is aided by the timely announcement of policy decisions, press conferences in which top ECB officials respond to questions, and the release of twice-yearly forecasts.

   d. The ECB's success is impaired by the fact that the minutes of its policy meetings are not published for 20 years.

Problems

1. For many years, Federal Reserve officials kept their policy decisions secret, claiming that surprises were more effective than announcements and that even accurate information could mislead financial markets. What do you think of this argument?

2. What are the Federal Reserve's goals? How are the Fed's officials held accountable for meeting them?

3. Go to the Federal Reserve Board's Web site and locate the FOMC's most recent statement. What did the committee members say at their last meeting regarding their two goals of price stability and sustainable economic growth? What is their current assessment of the balance of risks? Now read the committee's last two statements to see if the balance of risks has changed. If it has, can you figure out why?

4. What do you think would have happened if President Truman had sided with the Secretary of the Treasury in 1951? Describe how you think U.S. monetary policy since then would have differed and what the consequences would have been for growth and inflation.

5. Many people have argued that the FOMC should establish clear inflation objectives. How would such goals enhance internal deliberations, communication with the financial markets, and the accountability of the committee? If numerical inflation goals are set, do you think they should be determined by the FOMC or by Congress and the president? Why would the chair of the Board of Governors argue against setting such goals?

6. Some people have argued that the high inflation of the late 1970s was a consequence of the fact that Federal Reserve Board Chairman Arthur Burns did what President Richard Nixon wanted him to do. Explain the connection.

7. The Fed is very sensitive to the fact that Congress can always change the law that created it. One way it defends its independence is by using the Reserve Banks' boards of directors to lobby politicians. What do you think of this practice?

8. While the Chairman of the Federal Reserve Board has only one of 12 votes on the FOMC, he is never in the minority. What gives him the power to control the committee?

9. As Argentina's economy was collapsing, the governor of its central bank resigned and the president of the Republic of Argentina appointed a new one. Just months later, the new governor resigned after passage of a law that provided he could be put on trial for failure to perform his duties. What do you think of a system in which the governor of the central bank can be charged with such a crime?

10. What are the goals of the ECB? How are its officials held accountable for meeting them?

11. Go to the ECB's Web site and locate the most recent statement of the president of the ECB about monetary policy. What was the Governing Council's policy decision? How was it justified?

12. The Treaty of Maastricht gives the president of the Council of the European Union the right to attend ECB Governing Council meetings. In early 1999, German finance minister Oskar Lafontaine went to the meeting in an attempt to obtain an interest-rate reduction in his capacity as the official representative of the European Union. What do you think of the rule that allowed the finance minister to go to the meeting? What do you think of Lafontaine's decision to go? What do you think the outcome was?

13. Do you think the FOMC has an easier or a harder time agreeing on monetary policy than the Governing Council of the ECB? Why?

14. In 2001, Martin Mayer, a well-known financial commentator, wrote "The European Central Bank is run by a governing board of technocrats and has authority to set inflation for Europe without consulting any of the European governments." Evaluate this statement.

15. The Monetary Policy Committee (MPC) of the Bank of England is responsible for setting interest rates in the United Kingdom. Go to the bank's Web site at www.bankofengland.co.uk, and get as much information about the MPC as you can. How big is it? Who are its members? How often does it meet? What sort of announcements and publications does it offer? Is it independent of the United Kingdom's Parliament?

Chapter 17

The Central Bank Balance Sheet and the Money Supply Process

On the morning of September 11, 2001, four hijacked planes crashed: two into the World Trade Center Towers in New York City, one into the Pentagon in Washington, D.C., and one in a field in western Pennsylvania. Thousands of people died, and the world changed. The disruptions were enormous. All nonmilitary aircraft in the United States were immediately grounded and U.S. airspace was closed. In the Wall Street area, power and communications networks were shut down, closing the financial markets. Yet New Yorkers found they could still go to an ATM anywhere outside the immediate neighborhood of the attacks and withdraw cash. Despite the massive disruptions in the Wall Street area, the electronic network that processed the withdrawals continued to work.

Conditions were anything but normal inside the financial community, where the risk of a systemwide collapse was very real. But because of the immediate action of Federal Reserve officials, the financial system held together, and most of us never realized how close we came to catastrophe. At 11:45 a.m., three hours after the attacks began, the Federal Reserve Board issued a terse statement: "The Federal Reserve is open and operating. The discount window is available to meet liquidity needs." Over the next week, people throughout the Federal Reserve System made sure there was enough money circulating to keep the economy going. They bought nearly $100 billion worth of U.S. Treasury securities, extended tens of billions of dollars in loans to U.S. banks, and provided foreign central banks with the billions of dollars they needed to ensure that commercial banks in their countries could meet their obligations. They did it all from backup sites, since the Federal Reserve's primary operating site, two blocks from the World Trade Center, was inaccessible.

This was one of the great successes of modern central banking. In extraordinary circumstances, quick action by the Fed kept the financial markets afloat. While some institutions and individuals will never recover from the terrorist attacks, the financial system—one of the terrorists' primary targets—returned to near normal within weeks.

The story of September 2001 stands in stark contrast to what happened 70 plus years ago, when policy failures led to the collapse of the U.S. banking system, precipitating the Great Depression of the 1930s. At the time, Federal Reserve officials didn't fully understand how their actions affected the supply of credit in the economy. They failed to recognize the link between changes in the Fed's balance sheet and the growth rate of money. They thought that so long as they supplied more and more cash to the economy, and so long as commercial bank account balances at the Federal Reserve banks were growing, money and credit were easily available. They were wrong. The financial system collapsed because the Fed officials had failed to provide the liquidity that sound banks needed to stay in business. As a result, virtually no one could borrow; both the amount of credit and the quantity of money in the economy plummeted.

The Fed's policymakers did their best in the 1930s, and their best wasn't very good. But at least they did it in public, which is not always the case. When the economy is suffering, or when central bankers are taking actions they aren't supposed to, they have a tendency to hide what they are doing. At times, central bankers have delayed publication of statistics or distorted the information they did provide. That's what the central bank of Thailand did in 1997. The Bank of Thailand was committed to stabilizing the value of its currency, the Thai *baht*, at an exchange rate of about 26 to one U.S. dollar. To do so, officials had to convince foreign exchange traders that they had enough dollars to buy baht if market participants started to sell. To be convinced, currency traders had to see the numbers. But in summer 1997, officials at the Bank of Thailand refused to tell anyone, even their own Minister of Finance, how many dollars the bank held.[1] When the truth got out, and everyone learned that the cupboard was bare, the *baht* collapsed, ending 1997 at 50 to one dollar.

To appreciate what went right in September 2001—and what went wrong both in the United States in the 1930s and in Thailand in 1997—we need to understand how the central bank interacts with the financial system. What is it that central banks buy and sell? What are the assets and liabilities on their balance sheets? How do they control those assets and liabilities, and why might they want to hide them from the public? More to the point, how is the central bank's balance sheet connected to the money and credit that flow through the economy?[2] Where *do* the trillions of dollars in our bank accounts actually come from? In answering these questions, we will combine our knowledge of how central banks work with our understanding of commercial bank operations. Let's see how the system works.

The Central Bank's Balance Sheet

As the government's banker and the bankers' banker, the central bank engages in numerous financial transactions. It supplies currency, provides deposit accounts to the government and commercial banks, makes loans, and buys and sells securities and foreign currency. All these activities cause changes in the central bank's balance sheet. Because the balance sheet is the foundation of any financial institution, understanding the day-to-day operation of a central bank must start with an understanding of its assets and liabilities and how they change. The structure of the balance sheet gives us a window through which we can study how the institution operates.

Central banks publish their balance sheets regularly. The Federal Reserve and the European Central Bank both do so weekly; you can find the information on their Web sites.[3] Publication is a critical part of the transparency that makes monetary policy effective. The actual published data is complicated and includes items we don't need to worry about here. Instead, we'll focus on a stripped-down version of the balance sheet, one that has been reduced to the most important components. Figure 17.1 shows the major assets and liabilities that appear in every central bank's balance sheet in one form or another. Note that the entries are divided not only into columns, with assets on the left and liabilities on the right, but into categories as well. The top row shows the assets and liabilities the central bank holds in its role as the government's

---

[1]The Bank of Thailand hadn't actually sold its dollar reserves on the open market. Officials had engaged in forward transactions that committed them to sell the dollars in the future. Thus, they could claim to have dollars that in reality were committed to others. For a detailed description of this episode, see Paul Blustein, *The Chastening: Inside the Crisis That Rocked the Global Financial System and Humbled the IMF*, (New York: PublicAffairs, 2001).

[2]In 2004, the narrowest measure of money, M1, was around $1.3 trillion, while M2 was over $6 trillion. To gain some perspective on these numbers, we need to compare them to current-dollar GDP, which was $11.6 trillion at the time.

[3]The balance sheets can be a bit difficult to find since they don't have straightforward names. The Fed's is located in the H.4.1 release, which is called "Factors Affecting Reserve Balances." The ECB's can be found under the heading "Consolidated Weekly Financial Statement of the Eurosystem," in its Web site's Press Release section.

Figure 17.1 The Central Bank's Balance Sheet

	Assets	**Liabilities**
Government's Bank	Securities Foreign exchange reserves	Currency Government's account
Bankers' Bank	Loans	Accounts of the commercial banks (reserves)

bank, and the bottom row shows the assets and liabilities it holds as the bankers' bank. Let's examine each entry, starting with the assets.

Assets

The central bank's balance sheet shows three basic assets: securities, foreign exchange reserves, and loans. The first two are needed so that the central bank can perform its role as the government's bank; the loans are a service to commercial banks. Let's look at each in detail, focusing on its importance in the United States.[4]

1. *Securities* are the primary assets of most central banks. Though some central banks hold a wide variety of public and private debt, the Fed holds only U.S. Treasury securities.[5] The quantity of securities it holds (nearly $700 billion in 2004) is controlled through purchases and sales known as *open market operations*. It is important to emphasize that independent central banks, not fiscal authorities, determine the quantity of securities they purchase.

2. Foreign Exchange Reserves are the central bank's and government's balances of foreign currency. These are held in the form of bonds issued by foreign governments. For example, the Fed holds euro-denominated bonds issued by the German government as well as yen-denominated bonds issued by the Japanese government. These reserves are used in foreign exchange interventions, when officials attempt to change the market values of various currencies. (As we will see later, the Fed rarely intervenes in foreign exchange markets.) On the published balance sheet, these assets can be difficult to find. The Fed's foreign exchange reserves are buried in an entry called "other assets," so you can't figure out the exact amounts each week. But four times a year a report on foreign exchange operations is published that states the size of the reserves at the end of each quarter. In June 2004, it was just under $40 billion.[6]

---

[4] A detailed description of the Federal Reserve System's consolidated balance sheet appears in Appendix A of *The Federal Reserve System—Purposes & Functions*, available on the Federal Reserve Board's Web site.

[5] The Fed also holds small quantities of *Federal agency obligations* issued by U.S. government-sponsored enterprises such as the Federal National Mortgage Association. The government does not guarantee them, but they do have the highest credit rating.

[6] The report, called "Treasury and Federal Reserve Foreign Exchange Operations," is available on the Federal Reserve Bank of New York's Web site. Table 1, near the end, reports the foreign exchange positions of both the U.S. Treasury's Exchange Stabilization Fund and the Federal Reserve System. Together, they make up the U.S. foreign exchange reserves.

3. *Loans* are extended to commercial banks. There are several kinds, and their importance varies depending on how the central bank operates. In the United States, loans fall into two basic categories: *discount loans* and *float*.

   a. Discount loans are the loans the Fed makes when commercial banks need short-term liquidity. Except in extraordinary circumstances, discount loans are made in the millions of dollars.

   b. Float is a byproduct of the Fed's check-clearing business. The details are a bit complicated.[7] As the first step in clearing a check, the Fed credits the reserve account of the bank that presents it by the amount written on the check. It does so before debiting the reserve account of the bank on which the check is drawn. If the bank on which the check is drawn (the one whose account is to be debited) is located in a different Federal Reserve District from the bank that presented the check (whose account has been credited), then the check must be physically transported to the paying bank's district before that bank's reserve account is debited. To see how this process works, imagine you live in Los Angeles (in the 12th Fed District). You send a check to a friend in Philadelphia (in the 3rd District). Your friend deposits the check in a local bank, which presents it to its local Fed check-processing facility. That bank's reserve account is credited immediately. Then the Fed has to fly the check to California before your bank's reserve account is debited. The credit occurs before the debit. During the time it takes the check to get to California, the Fed in effect makes a loan to you and your bank—that's float. Since flying the checks around the country normally takes only a day, float rarely exceeds a few hundred million dollars.[8] (As we will see in Applying the Concept, the days immediately following September 11, 2001, were an exception.)

U.S. Treasury securities are the biggest, most important asset on the Federal Reserve's balance sheet. Through these holdings the Fed controls the federal funds rate and the availability of money and credit. Foreign exchange reserves, although they are sizable, play only a small role in policymaking, and loans are almost always modest. At other central banks, this ranking of assets often differs. In small countries, for instance, the primary focus is often on the level of foreign exchange reserves.

Before continuing, it is worth saying a word about gold. Gold reserves are an asset of many central banks, and you can find them listed on published balance sheets. Once crucial to the central bank's operations, in modern times they have become virtually irrelevant. The standard procedure in the United States is for the U.S. Treasury to issue gold certificates to the Federal Reserve, backed by gold that is stored at Fort Knox. The Fed credits the U.S. Treasury's account (on the liabilities side of the balance sheet) at a fixed price that does not vary with the market. When the Treasury's gold stock changes, so does the value of the Fed's gold certificates. But in the end, this is all just accounting. The amount of gold and its value on the Fed's balance sheet plays no role in modern monetary policy.

Liabilities

Turning to the liabilities side of the central bank's balance sheet, we see three major entries: currency, the government's deposit account, and the deposit accounts of the

---

[7]On the Federal Reserve System's consolidated balance sheet, float is the difference between two lines, "items in process of collection" minus "deferred availability cash items."

[8]With changes in technology, especially the advent of digital check imaging, the rules regarding when banks receive funds and when they pay them are evolving. It seems likely that as physical paper checks disappear, float will go with them.

commercial banks. Again, these can be divided into two groups based on their purpose. The first two items allow the central bank to perform its role as the government's bank, while the third allows it to fulfill its role as the bankers' bank. Let's look at each in turn, again using the example of the United States to illustrate some important details.

1. *Currency.* Nearly all central banks have a monopoly on the issuance of the currency used in everyday transactions. Take a look at the top of any dollar bill and you will see the words "Federal Reserve Note." Currency—really, currency circulating in the hands of the *nonbank* public—is a central bank's principal liability. Currency accounts for over 90 percent of the Fed's liabilities ($690 billion in 2004) and roughly 50 percent of the ECB's liabilities (€420 billion in 2004).[9]

2. *Government's account.* Governments need a bank account just like the rest of us. They have to have a place to deposit their income and a way to pay for the things they buy. The central bank provides the government with an account into which the government deposits funds (primarily tax revenues) and from which the government writes checks and makes electronic payments. The U.S. Treasury keeps deposits at commercial banks as well, transferring money to its Fed account to cover its purchases. The Treasury keeps its account balance at the Fed fairly constant; in recent years the target has been $5 billion.

3. *Commercial bank accounts (reserves).* Commercial bank reserves are the sum of two parts: deposits at the Fed *plus* the cash in the bank's own vault. *Deposits at the central bank* function like the commercial bank's checking account. In the same way that you can take cash out of a commercial bank, the bank can withdraw its deposits at the central bank. And just as you can write a check instructing your bank to transfer some part of your account balance to someone else, a commercial bank can transfer a portion of its deposit account balance to another bank. Vault cash is part of reserves; it is not part of item 1, which includes only cash held by the nonbank public. Because a bank's vault cash is available to meet depositors' withdrawal demands, it serves the insurance function for which reserves are designed. Reserves are assets of the commercial banking system and liabilities of the central bank. In 2004, U.S. commercial banking system reserves totaled roughly $45 billion; the reserves of commercial banks in the euro area were about €140 billion. One reason for this difference is that the Fed does not pay interest on reserves, while the ECB does.

While banking system reserves aren't the central bank's largest liability, they are the most important in determining the amount of money in the economy. Central banks run their monetary policy operations through changes in these reserves. Increases lead to a rise in deposits and to growth in the availability of money and credit; decreases do the opposite. As we saw in Chapter 12, there are two types of reserves: those that banks are required to hold, called required reserves, and those they hold voluntarily, called excess reserves. Originally, the government required banks to hold a certain level of reserves to ensure banks' safety and soundness. As described in *Tools of the Trade* later in this chapter, banks are no longer constrained by these reserve requirements. Today's bankers hold excess reserves both as insurance against unexpected outflows and for use in conducting their day-to-day business.

---

[9]The published balance sheets of central banks, like the one in the Federal Reserve System's weekly H.4.1 release, report cash as "currency in circulation," which combines currency in the hands of the public (part of M1) and vault cash (part of commercial bank reserves).

The Central Bank's Balance Sheet   Chapter 17 | 431

YOUR FINANCIAL WORLD
Why We Still Have Cash

For years experts have been predicting the demise of paper currency—cash. First credit cards were going to take over; now it is electronic forms of money. But still we have cash. In fact, we have more cash than ever. During the 1990s, as more and more people got hold of credit cards and clever people tried to introduce e-money, the volume of dollar bills outstanding rose 8 percent per year. To put it in concrete terms, the amount of U.S. currency in the hands of the public doubled in 10 years. By 2004, cash inside the country amounted to about $600 per U.S. resident.* Amazingly enough, Americans hold less cash than residents of other countries. Residents of the euro area, for example, hold about twice as much. Nothing seems to dissuade people from holding paper notes issued by the central bank.

There are a number of explanations for this phenomenon. First, there is convenience: the easiest way to repay $20 you borrowed from a friend is to use cash. Second, many people use cash to avoid paying taxes. Servers in restaurants, for instance,

don't want to pay income tax on their tips. Finally, there is the fact that cash provides anonymity. When you pay with cash, no one cares who you are and the transaction can't be traced back to you. This arrangement has obvious advantages for people engaged in drug dealing, smuggling, and other black-market activities. But if the demand for cash came solely from people engaged in illegal activities, the proper response would be to outlaw it. The fact is that law-abiding people use cash for legal transactions in which they would prefer to remain nameless. Surely we don't want to lose the ability to hide some of our purchases from public view.

Because cash is almost completely anonymous, there is little chance that electronic products will replace paper currency any time soon.

*The U.S. Treasury estimates that three-quarters of American currency circulates outside the United States and that the recent increase was shared between foreigners and U.S. residents. This means that of the $2400 per U.S. resident outstanding in 2004, roughly $600 was held inside the country. See *Applying the Concept* in Chapter 2.

The Importance of Disclosure

Buried in the mountain of paper that every central bank publishes is a statement of the bank's own financial condition. This balance sheet contains what is probably the most important information that any central bank makes public. Every responsible central bank in the world discloses its financial position regularly, most of them every week. In the same way that shareholders require a periodic accounting of the activities of the companies they own, we are all entitled to the information on our central bank's balance sheet. Without public disclosure of the level and change in the size of foreign exchange reserves and currency holdings, it is impossible for us to tell whether the policymakers are doing their job properly. Publication of the balance sheet is an essential aspect of central bank transparency. Delays, like those during the Mexican debt crisis of 1994–1995, are a clear sign of impending disaster.

Another sign of trouble is misrepresentation of the central bank's financial position. A particularly egregious case of lying by a central bank occurred in the Philippines in 1986, when then-President Ferdinand Marcos was desperate to remain in power. We know now that Marcos ordered the central bank to print enormous amounts of money so that he could try to buy enough individual votes to win the election. In the four months leading up to the election, the quantity of money circulating in the Philippine economy rose 40 percent. While a government can usually print money whenever it wants, that was not the case in the Philippines. As part of a loan agreement with the International Monetary Fund (IMF), the Central Bank of the Philippines had promised to limit the rate of money growth. Since Filipinos used currency for the vast majority of transactions, the easiest way for the IMF to enforce the agreement was to monitor the serial numbers on new bills. Because each bill has a unique serial number, figuring out how many of them are being printed shouldn't be difficult. But instead of printing one bill per serial number, the Philippine government printed bills in triplicate—three bills per serial number. And the central bank kept quiet about the scheme.[10]

The Monetary Base

Together, currency in the hands of the public and reserves in the banking system—the privately held liabilities of the central bank—make up the monetary base, also called high-powered money. As we will see in the next section, the central bank can control the size of the monetary base, the base on which all other forms of money stand. (The term *high-powered* comes from the fact that the quantity of money and credit in the economy is a multiple of currency plus banking system reserves.) As we will see later in this chapter, when the monetary base increases by a dollar, the quantity of money rises by several dollars.

To get some sense of the relationship between the monetary base and the quantity of money, we can look at a few numbers. In August 2004, the U.S. monetary base was $757 billion. At the same time, M1 was $1.3 trillion and M2 was $6.3 trillion. So M1 is almost twice the size of the monetary base, and M2 is more than 8 times as great as the monetary base. Later in the chapter we'll return to these relationships. But first, let's see how the central bank adjusts its balance sheet and changes the size of the monetary base.

Changing the Size and Composition of the Balance Sheet

Unlike you and me, the central bank controls the size of its balance sheet. That is, policymakers can enlarge or reduce their assets and liabilities at will, without asking anyone. We can't do that. To see the point, think about a simple transaction you engage in regularly, like buying $50 worth of groceries. When you arrive at the checkout counter, you have to pay for your purchases. Let's say you do it with a check. When the supermarket deposits your check in the bank, your $50 moves through the payments system. It is credited to the supermarket's account and, eventually, debited from yours. As long as you started with at least $50 in your checking account, the process works smoothly.[11] The grocery store's bank account is $50 larger and yours is $50 smaller.

Now think about a standard transaction in which the central bank buys a $1 million government security. What's the difference between this purchase and yours at the grocery store? First, there is its size. The central bank's transaction is 20,000 times as big as yours. But that's not all. To see another important difference, let's look at the mechanics of the security purchase. To pay for the bond, the central bank writes a $1 million check payable to the bond dealer who sells the bond. (In real life, the transaction is done electronically.) After the check is deposited, the dealer's commercial bank account is credited $1 million. The commercial bank then sends the check back to the central bank. When it gets there, something unusual happens. Remember, at the end of your check's journey, your bank debited your checking account $50. But

---

[10]Newspaper stories at the time documented what happened in the Philippines. See, for example, Chris Sherwell, "Banknotes in Triplicate Add to Filipino's Confusion," *Financial Times*, February 22, 1986.

[11]The fact that you may have *overdraft protection*, which allows you to write a check for more than your current balance and borrow the rest, adds a layer of complexity but doesn't change the basics.

when the central bank's $1 million check is returned, the central bank credits the reserve account of the bank presenting it $1 million. And that's it. The central bank can simply buy things (the $1 million bond, for instance) and then create liabilities to pay for them (the $1 million increase in reserves in the banking system). It can increase the size of its balance sheet as much as it wants.

Turning to the specifics of this process, we'll look at four types of transactions: (1) an *open market operation,* in which the central bank buys or sells a security; (2) a *foreign exchange intervention,* in which the central bank buys or sells foreign currency reserves; (3) the extension of a *discount loan* to a commercial bank by the central bank; and (4) the decision by an individual to *withdraw cash* from the bank. Each of these has an impact on both the central bank's balance sheet and the banking system's balance sheet. Open market operations, foreign exchange interventions, and discount loans all affect the *size* of the central bank's balance sheet and change the size of the monetary base. Cash withdrawals by the public are different. They shift components of the monetary base, changing the composition of the central bank's balance sheet but leaving its size unaffected.

To figure out the impact of each of these four transactions on the central bank's balance sheet, we need to remember one simple rule: When the value of an asset on the balance sheet increases, either the value of another asset decreases so that the net change is zero or the value of a liability rises by the same amount. What's true for assets is also true for liabilities. An increase in a liability is balanced either by a decrease in another liability or by an increase in an asset. The principle is the same regardless of whose balance sheet we are looking at.

In the following sections, we will discuss these transactions in the context of the Federal Reserve's institutional structure. As we go through the examples, remember that the securities and foreign exchange transactions are managed by the Federal Reserve Bank of New York, while discount loans are extended by all 12 Reserve Banks.

Open Market Operations

When the Federal Reserve buys or sells securities in financial markets, it engages in open market operations. These open market purchases and sales have a straightforward impact on the Fed's balance sheet. To see how the process works, take the common case in which the Federal Reserve Bank of New York purchases $1 billion in U.S. Treasury bonds from a commercial bank.[12] To pay for the bonds, the Fed transfers $1 billion into the reserve account of the seller. The exchange is done electronically. Figure 17.2 shows the change in the Federal Reserve's balance sheet. This is called a T-account. The left side shows the change in assets and the right side gives the change in liabilities. Figure 17.2 shows the impact of this open market purchase on the Fed's balance sheet: Its assets and liabilities both go up $1 billion, increasing the monetary base by the same amount.

What is the impact of the Fed's open market purchase on the banking system's balance sheet? The Fed exchanged $1 billion in securities for $1 billion in reserves, both of which are banking system assets. Figure 17.3 shows the balance-sheet effect of the exchange.

Note that there are no changes on the liabilities side of the banking system's balance sheet, and the changes on the asset side sum to zero.

Looking at Figures 17.2 and 17.3, you'll notice that reserves are an asset to the banking system but a liability to the Federal Reserve. This may seem confusing, but

---

[12]The Fed purchases securities from a list of *primary government securities dealers,* which includes a combination of commercial banks, investment banks, and securities dealers. While we could examine the mechanics of the Fed's purchase assuming the other side is either an investment bank or a dealer, it would complicate the analysis without providing additional insight.

Figure 17.2 Change in the Federal Reserve System's Balance Sheet following Purchase of a U.S. Treasury Bond

Assets		Liabilities	
Securities (U.S. Treasury bond)	+$1 billion	Reserves	+$1 billion

Figure 17.3 Change in the Banking System's Balance Sheet following the Fed's Purchase of a U.S. Treasury Bond

Assets		Liabilities	
Reserves	+$1 billion		
Securities (U.S. Treasury bond)	−$1 billion		

it shouldn't. It's like your own bank account. The balance in that account is your asset, but it is your bank's liability.

Before we move on, we should note that if the Fed *sells* a U.S. Treasury bond through what is known as an open market sale, the impact on everyone's balance sheet is reversed. All the credits in the two figures become debits and vice versa. The Fed's balance sheet shrinks, as does the monetary base; the banking system's reserves decline, while its securities holdings increase.[13]

Foreign Exchange Intervention

What happens if the U.S. Treasury instructs the Federal Reserve to buy $1 billion worth of euros? The answer is that the Federal Reserve Bank of New York buys German government bonds, denominated in euros, from the foreign exchange departments of large commercial banks and pays for them with dollars.[14] Like an open market bond purchase, this transaction is done electronically and the $1 billion payment

[13]In practice, the Fed virtually never sells securities. It always buys; the only question is how much. The Fed intentionally leaves itself in a position where it needs to buy securities on a temporary basis. The details are described in the *Tools of the Trade* in Chapter 18.

[14]As a technical matter, the Fed first purchases euro currency with dollars and then uses the proceeds to buy the German government bonds. But since it owns the euro currency for only a very short time, probably a few hours, we are ignoring that intermediate transaction.

Figure 17.4 Change in the Federal Reserve System's Balance Sheet following Purchase of Euro-denominated German Government Bonds

Assets		Liabilities	
Foreign exchange reserves (German government bonds in euros)	+$1 billion	Reserves	+$1 billion

Figure 17.5 Change in the Banking System's Balance Sheet following the Fed's Purchase of Euro-denominated German Government Bonds

Assets		Liabilities
Reserves	+$1 billion	
Securities (German government bonds)	-$1 billion	

is credited directly to the reserve account of the bank from which the bonds were bought. The impact on the Fed's balance sheet is almost identical to that of the open market operation, as Figure 17.4 shows. The Fed's assets and liabilities both rise by $1 billion, and the monetary base expands with them.

Since the Federal Reserve bought the euros from a commercial bank, the impact on the banking system's balance sheet is straightforward. The result, shown in Figure 17.5, is nearly identical to the impact when the Fed bought bonds through an open market purchase (see Figure 17.3). In both cases, the banking system's securities portfolio falls by $1 billion and reserve balances rise by an equal amount. The only difference is the exact assets that decline. In a standard open market operation, the reduction is in bank holdings of U.S. government bonds; here it is in their holdings of euro-denominated assets.

Discount Loans

The Federal Reserve does not force commercial banks to borrow money; the banks ask for loans. To get one, a borrowing bank must provide collateral, usually in the form of U.S. Treasury bonds.[15] Not surprisingly, when the Fed makes such a loan, it changes

[15]Remember, *collateral* is the term used to describe specific assets pledged by a borrower that a lender can seize in the event of nonpayment. To obtain a discount loan, a bank must identify specific assets (usually bonds) that the Fed can take if the bank doesn't repay the loan.

Figure 17.6 Change in the Federal Reserve System's Balance Sheet following a Discount Loan

Assets		Liabilities	
Discount loans	+$100 million	Reserves	+$100 million

Figure 17.7 Change in the Banking System's Balance Sheet following a Discount Loan

Assets		Liabilities	
Reserves	+$100 million	Discount loans	+$100 million

the balance sheet of both institutions. For the borrowing bank, the loan is a liability that is matched by an offsetting increase in the level of its reserve account. For the Fed, the loan is an asset that is created in exchange for a credit to the borrower's reserve account. The impact on the Federal Reserve's balance sheet is shown in Figure 17.6.

Note that the increase in loans is an asset to the Fed, while the change in reserves increases its liabilities. Once again, the impact on the Fed's balance sheet is the same as that of an open market purchase or an increase in foreign exchange reserves. The extension of credit to the banking system raises the level of reserves and expands the monetary base.

The impact on the banking system's balance sheet mirrors the impact on the Fed, with reserves and loans both increasing. In this case, however, commercial banks have increased the size of their balance sheet by borrowing from the Fed (see Figure 17.7).

In summary, open market purchases, an increase in foreign exchange reserves, and the extension of discount loans all increase the reserves available to the banking system, expanding the monetary base. We turn now to a different type of transaction, one that affects only the composition—not the size—of the monetary base.

Cash Withdrawal

The Federal Reserve can always shift its holdings of various assets, selling U.S. Treasury bonds and using the proceeds to buy Japanese yen, or engaging in an offsetting sale of a U.S. Treasury security after a bank takes out a discount loan. But the same is not true of its liabilities. Because the Fed stands ready to exchange reserves for currency on demand, it does not control the mix between the two. The nonbank public—the people who hold the cash—controls that.

You may be surprised to learn that when you take cash from an ATM, you are changing the Federal Reserve's balance sheet. The reason is that vault cash is part of reserves, while the currency holdings of the nonbank public—your cash and mine—are not. By moving your own assets out of your bank and into currency, you force a shift from reserves to currency on the Fed's balance sheet. The transaction is complicated, involving the nonbank public (you and me), the banking system, and the central bank, so understanding it means looking at three balance sheets.

Consider an example in which you withdraw $100 from your checking account. This transaction changes the composition of the asset side of your balance sheet, as shown in Figure 17.8. (Since there is no change in your liabilities, the changes in the asset side of your balance sheet must sum to zero.)

But that isn't all. By taking $100 out of the cash machine, you had an impact on your bank's balance sheet as well. Remember, cash inside the bank—vault cash—counts as reserves, so by withdrawing cash from your bank, you decreased the banking system's reserves. The change in the banking system's T-account is shown in Figure 17.9.

It should come as no surprise to you that when you take your money out of the bank, the bank's balance sheet shrinks. Here we see that your cash withdrawal forced the banking system to contract its balance sheet. Note that the change in bank assets equals the change in bank liabilities.

Finally, there is the Federal Reserve. Remember, the Fed controls the size of its own balance sheet, so your transactions can't affect that. But what you can do is change the composition of the Fed's liabilities. By withdrawing cash, you changed the amount of currency outstanding – a change that shows up on the Fed's balance sheet as a shift from reserves to currency. Both are liabilities. Figure 17.10 shows what the Fed's balance sheet looks like. Note that the monetary base hasn't changed.

Figure 17.8   Change in the Nonbank Public's Balance Sheet following a Cash Withdrawal

Assets		Liabilities
Currency	+$100	
Checkable deposits	-$100	

Figure 17.9   Change in the Banking System's Balance Sheet following a Cash Withdrawal

Assets		Liabilities	
Reserves	-$100	Checkable deposits	-$100

Figure 17.10   Change in the Federal Reserve System's Balance Sheet following a Cash Withdrawal

Assets	Liabilities	
	Currency	+$100
	Reserves	−$100

Remember that the monetary base equals currency plus reserves, and one went up while the other went down. But the *relative size* of each component of the monetary base has changed.

Table 17.1 summarizes the impact of each of the four transactions we have just studied on the size and composition of the Federal Reserve's balance sheet. Open market operations and foreign exchange interventions are both done at the discretion of the central bank, while the level of discount borrowing is decided by the commercial banks. The nonbank public decides how much currency to hold.

It is worth noting that there are countries where the process works differently. As we will see in Chapter 19, when a central bank wishes to control its country's exchange rate rather than the domestic interest rate, one way to do so is to stand ready to buy and sell

Table 17.1   Changes in the Size and Composition of the Federal Reserve's Balance Sheet and the Monetary Base

Transaction	Initiated by	Typical Action	Impact
Open market operation	Central bank	Purchase of Treasury bond	Increases reserves, the size of the Fed's balance sheet, and the monetary base
Foreign exchange intervention	Central bank	Purchase of German government bond	Increases reserves, the size of the Fed's balance sheet, and the monetary base
Discount loan	Commercial bank	Extension of loan to commercial bank	Increases reserves, the size of the Fed's balance sheet, and the monetary base
Cash withdrawal	Nonbank public	Withdrawal of cash from ATM	Decreases reserves and increases currency, leaving the size of the Fed's balance sheet and the monetary base unchanged

APPLYING THE CONCEPT
THE FED'S RESPONSE ON SEPTEMBER 11, 2001

On a normal day, U.S. banks have $40 billion worth of cash in their vaults and $10 billion in reserve deposits at Federal Reserve Banks. Their discount loan balance is virtually zero. And on a normal day, the Federal Reserve Bank of New York's trading desk buys $3 billion to $5 billion worth of bonds in temporary open market operations but does not intervene in the foreign exchange markets.

The days following September 11, 2001, were not normal. Airplanes were grounded, and the Wall Street area in lower Manhattan became inaccessible. The fact that civilian planes couldn't fly prevented the Fed from moving checks from one district to another. By Thursday, September 13, float had exploded, rising from its usual level of about $500 million to a whopping $50 billion. Meanwhile, people's inability to reach their offices in downtown New York had closed some very large banks. Though those banks could still receive payments from other banks, they couldn't make any payments to anyone. Funds were flowing into a few huge reserve accounts, but nothing was coming out. These banks were sucking up the lifeblood of the financial system, its liquidity, threatening to bring the payments system to a halt.

Fed officials saw the looming crisis and reacted immediately, providing reserves to anyone who needed them. A group of about 20 Fed employees slept in the Fed's building the night of September 11 so they could carry out open market operations the next morning. Then they moved to their contingency site across the Hudson River to continue their work.* On Thursday, September 13, and Friday, September 14, the Fed increased its securities holdings by between $70 and $80 billion, made $8 billion in discount loans, and bought almost $20 billion worth of euros. Adding these transactions to the nearly $50 billion in float, we see that over a two-day period the Fed increased banking system reserves by almost $150 billion.† This massive injection of reserves was quickly drained over the next week as the system got back to normal.‡ The banking system withstood the enormous shock, meeting its commitments and leaving people's finances more or less unaffected.

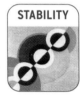

STABILITY

---

*The Fed has contingency sites in other places as well. Though most other central banks could not have done what the Fed did in September 2001, many of them can now.

†This is all described in detail in the Federal Reserve Bank of New York's annual report of Open Market Operations for 2001, available on the Bank's Web site at www.newyorkfed.org/markets/omo/omo2001.pdf.

‡The open market purchases were made as one-day repurchase agreements, in which the Fed exchanges reserves for securities from a bank one day with the promise that the transaction will be reversed the next day. The bank then returns the reserves, plus interest, in exchange for the securities. The euros were bought directly from the European Central Bank using a currency swap agreement of the type described in Chapter 9. These transactions were reversed almost immediately, as were the discount loans. As soon as the planes started flying again, float returned to normal levels.

foreign currency. In such cases, foreign exchange intervention is not truly under the central bank's control. Instead, the private sector decides when the purchases and sales are made and how large they are. That is essentially what the Bank of Thailand was doing in 1997, and when it started to run out of foreign currency reserves, the system collapsed.

The Deposit Expansion Multiplier

Central bank liabilities form the base on which the supplies of money and credit are built; that is why they are called the *monetary base*. The central bank controls the monetary base, causing it to expand and contract. But most of us don't focus much attention on the monetary base. Our primary interest is in the broader measures of money, M1 and M2 (defined in Chapter 2), which are multiples of the monetary base. This is the *money* we think of as available for transactions. What is the relationship between the central bank's liabilities and these broader measures of money? How do reserves become bank deposits? The answer is that the banking system makes them, in a process called multiple deposit creation.

Deposit Creation in a Single Bank

To see how deposits are created, let's start with an open market purchase in which the Federal Reserve buys $100,000 worth of securities from a bank called *First Bank*. While First Bank may have its own reasons for selling the securities, we are assuming that the Fed initiated the transaction. So if First Bank doesn't sell the securities, some other bank will.

The Fed's purchase leaves the bank's total assets unchanged, but it shifts $100,000 out of securities and into reserves, increasing reserves by the amount of the open market purchase. The impact on First Bank's balance sheet is shown in Figure 17.11. (It is similar to Figure 17.3).

What does First Bank do in response to this change in the composition of its assets? The bank's management must do something. After all, it just sold an interest-bearing U.S. Treasury bond to the Fed and received noninterest-bearing reserves in exchange. If it does nothing, the bank's revenue will fall, and so will its profits. With liabilities unchanged, the increase in First Bank's reserves doesn't affect the quantity of reserves the bank is required to hold, so it counts as an increase in *excess reserves*. Remember that banks hold reserves for two reasons: because regulators require them and because banks need them to conduct their daily business. But when reserves rise in response to the sale of a security, something profitable has to be done with the proceeds.

Figure 17.11 Change in *First Bank*'s Balance Sheet following the Fed's Purchase of a U.S. Treasury Bond

Assets		Liabilities
Reserves	+$100,000	
Securities	−$100,000	

Figure 17.12   Change in *First Bank*'s Balance Sheet following the Fed's Purchase of a U.S. Treasury Bond and Extension of a Loan

Assets		Liabilities
Reserves	+$100,000	OBI checking account +$100,000
Securities	−$100,000	
Loans	+$100,000	

Figure 17.13   Change in *First Bank*'s Balance Sheet following the Fed's Purchase of a U.S. Treasury Bond, Extension of a Loan, and Withdrawal by the Borrower

Assets		Liabilities
Reserves	$0	Checkable deposits $0
Securities	−$100,000	
Loans	+$100,000	

The most natural thing for a bank to do is to lend out the excess—and no more. To keep the example simple, assume that First Bank has just received a loan application from Office Builders Incorporated (OBI). OBI is seeking $100,000 to finance the continued construction of an office building. First Bank approves the loan and credits OBI's checking account with an additional $100,000. Figure 17.12 shows First Bank's balance sheet immediately after the loan is made.

OBI did not take out its $100,000 loan to leave it in First Bank's checking account. The company borrowed to pay suppliers and employees. So OBI's financial officer proceeds to write checks totaling $100,000. As First Bank makes good on OBI's checks, OBI's checking account balance falls, but so does First Bank's reserve account balance. When the entire $100,000 loan has been spent, First Bank's balance sheet looks like Figure 17.13.

In summary, following a $100,000 open market purchase of securities by the Fed, First Bank makes a loan equal to the amount of newly created excess reserves. That loan replaces the securities as an asset on First Bank's balance sheet.

Deposit Expansion in a System of Banks

First Bank's loan and OBI's expenditures can't be the end of the story because the suppliers and employees paid by OBI took their checks to the bank and deposited them.

As the checks made their way through the payments system, First Bank's reserves were transferred to the reserve accounts of the suppliers' and employees' banks. *Only the Fed (the central bank) can create and destroy the monetary base.* The nonbank public determines how much of it ends up as reserves in the banking system and how much is in currency; all the banks can do is move the reserves they have around among themselves. So, assuming cash holdings don't change following an open market purchase, the reserves created by the Fed must end up somewhere. Let's follow them to see where they go.

We'll start by making four assumptions that allow us to focus on the essential parts of the story. (1) Banks hold no excess reserves; (2) the reserve requirement is 10 percent of checking account deposits; (3) when the level of checking account deposits and loans changes, the quantity of currency held by the nonbank public does not; and (4) when a borrower writes a check, none of the recipients of the funds deposit them back in the bank that initially made the loan. Now, let's say that OBI uses the $100,000 loan to pay for steel girders from American Steel Co. American Steel deposits the $100,000 in its bank, Second Bank, which credits American's checking account. When OBI's check clears, Second Bank's reserve account at the Federal Reserve Bank is credited with $100,000. That's the transfer of reserves from First Bank. The result is shown in Figure 17.14.

The additional $100,000 in American Steel's checking account is costly for Second Bank to service. American Steel will want to receive interest on its idle balance as well as access to it for payments. And the reserves Second Bank just received don't pay any interest. In the same way that First Bank lent out its new reserves following the Fed's open market purchase, Second Bank will make a loan after American Steel has made its deposit. How large will the loan be? Since the reserve requirement is 10 percent, Second Bank must hold an additional $10,000 in reserves against the new $100,000 deposit. Individual banks can't make loans that exceed their excess reserves, so the largest loan Second Bank can make is $90,000—and that's what it does. (Remember, we're assuming banks hold no excess reserves.) If the borrower immediately uses the $90,000 loan, Second Bank's balance sheet will look like Figure 17.15.

This new loan, and the reserves that go with it, must go somewhere, too. Let's say that it is deposited in yet another bank, Third Bank, which makes a loan equal to 90 percent of the new deposit. The change in Third Bank's balance sheet is shown in Figure 17.16. (Recall, we're assuming that the owner of the checking account at Third Bank doesn't withdraw any cash.)

At this point, a $100,000 open market purchase has created $100,000 + $90,000 = $190,000 in new checking account deposits at Second Bank and Third Bank and

Figure 17.14 Change in *Second Bank*'s Balance Sheet following American Steel's Deposit

Assets		Liabilities
Reserves	+$100,000	American Steel's checking account +$100,000

Figure 17.15   Change in *Second Bank*'s Balance Sheet following a Deposit and Extension of a Loan

Assuming a 10 percent reserve requirement, banks hold no excess reserves, and there are no changes in currency holdings.

Assets		Liabilities
Reserves	+$10,000	American Steel's checking account
Loan	+$90,000	+$100,000

Figure 17.16   Change in *Third Bank's* Balance Sheet following a Deposit and Extension of a Loan

Assuming a 10 percent reserve requirement, banks hold no excess reserves, and there are no changes in currency holdings.

Assets		Liabilities
Reserves	+$9,000	Checking account +$90,000
Loan	+$81,000	

$100,000 + $90,000 + $81,000 = $271,000 in new combined loans at First Bank, Second Bank, and Third Bank. But the process doesn't stop there. The $81,000 loan from Third Bank is deposited into Fourth Bank, where it creates an additional $81,000 in checking account deposits. Fourth Bank then makes a loan that is 90 percent of $81,000, or $72,900, and the $72,900 is deposited. And so on, as shown in Figure 17.17.

Table 17.2 shows the consequences of a $100,000 open market purchase for the banking system as a whole. As the $100,000 in new reserves spreads through the banking system, it generates $1,000,000 in deposits and $1,000,000 in loans. With a 10 percent reserve requirement, each added dollar in reserves expands to $10 in deposits, increasing the quantity of money by a factor of 10.

With a bit of algebra, we can derive a formula for the deposit expansion multiplier—the increase in commercial bank deposits following a one-dollar open market purchase, (assuming there are no excess reserves in the banking system and no changes in the amount of currency held by the nonbank public).

There's an easy way and a hard way to figure out the size of the deposit expansion multiplier. Let's start with the easy way. Imagine that the entire banking system is

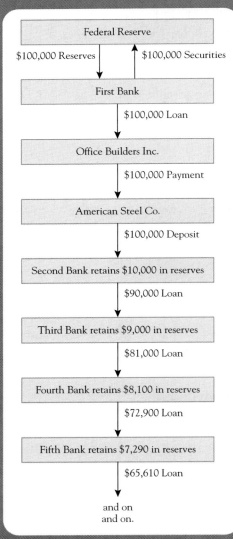

composed of a single bank—call it the Monopoly Bank. When the country's banking system is made up of just one bank, everyone has to use it. That means that any payment made from one person to another is just a transfer between two accounts in the Monopoly Bank. Because the managers of the Monopoly Bank know this, they don't need to worry about losing reserves when they make a loan.

So here's the question. For each dollar change in reserves arising from a transaction with the Fed, how much can the Monopoly Bank change its deposits? If we continue to assume that the Monopoly Bank holds no excess reserves and that there is no change in currency held by the nonbank public, then its level of reserves is just the **required** deposit **reserve ratio** r_D times its deposits. If required reserves are RR and deposits are D, the level of reserves can be expressed

$$RR = r_D D \qquad (1)$$

Any change in deposits creates a corresponding change in reserves, expressed as

$$\Delta RR = r_D \Delta D \qquad (2)$$

Now let's go back to the question we started with: What is the change in the level of deposits following a one-dollar change in reserves? From equation (2), we can see that the answer is

$$\Delta D = \frac{1}{r_D} \Delta RR \qquad (3)$$

So for every dollar increase in reserves, deposits increase by $(\frac{1}{r_D})$. This is the simple deposit expansion multiplier. If the reserve requirement is 10 percent, as it was in our example, then the simple deposit expansion multiplier equals $(\frac{1}{0.1}) = 10$, and a $100,000 open market purchase generates a $1,000,000 = 10 × $100,000 increase in the quantity of money. To see why this makes sense, note that if deposits rose by more than $1,000,000 following the addition of $100,000 in reserves, the banking system would violate the reserve requirement. And if deposits rose by less than 10 times the change in reserves, some banks would be holding excess reserves, which violates one of the assumptions we made at the outset.

The hard way to compute the simple deposit expansion multiplier is to look at Table 17.2 and add up the entries. Notice that starting with Third Bank, each entry in the column "Increase in Deposits" equals $(1-r_D)$ times the entry above it, where r_D is the reserve requirement (measured as a decimal). With a reserve requirement of 10 percent, $r_D = 0.10$, $(1-r_D) = 0.90$, so each entry is 0.90 times the one above it. For example, $90,000 equals 0.90 times $100,000; $81,000 equals 0.90 times $90,000. Thus, a one-dollar increase in reserves creates an increase in deposits equal to the sum of this series: $[1+ (1-r_D) + (1-r_D)^2 + (1-r_D)^3 + \ldots]$. Using a formula from Appendix 4, we can determine that this expression equals $(\frac{1}{r_D})$.

Table 17.2   Multiple Deposit Expansion following a $100,000 Open Market Purchase Assuming a 10% Reserve Requirement

Bank	Increase in Deposits	Increase in Loans	Increase in Reserves
First Bank	$ 0	$100,000	$ 0
Second Bank	$100,000	$90,000	$10,000
Third Bank	$90,000	$81,000	$9,000
Fourth Bank	$81,000	$72,900	$8,100
Fifth Bank	$72,900	$65,610	$7,290
Sixth Bank	$65,610	$59,049	$6,561
·	·	·	·
·	·	·	·
·	·	·	·
The Banking System	$1,000,000	$1,000,000	$100,000

Before we continue, it is important to emphasize that there is nothing magical about *increases* in reserves and deposit *expansion*. A *decrease* in reserves will generate a deposit *contraction* in exactly the same way. That is, a $100,000 open market sale, in which the Fed sells a security in exchange for reserves, will reduce the level of deposits. From equation (3), we see that with a 10 percent reserve requirement, the contraction in deposits is $10 \times \$100,000 = \$1,000,000$.

The Monetary Base and the Money Supply

We have made considerable headway in understanding the link between the central bank's balance sheet and the quantity of money in the economy. A change in reserves precipitates a significant change in the level of loans and checkable deposits in the banking system. But the simple deposit expansion multiplier is too simple. In deriving it, we ignored a few important details. First, we assumed that banks lent out the entirety of the reserves that were not required, leaving no excess reserves in the banking system. In fact, banks do hold some excess reserves, for other reasons besides supporting their deposit levels. Second, we ignored the fact that the nonbank public holds cash. As people's account balances rise, they have a tendency to hold more cash. From our discussion of the central bank's balance sheet, we know that when individuals change their cash holdings, they change the level of reserves in the banking system. Both these considerations affect the relationship among reserves, the monetary base, and the quantity of money in the economy. Let's look at the relationship in more detail.

Deposit Expansion with Excess Reserves and Cash Withdrawals

To see how important excess reserves and cash holdings are, we can go back through the deposit expansion story, this time taking them into account. Assume that banks want to hold excess reserves equal to 5 percent of checking account deposits and that the holder of a checking account withdraws 5 percent of a deposit in cash. Recall that the reserve requirement is 10 percent.

To understand the implication of these changes, let's go back to the example in the last section, in which the Fed purchased $100,000 worth of securities from First Bank (Figure 17.11), which proceeded to make a $100,000 loan to Office Builders Incorporated (Figure 17.12). OBI then used the $100,000 to purchase steel from American Steel, which withdrew the funds from First Bank and deposited them in a checking account in Second Bank. This brings us to the T-account in Figure 17.14. If American Steel takes some of the $100,000 in cash and Second Bank wishes to hold excess reserves, then the next loan cannot be $90,000.

Assuming that American Steel removes 5 percent of its new funds in cash, that leaves $95,000 in the checking account and $95,000 in Second Bank's reserve account. (Look back at Figure 17.9 to see the impact of a cash withdrawal on the banking system's balance sheet.) Since Second Bank wishes to hold excess reserves equal to 5 percent of deposits, it will want to keep reserves of 15 percent of $95,000, or $14,250. That means making a loan of only $80,750. Instead of Figure 17.15, Second Bank's balance sheet looks like Figure 17.18.

We can continue as before, following the proceeds of Second Bank's loan as it is deposited in Third Bank. Assuming that the depositor of the loan's proceeds wishes to hold 5 percent of the deposit in cash and that Third Bank wants to hold excess reserves equal to 5 percent of deposits, the increase in deposits will be $80,750 minus $4,037.50 equals $76,712.50, and Third Bank will make a loan of $65,205.63, keeping reserves of $11,506.87. Compare these numbers with the ones in Table 17.2 and you will see how much smaller the deposit expansion becomes if we take into account excess reserves and cash withdrawals.

In the last section, we derived the result that a one-dollar change in reserves created a change in deposits equal to one over the reserve requirement, or $(\frac{1}{r_D})$. So, for an r_D of 10 percent, a $1 change in reserves generated a $10 change in deposits. But now the analysis is more complicated and the deposit expansion is much smaller. The desire of banks to hold excess reserves and the desire of account holders to withdraw cash both reduce the impact of a given change in reserves on the total deposits in the system. The more excess reserves banks desire to hold, and the more cash the public withdraws, the smaller the impact. In fact, these two factors operate in the same way as an increase in the reserve requirement.

The Arithmetic of the Money Multiplier

To better understand the relationship between deposits and reserves, we can derive the *money multiplier*, which shows how

"God bless you, sir."

Figure 17.18   Change in *Second Bank*'s Balance Sheet following a Deposit and Extension of a Loan

Assuming excess reserves and cash holdings. Note: American Steel also has $5,000 in cash.

Assets		Liabilities
Required reserves	+$9,500	American Steel's checking account
Excess reserves	+$4,750	+$95,000
Loan	+$80,750	

the quantity of money (checking account deposits plus currency) is related to the monetary base (reserves in the banking system plus currency held by the nonbank public). Keep in mind that the monetary base is the quantity that the central bank can control.

If we label the quantity of money M and the monetary base MB, the money multiplier m is defined by the relationship

$$M = m \times MB. \tag{4}$$

To derive the money multiplier, we start with a few simple relationships: money equals currency (C) plus checkable deposits (D); the monetary base (MB) equals currency

YOUR FINANCIAL WORLD
Your Excess Reserves

Banks hold excess reserves to ensure that they have sufficient resources to meet unexpected withdrawals. Your bank guarantees that it will provide you with immediate access to the funds in your checking account, either by giving you cash or by honoring your check when it arrives. Sound business practice means having a little extra on hand, just in case people withdraw more money than usual. That is a cost of operating the bank.

In the same way that a bank holds excess reserves to insure itself against unexpectedly large withdrawals, individuals need to have an emergency fund to pay for unexpected expenses that can't be postponed. The appropriate size of the emergency fund varies from person to person; the exact amount depends on considerations like your tolerance for risk, the number of income earners in your household, the amount of your income, the deductible on your insurance policies, and the stability of your employment. Most financial planners recommend that individuals hold emergency funds equal to a minimum of three, and preferably six to nine, months' income in cash accounts. The accumulation of an emergency fund is the first step in any investment program. Unless you really like risk, make sure you have such a fund before you make any other investments. Like a bank, we all need excess reserves.

plus reserves in the banking system (R); and reserves equal required reserves (RR) plus excess reserves (ER). Writing these relationships as simple equations, we have

$$M = C + D, \quad \text{Money = Currency + Checkable deposits} \tag{5}$$

$$MB = C + R, \quad \text{Monetary base = Currency + Reserves} \tag{6}$$

$$R = RR + ER, \quad \text{Reserves = Required reserves + Excess reserves.} \tag{7}$$

RISK

These are just accounting definitions; the next step is to incorporate the behavior of banks and individuals. Starting with banks, we know that their holdings of required reserves depend on the required reserve ratio r_D. But what about excess reserves? In our earlier discussion, we assumed that banks hold excess reserves as a proportion of their deposits, and that *the amount of excess reserves a bank holds depends on the costs and benefits of holding them*. The cost of excess reserves is the interest on the loans that could be made with them, while the benefits have to do with safety should deposits be withdrawn suddenly. The higher the interest rate, the lower banks' excess reserves will be; the greater banks' concern over the possibility of deposit withdrawals, the higher their excess reserves will be.

Labeling the **excess reserve-to-deposit ratio** $\{ER/D\}$, we can rewrite the reserve equation (7) as

$$R = RR + ER \quad \text{Reserves = Required reserves + Excess reserves}$$
$$= r_D D + \{ER/D\}D \tag{8}$$
$$= (r_D + \{ER/D\})D.$$

That is, banks hold reserves as a proportion of their deposits.

Turning to the nonbank public, we need to take account of their currency holdings. Again, as in the preceding example, we assume that people hold currency as a fraction of their deposits. That is,

$$C = \{C/D\}D, \tag{9}$$

where $\{C/D\}$ is the **currency-to-deposit ratio**. The *decision of how much currency to hold depends on costs and benefits* in the same way as the decision to hold excess reserves. The cost of currency is the interest it would earn on deposit, while the benefit is its lower risk and greater liquidity. As interest rates rise, cash becomes less desirable. But if the riskiness of alternative holdings rises or liquidity falls, then cash becomes more desirable, and $\{C/D\}$ will rise.

Bringing all these elements together, we can rewrite the expression for the monetary base using the reserve and currency expressions. That gives us

$$MB = C + R \quad \text{Monetary base = Currency + Reserves}$$
$$= \{C/D\}D + (r_D + \{ER/D\})D \tag{10}$$
$$= (\{C/D\} + r_D + \{ER/D\})D.$$

We see now that the monetary base has three uses: required reserves, excess reserves, and cash in the hands of the nonbank public. But our interest is in the relationship between the quantity of money and the monetary base. To find this, we can solve equation (10) for the level of deposits.

$$D = \frac{1}{\{C/D\} + r_D + \{ER/D\}} \times MB \tag{11}$$

This expression tells us how much deposits change with a change in the monetary base. Notice that if we ignore excess reserves and cash withdrawals, so that $\{ER/D\}$ and $\{C/D\}$ both equal zero, we get the same result as in equation (3), that a change in deposits equals $(\frac{1}{r_D})$ times the change in the monetary base. For a reserve requirement of 10 percent, that meant that a $1 change in the monetary base increased deposits by $10. Adding the excess reserve-to-deposit and currency-to-deposit ratios that we used in the example after Figure 17.18, 5 percent each, this equation tells us that a $1 increase in the monetary base will increase deposits by [1/(0.10 + 0.05 + 0.05)] = 5.

Returning to the derivation of the money multiplier, we can take the expression for money and rewrite it as

$$M = C + D \qquad \text{Money = Currency + Checkable deposits}$$
$$= \{C/D\}D + D \tag{12}$$
$$= (\{C/D\} + 1)\, D.$$

Substituting D from equation (11) gives us the final answer:

$$M = \frac{\{C/D\} + 1}{\{C/D\} + r_D + \{ER/D\}} \times MB \tag{13}$$

Money = Money multiplier × Monetary base

This result is somewhat complicated, but it is worth studying. Equation (13) tells us that the quantity of money in the economy depends on four variables:

1. The monetary base, which is controlled by the central bank.
2. The reserve requirement that is imposed by regulators on banks that accept deposits.
3. The desire on the part of banks to hold excess reserves.
4. The demand for currency by the nonbank public.

To see how the quantity of money in the economy changes, we can look at the impact of each of these four elements. The first is the easiest. We know that if the monetary base increases, holding bank and public behavior constant, the quantity of money increases. Looking at the second and third elements—those factors affecting reserves—we see that an increase in either the reserve requirement or banks' excess reserve holdings decreases the money multiplier. So for a fixed level of the monetary base, an increase in either r_D or $\{ER/D\}$ reduces M.

Finally, there is the currency-to-deposit ratio. What happens when individuals increase their currency holdings at a fixed level of the monetary base? Since $\{C/D\}$ appears in both the numerator and the denominator of the money multiplier in equation (13), we can't immediately tell whether the change creates an expansion or a contraction. Fortunately, logic gives us the answer. When an individual withdraws cash from the bank, he or she increases currency in the hands of the public and decreases reserves, so the monetary base is unaffected. But the decline in reserves creates a multiple deposit contraction. (Remember, every dollar in reserves creates more than a dollar's worth of deposits, raising the quantity of money more than a dollar.) Because each extra dollar held in currency raises M by only a dollar, when reserves are converted to currency, the money supply contracts. Table 17.3 summarizes the effect of changes in the four components of the money supply.

A short numerical example illustrates the computation of the money multiplier.[16] In August 2004, banks held required reserves of $43.9 billion and excess reserves of $13.3 billion. Currency in the hands of the public was $686.2 billion, while deposit

[16]The example in the following paragraph is based on the Federal Reserve Board's H3 and H5 release that are neither seasonally adjusted nor adjusted for changes in reserve requirements. In addition, the excess reserve number used is not the official one, but includes "surplus vault cash," which serves the same economic purpose as conventionally calculated excess reserves.

accounts (demand deposits plus other checkable deposits) amounted to $645.2 billion. These amounts imply that the required reserve ratio r_D was (43.9/645.2) = 0.068; the excess reserve-to-deposit ratio {ER/D} was (13.3/645.2) = 0.021; and the currency-to-deposit ratio {C/D} was (686.2/645.2) = 1.064. Substituting these amounts into equation (13), we get the M1 money multiplier:

$$m = \frac{1+1.064}{0.068+0.021+1.064} = \frac{2.064}{1.153} = 1.79 \qquad (14)$$

As recently as 25 years ago, the currency-to-deposit ratio was much lower, so the multiplier was higher. In 1980, for example, currency was $105.1 billion, while deposits were $281.9 billion, so the ratio was 0.37. Replacing 1.064 with 0.37 in equation (14), we see that it raises the multiplier to 2.98.

TOOLS OF THE TRADE
The Irrelevance of Reserve Requirements

Since 1994, the Federal Reserve has allowed banks to use sophisticated computer software that dramatically reduces the required reserves they must hold. The software reclassifies a bank's liabilities by temporarily *sweeping* the balances in checking accounts (which are subject to reserve requirements) into savings accounts (which are not). The bank's customers don't even realize what is happening.

The details of deposit sweeping aren't all that complicated. The first step is to create a shadow savings account for each of the bank's checking accounts. While the checking account has unlimited monthly withdrawals, the shadow account allows only six withdrawals per month—any more, and the savings account becomes subject to a reserve requirement. The simplest version of the deposit-sweeping software shifts the balance in each checking account into a shadow savings account a minute or two prior to the close of business every Friday,* returning it on Monday morning, just after the bank opens. This procedure dramatically reduces the reserves a bank must hold for the simple reason that it has no checking account balances on its books when it closes on Friday, and Friday counts for three days in computing reserves. (Since all transactions made after the bank closes on Friday, including ATM cash withdrawals on Saturday and Sunday, are posted on Monday morning, the bank doesn't need to worry about customers trying to access their accounts over the weekend.) The bank sweeps its checking accounts every weekend,

reducing its required reserves by three-sevenths. More sophisticated software analyzes customers' deposit and withdrawal patterns to reduce the level of reserves even further.

At the same time that banks have been working to reduce the reserves they are required to hold, they have been increasing their use of automated teller machines to provide cash to customers. The cash that is loaded into ATMs at the close of business each day is classified as vault cash, which can be applied to meet reserve requirements. Thus, what is in the machines on Friday afternoon, when ATM cash levels are at their peak, counts for Friday, Saturday, and Sunday. So while banks have been reducing the level of reserves they are required to hold, they have been increasing the amount of cash in their vaults.†

Deposit sweeping and increased use of ATMs have had some interesting effects on both the structure of the Fed's balance sheet and the behavior of the monetary aggregates. Table 17.4 shows that from 1994 to 2004, required reserves

*In U.S. banking, the close of business occurs at 6:30 p.m. when the Federal Reserve's Fedwire transfer system closes.

†For more details, see Richard G. Anderson and Robert H. Rasche, "Retail Sweep Programs and Bank Reserves, 1994–1999," *Economic Review* of the Federal Reserve Bank of St. Louis, January/February 2001, pp. 51–72; Paul Bennett and Stavros Peristiani, "Are U.S. Reserve Requirements Binding?" *Economic Policy Review* of the Federal Reserve Bank of New York, May 2002; and Ann-Marie Meulendyke, *U.S. Monetary Policy & Financial Markets* (New York: Federal Reserve Bank of New York, 1998).

Table 17.3   Factors Affecting the Quantity of Money

Factor	Who Controls It	Change	Impact on M
Monetary base	Central bank	Increase	Increase
Required reserve-to-deposit ratio	Bank regulators	Increase	Decrease
Excess reserve-to-deposit ratio	Commercial banks	Increase	Decrease
Currency-to-deposit ratio	Nonbank public	Increase	Decrease

Table 17.4   Changes in Reserves and Money, 1994–2004
($ In Billions)

	Required Reserves	Vault Cash*	Commercial Bank Reserve Balances at the Fed	Monetary Base	Demand Deposits plus Other Checkable Deposits	M1	M2
January 1994	$60.6	$37.9	$27.8	$397.9	$810.5	$1,141.7	$3,490.6
August 2004	43.9	45.1	12.1	756.8	645.2	1,339.2	6,302.4

*Includes "surplus vault cash" not included in the official computation of either total reserves or excess reserves.

SOURCE: Data are from the Board of Governors of the Federal Reserve System, Release H3, and are neither seasonally adjusted nor adjusted for change in reserve requirements.

fell by one-quarter, from $60 billion to $44 billion and commercial bank reserve deposits at the Fed *shrank* by more than half, from $28 billion to $12 billion. While this was happening, the M1 measure of money was nearly constant, the monetary base *grew* by 90 percent, and M2 increased 80 percent.

The bottom line is that reserve requirements no longer have much of an impact on banks' behavior. In the jargon of the financial community, they do not *bind*. While a $1 increase in a checking account balance does obligate the bank to increase its reserve holdings by 10 cents—the *marginal reserve requirement*—virtually all banks hold more reserves than they need, so a change in the level of deposits has virtually no impact on their reserve position. The reserve requirements are still on the books in the United States, but a good case can be made for following the example of countries like Canada, where reserve requirements were eliminated in the early 1990s.

The Limits of the Central Bank's Ability to Control the Quantity of Money

At this point, we might discuss why the various factors affecting the quantity of money change over time. For example, market interest rates affect the cost of holding both excess reserves and currency. So as interest rates increase, we would expect to see both $\{ER/D\}$ and $\{C/D\}$ fall, increasing the money multiplier and the quantity of money. If these changes in the money multiplier were predictable, a tight link would exist between the monetary base and the quantity of money—a link the central bank might choose to exploit in its policymaking. While such a link made sense in a discussion of the U.S. economy in the 1930s (see *Applying the Concept: Monetary Policy in the 1930s*) and may still be important in developing countries, for countries with sophisticated

APPLYING THE CONCEPT
MONETARY POLICY IN THE 1930S

STABILITY

The notion of the money multiplier was originally developed to analyze U.S. monetary history from 1860 to 1960.* The 1930s were among the most turbulent years in that era. While we will never know what really caused the collapse of the U.S. economic and financial system during the Great Depression, we have learned some important lessons about how to run monetary policy. One of them is that central bankers need to look at both the monetary base and the money multiplier to figure out whether their policies are working.

In the early 1930s, Federal Reserve officials saw their balance sheet growing. From the beginning of 1931 to early 1934, currency plus reserves increased 14 percent, from $7 billion to $8 billion. That was more than double the annual growth rate during the 1920s boom. It really seemed as if the monetary base was growing very fast, and that was all that monetary policy could do. But what policymakers failed to understand was that, while their liabilities were growing, the money multiplier was plummeting. Beginning in late 1930, the ratio of M2 to the monetary base fell almost continuously, from $6\frac{1}{2}$ to $3\frac{1}{2}$. The wholesale collapse of banking and the financial system had increased the risk that bank deposits would not remain liquid, driving up both individual currency holdings and banks' excess reserve holdings. The result was that the quantity of money in the economy fell by roughly a quarter at the same time that the monetary base was growing! Figure 17.19 shows the pattern. In the top panel, you can see the monetary base increasing steadily while M2 collapses. The bottom panel displays the dramatic increase in the currency-to-deposit ratio that was largely responsible for the decline in the money multiplier that is also shown there.

*Almost everything you would ever want to know about this period in U.S. monetary history is contained in Milton Friedman and Anna J. Schwartz, *A Monetary History of the United States, 1867 to 1960* (Princeton, NJ: Princeton University Press, 1963).

continued on next page

continued from previous page

The conclusion is that the central bank needs to worry not just about its own balance sheet, but about the ability of the financial system to transform reserves into deposits. Failure of either one is disastrous.

Figure 17.19   Components of Money, 1928–1936

Data show that during the Great Depression, from mid-1929 to early 1934 the monetary base was growing while M2 was collapsing. The reason was that the money multiplier was falling because the currency/deposit ratio rose sharply as a result of bank panics.

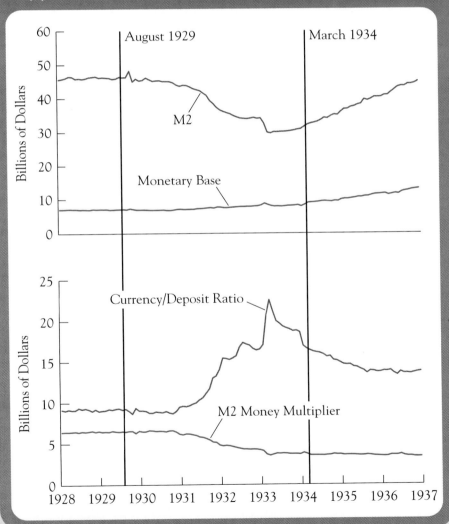

SOURCE: *Data compiled from Milton Friedman and Anna J. Schwartz,* A Monetary History of the United States. *(Princeton, NJ: Princeton University Press, 1963).*

San Francisco Chronicle

by Sam Zuckerman

July 16, 2003

The Bush administration forecast record budget deficits for the next two years plus shortfalls lasting through 2008, stoking fears that government red ink could raise interest rates and damage the economy.

The White House Office of Management and Budget projected that this year's deficit will reach $455 billion, $151 billion more than previously estimated.

The deteriorating fiscal picture stems from a weak economy that reduces the government's tax revenue, a costly war in Iraq, and the administration's tax cut package recently approved by Congress, officials said.

In 2004, the White House said, the budget gap will rise to $475 billion, $168 billion more than expected, before starting to shrink again as the pace of economic growth picks up.

Only a few years ago, the government ran surpluses amounting to hundreds of billions of dollars annually.

The latest deficit projections add fuel to a simmering debate over the Bush administration's economic program.

Administration critics warn that massive government borrowing needed to finance budget shortfalls would suck up capital and cause consumer and business interest rates to rise. Higher rates in turn could act as a drag that slows business and consumer spending and lowers economic growth.

"Although large in nominal terms and a legitimate subject of concern, these deficits are manageable if we continue pro-growth economic policies and exercise serious spending discipline," the White House argued in budget documents released Tuesday.

In an appearance before a congressional committee Tuesday, Federal Reserve Chairman Alan Greenspan said that rising deficits could push interest rates higher and slow economic growth. He urged Congress to reduce deficits by controlling spending.

In absolute terms, the deficits projected for 2003 and 2004 are the largest in history. But they aren't the biggest when measured as a percentage of the economy.

Shortfalls this year and next will equal between 4 and 5 percent of the nation's total production of goods and services. During the Reagan administration two decades ago, the deficit got as high as 6 percent of economic output.

Most economists believe that deficits can be helpful when business conditions are poor. The theory is that when business and consumer spending is weak, higher outlays by government can take up some of the slack.

"They lift aggregate demand and help the economy grow at a faster pace," said Christopher Wiegand, an economist with financial services giant Citigroup.

But problems arise when deficits continue year in and year out, through good times as well as bad. When the nation is prosperous, and households and businesses are clamoring for loans, the government can become an unwelcome competitor for credit.

Economists at the Federal Reserve recently estimated that a $100 billion increase in projected deficits would prompt long-term interest rates, such as mortgages, to rise by roughly one-quarter percentage point.

In its latest projection, the Bush administration estimated that deficits would fall sharply beginning in 2005, dropping to $213 billion in 2007 and then rising slightly in 2008. The smaller deficits will reflect faster economic growth and a winding down of Iraq war costs, officials said.

"People have become desensitized to big deficits because in the 1980s there were a lot of false claims about how ruinous they were going to be," said Stephen Moore, president of the Club for Growth, a conservative advocacy group.

Still, deficits could rise higher on the political radar screen if the economy remains lackluster and jobs stay hard to find.

"It's a risk for Bush to be running these big deficits," Moore said. "They keep on going up and up."

LESSONS OF THE ARTICLE

By increasing the supply of bonds, increased government borrowing drives down the price of bonds, raising interest rates. Federal Reserve Board Chairman Greenspan is concerned about this trend for two reasons. First, it makes the job of stabilizing interest rates more difficult. Second, it puts pressure on the Fed to purchase the bonds issued by the government. When the central bank purchases government-issued bonds, its action increases the monetary base and expands the quantity of money in the economy, which can eventually lead to inflation.

financial systems it no longer is.[17] In places like the United States, Europe, and Japan, the link between the central bank's balance sheet and the quantity of money circulating in the economy has become too weak and unpredictable to be exploited for policy purposes. The Fed, the ECB, and the Bank of Japan have very limited control over the quantity of money in their currency areas. So the money multiplier is really little more than an accounting mechanism that we can use to figure out the reasons for changes in M1 or M2 after they have already happened. To see the point, take a look at Figure 17.20, which shows U.S. monetary history over the last few decades.

For 20 years, the Federal Reserve was required to publish target ranges for the growth rate of the monetary aggregates. They were included in the Fed's biannual *Monetary Policy Report to Congress*, which contained target ranges for M2 and M3 over the coming year. Twice a year, we could count on getting a look at the FOMC's targets for money growth—until the July 2000 issue. Buried in a footnote of that report was this announcement: "At its June meeting, the FOMC did not establish ranges for growth of money and debt in 2000 and 2001. The legal requirement to establish and to announce such ranges had expired, and . . . for many years [they] have not provided useful benchmarks for the conduct of monetary policy."[18] While the FOMC surely controls the monetary base, committee members have given up on short-run control of the monetary aggregates.

In short, the theory of the money multiplier really isn't very useful—at least not in the U.S. Control of the monetary base doesn't give the Fed control of the money aggregates over the periods of two or three years that are important for policymaking. The problem is that the money multiplier is just too variable; you can see it in the data. Figure 17.20 plots the ratio of the M1 and M2 to the monetary base from 1980 to 2004. The results are striking. The M1 money multiplier—the one that is almost exactly analogous to our formula in equation (13)—was reasonably stable during the 1980s but then fell steadily over the next decade. From 1994 to 2004, the M1 multiplier fell from almost 3 to 1.8. Tools of the Trade describes one of the reasons: the change that allowed banks to classify their deposits in a way that avoids reserve requirements.

If the problem were confined to M1, policymakers could turn to controlling M2. But as Figure 17.20 shows, the M2 multiplier is volatile as well. It has followed roughly the same pattern as the M1 multiplier, falling from 12 at the end of the 1980s to 8 by the mid-90s. Further investigation reveals that even this amount of stability is misleading, since the definition of M2 changed several times over the period.

The conclusion is clear: The relationship between the monetary base and the quantity of money is *not* something that a central bank in a large industrialized economy can exploit for short-run policy purposes. Instead, as we will discuss in detail in Chapter 20, modern central banks keep an eye on trends in money growth, since that is what ultimately determines inflation. For short-run policy, however, interest rates have become the monetary policy tool of choice. That is the subject of the next chapter.

---

[17]A recent example proves the point. In the summer of 2003, the central bank of China raised the reserve requirement on bank deposits by one percentage point from 6 to 7 percent. Press reports suggested that policy officials did this in an effort to slow the growth of money and credit in the Chinese economy. While it might be difficult to predict the impact of such a move in the United States, Japan, or Germany, in China the effects may be more predictable.

[18]See footnote 2 in Section 1 of the report, available on the Federal Reserve Board's Web site at http://www.federalreserve.gov/boarddocs/hh/2000/July/ReportSection1.htm.

Figure 17.20 The M1 and M2 Multipliers, 1980–2004

M1 Money Multiplier

A.

M2 Money Multiplier

B.

SOURCE: *Board of Governors of the Federal Reserve System.*

Terms

central bank's balance sheet, 427
currency-to-deposit ratio, 448
deposit expansion multiplier, 443
discount loans, 429
excess reserves, 430
excess reserve-to-deposit ratio, 448
float, 429
foreign exchange intervention, 428
foreign exchange reserves, 428
high-powered money, 432

monetary base, 432
multiple deposit creation, 440
open market operations, 433
open market purchase, 433
open market sale, 434
required reserve ratio, 444
required reserves, 430
reserves, 430
T-account, 433
vault cash, 430

Chapter Lessons

1. The central bank uses its balance sheet to control the quantity of money and credit in the economy.

   a. The central bank holds assets and liabilities to meet its responsibilities as the government's bank and the bankers' bank.

   b. Central bank assets include securities, foreign exchange reserves, and loans.

   c. Central bank liabilities include currency, the government's account, and reserves.

   d. Reserves equal commercial bank account balances at the central bank plus vault cash.

   e. The monetary base, also called high-powered money, is the sum of currency and reserves, the two primary liabilities of the central bank.

2. The central bank controls the size of its balance sheet.

   a. The central bank can increase the size of its balance sheet, raising reserve liabilities and expanding the monetary base, through

      i. Open market purchases of domestic securities.

      ii. The purchase of foreign exchange reserves (in the form of bonds issued by a foreign government).

      iii. The extension of a loan to a commercial bank.

   b. The central bank can decrease the size of its balance sheet, lowering reserve liabilities and reducing the monetary base, through the sale of domestic or foreign securities.

   c. The public's cash withdrawals from banks shift the central bank's liabilities from reserves to currency and shrink the size of the banking system balance sheet.

3. Bank reserves are transformed into checkable deposits through multiple deposit creation. In the simplest case, this process is limited by the reserve requirement.

   a. When a bank's reserves increase, the bank makes a loan that becomes a deposit at a second bank.

www.mhhe.com/cecchetti1e

b. The second bank then makes another loan, but the amount of the loan is limited by the reserve requirement.

c. This process continues until deposits have increased by a multiple that is equal to one over the reserve requirement.

4. The money multiplier links the monetary base to the quantity of money in the economy.

a. The size of the money multiplier depends on

  i. The reserve requirement.

  ii. Banks' desire to hold excess reserves.

  iii. The public's desire to hold currency.

b. While the central bank controls the level of the monetary base, it cannot control the money multiplier.

c. Practices such as deposit sweeping have weakened the connection between the central bank's balance sheet and the quantity of money.

Problems

1. In an effort to diversify, the Central Bank of China has decided to exchange some of its dollar reserves for euros. Follow the impact of this move on the U.S. banking system's balance sheet, the Federal Reserve's balance sheet, and the European Central Bank's balance sheet. What is the impact on the U.S. and Chinese monetary bases?

2. The Fed buys $100,000 worth of U.S. Treasury bonds in an open market purchase. Assume that the reserve requirement is 10 percent, the banking system as a whole holds no excess reserves, and that the nonbank public is holding all the currency it wants. Show the impact of this injection of reserves, assuming that some banks in the system choose to purchase securities rather than to make loans with the increase in reserves.

3. Follow the impact of a $100 cash withdrawal through the entire banking system, assuming that the reserve requirement is 10 percent and that banks have no desire to hold excess reserves.

4. Compute the impact on the money multiplier of an increase in desired currency holdings from 10 percent to 15 percent of deposits when the reserve requirement is 10 percent of deposits and banks' desired excess reserves are 3 percent of deposits.

5. Consider an open market purchase by the Fed of $3 billion of Treasury bonds. Show the impact of the purchase on the bank from which the Fed bought the securities. Then, using the assumptions in problem 4, compute the impact on M1.

6. Recall that the definition of M2 is currency plus demand deposits plus time deposits. Assume that there is no reserve requirement on time deposits, but that individuals hold time deposits in a constant ratio to demand deposits called the time-deposit-to-demand-deposit ratio, or $\{TD/D\}$. Derive the M2 money multiplier and discuss its properties.

7. From the Web site of either the Federal Reserve Board or the Federal Reserve Bank of St. Louis, collect monthly data on the monetary base, M1, and M2 over

the past decade, seasonally adjusted and adjusted for changes in the reserve requirement. Compute the M1 and M2 money multipliers and plot them. Discuss the patterns you find.

8. List the factors that you suspect may have caused the Federal Reserve to lose control of the quantity of money in the economy. Explain your reasoning.

9. In fall 1999, people in the financial community were making their final plans for the beginning of the year 2000. Everyone was concerned about the Y2K problem—the fear that old computers would stop working because they used only 2 digits to record the year, so the year 2000 would be represented as "00" (the same as 1900). The primary concern was that the public would panic and remove significant amounts of cash from banks. What would you expect banks to do in anticipation of this problem? What was the appropriate response by the Fed? Can you figure out from the Fed's balance sheet at the time what was done?

10. The U.S. Treasury maintains accounts at commercial banks. What would be the consequences if the Treasury shifted funds from one of those banks to the Fed?

11. Suppose the Fed buys $1 billion in Japanese yen, paying in dollars. What is the impact on the monetary base? What would the Fed need to do to keep the monetary base from changing following the purchase?

12. Suppose the Fed purchases $1 billion in securities from First Bank. What is the impact on First Bank's balance sheet?

13. The Fed occasionally considers paying interest on reserves, following the example of central banks in a number of other countries. What impact would such a change have on excess reserve holdings and the money multiplier?

14. In 1937, the Fed's policymakers noticed the high level of excess reserves in the banking system and became concerned about the potential for the banking system to expand the quantity of money and spark inflation. As a result, the Fed raised the reserve requirement. Why were banks holding excess reserves in 1937? What do you think the banking system's response was to the increase in required reserves? What do you think happened to the quantity of money outstanding?

15. Footnote 17 mentions that the central bank of China raised the reserve requirement on deposits in the summer of 2003. Describe the likely impact of this action on the quantity of money in the Chinese economy.

www.mhhe.com/cecchettile

Chapter 18

Monetary Policy: Using Interest Rates to Stabilize the Domestic Economy

Central bankers have a long list of goals and a short list of tools they can use to achieve them. They are supposed to stabilize prices, output, the financial system, exchange rates, and interest rates, yet the only real power they have comes from their control over their own balance sheet and their monopoly on the supply of currency and reserves. To achieve their goals, policymakers can change the size of the monetary base by buying and selling assets—primarily government securities—and by making loans to banks. But as we saw at the end of the last chapter, modern central bankers cannot use these tools to control the *quantity* of money. Instead, they use them to control *interest rates*—both the market rate for reserves and the rate they charge for discount loans. These are the primary tools of monetary policy.

Interest rates play a central role in all of our lives. They are the cost of borrowing for those of us who need resources and the reward for lending to those of us with savings. Higher interest rates tend to restrict the growth of credit, making it harder for businesses to get financing and for individuals to find or keep jobs. Little wonder that everyone is preoccupied with interest rates and that the business press is constantly speculating about whether the Federal Open Market Committee will change its target.

In 2001, the FOMC lowered the target federal funds rate 11 times, once at each of its regularly scheduled meetings and three times between meetings. The committee cut the target for the *federal funds rate*, the rate at which banks lend each other reserves overnight, from $6\frac{1}{2}$ percent to $1\frac{3}{4}$ percent. This aggressive easing of interest rates was a direct consequence of policymakers' belief that the economy was faltering badly and that quick, forceful action was needed. GDP fell during the first three quarters of 2001; over the course of the year, the unemployment rate rose from 4 to 5.8 percent. In contrast, inflation continued at around $2\frac{1}{2}$ percent or less. Thus, the Fed focused on stabilizing growth; if inflation became a problem, the FOMC would deal with it later. In the end, GDP fell less than 1 percent, and the recession lasted only eight months. By the close of 2001, U.S. output was rising again. Growth was modest and the unemployment rate continued to rise gradually for another year and a half, but clearly conditions could have been much worse.

This episode is just one example of successful monetary policy stabilization. The Federal Reserve can also claim some of the credit for the low inflation and high growth the United States experienced during the 1990s. Around the world, many other industrialized and emerging-markets countries have seen impressive improvements in economic performance as inflation fell and growth rose. Much of the credit must go to monetary policymakers who were given both the tools and the support to do their jobs. Through changes in institutional structure, politicians gave central bankers a set of clear objectives and then left them alone.

We have emphasized on several occasions that we rely on the central bank to ensure the stability of the financial system when it is under stress. In Chapter 17, we saw that the Federal Reserve reacted to the terrorist attacks of September 11, 2001, by temporarily flooding the banking system with reserves. Episodes like that one underscore the importance of both the central bank's preparation for crises and its need for flexibility in responding to them. The extensive preparations for the century date change on January 1, 2000, provide another example of the importance of institutional design in ensuring that the financial system will function well. In anticipation of large increases in both the public's demand for currency and banks' demand for reserves, the Fed took two steps. It printed a large quantity of cash (more than would fit into its own vaults) and changed the rules governing lending. Rather than lend only when banks had no alternative source of funds, and at a low rate, the Fed lent to banks that were known to be in good shape, at a rate above the target federal funds rate. This new policy, which was based on a model that had been used in Europe for many years, worked so well that in 2002 the Fed abandoned the old approach.

We know, then, that policymakers set interest rates to meet their stabilization objectives. The purpose of this chapter is to study three links: the link from the central bank's balance sheet to its policy tools; the link from the policy tools to the policymakers' objectives; and the link from monetary policy to the real economy. We'll begin with the operational details that define the tools central bankers have at their disposal. Then we'll turn to a discussion of the relationship between those tools and the policymakers' objectives to explain why modern monetary policy is equivalent to interest-rate policy. Finally, we'll look at how the target interest rate is chosen. To keep the discussion manageable, we'll focus on monetary policy in large economies like the United States and the euro area. Chapter 19 will discuss exchange rates and issues that are important to central banks in small, open economies.

The Federal Reserve's Monetary Policy Toolbox

Like all central banks, the Federal Reserve can, if policymakers wish, control the quantity of reserves that commercial banks hold. Reserves are injected into the banking system through an increase in the size of the Fed's balance sheet, either because of a decision by the Fed to buy securities or because of a bank's decision to borrow from the Fed. Besides the quantity of reserves, the central bank can control either the size of the monetary base or the price of its components. Like most modern central banks, the Fed has chosen to focus its attention on prices. The two prices it concentrates on are the interest rate at which banks borrow and lend reserves overnight and the interest rate at which banks can borrow reserves from the Fed.

In examining day-to-day monetary policy, understanding the institutional structure of the central bank and financial markets is essential. What is true in one country may or may not be true elsewhere. Since cataloging the structure and tools of monetary policy around the world is too big a task, we will begin with the Federal Reserve and financial markets in the United States. In the next section, we will look at the ECB's operating procedures to see how they differ.

The Federal Reserve has three monetary policy tools, also known as *monetary policy instruments*.

1. The **target federal funds rate**, the interest rate at which banks make overnight loans to each other.
2. The **discount rate**, the interest rate the Fed charges on the loans it makes to banks.
3. The **reserve requirement**, the level of balances a bank is required to hold either as vault cash on deposit or at a Federal Reserve Bank.

We will examine each of these tools in detail. As we do, keep in mind that each has multiple purposes. That is, these tools are related to several of the central bank's functions and objectives.

The Target Federal Funds Rate and Open Market Operations

The target federal funds rate is the Federal Open Market Committee's primary policy instrument. Financial market participants are constantly speculating about movements in this rate. FOMC meetings always end with a decision on the target level, and the statement released after the meeting begins with an announcement of that decision. To a large extent, this *is* U.S. monetary policy. But because the federal funds rate is the rate at which banks lend reserves to each other overnight, it is determined in the market, not controlled by the Fed. With this qualification in mind, we will distinguish between the *target* federal funds rate set by the FOMC and the market federal funds rate, at which transactions between banks take place.[1]

The name *federal funds* comes from the fact that the funds banks trade are their deposit balances at Federal Reserve Banks. On any given day, banks target the level of reserves they would like to hold at the close of business. But as the day goes by, the normal flow of business may leave them with more or less reserves than they want to hold. This discrepancy between actual and desired reserves gives rise to a market for reserves, with some banks lending out their excess funds and others borrowing to cover a shortfall. Without this market, banks would need to hold substantial quantities of excess reserves as insurance against shortfalls. While transactions are often made through brokers (third parties who bring buyers and sellers together), they are all bilateral agreements between two banks. Since the loans are unsecured—there is no collateral to fall back on in the event of nonpayment—the borrowing bank must be creditworthy in the eyes of the lending bank, or the loan cannot be made.

MARKETS

If the Fed wanted to, it could force the market federal funds rate to equal the target rate all the time by participating directly in the market for overnight reserves, both as a borrower and as a lender. But as a lender, the Fed would need to make unsecured loans to commercial banks. And as a borrower, the Fed would in effect be paying interest on excess reserves. For several reasons the Fed has never done either of these. First, the Fed does not want the credit risk that comes with uncollateralized lending. Second, policymakers believe that the federal funds market provides valuable information about the health of specific banks. When a bank cannot get an overnight loan from any other bank, it's the first sign of trouble. As for paying interest on reserves, the Fed has stated that it will do so only at the request of Congress. Paying interest on reserves would reduce the income the Fed returns to the U.S. Treasury, shrinking the U.S. government's revenue. The more interest the Fed paid on reserves, the smaller its contribution to the U.S. Treasury would be, and the smaller the federal government's surplus (or the larger its deficit).

The Fed's approach places it in a somewhat awkward position. It targets an interest rate at the same time that it wants to allow an interbank lending market to flourish. Instead of adopting a strategy that would fix the interest rate at the target direct-

---

[1]The market federal funds rate is also referred to as the effective federal funds rate. Published daily by the Fed, it is the average of the interest rates on market transactions in federal funds, weighted by the size of the transactions.

ly, the Fed chooses to control the federal funds rate by manipulating the quantity of reserves. Using *open market operations,* the Fed adjusts the supply of reserves, with the goal of keeping the market federal funds rate close to the target rate. That is, the Fed buys or sells securities to add or drain reserves as required to meet the expected demand for reserves at the target rate.

We can use a standard supply-and-demand diagram to analyze the market in which banks borrow and lend reserves. The demand curve for reserves is downward sloping. Holding noninterest-bearing reserves is more costly at higher interest rates than at lower rates. Because keeping the market federal funds rate at the target rate means supplying what is demanded at that rate, the supply curve is horizontal (see Figure 18.1). Changing the target rate is straightforward: All it requires is a shift in the supply curve to the new target level.

Day-to-day control of the supply of federal funds is the job of the Open Market Trading Desk at the Federal Reserve Bank of New York. While the details are complicated, the fundamentals are not. Every morning, the members of the open market staff forecast the banking system's demand for reserves. Then they supply the quantity of reserves that will keep the market federal funds rate close to target. Their control is not precise because the Fed usually enters the market only once during the day, completing its open market operations by 10:00 a.m. Banks, in contrast, transfer funds into and out of their reserve accounts until 6:30 p.m. They may not know whether they will need to borrow or lend in the federal funds market until late afternoon. Because the Fed's morning forecast may turn out to be wrong, and since it is difficult to adjust the supply of reserves later in the day, some transactions may occur far above or below the target rate.

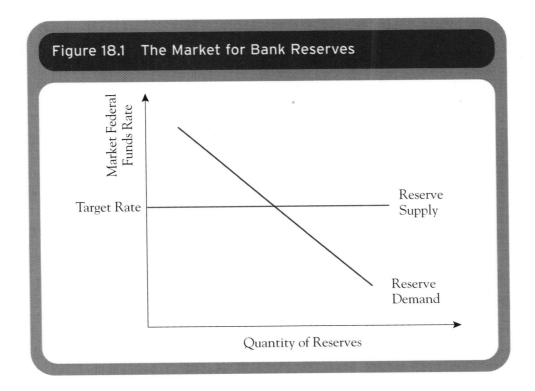

Figure 18.1   The Market for Bank Reserves

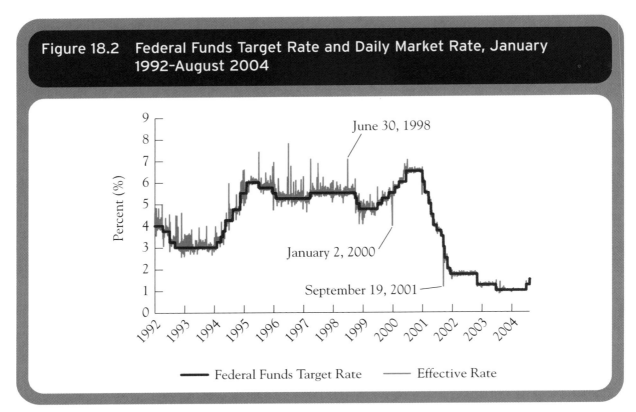

Figure 18.2 Federal Funds Target Rate and Daily Market Rate, January 1992–August 2004

SOURCE: *Board of Governors of the Federal Reserve.*

Let's take a moment to compare the FOMC's target rate with the market rate over the last few years, to see how well the Fed's staff has met its objective. Figure 18.2 plots both the target federal funds rate (the dark line that moves stepwise) and the market federal funds rate (the lighter line that jumps around) beginning in 1992. As you can see, the market interest rate was close to the target on most days. Every so often, though, the system seemed to go haywire, creating occasional spikes in the market interest rate. As information systems have improved, both within banks and at the Fed, there have been fewer of these surprises, and deviations from the target rate have become very small.[2] Changes made to the discount-lending program in 2002 appear to have stabilized the market rate even further.

Discount Lending, the Lender of Last Resort, and Crisis Management

When a central bank extends credit to commercial banks, its balance sheet changes. So by controlling the quantity of loans it makes, a central bank can control the size of reserves, the size of the monetary base, and ultimately interest rates. While the Fed could take this approach (and did for the first decade of its existence in the early 20th

---

[2]The easiest way to see this trend is to look at the daily standard deviation of the federal funds rate, available on the Federal Reserve Bank of New York Web site. While there once were days on which the standard deviation was near 1 percentage point, now it almost never rises higher than 0.3 percentage point.

YOUR FINANCIAL WORLD
What the Federal Funds Rate Means to You

On learning that the FOMC controls the federal funds rate, most people's reaction is, "I'm not a bank and I don't borrow overnight, so why should I care?" What they do care about is the interest rate they pay on student loans, or auto loans, or home mortgages. But since all interest rates move together, people who care about long-term interest rates must care about short-term interest rates.

Remember from our discussion of the term structure of interest rates in Chapter 7 that the long-term interest rate is the average of expected future short-term interest rates. Thus, the rate charged on a 30-year, fixed-rate home mortgage is the average of the expected one-year rates for the next 30 years. Those one-year interest rates, in turn, are averages of the expected one-day interest rates for the next 365 days. Unless everyone

expects the FOMC to keep interest rates at the same level for a very long time, the interest rates you care about will move—by less than the target federal funds rate, but they will move.

To see how important this is, we can look at the example of a 30-year mortgage. In December 2000, with the federal funds target at $6\frac{1}{2}$, the mortgage interest rate was $7\frac{1}{2}$, and the monthly payment on a $100,000 loan was $682. By November 2002, the FOMC had cut the federal funds rate to $1\frac{1}{4}$ percent, and the interest rate on a 30-year fixed rate mortgage had fallen to $5\frac{3}{4}$ percent. At the lower interest rate, the monthly payment on a $100,000 mortgage was $574—that's more than $100 a month lower! The lower interest rates mean that someone who could pay $700 a month would be able to afford to borrow $120,000.

century), today it does not. Lending by Federal Reserve Banks to commercial banks, called **discount lending**, is not an important part of the Fed's day-to-day monetary policy. During a normal week, the entire Federal Reserve System makes only a few hundred million dollars in loans. Instead of a way to control reserves, today discount lending is the Fed's primary tool for ensuring short-term financial stability, eliminating bank panics, and preventing the sudden collapse of institutions that are experiencing financial difficulties. When there is a crisis, discount lending explodes. On Wednesday, September 12, 2001, the first business day after the collapse of the World Trade Center, banks borrowed $45.5 billion from the Fed! In the preceding week, borrowing had averaged just over $100 million per day.

STABILITY

Recall that crises were the primary impetus for the creation of the Federal Reserve in the first place. The idea was that some central government authority should be capable of providing funds to sound banks to keep them from failing during financial panics. The knowledge that the central bank would not allow solvent banks to become illiquid—that depositors could always get their funds—became one of the important safeguards against bank runs. The central bank, then, is the **lender of last resort**, making loans to banks when no one else will or can. But a bank must show that it is sound to get a loan in a crisis. This means having assets that the central bank is willing to take as collateral, since the central bank does not make uncollateralized loans. A bank that does not have assets it can use as collateral for a discount loan is a bank that should probably fail.

For most of its history, the Federal Reserve has lent reserves to banks at a rate below the target federal funds rate. Borrowing from the Fed was cheaper than borrowing from another bank. Even so, no one borrowed, because the Fed required banks to exhaust all other sources of funding before they applied for a loan. Moreover, banks that used discount loans regularly faced the possibility of being denied loans in the future. Needless to say, these rules created quite a disincentive to borrow from the

Fed. Almost everyone was willing to pay high rates in the marketplace rather than ask the Fed for a loan; only banks with nowhere else to go went to the Fed. This creates problems like the one on June 30, 1998, when some banks paid 25 percentage points above the rate the Fed was charging to borrow funds (see Tools of the Trade box). By severely discouraging banks from borrowing, the Fed destabilized the interbank mar-

TOOLS OF THE TRADE
The Mechanics of Open Market Operations

The Markets Group works on the ninth floor of the Federal Reserve Bank of New York building, which takes up an entire city block in downtown Manhattan. These people are the eyes and ears of the Federal Reserve, listening to and watching the financial markets nearly 24 hours a day. Security is high, so you can't just walk in. If you could, you would see members of the group walking around wearing blue fleece jackets marked "FRBNY Markets." When the trading floor was renovated in the late 1990s, the old ventilation system posed a difficult challenge for the architects. They had a hard time keeping the newly designed floor at a comfortable temperature. Rather than go to the expense of trying to fix the building's heating system, the people in charge decided to give everyone a jacket.

Some of the people wearing jackets are the staff of the **Open Market Trading Desk**. Their job is to adjust the securities holdings in what is called the **System Open Market Account (SOMA)**, in order to stabilize the market federal funds rate at the target level. To do so, they manage the level of reserves in the banking system through both *permanent* and *temporary operations*. When the Fed forecasts a sustained increase in the demand for the monetary base, the manager directs the staff to make *outright* purchases in the U.S. Treasury securities market, buying bonds the Fed will hold until maturity.* These permanent operations take place as needed—in recent years, about once a week—and are announced publicly on the same day. Because the Fed's permanent securities holdings are almost always less than what it needs to provide to meet demand at the target federal funds rate, the Fed provides additional reserves through temporary operations. (In the parlance of the financial markets, the Fed always leaves itself short.)

Temporary operations occur almost every day and are accomplished through **repurchase agreements**, or **repos**. (Take a look back at Chapter 12 for a detailed explanation of repos.) The Fed buys a security in exchange for reserves, and the seller agrees to repurchase the security in a day or two. In other words, a repo is the exchange of a security for reserves combined with an agreement to undo the transaction on a specific future date. You may find it easier to think of it as a collateralized loan. While the term, or maturity, of a repo can be anywhere from one to 90 days, the Fed engages mainly in short-term repos of a day or two. In a **matched-sale purchase**, or **reverse repo**, the Fed sells the security in exchange for reserves, agreeing to buy it back in a day or two. Reverse repos are less common than repos.

Deciding what level of reserves to supply to the market each day is a complicated and difficult business requiring an accurate forecast of the demand and supply for reserves that day. The main inputs into the computation are an estimate of the size of the Fed's own balance sheet—the supply—and a forecast of how much the banks will need—the demand. Between 8:30 and 9:00 each morning, members of the open market staff, together with people at the Federal Reserve Board in Washington, D.C., collect information needed to estimate the banking system's demand for reserves. That means figuring out the level of float in the system, as well as the expected size of the balance in the U.S. Treasury's account at the end of the day.† (Remember that when the Treasury makes a deposit into its account at the Fed, it reduces bank reserves.) To assess market conditions, Fed staff members also speak with reserve managers at commercial banks and with dealers who buy and sell federal funds.

*The Fed does participate in U.S. Treasury auctions to replace only those bills, notes, and bonds that are maturing. The Federal Reserve Act requires that all net additions to the Fed's holdings must be made through purchases in the secondary market.

†It may surprise you to learn that the U.S. government doesn't know at 9:00 a.m. what its account balance will be at 5:00 p.m. But it doesn't, and that creates a problem for the Fed.

ket for reserves. Eventually, officials decided to make the process more rational. In 2002, they instituted the discount lending procedures that are in place today.

In addition to providing a mechanism for stabilizing the financial system, the current discount lending procedures also help the Fed meet its interest-rate stability objective. To see how this all works, we need to look at the details of how lending

By 9:15, a plan has been made for the day's temporary open market operation. At 9:20, everyone involved assembles for a conference call that includes the System Open Market Account manager, the director of monetary affairs of the Board of Governors (who is also Secretary of the FOMC), and one of the four Reserve Bank presidents outside New York who are voting members of the FOMC. The open market staff presents its analysis and proposes the day's action.

To conduct an open market operation, the Trading Desk sends an electronic message to dealers asking them to submit bids within the next 10 to 15 minutes. The message specifies the type of operation (one-day and three-day repos, for example) but not the size. The dealers submit their bids electronically, including the price and the quantity they are willing to buy or sell. When everyone has responded, a computer ranks the offers from cheapest to most expensive. The manager decides which ones to accept, the dealers are notified, the transactions completed, and the operation publicly announced. The whole process is finished by 10:00 a.m., and the reserve supply is effectively fixed for the day.[‡]

As the day wears on, the market may not behave as expected. Both the demand and supply for reserves could turn out to be above or below the Fed's forecast. If the open market staff has guessed wrong, federal funds market transactions will occur at interest rates that deviate from the target.[§] Fortunately, the people who do this work are very good at their jobs, and the market rate almost always stays close to target. But there are days when circumstances conspire against the open market staff and the market interest rate ends way above or below target.

June 30, 1998, was one such day. It was the last day of the fiscal year, so commercial banks were about to publish their close-of-business balance sheets in their annual reports. As a result, some large banks did not want to have any overnight loans on their books. They told the open market account staff that they would simply keep excess reserves that had accumulated during the day. With the bank's help, the open market staff tried to forecast the resulting increase in the demand for reserves and make allowances for it. But their estimates were wrong; much more went into these banks' reserve accounts than anyone had forecast. As a result, the reserves available to everyone else were more than $1 billion lower than expected. As Figure 18.2 shows, the target federal funds rate on that day was 5.5 percent, but the average rate at which trades occurred was 7.06 percent and the standard deviation was 3.41 percent. Some trades occurred at rates as high as 30 percent. (The discount lending procedures instituted in 2002 were designed to protect against such an event happening again.)

On other days, the market federal funds rate has fallen far below target. Figure 18.2 shows two deviations of this sort: the first business day of the year 2000 and during the week following the terrorist attacks of September 11, 2001. In both cases, hitting the federal funds rate target was not a priority. Instead, the Fed wanted to make sure the banking system had sufficient reserves to continue operating smoothly, so the staff erred on the side of providing too much liquidity.

[‡]Over the years, the Fed has moved the operating time earlier and earlier in the day in order to be in the repo market when it is most active. Most financial institutions settle their financing needs by 10:00 a.m., so it is difficult to find people who are willing to make such transactions later in the day.

[§]If we drew a supply-and-demand diagram for the federal funds market at the end of a day, it would have a vertical supply curve at the level set by the open market operation that morning and a downward-sloping demand curve. As a result, any unexpected shift in demand during the day would change the interest rate. See Applying the Concept: Choosing an Operating Instrument later in this chapter.

functions. The Federal Reserve makes three types of loans, called *primary credit, secondary credit,* and *seasonal credit.*[3] As with the target federal funds rate, the Fed controls the interest rate on these loans, not the quantity of credit extended. The banks decide how much to borrow, and the rules are not very complicated. Let's look at each one in turn.

Primary credit

Primary credit is extended on a very short-term basis, usually overnight, to institutions that the Fed's bank supervisors deem to be sound (as measured by the standardized ratings they produce).[4] Banks seeking to borrow must post acceptable collateral to back the loan.[5] The interest rate on primary credit is 100 basis points *above* the federal funds target rate. This is called the **primary discount rate**.[6] The term *discount rate* usually refers to this primary discount rate.

As long as a bank qualifies and is willing to pay the penalty interest rate, it can get the loan. The rules allow a borrowing bank to lend the funds again if it wishes. Primary credit is designed to provide additional reserves at times when the open market staff's forecasts are off and so the day's reserve supply falls short of the banking system's demand. In that case, the market federal funds rate will rise above the FOMC's target. Providing a facility through which banks can borrow at a penalty rate 100 basis points above the target puts a cap on the market federal funds rate. Banks will go to the discount window and borrow reserves from the Fed rather than go into the federal fund market and pay a rate above the primary discount rate. So the system is designed both to provide liquidity in times of crisis, ensuring financial stability, and to restrict the range over which the market federal funds rate can move, helping to maintain interest-rate stability.

Secondary Credit

Secondary credit is available to institutions that are not sufficiently sound to qualify for primary credit. Because secondary credit is provided to banks that are in trouble, the **secondary discount rate** is set 50 basis points above the primary discount rate, a spread that reflects the borrower's financial condition. There are two reasons a bank might seek secondary credit. The first is the standard one: a temporary shortfall in reserves. But short-run secondary borrowing is highly unusual. Banks that request secondary credit from the Fed are banks that can't borrow from anyone else. By offering to pay a rate above the primary discount rate, a bank signals other banks that it doesn't qualify for primary credit. By paying the Fed the secondary discount rate for funds, the bank advertises that it is in trouble. It is hard to see any but the most desperate banker doing this.

So who is secondary credit for, anyway? It is for banks that are experiencing longer-term problems that they need some time to work out. There are times when banks have serious financial difficulty that they can resolve without failing. A bank that takes a large loss from poor lending decisions will become undercapitalized, but it may be able to raise funds to continue operating if it is given enough time. Such a bank

---

[3]Prior to the 2002 change in procedures, primary credit was called *adjustment credit,* and secondary credit was called *long-term credit.*

[4]Banks with CAMELS ratings of 1 or 2 qualify for primary credit. The rating scheme is described in Chapter 14.

[5]The list of acceptable collateral is fairly broad, including not only government securities and investment-grade corporate bonds but consumer loans, commercial and agricultural loans, and some types of mortgage obligations.

[6]In the case of a financial emergency, defined as a significant disruption in the U.S. money market resulting from an act of war, military or terrorist attack, natural disaster, or other catastrophic event, the primary discount rate can be reduced to the target federal funds rate.

has nothing to lose by requesting secondary credit. Without it, it will fail anyway. But before the Fed makes the loan, it has to believe there is a good chance the bank will be able to survive. You can see why secondary credit is rare.

Seasonal Credit   Seasonal credit is used primarily by small agricultural banks in the Midwest to help in managing the cyclical nature of farmers' loans and deposits.[7] Historically, these banks had poor access to national money markets, so the Fed stepped in to provide credit, charging them a market-based interest rate.[8] In recent years, however, there has been a move to eliminate seasonal credit. While the Fed still extends several hundred million dollars of seasonal credit during the summer months, there seems little justification for the practice any longer. Banks that used seasonal credit in the past now have easy access to longer-term loans from large commercial banks.

Reserve Requirements

Reserve requirements are the third tool in the monetary policymaker's toolbox. Since 1935, the Federal Reserve Board has had the authority to set the reserve requirements, the minimum level of reserves banks must hold either as vault cash or on deposit at the Fed.[9] Required reserves equal the required reserve ratio times the level of deposits to which the requirement is applied. (In Chapter 17, we wrote this relationship as $RR = r_D D$.) As we saw in the last chapter, changes in the reserve requirement affect the money multiplier and the quantity of money and credit circulating in the economy. Increasing it reduces the deposit expansion potential of the banking system, lowering the level of money supported by a given monetary base. So, by adjusting the reserve requirement, the central bank can influence economic activity. Unfortunately, the reserve requirement turns out not to be very useful. One reason is that small changes in the reserve requirement have a large—really, too large—impact on the level of deposits. But there are other reasons it isn't a good way to control the quantity of money. To see why, we need to look at the details.

The method for computing required reserves is complex. Everything is based on two-week averages. The reserve requirement is applied to two-week average balances in accounts with unlimited checking privileges—*transaction deposits*. This reserve computation period ends every second Monday. The reserves a bank must hold are also averaged over a two-week period, called the *maintenance period*, which begins on the third Thursday after the end of the computation period. That may sound a bit complicated, but really it isn't. What it means is that the banks and the Fed both know exactly what level of reserves every bank is required to hold during a given maintenance period well *before* the period starts. All banks have 16 days to figure out their deposit balances before they even need to start holding reserves. This procedure is called lagged-reserve accounting, and it makes the demand for reserves more predictable.

In 1980, the Monetary Control Act changed the rules slightly so that the Fed can now set the reserve requirement ratio between 8 percent and 14 percent of these

---

[7]During spring and summer, as farmers plant and cultivate their crops, the demand for loans rises and deposits decline, driving down bank reserves. Harvests and crop sales bring repayment of loans and increases in deposits, raising bank reserves.

[8]The interest rate charged on seasonal credit is the average of the market (effective) federal funds rate and market rate on 90-day negotiable certificates of deposit, both averaged over the previous two weeks.

[9]Originally, the requirements were specified in the Federal Reserve Act and could not be changed. For a concise history of reserve requirements, see Joshua N. Feinman, "Reserve Requirements: History, Current Practice, and Potential Reform," *Federal Reserve Bulletin* 79, no. 6 (June 1993), pp. 569–589.

APPLYING THE CONCEPT
MAKING JANUARY 1, 2000, UNEVENTFUL

The New Year's Eve parties were big on December 31, 1999. Around the world, everyone celebrated the beginning of the new millennium—everyone, that is, except for central bankers. As midnight approached, William McDonough, president of the Federal Reserve Bank of New York, sat in his office. There was no champagne on his desk; there would be time for that later. For now, McDonough had his telephones, his computers, and his staff at the ready. Just in case there was nothing to do, he had brought in a few books. If everything went as planned, the evening would be uneventful.

For years, McDonough and people everywhere had been concerned about the *Year 2000*, or Y2K, problem—the fear that computers would stop working because they were programmed to record the year in only two digits, so 2000 would be recorded as "00"—the same as 1900. If computers could not tell that January 1, 2000, came after December 31, 1999, everything from ATMs to elevators might stop working. For some time, the financial community had been making preparations. Now everyone sat and waited to see if their planning had been sufficient. As it turned out, nothing happened. You won't read much about Y2K in textbooks, except perhaps those that describe the importance of adequate contingency planning.

The Fed was not alone in its concern about financial stability at the turn of the century. Many people were worried that their credit, debt, and ATM cards would stop working, so they were hoarding cash in their homes. Even though they had spent years preparing, banks wanted extra reserves just in case they had difficulty receiving payments from other

so-called transactions deposits. Since interest is not paid on reserve balances or vault cash, the reserve requirement is costly to banks. To reduce the burden of these costs on small banks, the law specifies a graduated reserve requirement that is similar to the graduated income tax. The first few million dollars in deposits are exempt; then the reserve requirement ratio rises to 3 percent for the next $40 million or so in deposits. For everything above $40 million, the rate is 10 percent.[10] The accounting rules allow banks to carry small amounts of excess reserves forward and backward one maintenance period to meet their reserve requirements.

The purpose of the reserve requirement has changed over the years. In the beginning, reserves were required to ensure banks were sound and to reassure depositors that they could withdraw currency on demand. With the advent of deposit insurance, the rationale for requiring reserves changed. Today, the reserve requirement exists primarily to stabilize the demand for reserves and help the Fed to maintain the market federal funds rate close to target. A critical element in the Fed's daily open market operations is an estimate of the reserve demand for the day. The better the forecast, the easier it is to keep the market federal funds rate close to the FOMC's target.

---

[10]The level at which the higher reserve requirement kicks in changes every year, based on the amount of demand deposits in the banking system. In 2004, the reserve requirement was zero for the first $6.6 million in deposits, 3 percent for deposits up to $45.4 million, and 10 percent above that.

continued from previous page

banks. To relieve these pressures that were developing in the financial system, the Fed took a number of steps. First, it increased the availability of cash everywhere. Second, it set up a Special Liquidity Facility that offered banks loans at 150 basis points above the target federal funds rate for however long the borrower wanted. Third, to address uncertainties associated with year-end financing and give banks easy access to the reserves they might need, the Fed sold options that gave holders the right to engage in an overnight repurchase agreement with the Open Market Trading Desk, at the same 150-basis-point spread as the loans. Financial institutions bought all the options the Fed had to offer.*

The banking system, and the rest of us, survived Y2K unscathed. While currency holdings went up $50 billion in the month before the year's end, banks had no trouble either getting cash to their customers or managing their reserve accounts. Borrowings from the Special Liquidity Facility peaked at $124 million, roughly the size of daily discount lending—a comparatively small number. And no one exercised any of the options that they had bought. A clear sign of the unqualified success of the Fed's contingency plan was the behavior of the market federal funds rate. The target was $5\frac{1}{2}$ percent, and while the market rate dipped to 4 percent on the last day of the year (see Figure 18.2), nothing out of the ordinary happened. President McDonough spent a boring New Year's Eve, just as he had hoped, and the Special Liquidity Facility became the model for the new lending procedures that were put in place two and a half years later.

*For a complete description of what the Fed did, you can read a summary written by the people who did it in Evangeline Sophia Drossos and Spence Hilton, "The Federal Reserve's Contingency Financing Plan for the Century Date Change," *Current Issues in Economics and Finance* of the Federal Reserve Bank of New York, December 2000.

Changes in the reserve accounting rules over the years have made the open market operations staff's job of estimating reserve demand easier. Before August 1998, the computation and maintenance periods overlapped. Banks had to manage their deposits and reserves at the same time, and the result was a volatile market federal funds rate; the average daily standard deviation was around 0.2 percentage point. Since summer 1998, with the implementation of the lagged-reserve accounting system, the average daily standard deviation of the market federal funds rate has dropped to less than half its prior level, about 0.1.

Today, the reserve requirement is administered in a way that makes reserve demand predictable. It is not used as a direct tool of monetary policy; the case against doing so is persuasive. An example will help to illustrate the pitfalls of using the reserve requirement as a policy tool. Following the banking crises of the Great Depression, U.S. banks began accumulating excess reserves. By the beginning of 1936, less than half of the $5.6 billion of reserves held in the banking system were required; the rest were excess reserves. The Federal Reserve Board was puzzled and became concerned that the high level of excess reserves could be used to support a rapid expansion of deposits and loans, which would lead to inflation. To head off the possibility, beginning in August 1936 the Fed used its newly acquired powers and in three steps doubled the reserve requirement. Suddenly, $3 billion in excess reserves

Table 18.1 The Tools of U.S. Monetary Policy

	What Is It?	How Is It Controlled?	What Is Its Impact?
Target Federal Funds Rate	Interest rate charged on overnight loans between banks.	Supply of reserves adjusted through open market operations to meet expected demand at the target rate.	Changes interest rates throughout the economy.
Discount Rate	Interest rate charged by the Federal Reserve on loans to commercial banks.	Set as a premium over the target federal funds rate.	Provides short-term liquidity to banks in times of crisis and aids in controlling the federal funds rate.
Reserve Requirement	Fraction of deposits that banks must keep either on deposit at the Federal Reserve or as cash in their vaults.	Set by the Federal Reserve Board within a legally imposed range.	Stabilizes the demand for reserves.

was reduced to $1 billion. Bank executives were not happy. They spent the next year rebuilding their reserve balances until excess reserves were back to the level where they had been before the reserve requirement was raised. The consequences for the economy were grim. While the monetary base remained relatively stable, the money multiplier plummeted, driving M1 and M2 down. As monetary aggregates fell, the economy went along with them. From its peak in spring 1937 to its trough less than a year later, real GDP fell more than 10 percent.

Operational Policy at the European Central Bank

Like the Federal Reserve's, the ECB's monetary policy toolbox contains an overnight interbank rate (equivalent to the federal funds rate), the rate at which the central bank lends to commercial banks (equivalent to the discount rate), and a reserve requirement. Since the ECB pays interest on reserve deposits, there is also a reserve deposit rate. The details are different, so let's have a look at them.

The ECB's Target Interest Rate and Open Market Operations

While the ECB occasionally engages in outright purchases of securities, it provides reserves to the European banking system primarily through what are called *refinancing operations*. The main refinancing operation is a weekly auction of two-week repurchase agreements in which the ECB, through the National Central Banks, provides reserves to banks in exchange for securities and then reverses the transaction two weeks later. The policy instrument of the ECB's Governing Council is the minimum interest rate allowed at these refinancing auctions, which is called the main refinancing operations **minimum bid rate**. This is the European equivalent of the Fed's target federal funds rate, so we will refer to it as the *target refinancing rate*. The main refinancing operations provide banks with virtually all their reserves and account for between 15 and 20 percent of the ECB's balance sheet.

While the ECB's refinancing operations are broadly similar to the Fed's daily open market operations, there are some differences. The most important one is that these operations are done at all the National Central Banks (NCBs) simultaneously. In 2004, there were 12 locations (and as the Eurosystem expands to include more countries, the number will grow). In the United States, everything is done at the Federal Reserve Bank of New York. And while the Fed solicits prices from a short list of 20 securities dealers in the course of its normal operations, literally hundreds of European banks participate in the ECB's weekly auctions. Finally, because of the differences in financial structure in different countries, the collateral that is accepted in refinancing operations differs from country to country. Under normal circumstances, the Fed takes U.S. government securities.[11] In contrast, some of the National Central Banks in the Eurosystem accept a broad range of collateral, including not only government-issued bonds but also privately issued bonds and bank loans.[12]

In addition to the weekly main refinancing operations, the ECB engages in both monthly long-term refinancing operations, in which it offers reserves for three months, and infrequent small operations that occur between the main refinancing operations, when policymakers want to fine-tune reserve levels.

The Marginal Lending Facility

The **Marginal Lending Facility** is the analog to the Federal Reserve's primary credit facility. Through this facility, the ECB provides overnight loans to banks at a rate that is normally well *above* the target-refinancing rate. The spread between the marginal lending rate and the target refinancing rate is set by the Governing Council and is currently 100 basis points. As in the case with discount borrowing from the Fed, commercial banks initiate these borrowing transactions when they face a reserve deficiency that they cannot satisfy more cheaply in the marketplace. Banks do borrow regularly, and on occasion the amounts they borrow are large. The similarity between this procedure and the Federal Reserve's primary credit facility is no accident, since the ECB's system (which is itself based on the German Bundesbank's) was the model for the 2002 redesign of the Fed's discount window.

The Deposit Facility

Banks with excess reserves at the end of the day can deposit them overnight in the **ECB's Deposit Facility** at an interest rate substantially *below* the target-refinancing rate. Again, the spread is determined by the Governing Council and is currently 100 basis points. While they are usually small, these deposits can be substantial, since they include all the excess reserves in the Eurosystem's banks. But what is important is that

---

[11]The Fed accepts both securities issued by the U.S. Treasury and those issued by government-sponsored agencies like the Federal National Mortgage Corporation but not commercial paper issued by private companies.

[12]In the spring of 2004, the Governing Council of the ECB started a process to make the list of eligible collateral uniform across the countries of the Eurosystem, thereby removing some of the inconsistencies that exist. The process is likely to be completed sometime in 2005.

the existence of the deposit facility places a floor on the interest rate that can be charged on reserves. Because a bank can always deposit its excess reserves in the deposit facility at a rate 100 basis points below the target refinancing rate, it will never make a loan at a lower rate.

Reserve Requirements

The ECB requires that banks hold minimum reserve levels based on the level of liabilities they hold. The reserve requirement of 2 percent is applied to checking accounts and some other short-term deposits. Deposit levels are averaged over a month, and reserve levels must be held over the following month. Unlike the Fed, the ECB pays interest on required reserves; the rate is based on the interest rate from the weekly refinancing auctions, averaged over a month, which is designed to be very close to the overnight interbank rate. As a result, the cost of meeting the reserve requirement is relatively low, and banks do not go out of their way to escape it.

The European system is designed to give the ECB tight control over the short-term money market in the euro area. And it works. Figure 18.3 shows the target refinancing rate, which is the minimum bid rate in the weekly auctions, as the heavy line running through the center of the graph, with the marginal lending rate 100 basis points above and the deposit rate 100 basis points below. The **overnight cash rate** is the European analog to the market federal funds rate, the rate banks charge each other for overnight loans. As you can see, this rate fluctuates quite a bit, but it always remains inside the 200-basis point band—the target refinancing rate plus or minus 100 basis points.

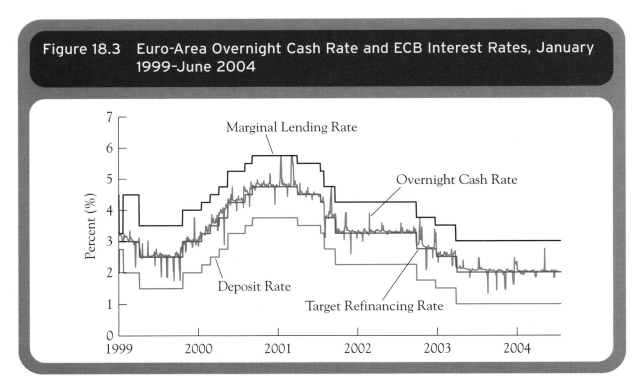

Figure 18.3 Euro-Area Overnight Cash Rate and ECB Interest Rates, January 1999–June 2004

SOURCE: *European Central Bank.*

This pattern contrasts starkly with that of the U.S. market federal funds rate. Looking back at Figure 18.2, we can see that the market federal funds rate occasionally moves more than 100 basis points above or below the target. In fact, over the twelve-and-one-half years plotted there, the funds rate was more than 100 basis points away from the target 28 times, or two to three times per year. The European system is clearly more successful in keeping the short-term interest rate close to target.

Linking Tools to Objectives: Making Choices

Monetary policymakers use the various tools they have to meet the objectives society gives them. Their goals—low and stable inflation, high and stable growth, a stable financial system, stable interest and exchange rates—are (or should be) given to them by their elected officials. But day-to-day policy is left to the technicians, who must then decide which tools are the best for the job.

Over the years, a consensus has developed among monetary policy experts, both inside and outside central banks, that (a) the reserve requirement is not useful as an operational instrument; (b) central bank lending is necessary to ensure financial stability; and (c) short-term interest rates are the tool to use to stabilize short-term fluctuations in prices and output. The logic of this conclusion is straightforward. To follow it, let's start by listing the features that distinguish good policy instruments from bad ones.

Desirable Features of a Policy Instrument

A good monetary policy instrument has three features.

1. It is easily *observable* by everyone.
2. It is *controllable* and quickly changed.
3. It is tightly *linked* to the policymakers' objectives.

These features seem obvious. After all, a policy tool wouldn't be very useful if you couldn't observe it, control it, or predict its impact on your objectives. But beyond the obvious, it is important that a policy instrument be easily observable to ensure transparency in policymaking, which enhances accountability. Controllability is important in both the short term and the long term. An instrument that can be adjusted quickly in the face of a sudden change in economic conditions is clearly more useful than one that takes time to adjust. And the more predictable the impact of an instrument, the easier it will be for policymakers to meet their objectives.

Requiring that a monetary policy instrument be observable and controllable leaves us with only a few options to choose from. The reserve requirement won't work. Since banks cannot adjust their balance sheets quickly, changes need to be announced some time in advance. Then there are the components of the central bank's balance sheet—commercial bank reserves, the monetary base, loans, and foreign exchange reserves—as well as their prices—various interest rates and the exchange rate. (Exchange rate policy is discussed in the next chapter.) But how do we choose between controlling quantities and controlling prices? Over the years, central banks have switched from one to the other. For example, from 1979 to 1982, the Fed did try targeting bank reserves, with an eye toward reducing inflation from double-digit levels. Inflation fell quickly, so in a sense the policy was a success. But one side effect of choosing to control reserves was that interest rates became highly variable, rising from 14 percent to over 20 percent and then falling to less than 9 percent, all in a period of less than six months.

APPLYING THE CONCEPT
CHOOSING AN OPERATING INSTRUMENT

We have emphasized that the Federal Reserve uses the federal funds rate as its operating instrument. This is not the only possibility. Since the central bank controls the size of its balance sheet, it could decide to use any quantity on that balance sheet as an operating instrument. Obvious possibilities include the level of reserves or the monetary base. It is important to understand two things. First, the Fed has to choose which operating instrument to use; second, an interest rate is the natural choice.

To understand why it needs to choose, recall that there is a market for reserves, and the Fed controls the supply. Controlling the quantity of reserves means holding supply constant at the target level. That's the vertical line in Figure 18.4. (Look back at Figure 18.1 to see how the picture looks when the Fed chooses to target the federal funds rate.) The consequences of choosing to target the quantity of reserves are immediately apparent. With reserve supply fixed, a shift in reserve demand changes the federal funds rate. When reserve demand increases, the market federal funds rate will go up; when reserve demand falls, the market federal funds rate will go down. If the Fed chooses to target the quantity of reserves, it gives up control of the federal funds rate.

From the discussion in Chapter 15, we can infer that in order to meet their objectives, central bankers will tend to adopt operating procedures that keep interest rates from becoming volatile. Interest rates are the primary link between the financial system and the real economy, so stabilizing growth means keeping interest rates from being overly volatile. In the context of choosing an operating target, that means keeping unpredictable changes in reserve demand from influencing interest rates and feeding into the real economy. The best way to do this is to target interest rates.*

*More than 30 years ago, William Poole first observed that the decision to target either interest rates or an aggregate like reserves or the monetary base depends on what is less predictable. Is it (1) the link from the monetary base to the money aggregates (the money multiplier from Chapter 17), or (2) the link from the monetary aggregates to the real economy (the velocity of money which we will discuss in Chapter 20)? Poole showed that if the money multiplier is less predictable, policymakers should target interest rates; otherwise, it is better to target the monetary base. See William Poole, "Optimal Choice of Monetary Policy Instruments in a Simple Stochastic Macro Model," *Quarterly Journal of Economics* 84, no. 2 (1970), pp. 197–216.

The consensus today is that the Fed's strategy of targeting reserves rather than interest rates in the period from 1979 to 1982 was a way of driving interest rates to levels that would not have been politically acceptable had they been announced as targets. Even in an environment of double-digit inflation, the FOMC could not explicitly raise the target federal funds rate to 20 percent. By saying they were targeting the quantity of reserves, the committee members escaped responsibility for the high interest rates. When inflation had fallen and interest rates came back down, the

continued from previous page

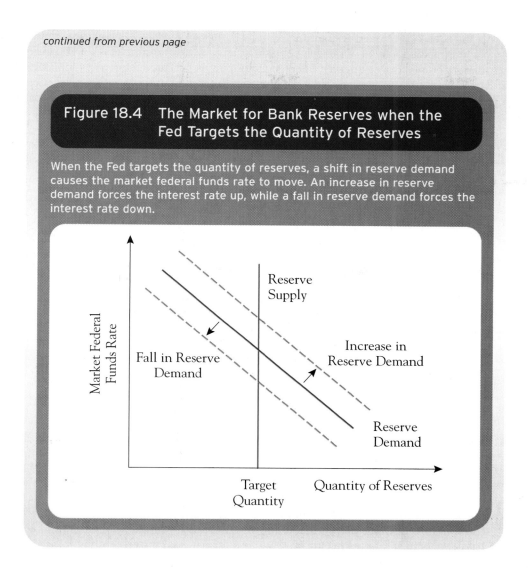

Figure 18.4   The Market for Bank Reserves when the Fed Targets the Quantity of Reserves

When the Fed targets the quantity of reserves, a shift in reserve demand causes the market federal funds rate to move. An increase in reserve demand forces the interest rate up, while a fall in reserve demand forces the interest rate down.

FOMC reverted to targeting the federal funds rate. And that is what it has done ever since. (Further details of this episode are discussed in Chapter 20.)

Operating Instruments and Intermediate Targets

Before continuing, we should pause to consider some terms and concepts that often crop up in discussions of central banking. Central bankers sometimes use the terms *operating instrument* and *intermediate target*. Operating instruments refer to actual tools of policy. These are instruments that the central bank controls directly. Every central bank can control the size of its balance sheet, for instance. It can choose to use this power to control the monetary base if it wishes, or to control the interest rate in the market for reserves, as the FOMC does. These are the operating instruments.

Central bankers use the term intermediate targets to refer to instruments that are not directly under their control but lie instead somewhere between their policymaking tools and their objectives (see Figure 18.5). The monetary aggregates are a prime example of intermediate targets. The idea behind targeting M2, for example, is that changes in the monetary base, or reserves, affect the monetary aggregates before they influence inflation or output. So in targeting M2, central bankers can more effectively meet their objectives. They don't actually care about money growth itself, in other words; it is just

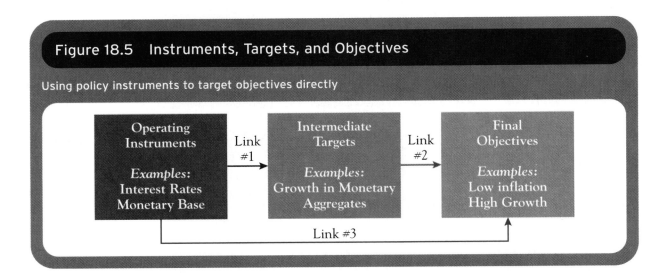

Figure 18.5   Instruments, Targets, and Objectives

Using policy instruments to target objectives directly

APPLYING THE CONCEPT
INFLATION TARGETING

If you can focus central bankers' attention clearly on a well-articulated objective, you will get better policy. The problem is how to do it. During the 1990s, a number of countries adopted a policy framework called inflation targeting in an effort to improve monetary policy performance. And it seems to have worked. Countries that embraced inflation targeting achieved both lower inflation and higher real growth.

Inflation targeting bypasses intermediate targets and focuses directly on the objective of low inflation. It is a monetary policy strategy that involves the public announcement of a numerical inflation target, together with a commitment to make price stability the central bank's primary objective to which all other objectives are subordinated. This approach creates an environment in which everyone believes policymakers will keep inflation low, so long-term expectations of inflation remain low, anchoring long-term interest rates and promoting growth. As we saw in Chapter 15, one of the keys to any successful central bank policy is for policymakers to convince the public that they will keep inflation low. Their commitment must be credible. Inflation targeting is designed to convince people that monetary policy will deliver low inflation.

Central banks that employ inflation targeting operate under what has been described as a *hierarchical mandate,* in which inflation comes first

a useful indicator. And announcing targets for money growth that can be monitored by the public increases policymakers' accountability.

Over the last two decades of the 20th century, central bankers largely abandoned intermediate targets, having realized that they didn't make much sense. There may be something special about money, and it may be particularly helpful in forecasting future economic developments and in guiding policy. But then again, it may not be helpful. More important, circumstances may change in ways that make an intermediate target unworkable. Link #1, between the operating instruments and the intermediate target, may shift (this is the problem described at the end of Chapter 16) or link #2, between money growth and the final inflation and growth objectives, may change (we will discuss this in Chapter 20). If either of these happened, the central bank would need to explain why it was changing its target and it would look as if policymakers don't know what they are doing.[13] So while people still do discuss intermediate targets, it is hard to justify using them. Instead, policymakers focus on how their actions directly affect their target objectives—link #3. A recent example of this is the practice of *inflation targeting*, which is discussed in Applying the Concept.

[13]Something similar happened to the Deutsche Bundesbank at the time of German reunification in 1990. The West German government decided to exchange East German currency at a rate roughly five times the black market exchange rate. The result was a huge increase in the quantity of money circulating in the reunified nation. This created a problem for the German central bank. For 20 years or so, policymakers had kept inflation under control with a very public policy focused on restraining money growth. Now money growth had exploded for political reasons, and there was nothing they could do about it. They had missed their targets for reasons outside their control and were forced to make excuses.

continued from previous page

and everything else comes second. The United Kingdom, Australia, Chile, and South Africa are among the growing number of countries that target inflation. Most observers put the ECB in the group as well. This approach contrasts with the Federal Reserve's *dual mandate,* in which inflation and growth are on an equal footing. Because of this dual mandate, the Fed has shied away from adopting inflation targeting.

To understand how inflation targeting works, let's look at the British example. The Bank of England Act of 1998 both granted the Bank of England independence and dictated its objective: to deliver price stability, as defined by the government's inflation target. A nine-member Monetary Policy Committee meets monthly to determine short-term interest rates in an effort to meet this objective, which has been defined as retail price inflation of 2.5 percent. Because transparency is a crucial part of inflation targeting, the Bank of England publishes the minutes of its Monetary Policy Committee's meetings, as well as quarterly forecasts of inflation in its *Inflation Report.*

By focusing on a clearly defined and easily observable numerical inflation statistic and requiring frequent communication with the public, inflation targeting increases policymakers' accountability and helps to establish their credibility. Not only do central bankers know what they are supposed to do, but everyone else does, too. The result is not just lower and more stable inflation but higher and more stable growth as well.

A Guide to Central Bank Interest Rates: The Taylor Rule

Interest-rate setting is about numbers. The members of the FOMC set the target federal funds rate at 3 or 4 or 5 percent; the Governing Council of the ECB chooses a specific level for the main refinancing rate. These policymakers don't just pick the number, they choose the day on which to make the changes. How do they do it? The answer is that they have large staffs—at the Fed and the ECB, hundreds of people—who distill huge amounts of information into manageable sets of policy recommendations. Committee members digest all the information, meet, and reach a decision. We could try to list all the factors they consider and explain how each influences the committee's decision, but that would take another book.

What we can do is study a simple formula that approximates what the FOMC does. Called the **Taylor rule** after the economist who created it, Professor John Taylor of Stanford University, it tracks the actual behavior of the target federal funds rate and relates it to the real interest rate, inflation, and output.[14] The formula is

$$\text{Target fed funds rate} = 2\tfrac{1}{2} + \text{Current inflation} + \tfrac{1}{2}(\text{Inflation gap}) + \tfrac{1}{2}(\text{Output gap}) \quad (1)$$

This expression assumes a long-term real interest rate of $2\tfrac{1}{2}$ percent, which is added to current inflation, the inflation gap, and the output gap. The inflation gap is current inflation minus an inflation target, both measured as percentages; the output gap is current GDP minus its potential level—that is, the percentage deviation of current output from potential output. (As Chapter 21 discusses in detail, potential output is what the economy is capable of producing when its resources are being used at normal rates.) When inflation exceeds the target level, the inflation gap is positive; when current output is above potential output, the output gap is positive.

The Taylor rule says that the target federal funds rate should be set equal to the current level of inflation plus a $2\tfrac{1}{2}$ percent real interest rate, plus a factor related to the deviation of inflation and output from their target levels. For example, if inflation is currently 3 percent, the target rate is 2 percent, and GDP equals its potential level so there is no output gap, then the target federal funds rate should be set at $2\tfrac{1}{2} + 3 + \tfrac{1}{2} = 6$ percent.

This rule makes intuitive sense: When inflation rises above its target level, the response is to raise interest rates; when output falls below the target level, the response is to lower interest rates. If inflation is currently on target and there is no output gap (current GDP equals potential GDP), then the target federal funds rate should be set at its neutral rate of target inflation plus $2\tfrac{1}{2}$.

[14]The Taylor rule first appeared in "Discretion versus Rules in Practice," *Carnegie-Rochester Conference Series on Public Policy* 39 (1993), pp. 195–214. Policy rules have quite a bit to recommend them. By removing policymakers' discretion, they remove the temptation to create inflation. Rules also enhance accountability, since it is easy to see whether they are being followed. Finally, rules may help to convince the public that central bankers are committed to fighting inflation and stabilizing growth, which should reduce expectations for inflation and make the central bankers' job easier.

THE AGE OF INNOCENCE

SOURCE: *The New Yorker Collection 1990 Kenneth Mahood from cartoonbank.com. All Rights Reserved.*

The Taylor rule has some interesting properties. Consider what happens if inflation rises by 1 percentage point, from 2 percent to 3 percent, and the inflation target is 2 percent (assume that everything else remains the same). What happens to the target federal funds rate? The increase in inflation affects two terms in the Taylor rule, current inflation and the inflation gap. Since the inflation target doesn't change, both these terms rise 1 percentage point. The increase in current inflation feeds one for one into the target federal funds rate, but the increase in the inflation gap is halved. *A 1 percentage point increase in inflation raises the target federal funds rate $1\frac{1}{2}$ percentage points.*

Significantly, the Taylor rule tells us that for each percentage point increase in inflation, the real interest rate, which is equal to the nominal interest rate minus expected inflation, goes up half a percentage point. Since economic decisions depend on the real interest rate, this means that higher inflation leads policymakers to raise the inflation-adjusted cost of borrowing, thereby slowing the economy and ultimately reducing inflation. If central banks failed to do this, if they allowed the real interest rate to fall following an increase in inflation, the result would be further increases in production and further increases in inflation.

The Taylor rule also states that for each percentage point output is above potential—that is, for each percentage point in the output gap—interest rates will go up half a percentage point.

The fractions that precede the terms for the inflation and output gaps—the halves in equation (1)—depend both on how sensitive the economy is to interest-rate changes and on the preferences of central bankers. The more central bankers care about inflation, the bigger the multiplier for the inflation gap and the lower the multiplier for the output gap. It is not unusual for central banks to raise the target interest rate by twice the increase in inflation while virtually ignoring the output gap.

Returning to the United States, we see that implementing the Taylor rule requires four inputs: (1) the constant term, set at $2\frac{1}{2}$ in equation (1); (2) a measure of inflation; (3) a measure of the inflation gap; and (4) a measure of the output gap. The constant is a measure of the long-term risk-free real interest rate, which is about 1 percentage point below the economy's growth rate. Since the U.S. economy has been growing at a rate of about $3\frac{1}{2}$ percent per year, we set this term at $2\frac{1}{2}$. But the number can and does change.

Next we need to add measures of current inflation and the inflation gap. What index should we use? While the CPI is widely known, economists and central bankers believe that the personal consumption expenditure (PCE) index is a more accurate measure of inflation. The PCE comes from the national income accounts and is based on the "C" in "Y = C + I + G + X – M." As for the inflation target to use in measuring the inflation gap, we will follow Taylor and use 2 percent, so the neutral target federal funds rate is $4\frac{1}{2}$ percent ($2\frac{1}{2}$ plus 2). For the output gap, the natural choice is the percentage by which GDP deviates from a measure of its trend, or potential.[15]

Figure 18.6 plots the FOMC's actual target federal funds rate, together with the rate predicted by the Taylor rule. The result is striking: The two lines are very close to each other.[16] The FOMC changed the target federal funds rate when the Taylor rule predicted it should. While the rule didn't match policy exactly, it did predict what policymakers would do in a general way. And what is really remarkable is that

---

[15]The easiest way to get the inputs to compute the current implications of the Taylor rule is to visit the Web site of the Federal Reserve Bank of St. Louis. This site maintains a database called FRED (Federal Reserve Economic Data) that allows you to download economic data directly into a spreadsheet.

[16]The average deviation of the Taylor rule from the FOMC's target rate was almost zero over the period, and the average distance (the mean absolute value of the deviation) was about one percentage point. The correlation between the two series is very high, 0.76.

Figure 18.6   The Taylor Rule, 1990–2004

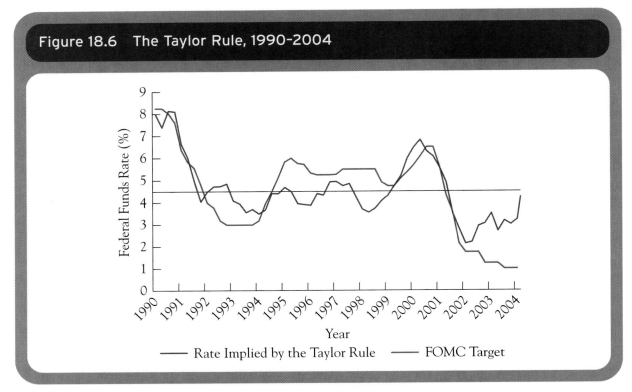

SOURCE: *Board of Governors of the Federal Reserve and author's calculations.*

Professor Taylor created his rule around 1992, at the beginning of the period shown in the graph.

Before we get carried away and replace the FOMC with an equation, or begin betting in the financial markets based on the Taylor rule's predictions, we should recognize some caveats. First, at times the target rate does deviate from the Taylor rule, and with good reason. The Taylor rule is too simple to take account of sudden threats to financial stability, such as the terrorist attacks of September 11, 2001.

Beyond that, there is another reason to question the practicality of the Taylor rule in making monetary policy: the lack of real-time data. Policy must be made based on the information available at the time. Figure 18.6 was drawn using data available in August 2004—data that were revised many times after their first release (see Your Financial World). So while we might be able to make good monetary policy for 1995 using the Taylor rule and the data available to us today, that ability really isn't of much practical use. Real-world policymakers have no choice but to make decisions based on information that is less than completely accurate. Their good judgment is the key to successful monetary policy.

In truth, central bankers have a nearly impossible job. They are supposed to stabilize the economy and financial system at the same time that they provide services to commercial banks and the government. To perform this task, we give them control over their own balance sheet, allowing them to buy and sell securities in the financial markets and make loans to banks. As we know, monopolists can choose between controlling the quantity of the product they sell or the price at which they sell it. Because the central bank is the monopoly supplier of currency and reserves, policymakers can control either the quantity or the price. Today they choose to control the price, which is an interest rate. Since movements in interest rates affect the entire economic system, control over interest rates gives monetary policymakers the leverage they need to stabilize inflation, growth, and the financial system. As we will see in detail in Part V, higher interest rates

YOUR FINANCIAL WORLD

Economic History Is Constantly Changing

The publication of new economic growth data makes headlines. Every three months, the Department of Commerce's Bureau of Economic Analysis publishes information on GDP for the preceding quarter. So at the end of April, we get the first estimate of growth for January through March, and news reporters trumpet it. Such attention would make sense except for the fact that the data are then revised numerous times. Only the initial estimates come out in April; in May, June, and July, they are revised as government statisticians slowly accumulate more information about what actually happened. And every July for the next three years they are revised again. By July 2005, GDP for the first quarter of 2002 will have been revised six times! Every five years after that, the data are revised yet again as new surveys of the population and business activity become available.

These revisions would be irrelevant if they were small, but they are not. An example will show how large the change can be. Figure 18.7 plots the progression of estimates of GDP growth for the third quarter of 1990, the trough of a mild recession.* The initial estimate, published in October 1990, suggested that the economy had grown +1.8 percent. The economy had been doing poorly, so this news was welcome. But as the data were revised, the story changed. Growth estimates dropped to -2 percent for a while, finally settling at about -0.03 percent in 2004.

What this means is that history is constantly changing. Our view of what really happened in the economy must be adjusted regularly. So when you see a headline announcing the publication of data on recent growth in GDP, remember that today's figure is just a rough estimate. Five years or more will pass before economists know what actually happened.

*These data come from a real-time database maintained by the Federal Reserve Bank of Philadelphia. For a description of the data, see Dean Croushore and Tom Stark, "A Funny Thing Happened on the Way to the Data Bank: A Real-Time Data Set for Macroeconomists," *Business Review* of the Federal Reserve Bank of Philadelphia, September/October 2000, pp. 15–27. The data themselves are available on the Bank's Web site at http://www.phil.frb.org/econ/forecast/readow.html.

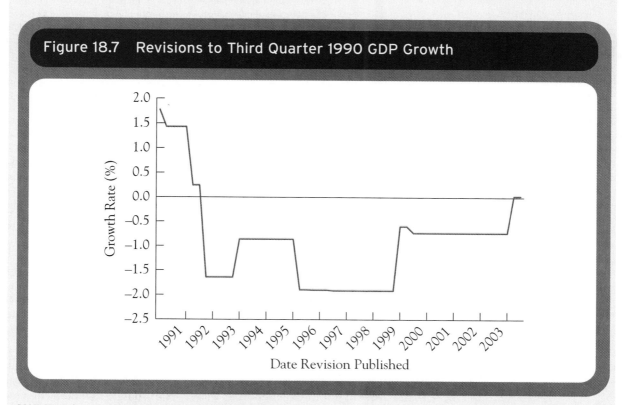

Figure 18.7   Revisions to Third Quarter 1990 GDP Growth

SOURCE: *Real-time database of the Federal Reserve Bank of Philadelphia.*

IN THE NEWS

Central Banks Move to Raise Rates as Inflation Fears Begin to Emerge

The Wall Street Journal

by G. Thomas Sims, Jason Booth, and Michael Williams

May 16, 2002

Central banks across the globe are beginning to raise interest rates, a sign they are confident the recovery is real and can now focus on its downside: inflation.

In recent weeks, central banks in South Korea, Australia, and Canada have raised their key rates a moderate quarter percentage point, in their first increases since last year's global economic slowdown. Sweden has already moved twice, while New Zealand's central bank Wednesday lifted the cost of borrowing for a third time this year.

Other central banks are also tilting toward higher rates. In the United Kingdom, economists say rates are likely to go up after a report from the central bank Wednesday predicted inflation would exceed its target if the bank were to leave rates alone. Its views are also believed to be shared by the European Central Bank. The Frankfurt-based bank is concerned inflation isn't easing fast enough, and has indicated it could act as soon as the economy steadies.

The trend marks a departure from the previous two tightening cycles, when the Federal Reserve led the pack. This time, Fed officials have signaled they intend to be patient,

for now leaving their short-term rate target at an "accommodative" 1.75 percent. The Fed has acknowledged that the rate target will have to rise, but it first wants to see sustained consumer spending and more business investment.

Like the Fed, central banks elsewhere cut rates last year to keep economies afloat, especially after September 11. Now that the danger of recession is over, some countries are returning to a more stringent monetary policy.

Major central banks that target inflation appear to be gearing up to raise interest rates in the months ahead. The Bank of England indicated it might be inclined to tighten policy in its quarterly inflation report published Wednesday. The bank warned that inflation is set to rise above its 2.5 percent target, to 2.6 percent within two years.

In the 12-nation euro zone, inflation has hovered above the ECB's 2 percent upper limit for 23 consecutive months. Some of the bank's top officials fear that the public will begin to doubt the young bank's ability to keep inflation as low as promised.

Several economists say the trend toward high rates won't put the global recovery at risk. "These are policy decisions to moderate growth, not choke it off," said Bruce Kasman, economist at JP Morgan Chase Bank. "Central banks are responding to a new macroeconomic situation."

Japan—mired in its third, and deepest, recession of the past decade—is likely to be a major exception to the trend of rising rates. This week, Finance Minister Masajuro Shiokawa said the economy had hit bottom, citing rising

slow inflation and growth by reducing the availability of credit; lower interest rates stimulate economic activity by making credit cheaper and easier to get.

Over the years, central bankers have learned from their mistakes, so today they do their job fairly well. They understand the importance of keeping the financial system running smoothly and have refined their ability to lend quickly in times of crisis. The result is a financial system that is much less prone to collapse and more conducive to growth. And because everyone understands the importance of keeping inflation low, we have designed our central banks to deliver price stability. The outcome is that inflation is lower now than it was from 1970 to 1995.

Today we have a set of principles that tells us how central banks should be designed and how they should use interest rates to stabilize their economy. But central bankers cannot do the job alone. Sound monetary policy must be combined with responsible fiscal policy to build a healthy economic and financial system. Moreover, with the fading economic importance of national borders, the time has passed when even large central banks could avoid taking international conditions into account. To fill this hole in our analysis, we turn in Chapter 19 to a study of exchange rate management and the international financial system.

continued from previous page

Figure 18.8   Heading Off Higher Prices

Central banks around the globe are engaged in a round of tightening in a bid to keep resurgent economies from overheating down the road.

As inflation threatens central banks...

Current inflation rates and central banks' upper limit or target

■ Current inflation
▨ Target inflation/upper limit

Interest rates are expected to rise

Current interest rates and expected interest rates for December 2002

■ Current rate
▨ Expected rate for December 2002

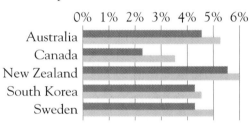

SOURCES: *National Central Banks and National statistics agencies, various countries; J.P. Morgan Chase.*

exports, a firming of the job market and an easing of price deflation. Still, the country faces no risk of inflation and so has no need for higher rates. Indeed, Japan's real demon is falling prices, and the Bank of Japan is expected to continue trying to aggressively expand the money supply as a way of combating price deflation.

The Japanese central bank has vowed to continue pumping cash into the economy until consumer prices stop falling or turn positive. The hope is that the extra money will eventually be spent by consumers on cars and houses or by investors on stocks, land, and other assets. To that end, the bank has been buying large amounts of Japanese government bonds and is ramping up the country's monetary base, the portion of the money supply that the bank controls most directly, by expanding the amount of reserves in the banking system. Price deflation moderated in March but remains severe, with the national consumer price inflation falling 1.2 percent from March of the previous year.

Meanwhile, the pre-emptive interest-rate increases by South Korea and Australia are less an indicator of the direction of monetary policy across Asia than an indicator of how these economies are outperforming most of their neighbors. And rather than facing inflation, some Asian

nations, notably China and Hong Kong, are grappling with persistent deflationary pressure. China, with its massive, low-cost production base and excess production capacity, is seen to be fueling falling producer prices in many of its neighboring economies.

Greg Ip contributed to this article.

Reprinted by permission of The Wall Street Journal, Copyright © 2002 Dow Jones & Company, Inc. All Rights Reserved Worldwide.

LESSONS OF THE ARTICLE

Policymakers lower interest rates when the economy is slowing and raise them when they believe inflation is likely to rise. Central banks that target inflation explicitly are more likely to raise interest rates quickly than those that don't. When faced with deflation, the Bank of Japan changed tack and moved from a policy of controlling interest rates to one of expanding the monetary base as quickly as possible.

Terms

discount lending, 465

discount rate, 461

ECB's Deposit Facility, 473

ECB's Main Refinancing Operations, 472

ECB's Marginal Lending Facility, 473

federal funds target rate , 461

inflation targeting, 478

intermediate targets, 477

lagged-reserve accounting, 469

lender of last resort, 465

market federal funds rate, 462

matched-sale purchase (or reverse repo), 466

minimum bid rate, 473

open market trading desk, 466

operating instruments, 477

overnight cash rate, 474

primary credit, 468

primary discount rate, 468

repurchase agreement (repo), 466

reserve requirement, 461

seasonal credit, 469

secondary credit, 468

secondary discount rate, 468

System Open Market Account (SOMA), 466

Taylor rule, 480

Chapter Lessons

1. The Federal Reserve has three monetary policy tools.

   a. The target federal funds rate is the primary instrument of monetary policy.

      i. Open market operations are used to control the federal funds rate.

      ii. The Fed forecasts the demand for reserves each day and then supplies the amount needed to meet the demand at the target rate.

   b. The discount lending rate is used to supply funds to banks primarily during crises.

      i. The Fed sets the primary lending rate 100 basis points above the target federal funds rate.

      ii. In setting the primary lending rate above the target federal funds rate, the Fed is attempting to stabilize the interest rate on overnight interbank lending.

      iii. The Fed also makes loans to banks in distress and to banks in need of seasonal liquidity.

   c. Reserve requirements are used to stabilize the demand for reserves.

      i. Banks are required to hold reserves against certain deposits.

      ii. Banks can hold either deposits at Federal Reserve Banks or vault cash, neither of which earns interest.

      iii. Reserves are accounted for in such a way that everyone knows the level of reserves required several weeks before banks must hold them.

2. The European Central Bank's primary objective is price stability.

   a. The ECB provides liquidity to the banking system through weekly auctions called refinancing operations.

   b. The minimum bid rate on the main refinancing operations, also known as the target refinancing rate, is the target interest rate controlled by the Governing Council.

c. The ECB allows banks to borrow from the marginal lending facility at an interest rate that is 100 basis points above the target refinancing rate.

d. Banks with excess reserves can deposit them at national central banks and receive interest at 100 basis points below the target refinancing rate.

e. European banks are required to hold reserves; they receive an interest rate on their balances that is equal to the average of the rate in recent refinancing operations.

3. Monetary policymakers use several tools to meet their objectives.

a. The best tools are observable, controllable, and tightly linked to objectives.

b. Short-term interest rates are the best tools for monetary policymaking.

c. Modern central banks do not use intermediate targets like money growth.

4. The Taylor rule is a simple equation that describes movements in the federal funds rate. It suggests that

a. When inflation rises, the FOMC raises the target interest rate by $1\frac{1}{2}$ times the increase.

b. When output rises above potential by 1 percent, the FOMC raises the target interest rate half a percentage point.

Problems

1. Recall from Chapter 15 that the central bank performs several functions. Describe how each tool of monetary policy is used in fulfilling each of those roles.

2. Suppose the demand for reserves became less stable. How would monetary policy be affected?

3. From 1979 to 1982, the FOMC used money growth as an intermediate target. To do so, the committee instructed the Open Market Trading Desk to target the level of reserves in the banking system. What was the justification for doing so? Explain why the result was unstable interest rates. Would you advocate a return to reserve targeting? Why or why not?

4. In 1992, the Bank of Canada eliminated the reserve requirement entirely. What do you think would happen if the Federal Reserve followed the same course? Alternatively, suppose that following an act of Congress, the Fed started to pay interest on required reserves. Would the change have an impact on the market for reserves?

5. Using economic data drawn from the Web site of the Federal Reserve Bank of St. Louis, plot the target federal funds rate and the Taylor rule for the past two years. Evaluate the result.

6. The Web site of the Federal Reserve Bank of New York contains information on the target federal funds rate. Find the data and describe the changes that have occurred over the past year. Using the data and information you can gather from the FOMC's press releases, discuss the justification for the changes you see.

7. In Applying the Concept: Making January 1, 2000, Uneventful, we discussed the Fed's planning for Y2K. What would have happened if the Fed had failed to provide the additional cash demanded by households?

8. Economists believe that central banks should be as transparent as possible, allowing the public to accurately forecast changes in interest policy. Explain the justification for this belief. What would happen if policymakers constantly surprised the public?

9. Suppose Congress banned discount lending. What would be the consequences?

10. The European Central Bank's Web site contains information on the interest rates under the bank's control. At what levels are they now and when did they last change? At the press conference held at the time of the last change, how did the Governing Council justify the action?

11. The ECB pays a market-based interest rate on required reserves and a lower rate on excess reserves. Explain why the system is structured this way.

12. Draw a supply-and-demand diagram for overnight interbank loans in Europe. Compare it to Figure 18.1.

13. During the 1970s, the Fed was much more concerned with growth than it is today. The result was that inflation climbed from less than 4 percent to over 10 percent. What do you think the coefficients in the Taylor rule might be for that period? Would the coefficients for the inflation and output gaps be larger or smaller than they are today?

14. Collect information on the current state of the economy—growth, unemployment, inflation, interest rates. Using this information, predict what you think the FOMC is likely to do over the next year. Explain your predictions.

15. As part of monetary policy strategy, the ECB continues to announce a "reference value" for the growth of M3 (which is roughly equivalent to the U.S. M2) in the euro area. In contrast, the FOMC has stopped announcing targets for growth in the monetary aggregates, stating: "The FOMC believes that the behavior of money and credit will continue to have value for gauging economic and financial conditions." Can you justify either or both of these strategies? How?

Chapter 19

Exchange-Rate Policy and the Central Bank

On the morning of September 22, 2000, the Federal Reserve Bank of New York's foreign exchange desk began buying euros for the first time since the currency came into existence 21 months earlier. Meanwhile, central bank officials in Frankfurt, London, Tokyo, and Ottawa (Canada) did the same. Among them, they bought between €4 and €6 billion. The Fed alone bought €1.5 billion for $1.34 billion. This was the Fed's second foreign exchange intervention in five years.[1]

The whole operation took about two hours; when it was over, the central banks announced what they had done. As the ECB wrote in its press release, they did it because of "shared concern about the potential implications of recent movements in the euro exchange rate for the world economy." Since its inception on January 1, 1999, the euro had fallen steadily from $1.18 to $0.85, a decline of more than 25 percent. Though its low value had made exports cheap, bolstering the foreign sales of European-made products, it had also forced up the prices of imports. ECB officials, charged with maintaining price stability, found the high price of imports particularly troubling since they really did not want to raise interest rates just to bolster the value of their currency (which is what they would have had to do). Experts debated whether the euro should be worth $1.10 or $1, but all agreed that $0.85 was too low.

The coordinated intervention in the foreign exchange market made headlines around the world. The euro did appreciate briefly, rising to $0.89 on the day of the intervention, but by mid-October, it had returned to $0.85. The action may have been dramatic, but it wasn't effective. To understand why the intervention didn't work—and why the Fed almost never engages in foreign currency transactions—we need to examine the mechanics of how a central bank manages its country's exchange rate.

Both the United States and Europe are huge and largely self-contained economies. Exports and imports account for 10 to 15 percent of GDP. For the most part, these economies produce what they consume and invest, so on most days policymakers at the Fed and the ECB are justified in concentrating on the domestic economy and letting their exchange rates take care of themselves. But in small countries, central banks do not have that luxury. These countries are much more exposed to what goes on in the rest of the world, so changes in their exchange rates can have a dramatic impact on them.

Argentina provides an interesting example of how external and domestic factors interact in the making of monetary policy. Over the years, Argentina has suffered from severe inflation. During the 1970s, inflation averaged about 100 percent, meaning that prices doubled every year, while the economy grew about 3 percent a year. By 1989, inflation had climbed to more than 2,000 percent per year and the price level was 60 *billion* times what it had been 20 years before. Needless to say, growth fell. In 1990, real GDP was below its 1973 level and Argentina's economy was at a standstill.

---

[1] In an attempt to stem the fall in the value of the Japanese yen, on June 17, 1998, U.S. and Japanese authorities both exchanged dollars for yen. U.S. authorities bought $633 million worth of the Japanese currency.

The cause of such high inflation is often a combination of failed fiscal policy and failed monetary policy. Politicians want to spend too much, so they lean on central bankers to print more money. To discipline policymakers, in 1991 Argentineans implemented a mechanism called a *currency board,* which had two important attributes. First, Argentina's central bank, the Banco Central de la Republica Argentina, guaranteed that it would exchange Argentinean pesos for U.S. dollars on a one-for-one basis; it fixed its exchange rate. Second, the central bank was required to hold dollar assets equal to its domestic currency liabilities, again at a one-to-one exchange rate. For every peso note that was issued and every peso in commercial bank reserves that it created, the Central Bank of Argentina had to hold one U.S. dollar.

The results were almost miraculous. Inflation fell immediately; after a few years, it had completely disappeared. But as we will see later, the victory didn't last. By early January 2002, the currency board had collapsed, GDP had fallen by a quarter, and inflation had risen to over 30 percent.

The examples of the ECB and Argentina suggest a connection between domestic monetary policy and exchange rate policy. To avoid raising domestic interest rates, the ECB organized a coordinated intervention to shore up the value of the euro. To control the inflationary impulses of fiscal and monetary authorities, Argentina fixed its exchange rate to the dollar. If exchange rate policy is inseparable from interest-rate policy, we have left something essential out of our analysis by ignoring cross-border transactions. To rectify the omission, we turn now to a discussion of exchange-rate regimes. Why is a country's exchange rate linked to its domestic monetary policy? Are there circumstances when exchange-rate stabilization becomes the overriding objective of central bankers? If so, should they try to fix the rate at which their currency can be exchanged for some other currency? Should a country even consider giving up its currency entirely?

Linking Exchange-Rate Policy with Domestic Monetary Policy

Exchange-rate policy is integral to any monetary policy regime. The city of Chicago, for instance, has a fixed exchange rate with the rest of the United States—both use the dollar—so it has no independent monetary policy. Because Chicago's monetary policy is made by the FOMC, interest rates in Chicago are the same as interest rates everywhere else in the United States. Any discrepancy between the price of a bond in Chicago and the price of the same bond in San Francisco is wiped out instantly by arbitrage, as investors buy the bond where it is cheap and sell it where it is expensive (all this is done electronically). What is true for Chicago is true for any country: *When capital flows freely across a country's borders, a fixed exchange rate means giving up domestic monetary policy.*

There are two ways to see the connection between exchange rates and monetary policy. The first comes from thinking about the market for goods and *purchasing power parity;* the second builds on the Chicago/San Francisco market arbitrage example. Purchasing power parity tells us about the long-run tendencies of exchange rates, while capital market arbitrage shows us how short-run movements in exchange rates are tied to the supply and demand in the currency markets. Let's look at each of these approaches in more detail.

Inflation and the Long-Run Implications of Purchasing Power Parity

In Chapter 10, we studied the long-run determinants of exchange rates starting with the *law of one price.* Ignoring transportation costs, the law of one price says that identical goods should sell for the same price regardless of where they are sold. That is, the same television set should sell for the same price in Philadelphia and St. Louis. The concept of purchasing power parity extends the logic of the law of one price to a basket of goods and services. As long as goods can move freely across international boundaries, one unit of domestic currency should buy the same basket of goods anywhere in the world.

This apparently simple idea has important implications. It means that when prices change in one country but not in another, the exchange rate will adjust to reflect the change. If Mexican inflation is higher than U.S. inflation, for instance, the Mexican peso should depreciate relative to the dollar. If everything in Mexico costs more pesos, dollars should cost more pesos, too. Figure 10.4 confirmed that this principle works well over periods of several decades. *In the long run, changes in the exchange rate are tied to differences in inflation.*

To understand how this works, recall that purchasing power parity means that

$$\text{Pesos per dollar} = \frac{\text{Peso price of basket of goods in Mexico}}{\text{Dollar price of basket of goods in U.S.}} \qquad (1)$$

Taking the percentage change of both sides of this expression, we get[2]

$$\begin{array}{l}\text{Percentage change in} \\ \text{number of pesos per dollar}\end{array} = \begin{array}{l}\text{Percentage change} \\ \text{in peso price of} \\ \text{basket of goods} \\ \text{in Mexico}\end{array} - \begin{array}{l}\text{Percentage change} \\ \text{in dollar price of} \\ \text{basket of goods in U.S.}\end{array} \qquad (2)$$

Since the percentage change in the basket of goods is the same as inflation, we can rewrite this expression as

$$\begin{array}{l}\text{Percentage change in} \\ \text{number of pesos per dollar}\end{array} = \text{Mexican inflation} - \text{U.S. inflation} \qquad (3)$$

Thus, when Mexican inflation is higher than U.S. inflation, the number of pesos needed to buy a dollar rises. When U.S. inflation is higher than Mexican inflation, the reverse is true. An example can help us to see how this works. Say we need 10 pesos to purchase a dollar (so a peso is worth 10 cents) at the beginning of the year. During the year, Mexican inflation is 5 percent, and U.S. inflation is 2 percent. At the end of the year we would expect the exchange rate to change so we need 3 percent more pesos to purchase a dollar, or 10.3 pesos per dollar.

Purchasing power parity has immediate implications for monetary policy. If the Banco de México, Mexico's central bank, wants to fix its exchange rate, then Mexican monetary policy must be conducted so that Mexican inflation matches U.S. inflation. Alternatively, if Mexico wants its inflation to diverge from U.S. inflation, the peso–dollar exchange rate must be allowed to vary. *The central bank must choose between a fixed exchange rate and an independent inflation policy; it cannot have both.*

We could stop here, except for the fact that purchasing power parity works only over long periods, like decades. That is, even though the exchange rate *eventually* adjusts to differences between prices at home and abroad, deviations from purchasing power parity can last for years. While this time lag in exchange-rate movements might appear to ease restrictions on monetary policy, in fact it does not. To understand why, we need to examine what happens in the capital markets when investors can move their funds freely across international boundaries.

[2]In going from equation (1) to equation (2), we are using the approximation that the percentage change in (X/Y) equals the percentage change in X *minus* the percentage change in Y. This approximation works best for small changes.

Interest Rates and the Short-Run Implications of Capital Market Arbitrage

In the short run, a country's exchange rate is determined by supply and demand. The exchange value of the dollar depends on factors such as the preferences of Americans for foreign assets and the preferences of foreign investors for U.S. assets. In the short run, investors play a crucial role, since they are the ones who can move large quantities of dollars, euros, pounds, or pesos across international borders. Assuming that governments allow funds to flow into and out of their countries, these movements can occur very quickly.

To understand the implications of international capital mobility, we need to look at how investors decide whether to purchase a foreign or a domestic bond. Given two bonds of equal risk, investors will always buy the one with the higher expected return. And when two otherwise identical bonds differ in yield, investors will bid up the price of the high-return bond and bid down the price of the low-return bond until the two converge. Thus, arbitrage in the capital market ensures that two equally risky bonds have the same expected return.

Like purchasing power parity, capital market arbitrage has immediate implications for monetary policy. Think about two bonds that are identical except that one is issued in Chicago and the other in San Francisco. The two bonds are equally risky, with the same time to maturity and the same coupon rate. Arbitrage ensures that they will sell for the same price and so have the same interest rate. Does it matter that both these bonds make payments in dollars?

To answer this question, we can substitute bonds issued in different countries that promise payments in their currencies. What happens if we compare a Chicago bond to an otherwise identical bond issued in London and denominated in pounds? At what interest rates will investors be indifferent between the Chicago bond and the London bond?

Consider a hypothetical case in which the Bank of England decides to fix the exchange rate at $1.50 per pound. If the pound–dollar exchange rate is fixed, and everyone expects that it will remain fixed, we can ignore the fact that the two investments are denominated in different currencies. Say a U.S. investor is considering what to do with $1,500 over the next year. The options are to buy a one-year Chicago bond with an interest rate we will call simply i or a one-year London bond with an interest rate i^f (the superscript f stands for *foreign*). Investing in London requires converting dollars to pounds and buying the bond at the beginning of the year, then taking the proceeds and reconverting them to dollars at the end of the year.

At a fixed exchange rate of $1.50 per pound, $1,500 becomes £1,000 (the "£" is the symbol used for the pound). After a year, this amount becomes £1,000 $(1 + i^f)$. Reconverting to dollars, again at the fixed exchange rate of $1.50 per £, the U.S. investor has $1,500 $(1 + i^f)$. In deciding which bond to buy, then, the investor should compare $1,500 $(1 + i^f)$ to the return from the Chicago bond, which is $1,500 $(1 + i)$. Because arbitrage in the capital market equates these two returns, under a fixed exchange rate:

$$\$1,500(1 + i^f) = \$1,500(1 + i) \tag{4}$$

and so

$$i^f = i. \tag{5}$$

Thus, investors will be indifferent between investing in a dollar-denominated bond in Chicago or a pound-denominated bond in London only when the interest rates in the two cities are the same. If interest rates differ in Chicago and London, and the dollar–pound exchange rate is fixed, investors will move funds back and forth, wiping out the difference. This example is analogous to the comparison between bonds sold in Chicago and in San Francisco. Since the dollar exchange rate between the two cities is fixed and capital is free to move between them, their interest rates must be the same.[3]

Capital Controls and the Policymakers' Choice

At first glance, it may seem as if policymakers can choose between stabilizing the domestic interest rate and stabilizing the exchange rate. But our discussion of interest rates and arbitrage in the last section depended critically on the ability of investors to move capital across international boundaries. If capital cannot flow freely between London and Chicago, there is no mechanism to equate interest rates in the two countries, and our logic falls apart. Thus, we need to revise our conclusion: So long as capital can flow freely between countries, monetary policymakers must choose between fixing their exchange rate and fixing their interest rate. A country *cannot*

- be open to international capital flows,
- control its domestic interest rate, *and*
- fix its exchange rate.

Policymakers must choose two of these three options.

Looking around the world, we see that different countries have made different choices. The United States, for example, has an open capital market, a controlled domestic interest rate, and a freely floating dollar. During the 1990s, Argentina maintained an open capital market but fixed its exchange rate with the dollar, giving up control of domestic interest rates. But these are not the only alternatives; there is another possibility that is worth exploring. If a country is willing to forgo participation in international capital markets, it can impose capital controls, fix its exchange rate, and still use monetary policy to pursue its domestic objectives.

Capital controls go very much against the grain of modern economic thinking. The consensus among economists is that open capital markets benefit everyone. In the same way that international trade allows countries to exploit their comparative advantage, internationally integrated capital markets ensure that capital goes to its most efficient uses. The free flow of capital across borders enhances competition, improves opportunities for diversification, and equalizes rates of return (adjusted for risk). As this view took hold in the late 20th century, countries removed the restrictions on the flow of capital that had been initiated earlier in the century.[4]

---

[3]Taking the analysis one step further, when the exchange rate is free to move, capital market arbitrage ensures that the return on bonds of similar maturity and risk will be the same when expressed in the same currency. This is the logic that leads to the interest-rate parity condition discussed in Appendix 10. That is, with flexible exchange rates, interest-rate differentials must equal the expected change in the exchange rate over the term of the bond. When capital moves freely across international boundaries, policymakers can choose a combination of an interest-rate differential and exchange-rate depreciation.

[4]Like central banks, controls on international capital flows are a 20th-century innovation. One of the hallmarks of the period between the world wars (the 1920s and 1930s) was the strong movement toward national autonomy. As the world economy collapsed during the Great Depression, countries tried to isolate themselves by instituting restrictions on both the trade in goods and services and the transfer of capital. Restrictions on the ability of foreigners to own domestic assets, and on everyone's ability to transfer currency or gold out of a country, became common. For example, in the 1930s, the Nazis severely restricted Germans' ability to take anything valuable out of the country. Many of these restrictions became part of the international financial system after World War II and were maintained by industrialized countries into the 1970s and beyond. Until 1979, the British government maintained controls on investments made abroad by U.K. residents. Until 1974, the United States taxed interest received by Americans on foreign bonds.

When we look at large industrialized countries, the benefits of open capital markets are easy to see. U.S. workers benefit from the jobs at Honda's assembly plant in Marysville, Ohio, and U.S. investors benefit from their access to French and German stocks (as discussed in the Chapter 10 Your Financial World on investing overseas). But for emerging-markets countries, this greater openness has come with certain risks. The problem is that capital that flows into a country can also flow out, and it can do so quickly. That means that countries with open capital markets are vulnerable to sudden changes in investor sentiment. Investors may decide to sell a country's bonds, driving their prices down and their interest rates up. They convert the proceeds of the sale into foreign currency, driving the value of the domestic currency down. If everyone loses confidence in a country at the same time, the result is similar to a bank run: All foreign investors leave at once, precipitating a financial collapse. Thailand in 1997 (discussed in Chapter 17) and Korea in 1998 (described in Chapter 10) are just two examples. (We will examine the mechanics of these crises in the next section of this chapter.)

It is tempting for government officials to try to avert such crises by restricting people's ability to move capital into and out of a country—by imposing controls on the flow of capital. There are two basic types of capital control. Inflow controls restrict the ability of foreigners to invest in a country; outflow controls place obstacles in the way of selling investments and taking funds out. During much of the 1990s, foreigners wishing to invest in Chile were required to make a one-year, zero-interest deposit of 20 percent of the investment at the central bank. This inflow control penalized short-term investments, encouraging investors to invest for a longer period.

Outflow controls include restrictions on the ability of domestic residents to purchase foreign assets, and often include prohibitions on removing currency from the country. In fall 1998, Malaysian citizens were prohibited from taking more than 1,000 *ringgit* in cash (worth a bit more than $250 at the time) out of the country, while foreigners could leave with at most the amount they had brought with them when they entered the country. Any nonresident who sold a Malaysian security was required to hold the proceeds in the country for at least 12 months before taking it out. These controls effectively cut Malaysia off from the world capital market.[5]

Mechanics of Exchange-Rate Management

Since both the Federal Reserve and the European Central Bank buy and sell securities to maintain their overnight interbank interest rates at target level, they must have given up control of their exchange rates.[6] No wonder their intervention on September 22, 2000, had almost no effect on the value of the euro. Even so, Fed and ECB policies *do* have an impact on the value of the dollar and the euro. And if either central bank chose to, it could give up controlling interest rates and target the exchange rate instead.

How would they do it? What are the mechanics of exchange-rate management and exchange-rate intervention? We have seen that everything the central bank does has

---

[5]For a detailed description of the Malaysian experience in 1998, see Ethan Kaplan and Dani Rodrik, "Did the Malaysian Capital Controls Work?" National Bureau of Economic Research Working Paper No. 8142, February 2001.

[6]If you read news reports carefully, you will discover a strange division of responsibility. In many countries, including the United States and the European Union, government officials will claim that the central bank is in charge of interest rates but the Finance Ministry or Treasury is in charge of exchange-rate policy. In the United States, for example, the Secretary of the Treasury is in charge of exchange-rate policy, while the FOMC makes interest-rate policy. If this division of responsibility sounds a bit strange, it is. As we have learned, domestic monetary policy and exchange-rate policy cannot be independent.

APPLYING THE CONCEPT
MALAYSIA IMPOSES CAPITAL CONTROLS

Following the financial crises that enveloped Thailand and Indonesia in 1997, then Korea and Russia in 1998, most emerging-markets countries suffered extreme stress. To reduce risk, foreign investors simply pulled out. They sold those countries' bonds, driving their prices down and their interest rates up, and then converted the proceeds into foreign currencies, driving the value of the domestic currencies down. As in a bank run, no one wanted to be last in line to sell; everyone rushed to leave at once. Plummeting exchange rates and skyrocketing interest rates brought these economies to their knees. Banks and industrial firms that had once been able to borrow easily became desperately short of funds.

The typical response of countries experiencing such a financial crisis is for the government to borrow from other countries and the IMF and use the borrowed funds to meet its obligations. Eventually, interest rates come down, the exchange rate recovers, foreign investors return, and the government repays the loans. But Malaysia adopted a different course. Believing there was nothing inherently wrong with the nation's economy and that the crisis resembled a bank run more than anything else, officials took the extreme step of implementing strict capital controls. By placing severe limits on investors' ability to remove money from the country, they ensured that foreign investments would remain there. More important, they could fix the value of their currency, the ringgit, and lower domestic interest rates.

At the time, Western economists condemned the policy, claiming that it would destroy the country's economy for years to come. While experts continue to argue about the wisdom of Malaysia's capital controls, their initial response was clearly mistaken. Malaysia's recovery took only two years, compared to five years for Thailand and Indonesia. Would the recovery have been even faster without the capital controls? We will never know for sure. But if countries start instituting capital controls every time there is a whiff of crisis, they will dramatically increase the risk of investing in emerging-market countries. Investors will become wary of putting money into foreign countries if they aren't sure they will be able to take it out whenever they want.

something to do with its balance sheet. Foreign exchange intervention is no exception. So to look at the mechanics of exchange-rate management, we'll start with the central bank's balance sheet. Once we understand the balance-sheet effects of foreign currency intervention, we can look more closely at what large central banks like the Fed and the ECB actually do.

The Central Bank's Balance Sheet

If all policymakers want to do is to fix the exchange rate, there is a simple way to do it: They can offer to buy and sell their country's currency at a fixed rate. For example, if officials at the Federal Reserve decided to fix the dollar–euro exchange rate at one to one, they would simply stand ready to exchange dollars for euros whenever anyone

YOUR FINANCIAL WORLD

Emerging-Markets Crises and You

One morning you awaken to news of a severe financial crisis in an emerging market country. As in Asia in 1997 and Latin America in 2002, some part of the developing world appears to be near collapse. The guardians of the financial system—officials from the central bank, the finance ministry, and international organizations like the IMF—are convening to decide what to do. In the meantime, the market value of investments in the emerging world is plummeting as traders flee to safety, moving their money into the United States and Europe. What should you do?

If you followed the advice in Chapter 10, some of your investments are in foreign stocks and bonds, so this crisis looks as if it may have an impact on you. Will it? The answer is it will have virtually no effect at all. Here's why. First, your portfolio should be well diversified, so you will be prepared for the possibility that some of your investments will do poorly. Second, these countries are small in an economic sense—the fact that they are "emerging" means they are at an early stage of development—

so your investments there will be small. To give some idea of just how small these countries are economically and financially, note that Malaysia's GDP is less than one one-hundredth the size of the U.S. GDP, and the Malaysian financial market is one five-hundredth the size of the U.S. financial market. In fact, if you diversified your investments internationally, purchasing stocks based on the size of each country's capital market, for each $100 you invested, you would put $54 in the United States, $28 in Europe, $9 in Japan, and 22 cents in Malaysia! So, even if the Malaysian stock market crashed by 50 percent, you would only lose 11 cents per $100 you had invested.

Finally, most of your investments are likely to be in a retirement account, which you probably won't need for decades. Over the years that you hold these investments, their value will go up and down; occasional losses are just bumps in the road. As long as you take a long-term perspective and diversify your holdings, these crises will have only a negligible impact on you.

asked. Buying euros wouldn't be much of a problem, since the Federal Reserve can print all the dollars it needs. But selling euros in exchange for dollars might pose some difficulty unless the Fed had a substantial euro reserve. We will ignore this complication for now and return to it in the next section, when we discuss the problem of speculative attacks.

In this example, as the Fed works to maintain a fixed dollar–euro exchange rate, its balance sheet shifts. When it buys euros, it increases its dollar liabilities; when it sells euros, it reduces its dollar liabilities (refer back to the section of Chapter 17 titled "Foreign Exchange Intervention"). These interventions have an impact on interest rates and, through the deposit expansion multiplier, on the quantity of money in the economy as well. Buying euros or selling dollars increases the supply of reserves to the banking system, putting downward pressure on interest rates and expanding the quantity of money. Remember that in taking these actions, the Fed responds to the market. The decision to buy and sell euros is made by financial market participants, not the Fed. Just by looking at the mechanics of the central bank's balance sheet, we can see that *controlling the exchange rate means giving up control of the size of reserves so that the market determines the interest rate.*

To see how this process works in practice, let's go back to September 2000, when the largest central banks in the world intervened to bolster the value of the euro. We'll focus on the Federal Reserve's decision to purchase €1.5 billion in exchange for $1.34 billion, ignoring the actions of the other central banks on that day as well as the open market operations that followed. When Fed employees bought euros, they did it the

Figure 19.1   Change in the Federal Reserve's Balance Sheet Immediately following a Purchase of Euros

Assets	Liabilities
Euro reserves +$1.34 billion (German government bonds)	Commercial bank reserves +$1.34 billion

same way they buy anything else: They created commercial bank liabilities. Then, as soon as they received the €1.5 billion from foreign exchange dealers, they spent it on bonds issued by euro-area governments. We will refer to these bonds as German government bonds, since that is primarily how the Fed holds its euro-denominated reserves.

The balance-sheet implications of this exchange are straightforward. Figure 19.1 shows the results of the intervention. Looking at the asset side, and following the standard convention of reporting the value of the central bank's foreign exchange reserves in domestic currency units, we see that the Fed has increased its euro-denominated foreign exchange reserve assets by $1.34 billion. On the liabilities side of the balance sheet, we see that commercial bank reserves have increased by the same amount.

This T-account should look familiar. If we focus on the liabilities side of the balance sheet, we see that the purchase of German government bonds is identical to a purchase of U.S. Treasury bonds. That is, the purchase of a security has added reserves to the banking system. The only difference is the issuer of the bond. Like any other change in reserves, this one has a direct impact on the quantity of money in the economy. In other words, it is expansionary, so it reduces domestic interest rates. *A foreign exchange intervention has the same impact on reserves as a domestic open market operation.*

Will this intervention change the exchange rate? Figure 19.2 shows what happens. Recall from Chapter 10 that the dollar exchange rate is determined by the supply of and demand for dollars. The Fed did supply dollars to the market through its intervention, but more important, the interest rate has fallen. Remember that whenever investing in the United States becomes less attractive relative to investing somewhere else, the result is a decrease in the demand for dollars that will be used by foreigners to purchase U.S. assets and an increase in the supply of dollars that will be used by Americans to purchase foreign assets. In this example, assuming that the Fed does nothing but purchase German government bonds, the U.S. interest rate will fall while European interest rates remain the same.[7] Foreign investors will want to buy fewer American bonds, and they will need fewer dollars to do it. As a result, the demand for dollars in the foreign exchange market falls. Meanwhile, U.S. investors will want to buy more foreign bonds, and they supply more dollars to do that. The demand and supply shifts shown in Figure 19.2 together drive the value of the dollar

MARKETS

[7]We could complicate the analysis in two ways. First, the Fed's purchase of German government bonds could drive up the price of those bonds, driving down European interest rates. Given the entire size of the European government bond market, this effect will be extremely small, so we will ignore it. Second, we could include the ECB's actions in our analysis as well. The ECB would sell U.S. Treasury bonds in exchange for euros, shrinking the size of euro-area commercial bank reserves and raising euro-area interest rates. Because this action would only reinforce the fall in U.S. interest rates *relative to* those in the euro area, we can safely ignore it.

Figure 19.2 Effect of a Decrease in U.S. Interest Rates Relative to Interest Rates in the Euro Area

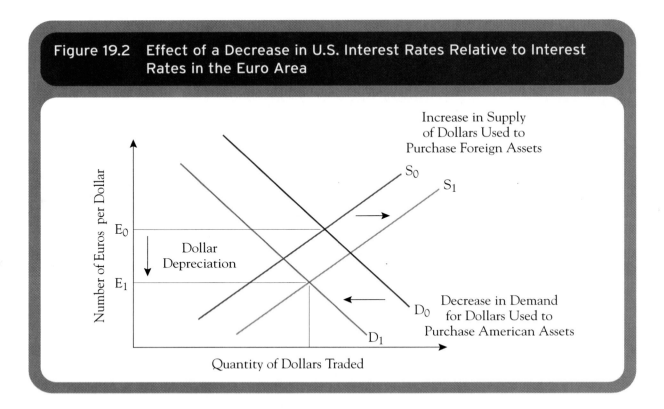

down and the value of the euro up. The dollar depreciates and the euro appreciates, reducing the number of euros offered per dollar in the foreign exchange market.

You may think there is something strange about this discussion. We started with a foreign exchange intervention in which the Fed purchased euros and noted its impact on the dollar–euro exchange rate. But the reason the exchange rate moved was that the domestic interest rate changed, shifting the demand for dollars in the foreign exchange market. By making domestic U.S. investment less attractive, the intervention prompted people to purchase fewer dollars, driving the price of dollars down. Our conclusion is that *a foreign exchange intervention affects the value of a country's currency by changing domestic interest rates*.

This conclusion has an important implication. It means that *any central bank policy that influences the domestic interest rate will affect the exchange rate*. The fact that we started with an exchange-rate intervention is irrelevant. An open market purchase or sale works exactly the same way. If the Federal Reserve bought U.S. Treasury bonds instead of euro-denominated bonds, the action would drive down U.S. interest rates, decreasing the demand for dollars in the foreign exchange market and causing a decline in the value of the dollar. There is nothing special about a foreign exchange intervention.

Sterilized Intervention

On September 22, 2000, when the ECB, the Federal Reserve, the Bank of Japan, the Bank of England, and the Bank of Canada all intervened to buy euros, none of them changed their domestic interest-rate targets. No wonder the value of the euro didn't change! But that means their transactions must have been different from the one we just studied. We assumed that when the Fed bought euros, it increased commercial bank reserves, which would reduce interest rates in the absence of any other action. Such a move is an example of an **unsterilized foreign exchange intervention**, one that changes central bank liabilities. But in large countries, central banks don't operate that way. Instead, they engage in **sterilized foreign exchange interventions**, in which a change in foreign exchange reserves alters the asset side of the central bank's balance sheet but the domestic monetary base remains unaffected.

A sterilized intervention is actually a combination of two transactions. First there is the purchase or sale of foreign currency reserves, which by itself changes the central bank's liabilities. But this is immediately followed by an open market operation of exactly the same size, designed to offset the impact of the first transaction on the monetary base. For example, the Fed's purchase of a German government bond, which would increase reserves, is offset by the sale of a U.S. Treasury bond. Together, these two actions leave the level of reserves unchanged. Such an intervention is sterilized with respect to its affect on the monetary base, or the size of the central bank's balance sheet. *An intervention is <u>unsterilized</u> if it changes the monetary base and <u>sterilized</u> if it does not change the monetary base.*

"If this doesn't help you don't worry, it's a placebo."

To see what happens in practice, let's go back to September 22, 2000, one last time. Between 7:11 a.m. and 9:20 a.m., the Federal Reserve Bank of New York sold $1.34 billion in exchange for €1.5 billion. We have already seen that the initial impact on the Fed's balance sheet was to increase the level of reserves in the banking system. But the FOMC had not changed the target federal funds rate, so the job of the Open Market Trading Desk was the same as it had been every day since May 17, when the prevailing $6\frac{1}{2}$ percent target rate had been put in place.

To do their job, the Federal Reserve Bank of New York staff entered the intervention numbers into their spreadsheet before estimating the size of the day's temporary operation. In figuring out what to do to keep the federal funds rate on target, they took account of the quantity of reserves their colleagues had already added. By 10:00 a.m., when the open market operations were completed, the impact of the foreign exchange intervention on the Fed's liabilities had disappeared.[8] The foreign exchange desk had purchased bonds issued by a euro-area government, paying for them with reserves, and the Open Market Desk had sold U.S. Treasury bonds to reverse the potential impact.

Figure 19.3 shows the result on the Fed's balance sheet. Notice two things. First, commercial bank reserves remain unchanged following a sterilized intervention, so domestic monetary policy does not change. Second, the intervention changes the *composition* of the asset side of the central bank's balance sheet. The Fed has swapped U.S. Treasury bonds for bonds issued by the German government—an action that has no impact on the exchange rate.

---

[8]Because foreign currency transactions take two days to settle, while temporary open market operations are settled the same day, the open market operation that sterilizes the foreign exchange intervention will be done the next day. Since the two transactions will settle at the same time, the intervention won't have an impact for even a few hours.

> ## Figure 19.3 Change in the Federal Reserve's Balance Sheet following a *Sterilized* Purchase of Euro-Denominated Bonds
>
> | Assets | | Liabilities |
> |---|---|---|
> | Euro Reserves (German Government Bonds) | +$1.34 billion | Commercial Bank Reserves unchanged |
> | Securities (U.S. Treasury Bonds) | –$1.34 billion | |

The Costs, Benefits, and Risks of Fixed Exchange Rates

STABILITY

Many countries allow their exchange rates to float freely, so that the value of their currencies is determined in the financial markets. But others—especially small, emerging-market countries—fix their exchange rates. That is, officials of the central bank and the finance ministry agree that the best policy is to maintain a predictable value for their currency, so they target the exchange rate. Why do some countries make that decision? Surely fixing the exchange rate has costs as well as benefits. We now turn to a brief discussion of the trade-offs.

Assessing the Costs and Benefits

The owners of the Blue Jays, Toronto's major league baseball team, probably wouldn't mind if the Bank of Canada decided to fix the exchange rate for the U.S. and Canadian dollars. They face a common problem for companies engaged in international trade: they pay most of their expenses in one currency and receive the bulk of their revenues in another. Specifically, the Blue Jays receive about 80 percent of their revenue in Canadian dollars but pay 80 percent of their expenses—including a $50 million annual payroll (in 2004) and the bills for chartered planes and fancy hotel rooms—in U.S. dollars. So if the Canadian dollar depreciates, as it did during the late 1990s, the Blue Jays incur a financial loss. Unless they hedge this exchange-rate risk, for each 10 percent drop in the value of the Canadian dollar they will lose something like $6 million. The more volatile exchange rates become, the worse the problem gets. If the exchange rates were fixed, the Blue Jays' risk would disappear.[9]

Goods and services aren't the only things that cross international borders; capital does, too. Fixed exchange rates not only simplify operations for businesses that trade internationally, they also reduce the risk that investors face when they hold foreign stocks and bonds. Think of what happens if you buy a Korean government bond. Unlike a U.S. Treasury bond, on which the interest rate tells you the return, a Korean

---

[9]The Toronto Blue Jays do hedge their foreign exchange risk in the derivatives market. In effect, they pay someone for insurance against moves in the exchange rate. Doing so makes their expenses and profits more predictable, but it isn't free.

YOUR FINANCIAL WORLD
Don't Bet on Exchange Rates

Lots of people have an opinion about the likely course of exchange rates. Should you listen to them to try to turn a profit on changes in the exchange rate? The answer is surely no. To see why, let's look at a recent episode in economic history. In 2002, U.S. imports exceeded exports by nearly 5 percent of GDP (that's a really big current account deficit); the economy was faltering; the stock market was declining; but still the dollar was strong. Moreover, the Japanese yen remained strong after a decade of stagnation and record low interest rates. Anyone who followed such matters would tell you that both the dollar and the yen should have depreciated. But having a good sense of what will happen over the long run doesn't help much in the short run. What the experts can't tell you is *when* the dollar will depreciate.

So how can you get a forecast of the future exchange rate? You can look at the *forward markets* for the major currencies. In these markets, foreign currency dealers agree today to a price at which they will sell euros (or yen or other major currencies) three months from now. Since they don't want to incur losses, the dealers will use all the information available to them (including interest rates) to make the most accurate forecast they can for the exchange rate on the day they agree to make the transaction. But if you look at the newspaper, you will discover that forward rates are virtually always within 1 or 2 percent of the current spot rate. In other words, the best forecast is that the exchange rate won't change much. (Take a look at the "Exchange Rates" column in the business section of a newspaper like *The Wall Street Journal* to confirm this claim.) This tendency holds true even if the Big Mac index (described in Chapter 10) or more sophisticated calculations based on purchasing power parity tell us that the exchange rate should move significantly in one direction or another.

The problem is that, in the short run, exchange rates are inherently unpredictable. No one has any idea what is going to happen over the next week, month, or even year. In short, the best forecast of the future exchange rate is usually today's exchange rate. Because you really can't do any better than that, betting on exchange rates is a bad idea.

bond involves the possibility that the dollar–Korean *won* exchange rate may change. An increase in the number of won needed to purchase one dollar—so that the dollar becomes more valuable—would reduce the return on the Korean bond by the amount of the dollar's appreciation.[10]

So fixed exchange rates seem to be a good idea for both businesses and investors. They also have another potential benefit. A fixed exchange rate ties policymakers' hands. Remember that in the long run, the exchange rate is determined by inflation differentials. In countries that are prone to bouts of high inflation, a fixed exchange rate may be the only way to establish a credible low-inflation policy. It enforces low-inflation discipline on both central bankers and politicians, and an exchange rate target enhances transparency and accountability.

There is one serious drawback to a fixed exchange rate, however. It *imports* monetary policy. Fixing your currency's value to that of another country means adopting the other country's interest-rate policy. When Argentina fixed the exchange rate of the peso to the U.S. dollar, policymakers gave up control of Argentinean interest rates and

---

[10]A numerical example helps clarify this point. Assume that a U.S. investor converts $1,000 into Korean won at a rate of 1,000 won per dollar and then buys a one-year, 10 percent Korean government bond. At the end of the year, the bond pays 1,100,000 won. If the exchange rate has not changed, this amount can be exchanged for $1,100. But if the dollar appreciates 10 percent during the year, so that the exchange rate rises to 1,100 won per dollar, then the American investor is left with only $1,000. The total return to holding the Korean bond equals the Korean interest rate minus the dollar's appreciation. Appendix 10 describes this phenomenon in more detail.

effectively handed it over to the FOMC. Needless to say, when the FOMC sets the target federal funds rate, committee members don't worry much about what is going on in Argentina. What this means is that a fixed exchange rate makes the most sense when the two countries involved have similar macroeconomic fluctuations. Otherwise, the country with the flexible exchange rate that is in control of monetary policy (e.g., the U.S.) might be raising interest rates to combat domestic inflation at the same time that the other country (e.g., Argentina) is going into recession.

In deciding whether to fix their country's exchange rate, policymakers should consider several additional matters. First, when a country fixes its exchange rate, the central bank is offering to buy and sell its own currency at a fixed rate. To honor this commitment to purchase currency, monetary policymakers will need ample currency reserves. For instance, a country that fixes its exchange rate to the dollar needs to hold dollars in reserve. Living up to this promise in a world of free-flowing capital requires a high level of foreign exchange reserves. For many countries, the billions of dollars required are both difficult to obtain and expensive to keep.

Second, since floating exchange rates act as automatic macroeconomic stabilizers, fixing the exchange rate means reducing the domestic economy's natural ability to respond to macroeconomic shocks. Imagine a country on the verge of recession. If monetary policymakers can, they will react by lowering interest rates in an attempt to keep the economy from slowing. Beyond the direct effect on investment and consumption, lower interest rates make domestic bonds less attractive to foreigners, reducing the demand for the domestic currency and driving down its value. The resulting currency depreciation drives down the price foreigners must pay for domestic exports, increasing the demand for them and amplifying the impact of the initial interest-rate reduction. With a fixed exchange rate, this stabilization mechanism is completely shut down.

The Danger of Speculative Attacks

While fixed exchange rates may have benefits for a country's economy, they are fragile and prone to a type of crisis called a speculative attack. To understand the nature of a speculative attack, imagine that a country is trying to maintain a fixed exchange rate. Now suppose that for some reason, financial market participants come to believe that the government will need to devalue its currency in the near future. They won't wait; instead, investors will attack the currency and force an immediate devaluation.

The mechanics of the attack are straightforward. Take the example of the attack on the Thai *baht* in 1997. Recall from Chapter 17 that, through the mid-1990s, the Bank of Thailand was committed to maintaining a fixed exchange rate of approximately 26 baht to the U.S. dollar. To do so, officials had to make sure foreign currency traders believed that the Bank of Thailand had enough dollars on hand to buy however many baht the traders wanted to sell. In summer 1997, financial market participants began to question whether the reserves at the central bank really were big enough, and they swung into action. Speculators borrowed baht at domestic Thai interest rates, took them to the central bank to convert them to dollars at the rate of 26 to one, and then invested the dollars in short-term, interest-bearing securities in the United States. The immediate impact of these transactions was to drain the Bank of Thailand's dollar reserves. The lower the dollar reserves, the less likely that the Thais would be able to meet further requests to convert baht into dollars. And the more baht speculators borrowed to convert into dollars, the further the reserves fell.

The details are instructive. Imagine that, anticipating a severe depreciation, you borrow 2.6 million baht. You take them to the Bank of Thailand and convert them into $100,000 at the fixed rate of 26 to one. With the proceeds, you buy U.S. Treasury bills. One week later, your expectations are realized and the baht depreciates by 10 percent. Now you need only $90,909 to obtain the 2.6 million baht with which to repay the loan. You've made an almost instant profit of over $9,000.[11] Since international currency speculators have very deep pockets, they can quickly drain billions of dollars from a central bank this way—and make a huge profit in the process.[12]

What causes a speculative attack? There are two possibilities. The first brings us back to fiscal policy: Remember that politicians can make the central banker's job impossible. Ensuring that a currency retains its value means keeping domestic inflation at the same level as that of the country to which your exchange rate is pegged. If investors begin to think that at current levels, government spending must ultimately increase inflation, they will stop believing that officials can maintain the exchange rate at its fixed level. This seems to have been an important part of what happened during the Asian crisis of 1997.

But speculative attacks can occur even when a country's fiscal and monetary policymakers are behaving

"Part of me wants to help you with your crisis, Hargraves, but part of me wants to go to lunch."

SOURCE: © The New Yorker Collection 1996. Leo Cullum from cartoonbank.com. All Rights Reserved.

responsibly. They can arise spontaneously out of nowhere. If by chance enough currency speculators simply decide that a central bank cannot maintain its exchange rate, they will attack it, mobilizing tens of billions of dollars virtually overnight. To make matters even worse, spontaneous speculative attacks are a bit like bank runs; they can be contagious.

Many observers suspect that in today's world, no central bank has the resources to withstand such an attack. It would take substantial foreign exchange reserves to even think about trying.

Summarizing the Case for a Fixed Exchange Rate

The easiest way to summarize this discussion is to make a list of the conditions under which adopting a fixed exchange rate makes sense for a country. A country will be better off fixing its exchange rate if it has all three of these:

- A poor reputation for controlling inflation on its own.
- An economy that is well integrated with the one to whose currency the rate is fixed, trading significantly with it and sharing similar macroeconomic characteristics.
- A high level of foreign exchange reserves.

Regardless of how closely a country meets these criteria, fixed exchange rates are still risky to adopt and difficult to maintain.

---

[11]This simple example ignores both the interest you would need to pay to borrow the baht and the interest you would receive on the Treasury bills. An exact calculation would take the difference between the two interest rates into account and would likely reduce the profit. But since such transactions are usually done over days or weeks at most, this adjustment would have only a modest impact on the return. The point is that this is a very profitable transaction.

[12]In September 1992, the Bank of England belonged to the European Exchange Rate Mechanism, which linked the exchange rates of many countries. It effectively pegged the pound to the then-independent German currency, the deutsche mark. In an attempt to contain domestic inflation, the Germans raised interest rates dramatically, a policy the British did not want to follow. When speculators realized that the situation was untenable—that the Bank of England could not fix its exchange rate and have a lower interest rate than the Germans—they attacked. George Soros is reputed to have made over $1 billion betting that the pound would be devalued.

APPLYING THE CONCEPT
THE GOLD STANDARD: AN EXCHANGE-RATE REGIME
WHOSE TIME HAS PASSED

If you take a dollar bill to the Federal Reserve, officials will give you a new one. Should they offer to give you gold instead? That would be returning to the time when the dollar was "as good as gold." Today, advocates of a return to the gold standard claim that it would eliminate inflation. As evidence, they point to the time before World War I, when the United States was on the gold standard and inflation averaged less than 1 percent per year. What these advocates don't advertise is that, while inflation was low *on average,* it was highly variable, fluctuating between +3¼ percent and -3¼ percent. (See Figure 19.4.) In fact, for much of the late 19th century, prices fell steadily. Only early in the 20th century did they rise back to a level not far above where they started in 1880.

The focus on past inflation obscures the long list of reasons why no economist today advocates a return to the gold standard. To begin with,

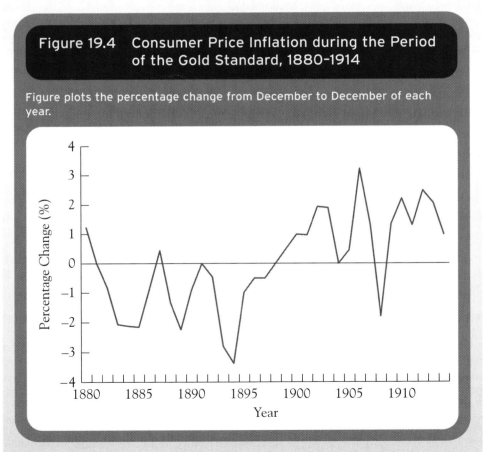

Figure 19.4   Consumer Price Inflation during the Period of the Gold Standard, 1880-1914

Figure plots the percentage change from December to December of each year.

SOURE: *Data from Jack W. Wilson and Charles P. Jones, "A Comparison of Annual Common Stock Returns: 1871–1925 and 1926–1985,"* Journal of Business 60, 1987, pp. 239–258. Chicago: University of Chicago Press, 1987.

continued from previous page

the gold standard obligates the central bank to fix the price of something we don't really care about. Instead of stabilizing the prices of the goods we buy and consume, the central bank fixes the dollar price of gold. In place of fluctuations in the market price of gold, there are fluctuations in the dollar price of goods.

Then there is the fact that, under the gold standard, the amount of money in the economy would depend on the amount of gold available. More gold equals more money. Since, in the long run, inflation is tied to money growth, this means that inflation depends on the rate at which gold is mined.* Why should monetary policy be determined by the rate at which South Africa and Russia dig gold from the ground? Moreover, any political disruption in those parts of the world could have dramatic monetary policy effects.

The case for gold grows even less persuasive when we realize that the gold standard is an exchange rate policy, too.[†] The promise to convert dollars into gold means that international transactions must be settled in gold. So when the value of imports does not exactly match the value of exports, gold is transferred from one country to another. Thus, a country with a current account deficit—whose imports exceed its exports—has to pay the difference by transferring gold to countries with current account surpluses. (See Appendix 19 for a brief description of balance-of-payments accounting.) With less gold, the country's central bank must contract its balance sheet, raising interest rates, reducing the quantity of money and credit in the economy, and driving domestic prices down. Under a gold standard, countries running current account deficits will be forced into deflation. Meanwhile, countries with current account surpluses can allow their gold inflows to generate inflation, but they need not. Under the gold standard, a central bank can have too little gold, but it can never have too much.

Economic historians believe that gold flows played a central role in spreading the Great Depression of the 1930s throughout the world. After World War I, all the major countries in the world worked to reconstruct the gold standard. By the late 1920s, they had succeeded. At the time, both the United States and France were running current account surpluses, absorbing the world's gold into their vaults. But instead of allowing the gold inflows to expand the quantity of money in their financial systems, authorities in both countries tightened monetary policy in an attempt to cool off their overheated, inflation-prone economies. The result was catastrophic, since it forced countries with current account deficits and gold outflows to tighten their monetary policies even more. The quantity of money available worldwide was shrinking, and the price level had to go down with it. The resulting deflation increased the likelihood that people would default on loans, destroying the economic and

*The fact that there were few gold discoveries in the 1870s and 1880s, followed by gold rushes in Alaska and South Africa in the 1890s, accounted for the historical pattern in the price data—deflation followed by inflation.

[†]Before the advent of paper money, prices everywhere were quoted in terms of gold or silver, so exchange rates were fixed.

continued on next page

continued from previous page

financial system in the United States and elsewhere.[‡] Economic historians place the blame squarely on the gold standard. What makes their argument truly convincing is the fact that the sooner a country left the gold standard and regained control of its monetary policy, the faster its economy recovered.

From our vantage point in the 21st century, the gold standard is a historical artifact that caused nothing but trouble. It is hard to understand why anyone would want to bring it back. We know enough today to design and implement a monetary and financial system that functions better than the gold standard did, one that keeps inflation low without risking deflation.

[‡]In Applying the Concept in Chapter 11, we discussed how deflation increases the adverse selection problems caused by information asymmetries. This is one of the mechanisms people today believe made the Depression of the 1930 so deep. For a more detailed discussion of the challenges deflation poses for modern central bankers, see Chapter 23.

Fixed Exchange-Rate Regimes

Our final task in this chapter is to study some examples of fixed exchange rate regimes, to see how they work. We will look at managed exchange-rate pegs, in which policymakers try to restrict the exchange rate to a certain range; at currency boards, in which the central bank holds foreign currency assets as backing for the domestic monetary base; and at dollarization, in which a country eliminates its own currency and begins using one issued by another country.

Exchange Rate Pegs and the Bretton Woods System

Despite the calamity of the 1930s, the world remained enamored of fixed exchange rates and the gold standard. So in 1944, a group of 44 countries agreed to form the Bretton Woods system. Named for the New Hampshire resort where the agreement was signed, it was a system of fixed exchange rates that offered more flexibility over the short term than had been possible under the gold standard.

The Bretton Woods system lasted from 1945 to 1971. Though the details of the system were complex, the basic idea is not. Each country maintained an agreed-upon exchange rate with the U.S. dollar—that is, it *pegged* its exchange rate to the dollar. To make the system work, every country had to hold dollar reserves and stand ready to exchange its own currency for dollars at the fixed rate. The dollar was what is known as a *reserve currency*, and it was convertible into gold at a rate of $35 per ounce. The choice of the dollar as the reserve currency was based on several factors. First, the United States was the biggest of the Allies (the victors in World War II), both economically and militarily. Second, dollars were relatively abundant.[13]

Since other countries did not want to adopt U.S. monetary policy, their fixed exchange rates required complex capital controls. Even so, countries had to intervene regularly, buying or selling dollars to maintain their exchange rates at the peg. Adjustments were made to the *exchange rate pegs*, but only in response to perceived

[13]In thinking about the mid-1940s, it is important to keep in mind that the United States was the only industrialized country whose capital stock had not been decimated by World War II.

YOUR FINANCIAL WORLD
Should You Buy Gold?

Since the gold standard isn't a workable system, central banks don't need to buy gold. But what about you? Americans have been legally allowed to own gold since 1974, but that doesn't mean it's a good idea. In fact, it's not. Gold doesn't pay interest like a bond or dividends like a stock, and its price is highly volatile. From 1974 to 1980, gold more than quadrupled in value, rising in price from $200 per ounce to $850 per ounce; more recently it has traded at $250 to $400 per ounce. These facts alone make gold both a high-risk and a low-return investment—not a good combination.

But that isn't all. Governments and central banks own about 30 percent of all the gold that has ever been taken out of the ground, over 900 million ounces. Because they have no use for it, governments are slowly selling it. Europeans are doing most of the selling, at a rate of about 50 million ounces per year. The fact that some of the largest holders of gold are now the biggest sellers just reinforces the metal's poor investment potential.

Some investment advisors might try to convince you to buy gold to reduce risk. What they will tell you is that gold rises in value when inflation goes up and falls when inflation goes down, so it can be used as a hedge against increases in nominal interest rates. Remember that higher inflation means higher interest rates, and higher interest rates mean lower bond prices. Gold appears to provide a hedge against inflation. While there may be some truth to this idea, it isn't very good investment advice. Not only is gold expensive to buy, sell, and store, but there are better ways to deal with inflation risk. After all, inflation risk is highest for long-term bonds. If inflation risk is what you are worried about, then buy short-term bonds; it's both cheaper and easier than buying gold.

While gold may be a reasonable investment for someone who is fleeing a homicidal dictator, the rest of us should stick to wearing it as jewelry. The best advice is to invest your savings in bonds and stocks.

long-term imbalances. What gave the system some flexibility was the *International Monetary Fund* (IMF). The IMF was created to manage the Bretton Woods System by making loans to countries in need of short-term financing to pay for an excess of imports over exports (see Tools of the Trade). For a number of years, the system worked reasonably well, but as capital markets started to open up, it came under increasing strain.

With a fixed exchange rate and the free movements of capital across international borders, countries could not have independent monetary policies. Recall the example of Mexico cited earlier in this chapter. The long-run implications of purchasing power parity meant that, if Mexican inflation deviated from U.S. inflation, the dollar–peso exchange rate had to change. In the late 1960s, the countries in the Bretton Woods system were in the same position as Mexico. Since their exchange rate was fixed to the dollar, participating countries were forced to adopt policies that resulted in the same amount of inflation as in the United States. When U.S. inflation began to rise in the late 1960s (yet another disastrous side effect of the Vietnam War), many countries balked; they didn't want to match the rise in inflation.

By 1971, the system had completely fallen apart. The response of American officials has been to allow the dollar to float freely ever since. Europeans took a different tack; for much of the time from the collapse of the Bretton Woods system to the adoption of the euro in 1999, they maintained various fixed exchange-rate mechanisms. Since capital flowed freely among these countries, that meant giving up their ability to set interest rates.

TOOLS OF THE TRADE
The Role of the International Monetary Fund Today

When the International Monetary Fund was created to manage the Bretton Woods system, it was given significant resources to do so. The idea was that the IMF would make loans to countries with balance-of-payments problems as well as give advice on how to avert future crises. Say a country's monetary authorities instituted a policy that created domestic inflation. With fixed exchange rates, inflation makes foreign goods cheaper for domestic consumers at the same time that it makes exports more expensive to foreigners.* As a result, imports would increase relative to exports, creating a current account deficit that needed to be financed. With capital controls in place, the funds would have to come from the central bank's dollar reserves. But because the stock of dollars is only so big, a country can maintain a current account deficit for only so long. Eventually, a liquidity crisis would ensue in which the country could not pay its bills. At this point, the IMF would step in with a loan, acting as a sort of lender of last resort. Along with a short-run loan, the IMF would provide advice on how to structure macroeconomic policy to eliminate long-run imbalances.

*Inflation means that domestic prices are higher and the domestic currency is worth less. With a lower-valued currency and a fixed exchange rate, foreign goods look cheap to domestic residents. But with domestic prices higher, domestic goods look expensive to foreigners.

Over the years, the international financial system has evolved, and the IMF has had to change with it. It continues to provide technical assistance, helping countries to design their financial and economic systems. And the IMF continues to provide loans to countries in crisis. But as countries liberalized their capital markets, increasing cross-border capital flows, the character of the crises changed. What were once current account imbalances (in which countries couldn't pay for all the goods they were importing) became capital account crises (in which countries couldn't repay foreign lenders).

The Korean experience during 1997–1998 provides an excellent example of what the IMF does today. When governments, corporations, and banks borrow abroad, they are usually forced to do so in dollars. While borrowing in domestic currency might be possible, lenders would require compensation for their exchange-rate risk, raising interest rates to exorbitant levels. Lending to the government of Korea in won would be unwise if the government could inflate the value of the currency before repaying the loans. When a government borrows in dollars, furthermore, it must repay in dollars.

By mid-fall 1997, it had become clear that Korean corporations and banks weren't going to have the dollars they needed to repay the loans they had taken on. Koreans were going to need more than $100 billion to pay off the loans coming

Hard Pegs: Currency Boards and Dollarization

STABILITY

The international monetary system took a big hit in 1971 when the Bretton Woods system collapsed. Since then, a consensus has developed that countries whose economies are open to international capital flows must choose between completely flexible, market-determined exchange rates and what have come to be known as hard pegs. In a hard-peg system, the central bank implements an institutional mechanism that ensures its ability to convert a domestic currency into the foreign currency to which it is pegged. The danger of a speculative attack means anything less is unworkable. In the words of the first deputy managing director of the International Monetary Fund, "pegs are not sustainable unless they are very hard indeed."[14]

[14]See Stanley Fischer, "Exchange Rate-Regimes: Is the Bipolar View Correct?" Distinguished Lecture on Economics in Government, American Economic Association and the Society of Government Economists, delivered at the Meetings of the American Economic Association, New Orleans, January 6, 2001. Available on the IMF's Web site at http://www.imf.org/external/np/speeches/2001/010601a.htm.

due in 1998. At the time, Korea's central bank had only $6 billion in foreign exchange reserves, and foreign banks were unwilling to extend enough additional credit for them to make the required payments. When financial market participants realized the full extent of the problem, they began pulling their investments out of Korea. As investors sold their securities and converted the proceeds to dollars to withdraw the money from the country, matters grew even worse.

That is when the IMF stepped in and arranged for a total of $55 billion in loans to the Korean government.[†] The idea was that the Korean government, together with the central bank, would lend dollars to corporations and banks that were short of funds, giving them the breathing space they needed to set their affairs in order. As it turned out, the promise of $55 billion wasn't enough; not until late December 1997, when foreign banks were pressured into offering long-term credit to Korean borrowers, did the crisis begin to subside. Even so, capital flight out of Korea continued until well into 1998.

While the IMF's crisis management seems to have worked well enough, the institution has been heavily criticized. All IMF loans come with strings attached. These typically include requirements for reform of the financial system to make it less crisis prone, as well as for tight monetary and fiscal policy to help the country's currency regain value and foreign investors regain confidence. While reform of the financial system was important and necessary, forcing Korea to adopt tight monetary and fiscal policy may not have been. Why should a country in the middle of a crisis be forced to raise its interest rates dramatically and cut back on its government spending, making the economy contract even more?

But criticism of these requirements is mild compared to criticism of the loans themselves. Many observers believe that, by bailing countries out, the IMF is allowing investors and governments to evade the consequences of the risks they have taken. As a result, countries can borrow internationally, behave irresponsibly, and avoid paying the price. Though the IMF claims there is little evidence of such moral hazard, many economists are not so sure.

We can be fairly certain that the IMF will continue to play an important role in the international financial community. But it is difficult to know what that role will be.

[†]Of the $55 billion, $21 billion came from the IMF, $10 billion from the World Bank, $4 billion from the Asian Development Bank, and the remaining $20 billion from the governments of large countries.

Only two exchange rate regimes can be considered hard pegs: currency boards and dollarization. With a currency board, the central bank commits to holding enough foreign currency assets to back domestic currency liabilities at a fixed rate. With dollarization, one country formally adopts the currency of another country for use in all its financial transactions. Let's look at examples of both systems.

Currency Boards and the Argentinean Experience Somewhere between 10 and 20 currency boards operate in the world today. The best known is the one in Hong Kong. The Hong Kong Monetary Authority (HKMA) operates a system whose sole objective is to maintain a fixed exchange rate of 7.8 Hong Kong dollars to one U.S. dollar. Since the HKMA holds roughly $125 billion in foreign currency (dollar) assets, it can issue 975 billion Hong Kong dollars in liabilities. The rules of the currency board provide that the HKMA can increase the size of Hong Kong's monetary base only if it can accumulate additional dollar reserves.

As this example suggests, with a currency board, the central bank's only job is to maintain the exchange rate. While that means that policymakers cannot adjust monetary policy in response to domestic economic shocks, the system does have its advantages. Prime among them is the control of inflation. As we noted in the introduction to this chapter, Argentina decided to adopt a currency board in April 1991 to end triple-digit inflation, and the approach worked. After three years, inflation had dropped to four percent; by 1998, it was nearly zero. Forgoing the ability to stabilize domestic growth seems like a small price to pay for this sort of inflation performance, especially in an inflation-prone economy.

But currency boards do have their problems. First, by giving up the ability to control the size of its balance sheet, the central bank loses its role as the lender of last resort to the domestic banking system. The Banco Central de la Republica Argentina solved this problem by establishing standby letters of credit (described in Chapter 12) from large U.S. banks. When the time came to make emergency loans to local banks, officials borrowed dollars from U.S. banks and then made loans in pesos. But their lending was limited to the amount of dollar credit that foreign banks were willing to extend.[15]

In 2001, the Argentinean currency board collapsed and authorities were forced to allow the peso to float. Within a few months, dollars that had once cost one peso apiece cost three. What caused the collapse? Entire books have been written to answer this question, but several points will take us a long way toward understanding what happened. First, the peso was pegged to the U.S. dollar, despite the fact that Argentina's economy doesn't have much to do with the U.S. economy. When the dollar appreciated in the 1990s, it made the peso more valuable as well. The overvalued peso priced Argentinean exporters out of their markets, which were not in the United States. Over a period of years, the fact that their exports were too expensive ended up severely damaging Argentina's economy.

But the overvalued exchange rate was only part of the story; fiscal policy was the other part. While the Argentinean economy grew at a healthy rate of nearly $4\frac{1}{2}$ percent per year through much of the 1990s, government spending rose even faster – so fast that the government needed to borrow an average of nearly 4 percent of GDP per year just to pay its bills. The more the government borrowed, the more wary lenders became of continuing to lend. Undeterred, politicians spent until they simply ran out of money.

The problem was worst at the provincial government level (analogous to the state governments in the United States), where borrowing became impossible even to meet the payroll. So provincial government officials began printing a sort of bond and using it to pay their employees. The bonds issued by the provincial government of Buenos Aires, called *patacones*, paid 7 percent interest and matured in one to five years (see the photo). What made them special was that they were the same physical size as currency and were issued in small denominations of one to 100 pesos in order to pay employees and retirees. Observers estimated that Argentina's provincial governments eventually issued 40 percent of the currency in circulation. When politicians began printing their own money, the claim that Argentinean inflation would roughly mirror U.S. inflation—a requirement for the long-run viability of the fixed exchange rate—was no longer credible and the currency board collapsed. Always remember, irresponsible politicians can undermine any monetary policy regime.

A 5-peso note issued by the government of the Province of Buenos Aires government in 2001.

[15]These standby letters of credit were not free. First, the central bank of Argentina had to obtain lines of credit they could call on when needed. Banks charge for these at rates of 0.25 percent or so. Then, should the Argentineans need the funds, they would have to pay interest on the loans themselves.

Dollarization in Ecuador

Some countries just give up and adopt the currency of another country for all their transactions, completely eliminating their own monetary policy. While this approach is commonly known as dollarization, it need not be based on the dollar. Monaco, the small country for the rich and famous on the southern coast of France, adopted the French franc in 1865 and uses the euro today.

Monaco is very small, covering less than 50 square miles (about twice the size of Manhattan), with a population of only 30,000. Ecuador, with a population of 13 million spread over 100,000 square miles, is another story. In 1999, Ecuador experienced a severe financial crisis. Real GDP fell more than 7 percent, inflation rose to 50 percent, the banking system nearly collapsed, and the currency, the *sucre*, went into freefall, losing two-thirds of its value relative to the dollar in a year. In January 2000, Ecuador officially gave up its currency. Within six months, the central bank had bought back all the sucres in circulation. Almost immediately, interest rates dropped, the banking system re-established itself, inflation fell dramatically, and growth resumed. Ecuador's move to dollarization was successful enough that, a year later, El Salvador followed suit. Panama has been dollarized since 1904.

Why would a country choose to give up its currency? In the case of a small emerging-market country, there are a host of reasons. First, with no exchange rate, there is no risk of an exchange-rate crisis—no possibility of either a large depreciation or a sudden capital outflow motivated by the fear of depreciation. Second, using dollars or euros or yen can help a country to become integrated into world markets, increasing its trade and investment. Finally, by rejecting the possibility of inflationary finance, a country can reduce the risk premium it must pay on loans and generally strengthen its financial institutions. But it does need to find some way to get the dollars it will need to keep the monetary base growing, which can prove to be a challenge.

The benefits of dollarization are balanced against the loss of revenue that comes from issuing currency—what is called *seignorage*. Remember, printing a $100 bill costs only a few cents. When Ecuador decided to dollarize, it gave those profits to the United States. Second, dollarization effectively eliminates the central bank as the lender of last resort because, again, the Federal Reserve prints dollars, not the Central Bank of Ecuador. If a banking emergency arises in Ecuador, the government will need to find some way to get dollars to provide the needed liquidity. (This is the problem Argentina solved by paying large U.S. banks for standby letters of credit.) Third, there is the loss of autonomous monetary or exchange-rate policy. But since foreign investors' lack of confidence in domestic policymakers was what created Ecuador's crisis, it is hard to see that loss as a serious one. Finally, any country that adopts the dollar as its currency gets U.S. monetary policy, like it or not. Obviously, this drawback is least worrisome for countries whose economies are closely tied to that of the United States. While it might make sense for countries like Mexico or Canada, for Ecuador the decision isn't so clear.

Note that dollarization is not the same as a monetary union. The decision by European countries to adopt a common currency, the euro, was fundamentally different from a country's decision to adopt the dollar. When the FOMC makes its decisions, the affairs of Ecuador and El Salvador carry no weight. And as we have already noted, dollarized countries forgo the revenue from issuing currency and are forced to make special arrangements to provide emergency loans to domestic banks. In contrast, all European countries participating in the monetary union take part in monetary policy decisions, and all share in the revenue that comes from printing euros. Europe's national banks still operate as lenders of last resort in making euro loans. In sum, a monetary union is shared governance; dollarization is not.

IN THE NEWS

The False Promise of Dollarization

Financial Times

by Sebastian Edwards

May 11, 2001

The recent crises in Argentina and Turkey have reignited the debate on exchange rate policies in emerging countries. A small but increasingly vocal group of economists argues that emerging nations should give up their currencies and adopt an advanced nation's currency as legal tender.

What started as an intellectual but impractical idea has become a genuine policy option. In 2000, in the middle of a crisis, Ecuador abolished its currency, the sucre, and adopted the U.S. dollar. On April 30 the dollar became legal tender in Guatemala, and El Salvador recently announced that it planned to adopt the dollar this year. Argentina has recently decided against it but its supporters consider this a temporary setback and expect the troubled South American nation soon to join the ranks of the dollarized.

This rather drastic piece of advice—giving up the national currency—is being dispensed on the basis of limited empirical and historical evidence. It is akin to a physician prescribing a drug without making clear what other steps the patient must take and without explaining the drug's side effects or its rate of success in clinical trials.

The economic record of dollarized nations leaves a lot to be desired and the recent push for dollarization is a typical case of misleading advertisement. Countries that give up their currencies, we are told, will be unable to engage in macroeconomic mismanagement. Public finances will stay in balance and external accounts will move within reasonable bounds. Dollarization-imposed macroeconomic stability is purported to bring lower interest rates, higher investment, and superior economic performance.

Twelve independent nations used another country's currency between 1970 and 1998—all very small countries with a median population in 1998 of 45,000. Many are city-states fully integrated into their neighbors' economies, such as Monaco, Liechtenstein, and Andorra. The largest dollarized countries in this period were Liberia and Panama.

The growth in gross domestic product per capita in these 12 countries has been significantly lower than in countries that use their own currencies. There is no evidence that nations that use other countries' currencies are more fiscally prudent. And in terms of current account imbalances, their behavior has been no different from that of countries with their own currencies. However, coun-

Terms

Chapter Lessons

1. When capital flows freely across a country's borders, fixing the exchange rate means giving up domestic monetary policy.

continued from previous page

tries that have given up their own currencies have had significantly lower inflation.

Supporters of dollarization point to Panama, which has low inflation, macroeconomic stability, and low interest rates.

But Panama has relied heavily on the International Monetary Fund in the past 35 years or so. The reason has been Panama's inability to control its public finances. Between 1973 and 1998 the fiscal deficit averaged 4 per cent of GDP and during 1973–87 it exceeded a remarkable 7 per cent of GDP. Why has the IMF accommodated Panama's repeated macroeconomic transgressions? Considerations of political economy—including the U.S. interest in maintaining the Canal Zone free of political turmoil—are surely part of the answer.

Contrary to what supporters of dollarization claim, Panama's cost of capital has not been the lowest in Latin America. The spread over Panamanian bonds has been systematically higher than that over Chile's sovereign bonds of similar maturity. But Chile has followed a different policy: its exchange rate has become more flexible. So dollarization does not by itself reduce country risk.

Robert Mundell's optimal currency areas analysis is the right approach for dealing with the dollarization question. Mundell argues that there are good reasons to think that very small countries that are highly integrated in terms of factor mobility and trade will benefit from having a common currency. The benefits could possibly compensate for the costs, including the loss of seignorage.

But dollarization is not appropriate for all countries. Large countries that face volatile terms of trade and are not deeply integrated into big economies are likely to incur net costs if they dollarize. They will have difficulties in accommodating external shocks while the alleged benefits of low costs of capital, fiscal discipline, and stability may continue to be elusive.

The writer is the Henry Ford II professor at UCLA's Anderson Graduate School of Management. Between 1993 and 1996 he was chief economist for Latin America at the World Bank.

Reprinted from The Financial Times 2001 © Sebastian Edwards.

LESSONS OF THE ARTICLE

Dollarization is a drastic step that is difficult to reverse. A country should give up its currency only if its economy is truly integrated with the economy of the country whose currency it is adopting. Because most Latin American economies are not strongly linked to the U.S. economy, adopting the dollar makes little sense for them.[*]

[*]Dollarization was discussed as part of the recent reconstruction of Iraq's economic and financial system. But since Iraq's primary external link is its oil sales to Europe, it was a poor candidate for dollarization. Instead, Iraqi authorities decided to issue their own currency.

---

  a. Purchasing power parity implies that in the long run, exchange rates are tied to inflation differentials across countries.

  b. Capital market arbitrage means that in the short run, the exchange rate is tied to differences in interest rates.

  c. Monetary policymakers can have only two of the following three options: open capital markets, control of domestic interest rates, and a fixed exchange rate.

  d. Countries that impose controls on capital flowing in and/or out can fix the exchange rate without giving up their domestic monetary policy.

2. Central banks can intervene in foreign exchange markets.

  a. When they do, it affects their balance sheet in the same way as an open market operation.

  b. Foreign exchange intervention affects the exchange rate by changing domestic interest rates. This is called unsterilized intervention.

c. A sterilized intervention is a purchase or sale of foreign exchange reserves that leaves the central bank's liabilities unchanged. It has no impact on the exchange rate.

3. The decision to fix the exchange rate has costs, benefits, and risks.

   a. Both corporations and investors benefit from predictable exchange rates.

   b. Fixed exchange rates can reduce domestic inflation by importing the monetary policy of a country with low inflation.

   c. Fixed exchange-rate regimes are fragile and leave countries open to speculative attacks.

   d. The right conditions for choosing to fix the exchange rate include

      i. A poor reputation for inflation control.

      ii. An economy that is well integrated with the one to whose currency the rate is fixed.

      iii. A high level of foreign exchange reserves.

4. There are a number of examples of exchange-rate systems.

   a. The Bretton Woods system, set up after World War II, pegged exchange rates to the U.S. dollar It collapsed in 1971 after U.S. inflation began to rise.

   b. Most fixed exchange-rate regimes are no longer thought to be viable.

   c. Two that may work are currency boards and dollarization.

   d. With a currency board, the central bank holds enough foreign currency reserves to exchange the entire monetary base at the promised exchange rate.

   e. Argentina's currency board collapsed when the regional governments began printing their own money.

   f. Dollarization is the total conversion of an economy from its own currency to the currency of another country.

   g. Several Latin American countries have adopted the dollar recently, with good results over the short run.

Problems

1. In June 1998, as the exchange rate was approaching 150 yen to the dollar, the Bank of Japan appealed to the Federal Reserve to engage in a coordinated exchange-rate intervention to prevent the yen from depreciating further.

   a. Discuss the possible justifications for such a foreign exchange intervention.

   b. What did the Bank of Japan and the Fed actually do? Show the impact of the intervention on each central bank's balance sheet.

   c. Do you think the intervention had an impact? Why or why not?

2. Go to the Web site of the Federal Reserve Bank of New York, www.newyorkfed.org. Click on "Publications." Under "Online Publications," click on "Quarterly and Annual" and finally on "Treasury and Federal Reserve FX Operations." Can you find the last time the Fed intervened in the FX (foreign exchange) market? How big was the intervention? In the full text of the report, or in news reports filed at the time, can you find the justification for the intervention?

3. How would you categorize the French, Italian, and German exchange rate regimes?

4. A number of people have suggested the creation of a Monetary Union of the Americas. What are the arguments for and against the countries of North and South America adopting a common currency? Should the United States favor or oppose the proposal?

5. Explain the mechanics of a speculative attack.

6. Define sterilized intervention and explain why economists believe it has no impact on the exchange rate.

7. Assume that the interest rate on one-year Japanese government bonds is 2 percent, one-year U.S. Treasury bills pay 3 percent, and the exchange rate is 100 yen per dollar.

   a. Assuming the yen–dollar exchange rate is fixed, explain how you could make a riskless profit.

   b. Assuming the yen–dollar exchange rate is floating, what would you expect it to be in one year?

8. If U.S. inflation were 2 percent, Mexican inflation 10 percent, and you could exchange 10 pesos for one dollar, what would you expect the dollar–peso exchange rate to be in one year? If U.S. and Mexican government bonds were equally risky, what would you expect the interest-rate differential to be?

9. In 1997, the Bank of Thailand was maintaining a fixed exchange rate at 26 Thai baht to the dollar. At the same time, Thai interest rates were substantially higher than those in the United States and Japan. Thai bankers were borrowing money in Japan and lending it in Thailand.

   a. Why was this transaction profitable?

   b. What risks were associated with this method of financing?

   c. Describe the impact of a depreciation of the baht on the balance sheets of Thai banks involved in these transactions.

10. During the time of the currency board, Argentinean banks offered accounts in both dollars and pesos, but loans were made largely in pesos. Describe the impact on banks of the collapse of the currency board.

11. Investors became nervous just before the 2002 Brazilian presidential election. As a result, the risk premium on Brazilian government debt increased dramatically and Brazil's currency depreciated significantly.

    a. How could concern over an election drive up the risk premium?

    b. How was the risk premium connected to the value of the currency?

12. During the Asian financial crisis in the summer and fall of 1997, investors became concerned that the Hong Kong Monetary Authority would not be able to maintain its currency board. As a result, the overnight interest rate in Hong Kong rose to about 200 percent. Explain this phenomenon.

13. Should Texas have its own currency? How would you evaluate whether the 50 states should remain "dollarized"?

14. When asked about the value of the dollar, the chair of the Federal Reserve Board answers, "The foreign exchange policy of the United States is the responsibility of the Secretary of the Treasury; I have no comment." Discuss this answer.

15. Explain the costs and benefits of dollarization. Could a dollarized regime collapse?

Appendix 19

What You Really Need to Know about the Balance of Payments

The international financial system exists to sustain the flow of capital and goods among countries. To understand how it works, we need to define three important terms connected with the international *balance of payments*. They are the current account balance, the capital account balance, and the official settlements balance.

The *current account* tracks the flow of payments across national boundaries. When an American purchases a television set made in Korea or a Japanese consumer buys a copy of Microsoft Windows, the transaction shows up as part of the U.S. current account. The *current account balance* is simply the difference between a country's exports and its imports of goods and services. A full accounting would include unilateral transfers, such as the money foreign workers send home to relatives, as well as investment income, such as the interest payments Americans receive on Mexican bonds. But we will ignore these and stick to the simple version: When a country's exports exceed its imports, its current account balance is positive. It has a *current account surplus*.

The *capital account* tracks the purchase and sale of assets—stocks, bonds, real estate, and the like—between countries. When a German buys shares of IBM stock or an American purchases a Brazilian government bond, the transaction appears in the capital account. The *capital account balance* is the difference between a country's capital inflows and capital outflows. When a country's capital account is in surplus, it has a net capital inflow. Its residents are either selling assets to foreigners or borrowing money from abroad.

Finally, the *Official Settlements Balance* is the change in a country's official reserve holdings. During the time of the gold standard, these reserves took the form of gold bars. It shows the change in the central bank's foreign exchange reserves (or gold reserves).

The international balance of payments is an accounting framework that relates these three pieces. Their relationship is simple: They must sum to zero.

$$\text{Current account balance} + \text{Capital account balance} + \text{Official settlements balance} = 0$$

This accounting identity has important implications. In Tools of the Trade in Chapter 10, we ignored the possibility of a change in official reserves and concluded that the current account balance plus the capital account balance sum to zero. So it appeared that a current account deficit must be matched by a capital account surplus, for example. If a country is importing more than it is exporting, it must either borrow from abroad or sell assets to foreigners to finance excess purchases.

When we add the official settlements balance, the analysis changes slightly. Now we see that if a country is running a current account deficit, there are two ways to pay for it. It can run a capital account surplus or it can draw down its foreign exchange reserves. That is, the central bank can convert enough domestic currency into foreign currency to finance the discrepancy between imports and exports. If capital controls are in place so that the capital account balance is zero, then drawing down foreign exchange reserves is the only option. Countries with current account deficits will lose reserves while those with current account surpluses will accumulate reserves. Finally, if foreigners want to sell their investments and take the proceeds home, they will force a country either to run a current account surplus—something it cannot do quickly—or to drain foreign exchange from the central bank's reserves.

Part V
Modern Monetary Economics

Chapter 20

Money Growth, Money Demand, and Modern Monetary Policy

Anyone who listens carefully to what central bankers say, or reads what they write, will form the clear impression that 21st-century monetary policy has very little to do with money, despite its focus on inflation. That impression is reinforced by the technical papers that monetary economists write. Everyone talks about interest rates and exchange rates; no one talks about money.

But digging deeper, you will find that central bankers and monetary economists *do* care about money. After decades of studying the economy, the Nobel Prize-winning economist Milton Friedman wrote, "inflation is always and everywhere a monetary phenomenon." Most economists would agree. We see concern for money, too, in statements made by officials of the European Central Bank (ECB). In Chapter 16, we discussed the stability-oriented strategy that the ECB's Governing Council adopted in fall 1998 to achieve the objective of price stability. The council's strategy assigned money a prominent role that was, in its members' words, "signaled by the announcement of a quantitative reference value for the growth rate of a broad monetary aggregate." The idea was that deviations of money growth from the reference value signaled a risk to European price stability.[1] Since then, the ECB's monthly announcements of its target interest rate have always mentioned money growth.

Obviously, money plays a central role in the formulation of European monetary policy. The contrast with the United States could not be more striking. In July 2000, after roughly a quarter century of publishing twice-yearly target ranges for the monetary aggregates, the Federal Open Market Committee (FOMC) stopped doing so, explaining that "these ranges [no longer] provide useful benchmarks for monetary policy."[2] While the Federal Reserve still collects and publishes data on the monetary aggregates, FOMC members now mention them only in passing. They rarely make any reference to money in public announcements of the federal funds target rate.[3]

What accounts for the distinctly different treatment of money growth in the two largest central banks in the world? Why does the ECB make regular public references to money growth, while the Fed never does? If money growth is tied to inflation, why don't central bankers in the United States pay more attention to it? The goal of this chapter is twofold. First, it examines the link between money growth and inflation in order to clarify the role of money in monetary policy. Second, it explains the logic underlying central bankers' focus on interest rates.

---

[1]At first the reference value was announced every year, in December. The practice was discontinued in 2003, when the Governing Council agreed that there was no reason to consider such frequent changes.

[2]This announcement appeared as a footnote in the biannual *Monetary Policy Report to Congress*.

[3]Governor Laurence H. Meyer has said that money "plays virtually no role in the conduct of monetary policy." See "Does Money Matter?" The 2001 Homer Jones Memorial Lecture, Washington University, St. Louis, Missouri, March 28, 2001.

Why We Care about Monetary Aggregates

We start with the single most important fact in monetary economics: the relationship between money growth and inflation. Figure 20.1 shows the average annual inflation and money growth in 167 countries over the roughly two decades from 1981 to 2003.[4] This graph is striking for two reasons. The first is its scale: some countries suffered inflation of more than 500 percent *a year* for two decades. Second, every country with high inflation had high money growth. History provides no examples of countries with high inflation and low money growth or with low inflation and high money growth.

One thing the figure does not show because of its scale is the huge number of points that fall very close to the origin, representing countries with both low inflation and low money growth. Figure 20.2 displays the data for the 129 countries that experienced moderate money growth (averaging less than 30 percent) over the two

[4]These figures are based on data from the International Monetary Fund's *International Financial Statistics*. Inflation was computed from each country's analog to the consumer price index; money is the rough equivalent of M2. Changing the definition of either inflation or money does not alter the graph.

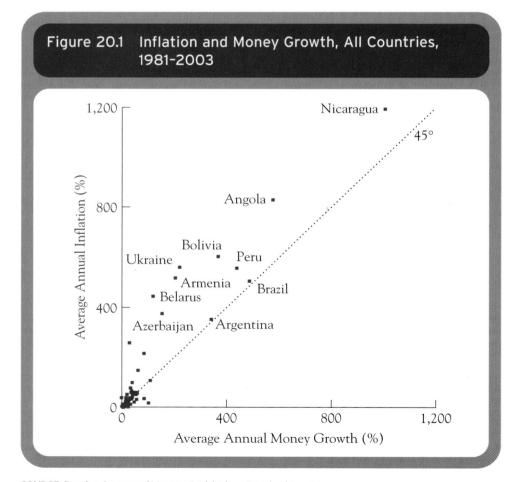

Figure 20.1 Inflation and Money Growth, All Countries, 1981-2003

SOURCE: *Data from International Monetary Fund database. Printed with permission.*

decades from 1981 to 2003. While the relationship between money growth and inflation is less striking—the correlation falls from 0.93 in Figure 20.1 to 0.49 in Figure 20.2—it is still clearly there.[5] The higher the rate of money growth is, the higher inflation is likely to be. The two variables move together. This evidence alone tells us that *to avoid sustained episodes of high inflation, a central bank must be concerned with money growth. Avoiding high inflation means avoiding rapid money growth.*

Figures 20.1 and 20.2 include a 45-degree line. Note that the points representing countries with very high inflation tend to lie above the line, while the points representing countries with moderate to low inflation tend to fall below it. As the simplified graph in Figure 20.3 shows, points lying above the 45-degree line represent countries where average inflation exceeds average money growth; points lying below the 45-degree line represent countries where money growth exceeds inflation. To

[5]Correlation is a measure of how closely two quantities are related. The numerical value ranges from +1 to –1. A positive correlation signifies that the two variables rise and fall together; a negative correlation means that they move in opposite directions.

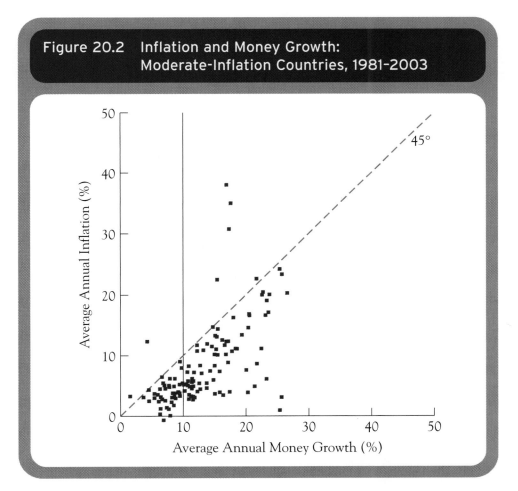

Figure 20.2   Inflation and Money Growth: Moderate-Inflation Countries, 1981-2003

SOURCE: *Data from International Monetary Fund database. Printed with permission.*

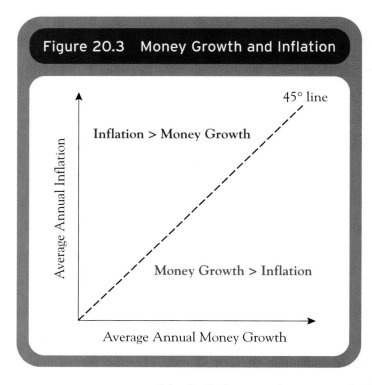

Figure 20.3 Money Growth and Inflation

understand this relationship, think about what would happen if inflation rose to 1,200 percent a year, as was the case in Nicaragua (see Figure 20.1). That means prices would be rising about 5 percent a week. When the currency that people are holding loses value that rapidly, they will work to spend what they have as quickly as possible.[6] As we will see shortly, spending money more quickly has the same effect on inflation as an increase in money growth.

Connecting this relationship to central bank policy is straightforward. Recall from Chapter 17 that the central bank controls the size of its own balance sheet. Policymakers can purchase as many assets as they want, issuing currency and commercial bank reserve liabilities to do so. Those liabilities, in turn, form the monetary base. Through the process of deposit expansion, the banking system turns the monetary base into the monetary aggregates. Thus, the monetary aggregates cannot grow rapidly without at least the tacit consent of the central bank. By limiting the rate at which they purchase securities, policymakers can control the rate at which aggregates like M2 grow. In other words, *it is impossible to have high, sustained inflation without monetary accommodation.*

Not surprisingly, evidence of the link between inflation and money growth is the foundation on which modern monetary policy is built. That is why the ECB pays close attention to growth in the monetary aggregates. But to use the link as a policy guide, central bankers must understand how it works. Looking back at Figures 20.1 and 20.2, we can see that all money growth is not created equal. Something beyond just differences in money growth accounts for the differences in inflation across countries. To see

---

[6]In some countries suffering from hyperinflation, workers may be paid more than once a day because cash loses value so quickly. Stories have been told about children traveling to their parents' workplace at midday to collect the morning's pay and spend it on food before its value declined.

This note, issued by the Central Bank of Hungary in 1946, is the highest-denomination currency note ever issued. Its face value is 100 million trillion *pengö* (that's a 1 followed by 20 zeros). The note was produced for use during one of the most extreme hyperinflations in history, which took place in Hungary following World War II. Starting in 1944, the amount of currency in circulation grew from 12 billion pengö (a number with 11 digits) to a 27-digit total in 1946. In two short years, the quantity of money had increased by a factor of about 10,000 trillion, reducing the value of this note to the equivalent of 20 cents.

the point, look at Figure 20.2 and note the vertical line drawn at the point where annual money growth averages 10 percent. Points lying on or near the line represent countries that experienced average annual inflation of between 2 percent and 9 percent. What accounted for the differences in inflation among those countries?

Still other questions arise. For instance, Figures 20.1 and 20.2 show average inflation and money growth over a 20-year period. The results suggest that money growth is a useful guide to understanding long-term movements in inflation. But what happens over shorter periods of a few months or years? Answering such questions requires moving beyond the simple statistical relationship shown in Figures 20.1 and 20.2.[7] We need to develop a deeper understanding of the link between money growth and inflation, one that is based on economic decisions.

The Quantity Theory and the Velocity of Money

What accounts for the fact that high money growth is accompanied by high inflation? Recall that during times of inflation, the value of money is falling. If we think about the value or purchasing power of money in terms of the goods needed to get money, the impact of inflation becomes clear. Normally, we think of how many dollars we need to buy a cup of coffee or a sandwich; that's the money price of the sandwich. But we can turn the question around and ask how many cups of coffee or sandwiches a person needs to buy one dollar. A fall in the number of cups of coffee it takes to buy one dollar represents a decline in the price, or value, of money.

If someone asked you how the price of a cup of coffee is determined, having learned your microeconomics, you would answer that it depends on the supply of and demand for coffee. When the supply of coffee rises but demand does not, the price falls. Not surprisingly, the same is true of the price of money: it is determined by supply and demand. Given steady demand, an increase in the supply of money drives the price of money down. That's inflation. If the central bank continuously floods the economy with large amounts of money, inflation will reach very high levels.

Velocity and the Equation of Exchange

To understand the relationship between inflation and money growth, we need to focus on money as a means of payment. Imagine a simple economy that is composed of four college students: One has $100 in currency; the second has two tickets to the weekend football game, worth $50 each; the third has a $100 calculator; and the fourth has a set of 25 high-quality drawing pencils that sell for $4 apiece. Each of these students wants something else. The one with the $100 in currency needs a calculator, so she buys it. The student who sold the calculator to her wants to see the football game, so he uses the cash she paid him to buy the two tickets. Finally, the student who sold the football tickets needs some pencils for a drawing class, so the cash changes hands again.

Let's analyze the effect of these transactions. Their total value is $100 × (1 calculator) + $50 × (2 football tickets) + $4 × (25 drawing pencils) = $300. In this

---

[7]The mere fact that two variables fluctuate together does not mean that movements in one *cause* movements in the other. So the fact that money growth and inflation are correlated does not mean that changes in money growth cause changes in inflation (or that a change in inflation causes a change in money growth). See the Tools of the Trade in Chapter 23 for an extended discussion of why correlation does not mean causality.

APPLYING THE CONCEPT

INFLATION AND THE COLLAPSE OF THE SOVIET UNION

In 1990, the Soviet Union collapsed, leaving in its place 15 independent countries known as the "former Soviet Republics." These new countries had several characteristics in common. One of them was their horrible inflation experience. In Latvia from 1991 to 1994, inflation averaged just below 300 percent per year—the lowest rate of the 15 countries. In Georgia in 1994, prices rose 15,600 percent, or roughly 10 percent per week.

The source of these extraordinary levels of inflation was not hard to find: It was rapid money growth. Because the governments of these countries were the successors to the Soviet Union, a command economy, they were responsible at first for controlling every aspect of their citizens' economic lives. Virtually everyone worked for and was paid by the government. But while these states were committed to extremely high levels of expenditure, they had virtually no sources of revenue. There was no way to collect taxes and no way to borrow. The only available source of revenue was to print money, so that is what government officials did. They printed lots of it, raising money growth rates to well over 100 percent a year. From 1992 to 1993, for example, the Ukrainian equivalent of M2 increased by a factor of 20. Not surprisingly, such high money growth was matched by high inflation. Ukraine's 2,000 percent rate of money growth was accompanied by 4,000 percent inflation.

Officials in these countries realized that inflation had to be brought under control, or people would revolt (again). So they made a number of changes. The most important was to take the authority to print money out of the hands of politicians and turn it over to an independent central bank. Together with vast economic reforms that shrank the size of most of the governments dramatically, this depoliticizing of monetary policy produced

four-person economy, the $100 was used three times, resulting in $300 worth of transactions. In general terms, we can write this calculation as

$$\text{(Number of dollars)} \times \text{(Number of times each dollar is used)} = \text{Dollar value of transactions} \qquad (1)$$

To interpret this expression, note that the number of dollars is the quantity of money in the economy. The number of times each dollar is used (per unit of time) is called the velocity of money. The more frequently each dollar is used, the higher the velocity of money.

Applying this same logic to the economy as a whole is straightforward, since virtually every transaction uses money at some stage. For our purposes here, we will restrict the analysis to sales and purchases of final goods and services produced in a country during a given period and measured at market prices. That is, we will focus on nominal gross domestic product. Every one of the purchases counted in nominal GDP requires the use of money. So by analogy with the four-student economy,

$$\text{(Quantity of money)} \times \text{(Velocity of money)} = \text{Nominal GDP} \qquad (2)$$

continued from previous page

Former Soviet Republics

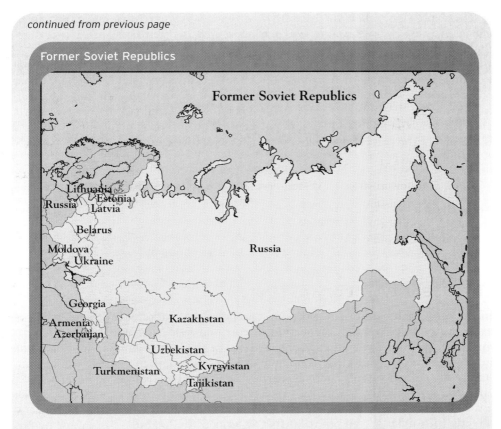

Former Soviet Republics

an amazing transformation. By 2001, inflation had dropped to less than 10 percent in nine of the fifteen countries; only Belarus had inflation of over 50 percent. As money growth fell, inflation dropped with it.

Since we have data on both the quantity of money and nominal GDP, we can use equation (2) to compute the velocity of money. Each definition of money—each monetary aggregate—has its own velocity. In August 2004, GDP equaled $11.6 trillion and M1 equaled $1.3 trillion, so M1 had a velocity of 8.9. In the same year, M2 equaled $6.3 trillion, so the velocity of M2 was 1.8. We will come back to this topic shortly.[8]

To manipulate the expression for velocity in equation (2), we can rewrite it using algebraic symbols. We'll use the letter M to represent money and V to represent velocity. Nominal GDP can be divided into two parts, the price level and the quantity of real output (or real GDP). Calling these two factors P and Y, we can state that nominal GDP = P times Y. Using this notation, we can rewrite equation (2) as

$$MV = PY \qquad (3)$$

---

[8]One way to think about equation (2) is as the definition of the velocity of money. That is, the velocity of money equals nominal GDP divided by the quantity of money.

This expression, called the equation of exchange, tells us that *the quantity of money multiplied by its velocity equals the level of nominal GDP*, written as the price level times the quantity of real output.

With money on the left-hand side and prices on the right, the equation of exchange provides the link between money and prices that we are looking for. But our real concern is with inflation, not the price level, and money growth, not the quantity of money. We need to manipulate equation (3) to allow for the percentage change in each factor. Noting that the percentage change of a product like *MV* or *PY* is the sum of the percentage changes in each factor,[9] we can write

$$\%\Delta M \quad + \quad \%\Delta V \quad = \quad \%\Delta P \quad + \quad \%\Delta Y$$

$$\text{(Money growth)} + \text{(Velocity growth)} = \text{Inflation} + \text{(Real growth)} \tag{4}$$

where the symbol "%Δ" stands for percentage change. We know that the percentage change in the quantity of money is money growth; the percentage change in the price level is inflation; and the percentage change in real GDP is real growth. So equation (4) tells us that *money growth plus velocity growth equals inflation plus real growth*.

The Quantity Theory of Money

In the early 20th century, the economist Irving Fisher wrote down the equation of exchange and derived the implication in equation (4). Next, he assumed that no important changes occur in payment methods or the cost of holding money. If the interest rate is fixed and there is no financial innovation, then velocity will be constant. Fisher also assumed that real output is determined solely by economic resources and production technology, so it too is fixed in the short run. In other words, Fisher assumed that $\%\Delta V = 0$ and $\%\Delta Y = 0$. He concluded that money growth translates directly into inflation, an assertion that is termed the quantity theory of money. According to Fisher's theory, changes in the aggregate price level are caused solely by changes in the quantity of money. So if the central bank pours more money into the economy, it drives up the prices of existing goods and services. Raising the quantity of money by 10 percent raises prices by 10 percent; doubling the quantity of money doubles the price level. As Milton Friedman said, *inflation is a monetary phenomenon*.

The fact that individuals require money to complete transactions means that we can reinterpret the quantity theory of money to describe the equilibrium between money demand and money supply. Note that in the classroom economy described earlier, the number of dollars needed equaled the total dollar value of the transactions divided by the number of times each dollar was used. That is, money demanded (M^d) equals the total value of transactions divided by the velocity of money. For the economy as a whole, the demand for money equals nominal GDP divided by velocity:

$$M^d = \frac{1}{V}PY \tag{5}$$

---

[9]This statement is based on the approximation that the change in the natural log of a variable x is approximately equal to its percentage change. To see how it works, first take the natural log of the product M_tV_t: $ln(M_tV_t) = ln(M_t) + ln(V_t)$. Now subtract $ln(M_{t-1}V_{t-1})$ from the left-hand side and $ln(M_{t-1}) + ln(V_{t-1})$ from the right-hand side to get $ln(M_tV_t) - ln(M_{t-1}V_{t-1}) = [ln(M_t) - ln(M_{t-1})] + [ln(V_t) - ln(V_{t-1})]$. This means that the change in the natural log of MV equals the change in the natural log of M plus the change in the natural log of V. Next, use the fact that the difference in the log is the log of the ratio, $[ln(M_t) - ln(M_{t-1})] = ln(M_t/M_{t-1})$. We can rewrite this as $ln[1 + (M_t-M_{t-1})/M_{t-1}]$, and use the fact that the natural log of one plus a small number equals the small number, so $ln(M_t/M_{t-1}) \approx (M_t-M_{t-1})/M_{t-1}$, which is the percentage change. Putting all of this together gives us the fact that the percentage change of a product is the sum of the percentage changes of the elements: $\%\Delta(MV) \approx \%\Delta M + \%\Delta V$.

Next, recall that the supply of money (M^S) is determined by the central bank and the behavior of the banking system. Equilibrium in the money market means that supply equals demand ($M^d = M^S$), which equals the quantity of money in the economy (M). Rearranging equation (5) gives us $MV = PY$. Assuming that velocity and real output are both constant, as Irving Fisher did, we can once again conclude that money growth equals inflation.

The quantity theory of money accounts for some important characteristics of the patterns shown in Figures 20.1 and 20.2. First, it tells us why high inflation and high money growth go together. Second, it explains the tendency for moderate- and low-inflation countries to fall below the 45-degree line in Figure 20.2. That is, money growth tends to be higher than inflation in those countries because they are experiencing real growth. Looking at equation (4), we can see that if velocity is constant, then money growth equals the sum of inflation and real growth. At a given level of money growth, the higher the level of real growth is, the lower the level of inflation will be. So in countries that are growing, inflation will be lower than money growth, causing their economies to fall below the 45-degree line in Figure 20.2.

The Facts about Velocity

If Irving Fisher was correct in assuming that the velocity of money is constant, his assumption would have important implications for monetary policy. Since the trend in real growth is determined by the structure of the economy and the rate of technological progress, countries could control inflation directly by limiting money growth. This logic led Milton Friedman to conclude that central banks should simply set money growth at a constant rate.[10] That is, policymakers should strive to ensure that the monetary aggregates like M1 and M2 grow at a rate equal to the rate of real growth plus the desired level of inflation. Friedman was aware that the central bank does not control the monetary aggregates precisely and that the link between the monetary base and M1 and M2 fluctuates over time. Policymakers cannot control the money multiplier since it depends both on how much currency individuals decide to hold and how much excess reserves banks decide to maintain. To make the rule viable, he suggested changes in regulations that would limit banks' discretion in creating money and tighten the relationship between the monetary aggregates and the monetary base, reducing fluctuations in the money multiplier. For example, an increase in the reserve requirement or restrictions on the number and types of loans banks could make would have such an effect.

But even if the relationship between the monetary base and the monetary aggregates were constant, Friedman's recommendation that the central bank should keep money growth constant would stabilize inflation only if velocity were constant. In countries with inflation above 10 or 20 percent per year, changes in velocity can probably be safely ignored. In those economies, lowering inflation really does require lowering money growth. But in countries where inflation is below 10 percent per year, changes in the velocity of money could have a significant impact on the relationship between money growth and inflation.

How much does the velocity of money fluctuate? To find out, we can look at some data. Panel A of Figure 20.5 shows the velocity of M1 and M2 from 1959 to 2004. While M1 has a clear upward trend, M2 looks very stable. But pictures can be deceiving. Since the fluctuations in M1 have been relatively large, the figure is drawn using a vertical scale that obscures the short-run movements in the velocity of M2.

STABILITY

---

[10]The original statement of what has come to be known as Friedman's *k-percent rule* is in Milton Friedman, *A Program for Monetary Stability* (New York: Fordham University Press, 1960).

YOUR FINANCIAL WORLD
Understanding Inflation Statistics

When people think about inflation, they usually have the consumer price index (CPI) in mind. The CPI is the most commonly used and closely watched measure of inflation in the United States.[*] Given its prominence, we should understand its limitations.

The CPI, published monthly by the Bureau of Labor Statistics, is used widely to make adjustments for inflation and to measure changes in the cost of living from month to month and year to year. The index is designed to answer the following question: How much more would it cost today to purchase the same basket of goods and services that was bought at some fixed point in the past? To calculate the CPI, every two years government statisticians ask a representative sample of people what they actually buy. Then they construct a representative "market basket" of goods and services and track how much it costs from month to month. Inflation, as measured by the CPI, is the percentage change in the price of this basket of goods.

The CPI systematically overstates inflation. That is, its estimates of the change in the cost of living are biased upward. There are several sources of bias. The first comes from the fact that consumers' *buying patterns* change all the time, while the Bureau of Labor Statistics' surveys are infrequent. (Figure 20.4 shows the relative weights used to divide the market basket among different types of expenditures in 2003.) Consumers tend to shift their purchases away from goods that have become relatively more expensive and toward those that have become less expen-

sive. Their willingness to make such substitutions lessens the impact of price changes on their standard of living. To the extent that statisticians fail to take such substitutions into account, the measure of consumer price inflation that they compile will overstate changes in the cost of living.

A second source of bias arises from the fact that statisticians have tremendous difficulty taking into account improvements in the *quality* of goods and services included in the consumer price index. Suppose, for example, that all cinemas introduce an elaborate new sound system that enhances the moviegoing experience, raising ticket prices at the same time. If consumers are willing to pay the higher ticket prices because they value the improved sound quality, statisticians may simply record the increase in ticket prices without accounting for the increase in quality.[†] The result is that inflation is overstated.

Economists estimate that the CPI overstates inflation by about 1 percentage point per year. So when the CPI rises by 2 percent, the real cost of living, correctly measured, rises only about 1 percent. While a bias of that size doesn't amount to much if prices are rising at 10 or 15 percent a year, it becomes significant to both policymakers and consumers at the low levels of inflation common in recent years. For central bankers who wish to maintain price stabil-

[*]Tools of the Trade in Chapter 2 describes other measures of inflation and gives a brief introduction to the CPI.

[†]New goods pose a problem similar to the one caused by changes in quality. While officials work hard to include new goods as they come out and eliminate old ones as they disappear, they aren't always successful. The result is that new goods, which typically have prices that fall during the first few years they are available, are not included as quickly as they might be. This introduces an additional upward bias in measured inflation.

To rectify this problem and give a more accurate picture of the fluctuations in M2 velocity, the lower panel of Figure 20.5 rescales the figure eliminating M1 velocity. Note two things. First, we can now see substantial short-run fluctuations. We will return to this shortly. For now, notice that in the long run, the velocity of M2 is stable, increasing only modestly from 1.72 to 1.82. That's an *average* annual growth rate of only 0.1 percent over 45 years. These historical data confirm Fisher's conclusion that *in the long run, the velocity of money is stable, so controlling inflation means controlling the growth of the monetary aggregates*.

But central bankers are concerned with inflation over quarters or years, not half a century. The monetary aggregates, even broad ones, can be useful guides to short-term policy only to the extent that they signal changes in inflation during the periods monetary policymakers care about. And the long-run view in Figure 20.5 masks some

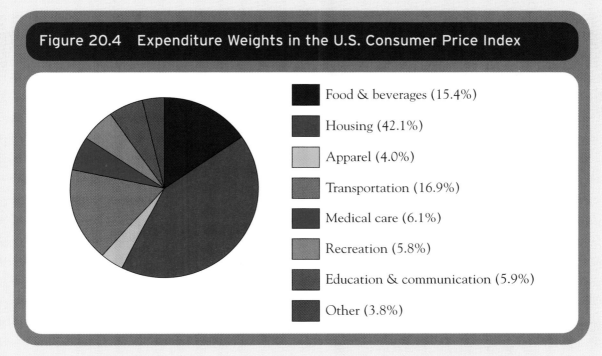

Figure 20.4   Expenditure Weights in the U.S. Consumer Price Index

- ■ Food & beverages (15.4%)
- ■ Housing (42.1%)
- □ Apparel (4.0%)
- ■ Transportation (16.9%)
- ■ Medical care (6.1%)
- ■ Recreation (5.8%)
- ■ Education & communication (5.9%)
- ■ Other (3.8%)

SOURCE: *Bureau of Labor Statistics, 2003.*

ity–zero inflation, correctly measured–the CPI's bias means that they need to systematically adjust their inflation objective, raising it about a percentage point. That is, rather than setting their objective at zero measured inflation, they must choose some positive rate above that. For the rest of us, the CPI's 1-percentage-point bias means that if the index goes up 3 percent a year, we need only a 2 percent raise to maintain our standard of living.**

[**]For a discussion of the biases associated with the computation of consumer prices, see David E. Lebow, and Jeremy B. Rudd, "Measurement Error in the Consumer Price Index: Where Do We Stand?" *Journal of Economic Literature* 41 (2003), pp. 159–201.

important short-run movements. To see them, we can look at the four-quarter (short-run) percentage change in M2 velocity shown in Figure 20.6. The shaded bars in the figure represent recessions. We can see that in the short run, velocity fluctuates quite a bit, sometimes by very large amounts. The scale of the figure runs from –8 to +8 percent!

From the point of view of policymakers who are trying to keep inflation low and stable, these fluctuations in velocity are enormous. To see why, assume for the moment that the Federal Reserve can accurately control the growth rate of M2 as well as accurately forecast real growth. With an inflation objective of 2 percent and a real growth forecast of $3\frac{1}{2}$ percent, equation (4) tells us that policymakers should set money growth equal to $5\frac{1}{2}$ percent minus the growth rate of velocity. If velocity increases by 3 percent, then money growth needs to be $2\frac{1}{2}$ percent. But if it falls by 3 percent, then money

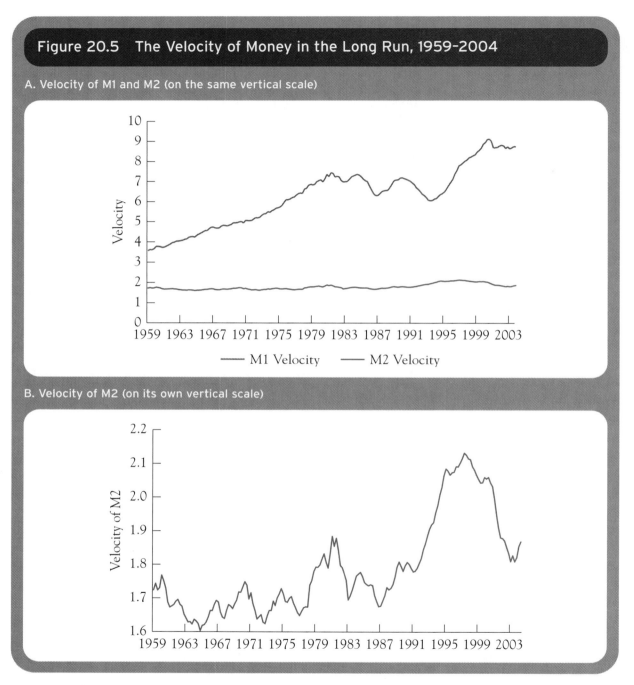

Figure 20.5 The Velocity of Money in the Long Run, 1959–2004

A. Velocity of M1 and M2 (on the same vertical scale)

B. Velocity of M2 (on its own vertical scale)

SOURCE: *Quarterly U.S. nominal GDP from the Bureau of Economic Analysis, divided by seasonally adjusted M1 and M2 from the Board of Governors of the Federal Reserve. Data on the monthly monetary aggregates were converted to quarterly averages.*

growth needs to be $8\frac{1}{2}$ percent. When inflation is low, short-run velocity growth can be several times the policymakers' inflation objective. Thus, to use money growth targets to stabilize inflation, policymakers must understand how velocity changes.

The first step in understanding short-run movements in velocity is to examine what happened in the past. Returning to Figure 20.5, notice the dramatic increase in velocity

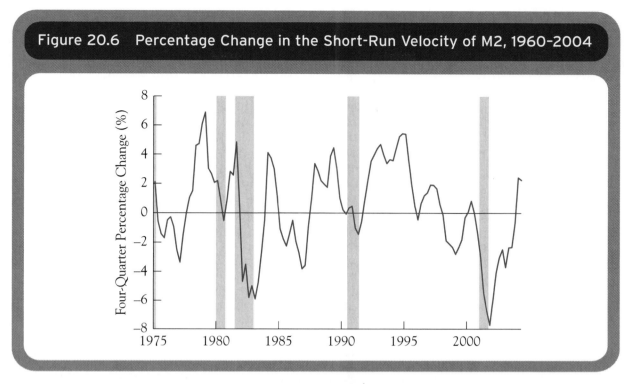

Figure 20.6   Percentage Change in the Short-Run Velocity of M2, 1960–2004

SOURCE: *Data are four-quarter percentage changes in the velocity of M2. Monetary aggregates are from the Board of Governors of the Federal Reserve; GDP, from the Bureau of Economic Analysis. The shaded areas denote recessions.*

MARKETS

in the late 1970s and early 1980s. This was a period of both high nominal interest rates, which peaked at over 20 percent, and significant financial innovations, including the introduction of stock and bond mutual funds that allow investors checking privileges. The first of these innovations made holding money very costly; the second allowed individuals to economize on the amount of money they held. Neither currency nor the checking accounts of the time paid interest, so with 20 percent inflation, the real rate of interest on money was –20 percent. Meanwhile, innovations like mutual funds outside of M2 (which allow for small-denomination withdrawals and provide transactions services similar to those of checking accounts) mean that individuals no longer needed to hold as much money. Together these reduced the amount of money individuals held for a given level of transactions, raising the velocity of money.

These data clearly suggest that fluctuations in the velocity of money are tied to changes in people's desire to hold money. To understand and predict changes in the velocity of money, then, policymakers must understand the demand for money. We turn to that topic next.

The Demand for Money

The best way to understand money demand, the determinants of the velocity of money, and the relationship between money and inflation is to ask why individuals hold money. What do they do with the money that is supplied to them? Recall from Chapter 2 that money can be a means of payment, a unit of account, and a store of value. While the unit-of-account function is crucial to the economy, it provides no justification for holding money, so we will ignore it here and focus on the first and third

APPLYING THE CONCEPT
THE ECB'S REFERENCE VALUE FOR MONEY GROWTH

The monetary policy strategy of the European Central Bank assigns a prominent role to money. Many of the ECB's practices are modeled on those of its predecessor, the German Bundesbank, widely viewed as one of the most successful central banks in the world. In the 1970s, as inflation rose into the double digits in the United States and throughout most of Europe, the Bundesbank kept inflation in Germany at levels that would be acceptable even today. Policymakers there did so by setting annual targets for the monetary aggregates. Several decades later, in the hope that the Bundesbank's reputation for controlling inflation would rub off on them, ECB policymakers decided to set a "quantitative reference value for the growth rate of a broad monetary aggregate."

For the first four years of its existence, the ECB announced what amounted to a target growth rate of $4\frac{1}{2}$ percent for euro-area M3 (the European equivalent of M2). Officials computed the rate using the percentage-change version of the equation of exchange (equation 4). That meant they had to make assumptions about real growth, velocity growth, and the desired level of inflation. They assumed the euro-area economy was growing at a rate of 2 to $2\frac{1}{2}$ percent per year, velocity was declining by $\frac{1}{2}$ to 1 percent per year, and inflation should be 1 to 2 percent annually. Substituting the midpoints of those ranges into equation (4), we get

$$Money\ growth - \tfrac{3}{4} = 1\tfrac{1}{2} + 2\tfrac{1}{4},$$
$$so\ Money\ growth = 4\tfrac{1}{2}\ percent.$$

The ECB was heavily criticized for its use of money growth targets. Observers claimed that the relationship between money growth and inflation was too unpredictable to be useful in the short run. They argued that the velocity of money in the newly created euro area would be difficult to forecast. For a new central bank with no proven record of controlling inflation, they charged, this was a potentially dangerous move that could damage policymakers' credibility. Possibly in response to their critics, in May 2003 ECB policymakers decided to downgrade the role of money growth in their strategy. From then on, money growth would be used as "a crosscheck," not a major part of their strategy. And the Governing Council would no longer review the reference value every year, emphasizing its usefulness only as a long-run benchmark.

functions. People hold money in order to pay for the goods and services they consume (the means-of-payment function) and as a way of holding their wealth (the store-of-value function). These two forms of demand are referred to as the transactions demand for money and the portfolio demand for money, respectively.[11] As we look at each of them, keep in mind that our objective is to understand fluctuations in the

---

[11]This framework for discussing the demand for money was originally developed by John Maynard Keynes and is known as Keynes's liquidity preference theory.

velocity of money. The more money individuals want to hold (all other things equal), the lower the velocity of money will be.

The Transactions Demand for Money

The quantity of money people hold for transactions purposes depends on their nominal income, the cost of holding money, and the availability of substitutes. The higher people's nominal income, the more they will spend on goods and services. The more they purchase, the more money they will need. This observation is the basis for the conclusion that nominal money demand rises with nominal income, part of the quantity theory of money (look back at equation (5)). Thus, *the higher nominal income is, the higher nominal money demand will be.*

Deciding how much money to hold depends on the costs and benefits of holding money. The benefits are easy to appreciate: holding money allows people to make payments. The costs are equally easy to understand. Because money can always be used to purchase an interest-bearing bond, the interest that people lose in not buying the bond is the opportunity cost of holding money. The nominal interest rate is the one that matters here. Compare money, which pays zero interest, to a bond that pays a nominal interest rate. The difference between the two is the rate that matters, and that's the nominal interest rate. Of course, the bond is not a means of payment; it must be converted into money before it can be used to pay for transactions. So the decision whether to hold money or bonds depends on how high the bond yield is and how costly it is to switch back and forth between the two.

Say, for example, that your employer deposits your take-home pay of $3,000 directly into your checking account on the first day of each month. While in reality your expenses for utilities, rent, groceries, and the like are staggered, let's simplify the example and assume that you spend $100 a day on each of the month's 30 days. If you do nothing else, your balance will decline to $1,500 just after the 15th of the month and to zero on the 30th day, just before your next paycheck is deposited. Your bank offers you a choice of leaving the entire $3,000 in the checking account or shifting funds back and forth between checking and a bond fund. The bond fund pays interest but adds a service charge of $2 for each withdrawal. How should you manage your account? If you choose to shift your funds back and forth between the bond fund and your checking account, how many times a month should you do it?[12]

To answer these questions, let's compare two alternative strategies (see Figure 20.7): in one, you leave your entire balance in your checking account. In the other, you split the $3,000 at the beginning of the month, taking half from your checking account and putting it into the bond fund. If you choose the second strategy, after 15 days you will have exhausted the $1,500 you left in your checking account and will need to transfer the balance from the bond fund into your checking account, at a cost of $2. Whether this choice is better than the other depends on the interest rate you receive on the bond fund. (If you receive interest on your checking account balance, then the difference in the two interest rates is what matters. That's the opportunity cost of holding money.) If the interest income is at least as much as the service charge, then you'll split your paycheck at the beginning of the month. But if the interest rate is less than this threshold, you won't want to invest in the bond fund.

---

[12]William Baumol and James Tobin worked out the answer to this question independently in the 1950s. Thus, the framework described here is often referred to as the Baumol-Tobin model. See William J. Baumol, "The Transactions Demand for Cash: An Inventory Theoretic Approach," *Quarterly Journal of Economics* 66 (1952), pp. 545–556; and James Tobin, "The Interest Elasticity of the Transactions Demand for Money," *Review of Economics and Statistics* 38 (1956), pp. 241–247.

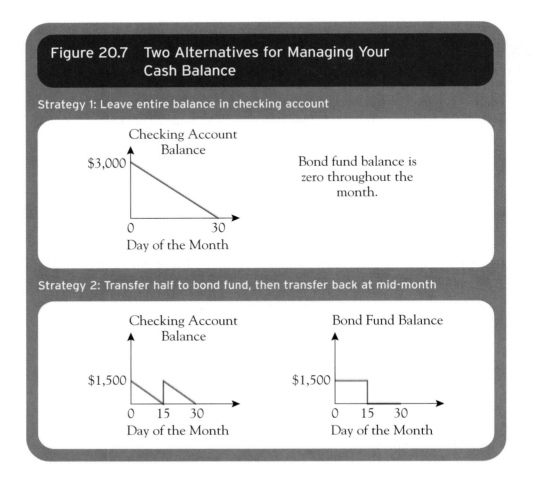

Figure 20.7 Two Alternatives for Managing Your Cash Balance

Strategy 1: Leave entire balance in checking account

Checking Account Balance

$3,000

0   30
Day of the Month

Bond fund balance is zero throughout the month.

Strategy 2: Transfer half to bond fund, then transfer back at mid-month

Checking Account Balance

$1,500

0   15   30
Day of the Month

Bond Fund Balance

$1,500

0   15   30
Day of the Month

Figuring out the interest rate above which you should shift your cash into the bond fund is straightforward. If you shift half your funds once, at the middle of the month, you'll have $1,500 in the bond fund during the first half of the month and $0 during the second half, so your average balance will be $750. Making the shift will cost you $2, so if the interest on $750 is greater than $2, you should make the shift. At a monthly interest rate of 0.27 percent, $750 will produce an income of $2 (2 ÷ 750 = 0.0027), so if the bond fund offers a higher rate, you should make the shift. Deciding whether to make a second shift is more complicated, but if the interest rate is high enough, doing so will be worthwhile. As the interest rate on the bond fund rises, you should consider two, three, or even more shifts between the bond fund and your checking account.

As the nominal interest rate rises, then, people reduce their checking account balances, shifting funds into and out of higher-yield investments more frequently. Knowing this, we can predict that the velocity of money will change with the interest rate. In our example, your annual income was $36,000 ($3,000 per month for 12 months). If you put it all into your checking account and simply spent it, your average money holding would be $1,500 and the velocity of your money would be $36,000/$1,500 = 24. But if the interest rate rose above 0.27 percent per month, your average money holdings would be cut to $750 and the velocity of your money would double, to 48.

The fact that the transactions demand for money falls as the interest rate rises has immediate implications for velocity. *The higher the nominal interest rate—the higher the opportunity cost of holding money—the less money individuals will hold for a given level of transactions, and the higher the velocity of money.*[13] This relationship explains why inflation tends to exceed money growth in the high-inflation countries shown in Figure 20.1. Why do the points representing high-inflation countries tend to lie above the 45-degree line? At high levels of inflation, when prices are rising at a rate of 1,000 or 1,500 percent a year, money is losing value very quickly, and the opportunity cost of holding money is equivalent to the cost of inflation, a real return of –1,000 or –1,500 percent a year. People respond to the high cost of holding money by keeping as little of it as possible, getting rid of their money as quickly as they can. They purchase durable goods that have a zero real return, which is quite a bit better than the real return of –1,000 percent they would get from holding money.[14] This frantic spending drives up the velocity of money. The quantity theory of money tells us that with national income held constant, inflation equals money growth plus growth in velocity. Since high inflation brings an increase in velocity, inflation must be higher than money growth in these countries, placing them above the 45-degree line in Figure 20.1.

Besides interest rates, *the transactions demand for money is affected by technology.* Financial innovation allows people to limit the amount of money they hold. Innovation can reduce the cost of shifting funds from a bond fund to a checking account. In our example, we assumed that the cost was $2 per transaction. The lower the transactions cost, the lower the interest rate at which people will shift money from their bond funds to their checking accounts, and the less money people will choose to hold.

To understand the impact of financial innovation on the transactions demand for money, suppose your bank offers a new kind of account that features free automatic transfers. You sign up for the account but continue using your old checks and debit card. As before, your take-home pay is $3,000 a month. Each time you make a purchase, your bank automatically shifts the amount of the purchase from your bond fund to your checking account, where it remains for one day before being paid to your creditor. Over a 30-day period, you spend $3,000 in this way. But your average money holding will be just $100, far below the $1,500 you would hold if you simply left the $3,000 in your checking account and spent it at a rate of $100 per day. So the lower the cost of shifting money from your bond fund to your checking account, the lower your money holdings at a given level of income and the higher the velocity of your money.

Thus, an increase in the liquidity of stocks, bonds, or any other asset reduces the transactions demand for money. The advent of ATMs and financial products that allow customers to make payments directly from their stock or bond mutual funds, often at no extra cost, means that today people don't need to hold as much cash in their wallets and their checking accounts as their parents and grandparents once did. This continued reduction in the cost of making payments accounts for the upward trend in the velocity of both M1 and M2 shown in Figure 20.5.

Finally, *we all hold money to insure ourselves against unexpected expenses.* We will include this form of demand, sometimes called the **precautionary demand for money,** as a part of transactions demand. Emergencies may arise that require immediate payments, for which we hold some amount of money in reserve. As we saw in Your Financial World in

[13]The fact that higher interest rates raise velocity means they put upward pressure on inflation. Yet, as we will see in the following chapters, monetary policymakers combat high inflation by raising interest rates. The apparent contradiction is resolved by the fact that, while interest-rate increases may drive velocity higher, they reduce real growth by even more—enough to make the overall effect the one that we have come to expect.

[14]You might think that people would invest in interest-bearing assets instead of durable goods. The problem is that the right kinds are often not available. At very high levels of inflation, inflation tends to be quite variable. The right investment in such an environment has a very short time to maturity. Any maturity longer than about a week becomes extremely risky and people will prefer to purchase durable goods instead.

YOUR FINANCIAL WORLD
Free Checking Accounts Are Rarely Free

Banks are always trying to attract new customers. To do so, some banks advertise free checking accounts. But are these accounts really free? The answer is almost surely no. In fact, bankers joke that *"free* checking" really means *"fee* checking" because of all the fees customers end up paying. While banks don't normally impose a monthly service charge on such accounts, that doesn't make them free.

Depending on the bank, customers with "free checking" may pay a fee to use the ATM or to visit a teller in person. They pay additional fees for notary public services, certified bank checks, and bounced checks. The insufficient funds charge is especially high for customers with "free checking," who are more likely than other customers to overdraw their accounts.

Overdrafts, in fact, are very profitable for banks. Here's why. If you write a check for $100 more than your account balance, the bank will cover it but will charge you a fee, usually $25 to $30. You will have only a week or so to pay back the overdraft. In other words, the bank is offering you a $100 loan at a weekly interest rate of 25 percent or more. While banks are normally required to disclose the interest rates they charge on loans, regulators have decided that overdrafts are not loans. As a result, banks don't have to tell people who overdraw their accounts that they are paying a compound annual interest rate of over 10,000,000 percent!

There are two lessons here. First, don't be fooled by offers of free checking. Before you open a checking account, figure out what services you are going to need and find the bank that meets your needs most cheaply. Second, don't overdraw your account. There is almost always a cheaper way to borrow money.

Chapter 17, an individual's rainy day fund is analogous to a bank's excess reserves. The level of precautionary balances we hold in such funds is usually related to our income and our level of expenditures. The higher our normal expenses, the larger our rainy day funds. The precautionary demand for money also rises with risk. While this effect is probably small, the higher the level of uncertainty about the future, the higher the demand for money and the lower the velocity of money.

The Portfolio Demand for Money

Money is just one of many financial instruments that we can hold in our investment portfolios. As a store of value, money provides diversification when held with a wide variety of other assets, including stocks and bonds. To understand the portfolio demand for money, note that a checking account balance or a money-market account is really just a "bond" with zero time to maturity. That means we can use the framework presented in Chapter 6, where we discussed the demand for bonds, to understand the portfolio demand for money.

Recall that the demand for bonds depends on several factors, including wealth, the return relative to alternative investments, expected future interest rates on bonds, risk relative to alternative investments, and liquidity relative to alternative investments. Each of these affects the portfolio demand for money. As wealth increases, individuals increase their holdings of all assets. A prudent person holds a diversified portfolio that includes stocks, bonds, real estate, and money. As wealth rises, the quantity of all these investments, including money, rises with it. So money demand varies directly with wealth. Note that this rule applies even at a fixed level of expenditures: a rich person who has the same expenses as a poor person will still hold more money.

In studying the demand for bonds, we noted that an investor's desire to hold any specific financial instrument depends on how well it compares with alternative investments. The higher the expected return relative to the alternatives, the higher the demand for an asset will be. The same is true for money: the higher its return relative to the alternatives, the higher the demand. Put slightly differently, a decline in bond yields will increase the portfolio demand for money.

Because expectations that interest rates will change in the future are related to the expected return on a bond, they will affect the demand for money as well. To understand why, remember that the price of a bond varies inversely with the interest rate. When interest rates rise, bond prices drop and bondholders suffer a capital loss. So if you think interest rates are likely to rise, bonds will become less attractive than money to you. (Recall that the prices of short-term bonds fluctuate less than the prices of long-term bonds. Money is the ultimate short-term bond because it has zero time to maturity.) As a result, you will sell the bonds in your portfolio and increase your money holdings—at least until interest rates stop rising. When interest rates are expected to rise, then, money demand goes up.

Next there is risk. In our discussion of bonds, we noted that a decline in risk relative to that of alternative investments increases the demand for bonds. While the riskiness of money can decrease, what usually happens is that the riskiness of other assets increases, driving up the demand for money.[15] Looking back at Figure 20.6, we can see that during the financial crises of the late 1990s, the velocity of M2 declined. The cause was an increase in uncertainty (risk), which drove investors to shift their funds into money.

Finally there is liquidity, a measure of the ease with which an asset can be turned into a means of payment. While some forms of money are more liquid than others, they are all closer to becoming a means of payment than other alternatives. If a sudden decrease in the liquidity of stocks, bonds, or other assets occurred, we would expect to see an increase in the demand for money.

Table 20.1 summarizes all of the factors that increase the demand for money.

Targeting Money Growth in a Low-Inflation Environment

So here is where we stand. In the long run, inflation is tied to money growth. In a high-inflation environment, where money growth and inflation are both running higher than 100 percent, moderate variations in the growth of velocity are a mere annoyance. What is important is the resolve of central bank officials (and politicians) to bring inflation down. There is no magic to it; the only solution is to reduce money growth.

In a low-inflation environment, controlling inflation is not so simple. The quantity theory of money tells us that our ability to use money growth as a policy guide depends on the stability of the velocity of money. In the United States, the velocity of the broad monetary aggregate M2 appears sufficiently stable for M2 to serve as a benchmark for controlling inflation over the long run—over periods of several decades. But in the short run, the velocity of money varies substantially. Yet the mere fact that velocity fluctuates is not reason enough to dismiss money growth as a policy target.

---

[15]To grasp why money can be risky, think of an example in which the nominal interest rate on money is zero (that is literally true for cash and nearly true for many bank deposits). When money pays no interest, its return is minus inflation. That is, money loses value at the rate of inflation. The less certain inflation is, the more uncertain the return on money, and the more risky it is. So inflation uncertainty increases the riskiness of holding money.

Table 20.1 Determinants of Money Demand: Factors That Cause Individuals to Hold More Money

Transactions Demand for Money

Nominal income	The higher nominal income, the higher the demand for money.
Interest rates	The lower interest rates, the higher the demand for money.
Availability of alternative means of payment	The less available alternatives means of payment, the higher the demand for money.

Portfolio Demand for Money

Wealth	As wealth rises, the demand for money goes up.
Return relative to alternatives	As the return on alternatives falls, the demand for money goes up.
Expected future interest rates	As expected future interest rates rise, the demand for money goes up.
Risk relative to alternatives	As the riskiness of alternatives rises, the demand for money goes up.
Liquidity relative to alternatives	As the liquidity of alternatives falls, the demand for money goes up.

As we saw in Chapter 18, an intermediate target can be useful when stable links exist between it and the policymakers' operating instrument, on the one hand, and their policy objective on the other. This statement implies two criteria for the use of money growth as a direct monetary policy target: (1) a stable link between the monetary base and the quantity of money and (2) a predictable relationship between the quantity of money and inflation. The first of these allows policymakers to predict the impact of changes in the central bank's balance sheet on the quantity of money. The second allows them to translate changes in money growth into changes in inflation. These criteria cannot be solely qualitative in nature; central bankers need numerical estimates of these relationships. Policymakers must be able to say that a 1 percent change in the monetary base will generate an x percent change in a monetary aggregate like M2, which will then translate into a y percent change in inflation, and over what time period. The relationship between money demand and its determinants listed in Table 20.1 must be stable and predictable—a problem for U.S. policymakers.

The Instability of U.S. Money Demand

To study the demand for money quantitatively, we will focus on the impact of the two factors that affect the transactions demand for money, nominal

"Forgive the mess. Warren just put everything into cash."

income and interest rates. Recalling the logic of the equation of exchange, we can conclude that the first factor, nominal income, is roughly proportional to money demand. Doubling people's nominal income means doubling the dollar value of the transactions they engage in, which requires double the original amount of money. That means we can focus on nominal income divided by the quantity of money, which equals velocity. This brings us to the second factor, interest rates (or more precisely, the opportunity cost of holding money). Is there a stable relationship between the velocity of money and the opportunity cost of holding it?

The data displayed in Figure 20.8 bear directly on this question. The figure shows the velocity of M2 on the vertical axis and the opportunity cost of holding M2 on the horizontal axis. The opportunity cost of M2 is defined as the yield on a three-month U.S. Treasury bill (an alternative asset) minus the return on holding M2, as computed by the Federal Reserve.[16] Note that this opportunity cost is a measure of the real return that individuals give up when they decide to hold M2 rather than a three-month Treasury bill. Each point on the figure represents a particular quarter. Notice that the points fall into two distinct groups. The first group, shown as blue squares, covers the decade of the 1980s. The second group, shown as beige squares, covers the 1990s. What we want to know is whether an increase in the opportunity cost of holding money can be used to forecast an increase in velocity. (Recall that higher interest rates raise the opportunity cost of holding money, reducing the demand for money at a given level of income and increasing its velocity.)

The answer to our question is yes, there is a relationship between the velocity of money and the opportunity cost of holding money, but that relationship shifted quite a bit between the two decades. To see how much it shifted, consider an increase from 1 to 2 percent in the opportunity cost of holding M2. In the 1980s, the implication of a 1 percent increase in opportunity cost was an increase of $1\frac{1}{2}$ percent in the velocity of M2, from roughly 1.73 to 1.76. In the 1990s, the same change in opportunity cost drove velocity up 6 percent, from 1.93 to 2.05. That is, the sensitivity of money demand to a change in the interest rate rose by a factor of four. The relationship between money demand and interest rates that held in the 1980s broke down in the 1990s. Using the relationship from the 1980s as a basis for policymaking in the 1990s would not have produced the desired result.

There are several possible explanations for the instability of U.S. money demand over the last quarter of the 20th century. The primary one has to do with the introduction of financial instruments that paid higher returns than money but could still be used as means of payment. While officials have tried to account for the new instruments by changing the composition of the monetary aggregates (see Applying the Concept), money demand continues to appear unstable.

A second explanation for the breakdown in the relationship between the velocity of M2 and its opportunity cost has to do with changes in mortgage refinancing rates. As long-term interest rates fell throughout the 1990s, they spurred periods of intense activity in the mortgage market. Because every mortgage comes with the right to repay early (the mortgage holder gets a put option), the holder of a conventional 30-year, fixed-rate mortgage can terminate the loan contract at any time by simply repaying the balance. When mortgage interest rates fall dramatically, large numbers of people pay off their old, high-interest mortgages and replace them with new, low-interest mortgages. The incentive to refinance a mortgage can be significant, even for what might seem a small decline in interest rates.

[16]Computing what is called the "own rate of return" on M2 is tricky. It requires measuring the interest rates on the different components of money and then weighting them according to the relative quantities people hold. The series is computed by the Federal Reserve and is available from the Federal Reserve Bank of St. Louis economic data service, FRED, at http://research.stlouisfed.org/fred2/series/M2OWN/.

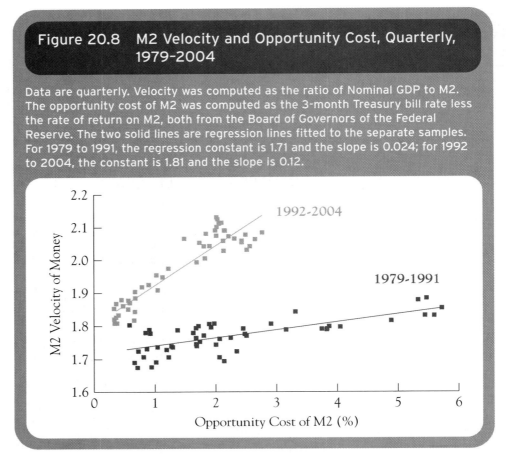

Figure 20.8   M2 Velocity and Opportunity Cost, Quarterly, 1979–2004

Data are quarterly. Velocity was computed as the ratio of Nominal GDP to M2. The opportunity cost of M2 was computed as the 3-month Treasury bill rate less the rate of return on M2, both from the Board of Governors of the Federal Reserve. The two solid lines are regression lines fitted to the separate samples. For 1979 to 1991, the regression constant is 1.71 and the slope is 0.024; for 1992 to 2004, the constant is 1.81 and the slope is 0.12.

SOURCE: *Board of Governors of the Federal Reserve, Federal Reserve Bank of St. Louis, and Bureau of Economic Analysis.*

When a mortgage is refinanced, it creates demand for money in several ways. Many people who are refinancing take the opportunity to remove some of their equity in their home. The proceeds go into liquid deposit accounts, which are part of M2, until they are spent on home renovations or other major purchases. In addition, funds for the new mortgage must be collected from investors and transferred to holders of the old mortgage. Along the way, they flow through an account that is part of M2. So when mortgage interest rates fall, M2 tends to grow rapidly. Once interest rates stabilize and the wave of refinancing subsides, M2 settles down and even shrinks. But in the meantime, velocity fluctuates.

The breakdown in the relationship between money demand and interest rates that occurred in the United States during the early 1990s drove researchers back to their computers to build better, more robust statistical models. The data for the 1990s shown in Figure 20.8 suggest that they should have been successful, and to some extent they were. Nevertheless, the debate over the stability of money demand in the United States serves as a cautionary note for policymakers.[17]

[17]To learn more about the debate over the stability of money demand in the United States, see Arturo Estrella and Frederick S. Mishkin, "Is There a Role for Monetary Aggregates in the Conduct of Monetary Policy?" *Journal of Monetary Economics* 40, no. 2 (1997), pp. 279–304.

TOOLS OF THE TRADE
Using Statistical Models in Policy Evaluation

For policymakers to do their jobs, they need to know how changes in policy will affect their objectives. An essential question in any monetary policy decision is how much to adjust interest rates in order to keep prices stable and economic growth high. Unlike theory, policymaking is about numbers; it requires quantitative estimates of the relative impact of alternative policies. These estimates are based on statistical models that summarize the correlations among economic variables. To obtain the necessary information, economists at the central bank collect historical information and analyze it in an attempt to determine how past changes in policy have affected the economy. Their estimates allow policymakers to answer questions such as "If we raise the federal funds rate from 4 to 5 percent, how much lower will inflation be two years from now?"

Such an exercise may seem straightforward, but it has pitfalls. For an economic prediction to be valid, it must be based on data drawn from a historical period in which the same set of policies was in place. If it isn't, the results can be seriously misleading. A sports analogy will help to make the point. In the United States, a football team has four downs to make 10 yards, but in Canada, a football team gets only three downs before being forced to give up the ball. As a result, Canadian football teams regularly kick the ball away on the third down. Needless to say, no one would think of using data from Canadian football games to predict third-down behavior in a U.S. game.

In the mid-1970s, Nobel Prize-winning economist Robert Lucas observed that what is true in sports is true in economics.[*] In the same way that altering the rules of a game will change the players' strategies, altering economic policy will

change people's economic decisions. For example, no one would use data from a fixed-exchange-rate period to model the impact of interest-rate policy in a floating-exchange-rate system. Nor would anyone use information from a period when central bankers targeted money growth, allowing interest rates to vary, to predict the impact of a shift to targeting interest rates. Economic and financial decisions, Lucas noted, are based on expectations about the future, including what policymakers will do. Any change in policymakers' behavior will change people's expectations, altering their behavior and the observed relationships among economic variables.

This observation, known as the Lucas critique, has had a profound influence on the way policymakers formulate their recommendations. It implies that in predicting the effects of a change in policy, policymakers must take into account how people's economic behavior will change with it. To understand the impact of policies never before implemented, Lucas emphasized, policymakers must rely heavily on economic theory, modeling people's reactions to changes in their environment.[†]

[*]The original Lucas critique is described in Robert E. Lucas, Jr., "Econometric Policy Evaluation: A Critique," Carnegie-Rochester Conference on Public Policy 1, 1976, pp. 19–46.

[†]Related to the fact that individuals adjust their behavior to policymakers' actions is the fact that, when policymakers choose to exploit a statistical relationship for policy purposes, they change the relationship. For example, if monetary policymakers find an indicator variable that allows them to perfectly predict the future path of inflation, they can use it to stabilize inflation. But if they do, inflation will in fact become stable, invalidating the correlation between the indicator and future data on inflation. Known as Goodhart's Law, this observation of the connection between statistical relationships and policy was first noted by the British monetary economist Charles Goodhart, who observed that money demand became unstable in the United Kingdom in the mid-1970s, immediately after the Bank of England's decision to target money growth. See K. Alec Chrystal and Paul D. Mizen, "Goodhart's Law: Its Origins, Meaning and Implications for Monetary Policy," in Paul Mizen, ed., *Central Banking, Monetary Theory and Practice: Essays in Honor of Charles Goodhart* 1 (Cheltenham, U.K.: Edward Elgar Publishing, 2003), pp. 221–243.

Targeting Money Growth: The Fed and the ECB

Though today virtually no central bank targets money growth, the practice was common in the 1970s. In the United States, the FOMC first adopted explicit objectives for money growth on January 15, 1970. Five years later, Congress passed a law directing the chair of the Federal Reserve Board to make quarterly appearances to testify to

APPLYING THE CONCEPT
FINANCIAL INNOVATION AND THE SHIFTING VELOCITY OF MONEY

In our discussion of the transactions demand for money, we emphasized the impact of financial innovations on the quantity of money demanded. By changing the amount of money people need to hold at a given level of income, financial innovations influence the velocity of money. While innovations like ATMs and bond mutual funds that offer check-writing privileges make people's lives easier, they create serious difficulties for statisticians who are trying to construct useful definitions of the monetary aggregates.

Recall from Chapter 2 that the different measures of money are defined based on the liquidity of available financial assets. For example, M2 includes all the assets in M1 plus some others that are less liquid; M3 includes all the assets in M2 plus some others that are even less liquid. But financial innovations can change the liquidity of the assets we hold. Ideally, the definitions of the monetary aggregates can be adjusted to take new financial instruments into account, but that task isn't easy.

To see the impact of financial innovations on measures of money, we can examine a particular historical episode: the introduction of the interest-bearing deposit account, including money-market mutual fund accounts, in the 1970s. As funds shifted from traditional checking accounts to these new instruments, the velocity of money appeared to rise, as the beige line in Figure 20.9 shows. That line represents the velocity of money according to the old definition of M2, which excluded money-market deposit accounts and money-market mutual fund accounts. Had the definition of M2 remained the same, velocity would have risen by a factor of two. Instead, statisticians redefined M2 to keep velocity fairly constant at 1.5 to 2, as the blue line in Figure 20.9 shows.

The monetary aggregates can always be adjusted after the fact to account for changes in the financial system. For monitoring long-run economic conditions, that is sufficient. The real difficulty is calculating the impact of such changes as they are occurring so that the information can be used for short-run policymaking. Could anyone have known before the fact precisely how the introduction of new interest-bearing deposit

the Fed's money growth targets for the coming year. And the Full Employment and Balanced Growth Act, passed in 1978, required the Fed to publish ranges for money growth in its twice-yearly *Monetary Policy Report to Congress*.

But announcing an objective is one thing; achieving it is something else. The FOMC rarely hit its money growth targets. Finally in July 2000, after the requirements of the 1978 legislation had expired, the committee stopped publishing them. A number of observers, including some inside the Federal Reserve, have argued that policymakers could have hit their money growth targets using procedures that were then in place. But to do so would have meant adjusting the federal funds rate target frequently, and by large amounts—something policymakers were unwilling to do. By

continued from previous page

Figure 20.9   Velocity of M2, Old and New Definitions, 1959–2003

Old definitions excluded other checkable deposits from M1. The old definition of M2 also excluded money-market deposit accounts and retail money-market mutual fund shares.

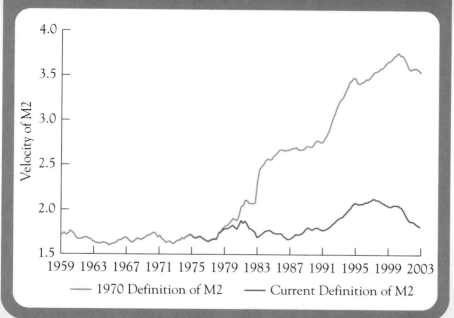

SOURCE: *Board of Governors of the Federal Reserve Board.*

accounts would influence money demand? Does the increase in velocity in the second half of the 1990s signal the need to redefine M2 once again? These are the sorts of questions that advocates of targeted money growth need to answer.

the summer of 2003, even Milton Friedman had given up. "The use of the quantity of money as a target has not been a success," he conceded. "I'm not sure I would as of today push it as hard as I once did."[18]

European monetary policymakers view matters differently. As we saw at the beginning of the chapter and in Applying the Concept: The ECB's Reference Value for

[18]Simon London, "Lunch with the FT: Milton Friedman," *Financial Times,* June 6, 2003. Interestingly, six weeks later, on August 19, 2003, Friedman published an article in *The Wall Street Journal* titled "The Fed's Thermostat," in which he claimed that the Federal Reserve's success in controlling inflation was due to its ability to respond accurately to changes in velocity. We should recognize, however, that if a central bank is successful in stabilizing inflation, it will appear after the fact to have been able to predict movements in velocity.

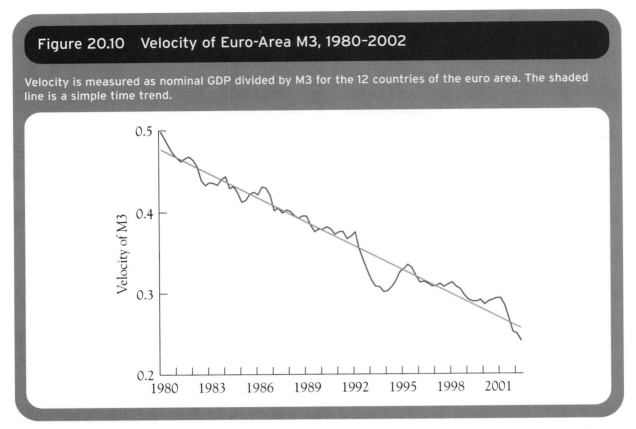

Figure 20.10   Velocity of Euro-Area M3, 1980-2002

Velocity is measured as nominal GDP divided by M3 for the 12 countries of the euro area. The shaded line is a simple time trend.

SOURCE: *The data are from Chart 1 of Klaus Masuch, Sergio Nicoletti-Altimari, Huw Pill, and Massimo Rostagno, "The Role of Money in Monetary Policy Making," in European Central Bank,* Background Studies for the ECB's Evaluation of its Monetary Policy Strategy, *(Frankfurt, Germany: European Central Bank, November 2003). All data are from the European Central Bank.*

Money Growth, the ECB's Governing Council periodically announces a money growth rate that is intended to serve as a long-run reference value. Large deviations from this reference value require an explanation. The difference of opinion between the Fed and the ECB on this matter can be traced to their divergent views on the stability of money demand. Researchers who study the demand for money in the euro area have concluded that it is stable, which implies that changes in velocity are predictable. This assumption is the justification for the ECB's emphasis on money in its monetary policy framework.[19]

The ECB's strategy is based on data like those shown in Figure 20.10. From 1980 to 2002, the velocity of euro-area M3 fell by half, from 0.50 to 0.25. While short-run fluctuations in velocity were significant, European policymakers point to the tendency of velocity to return to its long-run downward trend over periods of two to three years. (Recall that in computing the ECB's reference value for money growth, described in Applying the Concept, statisticians assumed that velocity would decline

[19]For a survey of studies of the stability of money demand in the euro area, see the discussion and references in Alessandro Calza and Joao Sousa, "Why Has Broad Money Demand Been More Stable in the Euro Area than in Other Economies? A Literature Review," in European Central Bank, *Background Studies for the ECB's Evaluation of its Monetary Policy Strategy* (Frankfurt, Germany: European Central Bank, November 2003).

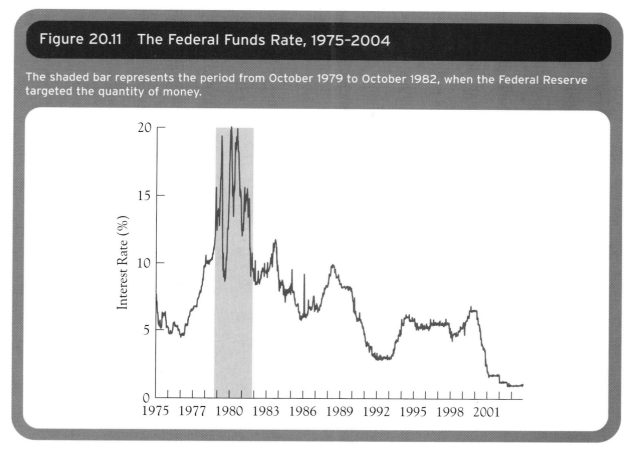

Figure 20.11   The Federal Funds Rate, 1975–2004

The shaded bar represents the period from October 1979 to October 1982, when the Federal Reserve targeted the quantity of money.

SOURCE: *Data are the effective federal funds rate, weekly, from the Board of Governors of the Federal Reserve.*

between $\frac{1}{2}$ and 1 percent a year.) Careful statistical analysis shows no evidence of instability in Euro-area velocity similar to that exhibited in the United States.[20]

Even given this difference in their emphasis on money growth, the ECB and the Fed have both chosen interest rates as their operating target. The reason is that interest rates are the link between the financial system and the real economy. Changes in interest rates are one of the primary tools central bankers have for influencing the economy. By keeping interest rates stable, policymakers can insulate the real economy from disturbances that arise in the financial system. For example, the payments system can change quickly. The introduction of more liquid financial instruments or newly configured electronic systems can have a direct impact on the way money is used and therefore on velocity. If policymakers wanted to, they could keep money growth constant in the face of such innovations. But doing so would create volatility in interest rates, which could destabilize the real economy. This point was made in Chapter 18, in Applying the Concept: Choosing an Operating Instrument, which discussed the rationale for choosing the interest rate rather than the quantity of

[20]While euro-area money demand is clearly stable, the velocity of European M3 does fluctuate significantly. In fact, the standard deviation of the four-quarter change in Figure 20.10 is 4.5 percentage points—nearly $1\frac{1}{2}$ times the equivalent number for the United States. The fact remains, however, that sophisticated statistical analysis shows tremendous instability in U.S. money demand but not in euro-area money demand.

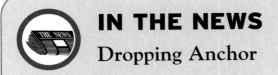

IN THE NEWS
Dropping Anchor

The Economist

September 23, 1999

It makes sense to set a medium-term inflation target, but don't ignore the money growth

CONSERVATIVELY dressed central bankers may not look like fashion victims, yet they are as prone to the latest craze as anybody else. Remember when monetarism was all the rage? Then central-bank independence became the "in" thing. The latest fashion is for inflation targets.

Most economists argue that monetary policy works best if central banks have some sort of nominal anchor to guide policy and to tie down inflationary expectations. The gold standard provided the firmest possible anchor, but at the cost of unacceptable swings in output. Modern anchors come in three main shapes. In the late 1970s and early 1980s most central banks adopted monetary targets. But then money-supply measures became distorted by financial deregulation and innovation, so central banks switched to exchange-rate or inflation targets.

Pegging a country's currency to that of a low-inflation economy such as Germany's, as under the European exchange-rate mechanism (ERM), was an easy rule to fol-

low, and it certainly helped countries such as France and Britain to reduce inflation. But in a world of highly mobile capital flows, pegged exchange rates are vulnerable to speculative attacks.

This leaves inflation targets as the last effective anchor. They are clearly becoming more popular. A survey by the Bank of England of 91 central banks in developed and emerging economies found that 54 had an explicit inflation target in 1998, compared with eight in 1990.

An inflation target is easier for the public to understand than a target for money or the exchange rate. That, it is argued, may make it more effective in reducing inflationary expectations. But perhaps the most important feature of inflation targets is the emphasis they put on transparency and accountability. Inflation targets are not rigid; they allow a central bank to make use of all available information, giving it considerable discretion in setting policy, so transparency in its decision making is vital. Because it is easier to judge whether policy is on track, inflation targets make central banks more accountable, which, in turn, helps to build public support for their independence.

Ideally, central banks should target a broad price index, including asset prices. In practice, however, such an index would be tricky to calculate. Probably the best option is for a central bank to set a medium-term inflation target, but to keep a close eye on asset prices, and be prepared to undershoot the target temporarily—and to

reserves as an operating instrument. There we noted that the best way to keep changes in reserves from influencing interest rates and affecting the real economy is to target interest rates. While inflation is tied to money growth in the long run, interest rates are the tool policymakers use to stabilize inflation in the short run.

The idea that targeting money growth destabilizes interest rates is not just a theoretical possibility. For roughly three years from October 1979 to October 1982, as part of the effort to reduce inflation from well over 10 percent the FOMC used reserves to target money growth, allowing the federal funds rate to fluctuate.[21] Figure 20.11 shows the results. The shaded area represents the period when the FOMC targeted the quantity of money. Notice how volatile the interest rate was during that three-year period. In fact, over intervals as short as three to four months, the federal funds rate fluctuated as much as 10 percentage points, rising from $11\frac{1}{2}$ percent in September 1979 to 20 percent in March 1980, then falling to 10 percent in July 1980 before

[21]For a discussion of this period, see the Federal Reserve Bank of San Francisco's Web site: http://www.frbsf.org/education/activities/drecon/2003/0301.html.

explain why—if share prices bubble over. In normal circumstances an inflation target is an excellent guide for monetary policy, but it should not be applied too rigidly. Central banks need to keep their eyes open for other signs of excess.

Share prices are one sign of excess; money is another. Back in August 1977, *The Economist* published a signed article by Alan Greenspan, then a private economist, with a list of five economic don'ts. One of them was: "Don't allow money-supply growth to spiral out of hand."

The notion that persistent rapid growth in the money supply leads to higher prices is one of the oldest propositions in economics. The Bundesbank was the first central bank to introduce money targets, in 1974, and most other countries followed suit. But as the link between money and inflation appeared to weaken, strict money targets were abandoned by virtually all except the Bundesbank. Or, as Gerald Bouey, a former governor of the Bank of Canada, put it, "We didn't abandon the monetary aggregates, they abandoned us." Financial deregulation and innovation, and the blurring of boundaries between banks and other financial institutions, have made money-supply figures hard to understand.

But central banks may have thrown the baby out with the bathwater. Today most of them pay little attention to money; it is not even included in banks' models for forecasting inflation. Only the ECB has refused to join this trend. The bank's chief economist, Otmar Issing (who used to do the same job at the Bundesbank), insists that money still matters. All past inflations, he says, have been preceded or accompanied by rapid monetary growth.

Money may be a fickle guide to the economy over the next year or so, but over long periods there is still a close link between money growth and inflation. The financial revolution may mean that rigid monetary targets are no longer practical, but this is no reason to ignore money completely. When money growth is unusually fast, as it currently is in America, a central bank should ask why. It might be signaling a future rise in inflation, or if inflation remains low, it may signal an asset-price bubble. For example, Japan's broad money expanded at an annual rate of more than 10 percent during its late-1980s bubble. Central banks cannot use the money growth rate to sail on autopilot, but they would be foolish to ignore its warning lights.

LESSONS OF THE ARTICLE

Even though targeting money growth is no longer a viable monetary policy, the monetary aggregates still contain information that policymakers can use in the pursuit of low, stable inflation. Central bankers need to be vigilant, watching for any telltale signs that inflation may return. In the long run, controlling inflation means ensuring that money growth doesn't get out of hand.

climbing back to 20 percent in December 1980. This sort of volatility, caused by policymakers' inability to forecast shifts in the velocity of money, would surely damage the real economy. Realizing the problem, policymakers have turned to the only viable alternative: targeting and smoothing fluctuations in interest rates. In the next chapter, we will study how they use interest rates to stabilize inflation and growth.

Terms

equation of exchange, 526

Lucas critique, 541

nominal gross domestic product, 524

portfolio demand for money, 532

precautionary demand for money, 535

quantity theory of money, 526

transactions demand for money, 532

velocity of money, 524

Chapter Lessons

1. There is a strong positive correlation between money growth and inflation.

    a. Every country that has had high rates of sustained money growth has experienced high inflation.

    b. At very high levels of inflation, inflation exceeds money growth.

    c. At moderate to low inflation, money growth exceeds inflation.

    d. Ultimately, the central bank controls the rate of money growth.

2. The quantity theory of money explains the link between inflation and money growth.

    a. The equation of exchange tells us that

        i. The quantity of money times the velocity of money equals the level of nominal GDP.

        ii. Money growth plus velocity growth equals inflation plus real growth.

    a. If velocity and real growth were constant, the central bank could control inflation by keeping money growth constant.

    b. In the long run, velocity is stable, so controlling inflation means controlling money growth.

    c. In the short run, velocity is volatile.

3. Shifts in velocity are caused by changes in the demand for money.

    a. The transactions demand for money depends on income, interest rates, and the availability of alternative means of payment.

    b. The portfolio demand for money depends on the same factors that determine the demand for bonds: wealth, expected future interest rates, and the return, risk, and liquidity associated with money relative to alternative investments.

4. The quantity theory of money and theories of money demand have a number of implications for monetary policy.

    a. Countries with high inflation can reduce inflation by controlling money growth.

    b. Countries with low inflation can control inflation by targeting money growth only if the demand for money is stable in the short run.

    c. In the United States, the relationship between the velocity of M2 and its opportunity cost (the yield on an alternative investment) has proven unstable over time.

    d. The instability of money demand in the United States has caused policymakers at the Federal Reserve to pay less attention to money growth than to interest rates.

    e. In the euro area, money demand is stable, which has caused the ECB's policymakers to pay more attention to money growth than the Fed does.

    f. Regardless of the stability of money demand, central banks target interest rates to insulate the real economy from disturbances in the financial sector.

Problems

1. Why is inflation higher than money growth in high-inflation countries and lower than money growth in low-inflation countries?

2. Explain how the central bank can control the growth rate of money.

3. If velocity were constant at 2 while M2 rose from $5 trillion to $6 trillion in a single year, what would happen to nominal GDP? If real GDP rose 3 percent, what would be the level of inflation?

4. If velocity were predictable but not constant, would a monetary policy that fixed the growth rate of money work?

5. Nobel-prize winning economist Milton Friedman suggested that the Federal Reserve could control the quantity of money more accurately by changing certain financial regulations. Describe the changes he suggested and explain the effects they might have. Do you think such changes would have an impact on velocity? Why or why not?

6. Using data from the Federal Reserve Bank of St. Louis Web site, compute the velocity of M2 over the past five years. To do so, convert the monthly, seasonally adjusted M2 data to quarterly data by averaging the three months in each quarter together. Plot the points you have computed and discuss the likely causes of recent fluctuations.

7. Using the numbers in the example on page 533, compute the monthly interest rate above which a twice-monthly shift in funds from your interest-bearing bond fund to your checking account would become worthwhile.

8. If the interest rate on bonds dropped to zero, what would happen to the transactions demand for money?

9. Suppose that expected inflation rises by 3 percent at the same time that the yields on money and on nonmoney assets both rise by 3 percent. What will happen to the demand for money? What if expected inflation rises by only 2 percent? What if the yield on nonmoney assets rises by 4 percent?

10. Do you think money demand is likely to be higher in cities or in rural areas? Explain your answer.

11. If people suddenly lost faith in the banking system, what would happen to the demand for money? What impact would their loss of confidence have on inflation?

12. Provide arguments both for and against the Federal Reserve's adoption of a target growth rate for M2. What assumptions would be necessary to compute such a target rate?

13. Using data from FRED II at the Federal Reserve Bank of St. Louis, compute M1 and M2 velocity over the past year. (You will need to convert the monthly M1 and M2 data to quarterly data. Do this by taking the middle month of each quarter.)

14. Describe the impact of financial innovations on the demand for money and velocity.

15. Comment on the ECB's use of the reference value for money growth.

Chapter 21

Modern Monetary Policy and Aggregate Demand

Governments publish economic data constantly. Almost every day we receive new information on some aspect of the economy. And the news stories follow, quoting experts on what it all means. Is inflation on the way up? Is the economy on the verge of recession? An important part of such analyses is speculation about the impact of the new data on monetary policy. In our discussion of central banking, we noted that conjecture about policymakers' likely reaction fills the financial news. And no wonder, for members of the committees that set interest rates—the FOMC in the United States and the Governing Council in the euro area—always tie their policy actions to current and future economic conditions.

Everyone is preoccupied with monetary policy. While traders in the financial markets are trying to outguess each other, to make a profit by betting on the next move in interest rates, the rest of us are just hoping the central bank will succeed in keeping inflation low and growth in real output high. How do policymakers do it? What is the mechanism through which changes in the interest rate influence inflation and output? And what are the limits of policymakers' power to control the economy?

Our purpose in Chapters 21 and 22 is to construct a framework that will show how interest rates, inflation, and real growth are linked. To do it, we need to develop a macroeconomic model of fluctuations in the business cycle in which monetary policy plays a central role. What are the sources of movements in inflation and output, and how can central banks stabilize them? The answer is that short-run movements in inflation and output can arise from two sources: changes in aggregate demand (that is, changes in consumption, investment, government spending, or net exports) and changes in aggregate supply (that is, changes in the costs of production). Modern monetary policymakers work to eliminate the volatility that such changes cause by adjusting their target interest rate, which influences the components of aggregate demand. As we have already seen, in the long run, output is determined by technological factors, while inflation is determined by the rate of money growth. But we are interested in the short-run economic effects of money and monetary policy.

We will develop our macroeconomic model in two steps.[1] This chapter describes the aggregate demand curve, which shows the quantity of real output demanded at each level of inflation. Here we will see a role for monetary policy. The next chapter will introduce aggregate supply—the level of real output supplied by firms at each level of inflation. As we will see, there is both a short-run and a long-run version of the aggregate supply curve. In the short run, equating aggregate demand with aggregate supply gives us current output and inflation. Business cycles are movements in this short-run equilibrium.

---

[1]The development in Chapters 21 and 22 is a simplified version of the model described by David H. Romer in "Keynesian Macroeconomics without the LM Curve," *Journal of Economic Perspectives* 14 (Spring 2000), pp. 149–169. A complete treatment is available in "Short-Run Fluctuations," unpublished manuscript, Department of Economics, University of California at Berkeley, revised August 2002, on Professor Romer's Web site, http://emlab.berkeley.edu/users/dromer/index.shtml.

This chapter begins with a description of long-run equilibrium and then goes on to present aggregate demand. As we proceed through the chapter, keep in mind that our ultimate objective is to understand how modern central bankers set interest rates. When policymakers change the target interest rate, what are they reacting to?

Output and Inflation in the Long Run

The best way to understand fluctuations in the business cycle is as deviations from some benchmark or long-run equilibrium level. The booms and recessions that make up business cycles are temporary movements away from this long-run equilibrium level. So we begin with the following question: What would the levels of inflation and output be if nothing unexpected happened for a long time? In the long run, current output equals *potential output*—full-employment output—and inflation equals the level implied by the rate of money growth.

Potential Output

Potential output is what the economy is capable of producing when its resources are used at normal rates. Imagine you are running a company that produces baseball bats for the Milwaukee market. You have estimated the demand for bats based on the information available to you, purchased machines, and hired workers to operate them. If everything goes according to plan, you'll make a nice profit. But suddenly the Milwaukee Brewers, a team that hasn't won a championship for a long time, win the World Series. As a result, the number of kids who play baseball in your area increases dramatically, and your bat sales skyrocket. To meet the increased demand, you begin running your factory around the clock.

What happened? The fact that the Brewers won the World Series drove your output above the normal level—that is, above potential output. Now, what if the local pro basketball team, the Milwaukee Bucs, were suddenly successful? This would create a boom in the sale of basketballs at the expense of baseball equipment, forcing you to cut back on production. The reduction in the rate at which you use your resources would drive your output level below potential.

Over time, conditions at your baseball bat factory are likely to change. First, if you come to believe that an increase or decrease in the demand for your product is permanent, you will change the scale of your factory, redesigning it to enlarge or reduce its size. Second, technological improvements will allow you to increase the factory's production at given levels of capital and labor. In other words, your factory's normal level of output will change over time, usually going up but occasionally going down.

What is true for the Milwaukee bat manufacturer is true for the economy as a whole. There is a normal level of production that defines potential output. But potential output is not a fixed level. Because the amount of labor and capital in an economy can grow, and improved technology can increase the efficiency of the production process, potential output tends to rise over time. Furthermore, unexpected events can push current output away from potential output, creating an output gap. When current output climbs above potential it creates an expansionary gap; when it falls below potential it creates a recessionary gap. These gaps close naturally, however, canceling each other out over time. *In the long run, current output equals potential output.*

STABILITY

Long-Run Inflation

The other key to long-run equilibrium is inflation. In the last chapter, we saw that the equation of exchange implies that money growth plus the change in the velocity of money equals inflation plus real growth. (Look back at equations (3) and (4) in Chapter 20.) We can restate the equation of exchange in terms of potential output. In the long run, since current output equals potential output, real growth must equal growth in potential output. *Ignoring changes in velocity, in the long run, inflation equals money growth minus growth in potential output.*

While central bankers focus their attention on controlling short-term nominal interest rates, they keep an eye on money growth. They know that when they adjust the level of reserves in the banking system to meet their target nominal interest rate, their action affects the rate at which money grows. That is what ultimately determines inflation. So concern for money growth is never far from their minds.

We turn now to the primary topic of this chapter, the role of monetary policy in the determination of current output. To understand that role, we need to develop a simple macroeconomic model—a shorthand description of the economy that will help us to organize our thinking.

Money Growth, Inflation, and Aggregate Demand

Aggregate demand tells us how spending (demand) by households, firms, the government, and foreigners changes as inflation goes up and down. The level of aggregate demand is tied to monetary policy through the equation of exchange, $MV = PY$. Households and firms need money to purchase the economy's output (Y). Because the amount of money in the economy limits their ability to make payments, aggregate demand for real output depends on the amount of money in circulation. To see what this means, we can rewrite the equation of exchange as

$$Y^{ad} = \frac{MV}{P} \qquad (1)$$

where Y^{ad} = aggregate demand,

M = the quantity of money,

V = the velocity of money, and

P = the price level.

This expression tells us that aggregate demand equals the ratio of the quantity of money divided by the price level (that's the purchasing power of the money in circulation) times velocity.

Now consider a one-time rise in the price level, P, that does not change either the quantity of money or its velocity. Looking at equation (1), we know that this rise in the price level forces the right-hand side of the expression down ($P\uparrow$ means $\frac{MV}{P}\downarrow$). The higher price level reduces the purchasing power of the money in circulation. Put another way, the level of real money balances falls. With constant velocity, this lower level of real money balances means that individuals and firms can make fewer purchases. Their reduction in purchases drives aggregate demand down. The conclusion is that an overall increase in the prices of goods and services ($P\uparrow$), at a fixed velocity and quantity of money (MV fixed), reduces the amount of goods and services individuals can purchase, depressing aggregate demand (Y^{ad}). That is, an increase in the price level leads to a decline in real money balances and a reduction in aggregate demand.[2]

Thus far, our discussion has been about the price level. A modern central bank's objectives are stated in terms of inflation, of *increases* in the price level, not the price level per se. That makes sense, since even over short periods the quantity of money and the level of prices are likely to change. That means that we need to shift the focus to inflation.

To see how to transform our model from one based on the price level to one focused on inflation, let's begin with the long-run case in which inflation equals money growth and both are 5 percent per year. We'll continue to assume that velocity is constant. Thus, while the numerator and denominator of $\frac{M}{P}$ are both rising, they are rising at the same rate. If money growth and inflation are equal, the level of real money balances in the economy remains the same.[3]

Now consider a case in which inflation exceeds money growth, again with velocity held constant. If, for example, inflation equals 6 percent while money is growing at only 5 percent, then $\frac{M}{P}$ will be falling. Should this situation continue for a full year, at the end of the year $\frac{M}{P}$ will be 1 percent lower than it was at the beginning of the year. And when velocity is fixed, a 1 percent fall in the purchasing power of the money in circulation generates a 1 percent decline in aggregate demand.[4]

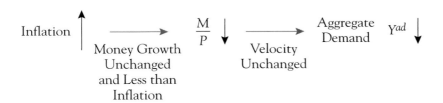

The result, a downward-sloping aggregate demand curve, is shown in Figure 21.1.

In summary, the equation of exchange tells us that when inflation rises, real money balances $\frac{M}{P}$ fall, so aggregate demand must fall as well.

Before continuing, we should say a word about interest rates. This description of the aggregate demand curve focuses on the impact of inflation on real money balances and ignores interest rates altogether. In fact, "real-money-balance effects" will impart a downward slope to the aggregate demand curve even if real interest rates (nominal interest rates minus expected inflation) remain unchanged as inflation varies. As we will see shortly, the ability to change the real interest rate is the tool that allows policymakers to influence economic activity. And these changes in the real interest rate provide an additional mechanism for aggregate demand to slope down.

[2]Many economics principles textbooks refer to this relationship between the quantity of aggregate demand and the price *level* as the aggregate demand curve. We will follow the lead of some newer principles books and present an alternative version that relates quantity to *inflation*.

[3]We are explicitly ignoring that the economy is constantly growing and that velocity is changing with it. As will become clear later in the chapter, our major concern (and that of policymakers) is deviations of current output from potential output. Though both are always growing, when current output and potential output grow at different rates, the result is an output gap.

[4]Recall from Chapter 20 that the equation of exchange implies that real growth (%ΔY) = (money growth) (%ΔM) + (velocity growth) (%ΔV) − inflation (%ΔP). With velocity constant, %ΔY = 5% − 6% = −1%.

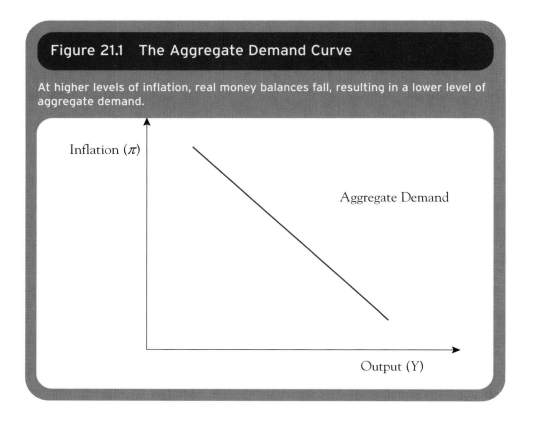

Figure 21.1 The Aggregate Demand Curve

At higher levels of inflation, real money balances fall, resulting in a lower level of aggregate demand.

YOUR FINANCIAL WORLD
Using the Word *Inflation*

Everyone talks about inflation, but what do they mean? In normal conversation, when people use the word *inflation*, they are referring to price increases. If the price of gasoline or the cost of a basket of groceries rises, that's inflation. When *The Wall Street Journal* reports that inflation was one- or two-tenths of one percent over the past month, it means that the average price level went up. As it is commonly used, the word *inflation* does not distinguish a one-time change in the price level from a situation in which prices are rising continuously.

Economists use the term more precisely. To them, inflation means a *continually rising price level*. It refers to a *sustained rise* that continues day after day, month after month, year after year. Economists emphasize the distinction between *temporary* and *permanent* changes in inflation. A

temporary increase is a one-time adjustment in the continuously rising price level, while a permanent change is a rise or fall in the long-run course of inflation.

To see the difference, consider an example in which inflation is running at the central bank's target level of zero percent. Then something forces inflation up to 5 percent for one year. (In Chapter 22, we will refer to that as a *positive inflation shock*.) After a year, policymakers succeed in bringing inflation back down to zero percent. At the end of this episode, inflation is back where it started, at zero, but the price level is 5 percent higher than it would have been otherwise. Temporary changes in inflation lead to adjustments in the price level. Only changes in monetary policy can cause permanent increases in inflation.

The Monetary Policy Reaction Curve

Policymakers know that money growth is an important benchmark for tracking long-run inflation trends, so they pay close attention to it. In fact, when faced with very high inflation, central bankers will focus almost exclusively on controlling money growth. Reducing the growth of the money supply is the only way to bring down inflation of 50 or 100 percent per year.

But with 1 or 2 or even 10 percent inflation, money growth is not the objective of short-run policy considerations. Instead, modern central bankers concentrate on manipulating interest rates to keep inflation low and close the gap between current and potential output. Thus, the Federal Open Market Committee's policy statements refer to inflation and growth when announcing and explaining interest-rate decisions. They make virtually no mention of money growth. If we want to understand the role of central bankers in stabilizing the economy—particularly how policymakers themselves think about their role—we need, to examine the connection between short-term interest rates and policymakers' inflation and output targets.

Monetary Policy and the Real Interest Rate

As we saw in Chapter 18, central bankers control short-term *nominal* interest rates by controlling the market for reserves. The Federal Reserve adjusts the level of reserves in the U.S. banking system in order to meet the federal funds target rate (the overnight interest rate at which banks make loans to each other). But the economic decisions of households to save and of firms to invest depend on the *real* interest rate, not the nominal interest rate. Controlling the nominal interest rate is not sufficient, then. To alter the course of the economy, central banks must influence the real interest rate as well.

In the short run, when monetary policymakers change the nominal interest rate, they change the real interest rate. To see why, recall from Chapter 4 that the nominal interest rate, i, equals the real interest rate, r, plus expected inflation, π^e. So

$$r = i - \pi^e \tag{2}$$

That is, the real interest rate equals the nominal interest rate minus expected inflation. As we will see in more detail in Chapter 22, both inflation expectations and inflation itself adjust only slowly in response to changes in economic conditions. Because inflation is slow to respond, when policymakers change the nominal interest rate, they change the real interest rate.

That movements in the short-term nominal interest rate are also movements in the short-term real interest rate is clear from data gathered over the past two decades. Figure 21.2 plots the nominal federal funds rate—the one the FOMC controls—against a measure of the real federal funds rate, constructed using survey data on expected inflation. (See Tools of the Trade for a discussion of inflation expectations.) The figure shows clearly that the nominal and real federal funds rates rise and fall together; the correlation between the two is 0.97. The clear conclusion is that when the Federal Reserve raises the nominal federal funds rate, it raises the real federal funds rate as well. And when the Fed lowers the nominal federal funds rate, it lowers the real federal funds rate with it.

The real interest rate, then, is the lever through which monetary policymakers influence the real economy. In changing real interest rates, they influence aggregate demand. Our task in the next section is to understand how this works.

Aggregate Demand and the Real Interest Rate

To understand the impact of monetary policy on the economy, we need to link the real interest rate to the level of output. This task requires a more detailed description

Figure 21.2 The Nominal and Real Federal Funds Rates, 1983–2004

The real federal funds rate is computed as the monthly nominal effective federal funds rate minus expected inflation for the next year from the University of Michigan's Survey of Consumers, described in Tools of the Trade.

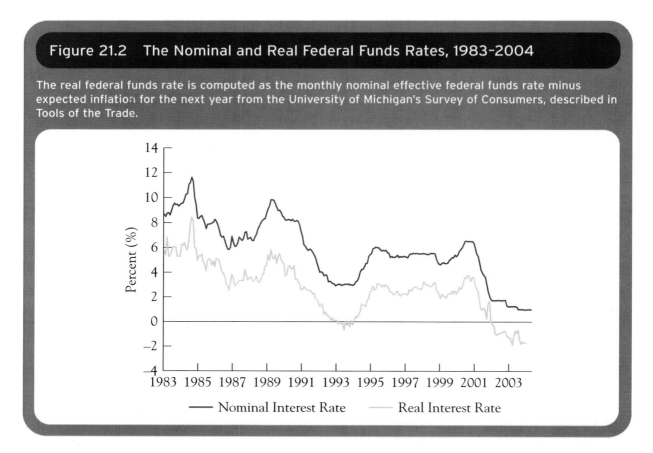

SOURCE: *Federal funds rate data were drawn from the Federal Reserve Board Web site, www.federalreserve.gov; inflation expectations data were drawn from the median expected change in prices during the next 12 months, Table 19 of the Michigan Survey, available at www.sca.isr.umich.edu.*

of aggregate demand and its relationship to the real interest rate. The best way to start is by analyzing the uses of the economy's output. Doing so allows us to divide aggregate demand into four parts:

$$\begin{array}{ccccccccc} \text{Aggregate} \\ \text{demand} \end{array} = \text{Consumption} + \text{Investment} + \begin{array}{c}\text{Government}\\ \text{purchases}\end{array} + \text{Net exports}$$

$$Y^{ad} = C + I + G + NX \qquad (3)$$

The terms in this equation are defined as follows:

1. **Consumption** (C) is spending by individuals for items like food, clothing, housing, transportation, entertainment, and education.
2. **Investment** (I) is spending by firms for additions to the physical capital they use to produce goods and services. Examples include new buildings and equipment. The cost of newly constructed residential homes and the change in the level of business inventories are also included in this category.[5]

[5]Remember that economists use the term *investment* differently from the business press. In *The Wall Street Journal*, an investment is a financial instrument like a stock or bond that people use as a means of holding their wealth. Importantly, though, people who make such a "financial investment" aren't creating anything new; they are buying something that already exists. To an economist, investment is the creation of new physical capital.

3. Government purchases (G) is spending on goods and services by federal, state, and local governments. New military equipment and schools fall into this category, as do the salaries of public school teachers, police officers, and firefighters.[6]

4. Net exports (NX) equals *exports* minus *imports*. Remember that exports are goods and services produced in one country and sold to residents of another country; imports are purchases of foreign-made goods and services. The difference between the two represents an addition to the demand for domestically produced goods. (Net exports are often referred to as the *current account surplus*; see the Tools of the Trade box in Chapter 10, page 242.)

To get some sense of the size of these four components of spending, we can compute the percentage of total output that each accounts for. In other words, we can divide GDP into four shares. From 1985 to 2004, consumption averaged two-thirds of GDP. Government purchases averaged nearly 20 percent of GDP and investment 16 percent. Net exports were negative, averaging –2.2 percent of GDP.

For our purposes, it is helpful to think of aggregate demand as having two parts, one that is sensitive to changes in the real interest rate and one that is not. Among the components of aggregate demand that are sensitive to changes in the real interest rate, investment is the most important. Deciding whether to replace an existing machine or purchase a new one is a complicated matter, dependent on a comparison of the revenue generated by the investment with the cost of financing it. In Chapter 4 we saw that this decision boils down to a comparison of the internal rate of return on the investment and the cost of borrowing to finance it. An investment can be profitable only if its internal rate of return exceeds the cost of borrowing. We can conclude that the higher the cost of borrowing, the less likely that an investment will be profitable. Since borrowers and lenders both care about the real return, we see immediately that the higher the real interest rate, the lower the level of investment.

While investment may be the most important component of aggregate demand that is sensitive to real interest rates, it isn't the only one. Consumption and net exports also respond to the real interest rate. What is true for a business considering an investment, for example, is true for a family thinking about buying a new car. Higher real interest rates mean higher inflation-adjusted car-loan payments, which make new cars more costly. Furthermore, as the real interest rate rises, the reward to saving goes up. More saving means lower consumption.[7]

[6]Social Security and unemployment insurance payments are not part of government purchases; rather, they are transfers from the group that pays the payroll taxes to the people who receive benefits.

[7]Increases in real interest rates influence decisions about saving in a second way. Consider someone who is saving for retirement. The higher the real interest rate, the less the person needs to save in order to achieve a given retirement goal. This effect makes the net impact of an increase in the real interest rate on consumption ambiguous, at least in theory. In practice, however, evidence tells us that higher real interest rates result in lower consumption and more saving.

"How many times have I asked you not to discuss stubbornly high interest rates in front of the children?"

SOURCE: © *The New Yorker Collection 1991. Lee Lorenz from cartoonbank.com. All Rights Reserved.*

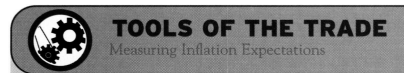

TOOLS OF THE TRADE
Measuring Inflation Expectations

Inflation expectations are central to many economic decisions. Any agreement that includes future monetary payments must be evaluated using some measure of expected inflation. Computing the real interest rate on a bond means subtracting expected inflation from the nominal interest rate. Figuring out whether an annual pay raise increases your purchasing power means estimating inflation over the next year. And as we will see in Chapter 22, monetary policymaking requires a measure of inflation expectations. So how do we measure expected inflation?

There are two ways. One is to survey people, asking about their inflation expectations; the other is to look at the prices of certain bonds in the financial markets. Surveys are of two types. First, there are consumer surveys like those done by the University of Michigan's Survey Research Center. Every month, as part of the Michigan Survey of Consumers, researchers ask hundreds of people across the United States how much inflation they expect over the coming 12 months. (Data and methods are available at www.sca.isr.umich.edu/main.php, Table 19.) Second, there are surveys of professional economic forecasters. For example, in the Survey of Professional Forecasters, researchers for the Federal Reserve Bank of Philadelphia ask professional economists what they think inflation will be over the next year. (See www.phil.frb.org/econ/spf/index.html.)

We can also look to the financial markets for measures of expected inflation. In Chapter 6, we discussed a type of U.S. Treasury bond that is guaranteed to beat inflation. Called Treasury Inflation Protection Securities (TIPS), these bonds are structured so that the owner receives payments equal to a real interest rate plus the change in the consumer price index. If you look in the newspaper, you will see that the yield reported on these bonds is the real interest rate. Traditional U.S. Treasury bonds promise nominal payments that do not change with inflation, so the rates reported in the newspaper are nominal interest rates. Since the nominal interest rate equals the real interest rate plus expected inflation, we can get an estimate of expected inflation by subtracting the real interest rate on TIPS from the nominal interest rate on traditional Treasury bonds. Because traditional Treasury bonds often have fairly long terms (five- and ten-year terms are common) this method allows us to compute expected inflation over an extended horizon.

What about the results? In April 2004, surveys predicted that expected inflation would be roughly 3 percent over the next year. U.S. Treasury yields gave a similar answer. The difference between the nominal and real yields would be 2.5 percent for the coming 5 years.

Interestingly, the Michigan survey data are broken down by demographic group. Looking at the details, economists have noticed that women expect higher inflation than men, often several percentage points higher. (Men's expectations are more accurate.) Researchers have speculated that the discrepancy could arise from the different types of goods women and men purchase or the fact that women shop more frequently than men. But after careful study, the fact that women expect more inflation than men remains a puzzle.*

*For a description of the difference between women's and men's inflation expectations and an examination of the possible reasons for it, see Michael F. Bryan and Guhan Venkatu, "The Curiously Different Inflation Perspectives of Men and Women," *Economic Commentary of the Federal Reserve Bank of Cleveland*, November 2001.

The case of net exports is more complicated. Recall from Chapter 10 that, when the real interest rate in the United States rises, U.S. financial assets become more attractive to foreigners. This rise in the desirability of U.S. assets to foreigners increases the foreign demand for dollars, causing the dollar to appreciate. The higher the value of the dollar, the more expensive U.S. exports will be, and the cheaper U.S.

YOUR FINANCIAL WORLD
It's the Real Interest Rate That Matters

In mid-2003, with 10-year U.S. Treasury bonds yielding less than 4 percent, business reporters were writing columns about people who were yearning for the days 25 years earlier when nominal interest rates were closer to 20 percent. *The Wall Street Journal* interviewed retirees living off the interest income who were having a hard time.* With money-market mutual fund account yields 1 percent or less, they were having trouble paying their bills. If only (nominal) interest rates were as high as they had been several decades earlier, the retirees complained, their lives would be easier.

While nominal interest rates were extremely low in mid-2003, no one should be wishing for a return to the high interest rates of the late 1970s. Those high nominal interest rates were high because inflation was high. In fact, in 1979, when nominal interest rates were at their peak, real interest rates were less than zero! (See Figure 4.3, page 82.) It's the real interest rate that matters.

An example shows the importance of focusing on the real interest rate. Consider a retired person who is living off the income from a $500,000 savings account. Say that inflation and the nominal interest rate have both been stable for some time, at 7 percent and 10 percent, respectively. At a 10 percent nominal rate, the annual interest income on half a million dollars would be $50,000. But what would happen if the retiree spent the entire $50,000 in annual income? Each year, the purchasing power of the income would fall 7 percent because of inflation. After 10 years, the person's real income would be only half what it was initially (remember the rule of 72).

To avoid such a reduction in purchasing power, it is important not to spend all the interest income. Instead, the retiree should save a portion of the income, increasing the size of the savings account at the same rate as inflation. In this case, maintaining the inflation-adjusted value of the savings account means increasing the balance by 7 percent each year. Of the first year's income of $50,000, then, $35,000 must be returned to the savings account; only $15,000 can be spent. Notice that in this example, the real interest rate is 3 percent, and $15,000 exactly equals 3 percent of the $500,000 balance. The result would be no different if the interest rate was 5 percent and inflation was 2 percent. The real interest rate would still be 3 percent, which is the maximum that can be spent without eroding the purchasing power of the savings account balance.[†]

High nominal interest rates can be misleading. They fool people into thinking that their incomes are high. But since high nominal rates almost always result from high inflation, spending all the interest income causes a gradual decline in the purchasing power of one's savings. To maintain the real purchasing power of their interest income, retirees can spend only the real return. For this reason, high interest rates are almost never a good thing; low inflation is.

---

[*]Kelley Green, "As the Fed Cuts Rates, Retirees Are Forced to Pinch Pennies," *The Wall Street Journal*, July 7, 2003, p. A1.

[†]Because of the way the income tax system works, the effect of high nominal interest rates is even worse than this example suggests. The problem is that income tax is computed on nominal interest income. Consider the example of a bond with a 10 percent nominal yield in an economy with 7 percent inflation. Someone whose income is taxed at a 25 percent rate would receive a $7\frac{1}{2}$ percent after-tax nominal return on the bond. But since inflation is 7 percent, the after-tax real return on the bond would be just $\frac{1}{2}$ percent. In other words, if the nominal interest rate is 10 percent and inflation is 7 percent, a $500,000 investment would deliver only a $2,500 return.

---

imports will be. Together, lower exports and higher imports mean lower *net exports*. Again, the higher real interest rate has reduced a component of aggregate demand.

Finally, there is government expenditure. While changes in the real interest rate may have an impact on the government's budget by raising the cost of borrowing, the effect is likely to be small, so we will ignore it.

For three of the four components of aggregate demand, then, our conclusion is the same: When the real interest rate rises, consumption, investment, and net exports fall. (Table 21.1 summarizes this discussion.) Thus, *a rise in the real interest rate reduces aggregate demand.* Bear in mind, though, that the components of aggregate demand can change for other, unrelated reasons. Consumption or investment can rise because individuals or businesses become more confident about their future income or sales. Government purchases can increase because of a change in fiscal policy, and net exports can climb because of movement in the exchange rate. Any of these circumstances can drive current output above potential output.

STABILITY

We can see immediately how the relationship between the real interest rate and aggregate demand helps central bankers to achieve one of their objectives: stabilizing current output at a level close to potential output. When economic activity speeds up or slows down and current output moves above or below potential output, policymakers can adjust the real interest rate in an effort to close the gap. But as we have emphasized repeatedly throughout our study of monetary policy, central bankers spend much of their time working to keep inflation low.

APPLYING THE CONCEPT
INVESTMENT AND THE BUSINESS CYCLE

Fluctuations in investment are one of the most important sources of movement in aggregate demand. Over short periods of a quarter or a year, consumption and government purchases tend to be fairly stable, and net exports are just too small to account for much of the movement in aggregate output. So understanding fluctuations in the business cycle means understanding changes in investment.

To grasp this point, take a look at Figure 21.3, which plots the ratio of investment to gross domestic product over roughly the last half century. The shaded bars designate recessions. Note that over the period from 1947 to 2004, investment fluctuated from less than 13 percent of GDP to over 20 percent of GDP. More to the point, during every recession investment itself falls by between 2 and 5 percent of GDP, which is roughly the same size as the fall in GDP itself. In other words, when we talk about a recession, what we are really talking about is a drop in investment.

What causes the level of investment to change? The tools we have developed suggest two answers: changes in the real interest rate and changes in expectations about future business conditions. Recall from Chapter 4 that an investment is profitable when its real internal rate of return exceeds its real cost of financing. Once again, the real interest rate is what matters in economic decisions. The higher the real cost of financing, the less likely an investment will be profitable. And the lower the expected future revenue from an investment is, the lower the real internal rate of return will be. So the higher the real interest rate and the less optimistic business people are about the future, the fewer investments firms will undertake, and the more likely the economy will fall into recession.

Table 21.1   Impact of Rise in the Real Interest Rate on Components of Aggregate Demand

Component of Aggregate Demand	Effect of a Rise in the Real Interest Rate	Impact on Component of Aggregate Demand
Consumption *(C)*	Reward to saving rises	Consumption *falls*
Investment *(I)*	Cost of financing rises	Investment *falls*
Net Exports *(NX)*	Demand for domestic assets rises, causing a currency appreciation, raising the price of exports and reducing the cost of imports	Exports fall; imports Rise; net exports *fall*
Aggregate Demand *(Y^{ad})*	*C, I,* and *NX* all fall	Aggregate demand falls

continued from previous page

Figure 21.3   Investment and the Business Cycle: The Ratio of Investment to GDP, 1947–2004

Gross private investment and gross domestic product, current dollars, seasonally adjusted at an annual rate.

SOURCE: *Computed by the Department of Commerce, Bureau of Economic Analysis. Shaded bars denote recessions, dated by the National Bureau of Economic Research.*

The Long-Run Real Interest Rate

Before getting into a discussion of the relationship between monetary policy and inflation, there is one more thing we must do. We need to figure out what happens to the real interest rate in the long run. At the beginning of this chapter we discussed the concept of potential output and noted the economy's tendency to move toward that normal level over time. In this section we have examined how various components of aggregate demand respond to the real interest rate. We have seen that higher real interest rates are associated with lower levels of aggregate demand. Putting these two together, we can conclude that there must be some level of the real interest rate at which aggregate demand equals potential output. This concept is important enough that we will give it a name, the **long-run real interest rate**. *The long-run real interest rate equates aggregate demand with potential output.*

Calculating the level of the long-run real interest rate is complicated because it is related to the return on capital investment (adjusted for risk) for the economy as a whole. In the United States, the long-run real interest rate is between 2 and 3 percent.[8] Our concern is less the exact level of the rate than what will cause it to change. There are two possibilities. One is that a component of aggregate demand that is not sensitive to the real interest rate goes up or down. The other is that potential output changes.

First, take the case in which the level of potential output remains fixed but some of the components of aggregate demand that do *not* respond to the real interest rate vary. For example, an increase in government purchases (all other things held equal) will raise aggregate demand at every level of the real interest rate. For aggregate demand and potential output to remain equal, one of the interest-sensitive components of aggregate demand must fall. And for that to happen, the long-run real interest rate must rise.[9] Besides government purchases, some components of consumption, investment, and net exports are not sensitive to the real interest rate. If any of those components rises, driving aggregate demand up at every level of the real interest rate, the long-run real interest rate must go up.

What about the second case, in which a change in potential output causes a change in the long-run real interest rate? A change in potential output has an inverse effect on the long-run real interest rate. When potential output rises, aggregate demand must rise with it. But an increase in aggregate demand requires a decline in the real interest rate. So when potential output goes up, the long-run real interest rate must fall.

In summary, the long-run real interest rate is that level at which aggregate demand equals potential output. When components of aggregate demand that are not sensitive to the real interest rate rise, the long-run real interest rate rises with them. But when potential output rises, the long-run real interest rate falls.

Inflation, the Real Interest Rate, and the Monetary Policy Reaction Curve

In the fall of 2003, consumer price inflation in the United States was just 1 percent, and current output was running 1 to 2 percentage points below potential output. That is, current inflation was very low and there was a sizable negative output gap.

---

[8]For a more detailed discussion of how to compute the long-run real interest rate, see John C. Williams, "The Natural Rate of Interest," *Federal Reserve Bank of San Francisco Economic Letter,* 2003-32, October 31, 2003.

[9]This effect is related to what is sometimes called *crowding out,* in which government spending takes the place of investment. The more common type of crowding out occurs when the government borrows funds to increase spending, thereby increasing the supply of bonds. Recall from Chapter 6 that an increase in the supply of bonds drives the price of bonds down and the interest rate up.

Following a meeting on December 9, 2003, with the federal funds rate target set at 1 percent, the Federal Open Market Committee released a statement that included the following sentence: "[W]ith inflation quite low and resource use slack, the Committee believes that policy accommodation can be maintained for a considerable period." That is, FOMC members had concluded that economic conditions justified keeping nominal interest rates low so that they could keep the real interest rate down in an effort to raise aggregate demand and close the recessionary output gap. The announcement also made clear that in practice, the FOMC sets policy and then waits a while to see if it works.

Comments made by the European Central Bank's Governing Council after its monthly meetings reveal similar thinking. On June 5, 2003, the ECB reduced its target overnight interest rate by 50 basis points, from $2\frac{1}{2}$ to 2 percent. The statement that announced the change read in part, "This decision is in line with our monetary policy strategy, including the aim of maintaining inflation below but close to 2 percent over the medium term. At the same time, this nominal interest rate reduction takes into account the downside risks to economic growth." While the specifics of the FOMC's and the Governing Council's statements may differ, both clearly indicate that policymakers set their short-run nominal interest-rate targets in response to economic conditions in general and inflation in particular.[10] Low inflation leads to low nominal and real interest rates.

Looking at the details of the two statements, we can conclude that when current inflation is high or current output is running above potential output, central bankers will raise nominal interest rates; when current inflation is low or current output is well below potential, they will lower interest rates. Importantly, central bankers envision themselves as reacting to changes in the economic environment. And while they state their policies in terms of nominal interest rates, they do so knowing that changes in the nominal interest rate will eventually translate into changes in the real interest rate. It is these changes in the real interest rate that influence the economic decisions of firms and households.

STABILITY

Our objective here is to incorporate the nature of these interest-rate reactions into a macroeconomic model. To do it, we will once again note the words of the policymakers. In an address given on January 3, 2004, Federal Reserve Chairman Alan Greenspan stated: "[R]ules that relate the setting of the federal funds rate to deviations of output and inflation from their respective targets . . . do seem to capture the broad contours of what we did over the past decade and a half."[11] In commenting on the chairman's address, Bank of England Governor Mervyn King agreed with Greenspan when he noted that "any (coherent) monetary policy can be written as an inflation target plus a response to supply shocks."[12] As we will see in Chapter 22, the "supply shocks" to which Governor King referred are changes in production costs that drive current inflation away from target inflation; we will call these inflation shocks. Importantly, Governor King was saying that even if a central bank does not have an explicit, publicly announced inflation target (as the Bank of England does but the Federal Reserve does not), it must have an implicit inflation target that can be inferred from its actions.

[10] The fact that policy does not have an immediate impact on either inflation or output complicates matters substantially. In fact, interest-rate changes must anticipate changes in inflation and output, so they must be based on forecasts of inflation as much as on current levels. That is why, in their public statements, central bankers nearly always refer to likely future developments. We will ignore that distinction here.

[11] Alan Greenspan, "Risk and Uncertainty in Monetary Policy," *American Economic Review* 94, no. 2, May 2004, pp. 33–40.

[12] Mervyn King, "Comments on 'Risk and Uncertainty in Monetary Policy' by Alan Greenspan," *American Economic Review* 94, no. 2, May 2004, pp. 43–45.

Deriving the Monetary Policy Reaction Curve We have seen that central bankers set nominal interest-rate targets in response to changes in current inflation and current output. In other words, they react to economic conditions. And as we have already noted, when policymakers change the nominal interest rate, they are changing the real interest rate. We can summarize all of this in the form of a monetary policy reaction curve that approximates the behavior of central bankers.

To see what the monetary policy reaction curve looks like, let's start with the central bankers' own statements. They are clearly saying that *higher current inflation requires a policy response that raises the real interest rate*. To ensure that deviations of inflation from the target rate are only temporary, monetary policymakers respond to changes in inflation by changing the real interest rate in the same direction. When inflation rises above the target level, for example, policymakers raise the real interest rate to restrain aggregate demand and lower inflationary pressures. That means the monetary policy reaction curve must slope upward, as shown in the top panel of Figure 21.4.

How do we draw the reaction curve—that is, how do we determine its location and slope? The location depends on where policymakers would like the economy to end up in the long run. What is the equilibrium point toward which the economy will tend over time? For the real interest rate, the economy will move toward the long-run real interest rate that equates aggregate demand with potential output. That interest rate is shown as r^* in the top panel of Figure 21.4. For inflation, the answer is the central bank's target level (π^T). *The monetary policy reaction curve is set so that when current inflation equals target inflation, the real interest rate equals the long-run real interest rate.* That is, $r = r^*$ when $\pi = \pi^T$. Importantly, we can draw such a curve even for central banks that do not explicitly target inflation. As Governor King of the Bank of England suggests, every central bank must have a long-term inflation objective that anchors its policy decisions. That is what we mean by an inflation target.

The monetary policy reaction curve is a version of the Taylor rule introduced in Chapter 18.[13] There we noted that the target nominal federal funds rate is related to the long-run real interest rate, current inflation, the gap between current and target inflation, and the output gap. To keep our derivation of the policy reaction curve manageable (so we can draw it on a piece of paper), we have assumed that the real interest rate depends only on the gap between current and target inflation and is not sensitive to the output gap. While central bankers clearly set policy with both output and inflation in mind, ignoring output does not change our analysis in any important way because there is a direct relationship between the output gap and inflation. Specifically, a positive output gap tends to force inflation higher. (We will defer discussion of the relationship between the output gap and changes in inflation to Chapter 22.)

To see how the monetary policy reaction curve works, let's look at the case of the FOMC. In the United States, the long-run real interest rate is roughly $2\frac{1}{2}$ percent, and the Fed behaves as if its inflation target is roughly 2 percent. So if current inflation is 2 percent, policymakers will set the nominal interest rate at $4\frac{1}{2}$ percent. Estimates suggest that a one-percentage point increase in current inflation leads the FOMC to increase the real interest rate by half a percentage point in an effort to ensure that the increase in inflation will be temporary. That means that if current inflation rises from 2 to 3 percent, policymakers will raise the real interest rate from $2\frac{1}{2}$ percent to 3 percent. They will do so by raising the nominal federal funds rate target from $4\frac{1}{2}$ percent

---

[13]While the reaction curve is sometimes referred to as a "rule," it is not a rule in any mechanical or legal sense. Central bankers are free to deviate from it and often do.

Figure 21.4   Monetary Policy

A. The Monetary Policy Reaction Curve

Monetary policymakers react to changes in current inflation by changing the real interest rate. Increases in current inflation lead them to raise the real interest rate, while decreases lead them to lower it. The monetary policy reaction curve is located so that the central bank's target inflation is consistent with the long-run real interest rate, which equates aggregate demand with potential output.

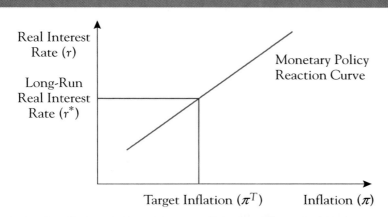

B. Movements Along the Fed's Monetary Policy Reaction Curve

The long-run real interest rate in the United States is roughly 2.5 percent, and the Federal Reserve's implicit inflation target is approximately 2 percent. The Fed's monetary policy reaction curve implies that a one-percentage-point increase in inflation calls for a half-percentage-point increase in the real interest rate—a movement along the monetary policy reaction curve. That means that an increase in inflation from 2 to 3 percent calls for an increase in the real interest rate from 2.5 to 3 percent.

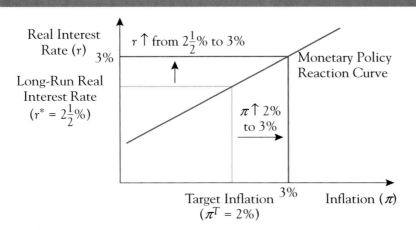

to 6 percent (that is, they will add a 3 percent long-run real interest rate to the 3 percent inflation). The resulting movement along the monetary policy reaction curve is shown in the bottom panel of Figure 21.4.

What about the slope of the monetary policy reaction curve? Is it steep or flat? The answer is that the slope depends on policymakers' objectives. When central bankers decide how aggressively to pursue their inflation target and how willing they are to tolerate temporary changes in inflation, they are determining the slope of the monetary policy reaction curve. They are deciding whether to respond to deviations of current inflation from target inflation with small or large changes in the real interest rate.

Policymakers who are aggressive in keeping current inflation near target will have a steep monetary policy reaction curve, like the one shown in the top panel of Figure 21.5. A steep curve means that a small change in inflation will be met with a large change in the real interest rate. The steeper the curve is, the larger the policymakers' reaction will be. Conversely, the flatter the curve is, the smaller the reaction to a given change in inflation will be. A relatively flat curve, like the one shown in the bottom panel of Figure 21.5, means that central bankers are less concerned than they might be with keeping current inflation near target over the short term. They are more willing to allow temporary fluctuations in inflation. Interestingly, most estimates of the monetary policy reaction curve suggest that the ECB and the Fed have roughly similar reactions to inflation. That is, both react to a one-percentage-point increase in inflation by raising the real interest rate half a percentage point.[14]

The monetary policy reaction curve is based on the view that central bankers can influence aggregate demand and ultimately inflation by adjusting the real interest rate. That assumption is consistent with our conclusion that in the long run, inflation is determined by money growth. Recall that the central bank controls the real interest rate by adjusting the size of its balance sheet. To hit their interest-rate target, policymakers adjust the supply of reserves in the commercial banking system. While changes in commercial bank reserves may not have much to do with money growth in the short run, in the long run they do. Money growth depends on the willingness of commercial banks to expand their balance sheets for the long run. Thus, growth in reserves eventually leads to growth in the money supply. And in the long run, growth in the money supply brings inflation. So policymakers can both choose the level of the real interest rate in the short run and control inflation in the long run.

Shifting the Monetary Policy Reaction Curve

When policymakers adjust the real interest rate, they are either moving along a fixed monetary policy reaction curve or shifting the curve. A movement along the curve is a reaction to a change in current inflation. A shift in the curve represents a change in the level of the real interest rate at every level of inflation. To see what can shift the monetary policy reaction curve, we need to examine the variables we held constant when we drew the curve in Figure 21.4. In that analysis, we held both target inflation π^T and the long-run real interest rate r^* fixed. If either of those variables changes, the entire curve will shift.

Let's start with a change in the inflation target, π^T. A change in π^T reflects a change in the preferences of monetary policymakers. The top panel of Figure 21.6 shows the result of an *increase* in the central bank's inflation target, from the old level (π_0^T, to the new, higher level π_1^T. *With a higher inflation target, the central bank will set a lower current real interest rate at every level of current inflation.* This change in the real

---

[14]Many studies have compared U.S. and European monetary policy. One example is Stefan Gerlach and Gert Schnabel, "The Taylor Rule and Interest Rates in the EMU area," *Economic Letters* 67, 2000, pp. 165–171.

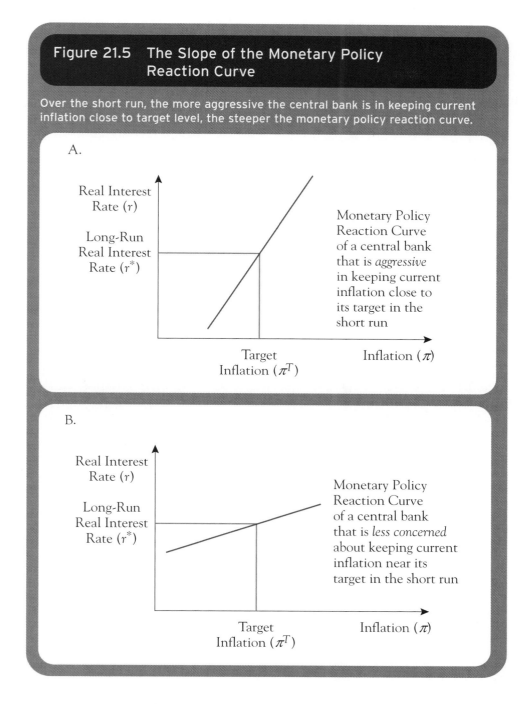

Figure 21.5   The Slope of the Monetary Policy Reaction Curve

Over the short run, the more aggressive the central bank is in keeping current inflation close to target level, the steeper the monetary policy reaction curve.

A.

Real Interest Rate (r)

Long-Run Real Interest Rate (r^*)

Monetary Policy Reaction Curve of a central bank that is *aggressive* in keeping current inflation close to its target in the short run

Target Inflation (π^T)

Inflation (π)

B.

Real Interest Rate (r)

Long-Run Real Interest Rate (r^*)

Monetary Policy Reaction Curve of a central bank that is *less concerned* about keeping current inflation near its target in the short run

Target Inflation (π^T)

Inflation (π)

interest rate shifts the monetary policy reaction curve to the right.[15] A reduction in the inflation target would have the opposite effect, increasing the level of the real interest rate at each level of current inflation and shifting the monetary policy reaction curve to the left.

[15]In the long run, this effect will be achieved through higher money growth. With a higher inflation target, money growth must be higher.

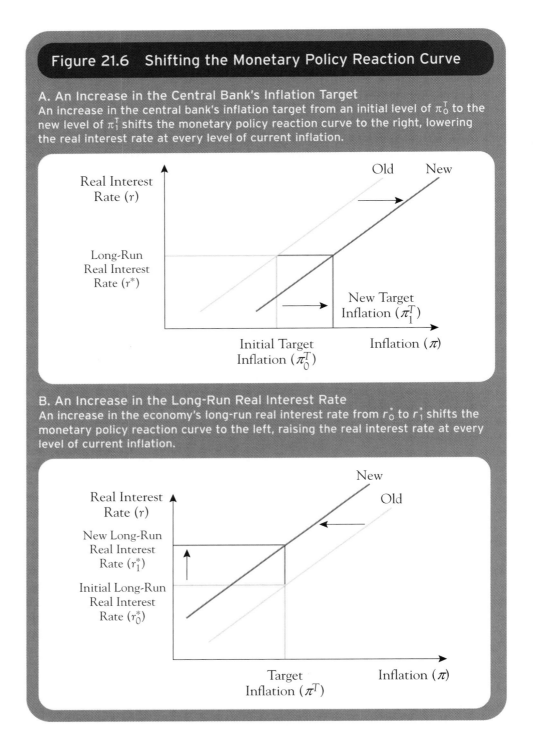

Figure 21.6 Shifting the Monetary Policy Reaction Curve

A. An Increase in the Central Bank's Inflation Target
An increase in the central bank's inflation target from an initial level of π_0^T to the new level of π_1^T shifts the monetary policy reaction curve to the right, lowering the real interest rate at every level of current inflation.

B. An Increase in the Long-Run Real Interest Rate
An increase in the economy's long-run real interest rate from r_0^* to r_1^* shifts the monetary policy reaction curve to the left, raising the real interest rate at every level of current inflation.

Going back to the example of the Federal Reserve, we can ask: What would happen if the Fed raised its long-term inflation target from 2 to 3 percent? Assuming that the long-term real interest rate remains at $2\frac{1}{2}$ percent, such a change implies a shift to the right in the monetary policy reaction curve. In terms of the federal funds rate, the result would be a rise of 1 percentage point, from $4\frac{1}{2}$ to $5\frac{1}{2}$ percent. (Recall that the

Table 21.2 The Monetary Policy Reaction Curve

What is it?	The relationship between current inflation and the real interest rate set by monetary policymakers.
What determines its location?	Drawn so that, when current inflation equals target inflation, policymakers will set the real interest rate equal to the long-run real interest rate.
What determines its slope?	Policymakers' attitude toward inflation. The more aggressive policymakers are in keeping current inflation close to target level, and the less tolerant they are of temporary changes in inflation, the steeper the slope.
When does it shift?	In response to changes in either the long-run real interest rate or the central bank's inflation target. An increase in the long-run real interest rate shifts the curve to the left. An increase in the inflation target shifts the curve to the right.

long-term nominal federal funds rate equals the long-run real interest rate of $2\frac{1}{2}$ percent plus the inflation target, which is now 3 percent.)

We said in our earlier discussion that monetary policymakers cannot choose the long-run real interest rate (r^*); it is determined by the structure of the economy. What if r^* rose as a consequence of an increase in government purchases or some other component of aggregate demand that is not sensitive to the real interest rate? The result of such an increase is a shift to the left in the monetary policy reaction curve. Remember that the curve is drawn so that the real interest rate equals its long-run level at the point where inflation meets the central bank's target. An increase in the long-run real interest rate means that policymakers have set a higher real interest rate at every level of current inflation (see the bottom panel of Figure 21.6). Assuming that policymakers have not changed their inflation target, this shift means that the long-run nominal interest rate will rise as well.

Any shift in the monetary policy reaction curve can be characterized as either a change in target inflation or a shift in the long-run real interest rate. Suppose nothing has happened that would lead to a change in the long-run real interest rate. Regardless of what policymakers might say, under such circumstances a move to a more accommodating policy would reveal an implicit increase in target inflation. We know that must be the case because they have shifted the monetary policy reaction curve to the right, leaving r^* unchanged. The top panel in Figure 21.6 shows such an increase in π^T. To paraphrase the Bank of England's Governor King once again, any monetary policy can be characterized by the location and slope of the monetary policy reaction curve. The curve's location is determined by policymakers' implicit or explicit inflation target. Its slope is determined by how aggressive policymakers are in responding to deviations from target inflation.

Exchange-Rate Targeting In Chapter 19 we saw that, in a world with open capital markets, policymakers must choose between controlling the domestic interest rate and fixing the exchange rate. Central bankers can adjust their balance sheet to meet either a target interest rate or a target exchange rate, but not both. What happens if policymakers decide to target the exchange rate instead of the interest rate? The answer we gave in Chapter 19 was that when a country's exchange rate is fixed, its interest rate and inflation are determined by the monetary policy in the country to whose currency the exchange rate has been pegged. For example, the decision by a Latin American country to maintain a fixed dollar-exchange rate would mean adopting the monetary policy set by the FOMC. That is what Argentina's currency board did in the 1990s. In the context of this discussion, we can say that *a decision to fix the exchange rate means adopting the monetary policy reaction curve of the country to whose currency the exchange rate has been pegged.*

The Aggregate Demand Curve

We are now ready to construct an aggregate demand curve that accounts for modern monetary policy—that is, for the fact that policymakers respond to changes in current inflation by changing the interest rate. To do so, we need to examine what happens to aggregate demand when current inflation changes. From our earlier discussion, we know that policymakers will respond to an increase in current inflation by raising the real interest rate. That decision represents a movement along the monetary policy reaction curve shown in Figure 21.4. We also know that a higher real interest rate will reduce investment, consumption, and net exports. In other words, it lowers aggregate demand. Putting these two concepts together, we can conclude that inflation and aggregate demand move in opposite directions. When current inflation rises, aggregate demand falls, and vice versa. Extending the relationship to all levels of inflation and output yields the aggregate demand curve shown in Figure 21.1. The difference is that we know there is a central role for the real interest rate that is controlled by monetary policymakers.

Output, Inflation, and the Aggregate Demand Curve

To understand this version of the aggregate demand curve, think about what happens when current inflation rises. In response to higher current inflation, monetary policymakers raise the real interest rate, moving upward along the monetary policy reaction curve. The higher real interest rate reduces consumption, investment, and net exports (the interest-sensitive components of aggregate demand), causing aggregate demand (output) to fall. Thus, higher current inflation means lower aggregate demand. In contrast, in response to lower current inflation, policymakers lower the real interest rate, moving downward along the monetary policy reaction curve. Their action raises consumption, investment, and net exports, causing aggregate demand (output) to rise. Thus, *changes in current inflation move the economy along a downward-sloping aggregate demand curve* (see Figure 21.7).[16]

We should emphasize that this relationship between monetary policy and real interest rate is only part of the reason why inflation and output are negatively related. Higher

---

[16]Some observers have noted historical episodes in which central banks appear to have reacted to higher inflation by *lowering* the real interest rate. That is, they increased the nominal interest rate by less than the rise in inflation. That would mean that the monetary policy reaction curve slopes downward. Unless the accompanying effect on real money balances is sufficiently strong, the result would be an upward-sloping aggregate demand curve. When the aggregate demand curve slopes upward, deviations of inflation from the central bank's target rate generate ever larger movements away from long-run equilibrium. The estimates in Richard Clarida, Jordí Galí, and Mark Gertler, "Monetary Policy Rules: Evidence and Some Theory," *Quarterly Journal of Economics*, February 2000, show that before 1979, the Federal Reserve did react to increases in inflation by lowering the real interest rate, suggesting the possibility of this sort of unstable upward inflation spiral. Even when the accompanying effect on real money balances is weak, however, a more complex model (in which real interest rates respond to the output gap in addition to the deviation of inflation from target) shows that if the reaction to the output gap is strong enough, aggregate demand will slope downward regardless of policymakers' reaction to inflation.

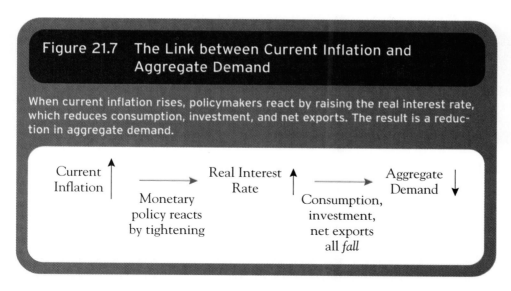

Figure 21.7   The Link between Current Inflation and Aggregate Demand

When current inflation rises, policymakers react by raising the real interest rate, which reduces consumption, investment, and net exports. The result is a reduction in aggregate demand.

Current Inflation ↑ → Monetary policy reacts by tightening → Real Interest Rate ↑ → Consumption, investment, net exports all *fall* → Aggregate Demand ↓

inflation reduces output *both* because of the monetary policy reaction curve *and* because of its effect on real money balances, emphasized earlier in the chapter (page 553).

The Slope of the Aggregate Demand Curve

The slope of the aggregate demand curve tells us how sensitive current output is to a given change in current inflation. If a change in current inflation creates a large movement in current output—that is, if current output is very sensitive to inflation—the aggregate demand curve will be relatively flat. If it creates only a small movement—if current output is not very sensitive to inflation—the aggregate demand curve will be relatively steep. The less sensitive current output is to a change in current inflation, the steeper the aggregate demand curve.

Three factors influence the sensitivity of current output to changes in inflation and thus determine the slope of the aggregate demand curve. They are (1) the strength of the effect of inflation on real money balances, (2) the extent to which monetary policymakers react to a change in current inflation, and (3) the size of the response of aggregate demand to changes in the interest rate. The larger each of these factors, the greater the move in current output when inflation changes, and the flatter the aggregate demand curve.

Given our focus on monetary policy, we will concentrate on the second factor. We want to know how the slope of the monetary policy reaction curve affects the slope of the aggregate demand curve. Consider a case in which an aggressive policymaker reacts to a movement of current inflation away from its target level with a large change in the real interest rate. In that case, the monetary policy reaction curve is steep, as was shown in the top panel of Figure 21.5. This large change in the real interest rate will have a large impact on current output. So when the monetary policy reaction curve is steep, small changes in inflation lead to large changes in current output. Thus, the aggregate demand curve is flat, as shown in the top panel of Figure 21.8.

A policymaker who is less concerned with keeping current inflation close to target will respond more cautiously, raising the real interest rate in small increments. That was the case in the bottom panel of Figure 21.5. Since the real interest rate doesn't move much, neither does current output. When the monetary policy reaction curve is flat, large changes in inflation lead to small changes in current output, and the aggregate demand curve is steep, as shown in the bottom panel of Figure 21.8.

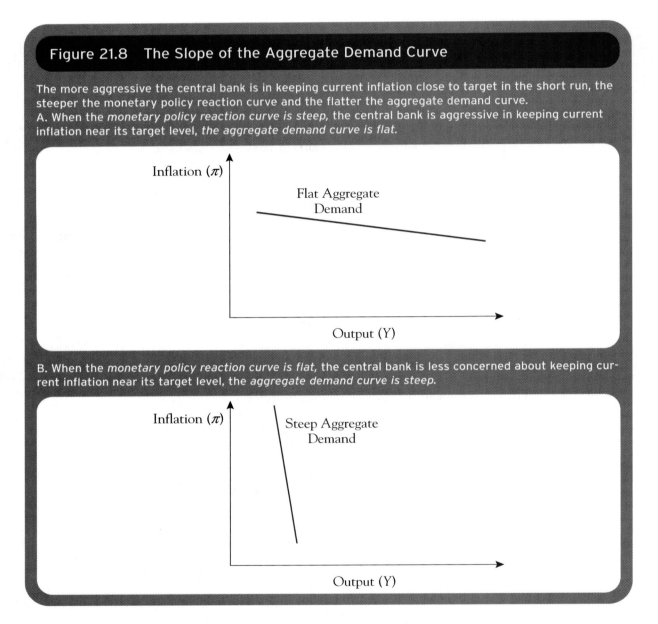

Figure 21.8   The Slope of the Aggregate Demand Curve

The more aggressive the central bank is in keeping current inflation close to target in the short run, the steeper the monetary policy reaction curve and the flatter the aggregate demand curve.
A. When the *monetary policy reaction curve is steep,* the central bank is aggressive in keeping current inflation near its target level, *the aggregate demand curve is flat.*

B. When the *monetary policy reaction curve is flat,* the central bank is less concerned about keeping current inflation near its target level, the *aggregate demand curve is steep.*

The important point here is that the slope of the aggregate demand curve depends in part on the preferences of the central bank—on how aggressive policymakers are in responding to deviations of inflation from target level. Their reaction to these movements in inflation is what the Bank of England's Governor King was referring to in his description of monetary policy.

Why the Aggregate Demand Curve Slopes Down

To recap, there are two reasons why the aggregate demand curve slopes down. The first has to do with the relationship between inflation and money growth: The higher the rate of inflation for a given level of money growth, the lower the level of output implied by the equation of exchange. With a lower level of real money balances, people purchase fewer goods. Added to this effect is a second reason, the reaction of the central bank. Higher current inflation induces policymakers to raise the real interest rate, depressing various components of aggregate demand. Even if the monetary policy reaction curve is flat, however, the effect of inflation on real money balances will cause the aggregate demand curve to slope down.

Economists have suggested a number of more subtle reasons why rising inflation drives aggregate demand down. One is that higher inflation reduces wealth, which in turn lowers consumption. It does so in two ways. First, inflation means that the money everyone holds is gradually declining in value (an idea that is an extension of the effect on real money balances discussed earlier). Second, inflation is bad for the stock market since as it rises, uncertainty about inflation rises with it, rendering equities a relatively more risky and hence less attractive investment. A drop in the value of stocks reduces wealth.

Yet another reason for the downward slope of the aggregate demand curve is that inflation can have a greater impact on the poor than it does on the wealthy, redistributing income to those who are better off. For example, minimum-wage workers tend to have incomes that are fixed in dollar terms, so inflation erodes their purchasing power. And since the rich consume a smaller portion of their income than others, saving a greater portion than the poor (who can't afford to save at all), this redistribution lowers consumption in the economy as a whole, reducing aggregate demand. Then there is the fact that inflation creates risk; the higher inflation is, the greater the risk will be. (See Your Financial World: Why Inflation Is Bad for You in Chapter 15.) Most people want to insure themselves against risk, and that means increased saving, just in case. More saving means lower consumption and lower aggregate demand. Finally, there is the fact that rising inflation makes foreign goods cheaper in relation to domestic goods, driving imports up and net exports down. In every case, higher inflation means lower aggregate demand, causing the aggregate demand curve to slope downward.

Shifting the Aggregate Demand Curve

In deriving the aggregate demand curve, we saw that increases and decreases in inflation bring a monetary policy response that raises or lowers the real interest rate. Those movements in the real interest rate, in turn, cause changes in the components of aggregate demand. In our derivation we held constant both the location of the monetary policy reaction curve and those components of aggregate demand that do not respond to the real interest rate. Changes in any of those components, as well as changes in the location of the monetary policy reaction curve, *shift* the aggregate demand curve. As we will see in detail in Chapter 22, shifts in aggregate demand are one possible source of fluctuations in the business cycle. When aggregate demand falls, the economy tends to go into recession. Conversely, increases in aggregate demand can raise the level of economic activity, generating a boom.

Shifts in the Monetary Policy Reaction Curve Whenever the monetary policy reaction curve shifts, the aggregate demand curve will shift as well. To see why, consider an increase in the central bank's inflation target, like the one you saw in the top panel of Figure 21.6. This rise in the inflation target shifts the monetary policy reaction curve to the right, lowering the real interest rate that policymakers set at every level of inflation. (Some people might characterize this move as a permanent easing of monetary policy.) At the new, higher inflation target, the lower real interest rate increases aggregate demand at every level of inflation, shifting the aggregate demand curve to the right (see Figure 21.9). Thus, an increase in the central bank's inflation target shifts both the monetary policy reaction curve and the aggregate demand curve to the right.

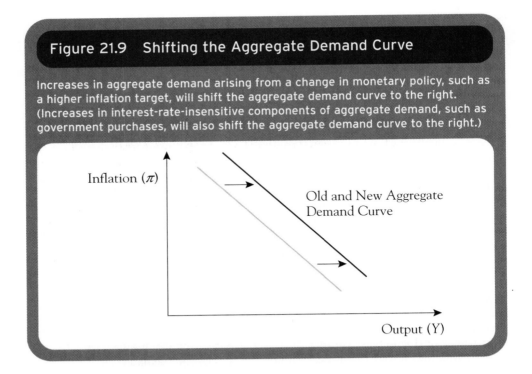

Figure 21.9   Shifting the Aggregate Demand Curve

Increases in aggregate demand arising from a change in monetary policy, such as a higher inflation target, will shift the aggregate demand curve to the right. (Increases in interest-rate-insensitive components of aggregate demand, such as government purchases, will also shift the aggregate demand curve to the right.)

In fact, any shift in the monetary policy reaction curve will shift the aggregate demand curve in the same direction. That means that changes in the long-run real interest rate will shift aggregate demand as well. To see why, suppose the level of potential output goes up. Because the long-run real interest rate equates aggregate demand with potential output, when potential output rises, the long-run real interest rate must fall, driving up the interest-rate-sensitive components of aggregate demand. (Recall that policymakers cannot choose the long-run real interest rate. It is a consequence of the structure of the economy.) This fall in the long-run real interest rate has the same effect on the monetary policy reaction curve as an increase in policymakers' inflation target. It shifts the curve to the right, reducing the real interest rate policymakers set at every level of inflation and shifting the aggregate demand curve to the right.

To complete the analysis, think about the consequences of either a fall in target inflation or a rise in the long-run real interest rate. Both of these events will shift the monetary policy reaction curve to the left, increasing the real interest rate policymakers set at every level of inflation (review the bottom panel of Figure 21.6). Because a higher real interest rate means lower aggregate demand, the aggregate demand curve shifts to the left.

In summary, when the monetary policy reaction curve shifts, the aggregate demand curve shifts in the same direction. If the central bank's inflation target goes up or the long-run real interest rate goes down, the monetary policy reaction curve will shift to the right, causing the aggregate demand curve to shift rightward as well. If the central bank's inflation target goes down or the long-run real interest rate goes up, the monetary policy reaction curve will shift to the left, causing the aggregate demand curve to shift to the left.

Changes in the Components of Aggregate Demand   Besides a shift in the monetary policy reaction curve, any change in a component of aggregate demand that is caused by a factor *other* than a change in the real interest rate will shift the aggregate demand curve. That is, changes in consumption, investment, government purchases, or net exports that are unrelated to changes in the real interest rate will shift the aggregate demand curve.[17]

A few examples will illustrate these sources of shifts in the aggregate demand curve. Let's start with business investment. Decisions to invest depend as much on forecasts of future revenues as on the cost of financing. When firms become more optimistic about the future, their estimate of the internal rate of return on a particular investment goes up. At a fixed real interest rate, this change in the internal rate of return will raise investment, increasing aggregate demand. We can conclude that an improved business climate increases aggregate demand at every level of inflation, shifting the aggregate demand curve to the right (see Figure 21.9).

The same effect happens when consumers' confidence in the economy rises. When people perceive that the risks they face have diminished, they tend to save less. Someone who is less concerned about being laid off is surely more likely to purchase a new car or go on an expensive vacation. Thus, increases in *consumer confidence* tend to raise consumption at every level of the real interest rate, increasing aggregate demand and shifting the aggregate demand curve to the right.[18]

Changes in government purchases affect aggregate demand at every level of inflation as well. Legislators may increase their spending on goods and services for a variety of reasons. They may wish to strengthen national security, expand health insurance for retirees, or improve the quality of public education. Regardless of the reason, any rise in government spending on goods and services will increase aggregate demand. A

---

[17]In some textbooks, these components of aggregate demand are referred to as *autonomous components*. In our model, they are those components that are not sensitive to either the level of income or the real interest rate.

[18]An increase in the value of stocks that is unrelated to changes in inflation will also raise wealth and consumption, shifting the aggregate demand curve to the right as well.

Table 21.3   Factors That Shift the Aggregate Demand Curve to the Right

Changes That Shift the Monetary Policy Reaction Curve to the Right

- An *increase* in the central bank's inflation target
- A *decline* in the long-term real interest rate

Changes That Shift the Components of Aggregate Demand to the Right

- An *increase* in consumption unrelated to a change in the real interest rate
- An *increase* in investment unrelated to a change in the real interest rate
- An *increase* in government purchases
- A *decrease* in taxes
- An *increase* in net exports unrelated to a change in the real interest rate

decrease in taxes will have the same effect. Lowering the taxes that individuals pay raises their take-home pay and increases their consumption; lowering the taxes that businesses pay leaves them with more income, raising their investment. All these things will raise aggregate demand at every level of inflation and the real interest rate.

Finally, there are net exports. Increases in net exports that are unrelated to changes in real interest rates will shift the aggregate demand curve to the right. A rise in the foreign demand for domestically produced goods and services because of a technological improvement or even just a fad could increase exports without influencing imports. The result would be higher aggregate demand at every level of inflation. (Table 21.3 summarizes the factors that shift the aggregate demand curve to the right.)

Monetary Policy and Aggregate Demand   We have seen that shifts in the monetary policy reaction curve, as well as changes in components of aggregate demand that are unrelated to changes in the real interest rate, can shift the aggregate demand curve. This brings up the possibility that monetary policy can cause recessions. When policymakers lower their inflation target, they shift the monetary policy reaction curve to the left, shifting the aggregate demand curve to the left with it. At the new, lower inflation target, aggregate demand is reduced at every level of inflation. The drop in aggregate demand can drive down current output, creating a recessionary output gap.

The data shown in Figure 21.10 certainly suggest that the Federal Reserve's actions might have caused some recessions. Note that the line representing the three-month Treasury bill rate tends to rise just to the left of the shaded bars indicating recessions.

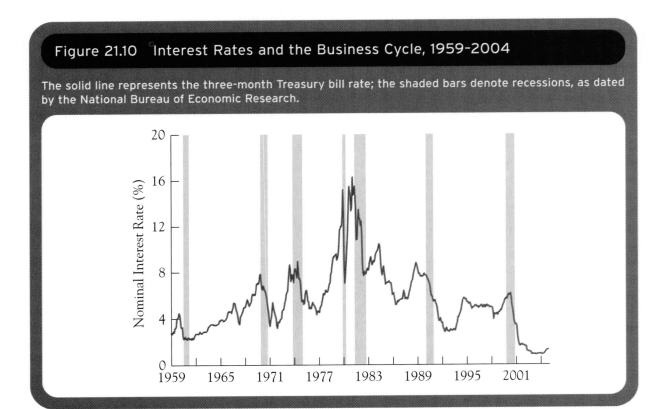

Figure 21.10   Interest Rates and the Business Cycle, 1959-2004

The solid line represents the three-month Treasury bill rate; the shaded bars denote recessions, as dated by the National Bureau of Economic Research.

That is, the interest rate tends to rise shortly before a recession. Recall that inflation expectations don't change quickly, so in the short run, a change in the nominal interest rate means a change in the real interest rate. And since policymakers can control the real interest rate, the pattern seems to suggest that monetary policy can lead to recessions.[19]

If policymakers can cause recessions, they can probably avoid them as well. Monetary policy can neutralize shifts in the aggregate demand curve that arise from other sources, reducing or even eliminating output gaps. For example, if businesspeople become pessimistic about the future, their reduced confidence will shift the aggregate demand curve to the left. In the absence of a policy response, the result will be a recessionary output gap. But policymakers have the ability to stabilize the economy and prevent current output from falling. By shifting the monetary policy reaction curve to the right in response to the decline in aggregate demand, central bankers can keep current output close to potential output.

Thus far, we have ignored the fact that inflation changes over time. In fact, in discussing the possibility that policymakers can both cause recessions and neutralize recessionary shifts in aggregate demand, we have assumed that inflation doesn't change. Our analysis is incomplete. A complete description of fluctuations in the business cycle would include an understanding of the fact that inflation and output are jointly determined and that monetary policy plays a role in the short-run movements of both. For this part of the analysis, we must turn to the behavior of firms in making their production decisions. That is, we need to introduce the supply side of the economy, the topic of Chapter 22.

STABILITY

APPLYING THE CONCEPT
THE REMARKABLE 1990S

By any measure, the 1990s were a remarkable decade. Information technology came of age, bringing the benefits of computerization into our lives through everything from cars to dishwashers. Because of the Internet, incredible libraries are now available to us in our homes and offices.

What may be even more extraordinary is that the 1990s brought unprecedented economic stability. In the 10 years from 1991 to 2001, the U.S. economy did not suffer a single decline in output. During these 10 years of phenomenal growth, inflation fell steadily, from more than 5 in 1991 to less than 2 percent by the end of the decade. Comparing the 1980s with the 1990s, researchers find that the volatility of growth and inflation dropped by more than half.*

*This decline in volatility is documented in detail by Margaret M. McConnell and Gabriel Perez Quiros in "Output Fluctuations in the United States: What Has Changed Since the Early 1980s?" *American Economic Review* 90 (December 2000), pp. 1464–1476.

continued on next page

[19]The interest-rate pattern in Figure 21.10 does not by itself establish that monetary policy causes recessions. In fact, a number of interest-rate increases were not followed by recessions. Three examples are apparent in the figure: the 2-percentage-point increase during 1965–66; the 3-percentage-point increase in 1988–89; and the greater than 2-percentage-point increase in 1993–94. Without further evidence that particular interest-rate increases resulted from policies intended to slow the economy, the evidence is only suggestive. For a thorough discussion of this issue, see the Chapter 23 Tools of the Trade on the difference between correlation and causality.

continued from previous page

The amazing prosperity and stability were shared across the industrialized world. In a broad cross-section of the 63 countries for which we have reliable data, inflation dropped dramatically between the 1980s and 1990s. Median inflation fell from an average annual rate of 7 percent in the period 1985–1994 to 3 percent in 1995–1999. The decline in average inflation was even sharper, from 83 percent to just $8\frac{1}{2}$ percent. Inflation rose in only 10 of the 63 countries.[†]

There are three possible explanations for this phenomenal worldwide economic performance. One is that everyone was extremely lucky and the 1990s were simply an exceptionally calm period. The second is that economies have become more flexible in responding to external economic shocks (unexpected changes in the economic environment). And third, maybe monetary policymakers have finally figured out how to do their job more effectively. Which one of these explanations is most likely?

It's difficult to argue that the stability of the 1990s was mere good fortune. Surely the decade was not a calm one for the financial markets. Major economic crises occurred in Latin America and Asia, and Long-Term Capital Management nearly collapsed, paralyzing the bond markets. Raw materials prices fluctuated wildly. The price of oil spiked at more than $35 a barrel late in 1990, then plunged below $12 a barrel at the end of 1998 before beginning a steady rise to $30 a barrel by 2000.

If the size and frequency of external shocks did not diminish, something must be cushioning the blows. Advances in information technology have increased manufacturers' flexibility in responding to changes in demand. The result has been a dramatic decline in inventories at every stage of the production process. In durable manufacturing, the new supply method called *just in time* cut the ratio of inventories to sales in half from the early 1990s to the beginning of 2002. Today an automobile assembly plant keeps only a few hours' worth of parts on hand; the rest are in transit to the factory, timed to arrive at just the right moment. Similarly, a supermarket or superstore like Wal-Mart or Target holds only one to two days' supply of most products. The result is a great deal of flexibility in responding to changes in demand and sales.

While improvements in inventory management are surely part of the explanation for the long period of prosperity in the 1990s, every description of the recession that began in March 2001 points to the impact of an inventory adjustment. The most persistent problems have emerged in the high-technology sector—semiconductors, computers, and communications equipment. So while the U.S. economy has surely become more flexible, it hasn't changed enough to prevent fluctuations caused by unexpected events.

That leaves monetary policy as the only remaining explanation for the improved economic performance. Economists now have a much better understanding of how to implement monetary policy than they did as recently as 20 years ago. To succeed in keeping inflation low and stable

[†]See Stephen G. Cecchetti and Stefan Krause, "Central Bank Structure, Policy Efficiency and Macroeconomic Performance: Exploring Empirical Relationships," *Economic Review of the Federal Reserve Bank of St. Louis* 84 (July/August 2002), pp. 47–59.

continued from previous page

while at the same time keeping real growth high and stable, central bankers must focus on raising interest rates when inflation goes up and lowering them when inflation goes down. That is, they must adopt a monetary policy reaction curve like the one in Figure 21.4. By focusing on long-run inflation, policymakers have succeeded in bringing inflation down and keeping it low.

Figure 21.2 suggests the Federal Reserve had a hand in creating the long period of prosperity. Notice that interest rates, both nominal and real, were quite variable in the 1990s even though inflation was not. A boom lasted the entire decade. In other words, the Fed successfully adjusted the real interest rate to stabilize inflation and keep current output close to potential.

IN THE NEWS
On Presidential Politics, the Fed Walks a Tightrope

The New York Times

by Eduardo Porter

January 28, 2004

Many Democrats are certain the Federal Reserve has a Republican bias. They point out that the Fed raised interest rates six times from June 1999 to May 2000, holding the economy back while Al Gore was running for president, but lowered them 13 times once George W. Bush defeated him.

Some Republicans have a chip on their own shoulders. They contend that in 1992, the Fed helped Bill Clinton defeat President Bush's father by not lowering interest rates fast enough in the face of a sluggish economic recovery.

Most economists dismiss such complaints of political favoritism. But the Fed is not totally above the fray. Indeed, there seems to be one clear political pattern in interest-rate decisions—one particularly relevant to today's circumstances. Precisely because of the potential impact of changes in monetary policy, the Fed tries not to start raising interest rates in the months before a presidential election.

"The Fed considers itself apolitical, but that does not mean ignoring politics; rather, it means trying to avoid becoming a political issue itself," said Laurence H. Meyer, a former Fed governor who advises investors on monetary policy. "It tries to do this by avoiding actions that are unnecessarily provocative."

This year, avoiding provocation could be awkward. With the economy perking up and interest rates at historic lows, there is little doubt that the Fed's next move will be to raise rates, for the first time since May 2000.

But when? Starting to raise rates in September, at the last meeting of the Federal Open Markets Committee before the election, could be seen as a slap at President Bush. Raising rates at the November meeting, a week after the election, might elicit charges that the Fed waited to avoid harming Mr. Bush's electoral chances by putting the brakes on the economy. The committee meets again in December, but few economists expect sharp policy changes in a month when financial market activity traditionally tails off.

So if the Fed does not move by August, the betting is that it is not likely to do anything until next January. The futures markets are predicting that short-term rates will rise from the current 1 percent to 1.25 percent by the summer.

Evidence of the Fed treading carefully before presidential elections extends back at least 40 years. Gary Hufbauer and Paul Grieco of the Institute for International Economics found that from November 1959 to October 2003, the Fed changed interest rates only about half as frequently in the six months before an election as in other six-month periods. Most of the Fed's moves in the months before an election have involved staying a previously set course of raising or lowering rates.

"The Fed wants to maximize its long-term independence," Mr. Hufbauer explained. "The way to keep your long-term independence is you don't do anything that seems highly political around the elections."

continued on next page

continued from previous page

Mr. Meyer—who expects the Fed to raise interest rates in January of 2005—stresses that electoral considerations would not keep the Fed from acting if something drastic were to change in the economy, say a spike in inflation.

Dick Rippe, chief economist at Prudential Equity Group, noted that under Chairman Paul A. Volcker, the Fed reversed course on monetary policy and started a period of steep interest rate increases in September 1980. That move gets at least some of the credit—or blame, depending on your politics—for Ronald Reagan's defeat of President Jimmy Carter that November.

Mr. Rippe noted that Mr. Volcker's Fed acted during a period of very high inflation that could justify drastic action. "Barring some sort of emergency," Mr. Rippe said, "once beyond Labor Day, it would be hard to make a move. It would inject the Fed into the political debate in a way that they would not like."

Do these political considerations matter in 2004? Alice M. Rivlin, a former vice chairwoman of the Fed who is now at the Brookings Institution in Washington, said that given the sluggish job growth and the virtual absence of inflation, the Fed has no reason to tighten monetary policy for quite awhile, regardless of the electoral calendar.

LESSONS OF THE ARTICLE

Central bank independence is supposed to free monetary policymakers from political pressure. Yet it offers only partial protection, especially before a presidential election. The higher the level of output and employment, the more likely an incumbent president is to win re-election. But increases in interest rates slow the economy, reducing aggregate demand. Thus, raising interest rates just before an election—even if it is justified by economic conditions—puts the central bank on a collision course with politicians.

Terms

Chapter Lessons

1. In the long run
   a. Current output equals potential output, which is the level of output the economy produces when its resources are used at normal rates.
   b. Inflation equals money growth minus growth in potential output (ignoring changes in velocity).
2. The aggregate demand curve is a downward-sloping relationship between inflation and output. The higher the level of inflation, the lower the economy's output. One explanation for this relationship is that with constant money growth, higher inflation lowers the level of real money in the economy, reducing the quantity of goods and services people can buy and thus reducing real aggregate demand.

3. Another explanation for the downward-sloping aggregate demand curve is based on the following logic:

   a. Aggregate demand is composed of consumption, investment, government purchases, and net exports.

   b. Consumption, investment, and net exports fall when the real interest rates rises.

   c. The long-run real interest rate equates aggregate demand with potential output.

   d. When policymakers change the nominal interest rate, they change the real interest rate as well, because inflation doesn't change quickly.

   e. So when policymakers change the nominal interest rate, they influence aggregate demand.

4. Monetary policy is described by an upward-sloping monetary policy reaction curve.

   a. To meet the goal of low, stable inflation, policymakers react to a rise in current inflation by raising the real interest rate.

   b. The monetary policy reaction curve is set so that the central bank's inflation target is consistent with the long-run real interest rate.

   c. An increase in target inflation or a decrease in the long-run real interest rate shifts the monetary policy reaction curve to the right.

   d. When target inflation goes down, or the long-run real interest rate goes up, the monetary policy reaction curve shifts to the left.

   e. The slope of the monetary policy reaction curve depends on how intent policymakers are on keeping current inflation close to target inflation.

      i. A steep monetary policy reaction curve signals that policymakers are determined to eliminate deviations of current inflation from target inflation.

      ii. A flat monetary policy reaction curve means that policymakers are relatively tolerant of temporary movements in current inflation.

5. Combining the fact that aggregate demand falls when real interest rates rise with policymakers' tendency to raise the real interest rate when inflation rises gives us a downward-sloping aggregate demand curve.

   a. Movements along the aggregate demand curve occur when monetary policymakers react to changes in inflation by adjusting the real interest rate.

   b. The aggregate demand curve shifts when

      i. An increase in consumer confidence, business optimism, government purchases, or net exports shifts the aggregate demand curve to the right.

      ii. The monetary policy reaction curve shifts to the right, shifting the aggregate demand curve to the right.

   c. The aggregate demand curve becomes flatter when

      i. The monetary policy reaction curve becomes steeper, and

      ii. The interest-rate-sensitive components of aggregate demand become more sensitive to changes in the real interest rate.

www.mhhe.com/cecchettile

Problems

1. Using the equation of exchange, derive an aggregate demand curve.

2. Explain the determinants of potential growth.

3. What are the determinants of the long-run real interest rate, and how might you use data to figure out what it is?

4. Explain how and why the components of aggregate demand depend on the real interest rate. Be sure to distinguish between the real and nominal interest rates and explain why the distinction matters.

5. Suppose the value of the stock market suddenly drops 20 percent. What will happen to the aggregate demand curve. Why?

6. The European Central Bank's primary objective is price stability. Policymakers interpret this objective to mean keeping inflation close to 2 percent, as measured by a euro-area consumer price index. In contrast, the FOMC has a dual objective of price stability and high economic growth. How would you expect the monetary policy reaction curves of the two central banks to differ? Why?

7. In the United Kingdom, the Chancellor of the Exchequer (equivalent to the Secretary of the Treasury in the United States) sets the Bank of England's inflation target. For years, the Chancellor set the target rate at $2\frac{1}{2}$ percent, but after a new government was elected, the new Chancellor set the rate at $3\frac{1}{2}$ percent. Describe the impact of this change in the inflation target on

   a. The monetary policy reaction curve.

   b. The aggregate demand curve.

8. Suppose foreign investors suddenly lose faith in their U.S. investments and begin to dispose of them, driving down the value of the U.S. dollar. Describe how this would affect aggregate demand. What sort of monetary policy response would be appropriate in this situation?

9. Collect the following information for the years 1960 to the present from the Internet sources provided:

   • The NBER Business Cycle Reference Dates since 1960, from www.nber.org

   • Real GDP, from www.bea.gov

   • The federal funds rate, from www.frb.gov

   Using these data, construct a table that shows the change in GDP and the federal funds rate during each recession since 1960. Comment on any interesting patterns you find.

10. Plot the interest-rate data you collected in Problem 9. Note the behavior of the federal funds rate just before each recession began. Did interest rates rise or fall before peaks in the business cycle? Do your findings suggest that monetary policy causes recessions?

11. Describe the determinants of the long-run real interest rate and speculate on the sorts of events that would make it fluctuate. Given your answer, do you think the real interest rate is more likely to have gone up or down over the past five years?

12. In the United States, inflation fell from 12 percent in 1980 to 4 percent in 1983. Describe the likely effect on the monetary policy reaction curve and the aggre-

gate demand curve. What would you expect happened to output over the period? Can you find data to substantiate your answer?

13. The Federal Reserve has refused to announce an explicit inflation target. Do FOMC members behave as if they do have a target? Explain how to determine what their implicit target is and examine some data to evaluate the method.

14. Discuss the impact of each of the following variables on aggregate demand. (Consider each individually.)

   a. An increase in individual taxpayers' contribution to Social Security (a rise in the payroll tax).

   b. A depreciation of the dollar.

   c. A rise in the federal government's defense spending.

   d. A tax credit for new corporate investment.

   e. An increase in foreign demand for U.S. goods.

15. Consider a case where, in response to an increase in inflation, monetary policy-makers raise the nominal interest rate by less than one percent. What happens to the monetary policy reaction curve and the aggregate demand curve?

Chapter 22

Understanding Business Cycles

In 1965, the aggregate price level in the United States was rising at a rate of just $1\frac{1}{2}$ percent per year. Fifteen years later, consumer price inflation had climbed more than 10 percentage points, peaking at nearly 14 percent. For the next decade it fell, at first sharply and then more slowly. By 1991, prices were increasing at a rate of less than 4 percent per year. Ten years later, the rate of increase was half that. These long-run trends are apparent in Figure 22.1, which shows consumer price inflation over the last half century.

In addition to data on inflation, Figure 22.1 shows a series of shaded bars representing recessions. Note that inflation tends to fall during recessions and rise just prior to peaks in the business cycle (the left-hand edges of the shaded bars). There are some exceptions to this pattern. During 1974–75, for example, inflation rose dramatically even as the economy was slumping. And during much of the boom of the 1990s, inflation remained below its level at the end of the last recession. But in general, growth and inflation appear to be connected. Note, too, that the frequency of recessions has fallen markedly over the past half century. In the 30 years from 1955 to 1984, there were six recessions; in the 20 years since then, there have been only two. Recessions used to occur once every five years; now they occur only once in a decade.

Figure 22.1 Inflation and the Business Cycle, 1955–2004

This graph shows the 12-month change in consumer prices, calculated by the Bureau of Labor Statistics. The shaded bars represent recessions, as dated by the National Bureau of Economic Research.

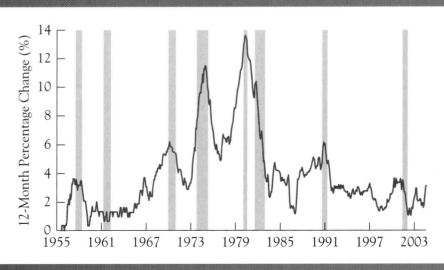

In Chapter 20 we learned that, in the long run, inflation is tied to money growth. Over periods of several decades, high money growth leads to high inflation. But over shorter periods of months or years, changes in the rate of money growth tell us little about future movements in inflation. That is especially true when inflation is low, as it has been throughout much of the industrialized world over the past decade or two. The objective of this chapter is to explain the rise in inflation that began in 1966, the drop 15 years later, and its low level since the mid-1990s. To figure out these trends, we will need to understand the relationship between inflation and real output.

In the last chapter, we took the first step toward explaining the connection between inflation and output. There we examined the determinants of aggregate demand and their connection to monetary policy. Recall that various components of aggregate demand, especially investment, are sensitive to the real interest rate. Central bankers adjust the real interest rate in response to deviations of current inflation from its target level. Specifically, they raise the real interest rate in response to increases in inflation. Increases in the real interest rate reduce the level of investment, consumption, and net exports, lowering the economy's output.

In this chapter, we will finish the job we started in Chapter 21. To do it, we need to examine the pricing and production decisions firms make. These form the basis for the aggregate supply curve. Putting aggregate demand and aggregate supply together will show us how inflation and real output are determined, as well as what causes their levels to change over time. And because we have built monetary policy into the model, we will see how modern central banks can use their policy tools to stabilize the economy.

The Aggregate Supply Curve

We know that the aggregate demand curve is a downward-sloping relationship between aggregate demand and inflation. Higher inflation is associated with lower levels of aggregate demand. That relationship doesn't tell us how inflation and output are determined, however. To understand that, we need to introduce an aggregate supply curve. The *aggregate supply curve* tells us where on the aggregate demand curve the economy will end up, explaining the relationship between inflation and real output in the process. Critically, there are two versions of the aggregate supply curve, a short-run and a long-run curve. The short-run aggregate supply curve tells us where the economy will settle at any particular time; the long-run curve tells us the levels of inflation and output the economy is moving toward. Inflation doesn't change much in the short run, but in the long run its level adjusts.

Inflation Persistence and the Short-Run Aggregate Supply Curve

Looking back at Figure 22.1, we can see that inflation tends to change slowly. When inflation is low one year, it tends to be low the next, and when it is high, it tends to stay high. Economists refer to this phenomenon as **inflation persistence**. What is true for the United States is true for other low-inflation countries as well. Figure 22.2 shows the persistence of European inflation throughout the 1990s. While inflation did fall gradually and then rise again, the overall pattern was relatively smooth.

Figures 22.1 and 22.2 display the changes in inflation over several years or decades. But over periods of several months, inflation remains steady while real output adjusts. That means the **short-run aggregate supply curve (SRAS)** must be flat at the current level of inflation. We need to understand why.

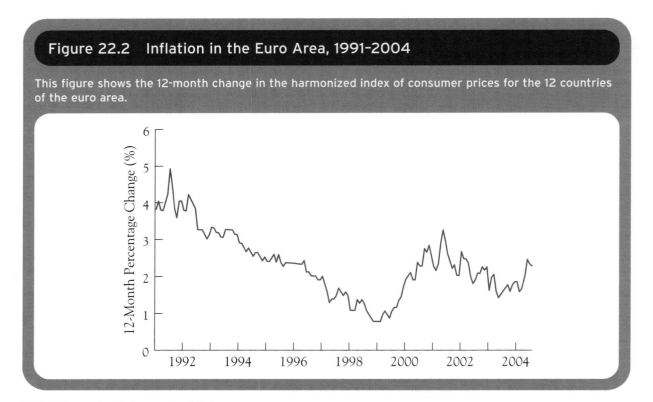

Figure 22.2 Inflation in the Euro Area, 1991–2004

This figure shows the 12-month change in the harmonized index of consumer prices for the 12 countries of the euro area.

SOURCE: *Data are from the European Central Bank.*

The Sources of Inflation Persistence

Inflation is persistent for two related reasons. First, when people expect inflation to continue, they adjust their prices and wages accordingly. Second, not all wage and price decisions are made at the same time. The result is that today's inflation tends to be very nearly what yesterday's was.

Suppose you own a shoe company and are deciding how much to charge for your shoes over the next six months. If current inflation is 2 percent per year, you can expect your competitors—other shoe producers—to increase the price of their shoes by 2 percent. To keep your price near those of your competitors, you will raise your price by 2 percent as well. Since everyone is taking the same action, inflation remains at a steady 2 percent.

What is true for prices is also true for wages. To see why, think about your shoe company's wage decision. You need to make sure that what you are paying your employees is close to the wage your competitors are paying. If the wages you pay are too low, your employees will quit and go to work elsewhere; if the wages you pay are too high, your profits will go down. Keeping wages near the level paid by your competitors means giving your employees increases that are similar to the increases offered by other shoe manufacturers. If your competitors raise the wages they pay by 4 percent, then you will be forced to do the same. When you see wages rising elsewhere, you will follow suit.

Your decisions regarding prices and wages depend on what you think other manufacturers will do. That means that decisions to raise prices or wages depend on *expected inflation*. When everyone expects inflation, they raise wages and prices in a way

MARKETS

that creates the inflation they expect. The more inflation they expect, the more they will raise wages and prices, and the higher inflation will climb. Thus, current inflation is at least partially determined by expected inflation. When expected inflation changes, current inflation does, too. Higher expected inflation produces an increase in current inflation; lower expected inflation produces a decline in current inflation. Still, the fact that inflation expectations depend in large part on current inflation imparts inertia to current inflation.

Expected inflation plays an important role in many decisions. Just as firms that expect inflation in the prices of competitors' products will raise the prices of their products, workers who expect inflation in consumer prices will demand an increase in wages. And since workers care about the purchasing power of their wages, the higher they expect inflation to rise, the larger the wage increases they will demand. Wages generally increase more rapidly than expected inflation, so that the real wage goes up. If everyone expects inflation to be 2 percent, wage increases may turn out to be 4 percent. In the long run, however, real wages rise at the same rate as worker productivity.

Expectations that inflation will continue are only one reason for the persistence of inflation. The other is the fact that across the economy, prices and wages change at different times. Just by looking around, we can see that the price of a cup of coffee or a muffin at the local diner does not change at the same time as the price of a pair of shoes at the store across the street. People's wages change at different times, too. Across the economy, price and wage adjustments are staggered. Not only do these changes occur at different times, but they are infrequent. Prices tend to remain stable for several months or more, and many people's wages rise only once a year.

TIME

The fact that wages and prices change infrequently and at different times of the year slows down the adjustment process considerably, causing persistence in inflation. To see why, let's return to the example in which you are setting the prices of the shoes you manufacture and the wages of the workers you employ. In deciding how much to increase your prices and wages, you consider what other firms like yours have done recently. If they have raised prices by 2 percent and wages by 4 percent, you will know about it, and because you want to keep your own prices and wages competitive, you will tend to take the same actions. The implication is that today's price and wage decisions depend on the price and wage decisions that were made just a few days or weeks ago.

These staggered price and wage adjustments, combined with expectations that current inflation will continue, keep today's inflation close to yesterday's inflation. Even so, inflation does change from time to time in response to changes in the environment. But the fact that today's decisions depend on yesterday's means that these changes occur slowly.

Deriving the Short-Run Aggregate Supply Curve
What does the persistence of inflation mean for the relationship between inflation and the quantity of output supplied? The fact that inflation is persistent means that it is fixed in the short run. From this we can conclude that the *short-run aggregate supply curve*, which relates inflation to the level of aggregate output supplied, is horizontal at the current level of inflation (see Figure 22.3).[1] Firms simply do not adjust the rate of their price increases in the short run; instead, they adjust the quantities they produce and sell. Of course, over periods of several years or more, inflation does change, shifting the short-run aggregate supply curve up or down.

---

[1]Assuming that the short-run aggregate supply curve is flat is a good approximation. In reality, it probably has some upward slope.

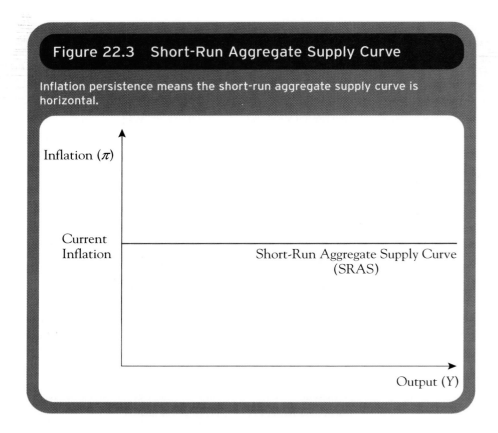

Figure 22.3 Short-Run Aggregate Supply Curve

Inflation persistence means the short-run aggregate supply curve is horizontal.

Inflation (π)

Current Inflation

Short-Run Aggregate Supply Curve (SRAS)

Output (Y)

Shifts in the Short-Run Aggregate Supply Curve

There are two reasons why the short-run aggregate supply curve can shift. The first has to do with deviations of current output from potential output. That is, when an output gap develops, inflation changes. The second reason concerns changes in external factors, which can drive up production costs. We will consider each in turn.

Output Gaps When current output equals potential output, so that there is no output gap, the short-run aggregate supply curve remains stable. But when current output rises above or falls below potential output, so that an output gap develops, inflation will rise or fall. To understand why, recall that potential output is that level at which firms are using labor and capital at normal rates. But when current output falls below potential output, creating a recessionary output gap, part of the economy's capacity is idle. Firms have little trouble hiring new workers under these conditions, and their plants and equipment are underutilized. As a result, firms tend to raise their prices and wages less than they did before, when current output equaled potential output.

When current output exceeds potential output, creating an expansionary output gap, the opposite happens. Firms have difficulty hiring new workers and retaining those already on the payroll. They pay overtime to their employees and use their plants and equipment at levels they can maintain only temporarily. Under these circumstances, firms will increase their prices and wages more than they would if they were operating at normal levels.

We can conclude that when current output deviates from potential output, inflation adjusts. The process is shown in Figure 22.4. A recessionary output gap, in which

Figure 22.4   Shifts in the Short-Run Aggregate Supply Curve
Response to an Output Gap

When current output rises above potential output, creating an expansionary output gap, the short-run aggregate supply curve shifts upward. When current output falls below potential output, creating a recessionary output gap, the short-run aggregate supply curve shifts downward.

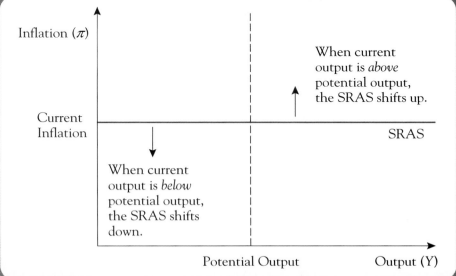

current output falls below potential output, forces inflation down; an expansionary output gap, in which current output rises above potential output, drives inflation up. Looking back at the historical inflation data in Figure 22.1, as well as at the data on inflation and the output gap in Figure 22.5, we can see that this model of inflation fits the facts fairly well.

Figure 22.5 plots changes in inflation (the blue line) against changes in the output gap, lagged six quarters (the beige line) over the period 1988 to 2004.[2] As it shows, inflation tends to fall during recessions and rise during expansions. Importantly, an output gap has little immediate impact on inflation; its effect takes roughly a year and a half to be felt. By looking closely at the data in the figure, we can estimate that a 1 percent recessionary output gap (current output that is 1 percent below potential) will drive inflation down 0.2 percentage points over the next 18 months.[3]

How quickly does the short-run aggregate supply curve respond to an output gap? Does inflation respond slowly or rapidly? Economists differ markedly in their answers

---

[2]This period coincides roughly with the period during which Alan Greenspan has been chairman of the Federal Reserve Board.

[3]What is true in the United States is true in other industrialized countries as well. Laurence Ball finds that periods of below-normal output are associated with falling inflation in a sample of 19 countries. See "What Determines the Sacrifice Ratio?" in N. Gregory Mankiw, ed., *Monetary Policy*, (Chicago: University of Chicago Press, 1994), pp. 155–182.

Figure 22.5 Inflation and the Output Gap, 1988–2004

In this figure the output gap is measured as the percentage deviation of current real gross domestic product from potential real GDP. The change in inflation is measured as the year-to-year change in the two-year consumer price index, excluding food and energy.

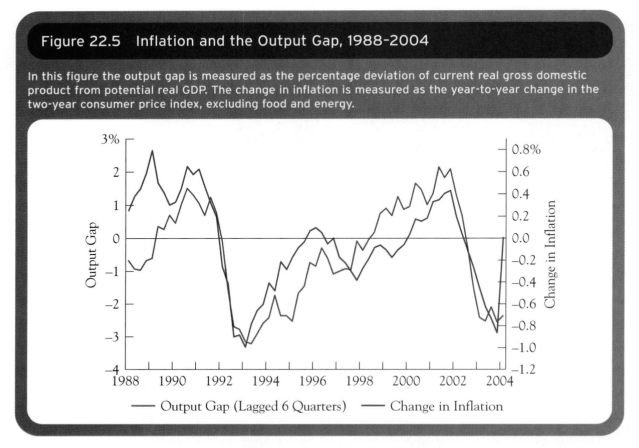

—— Output Gap (Lagged 6 Quarters)   —— Change in Inflation

SOURCES: *Real GDP data are from the Bureau of Economic Analysis; potential real GDP data, from the Congressional Budget Office; and consumer price data from the Bureau of Labor Statistics. All are available on the Web site of the Federal Reserve Bank of St. Louis: research.stlouisfed.org/fred2.*

to these questions. One group believes that prices are flexible, so inflation reacts quickly to deviations of output from potential. If this group is right, the short-run aggregate supply curve shifts quickly to eliminate any output gaps. The other group emphasizes the fact that many price and wage decisions are based on long-term contracts, which are both difficult and costly to change. If price and wage inflation are "sticky" rather than flexible, the short-run aggregate supply curve will respond only sluggishly to gaps between current and potential output.

Inflation Shocks Deviations of current output from potential output are only one reason that the short-run aggregate supply can shift. We drew the short-run aggregate supply curve in Figure 22.3 by holding a number of factors constant, including the cost of labor, the prices of raw materials used in production, and expected inflation. If any of these factors changes, the short-run aggregate supply curve will shift. We will call changes in these production factors **inflation shocks**.

An *inflation shock*, then, is a change in the cost of producing output. Changes in the cost of raw materials or labor are two examples, but the most common inflation shock is a change in the price of energy. When oil prices rise, increasing the cost of production, firms are forced to raise the prices of their products. The sharp increases in oil prices in the 1970s, from $3.50 a barrel in 1973 to $10 a barrel in 1976 and $39 a barrel in 1980, were a major cause of inflation during that decade. Conversely, when oil

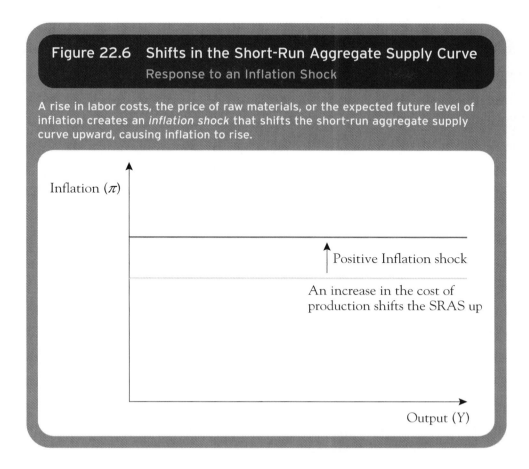

Figure 22.6   Shifts in the Short-Run Aggregate Supply Curve
Response to an Inflation Shock

A rise in labor costs, the price of raw materials, or the expected future level of inflation creates an *inflation shock* that shifts the short-run aggregate supply curve upward, causing inflation to rise.

Inflation (π)

Positive Inflation shock

An increase in the cost of production shifts the SRAS up

Output (Y)

prices fall, as they did in 1986 and again in 1999, inflation tends to fall. The short-run aggregate supply curve also shifts up when labor costs rise, as they do when payroll taxes increase or the cost of employer-provided health insurance rises. *A positive inflation shock causes the short-run aggregate supply curve to shift upward*, as shown in Figure 22.6.

The Long-Run Aggregate Supply Curve

The final task in constructing our model of the fluctuations in output and inflation is to examine what happens in the long run. What happens after everyone has had time to make the adjustments that bring output and inflation back to normal? The economy moves to the point where current output equals potential output, while inflation is determined by money growth. The implications of this answer are that in the long run, current output *must* equal potential output, and inflation must be determined by monetary policy. That is, in the long run, output and inflation are unrelated. As Figure 22.7 shows, *the long-run aggregate supply curve (LRAS) is vertical at the point where current output equals potential output.*

Looking ahead, we will see that this conclusion makes sense for another reason. From our earlier discussion, we know that the short-run aggregate supply curve shifts whenever current output rises above or falls below potential output, creating an output gap. When current output equals potential output, the short-run aggregate supply curve does not shift. The fact that the short-run aggregate supply curve is stable when there is no output gap suggests that the long-run aggregate supply curve is vertical at that point.

YOUR FINANCIAL WORLD
The Problem with Measuring GDP

Looking at the economy as a whole, we know that expenditures must equal income. Eventually, every dollar that is earned as income must be spent on something. In thinking about gross domestic product, then, we usually divide it into the components on which it is spent—consumption, investment, government purchases, and net exports. So one way to calculate GDP is to measure expenditures in all these categories.

But the fact that expenditures equal income means that there is another, equally important way to think about GDP. If one person's expenditure is another person's income, we can also measure GDP by dividing income into categories and computing what economists call gross domestic income (GDI). Income categories include wages, rental income, interest income, and dividend income. And since everyone is supposed to pay taxes on his or her income, measuring it should be straightforward.

The fact that income and expenditures are supposed to be equal doesn't mean that when we go to measure them they are, however. And they're not. Looking at the tables constructed by the Department of Commerce's Bureau of Economic Analysis, we find

a line labeled "Statistical Discrepancy."[*] The amount on this line, which represents GDI computed from the income data minus GDP calculated from expenditures data, is quite large. From 1998 to 2004, the statistical discrepancy between the two measures averaged about two-thirds of 1 percent of nominal GDP and often exceeded 1 percent. Since nominal GDP grows at a rate of about 5 percent a year (that is the sum of inflation plus real growth) changes in the statistical discrepancy can have a big impact on official estimates of overall economic performance.

In Chapter 18, we saw that the government continues to revise its estimates of GDP for many years, and the revisions tend to be large (see Your Financial World: Economic History Is Constantly Changing). Attempts by government statisticians to get rid of the discrepancy between the income- and expenditure-based estimates of GDP are one explanation for these revisions.

[*]You can find the statistical discrepancy by going to the website www.bea.gov and locating the National Income and Product Accounts Table 1.7.5, Relation of Gross Domestic Product, Gross National Product, Net National Product, National Income, and Personal Income. The statistical discrepancy is on line 15.

In deriving the short-run aggregate supply curve, we noted that inflation depends on inflation expectations. That is, when workers and firms make the wage and price decisions that determine today's inflation, they do it with an eye toward future inflation. While we have not emphasized the following fact, changes in expected inflation operate like cost shocks, shifting the short-run aggregate supply curve. Increases in expected inflation shift the short-run aggregate supply curve upward; decreases shift it downward.

To see why inflation expectations have this effect, recall that wages and prices are set based on expected inflation. For example, a rise in expected inflation causes workers to demand, and employers to grant, higher-than-normal wage increases, which drive up production costs. Turning to prices, remember that the higher the shoe manufacturer expects inflation to be, the more he or she will raise the price of shoes. Suppliers behave in the same way. Expecting more inflation, they raise their prices to compensate, increasing the cost of the materials manufacturers need to produce their products. Rising inflation expectations raise the cost of production just as an inflation shock does.

To summarize, the short-run aggregate supply curve shifts *both* when current output deviates from potential output *and* when expected inflation deviates from current inflation. For the economy to remain in long-run equilibrium, then, in addition to current output equaling potential output, current inflation must equal expected inflation. So *at any point along the long-run aggregate supply curve, current output equals potential output and current inflation equals expected inflation.*

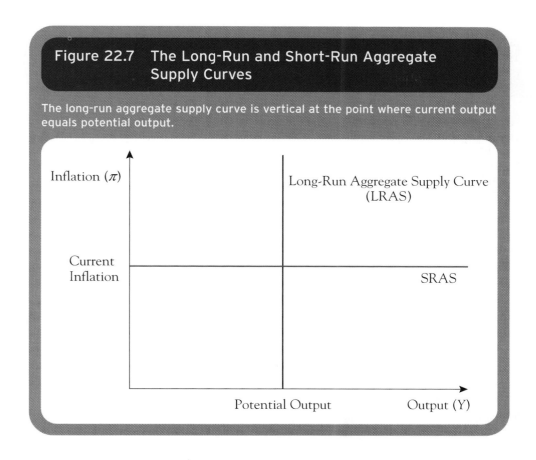

Figure 22.7   The Long-Run and Short-Run Aggregate Supply Curves

The long-run aggregate supply curve is vertical at the point where current output equals potential output.

Up to this point our entire discussion has been cast in terms of current output, potential output, and the output gap. But the economy is constantly growing. Investment increases the size of the capital stock used in production, and new hires raise the number of people working. And then there are technological improvements: Inventions and innovations are constantly increasing individual productivity. Increases in the available amounts of capital and labor, together with improvements in productivity, are the sources of economic growth. And because economic growth implies an increase in the normal output level, potential output is constantly rising.

Such changes in the economy's productive capacity will shift the long-run aggregate supply curve. Increases in either the inputs into the production process or the amount of output per unit of inputs will raise potential output, shifting the long-run aggregate supply curve to the right. Declines in the economy's productive capacity do occur on occasion, and when they do they shift the long-run aggregate supply curve to the left. We will return to this topic later in the chapter.

"Please stand by for a series of tones. The first indicates the official end of the recession, the second indicates prosperity, and the third the return of the recession."

TOOLS OF THE TRADE
Defining a Recession: The NBER Reference Cycle

From reading the business press, you might conclude that a recession is any episode in which real gross domestic product declines for two consecutive quarters. While that casual definition may work in most instances, it does have some drawbacks. One is that because GDP is computed and published quarterly, a definition that is based on GDP cannot indicate the specific months in which a recession started and ended. To determine that information, we need a definition that is based on measures like production, employment, sales, and income—all of which are available monthly.

In the end, though, there is no hard and fast definition of a recession. An American recession is what the National Bureau of Economic Research (NBER) says it is. The NBER, which was founded in 1920, is a research organization that is devoted to studying how the economy works. Early work at the NBER led to the construction of much of the economic data we use today. Two of the NBER's pioneering researchers, Wesley Mitchell and Arthur Burns, dated the beginning and end of all the recessions in the United States from the Civil War through World War II. In their book *Measuring Business Cycles* (1946), they called this dating a "reference cycle."

Over the years, the NBER's Business-Cycle Dating Committee has become the unofficial arbiter for the time at which the economy has reached a peak or a trough. Its definition of a recession is as follows:

"A recession is a significant decline in activity spread across the economy, lasting more than a few months, normally visible in real GDP, real income, employment, industrial production, and wholesale-retail sales. A recession begins just after the economy reaches a peak of activity and ends as the economy reaches its trough. Between trough and peak, the economy is in an expansion. Expansion is the normal state of the economy; most recessions are brief and they have been rare in recent decades."

Table 22.1 Recent NBER Business-Cycle Reference Dates

Peak	Trough	Length of Recession in Months Peak to Trough	Length of Expansion in Months Previous Trough to Peak
November 1948	October 1949	11	37
July 1953	May 1954	10	45
August 1957	April 1958	8	39
April 1960	February 1961	10	24
December 1969	November 1970	11	106
November 1973	March 1975	16	36
January 1980	July 1980	6	58
July 1981	November 1982	16	12
July 1990	March 1991	8	92
March 2001	November 2001	8	120

SOURCE: *www.nber.org.*

continued from previous page

Figure 22.8   Growth in Real GDP over the Business Cycle, 1948–2004

The curve shows the four-quarter percentage change in real GDP. The shaded bars represent recessions, as determined by the NBER.

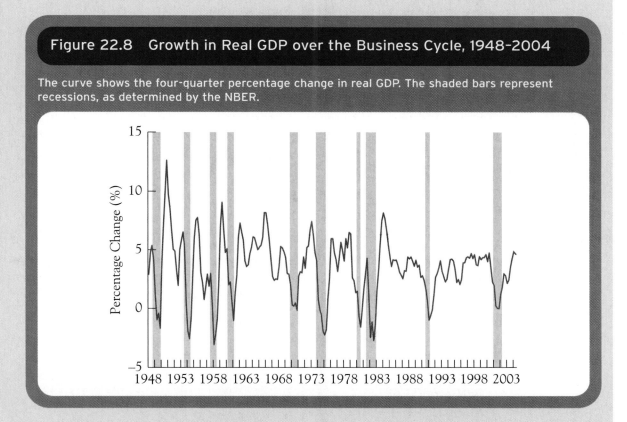

This definition has three important implications. First, a recession is a decline in activity, not just a dip in the growth rate. Second, the exact length of the economic contraction is ambiguous. A severe decline in economic activity that lasted less than two quarters could still be considered a recession according to this definition. Third, since key economic indicators often change direction at different times, there is an element of judgment in dating the peaks and troughs of business cycles. As a result, the NBER's Business-Cycle Dating Committee takes its time in declaring the beginning and end of a recession. Delays of six months to a year are common.

The term *business cycle* is somewhat misleading when used to refer to fluctuations in economic activity. The word *cycle* calls up images of recurring waves that rise and fall in a periodic pattern. Economic fluctuations aren't like that. Both the length of recessions and the time between them are irregular. As Burns and Mitchell wrote in their book, "A cycle consists of expansions . . . followed by contractions and revivals which merge into the expansion phase of the next cycle; this sequence of changes is recurrent but not periodic. . . ."

Table 22.1 displays the results of the NBER's analyses of the business cycle since the end of World War II. Figure 22.8 plots the bureau's business-cycle reference dates against the growth in real GDP over the period. The figure clearly shows the tendency for real growth to be low—usually below zero—during recessions. The table illustrates the remarkable fact that recessions are much shorter than expansions in the U.S. economy. Most people credit this fact to a combination of successful policy and the economy's capacity for self-correction.

For more information on the procedures used by the NBER's Business-Cycle Dating Committee, go to the bureau's website at www.nber.org.

Equilibrium and the Determination of Output and Inflation

Short-Run Equilibrium

We now have all the tools we need to understand both the determination of output and inflation over the long run and their movements in the short run. Short-run equilibrium is determined by the intersection of the aggregate demand curve (AD) with the short-run aggregate supply curve. That is, we draw the aggregate demand curve from Figure 21.1 (page 554) on the same diagram as the short-run aggregate supply curve from Figure 22.3. The result is shown in Figure 22.9.

Adjustment to Long-Run Equilibrium

What happens when current output does not equal potential output? To see, let's examine two cases; one in which current output is above potential and one in which it is below potential. When current output exceeds potential, the resulting expansionary gap exerts upward pressure on inflation, shifting the short-run aggregate supply curve upward. This process continues until output returns to potential, as shown in the top panel of Figure 22.10. At first, aggregate demand equals short-run aggre-

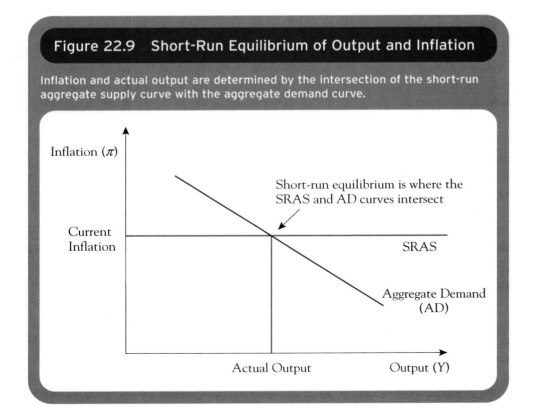

Figure 22.9 Short-Run Equilibrium of Output and Inflation

Inflation and actual output are determined by the intersection of the short-run aggregate supply curve with the aggregate demand curve.

gate supply at point 1, where current output exceeds potential output. The resulting expansionary output gap pushes the short-run aggregate supply curve up until it reaches point 2, where current output equals potential output and there is no output gap. Only at this point does inflation stop changing.

Now consider the second case, in which current output is lower than potential output. The resulting recessionary gap places downward pressure on inflation, causing the short-run aggregate supply curve to shift downward. Again, the process continues until current output returns to potential, as shown in the bottom panel of Figure 22.10. At first, aggregate demand equals short-run aggregate supply at point 1, where current output falls short of potential output. The resulting recessionary gap causes the short-run aggregate supply curve to shift downward. As aggregate supply falls, current output increases until it equals potential output at point 2. At this point, inflation remains steady.

This example has several important implications. First, it shows that the economy does indeed have a self-correcting mechanism. When current output moves away from its long-run level equal to potential output, the short-run aggregate supply curve shifts the economy back to the point where it began, eliminating the output gap. Second, the manner in which the short-run aggregate supply curve shifts in response to output gaps reinforces our conclusion that the long-run aggregate supply curve is vertical.

Long-run equilibrium has some other important properties. As we noted earlier, in the long run, current inflation must equal expected inflation. Recall from Chapter 21 that, when current output equals potential output, the real interest rate equals the long-run real interest rate. And going back to the monetary policy reaction curve, we know that policymakers set the real interest rate equal to this long-run level when current inflation equals their inflation target. So the conditions for long-run equilibrium are that (a) current output equals potential output and (b) current inflation is steady and equal to target inflation, which equals expected inflation.

The Impact of Shifts in Aggregate Demand on Output and Inflation

With our understanding of the determinants of short-run and long-run equilibrium, we can now study the consequences of shifts in the various curves: aggregate demand, short-run aggregate supply, and long-run aggregate supply.[4] Let's look at the effects of a shift in each, starting with an increase in aggregate demand. Recalling our discussion in Chapter 21, we know that a shift in the aggregate demand curve can be caused by both a shift in the monetary policy reaction curve and a change in factors such as consumer confidence and government purchases. Let's look at a case in which government purchases rise, so the aggregate demand curve shifts to the right.

The result of this shift is shown in the top panel of Figure 22.11. When the aggregate demand curve shifts from its original position to its new position, the economy moves from the original short-run equilibrium point, labeled 1, to the new short-run equilibrium point, 2. At first, current output rises but inflation does not change. Since potential output has not changed, the new, higher level of current output implies an expansionary gap. To return to long-run equilibrium, the economy must move from this point. With current output above potential output, the short-run aggregate supply curve begins to shift upward, and inflation begins to rise. Higher inflation moves

---

[4]Shifts in the short-run and long-run aggregate supply curves are sometimes called *supply shocks*.

Figure 22.10 Adjustment to Long-Run Equilibrium

A. Adjustment when Current Output Is *Greater* than Potential Output
At the initial short-run equilibrium point 1, current output is *greater* than potential output, creating an *expansionary* output gap that exerts upward pressure on inflation. From here, the short-run aggregate supply curve will shift upward. The process continues until the economy reaches point 2, where current output and potential output are equal.

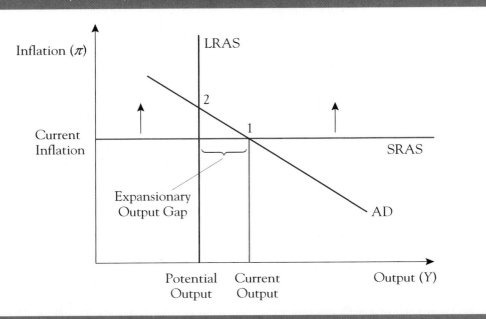

B. Adjustment when Current Output Is *Less* than Potential Output
At the initial short-run equilibrium point 1, current output is *lower* than potential output, creating a *recessionary* output gap that exerts downward pressure on inflation. From here, the short-run aggregate supply curve will shift downward. The process continues until the economy reaches point 2, where current output and potential output are equal.

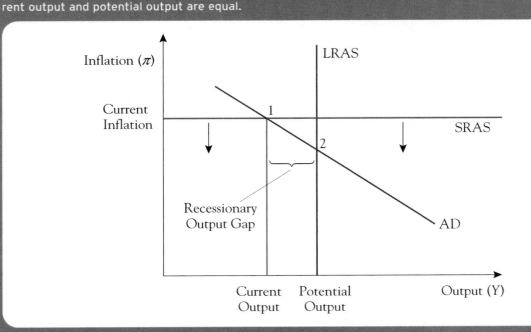

Figure 22.11   The Impact of a Shift in Aggregate Demand on Output and Inflation

A. Short-Run Equilibrium Inflation and Output Following an Increase in Aggregate Demand

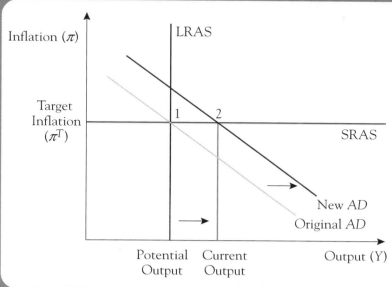

1. Start at long-run equilibrium
   Y = Potential output
   π = Target inflation

2. Aggregate demand shifts right
   Original AD shifts to new AD
   Y > Potential output
   Inflation is unchanged

3. Short-run equilibrium moves
   from point 1 to point 2

B. Adjustment of Short-Run Equilibrium Inflation and Output Following an Increase in Aggregate Demand

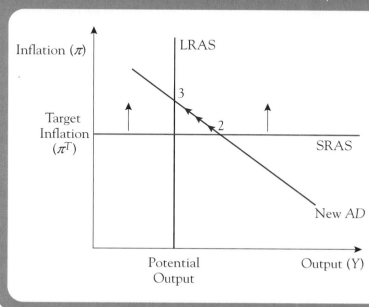

1. At short-run equilibrium
   point 2: Y > Potential output

2. SRAS begins to shift up
   Output begins to fall
   Inflation begins to rise as
   economy moves along new AD

3. With no policy response, economy
   moves to point 3, where
   Current inflation > Target inflation

monetary policymakers along their reaction curve, leading them to raise the real interest rate and move the economy upward *along* the new aggregate demand curve. As a result, output begins to fall back toward its long-run equilibrium level, potential output, as shown in the bottom panel of Figure 22.11.

Unless something else happens, the economy will ultimately settle at point 3 in the bottom panel of Figure 22.11, where the new aggregate demand curve crosses the long-run aggregate supply curve, and current output once again equals potential output. It is extremely important to realize that at point 3, inflation is above where it started at point 1, so it is above the policymakers' original target. If central bankers simply sit and watch as the aggregate demand curve shifts to the right, inflation will rise.

While policymakers could allow the increase in government purchases to drive up their inflation target, permanently increasing inflation and the monetary growth rate, that course of action seems unlikely. So long as monetary policymakers remain committed to their original inflation target, they will need to do something to get the economy back to the point where it began—point 1 in the top panel of Figure 22.11, at the intersection of the original aggregate demand curve with the long-run aggregate supply curve. This is the point where current output equals potential output and current inflation equals their original inflation target.

In Chapter 21, we emphasized that an increase in government purchases raises the long-term real interest rate. The higher the level of government purchases, the higher the level of the real interest rate needed to equate aggregate demand with potential output. Realizing this, policymakers will compensate by shifting their monetary policy reaction curve to the left, increasing the real interest rate at every level of inflation (look back at the bottom panel of Figure 21.6, page 568). When the monetary policy reaction curve shifts, the aggregate demand curve shifts with it. In this case, the aggregate demand curve will shift to the left, bringing the economy back to long-run equilibrium.

We can summarize the path the economy takes after an increase in government purchases as follows. Output rises above potential output and then falls back to long-run equilibrium. Inflation rises and then returns to the central bank's target level. From this we can conclude that, without a change in target inflation, *an increase in government purchases causes a temporary increase in both output and inflation.* The same is true for any factor that shifts the aggregate demand curve to the right. Immediately following such a shift, output rises but inflation remains unchanged. With time, the expansionary output gap causes the short-run aggregate supply curve to shift upward, moving the economy upward along the new aggregate demand curve. This movement drives up inflation as current output begins to fall toward potential output.

A decline in aggregate demand, perhaps caused by a fall in consumer or business confidence, has the opposite impact. Aggregate demand shifts to the left, driving output down. The immediate effect of this shift is to place downward pressure on inflation, inducing policymakers to lower the real interest rate. The monetary policy reaction curve shifts to the right, reducing the real interest rate that policymakers set at every level of inflation and ultimately bringing aggregate demand back to where it started. Thus, *a decline in aggregate demand causes a temporary decline in both output and inflation.* Immediately following such a shift in the aggregate demand curve, output falls but inflation remains unchanged. With time, the recessionary output gap causes the short-run aggregate supply curve to shift downward, moving the economy downward along the new aggregate demand curve. This movement drives inflation down, and current output begins to rise toward potential output.

Over the years, policymakers have reacted to shifts in aggregate demand in different ways, with differing results. In response to increases in government spending during the

APPLYING THE CONCEPT
INFLATION AND THE VIETNAM WAR

Without a shift in the monetary policy reaction curve, an increase in government purchases leads to a permanent increase in inflation. That is one explanation for why inflation rose in the United States in the late 1960s and early 1970s. As we noted at the beginning of this chapter, inflation rose from less than 2 percent in 1965 to over 5 percent in 1970.

The story goes like this. As the Vietnam War escalated, military spending increased sharply. From 1965 to 1968, the U.S. government's defense budget rose from 7.4 percent of GDP to 9.4 percent. To put this increase in perspective, notice that over a three-year period, government spending on the military alone rose by 2 percent of GDP. In recent years, the nation's entire defense budget has amounted to between 3 and 4 percent of GDP.

In addition to the steep increase in military expenditures, Presidents Johnson and Nixon raised spending on social programs. From 1965 to 1972, total U.S. government expenditures rose from 16 percent to 20 percent of GDP. The huge increase contributed to an economic boom, driving current output above potential output and creating an expansionary gap like the one shown in Figure 22.11. We know that to keep inflation from rising after a shift in aggregate demand, policymakers need to adjust their policy accordingly. They must react to the increase in government spending by shifting their monetary policy reaction curve to the left, raising the real interest rate at every level of inflation.

But the policymakers at the Federal Reserve failed to take action. Instead, they allowed what could have been a temporary increase in inflation to become a permanent one. It is difficult to know exactly why they chose this course. Did they fail to understand the need for a tighter monetary policy? Were they afraid to confront politicians with the consequences of their actions? Regardless of the reason, the Fed's inaction marked the beginning of a period of inflation that lasted for a decade. Proponents of explicit, publicly announced inflation targets point to episodes like this one as evidence of what can happen when central bankers are not held publicly accountable for checking inflation.

escalation of the Vietnam War in the late 1960s, the Fed simply allowed inflation to rise. What could have been a temporary increase in inflation became a permanent one, in effect increasing the Fed's inflation target to the point where the new aggregate demand curve intersected the long-run aggregate supply curve. (See Applying the Concept for a discussion of this episode.) The 1980s and 1990s were different. Then the Fed's policymakers took advantage of the downward pressure on inflation to reduce their inflation target in a process that some central bankers have called *opportunistic disinflation*. Disinflation is the term used to describe declines in inflation; the word *opportunistic* indicates that an opportunity to reduce the target inflation level arose naturally.[5]

---

[5]Disinflation is a very different term from deflation, which is the opposite of inflation. *Deflation* means that *aggregate prices* are consistently falling; *disinflation* means falling *inflation*.

YOUR FINANCIAL WORLD
Keeping Track of the Tax Code

Tax cuts are always popular, especially when the economy is in trouble. They are the politicians' way of addressing a recessionary output gap. To implement a tax cut, legislators change the tax code, the rules people have to follow in figuring out how much money they owe the government. To make sure you get the best tax break possible, you need to keep track of these changes in the tax code and change your behavior accordingly.

Let's take an example. In the spring of 2003, Congress passed a new law that reduced the maximum tax rate on stock dividends and long-term capital gains to 15 percent, but left the tax rate on interest income unchanged. The interest income from bonds is taxed at the ordinary income rate, which is higher than 15 percent for nearly everyone. In 2003, an individual whose income is as low as $28,400 pays a tax rate of 25 percent on

income over that amount. (Married couples pay 25 percent on income over $56,800.)

These changes in the tax law should have an impact on whether you hold bonds and stocks in your tax-deferred retirement account or your taxable savings account. Retirement accounts are *tax-advantaged;* neither the deposits you make nor the subsequent increases in their value are taxed until you withdraw your money after retirement.

The benefits of diversification mean that you will want to hold some stocks and some bonds, but you will want to divide your investments so as to minimize your tax bill. With the tax on interest income so much higher than the tax on stock returns, keeping your tax bill low means investing your retirement funds in bonds and your taxable savings in stocks. But if the tax rules change, this advice might change, too.

This discussion implies that whenever we see a *permanent* increase in inflation, it must be the result of monetary policy. That is, if inflation goes up or down and remains at its new level, the only explanation is that central bankers are allowing it to happen. They have changed their inflation target, whether or not they acknowledge the change explicitly.

The Impact of Inflation Shocks on Output and Inflation

An inflation shock shifts the short-run aggregate supply curve. Using the aggregate demand/aggregate supply diagram, we can trace the effects of such a shock. The immediate effect of a positive inflation shock, such as an oil price increase, is to move the short-run aggregate supply curve to a higher level, as shown in Figure 22.12. Short-run equilibrium—the point where the short-run aggregate supply and aggregate demand curves intersect—moves to point 2 in the figure, where output is lower and inflation is higher. This situation is sometimes referred to as *stagflation*—inflation coupled with economic stagnation.

Following the initial increase in inflation, the accompanying decline in output exerts downward pressure on inflation. As a result, the short-run aggregate supply curve begins to shift downward, driving inflation down and output up. Inflation falls and output rises until the economy returns to the point where current output equals potential output and inflation equals the central bank's target level.

Like the change in government purchases (Figure 22.11), an inflation shock has no effect on the economy's long-run equilibrium point. Only a change in potential output or a change in the central bank's inflation target can accomplish that. Instead, the inflation shock moves output and inflation temporarily away from potential output and the inflation target. Over time, the recessionary output gap causes the short-run aggregate supply curve to shift downward. As it does, the economy moves along the aggregate

Figure 22.12 The Effects of a Positive Inflation Shock on Short-Run Equilibrium

A positive inflation shock shifts the short-run aggregate supply curve upward, moving short-run equilibrium from point 1 to point 2. Inflation rises and output falls.

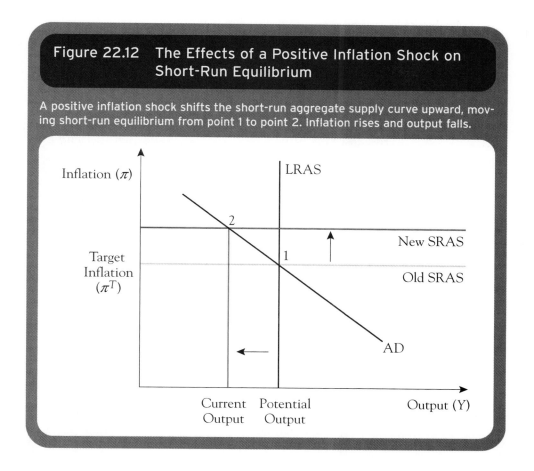

demand curve until output and inflation finally return to the initial equilibrium point, labeled 1 in Figure 22.12. Thus, an inflation shock causes inflation to rise temporarily and then fall, at the same time that current output falls temporarily and then rises.[6]

Shifts in Potential Output and Real Business Cycle Theory

So far we have ignored the possibility of changes in potential output in order to concentrate on the impact of shifts in the aggregate demand and short-run aggregate supply curves. But potential output does change, and the consequences of such a change are important to understand. *Changes in potential output shift the long-run aggregate supply curve*, as Figure 22.13 shows. At first this shift in long-run aggregate supply has no impact on the short-run aggregate supply curve, so inflation and output remain stable. But with time, the increase in potential output will mean that current output is now below potential output, creating a recessionary output gap. This gap puts downward pressure on inflation, shifting the short-run aggregate supply curve downward.

---

[6]The economy's path of adjustment following a positive inflation shock is the same as the path it follows after a leftward shift in the aggregate demand curve. In both cases, inflation eventually falls and output eventually rises. The difference is in the initial impact of the shock on inflation. An inflation shock drives inflation up at first; a shift in aggregate demand leaves it unchanged.

Figure 22.13 The Effects of an Increase in Potential Output on Inflation and Output

An increase in potential output shifts the long-run aggregate supply curve (LRAS) to the right. In the short run, current output remains unchanged. But since current output is now below potential output, the resulting recessionary gap places downward pressure on inflation, and output eventually begins to rise.

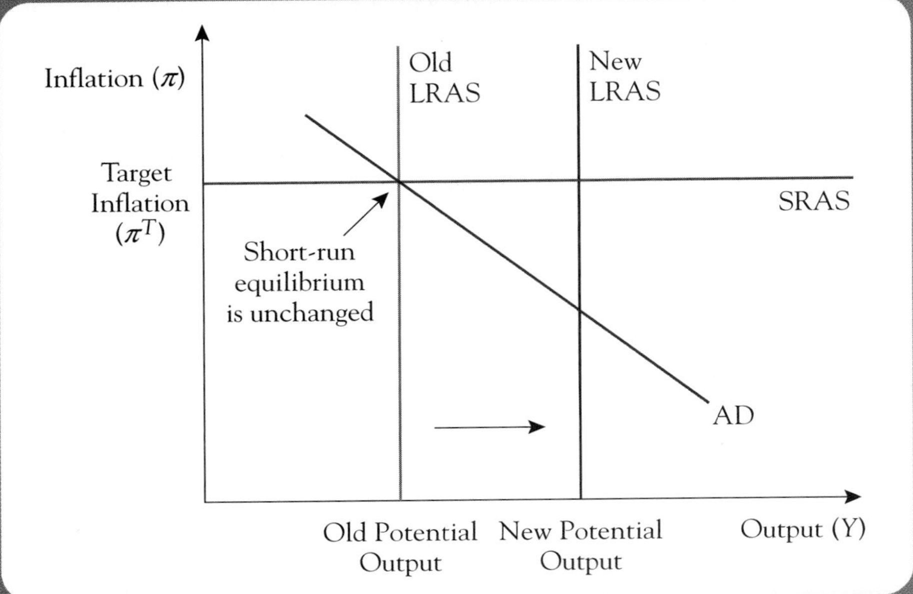

What happens next depends on what monetary policymakers do. They can take advantage of the downward pressure on inflation to reduce their inflation target, or they can initiate actions to ensure that inflation does not fall. In either case, policymakers will need to recognize that the higher level of potential output means a lower long-term real interest rate.

Throughout this discussion of business-cycle fluctuations, we have assigned a major role to aggregate demand. Our model indicates that output is determined by shifts in the aggregate demand curve that change its point of intersection with a flat short-run aggregate supply curve. An alternative explanation for business-cycle fluctuations focuses on shifts in potential output. This view, known as **real-business-cycle theory**, starts with the assumption that prices and wages are flexible, so inflation adjusts rapidly. In other words, the short-run aggregate supply curve shifts rapidly in response to deviations of current output from potential output. This assumption has dramatic implications. First, it renders the short-run aggregate supply curve irrelevant. Equilibrium output and inflation are determined by the point on the aggregate demand curve where current output equals potential output. Thus, any shift in the aggregate demand curve, regardless of its source, will change inflation but not output. Neither changes in aggregate demand nor changes in monetary policy will have any impact on the level of output.

Since inflation ultimately depends on the level of money growth, it is determined by monetary policy.

To explain recessions and booms, real-business-cycle theorists look to fluctuations in potential output. They focus on changes in productivity and their impact on GDP. Productivity is a measure of output at a fixed level of inputs. An increase in productivity means an increase in GDP for a given quantity of capital and number of workers. Shifts in productivity can be either temporary or permanent. Examples of such shifts include changes in the availability of raw materials, changes in government regulation of labor and product markets, and inventions that improve the economy's productive capacity. Any of these events will shift potential output. According to real-business-cycle theory, they are the only sources of fluctuations in output.

Table 22.2 summarizes our discussion of the impact of shifts in aggregate demand and aggregate supply.

Table 22.2   Impact of Shifts in Aggregate Demand and Aggregate Supply on Output and Inflation

	Increase in Aggregate Demand	Positive Inflation Shock	Increase in Potential Output
Source	Consumer confidence up Business optimism up Government purchases up Taxes down Exchange rate depreciates	Labor costs up Raw materials prices up Expected inflation up	Capital in production up Labor in production up Productivity up
Short-Run Effects	Y increases π is unchanged	Y falls π rises	Y unchanged π is unchanged
Path of Adjustment	1. Expansionary output gap puts upward pressure on inflation. 2. As inflation begins to rise, output begins to fall.	1. Recessionary output gap puts downward pressure on inflation. 2. As inflation begins to fall, output begins to rise.	1. Recessionary output gap puts downward pressure on inflation. 2. As inflation begins to fall, output begins to rise.
Long-Run Effects	Y = original potential π = target (may change)	Y = original potential π = target (may change)	Y = new potential π = target (may change)
Effects of Monetary Policy	Inflation will rise temporarily unless the central bank changes its inflation target.	Inflation will rise temporarily unless the central bank changes its inflation target.	Inflation will fall temporarily unless the central bank changes its inflation target.

Short-run equilibrium: Aggregate demand (AD) intersects short-run aggregate supply (SRAS)

Long-run equilibrium: Current output = potential output; inflation = target inflation

APPLYING THE CONCEPT
WHAT CAUSES RECESSIONS?

For years, economists have argued over the cause of recessions. The debate has focused on two possibilities: (1) a change in monetary policy that shifts the aggregate demand curve to the left and (2) an increase in oil prices that causes an inflation shock, shifting the short-run aggregate supply curve upward. Which is it? The answer is that both probably contribute to recessions.

We can use the aggregate demand/aggregate supply model to get some insight into the debate, since it shows how macroeconomic variables change following each disturbance. Remember, after a shift in aggregate demand, output and inflation move in the same direction (see Figure 22.11); after a shift in short-run aggregate supply, output and inflation move in opposite directions (see Figure 22.12). So if monetary policy is the cause of recessions, we should see inflation fall as the result of a shift in aggregate demand. And if oil price increases are the cause of recessions, we should see inflation rise as the economy slows down.

Table 22.3 lists the dates of the recessions that have occurred since the mid-1950s (see Tools of the Trade for a description of how recessions are dated). The peak (column 1) is the beginning of the recession, when economic activity was at its highest before beginning to slow. The trough (column 2) is the lowest point of the recession, when economic activity began to rise. The third column of the table shows the change in inflation from the beginning to the end of the recession. Note that inflation fell in six of the past seven recessions; it rose in only one. The recession of 1973–1975 was the exception. Oil prices tripled in 1973, creating an enormous inflation shock. The results were a protracted recession and a dramatic increase in inflation.

Besides this evidence for the role of monetary policy in creating recessions, it turns out that interest rates rose just before almost every one

STABILITY

Stabilization Policy

The aggregate demand/aggregate supply model is useful in understanding how monetary and fiscal policymakers seek to stabilize output and inflation. In this section we will examine how both groups pursue what is called stabilization policy.

Monetary Policy

In thinking about the way monetary policy can be used to stabilize the economy, we must remember that movements in output and inflation can be caused both by shifts in the aggregate demand curve and by inflation shocks. Policymakers can shift the aggregate demand curve by shifting their monetary policy reaction curve, but they cannot shift the short-run aggregate supply curve. Thus, they can neutralize move-

continued from previous page

Table 22.3   Inflation during Recessions

Peak	Trough	Inflation Change
August 1957	April 1958	3.6 to 3.5 ↓
April 1960	February 1961	1.7 to 1.4 ↓
December 1969	November 1970	5.7 to 5.4 ↓
November 1973	March 1975	7.9 to 10.0 ↑
January 1980	July 1980	13.0 to 12.4 ↓
July 1981	November 1982	10.3 to 4.4 ↓
July 1990	March 1991	4.7 to 4.7 =
March 2001	November 2001	2.9 to 1.8 ↓

SOURCE: *Inflation is the 12-month change in the all-items CPI-U from the Bureau of Labor Statistics. Business-cycle peaks and troughs are from the NBER.*

of them. All this suggests that monetary policy bears the primary responsibility for the occurrence of recessions. But why would policymakers have chosen to cause these recessions? They did it to bring down inflation. Especially after 1980, when inflation was running at close to 15 percent per year, something had to be done. The only thing the Fed could do under such circumstances was to raise interest rates, reducing aggregate demand in the process and triggering a recession. The low inflation we enjoy today is the result of the Fed's tough policy decisions.

ments in aggregate demand, but they cannot eliminate the effects of an inflation shock. And as we will see, increases in productivity that shift the long-run aggregate supply curve provide policymakers with an interesting opportunity.

Shifts in Aggregate Demand   To see how monetary policy can stabilize the economy following a shift in the aggregate demand curve, consider what happens when households and businesses suddenly become more pessimistic about the future. This change in sentiment drives down aggregate demand, shifting the aggregate demand curve to the left. In the absence of any change in monetary policy, this sudden drop in consumer and business confidence would surely cause a recession. As the aggregate demand curve shifts to the left, the economy moves to a new short-run equilibrium point where current output falls short of potential output (see Figure 22.14).

Figure 22.14 Stabilizing a Shift in Aggregate Demand

Following a drop in consumer or business confidence, aggregate demand shifts to the left. To stabilize the economy, the central bank can ease policy, shifting the monetary policy reaction curve to the right. This reduces the real interest rate at every level of inflation and shifts the aggregate demand curve back to where it started. Their action leaves current output and inflation unchanged.

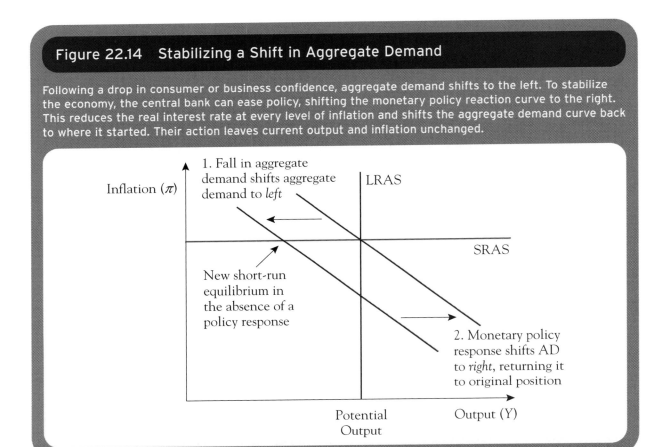

Realizing that household and business confidence has fallen, policymakers will conclude that the long-run real interest rate has gone down. Assuming that their inflation target remains the same, the drop in aggregate demand prompts them to shift their monetary policy reaction curve to the right, reducing the level of the real interest rate at every level of inflation. Recall that when the monetary policy reaction curve shifts, the aggregate demand curve shifts in the same direction. The result is that the policymakers' action shifts the aggregate demand curve back to its initial point, shown in Figure 22.14. In the absence of a policy response, output would fall. Instead, when aggregate demand shifts back to its initial position, output remains steady, along with inflation. Policymakers have neutralized the shift in aggregate demand, keeping current output equal to potential output and current inflation equal to target inflation.

Inflation Shocks and the Policy Trade-off For policymakers, an inflation shock is an entirely different story. Take the case of a positive inflation shock, whose immediate effect is to drive output down and inflation up (refer back to Figure 22.12). Now consider the tools that are available to policymakers. By shifting the monetary policy reaction curve, they can shift the aggregate demand curve, relying on the economy's natural response to an output gap to bring inflation back to target. Is there any way to use this tool to bring the economy back to its original long-run equilibrium point? The answer is no. Monetary policy can shift the aggregate demand curve but not the short-run aggregate supply curve. And there is no shift in aggregate demand that can quickly move the economy back to its original equilibrium point, where current output equals potential output and current inflation equals the central bank's target.

But that isn't the end of the story. In Chapter 21, we learned that monetary policymakers can choose the slope of their monetary policy reaction curve, which in turn affects the slope of the aggregate demand curve. The more aggressive policymakers are in keeping current inflation close to target, the steeper their monetary policy reaction curve and the flatter the aggregate demand curve. So by choosing how steep or flat to make the monetary policy reaction curve, policymakers can control the slope of the aggregate demand curve. In this way they can choose the extent to which inflation shocks translate into changes in output or changes in inflation.

To see how this works, look at Figure 22.15. The top panel shows the case of a central bank that has chosen to respond aggressively to deviations of current inflation from the target level. These policymakers have a steep monetary policy reaction curve: small deviations in inflation from the target level elicit large changes in the real interest rate. (Take a look back at Figure 21.8.) As a result, the aggregate demand curve is flat, which means that an inflation shock will create large changes in current output. So a positive inflation shock like the one shown in Figure 22.15 will drive output down sharply, opening up a large recessionary output gap. We can assume that the larger the output gap, the greater the pressure on inflation. A large recessionary gap should force inflation down faster than a small recessionary gap. In fact, policymakers are counting on that mechanism when they choose to follow this path. By reacting aggressively to inflation shocks, they force current inflation back to target quickly. The cost of following this path, however, is that it causes output to fall substantially.

The bottom panel of Figure 22.15 shows what happens when policymakers are less concerned about keeping inflation close to target in the short run. When policymakers worry more about fluctuations in output than about temporary movements in inflation, they will choose a relatively flat monetary policy reaction curve in which movements in the real interest rate are small, even when inflation strays far from its target level. The result is a steep aggregate demand curve like the one in the bottom panel. Notice what happens in this case following an inflation shock. Once more, inflation rises, creating a recessionary output gap. But the output gap is small, so the downward pressure on inflation is relatively weak. As a result, inflation adjusts slowly, remaining high for a longer period than it would have if policymakers had reacted more aggressively.

In Chapter 21, we quoted the Bank of England's Governor Mervyn King, who said that monetary policy can be characterized as an inflation target plus a response to inflation shocks. The second part of Governor King's statement is now clear. When choosing how aggressively to respond to inflation shocks, central bankers are deciding how to conduct *stabilization policy*. Do they want to ensure that inflation remains near target or that output remains close to potential? When faced with an inflation shock, policymakers cannot stabilize both output and inflation; they must choose one or the other.

Opportunities Created by Increased Productivity

Finally, let's consider what happens when productivity is rising, increasing potential output. This increase in potential output shifts the long-run aggregate supply curve to the right, as shown in Figure 22.13. As we noted earlier, short-run equilibrium is unaffected by this change; inflation and output do not change at first. But eventually the increase in

Figure 22.15 The Policymakers' Choice

A. Respond Aggressively to Keep Current Inflation near Target Inflation
Policymakers who are concerned about keeping current inflation near their target level will choose a steep monetary policy reaction curve. When small changes in inflation generate large changes in the real interest rate, the aggregate demand curve will be relatively flat. Thus, when a positive inflation shock causes the short-run aggregate supply curve to shift upward, current output drops substantially, creating a large recessionary gap that quickly pushes inflation back to target level.

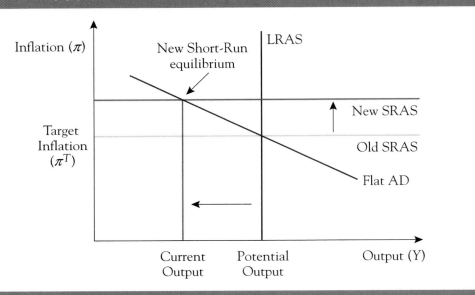

B. Respond Cautiously to Minimize Deviations of Current Output from Potential Output
Policymakers who are concerned about keeping current output near potential output will choose a flat monetary policy reaction curve. When large changes in inflation generate small changes in the real interest rate, the aggregate demand curve will be relatively steep. Thus, when a positive inflation shock causes the short-run aggregate supply curve to shift upward, current output drops only slightly, creating a small recessionary gap that pushes inflation slowly back to target level.

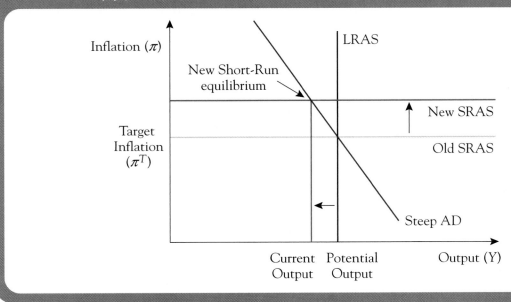

potential output creates a recessionary gap, which exerts downward pressure on inflation. The interesting thing about this situation is that it gives policymakers the opportunity to guide the economy to a new, lower inflation target without inducing a recession.

Policymakers' standard mechanism for reducing inflation is to tighten their monetary policy. In the context of our model, they reduce their inflation target, shifting both the monetary policy reaction curve and the aggregate demand curve to the left. This contractionary policy drives down current output, opening up a recessionary gap that puts downward pressure on inflation. As a result, inflation falls to the new, lower target level. In Chapter 21, we discussed the possibility that monetary policy could be the source of recessions. This is the mechanism that links monetary policy to economic downturns.

When increases in productivity shift the long-run aggregate supply curve to the right, inflation falls even as output rises. Under such circumstances, central bankers can reduce their inflation target without inducing a recession. But they have an alternative. Recall that an increase in potential output lowers the long-run real interest rate. Rather than reducing their inflation target, then, policymakers can simply shift their monetary policy reaction curve to the right, which shifts the aggregate demand curve to the right as well. This action will increase current output quickly, leaving inflation unchanged at the old target level.

Looking back at the 1990s (see Figure 22.1), we see that inflation fell gradually from 5 percent at end of the 1990–91 recession to $1\frac{1}{2}$ percent in 1998. This drop in inflation occurred during an economic boom. Over the last half of the 1990s, economic growth averaged $4\frac{1}{2}$ percent per year, which is one and one-half percentage points above the rate for the preceding 20 years. That is, U.S. productivity grew more rapidly from 1996 to 1999 than it did from 1975 to 1995. In effect, the economy's long-run aggregate supply curve shifted to the right, and when it did the Federal Reserve took the opportunity to allow inflation to fall. Rather than maintain the Fed's implicit inflation target near 5 percent, the FOMC slowly reduced it until it fell below 2 percent.

Fiscal Policy

Central bankers are not the only government officials who can stabilize output and inflation. The people who control the government's tax and expenditure policies can, too. To some extent, changes in fiscal policy can influence aggregate demand. Either a rise in government purchases or a decrease in taxes will increase aggregate demand, shifting the aggregate demand to curve to the right. Thus, fiscal policy can be used just like monetary policy to neutralize shocks to aggregate demand and stabilize inflation and output. In fact, it has been used in exactly that way on a number of occasions. In 2001 and 2002, for example, tax cuts clearly boosted aggregate demand, helping to moderate the recession.

At least in principle, then, fiscal policy would seem to offer a clear alternative to monetary policy. On closer examination, however, we can see that it has at least two defects: It works slowly and is almost impossible to implement effectively. First, most recessions are short, lasting a year or less. The longest post–World War II recession in the United States spanned 16 months (see Table 22.1). Furthermore, since economic data only become available several months after they are collected, we are often halfway through a recession before a consensus has developed on whether a recession has actually started. Under even the best of circumstances, Congress can't pass new legislation in less than several months. And fiscal policies do not have an immediate impact. Even after a tax cut has been passed, individual consumption and corporate

APPLYING THE CONCEPT
DO TAX CUTS REALLY STIMULATE THE ECONOMY?

Whenever a recession begins, causing incomes to fall and people to lose their jobs, politicians think they should do something about it. To raise output and employment, legislators look for ways to shift the aggregate demand curve upward and to the right. Since they control fiscal policy, they typically attempt to cut taxes. The logic of the last section of this chapter suggests that such an approach should work. Tax cuts raise people's disposable income—that's their after-tax income—spurring consumption, a component of total spending. Thus, they should increase aggregate demand.

But a closer look suggests that the solution isn't so simple. The fact is, cutting taxes may or may not stimulate the economy. To understand why, we need to realize that tax cuts increase the government's deficit. After all, no politician would cut taxes *and* spending during a recession. A larger deficit means more government borrowing, and that's the problem. To finance the deficit, the government issues bonds that will have to be repaid. Government bonds are, in essence, a promise to raise taxes at some future date. So while a deficit-financed tax cut may raise taxpayers' disposable income today, it means higher taxes and lower disposable income tomorrow.* If people realize that, they will conclude that the tax cut has no real impact on their well-being, and they won't change their spending plans.

Another way to think about this is to take a simple economy in which everyone is the same, so we can consider a single representative individual—you. Like everyone else, you work, receive income, and pay taxes. Now think about what happens when the government cuts your taxes. To finance the tax cut, the government must borrow money by issuing a bond. Since you're the only person in our simplified economy, you must buy the government's bond. Remember, a bond is a promise by the issuer to repay the principal plus interest to the holder. So the bond is the government's promise to repay you. But taxes are the government's only source of revenue, and you are the only taxpayer in the economy. So the bond is the government's promise to tax you in order to repay you. How could that arrangement possibly affect your behavior?

This example is extreme, but there is some truth to it. The fact that individuals understand that government bonds represent an increase in future taxes does reduce the impact on aggregate demand of a deficit-financed increase in government purchases. Inevitably, some people will compensate for the expected increase in future taxes by refusing to change their behavior. But people differ. Some may not have to pay higher taxes in the future, when the bonds come due, so they will increase their consumption, raising aggregate demand in the process. In short, tax cuts do stimulate the economy, but their impact is blunted by people's understanding of what government bonds represent.

*The value of the bonds that are issued to finance the government's deficit is exactly equal to the present value of the future taxes, so in present-value terms, the bonds offset the tax cut perfectly.

investment tend to remain sluggish. Odds are that, by the time the spending does start, the recession will be over.

The problems with fiscal policy don't end there, because economists don't write economic stimulus packages; politicians do. And economics clearly collides with politics where fiscal stimulus is concerned. Economists prefer policies that influence a few key people to do something they were not doing. They try to avoid paying people to do what they would have done anyway. Thus, economists advocate temporary investment incentives and income tax reductions targeted toward those who are less well off. In contrast, politicians look for programs that reward the largest number of people possible, to ensure their re-election. Their economic stimulus packages are based more on political calculation than on economic logic. Though we can't hold public officials' opportunism against them, we need to recognize its existence. Because politicians want to remain popular with their constituencies, economic slowdowns—when some voters are suffering and the rest are worried—play to their worst instincts. In short, discretionary fiscal policy is an extraordinarily poor stabilization tool. While an economically sensible stimulus package can be designed, such legislation does not often become law.

Under most circumstances, then, stabilization policy should be left to the central bankers, who have both the ability to act quickly and the independence to put the economy before politics. Fiscal policy does have a role in economic stabilization, but only after monetary policy has run its course—when conditions are so bad that using every available tool makes sense.

IN THE NEWS
The Real Threat of Stagnation

Financial Times

August 31, 2002

Markets and economies never move exactly in tandem. But this year it has been even harder than usual to link equity markets with economic prospects.

Until midsummer, optimism about global economic recovery had been running high. Markets, though, were distinctly unimpressed, stagnating until May and falling rapidly in June and July. Since the U.S. equity market trough on July 23, stock markets have staged a robust recovery. The S&P 500 index of U.S. shares has risen about 16 percent and European stock markets are up a little more than 10 percent. But investors' joy has coincided with a new bout of pessimism among economists.

Growing concerns are reflected in the theme of this year's gathering of central bankers and academic economists in the Rocky Mountain resort of Jackson Hole. Discussions this weekend are centered on "rethinking stabilization policy."

In part, the darker economic picture is a simple reflection of recent troubles in the equity and corporate bond markets. But more important have been the disappointing economic data that have emerged since the spring, fears of war in the Gulf, and a nervousness that past excess in the financial markets of the late 1990s may leave long-lasting economic scars.

The large economies are simply not growing as fast as had been hoped this year, despite extremely low interest rates across the developed world. Growth in the U.S. has slowed sharply. In the second quarter, it managed to grow at an annualized rate of only 1.1 percent; and even that rate was flattered by companies rebuilding their inventories. With investment continuing to fall, the prospects for fast productivity growth have deteriorated.

In Europe, domestic demand refuses to take off as hoped. Consumers and companies show no sign of increasing their spending. Instead, growing unemployment dominates the public debate.

Although there has been a welcome rebound in growth in east Asia, Japan's stagnation continues.

continued on next page

continued from previous page

Yesterday a massive downward revision to Japan's economic growth figures dashed hopes of a rebound. Rather than an economy growing at an annual rate of 5.8 percent in the first quarter, authorities now believe there was no growth at all.

Disappointing data this summer have been compounded by rising oil prices stemming from fears of war in Iraq. So the unintended consequence of growing U.S. pressure on the Iraqi regime has been to increase the costs of doing business at home.

And perhaps the greatest cause for concern is that in many advanced economies, consumer spending can no longer be relied on to keep driving economic growth. If, as seems increasingly likely, the excesses of the 1990s encouraged spending to grow faster than was sustainable, the subsequent return to reality will persuade many consumers to increase their savings. Such an adjustment could have extremely destabilizing effects; you need look no further than Japan to see how difficult asset price declines can be to manage.

So none of the central bankers at Jackson Hole should be under any illusion about the balance of risks in the global economy. Inflationary risks are minimal. In fact, a little more inflation would help mitigate the debt burden of overextended households and companies. But the risk of long-term stagnation has grown.

If monetary policy was appropriate in the spring, it must be too tight now. It would be better to risk interest rates falling to zero to avoid stagnation than to ensure that outcome by doing nothing.

Governments, too, should allow their budget deficits to rise as tax revenues fall below forecast and spending on Social Security grows. If that means embarrassment for the European stability and growth pact, which attempts to limit budget deficits to 3 percent of gross domestic product, so be it.

Further fiscal action should be avoided, though, because its effects are ambiguous and often ill timed and government budgets are not as healthy as was thought. The U.S. administration's talk of further capital gains tax reductions, for example, would do nothing for immediate economic prospects but would damage its credibility for long-term budget management.

Steady, sustainable economic growth is the ambition of all policymakers. It also provides the best conditions for healthy investment returns. But in the current economic climate, with the forces of stagnation strong, achieving decent rates of growth will be difficult. Stability alone is perhaps an investor's best hope until the hangover from the 1990s is fully past.

LESSON OF THE ARTICLE

In the summer of 2002, as the global economy continued to sputter, the major threat to the economy was the possibility that economic growth would remain low. Consequently, both monetary and fiscal policymakers needed to do whatever they could to get the economy moving again. Central banks were advised to reduce interest rates, which they did. Governments were advised to allow the decline in tax receipts to increase the deficit, which they did. By and large, this approach worked well, since the world economy regained some of its momentum the following year and economic growth increased.

Terms

disinflation, 601

inflation persistence, 585

inflation shock, 590

long-run aggregate supply curve (LRAS), 591

real-business-cycle theory, 604

short-run aggregate supply curve (SRAS), 585

stabilization policy, 606

Chapter Lessons

1. The aggregate supply curve tells us the amount of output producers are willing to supply at given levels of inflation.

    a. The short-run aggregate supply curve is flat because of inflation persistence.

    b. Inflation is persistent because

        i. People expect that future inflation will be the same as past inflation.

        ii. Not everyone changes prices and wages simultaneously.

    c. The short-run aggregate supply curve shifts when current output deviates from potential output, creating an output gap.

        i. When output rises above potential, the short-run aggregate supply curve shifts upward.

        ii. When output falls below potential, the short-run aggregate supply curve shifts downward.

    d. The short-run aggregate supply curve shifts upward in response to an inflation shock—a higher-than-expected increase in the costs of production.

    e. The long-run aggregate supply curve is vertical at potential output.

        i. Along the long-run aggregate supply curve, expected inflation equals current inflation.

        ii. The long-run aggregate supply curve shifts (1) when the amounts of capital and labor used in the economy change and (2) when productivity changes.

2. Equilibrium output and inflation are determined by the intersection of the aggregate demand curve with the short-run or long-run aggregate supply curve.

    a. The short-run equilibrium point is located where the aggregate demand curve intersects the short-run aggregate supply curve.

    b. The long-run equilibrium point is located where the aggregate demand curve intersects the long-run aggregate supply curve. At that point, current output equals potential output and inflation equals the inflation target, which equals expected inflation.

    c. An increase in aggregate demand shifts the aggregate demand curve to the right.

        i. In the short run, this shift in aggregate demand increases output but leaves inflation unchanged.

        ii. In the long run, such a shift creates an expansionary output gap, exerting upward pressure on inflation.

        iii. To keep inflation from rising, monetary policymakers respond to the shift by raising the real interest rate.

        iv. Unless the central bank's target inflation changes, the economy will eventually return to its original long-run equilibrium point.

    d. A positive inflation shock shifts the short-run aggregate supply curve upward.

        i. In the short run, this shift in aggregate supply decreases output and increases inflation.

        ii. In the long run, such a shift creates a recessionary output gap that places downward pressure on inflation.

    iii. Unless the central bank's target inflation changes, the economy will eventually return to its original long-run equilibrium point.

  e. An increase in potential output shifts the long-run aggregate supply curve to the right.

    i. In the short run, output and inflation remain unchanged.

    ii. In the long run, such a shift in aggregate supply creates a recessionary output gap, exerting downward pressure on inflation.

    iii. Over time, output will begin to rise and inflation to fall.

    iv. In the long run, current output will rise to the new level of potential output.

    v. Unless the central bank's target inflation changes, inflation will eventually return to its original level.

3. Stabilization policy is the use of monetary and fiscal policy tools to stabilize output and inflation.

  a. Monetary policy can be used to shift the aggregate demand curve in order to neutralize changes in aggregate demand.

  b. When faced with an inflation shock, monetary policymakers must choose whether to stabilize output or inflation; they cannot stabilize both.

  c. Like monetary policy, fiscal policy can be used to shift the aggregate demand curve in order to neutralize changes in aggregate demand. Fiscal policy can be implemented through a change in taxes and/or government purchases.

  d. Unlike monetary policy, fiscal policy is difficult to implement quickly and effectively.

Problems

1. The economy has been sluggish, so in an effort to increase growth, government officials have decided to cut taxes. They are considering two possible tax cuts of equal size. The first would reduce the taxes everyone pays by 10 percent. The second would eliminate taxes on people in the lowest income bracket, leaving everyone else's taxes the same. Does it matter which one of these plans the government implements? Why or why not?

2. Assume that current output is below potential output. Draw this situation on an aggregate demand/aggregate supply diagram. On the same diagram, show what will happen to inflation and output over time. Describe why the curves you have drawn will shift in the way you have described.

3. Interest rates tend to rise just before a recession. Is this phenomenon evidence that monetary policymakers are responsible for the business cycle? Why or why not?

4. Define the term *stabilization policy* and describe how it can be used to reduce the volatility of economic growth and inflation. Do stabilization policies improve everyone's welfare? Should government authorities pursue economic stabilization? Why or why not?

5. Congress has decided to change the tax system by eliminating the personal income tax and replacing it with a national sales tax. How would such a change affect aggregate demand and aggregate supply?

6. There are two possible sources of inflation, shifts in aggregate demand and inflation shocks. Describe each source in detail and illustrate how it influences inflation using the aggregate demand/aggregate supply diagram.

7. Germany has been suffering from a chronically high level of unemployment. Economists have identified two causes of this problem: the high taxes German companies must pay whenever they hire a new worker and the fact that firing workers is nearly impossible. After listening to the economists' advice, German politicians have decided to change the tax law to reduce the cost of employing workers. What will be the immediate and long-term impacts of this change in taxes on output and inflation?

8. The president has requested, and Congress has passed, a dramatic cut in taxes, but it has left government expenditures unchanged, thus increasing the budget deficit. Using the tools presented in this chapter, explain what would happen in each of the following cases.

   a. Everyone concludes that in the future, the government will need to raise taxes in order to pay off the bonds it is issuing to finance the tax cut.

   b. Everyone suspects that the government's new bonds will be purchased by the Federal Reserve and inflation will rise as a result.

9. One morning you wake up to the startling news that scientists have perfected a process called cold fusion, through which they can generate power directly from water. Instead of going to the gas station, car owners will soon be able to fill their tanks with a garden hose and homeowners will be able to run their appliances on tap water. Describe the immediate and long-term impacts of this technological innovation on output and inflation.

10. Foreign investors suddenly lose faith in their U.S. investments and begin to sell them, driving down the value of the U.S. dollar. Describe how this change in investment will affect total spending, aggregate demand, output, and inflation. Design a policy response that will stabilize the economy.

11. After years of double-digit inflation, the central bank of the small Pacific island nation of Ganji announces a new anti-inflation policy. Ganjians believe the new policy will work, so they lower their expectations of future inflation almost immediately. What will happen to aggregate demand, aggregate supply, output, and inflation as a result? What would happen if the central bankers lacked credibility so that no one in Ganji believed them?

12. Will changes in technology affect the rate at which the short-run aggregate supply curve shifts in response to an output gap? Why or why not? Provide some specific examples of how technology will change the rate of adjustment.

13. Examine the American inflation experience beginning in 1990. Using the aggregate demand/aggregate supply model, provide at least one explanation for the path you see.

14. Go to FRED II at http://research.stlouisfed.org/fred2/ and collect data on output per hour in U.S. nonfarm business since 1990. Compute the percentage change in productivity. Compare this plot to the plot of inflation data at the beginning of this chapter. Is this an example of opportunistic disinflation?

15. The 2001 U.S. recession was extremely mild. Can you explain why? Be sure to use information on the path of interest rates in your answer.

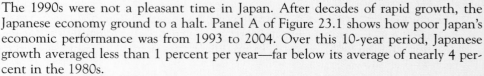

Chapter 23

Monetary Policy, Output, & Inflation in the Short Run

The 1990s were not a pleasant time in Japan. After decades of rapid growth, the Japanese economy ground to a halt. Panel A of Figure 23.1 shows how poor Japan's economic performance was from 1993 to 2004. Over this 10-year period, Japanese growth averaged less than 1 percent per year—far below its average of nearly 4 percent in the 1980s.

Japanese policymakers took action, lowering interest rates throughout the decade. Panel B of Figure 23.1 shows the downward path of the overnight cash rate, the Bank of Japan's policy instrument. Finally, in the winter of 1999, the Bank's policy board lowered the target interest rate to zero. Still, growth didn't pick up. With the interest rate at zero, there didn't appear to be much more the Bank of Japan could do. Nominal interest rates can't fall below zero.

Japan's experience in the 1990s contrasted sharply with that of the United States. While Japan's economy was floundering, the U.S. economy was booming: growth averaged nearly 4 percent per year from 1995 to 2000 (see Panel A of Figure 23.2). During this period, the Fed eased policy several times, and growth appeared to respond. As Panel B of Figure 23.2 shows, the FOMC lowered the targeted federal funds rate in the fall of 1998, in response to world financial crises,[1] and then raised it two years later in an effort to keep inflation from rising. When the economy finally did slow in 2001, the FOMC reduced the interest rate. The result was a quick recovery: in less than a year, the recession was over. Still, disappointed with the level of growth, the FOMC continued to ease rates until on June 25, 2003, the target federal funds rate hit 1 percent. At that point, people began to voice concern that U.S. policymakers might be traveling down the same road as the Bank of Japan. Were they?

The aggregate demand/aggregate supply framework described in Chapters 21 and 22 helps us to understand the sources of inflation and fluctuations in the business cycle, as well as how stabilization policy works. But it cannot explain what happened in Japan in the 1990s, nor did it provide any guide for the FOMC when the federal funds rate dropped near zero. To understand these cases, we must return to the question of how monetary policy affects the economy.

We know from Chapter 17 that policymakers' ability to influence the economy comes from their control over the size of the central bank's balance sheet. And we know from Chapter 18 that they can use their power over the balance sheet to control the interest rate banks charge each other for overnight loans. Because inflation is persistent, changing only slowly, policymakers can use this tool to influence the short-run real interest rate. In Chapter 21, we saw that the components of aggregate expenditure are sensitive to the real interest rate, so by changing the real interest

---

[1]The crises of 1997 and 1998 have been mentioned at various points in this book. They first began in the summer of 1997 with problems in Thailand (described in Chapters 17 and 19) and Indonesia, then spread to Korea by the end of the year (see Chapter 10). In 1998, the Fed reduced the interest rate in response to problems caused by the Russian government's bond default (discussed in Chapter 6) and the collapse of Long-Term Capital Management (examined in Chapter 9).

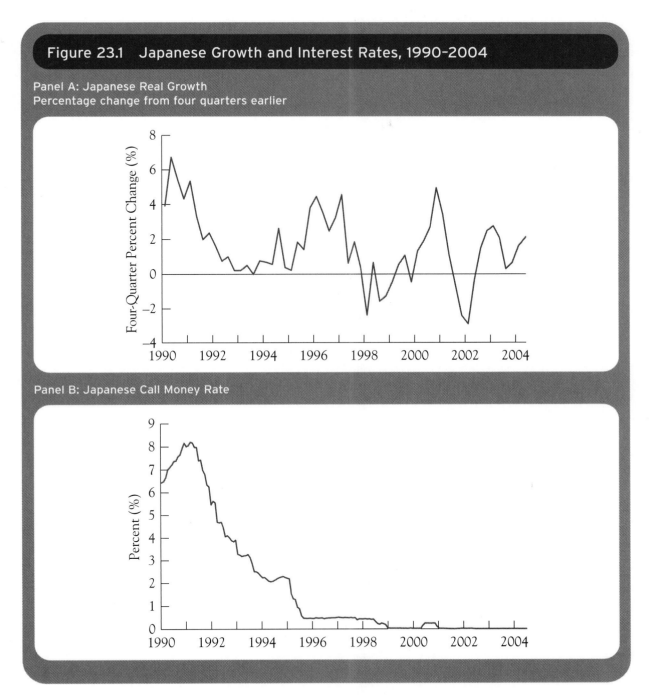

Figure 23.1   Japanese Growth and Interest Rates, 1990-2004

Panel A: Japanese Real Growth
Percentage change from four quarters earlier

Panel B: Japanese Call Money Rate

SOURCE: *Bank of Japan.*

rate, policymakers can influence real economic activity. Yet the Japanese experience suggests that this standard policy tool doesn't always work. To see why, we need to look at all the ways monetary policy actions can affect economic activity. That means recalling the role of financial intermediaries in solving the information problems that keep lenders and savers apart.

Figure 23.2 U.S. Growth and Interest Rates, 1990-2004

Panel A: U.S. GDP Growth
Percentage Change from Four Quarters Earlier

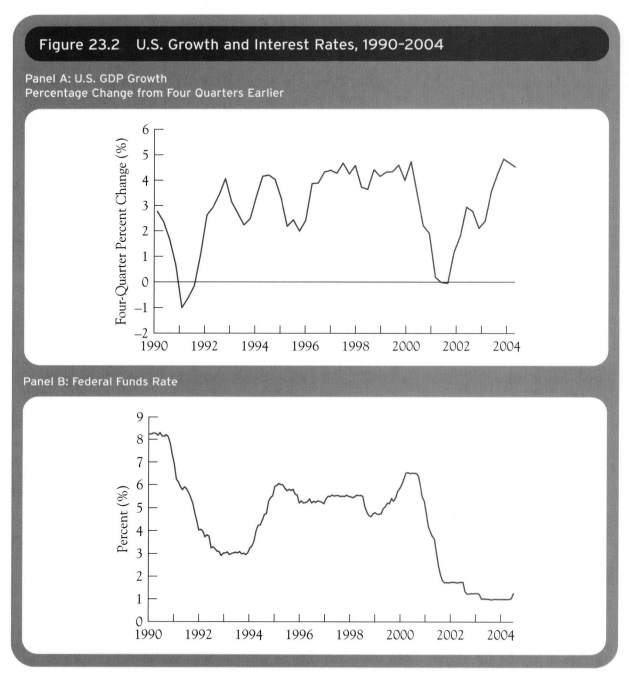

Panel B: Federal Funds Rate

SOURCE: *U.S. GDP data are from the Bureau of Economic Analysis, and federal funds data are from the Federal Reserve.*

The purpose of this chapter is twofold. First, we will examine all the ways that monetary policy affects real economic activity—that is, all the channels through which monetary policy is transmitted. Second, we will look at the challenges central bankers face today. What are the factors that make modern monetary policy so difficult?

The Monetary Policy Transmission Mechanism

Any time the central bank alters the size of its balance sheet, the effects ripple through the economy, changing nearly everyone's behavior. Households adjust their spending on houses and cars. Companies rethink their decisions about how much and how fast to grow. Exchange rates change, bond and stock prices move, and banks adjust their balance sheets. In fact, we would be challenged to find a financial or economic decision that is unaffected. To fully appreciate how monetary policy works, then, we need to examine all the ways in which it affects the economy. These are referred to collectively as the channels of the **monetary policy transmission mechanism**. We will begin with the traditional **interest-rate** and **exchange-rate channels**. Next we will study the importance of stock price movements and finally the role of banks.

The Traditional Channels: Interest Rates and Exchange Rates

Central banks, such as the Federal Reserve, the European Central Bank, and the Bank of Japan, target a very short-term (usually overnight) interest rate. In the Fed's case, for example, a policy change is a change in the target federal funds rate. And as we saw in Chapter 21, a change in the monetary policymakers' target interest rate represents a change in the real interest rate, which has a direct effect on total spending. The lower the real interest rate, the higher investment, consumption, and net exports will be.

Let's review this process. As the real interest rate falls, financing becomes less expensive, so firms become more likely to undertake investment projects and families more likely to purchase new cars. Changes in the real interest rate also affect the exchange rate. When the real interest rate falls, investor demand for U.S. assets falls with it, lowering the demand for and increasing the supply of dollars, reducing its value (see Chapter 19, Figure 19.2). That is, an easing of monetary policy—by which we mean a decrease in the target nominal interest rate, which lowers the real interest rate—leads to a depreciation of the dollar. A less valuable dollar, in turn, drives up the cost of imported goods and services, reducing imports from abroad. At the same time, however, the lower value of the dollar makes U.S. goods and services cheaper to foreigners, so they will buy more of them. Together, lower imports and higher exports mean higher net exports, or an increase in total spending.

While these traditional channels of monetary policy transmission make sense theoretically, they present a practical problem. Though changes in monetary policy do influence firms' decisions to purchase new equipment and build new buildings, the interest-rate channel appears to be a weak one. That is, data suggest that the investment component of total spending isn't very sensitive to interest rates, which should not be a surprise to us. At the end of our discussion of financial intermediation in Chapter 11, we saw that information problems often make external financing too difficult and costly for firms to undertake, either directly in the financial markets or indirectly through institutions. As a result, the vast majority of investments are financed by businesses themselves, through their own funds. So while a change in the interest rate does change the cost of external financing, it doesn't have much of an effect on investment decisions, because not many companies obtain their funds that way.

The impact of short-term interest rates on household decisions is also rather modest. The problem is that people's decisions to purchase cars or houses depend on longer-term interest rates rather than the policymakers' short-run target rate. So household consumption decisions will change only to the extent that changing the target interest rate affects long-term interest rates. And the overall effect isn't that large.

As for the effect of monetary policy on the exchange rate, once again, theory and practice differ. In the real world, the policy-controlled interest rate is just one of many factors that shift the demand and supply for the dollar on foreign exchange markets. The rather long list, described in Chapter 10, includes a change in the riskiness of domestic investment relative to foreign investment; a change in the preference of U.S. consumers for foreign-produced goods and services; and a change in foreigners' income and wealth. The influence of these other factors renders the impact of monetary policy on the exchange rate and net exports unpredictable.

Thus, after careful analysis, we must conclude that the traditional channels of monetary policy transmission aren't very powerful. Yet evidence shows that monetary policy *is* effective. Something else must be amplifying the impact of monetary policy changes on real economic activity. Otherwise, no one would care about the central bank's periodic policy statements. To figure out what that link might be, we turn now to a discussion of two alternative transmission channels: the stock and real estate markets, and the behavior of banks.

Asset Price Channels: Wealth and Investment

When the interest rate moves, so do stock prices. Specifically, a fall in the interest rate tends to push stock prices up. This relationship between the interest rate and the stock market is referred to as the asset price channel of monetary policy transmission. To understand it, we must first figure out why a change in the interest rate might cause a movement in stock prices. Then we must explain how a change in stock prices can influence aggregate demand.

To see how the interest rate influences stock prices, recall from Chapter 8 that the fundamental value of a stock is the present value of the stream of its future dividends. The lower the interest rate is, the higher the present value is and, therefore, the higher the stock price will be. Added to this relationship is the fact that an easing of monetary policy might well improve consumer and business confidence in the prospects for future growth. More growth means more revenue and higher profits and that, too, will drive up stock prices. In fact, stock prices will rise in anticipation of a cut in the interest rate.[2]

Monetary policy affects real estate markets in the same way that it influences stock markets. The mechanism is straightforward. When policymakers reduce their interest-rate target, it drives the mortgage rate down (see Your Financial World: What the Federal Funds Rate Means to You in Chapter 18). Lower mortgage rates mean higher demand for residential housing, driving up the prices of existing homes.

In short, when the central bank reduces its target interest rate, the stock and real estate markets are likely to boom. Then what? Stock and property prices affect both individual consumption and business investment. For individuals, a rise in stock and real estate prices means an increase in wealth. The richer people become, the more they will consume. If stock values go high enough, shareholders can actually buy the luxury cars they have been wanting, or take the fancy vacations they've been dreaming of, or maybe both. The conclusion is that higher asset prices mean increased wealth and raised consumption.

[2]Because current stock prices are based largely on expectations for future growth and future interest rates, they tend to rise before an easing of monetary policy. The business news often contains reports of a rise in the stock market after a cut in the interest rate becomes more likely, in the judgment of financial market participants.

TOOLS OF THE TRADE
Correlation Does Not Imply Causality

Suppose we notice that the higher the crime rate in a neighborhood, the more often police are present. Should we infer that the police are causing crime? Surely not. Nor should we conclude from the fact that hospitals are filled with doctors that doctors make people ill. A fundamental principal of sound logical reasoning is that correlation does not imply causality. The fact that two events happened together does not indicate a causal link.[*]

In the physical sciences, where researchers can conduct controlled experiments, establishing a causal link is not a serious challenge. We know from scientific trials that antibiotic drugs really do eliminate infections. It's not just chance that the people who take them feel better. But in economics, establishing a causal relationship is much more difficult. How can we be sure that monetary policy affects real economic activity? Our theories tell us that when policymakers raise the nominal interest rate, the real interest rate goes up, depressing aggregate demand and lowering real economic activity. But do we have any hard and fast evidence of this relationship?

The answer is that we do have some evidence that higher interest rates are associated with lower levels of real growth. Look back at Figure 21.10 (page 576), and you'll see the pattern: when interest rates rise, growth falls. But does that mean that increases in the interest rate *cause* recessions? What if, simultaneously, an increase in oil prices depresses real growth, causing policymakers to raise the interest rate in order to head off rising inflation? That is, what if some third factor drives up the interest rate, driving growth down at the same time? In that case, the interest rate becomes another implication of the fundamental cause of recession, an increase in oil prices.

How can we eliminate this problem and determine the extent to which monetary policy actually causes economic fluctuations? The answer is that

we need to look for clear evidence that particular monetary policy actions are unrelated to this sort of third factor. Some years ago, Christina Romer and David Romer of the University of California at Berkeley read through the records of the Federal Reserve's interest-rate decisions since 1946. They identified a series of dates on which FOMC members stated unambiguously that they were raising interest rates to combat inflation. Each of these episodes was followed by a recession. Romer and Romer argued that, because the intention in each of these instances was to fight inflation, the FOMC's actions were not the result of the level of GDP at the time. That is, the committee's policy actions were independent of output conditions.[†]

While most economists today accept the proposition that monetary policy can affect the real economy, Romer and Romer's evidence is open to interpretation. Critics argue that they failed to establish a true causal link between monetary policy and the real economy, since the decisions taken on the dates they identified could have been predicted from economic conditions. Policymakers were not running an experiment to see whether they could cause a recession; they were reacting to the economic environment. And events like a change in oil prices could well cause interest rates to rise and output to fall. In economics, finding clear and indisputable evidence of causality is extremely difficult.

---

[*]Similarly, the fact that two events are *not* correlated does not mean that one does not cause the other. If, for example, policymakers are completely successful in stabilizing inflation, holding it literally constant, then inflation will be uncorrelated to other economic variables.

[†]See Christina D. Romer and David H. Romer, "Does Monetary Policy Matter? A New Test in the Spirit of Friedman and Schwartz," in O. J. Blanchard and S. Fischer, eds., *NBER Macroeconomic Annual* (Cambridge, MA: MIT Press, 1989), pp. 121–170. Romer and Romer's work takes after the classic work that established the importance of monetary policy, *A Monetary History of the United States*, by Milton Friedman and Anna Schwartz (Princeton, NJ: Princeton University Press, 1963). Friedman and Schwartz proposed that monetary policy is an important determinant of output and inflation. They showed first that money growth is associated with growth in output and then found examples of events that established the causal link between monetary policy and output. The most important of these examples was an increase in the reserve requirement in 1937, which reduced the quantity of money in the economy and led to a contraction in real economic activity.

Just as consumption is affected by stock price movements, so is investment. As stock prices rise, firms find it easier to raise funds by issuing new shares. That is, they gain access to financing in the primary capital market. To see why, think of a simple example in which the price of a company's stock suddenly increases. In the meantime, nothing has happened to the cost of a new investment and hence to its internal rate of return. But at the higher stock price, financing is now cheaper. This story should sound familiar. Recall the way in which the traditional *interest-rate channel* influences investment: a lower real interest rate means a lower cost of financing, which raises the profitability of investment projects. As a result, borderline investment projects suddenly become profitable when real interest rates fall. The same thing happens when stock prices rise. As financing becomes less expensive, more investments become profitable. In short, when asset markets boom, so does business investment in new equipment and buildings.[3]

Bank Lending and Balance-Sheet Channels

Four times a year the Federal Reserve conducts an opinion survey on bank lending practices. Addressed to the senior loan officers who oversee lending policies at the 60 or so largest banks in the country, the survey contains questions about both the demand for and the supply of loans. On the demand side, the questions have to do with the quantity and quality of loan applications. On the supply side, they have to do with the relative difficulty of getting a loan, as well as the rates borrowers must pay. This survey provides important information to monetary policymakers. Without it, they would not be able to tell whether a change in the quantity of new loans granted resulted from a shift in supply or a shift in demand. Was a drop in the quantity of new loans the result of fewer applications or a tightening of credit standards? Did interest-rate spreads climb because the quality of borrowers declined or because banks became more stingy? Policymakers at the Fed care about the answers to these questions because if banks stop making loans, businesses can't borrow to finance their investment projects, and economic growth will slow.

The fact is that banks are essential to the operation of a modern industrial economy. They direct resources from savers to investors and solve problems caused by information asymmetries. In Chapter 11, we noted that financial intermediaries specialize in screening borrowers to ensure they are creditworthy. Financial institutions also monitor loan recipients to guarantee that they use borrowed funds as they said they would. But banks are not only the hub of the financial system; they are also the conduit through which monetary policy is transmitted to the economy. When policymakers change the size of the central bank's balance sheet, their action has an immediate impact on commercial bank balance sheets because it affects the level of reserves they hold. To understand monetary policy changes completely, then, we need to look carefully at how they affect the banking system. That means we need to examine the impact of policy changes on banks and bank lending.

Banks and Bank Lending

For the vast majority of individuals and firms, the cost of issuing either stocks or bonds is prohibitive. These borrowers do not have access to direct capital market financing; instead, they must go to banks, which step

---

[3]This line of reasoning, known as *Tobin's q-theory*, was originally developed by the Nobel Prize-winning economist James Tobin. Tobin pointed out that the question of whether or not a firm invests should depend on the ratio of the market value of its shares to the replacement cost of its plant and equipment, which he called q. When q is greater than one—that is, when a firm's stock-market value exceeds its cost of rebuilding—investment in new plant and equipment is cheap relative to the value placed on it in the financial markets. When q is less than one, embarking on new investments isn't worthwhile.

in to reduce the information costs small borrowers face. A small business that is denied a bank loan has nowhere else to turn, so the project it wishes to undertake goes unfunded. When banks stop lending, then, a large class of borrowers simply can't obtain financing. Thus, bank lending is an important channel through which monetary policy affects the economy.[4] By altering the supply of funds to the banking system, policymakers can affect banks' ability and willingness to lend. This policy mechanism is referred to as the bank lending channel of monetary policy transmission.

To see how the banking lending channel works, think about the immediate consequences of an open market purchase (see Figure 17.3 on page 434). Recall that an open market operation involves an exchange of securities for reserves between the banking system and the central bank. When the central bank purchases securities from commercial banks, it pays for them with reserves. So after an open market purchase, banks have fewer interest-bearing securities and more noninterest-bearing reserves. Unless bank managers do something, their revenues will fall. The natural reaction of the banks is to lend the new funds. These new loans work their way through the banking system through the process of multiple deposit creation, increasing the supply of loans throughout the economy. (Take a look back at the section on the deposit expansion multiplier in Chapter 17, pages 440–445.) In short, an open market purchase has a direct impact on the supply of loans, increasing their availability to those who depend on banks for financing.

Monetary policymakers are not the only people who can influence bank lending practices. Financial regulators can, too. Changes in financial regulations, such as an

---

[4]Studies of how and why monetary policy is transmitted through bank lending and balance sheets include Ben Bernanke and Mark Gertler, "Inside the Black Box: The Credit Channel of Monetary Policy Transmission," *Journal of Economic Perspectives* 9 (Fall 1995), pp. 27–45; and Anil K Kashyap and Jeremy Stein, "Monetary Policy and Bank Lending," in N. Gregory Mankiw, ed., *Monetary Policy*, (Chicago, IL: University of Chicago Press for NBER, 1994), pp. 221–256.

YOUR FINANCIAL WORLD
Don't Count on Inflation to Bail You Out

When policymakers lower interest rates, their aim is to encourage people to borrow. Central bankers know that low-interest mortgages make it possible for people to buy homes they otherwise couldn't afford. And low-interest car loans allow them to buy a new car earlier than they would otherwise. In lowering interest rates, the FOMC is counting on a surge in borrowing to drive output higher. But while the increase in debt may help the economy as a whole, it can be dangerous for individuals. They may borrow too much and end up with more debt than they can manage.

The problem with debt is that it must be repaid. Making sure you can repay your debts means carefully calculating what you can afford—not just now but over the entire term of the loan. To avoid overextending yourself, don't borrow on the assumption

that your income is going to rise rapidly. While you will almost surely receive annual increases in your real wage (adjusted for inflation), they are likely to be fairly modest. In fact, for the economy as a whole, pay raises tend to match the rate of productivity growth, which is usually between 2 and 3 percent. So don't be tempted into thinking that, though your budget may be tight when you take out a loan, future salary raises will remedy the problem.

The strategy of counting on salary increases to help eliminate debt amounts to counting on inflation to bail you out. It's true that inflation can be helpful to people who are in debt because it reduces the burden of repayment. But if policymakers at the Fed are doing their job, which is to keep inflation low, hoping inflation will help you pay off your loans is a strategy that is likely to backfire.

increase or decrease in the amount of capital banks are required to hold when they make certain types of loans, will have an impact on the amount of bank lending as well. In 1980, for example, President Jimmy Carter authorized the Federal Reserve to impose a series of credit controls in an attempt to reduce bank lending and, with it, aggregate demand and inflation. A mild recession followed. In the early 1990s, the economy failed to make a strong recovery from the recession after the first Gulf War. Careful examination of the historical record suggests that the disappointing economic performance was a direct consequence of a slowdown in bank lending. At the time, bank balance sheets were very weak, having been eroded by large loan losses during the banking crises of the 1980s. When an increase in capital requirements was added to the banks' already heavy burden, the result was a reduction in lending.

Firms' Balance Sheets and Household Net Worth

Besides its influence on the willingness of banks to lend, monetary policy has an important effect on the creditworthiness of borrowers—or at least on their perceived creditworthiness. This balance-sheet channel of monetary policy transmission works because monetary policy has a direct influence on the net worth of potential borrowers. Specifically, an easing of monetary policy improves firms' and households' balance sheets, increasing their net worth. In turn, these increases in net worth reduce the problems of moral hazard and adverse selection, lowering the information costs of lending and allowing borrowers to obtain financing more easily. Recall from Chapter 11 that the higher the net worth of a borrower, the more likely that the lender will be repaid.

There are two ways in which a monetary policy expansion can improve borrowers' net worth. First, as we have already discussed, an expansionary policy drives up asset prices, increasing the value of firms and the wealth of households. Higher equity and property prices mean higher net worth, which implies lower information costs and greater ease in obtaining financing. The increase in home equity loans that follows a real estate boom is an example of this process. With an increase in household wealth, banks are willing to step up their lending.

The second way that a monetary policy expansion can improve borrowers' net worth has to do with the drop in interest rates. Most borrowers already have loans that they are in the process of repaying; lower interest rates reduce the burden of repayment. For a firm, the drop in the cost of financing increases the difference between revenues and expenses, raising profits and increasing the firm's value. Something similar happens for individuals. When interest rates fall, people who hold variable-rate loans enjoy lower interest payments. This drop in the cost of their financing reduces the information problems that plague the lending relationship. Why? To evaluate a borrower's creditworthiness, banks look at the percentage of a person's income that is devoted to loan payments. At lower interest rates, that percentage will be lower, so individuals will qualify for larger loans. The conclusion is that *as interest rates fall, the supply of loans increases.*[5]

It is worth pausing to emphasize that information is the driving force in the bank lending and balance-sheet channels of monetary policy transmission. Information services are central to banks' role in the financial system because they help to address the problems of adverse selection and moral hazard. The primacy of information in

---

[5]There is a second, more subtle effect of interest rates on lending. If a borrower is willing to pay a high interest rate, the bank has reason to be suspicious. How can the borrower afford it? The borrower is planning to undertake a risky investment project. Should the risky project succeed, the borrower, not the bank, will be the primary beneficiary. Using the terminology of Chapter 11, the higher the interest rate is, the worse the adverse selection problem is likely to be and the higher the risk of the average borrower willing to accept a loan on those terms. As interest rates fall, the degree of risk diminishes and the adverse selection problem abates.

banking has some important implications for our understanding of the link between the financial system and the real economy. It means that financial instability, which is characterized by large and unpredictable moves in asset prices, accompanied by widespread bankruptcy, will reduce lenders' willingness to supply financing. It also means that accounting scandals, such as the ones that plagued U.S. companies in 2001 and 2002, will have an effect on the economy as a whole. When bankers are worried about the accuracy of accounting information, they will be less willing to make loans to anyone. Inferior information leads to an increase in adverse selection, reducing bank lending, lowering investment, and ultimately depressing aggregate demand.

The channels of monetary policy transmission depend on the structure of the financial system. To the extent that banks are unimportant sources of funds for firms and individuals, the bank lending channel is not tremendously important. As we will see at the end of this chapter, with the growth of loan brokers and asset-backed securities, we expect the bank lending channel to become less important than it once was. But information problems and the balance-sheet effects they create seem likely to persist for some time. While technology has made the processing of increasing amounts of information easier and cheaper, it seems unlikely to solve the problems of adverse selection and moral hazard, which make net worth such an important determinant of a borrower's creditworthiness.

Table 23.1 summarizes the various channels through which the monetary policy transmission mechanism works.

Table 23.1   The Monetary Policy Transmission Mechanism

Channel	Mechanism
Interest rates (traditional channel)	Lower interest rates reduce the cost of investment, making more projects profitable.
Exchange rates (traditional channel)	Lower interest rates reduce the attractiveness of domestic investment, depressing the value of the currency and increasing net exports.
Asset prices	Higher stock prices and real estate values fuel an increase in both business investment and household consumption.
Bank lending	An easing of monetary policy raises the level of bank reserves and bank deposits, increasing the supply of funds.
Firms' balance sheets	Lower interest rates raise firms' profits, increasing their net worth and reducing the problems of adverse selection and moral hazard.
Household net worth	Lower interest rates raise individuals' net worth, improving their creditworthiness and allowing them to increase their borrowing.

The Challenges Modern Monetary Policymakers Face

Having looked at the myriad of ways in which a central bank can influence economic activity, we could easily come away from this discussion with the impression that monetary policy can be distilled to a hard and fast science—that a few equations, coupled

APPLYING THE CONCEPT
WHAT HAPPENED IN JAPAN?

At this point, you may still be wondering about the deep recession that occurred in Japan during the 1990s (see the chapter opener). Why did the Japanese economy fail to respond to the Bank of Japan's long sequence of interest-rate reductions? Solving the mystery requires that we look at various channels of monetary policy transmission—in this case, asset prices and bank lending.

Figure 23.3 provides the first piece of the puzzle, the collapse of the Japanese stock market. From a peak of nearly 40,000 at the end of 1989, the Nikkei 225 index (the Japanese equivalent to the S&P 500) fell by more than half, to 16,000 in 1992. Property prices fell with it. The impact

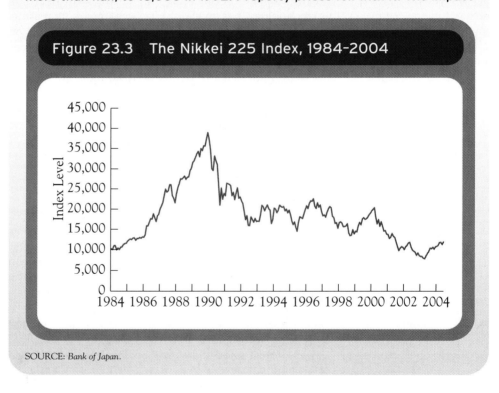

Figure 23.3   The Nikkei 225 Index, 1984–2004

SOURCE: *Bank of Japan.*

with some statistical analysis, will do. Unfortunately, that isn't true. To do their job well, central bankers need a detailed understanding of how both the financial system and the real economy will react to their policy changes. That would be tough enough in a world that is standing still, but the constant change that is a feature of today's economy makes the job all the more difficult. In fact, policymakers face a series of daunting challenges. In this section, we will look at four that loom large in the early 21st century. First, there is the fact that the economy's sustainable growth rate fluctuates. Second, policymakers' options are limited, as we have seen, by the fact that the nominal interest rate cannot fall below zero. Third, stock prices and property values have a tendency to go through cycles of booms and busts. And finally, the structures of the economy and the financial system are constantly evolving.

continued from previous page

of this decline in asset prices was severe. Beyond its direct effects on consumption and investment, both of which collapsed, the crash did considerable damage to both the creditworthiness of borrowers and banks' balance sheets. Borrowers' net worth fell with the collapse of equity and property values, worsening information problems and depressing aggregate demand even further.

When real growth slowed to a standstill, firms were no longer able to repay their loans. The quantity of nonperforming loans skyrocketed, eroding bank capital and causing loan officers to become extremely wary of extending new loans. By 2000, bad loans accounted for 14 percent of outstanding loans, up from 3 percent in 1993. Bank capital fell from a relatively low $5\frac{1}{4}$ percent of assets early in the 1990s to less than $2\frac{1}{2}$ percent in 2000.*

The dramatic rise in the number of nonperforming loans was compounded by the fact that many were backed by assets whose value had collapsed. As a result, many banks had virtually no capital left. They should have been shut down but, for political reasons, closing them was impossible. So they were allowed to continue operating, just as the U.S. savings and loans were permitted to stay in business in the 1980s. (See Applying the Concept in Chapter 14, page 368). Unlike the zombie S&Ls, however, the insolvent Japanese banks were unwilling to make new loans.[†]

Given the large numbers of both bankrupt firms and impaired banks, it was no wonder that the Bank of Japan's monetary policy had virtually no impact. The fact that the interest rate was zero simply didn't matter, because the channels through which interest-rate reductions would normally have influenced real economic activity were almost completely blocked. There was no way for borrowers to obtain financing. Thus, policymakers had little ability to shift the aggregate demand curve or even to influence its slope. To clean up the mess, the banking system would need to be put back on a solid footing.

The state of Japan's banking system explains the contrast between the U.S. and Japanese economies described at the beginning of this chapter. When the Internet bubble burst in 2000, the U.S. economy did not follow the same path as Japan's. Though Americans suffered many of the same consequences as the Japanese—their wealth declined, reducing consumption and investment and damaging borrowers' balance sheets—U.S. banks were well capitalized and were able to continue lending. A healthy banking system makes all the difference.

*For a thorough discussion of the problems in the Japanese financial system during the 1990s, see Anil K Kashyap, "Sorting Out Japan's Financial Crisis," *Economic Perspectives of the Federal Reserve Bank of Chicago*, 2000, 4th Quarter, pp. 42–55.

[†]A striking feature of the Japanese experience in the 1990s is that regulators and supervisors failed to enforce prudential regulations that would have forced many banks to close for lack of adequate capital. The reasons for their "regulatory forbearance" are complex, but two are particularly noteworthy. First, without a fully developed deposit insurance system, it was unclear to regulators how depositors would be compensated when banks were liquidated. Second, and possibly more important, shutting the doors on banks would have meant foreclosing on defaulted borrowers. Not only were many depositors supporters of the political party that held power at the time, but it was commonly believed that some were members of organized crime who were prone to violence. See Mitsuhiro Fukao, "Japan's Lost Decade and Its Financial System," *The World Economy* 26, no. 5 (March 2003), pp. 365–384.

Estimating Potential GDP

Modern monetary policymakers can't do their jobs without estimates of both the level and growth rate of potential output. The reason is that interest-rate adjustments depend on the difference between current and potential output, referred to in earlier chapters as the output gap. Recall from Chapter 22 that inflation goes up or down depending on whether the output gap is positive (real output greater than potential) or negative (real output less than potential). Thus, stabilizing inflation means adjusting monetary policy to the output gap by raising interest rates when the gap is positive and lowering them when the gap is negative. When we say that central bankers strive to stabilize growth at a high level, what we mean is that they try to keep the economy growing at the same rate as potential output. The growth rate of potential output is the economy's sustainable growth rate. This logic provides the foundation for the Taylor rule (introduced in Chapter 18) and the monetary policy reaction curve (described in Chapter 21).

The policymaker's challenge is to distinguish movements in measured GDP that represent a change in the output gap from movements that represent a change in potential output. To understand why this is such an important task, consider an unexpected increase in GDP. If potential output has not changed, the correct response to the rise in real output is to tighten policy, raising interest rates in order to reduce aggregate demand and keep inflation from rising. But if the rise in GDP is permanent and sustainable, so that it represents an increase in potential output, the appropriate response is to allow aggregate demand to climb to a new long-run level while stabilizing inflation.

The problem is, telling the difference between temporary and permanent changes in real growth is extremely difficult. The 1990s provided a good example of just how hard the task is. Look back at Panel A of Figure 23.2, which shows growth in U.S. GDP from 1990 to 2004. In the latter half of the 1990s, growth was an average of more than $1\frac{1}{2}$ points higher than in the first half of the decade. In hindsight we can see the difference.[6] But the danger is that policymakers will raise interest rates when they see output rise, not realizing that potential output has risen.

In the terminology of Chapter 22, policymakers may not be able to tell the difference between a rightward shift in the aggregate demand curve (shown in Figure 22.11, page 599) and a rightward shift in the long-run aggregate supply curve (shown in Figure 22.13, page 604). These two shifts require very different policy responses. An increase in aggregate demand that does not represent a change in potential GDP creates an expansionary (positive) output gap and pushes up the long-run real interest rate. The proper response is a shift in the monetary policy reaction function to the left, increasing the real interest rate at all levels of inflation. A shift in long-run aggregate supply, on the other hand, represents an increase in potential output, which creates a recessionary (negative) output gap at the same time that it lowers the long-run real interest rate. In this case, the correct response is to lower the real interest rate at all levels of inflation, shifting the monetary policy reaction curve to the right. The question is, when output rises unexpectedly, should policymakers raise or lower the target interest rate?

To get some sense of how hard it is to tell the difference between changes in aggregate demand and changes in potential output, we can look at the forecasters' record during the latter half of the 1990s. Figure 23.4 plots the level of GDP (on a log scale) against a series of *consensus forecasts*—the median forecasts of a broad survey of professional economists who specialize in predicting GDP growth. For each quarter, the chart shows the forecast-

---

[6]The difference in the two growth rates varies depending on how output is measured. For example, if we looked only at "nonfarm business output," the difference would be more than 2 percent.

ed path of GDP over the next two years. In the first quarter of 1996, for example, the figure shows the actual data point plus the forecast for the next eight quarters. Note that actual GDP followed a steeper path than forecasted GDP throughout the period, meaning that forecasters consistently underestimated GDP growth. This systematic underestimation of the growth rate is a clear sign that forecasters were slow to recognize that part of the acceleration in productivity was permanent and so a portion of the unexpected increase in actual output was a result of a shift in potential. Not surprisingly, their series of underestimates of GDP were accompanied by a series of overestimates of inflation.

The difficulty of estimating the growth trend of potential GDP extends beyond the tumultuous years of the late 1990s. When potential growth slowed in the early 1970s, analysts took years to realize it. The dramatic rise in inflation during that decade is now thought to be a result of the Fed's failure to realize that the growth rate of potential GDP had fallen and its attempt to keep output growing at an unsustainably high level.

Then there is the difficulty posed by data revisions. In Chapter 18, we saw that GDP data are revised for years after they are published. That means that the output gap must be revised as well. These revisions occur virtually all the time. In one study, researchers compared the initial estimates of the output gap, available to policymakers at the time they were making their decisions, with subsequent revisions over the

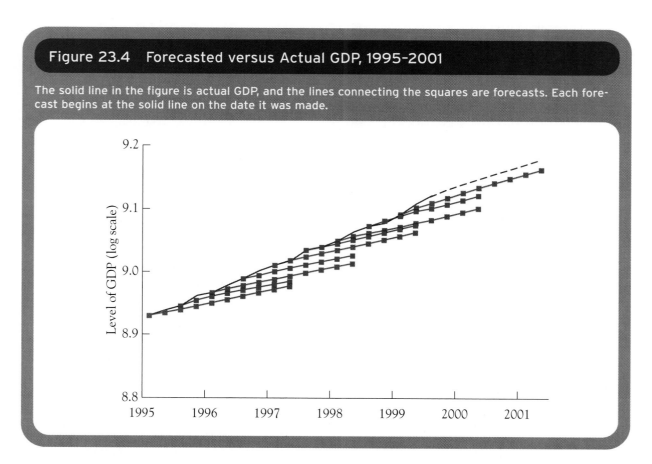

Figure 23.4 Forecasted versus Actual GDP, 1995–2001

The solid line in the figure is actual GDP, and the lines connecting the squares are forecasts. Each forecast begins at the solid line on the date it was made.

SOURCE: *The forecasts are from Blue Chip Forecasts.*

IN THE NEWS

When It Comes to Crystal-Ball Gazing, the Fed Trounces the Private Sector

The New York Times

by Hal R. Varian

November 21, 2002

The Fed gave the economy a flu shot earlier this month by cutting interest rates half a point. But it was quick to point out that, as with a real flu shot, this was intended only as a preventive measure.

"The economy's most likely projection is to come out of this soft spot and to start accelerating," the Federal Reserve chairman, Alan Greenspan, told Congress.

Other Fed officials are also positive about the economy. Gary H. Stern, president of the Federal Reserve Bank of Minneapolis, said, "There is no question that an economic expansion, an economic recovery, is under way."

Unfortunately, business leaders do not share the Fed's optimism. According to a report by the Business Roundtable, 60 percent of executives surveyed said they planned to eliminate jobs next year, while only 11 percent thought they would add jobs.

Whom should we believe: the Fed or the executives? After all, the executives are actually making economic decisions, while the Fed is only trying to forecast what they will do. What do those guys in Washington know, anyway?

Plenty, it turns out.

For evidence, turn to "Federal Reserve Information and the Behavior of Interest Rates," a paper in the *American Economic Review* in June 2000 by Christina and David Romer, two economists at the University of California at Berkeley.

The Romers ask whether the Fed has an advantage in predicting economic variables and, if so, what the source of that advantage is. The answer to the first question is a resounding yes. The answer to the second is a bit more tentative: the Fed is better at forecasting than the private sector, but we're not sure why.

Forecasts for both inflation and output growth are prepared by the Fed staff before each meeting of the Federal Open Market Committee, which uses these forecasts to help set economic policy. The forecasts are closely guarded secrets and are released to the public only after five years.

How good are the Fed's forecasts? To answer this question, the Romers compare the forecasts from 1965 to 1991 with those of several private forecasting services.

period 1980 to 1992. They found that over the 13-year period, estimates of the gap that were available to policymakers at the time they had to act averaged –3.99 percent of potential GDP, nearly 4 percent below potential output. Subsequent revisions of both current and potential output led to large changes in the estimated output gap. By 1994, the revised figures implied an average output gap of only –1.64 percent. In other words, the revised output gap was an average of 2.35 percentage points smaller than the estimated output gap available to monetary policymakers at the time they were making their decisions.[7]

The message is clear. During periods when the growth rate of potential GDP is changing, central bankers face challenges that are even more daunting than usual. Failing to react to a decline in potential output growth, as policymakers at the Fed did in the 1970s, can result in an extended episode of undesirably high inflation, which can be costly to eliminate. But tightening policy in the face of an increase in potential growth can prevent growth from occurring. The challenge is to figure out, as quickly and accurately as possible, the true growth rate of potential GDP.

[7]See Athanasios Orphanides, "Monetary Policy Evaluation with Noisy Information," Finance and Economics Discussion Paper 1998-50, Board of Governors of the Federal Reserve System, November 1998.

The Romers first look at how well private forecasts have predicted inflation, then ask whether the forecasters could have improved their performance if they had been given access to the Fed forecasts. The researchers find that the Fed forecasts offer big improvements over the private ones. In fact, if you had access to both forecasts, a good rule of thumb would be to rely exclusively on the Fed and ignore the private predictions.

Why are the Fed's forecasts so much better? The most likely explanation for their superiority in forecasting inflation, the Romers say, is that the Fed devotes "far more resources to forecasting than even the largest commercial forecasters."

It's not that it has better information about the state of the economy, or secret forecasting methods—it simply looks at a lot more information, has a lot more staff, and has a lot more experience. So it is not too surprising that the Fed does better.

These days the big economic uncertainty is not so much about inflation (or deflation) but about output. Everyone wants to know when the economy will resume robust growth. Does the Fed's forecasting superiority extend to GDP growth?

The answer is yes: the researchers find that the Fed is also substantially better at predicting output growth than the private sector. But the Fed's advantage in this case is not as large as with predicting inflation. In the case of output growth, the optimal forecast would combine both the private and the Fed forecasts, though it would give more weight to the Fed's forecast.

In the case of output forecasting, the Romers suggest that the Fed's advantage may in fact be, at least in part, a result of better access to data since the Fed manages the collection of information used to compute the index of industrial production.

Note that the Berkeley economists' study is mostly pre-Greenspan; Mr. Greenspan joined the Fed in August 1987, while the Romers' data ends in 1991. Mr. Greenspan is well known for reading a variety of economic tea leaves, but most of the data he uses appears to come from reports available to the private sector. His forecasting success seems to come not from special ingredients, but from a finely tuned sense of how ordinary ingredients should be combined.

LESSONS OF THE ARTICLE

Forecasts are an essential ingredient in any policy process. The need for high-quality forecasts in determining monetary policy seems obvious. Setting the target federal funds rate requires reliable forecasts of both inflation and growth under various interest-rate scenarios. As a result, the Federal Reserve devotes substantial resources to producing forecasts. Evidence shows that the strategy works: The Fed's forecasts are significantly better than those of private-sector economists.

Deflation and the Zero Nominal-Interest-Rate Bound

Since investors can always hold cash, bonds must have positive yields. Thus, nominal interest rates cannot be negative. Put another way, there is a zero nominal-interest-rate bound, which prevents the price of a zero-coupon bond from exceeding par.[8] While this point may strike you as something only investors should worry about, it is not. The fact that nominal interest rates can't fall below zero places a significant restriction on what monetary policymakers can do. Look back at Panel B of Figure 23.1 and you will see that beginning in mid-1999, the Bank of Japan's target interest rate was set at zero. Even though real economic growth remained low in Japan (see Panel A of Figure 23.1), policymakers couldn't lower the rate any further.

[8]On rare occasions, bond prices have exceeded par by small amounts. From 1939 to 1941, for instance, the yield on U.S. Treasury bills was slightly negative. An explanation for this apparent anomaly can be found in the structure of the era's financial institutions. At the time, some U.S. states taxed wealth but exempted U.S. Treasury securities. In addition, banks that wished to hold U.S. government deposits were required to post Treasury bonds, notes, or bills as collateral. If you ever see a negative nominal interest rate, look deeper for an explanation. For an extensive discussion of these issues, see Stephen G. Cecchetti, "The Case of the Negative Nominal Interest Rates: New Estimates of the Term Structure of Interest Rates during the Great Depression," *Journal of Political Economy*, 96 (December 1988), pp. 1111–1141.

APPLYING THE CONCEPT
INFLATION AND SLOW GROWTH IN THE 1970S

When Arthur Burns became chairman of the Federal Reserve Board in 1970, inflation exceeded 6 percent. By the time he retired in early 1978, it was on its way to a level nearly twice that. As Figure 23.5 shows, inflation continued to rise, peaking at nearly 14 percent in 1980. What caused this steep climb in inflation?

A number of things did. At the beginning of the decade, the Federal government was engaged in a costly war in Vietnam, which placed extremely high demands on the nation's resources. Then between 1973 and 1979, oil prices rose by a factor of 10, creating huge inflation shocks. In the language of the macroeconomic model presented in the last two chapters, the rise in government expenditures to finance the war increased aggregate demand at the same time that a steep rise in oil prices created an inflation shock. Both these events placed upward pressure on inflation.

Chairman Burns and his colleagues on the FOMC could have slammed on the brakes, raising the target federal funds rate in an effort to reduce

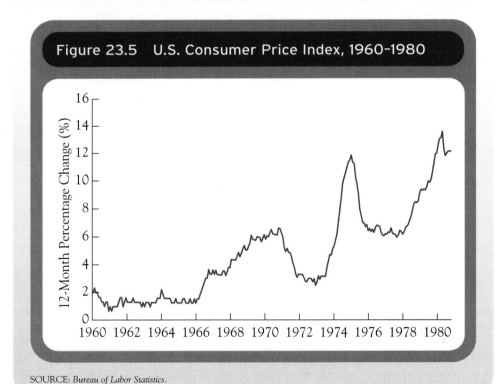

Figure 23.5 U.S. Consumer Price Index, 1960-1980

SOURCE: *Bureau of Labor Statistics.*

continued from previous page

aggregate demand and keep inflation from rising. But they didn't. Why? Looking at Figure 23.6, we can see that from 1960 to 1973, growth in real GDP averaged just over 4 percent per year. Then, sometime around 1973, growth slowed by nearly a full percentage point. Believing that the fall in real growth had opened up a recessionary output gap, the FOMC decided to keep interest rates low.

The FOMC failed to understand what was happening to potential GDP. Today we know that growth in potential GDP had fallen, so the long-run equilibrium real interest rate must have risen. That was what members of the FOMC would have had to know in order to keep inflation from rising. Instead, Chairman Burns and his colleagues consistently overestimated potential GDP, assuming that it was still growing at a rate of 4 percent per year. As a result, they mistakenly believed there was a recessionary output gap.

The outcome was a substantial increase in inflation. At least five years passed before policymakers were convinced that growth had slowed, by which time inflation was headed over the 10 percent mark. Not until Paul Volcker became chair of the Federal Reserve in 1979 did the FOMC become serious about fighting inflation.

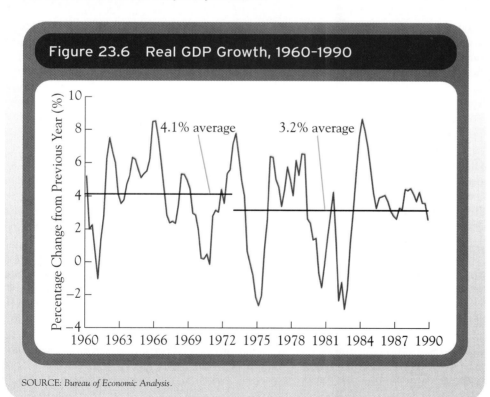

Figure 23.6   Real GDP Growth, 1960–1990

SOURCE: *Bureau of Economic Analysis.*

The risk of becoming caught in such a predicament concerns central bankers around the world. The FOMC has had to consider the implications of the zero nominal-interest-rate bound as well. Look back at Panel B of Figure 23.2 and you will see that, by the summer of 2003, the target federal funds rate was 1 percent. There wasn't much room left for further easing—at least not in the form of interest-rate reductions.

The problem posed by the zero nominal-interest-rate bound is a serious one. To understand why, we can do an exercise based on the macroeconomic model presented in Chapters 21 and 22. Think about the consequences of a shock that depresses aggregate demand, shifting the aggregate demand curve to the left and driving real output down. The shock could be caused by a decline in investment due to a fall in business prospects; by an appreciation of the dollar due to a deteriorating investment climate abroad, which has increased foreign demand for dollars; or by a decline in individuals' confidence in the future. Regardless of the source, the slowdown drives spending down at every level of inflation and the real interest rate, shifting the aggregate demand curve to the left (see Figure 22.14, page 608). The immediate consequence of this drop in aggregate demand is that real output falls below potential output, creating a recessionary output gap that puts downward pressure on inflation. Under normal circumstances, monetary policymakers would react to the decline in inflation by cutting the nominal interest rate enough to lower the real interest rate. Their action would increase spending, raise real output, and eliminate the output gap.

Now let's make a small adjustment to this story and assume that, when the shock occurs, inflation is zero and the target nominal interest rate that central bankers control is close to zero. Under these conditions, the decline in aggregate demand still drives real output below potential output, placing downward pressure on inflation. But when inflation falls, it drops below zero so that on average, prices are falling. The result is **deflation**.

Deflation isn't necessarily a problem, unless the shock that moves the economy away from its long-run equilibrium is big enough to reduce aggregate demand to the point where policymakers can't shift it back, even by setting their nominal interest rate target to zero. At that point we have arrived at one of the central banker's worst nightmares: a nominal interest rate of zero accompanied by deflation and real output that is below potential. The recessionary output gap places further downward pressure on prices, driving deflation down even more. Because the nominal interest rate is already zero, policymakers cannot counter the worsening deflation by lowering it. Instead, the real interest rate rises, reducing spending, shifting aggregate demand downward, and expanding the output gap even more. The result is a *deflationary spiral* in which deflation grows worse and worse.

Recall from Chapter 11 that deflation aggravates information problems in ways that inflation does not. Deflation makes it more difficult for businesses to obtain financing for new projects. Without financing there is no investment; without investment there is no growth. The primary reason this happens is that debt is measured in fixed dollars, and deflation makes those dollars more valuable. Thus, deflation increases the real value of a firm's liabilities without affecting the real value of its assets. (See Applying the Concept: Deflation, Net Worth, and Information Costs, page 277). At a lower net worth, companies are suddenly less creditworthy.

In short, deflation and the zero nominal-interest-rate bound can have a devastating impact on growth by short-circuiting the process that normally stabilizes the economy.[9] Can policymakers do anything to avoid this pitfall? The answer is yes;

[9]With some difficulty, we could explain this process using a version of the aggregate demand/aggregate supply model introduced in Chapters 21 and 22. The details quickly become complicated, but the essence of the explanation is that with deflation, the aggregate demand curve slopes upward, so the economy is no longer self-correcting and does not return to long-run equilibrium on its own.

there are ways to minimize the chances of this sort of catastrophe. Policymakers can choose from three strategies. First, they can set their inflation objective with the perils of deflation in mind; second, they can act boldly when there is even a hint of deflation; and third, they can adopt what are known as "unconventional" policies.

The difficulties posed by the zero nominal-interest-rate bound arise only when central bankers have achieved their objective of low, stable inflation. When inflation is high, so is the nominal interest rate; chances are therefore remote that the interest rate will hit the zero bound. This observation suggests that central bankers should set their inflation objective high enough to minimize the possibility of a deflationary spiral. The consensus is that an inflation objective of 2 to 3 percent gives policymakers enough latitude to avoid the problems caused by deflation.

"I had no idea our marriage was so interest-rate sensitive."

Reducing the interest rate significantly and rapidly when faced with the possibility of hitting the zero nominal-interest-rate bound is another approach to avoiding deflation. Central bankers call this strategy "acting preemptively," which means working hard to avoid ever reaching the point where interest rates hit zero. Acting preemptively was one reason why the FOMC reduced the target federal funds rate by $4\frac{3}{4}$ percentage points (from $6\frac{1}{2}$ to $1\frac{3}{4}$ percent) in a series of 11 cuts taken between January and November 2001. Dramatic actions of that sort are meant to ensure that the economy will recover before deflation can take hold.

Finally, central bankers have at their disposal a set of unconventional policy options that can be adopted when the traditional interest-rate target, an overnight rate, hits zero. The mechanics are straightforward and are based on the fact that policymakers can control the size of the central bank's balance sheet, altering its assets and liabilities to influence the economy. All monetary policy, conventional or not, is based on balance-sheet manipulation. During normal times, policymakers control the supply of their reserve liabilities in order to meet a target interest rate. But even if the short-run target interest rate drops to zero, monetary policymakers retain their ability to expand their balance sheet. They can continue to purchase securities in order to increase the size of the monetary base.

The most effective way to expand the monetary base when the overnight interest rate has fallen to zero is to shift to targeting longer-term rates. For example, the FOMC can instruct the Open Market Trading Desk to ensure that the interest rate on U.S. Treasury securities with maturities of two, three, or even ten years doesn't rise above some predetermined level. The committee might put a 2 percent ceiling on the 10-year Treasury bond while holding the federal funds rate steady at zero. Operationally, this strategy involves decisions about which assets the central bank should hold. The Fed simply stands ready to purchase the securities at a price that is consistent with the target interest rate. Eventually the market price may rise above that cap, so that the interest rate is even lower than the target rate. But in the meantime, the Fed will begin to accumulate bonds, and the monetary base will expand.[10]

---

[10]Another way to force the long-term interest rate down would be for the Fed to commit to a target federal funds rate of zero for a significant period. The expected short-term interest rate would then be zero. Since the long-term interest rate is an average of the expected short-term interest rates, the long-term rate would be driven down.

While everyone agrees that unconventional policy options like these are feasible, central bankers are not eager to try them. The primary reason is that they lack any experience with them. Monetary policymaking rests on quantitative estimates of the impact of a change in the target interest rate on the central bank's objectives. While policymakers have some idea of how a 25- or 50-basis-point reduction in the federal funds rate would affect output and inflation over the next year or two, they don't know what the quantitative impact of an unconventional policy option would be. What would happen if they reduced the 10-year Treasury bond rate by 25 basis points while holding the funds rate at zero? While policymakers can be sure which direction the economy will move, they can't tell how far or how fast.[11]

Booms and Busts in Equity and Property Prices

Nearly everyone agrees that we would all be better off without skyrocketing increases in stock and property prices followed by sudden collapses. Abrupt changes in asset prices, like the ones that occurred during the Internet boom of the late 1990s, affect virtually every aspect of economic activity. Looking back at the first part of this chapter, we can see that changes in asset prices have a direct impact on both consumption and investment. Bubbles that inflate and then burst are particularly damaging because the wealth effects they create cause consumption to explode and then contract just as rapidly. The associated increases in equity prices allow firms to finance new projects more easily, causing investment to boom—and then bust. Because the collateral that is used to back these loans is overvalued, the subsequent collapse in prices impairs the balance sheets of the financial intermediaries that made the loans.

A major question modern monetary policymakers face is whether they should react to equity and property price bubbles. Should the Federal Reserve have raised interest rates between 1997 and 1999, when the Nasdaq Index was soaring from 1,000 to 5,000 (see Figure 23.7)? Arguments can be made on both sides. Proponents of such a policy say that stabilizing inflation and real growth means raising interest rates to discourage bubbles from developing in the first place. If successful, this policy would reduce the consumption and investment booms that accompany bubbles, along with the busts that inevitably follow.

Opponents of this interventionist view claim that a bubble is virtually impossible to identify while it is developing. That may be true, but the fact that an economic phenomenon is difficult to measure is no excuse for ignoring it. As we saw earlier, the output gap is extremely hard to measure, yet an estimate of the gap is essential to the conduct of monetary policy. Furthermore, as should be clear from our earlier discussion of the monetary policy transmission mechanism, macroeconomic forecasts rest on estimates of future wealth and stock prices. Without them, there is no way to forecast either consumption or investment.[12]

---

[11]For a detailed discussion of unconventional monetary policy options, see Federal Reserve Board Governor Ben S. Bernanke's article "Deflation: Making Sure 'It' Doesn't Happen Here," remarks before the National Economists Club, Washington, D.C., November 21, 2001. The speech is available on the Federal Reserve Board's Web site at www.federalreserve.gov.

[12]The case for intervention is summarized in Stephen G. Cecchetti, Hans Genberg, and Sushil Wadhwani, "Asset Prices in a Flexible Inflation Targeting Framework," in William C. Hunter, George G. Kaufman, and Michael Pomerleano, editors, *Asset Price Bubbles: Implications for Monetary, Regulatory, and International Policies*, (Cambridge, MA: MIT Press, 2002), pp. 427–444. For the case against, see Ben Bernanke and Mark Gertler, "Should Central Banks Respond to Movements in Asset Prices?" *American Economic Review*, May 2001, pp. 253–257.

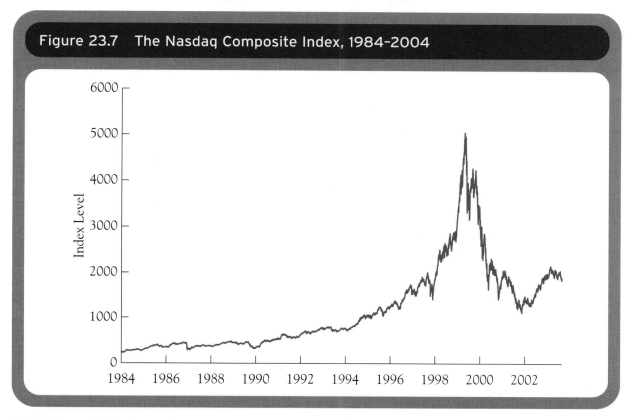

Figure 23.7   The Nasdaq Composite Index, 1984–2004

SOURCE: *Data compiled from Thompson Datastream.*

The Evolving Structure of the Financial System

Monetary policy works through its effects on the financial system. Thus, differences in financial structure across countries may help to explain differences in the effectiveness of monetary policy. By extension, changes in financial structure will change the impact of monetary policy. Recall from the first part of this chapter that one of the primary channels through which monetary policy influences real output and inflation is its impact on the supply of bank loans. By influencing bank lending, policymakers can affect the ease with which individuals and firms obtain financing.

Banks are crucial to this mechanism. As the nature of banking changes, we would expect the importance of this channel of monetary policy transmission to change along with it, and that has been the case. Specifically, banks are no longer as important a source of financing as they once were. Figure 23.8 shows bank loans as a percentage of total credit in the U.S. economy from 1983 to 2003. As you can see, in 1983, bank loans accounted for virtually all the credit extended in the U.S. economy. Twenty years later, the percentage was below 60 percent.

As banks have declined as a source of financing, the asset-backed securities discussed in Chapter 3 have increased in importance. Mortgage-backed securities held by government-sponsored enterprises like Fannie Mae and Freddie Mac (described in Chapter 13) are the most prominent example. To create these financial instruments, a mortgage broker bundles together a large number of home mortgages and then sells shares in the pool. Investors in mortgage-backed securities purchase shares in the revenue from the

MARKETS

YOUR FINANCIAL WORLD
Know the Level of Inflation

By now, you're probably convinced that inflation is bad for everyone, including yourself. The first step in dealing with inflation is to become informed. Casual observation of the prices we pay from day to day is an unreliable way to evaluate inflation, because most of us have fairly selective memories and are prone to remember price increases more than price decreases. Surveys like the ones described in Chapter 21's Tools of the Trade, indicate that most people overestimate inflation. So economic statistics are more reliable. The Bureau of Labor Statistics, the government agency that computes the consumer price index, provides information about inflation on its Web site, www.bls.gov/cpi/.

What should you look for on the BLS Web site? First, don't pay much attention to monthly measures of inflation; they aren't very reliable as indicators of the long-term inflation trend. Instead, focus on 12-month changes, especially measures that exclude food and energy. These so-called core measures of inflation omit parts of the price index that tend to be extremely volatile, making sharp movements that are likely to be reversed in a few months.[*] Because gasoline prices rise and fall from one month to the next, for example, removing

them smoothes inflation, making the core measure more representative of the long-term trend.

Knowing the level of inflation is essential to managing your finances. If you don't know the level of inflation, you won't know whether the interest rate you receive on your savings is high or low, or whether the interest rate you are paying on your loans is high or low. Nor will you be able to evaluate properly the next raise you receive. Stay informed about inflation so that you can adjust for it. Know the real interest rate you receive or pay and how much your real wage is changing.[†]

---

[*]Some other measures of core inflation are as useful as the CPI with food and energy excluded. A particularly good one is the Median CPI, computed monthly by the Federal Reserve Bank of Cleveland and available on its Web site at www.clevelandfed.org.

[†]In addition to knowing what the level of inflation is today, you'll need some idea of what it is likely to be in the future. That is, forecasts of inflation are useful, particularly when your goal is to compute the real interest rate. Remember that the real interest rate is the nominal interest rate minus *expected* inflation. While forecasting inflation accurately is extremely difficult, getting a rough idea of what it is likely to be is easy. Since inflation tends to be persistent, a good forecast of the future inflation level would be the average core inflation level over the past year. The percentage change over the past 12 months in the CPI with food and energy excluded will give you a good idea of what the inflation level is likely to be in the next year or two.

underlying financial instruments—in this case, the pooled mortgage payments made by home buyers. Borrowers obtain a form of financing that is almost equivalent to direct capital market financing. Over the years, the list of assets included in asset-backed securities has grown; it now includes car loans, credit card debt, student loans, equipment leases, and even movie box-office receipts.

The shift away from bank financing and toward direct financing in the capital markets means that the bank lending channel of monetary policy transmission is likely to become less and less important. The trend presents a significant challenge to central bankers, who need to know the quantitative impact their policies are likely to have. But as the structure of the financial system evolves, the effect of a 25- or 50-basis-point change in the federal funds rate will doubtless change with it. In fact, the structure of the financial system will always be changing. As financial instruments, markets, and institutions evolve, the central bank's balance sheet will change with them, along with the monetary transmission mechanism.

The changing nature of the financial system is important for individuals as well as policymakers. As the nature of money, banks, and loans evolves, we will all adjust how we pay for our purchases, how we hold our wealth, and how we obtain our financ-

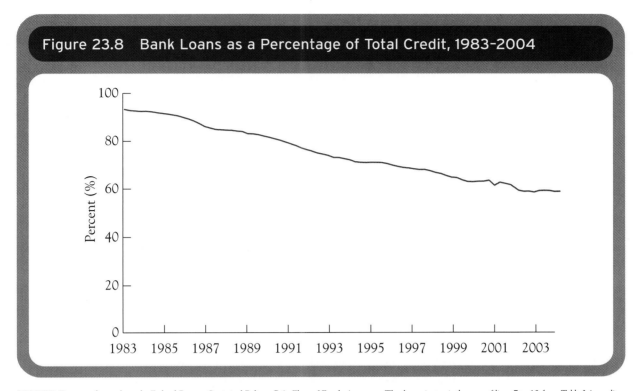

Figure 23.8   Bank Loans as a Percentage of Total Credit, 1983–2004

SOURCE: *Data are drawn from the Federal Reserve Statistical Release Z.1, Flow of Funds Accounts. The denominator is the sum of lines 7 to 10 from Table L4; credit market debt includes bank loans not elsewhere classified, other loans and advances, mortgages, and consumer credit. The numerator of the series is the denominator minus the sum of Tables L126 line 1 and L127 line 1, financial assets of federally related mortgage pools plus financial assets of private issuers of asset-backed securities.*

ing. Our use of currency will likely decline, and banks will likely reduce their reserves. No one can predict exactly when these changes will occur, but since you have reached the end of this book, you now know how to think about them. You understand the economic role of financial institutions, as well as what a central bank is and how it operates. Together with the aggregate demand/aggregate supply model, this knowledge gives you a framework with which to comprehend the evolution of the financial system, its effects on monetary policy, and its effects on you personally.

Terms

asset price channel, 622
balance-sheet channel, 626
bank lending channel, 625
deflation, 636
exchange-rate channel, 621

interest-rate channel, 621
monetary policy transmission
    mechanism, 621
zero nominal-interest-rate bound, 633

www.mhhe.com/cecchettile

Chapter Lessons

1. Monetary policy influences the economy through several channels.

   a. The traditional channels of monetary policy transmission are interest rates and exchange rates.

      i. Interest rates influence consumption and investment.

      ii. Exchange rates affect net exports.

   b. The asset price channel of monetary policy transmission works through stock and real estate prices.

      i. Stock and property prices influence household wealth and consumption.

      ii. Stock prices also affect businesses' ability to raise funds and make investments.

   c. Monetary policy affects the supply of bank loans, changing the availability of bank financing to firms and individuals.

   d. Monetary policy can change firms' and households' net worth, affecting their creditworthiness as borrowers.

2. Monetary policymakers face significant challenges. To be successful, they require

   a. Accurate estimates of potential GDP, even when its growth trend is shifting.

   b. An understanding of how to cope with the problems created by the zero nominal-interest-rate bound and the possibility of deflation.

   c. A knowledge of how and when to react to the possibility of a stock or real estate boom (and bust).

   d. An awareness of the changing structure of the financial system and a knowledge of how to react to it.

Problems

1. In Chapter 3, we discussed the relationship between financial development and economic growth. Can causality be established in either direction? What type of information would prove convincing?

2. Explain in detail how monetary policy influences banks' lending behavior. Show how an open market purchase affects the banking system's balance sheet. Discuss the impact on the supply of bank loans. (You may wish to refer to Chapter 17 in answering this question.)

3. Suppose banks discover a low-cost, convenient way to obtain deposits for which they are not required to hold additional reserves. Will this discovery alter the effectiveness of monetary policy? Why or why not?

4. The chair of the Federal Reserve Board gives a speech and says that interest rates are unlikely to rise for the next few years. Will this statement have any impact on the economy? Which channels of monetary policy transmission will be affected by the announcement? Will the speech pose any difficulties when the FOMC finally raises the interest rate?

5. From the senior loan officers' survey, FOMC members learn that banks are tightening their lending standards. Why should policymakers care about this change? What action are they likely to take, and why?

6. New developments in information technology have simplified the assessment of individual borrowers' creditworthiness. What are the likely consequences for the structure of the financial system? For monetary policy?

7. In the late 1990s, the rate of economic growth in the United States rose suddenly and unexpectedly. Was it important for the FOMC to recognize the change? What happens if policymakers do not recognize such a change and continue to assume that the economy is growing at the old rate? In answering this question, use the aggregate demand/aggregate supply analysis presented in Chapters 21 and 22.

8. From 1930 to 1932, prices in the United States fell nearly 10 percent per year. Many economists blame the deflation for the collapse of the U.S. financial system and economy. How can deflation cause a drop in real output? Why might it cause a financial collapse?

9. Seeing inflation rise, policymakers at the FOMC realize that they need to raise the interest rate. What will happen if they think inflation has gone up 1 percentage point when it has actually risen by 2 percentage points?

10. The "In the News" article in this chapter presents evidence that the FOMC's forecasts are better than private-sector forecasts. Why might they be better? Should the Fed release its forecasts publicly so that everyone can use them?

11. Many economists have argued that Japan's economic problems during the 1990s were caused largely by bank failures and the refusal of the Japanese government to clean up the banking system. Explain how a collapse of the banking system could cause a fall in real output. Can monetary policymakers do anything to revive the economy under such circumstances?

12. The government decides to place limits on the interest rates banks can pay their depositors. Seeing that alternative investments pay higher interest rates, depositors withdraw their funds from banks and place them in bonds. Will their action have an impact on the economy? If so, how?

13. Describe the economic impact of a widespread corporate accounting scandal. Can central bankers do anything to counteract it?

14. Why might the zero nominal-interest-rate bound lead policymakers to raise their inflation objective?

15. Describe the impact of an asset price bubble on consumption and investment, both on the way up and on the way down. How might monetary policy reduce the instability caused by such a bubble?

Glossary

A

accommodating monetary policy A policy that is aimed at increasing output and raising inflation, usually a lowering of the central bank's interest-rate target. (15)

accountability The idea that central bankers should be held responsible for their policies. (15)

adverse selection The problem of distinguishing a good risk from a bad one before making a loan or providing insurance; it is caused by asymmetric information. (11)

aggregate demand The total demand for the economy's production; the sum of consumption, investment, government purchases, and net exports. (21)

aggregate demand (AD) curve The graph of the relationship between inflation and the quantity of spending on domestically produced goods and services. (21)

American option An option that can be exercised any time up to the expiration date, in contrast to a *European option*. (9)

appreciation The increase in the value of a country's currency relative to the value of another country's currency. (10)

arbitrage The practice of simultaneously buying and selling financial instruments to benefit from temporary price differences; eliminates a riskless profit opportunity. (9)

arbitrageurs People who engage in arbitrage. (9)

asset Something of value that can be owned; a financial claim or property that serves as a store of value. (3)

asset price channel The channel of the monetary policy transmission mechanism where changes in policy affect consumption and output through their impact on stock prices and the value of real estate. (23)

asset-backed securities Shares in the returns or payments arising from a specific asset or pool of assets, such as home mortgages or student loans. (3)

asymmetric information The fact that the two parties to a transaction have unequal knowledge about each other. A borrower, for example, has more information about his or her abilities and prospects than a lender. (11)

at-the-money option An option whose strike price equals the current market price for the underlying instrument. (9)

automated clearinghouse (ACH) transaction The most common form of electronic funds transfers. (2)

average See *expected value*. (5)

B

balance of payments An accounting system for tracking both the flows of goods and services and the flow of assets across international boundaries. (19)

balance sheet The list of assets and liabilities that shows an individual's or firm's financial position. (3)

balance-sheet channel The channel of the monetary policy transmission mechanism where changes in policy affect consumption and output through their impact on household and firm balance sheets. (23)

bank See *depository institution*. (1)

bank capital Bank assets minus bank liabilities. The net worth of the bank. The value of the bank to its owners. (12)

bank charter The license authorizing the operation of a bank. (13)

bank holding company A company that owns one or more banks and possibly other nonbank subsidiaries. (13)

bank lending channel The channel of the monetary policy transmission mechanism in which changes in policy affect consumption and output through their impact on banks' willingness to make loans. (23)

bank panic The simultaneous failure of many banks during a financial crisis. (14)

bank run An event when depositors lose confidence in a bank and make withdrawals, exhausting the bank's reserves. (14)

bank supervision Government oversight of commercial banks; see also *supervision*. (14)

Basel accord An agreement requiring internationally active banks to hold capital equal to or greater than 8 percent of their risk-adjusted assets. (14)

basis point One one-hundredth of a percentage point. (4)

benchmark bond A low-risk bond, usually a U.S. Treasury bond, to which the yield on a risky bond is compared to assess its risk. (7)

Big Mac index The index used to estimate whether currencies are under- or over-valued that is based on the price of the Big Mac in various countries. (10)

Board of Governors of the Federal Reserve System The seven-member board that oversees the Federal Reserve System, including participation in both monetary policy and financial regulatory decisions. (16)

bond A financial instrument that promises a series of future payments on specific dates. Also known as a fixed-income security. (4)

bond coupon payment Yearly payment made to the holder of a coupon bond. Also known as a coupon payment. (4)

bond coupon rate Annual interest rate equal to the yearly coupon payment divided by the face value of a coupon bond. Also known as coupon rate. (4)

bond market A financial market in which debt instruments with a maturity of more than one year are traded. (3)

bond principal value The final payment made to the holder of a bond; also known as the *par value* and the *face value*. (4)

Bretton Woods system The international monetary system in place from 1945 to 1971, in which exchange rates were fixed to the U.S. dollar, and the dollar was convertible into gold at $35 per ounce. (19)

brokerage firm Financial intermediary that provides accounting and custody services, access to secondary markets, liquidity, loans, and advice. (13)

British pound The name of the currency used in the United Kingdom. (10)

bubble A persistent and expanding gap between actual stock prices and those warranted by the fundamentals; usually created by mass enthusiasm. (8)

business cycles The periodic fluctuations in aggregate economic output. (1)

C

call option A contract that confers the right, but not the obligation, to purchase a financial instrument at a predetermined price on or prior to an agreed upon date. (9)

call reports The detailed financial reports banks are required to file every three months. Officially known as the *Consolidated Reports of Conditions and Income*. (14)

callable bond A bond that the issuer has the option of repaying before the maturity date. (6)

CAMELS The system used by U.S. bank examiners to summarize their evaluation of a bank's health. The acronym stands for Capital adequacy, Asset quality, Management, Earnings, Liquidity, and Sensitivity to risk. (14)

capital account The part of the balance of payments accounts that measures the flow of assets among countries; also called the financial account. (10)

capital account deficit/surplus A country's capital inflows minus its capital outflows. (10)

capital controls Government-imposed barriers to investment across international boundaries; restrictions on the ability of foreigners to buy and sell domestic assets. (19)

capital gain The difference between the price that has been paid for an asset and the higher price at which it is sold; contrasts with a *capital loss*, where the price paid exceeds the price at which the asset is sold. (6)

capital inflow controls Government restrictions that restrict the flow of funds into a country to purchase domestic assets. (19)

capital loss The difference between the price that has been paid for an asset and the lower price at which it is sold; contrasts with *capital gain*. (6)

capital market See *bond market*. (8)

capital outflow controls Government restrictions on the flow of funds out of a country to purchase foreign assets. (19)

cash items in process of collection Checks and transfers due to a bank that have not yet been collected; a bank asset. (12)

central bank The financial institution that manages the government's finances, controls the availability of money and credit in the economy, and serves as the bank to commercial banks. (15)

central bank credibility The idea that everyone trusts central bankers to do what they say they are going to do. (15)

central bank independence The central bank's freedom from political pressure. (15)

central bank's balance sheet The statement of the assets and liabilities of the central bank. (17)

centralized exchange A financial market in which financial instruments are traded in a single physical location. (3)

check An instruction to the bank to take funds from one account and transfer them to another. (2)

clearing corporation The institution that acts as the counterparty to both sides of all futures market transactions, guaranteeing that the parties to the contract will meet their obligations. (9)

collateral Assets pledged to pay for a loan in the event that the borrower doesn't make the required payments. (3, 11)

commercial banks Financial intermediaries that provide banking services to businesses and households, allowing them to deposit funds safely and borrow them when necessary. (2)

commercial paper Short-term, privately issued zero-coupon debt that is low risk and very liquid and usually has a maturity of less than 270 days. (7)

commodity money Precious metals or other items with intrinsic value that are used as money. (2)

common stock Ownership shares in a firm; also called just *stock* and *equity*. (8)

compound interest The interest you get on interest as it accumulates over time. (4)

consol A coupon bond in which the issuer makes regular interest payments forever, never repaying the principal; a coupon bond with infinite time to maturity. (6)

consumption Spending by individuals for items like food, clothing, housing, transportation, entertainment, and education. (21)

contagion When the failure of one bank causes a run on other banks. (14)

counterparty The person or institution that is on the other side of a financial contract. (3)

coupon bond A bond offering annual coupon payments at regular intervals until the maturity date, at which time the principal is repaid. (4)

credit card A promise by a bank to lend the cardholder money in order to make purchases. (2)

credit risk The probability that a borrower will not repay a loan; see also *default risk*. (12)

credit union A nonprofit depository institution that is owned by people with a common bond, such as members of police associations, union members, university students, and employees (12)

currency Paper money; dollar bills or euro notes. (2)

currency board A fixed-exchange-rate system in which the central bank commits to holding enough foreign currency assets (often dollars) to back domestic currency liabilities at a fixed rate. (19)

currency in the hands of the public The quantity of dollar bills held by the nonbank public; part of M1. (2)

currency-to-deposit ratio The ratio of publicly held currency to demand deposits held at commercial banks. (17)

current account The part of the balance-of-payments account that measures the flow of currently produced goods and services among countries. (10)

current account deficit/surplus A country's goods and services exports minus its goods and services imports. (10)

current output The level of goods and services currently being produced in an economy. (21)

current yield A bond's yearly coupon payment divided by its current market price. (6)

D

debit card A card that provides instructions to the bank to transfer funds from the cardholder's account directly to a merchant's account. (2)

debt A loan obligating the borrower to make payments to the lender. (2)

debt market A financial market where bonds, loans, and mortgages are traded. (3)

default Failure to meet an obligation; in the case of a debt, the failure of the borrower to make required payments to the lender. (5)

default risk The probability that a borrower will not repay a loan; see also *credit risk*. (6)

defined-benefit pension plan A pension plan in which beneficiaries receive a lifetime retirement income based on the number of years they worked at the company and their final salary. (13)

defined-contribution pension plan A pension plan in which beneficiaries make payments into an account and then receive the accumulation, plus the investment income, on retirement, at which time they must decide what to do with the funds. The options include accepting a lump sum, removing small amounts at a time, or converting the balance to a fixed monthly payment for life by purchasing an annuity. (13)

deflation A sustained fall in the general price level; the opposite of *inflation*. (11, 23)

demand deposits Standard checking accounts that pay no interest; part of M1. (2)

demand for dollars Dollars demanded in the foreign exchange market as a function of the nominal exchange rate. (10)

deposit expansion multiplier The formula for the increase in commercial bank deposits following a one-dollar increase in reserves. (17)

deposit insurance The government guarantee that depositors will receive the full value of their accounts should a financial institution fail. (14)

depository institution A financial institution that accepts deposits and makes loans. (12)

depreciation The decrease in the value of a country's currency relative to the value of another country's currency. (10)

derivative See *derivative instrument*. (9)

derivative instrument A financial instrument, such as a futures contract or an option, whose value and payoff are "derived from" the behavior of underlying instruments. (3)

direct finance Financing in which borrowers sell securities directly to lenders in the financial markets. (3)

discount lending Lending by the Federal Reserve to commercial banks. (18)

discount loans A loan from the Federal Reserve to a commercial bank. (12, 17)

discount rate The interest rate at which the Federal Reserve makes discount loans to commercial banks. (16, 18)

discount yield See *yield on a discount basis*. (6)

disinflation The term used to describe declines in inflation. (22)

diversification Splitting wealth among a variety of assets to reduce risk. (5)

dividend-discount model The theory that the fundamental value of a stock equals the present value of expected future dividend payments. (8)

dividends The payments made to a company's stockholders when the company makes a profit. (8)

dollarization One country's formal adoption of the currency of another country for use in all its financial transactions. (19)

Dow Jones Industrial Average The best-known index of stock market performance, it measures the average price of a single share in 30 very large and well-known American companies. (8)

dual banking system The system in the United States in which banks supervised by federal government and state government authorities coexist. (13)

E

ECB's deposit facility Where euro-area banks with excess reserves can deposit them overnight and earn interest. (18)

ECB's Main Refinancing Operations The weekly auction of two-week repurchase agreements in which the ECB, through the National Central Banks, provides reserves to banks in exchange for securities. (18)

ECB's Marginal Lending Facility The facility through which the ECB provides overnight loans to banks; the analog to the Federal Reserve's primary credit facility. (18)

economies of scale When the average cost of producing a good or service falls as the quantity produced increases. (11, 13)

economies of scope When the average cost of producing a good or service falls as the number of different types of goods produced increases. (13)

electronic funds transfer (EFT) Movements of funds directly from one account to another over an electronic network. (2)

e-money Private money, as represented by a claim on the issuer, which is (1) stored on an electronic device, (2) issued on receipt of funds, and (3) accepted as a means of payment by persons other than the issuer. (2)

equation of exchange The equation stating that nominal income equals the quantity of money times the velocity of money; $MV = PY$. (20)

equity Ownership shares in a firm; also called *stock* and *common stock*. (8)

equity market A financial market where stocks are bought and sold. (3)

euro The name of the currency used in the countries of the European Monetary Union. (10)

euro area The countries in Europe that use the euro as their common currency. (16)

eurodollars Dollar-denominated deposits outside the U.S.; eurodollars held by U.S. citizens are part of M3. (2, 13)

European Central Bank (ECB) The central authority, located in Frankfurt, Germany, which oversees monetary policy in the common currency area. (16)

European option An option that can be exercised only on the expiration date, not before, in contrast with an *American option*. (9)

European System of Central Banks (ESCB) The European Central Bank plus the National Central Banks of all the countries in the European Union, including those that do not participate in the monetary union. (16)

Eurosystem The European Central Bank plus the National Central Banks of participating countries; together, they carry out the tasks of central banking in the euro area. (16)

examination (of banks) The formal process by which government specialists evaluate a bank's financial condition. (14)

excess reserves Reserves in excess of required reserves. (12, 17)

excess reserve-to-deposit ratio The ratio of banks' excess reserves to their demand deposit liabilities. (17)

exchange rate See *nominal exchange rate*. (10)

exchange-rate channel The channel of the monetary policy transmission mechanism where changes in policy affect consumption and output through their impact on exchange rates. (23)

exchange-rate stability One of the objectives of the central bank is to reduce exchange-rate fluctuations making it stable. (15)

Executive Board of the ECB The six-member body in Frankfurt that oversees the operation of the European Central Bank and the Eurosystem. (16)

exercise price The predetermined price at which a call or put option specifies that the underlying asset can be bought (call) or sold (put); also called the *strike price*. (9)

expansionary gap When current output exceeds potential output; the gap puts upward pressure on inflation. (21)

expectations hypothesis of the term structure The proposition that long-term interest rates are the average of expected future short-term interest rates. (7)

expected return The probability-weighted sum of possible returns to an investment. (5)

expected value The probability-weighted sum of possible values of an investment; also known as the mean or average. (5)

F

face value See *bond principal value*. (4)

fallen angel A low-grade bond that was initially a high-grade but whose issuer fell on hard times. (7)

Fannie Mae The Federal National Mortgage Association; a government-sponsored entity that aids in the financing of home mortgages. (13)

federal funds market The market where banks lend their excess reserves to other banks; the loans are unsecured. (12)

federal funds rate The interest rate banks charge each other for overnight loans on their excess deposits at the Fed; the interest rate targeted by the FOMC. (16)

Federal Open Market Committee (FOMC) The 12-member committee that makes monetary policy decisions in the United States. Members include the seven members of the Board of Governors, the president of the Federal Reserve Bank of New York, and the presidents of four Federal Reserve Banks. (16)

Federal Reserve Banks The 12 regional banks in the Federal Reserve System. (16)

Federal Reserve System The central bank responsible for monetary policy in the United States. (16)

fiat money Currency with no intrinsic value, it has value as a consequence of government decree. (2)

finance company Nondepository financial institution that raises funds directly in financial markets to provide loans to businesses and households. (13)

financial holding company A company that owns a variety of financial intermediaries. (13)

financial institutions Firms, such as banks and insurance companies, that provide access to the financial markets, both to savers who wish to purchase financial instruments directly and to borrowers who want to issue them; also known as financial intermediaries. (3)

financial instrument The written legal obligation of one party to transfer something of value (usually money) to another party at some future date, under certain conditions. (3)

financial market   The part of the financial system that allows people to buy and sell financial instruments quickly and cheaply. (1)

financial stability   One objective of the central bank is to eliminate financial system volatility, ensuring that it remains stable. (15)

financial system   The system that allows people to engage in economic transactions. It is composed of five parts: money, financial instruments, financial markets, financial institutions, and central banks. (1)

fiscal policy   The government's tax and expenditure policies, usually formulated by elected officials. (15)

fixed-payment loan   A type of loan that requires a fixed number of equal payments at regular intervals; home mortgages and car loans are examples. (4)

fixed-rate payer   The party to an interest-rate swap that is making fixed payments. (9)

flexible-rate payer   The party to an interest-rate swap that is making variable payments. Also called floating-rate player. (9)

flight to quality   An increase in the demand for low-risk government bonds, coupled with a decrease in the demand for virtually every risky investment. (7)

float   A loan from the Federal Reserve to the commercial banking system that is the result of the workings of the check-clearing process. (17)

FOMC statement   The press release that immediately follows every FOMC meeting; usually contains an announcement of the federal funds rate target, an evaluation of the current economic environment, and a statement of the risks to the economy. (16)

forbearance   Political pressure on regulators to allow banks with insufficient capital to continue to operate. (14)

foreign exchange intervention   The purchase or sale of foreign exchange by government officials with the intention of moving the nominal exchange rate. (10, 19)

foreign exchange reserves   Assets of the central bank denominated in foreign currency. (17)

foreign exchange risk   The risk arising from holding assets denominated in one currency and liabilities denominated in another. (12)

forward contract   An agreement to exchange an asset for money in the future at a currently agreed upon price. (9)

free rider   Someone who doesn't pay the cost but still gets the benefit of a good or service. (11)

fundamental value   The present value of the expected future returns to owning an asset, which equals the asset's price in an efficient market. (8)

future value   The value on some future date of an investment made today. (4)

futures contract   A standardized agreement specifying the delivery of an underlying asset (commodity or financial instrument) at a given future date for a currently agreed-upon price. (9)

G

gold standard   A fixed-exchange-rate regime in which the currencies of participating countries are directly convertible into gold. (19)

Governing Council of the ECB   The (currently) 18-member committee that makes monetary policy in the common currency area. (16)

government purchases   Spending on goods and services by federal, state, and local governments. (21)

government-sponsored enterprises (GSEs)   Federal credit agencies that provide loans directly for farm and home mortgages as well as guaranteeing programs that insure the loans made by private lenders. (3)

gross domestic product (GDP)   The market value of final goods and services produced in the economy during a year. (2)

H

hard peg   An exchange-rate system in which the central bank implements an institutional mechanism that ensures its ability to convert a domestic currency into the foreign currency to which it is pegged. (19)

hedge funds   Private, largely unregulated, investment partnerships that bring together small groups of people who meet certain (high) wealth requirements. (13)

hedger   Someone who uses financial instruments, like derivatives, to reduce risk. (9)

hedging   Reducing overall risk by investing in two assets with opposing payoffs. (5)

high-powered money   See *monetary base*. (17)

holding period return   The return from purchasing and selling a bond (applies to bonds sold before or at maturity). (6)

hyperinflation   Very high inflation; when prices double every two to three months. (15)

I

idiosyncratic risk   Risk affecting a small number of people (a specific firm or industry). (5)

illiquidity   The inability to meet immediate payment obligations. For a bank, reserves are insufficient to honor current withdrawal requests. (14)

in-the-money option   An option that would yield a profit if exercised immediately. A call option is in the money when the strike price is *less* than the current market price for the underlying instrument. (9)

indirect finance   An institution like a bank stands between the lender and the borrower, borrowing from the lender and providing the funds to the borrower. (3)

inflation   A sustained rise in the general price level; a situation in which the price of everything goes up more or less at the same time. (2)

inflation-indexed bonds   A bond whose yield equals a fixed real interest rate plus realized (as opposed to expected) inflation. (6)

inflation persistence   A term used to describe the phenomenon that when inflation is low one year, it tends to be low the next, and when it is high, it tends to stay high. (22)

inflation risk   The risk that the real value of the payments from owning a bond will be different from what was expected; that the real interest rate on a bond will differ from what was expected. (6)

inflation shock   A change in the cost of production that shifts the short-run aggregate supply curve. (22)

inflation targeting   A monetary policy strategy that involves the public announcement of a numerical inflation target, together with a commitment to make price stability the central bank's primary objective to which all other objectives are subordinated. (18)

information   A collection of facts. The basis for the third core principle of money and banking: Information is the basis for decisions. (1)

information costs   The costs lenders must pay to screen potential borrowers to determine their creditworthiness and monitor how they use the loans. (3)

insolvency   When the value of a firm's or bank's assets is less than the value of its liabilities; negative net worth. (14)

insurance company   A financial intermediary that accepts premiums, which it invests in securities and real estate (its assets) in return for promising compensation to policyholders should certain events occur (its liabilities). (3)

interest rate   The cost of borrowing and the reward to lending. See also *yield*. (4)

interest-rate channel   The traditional channel of the monetary policy transmission mechanism where changes in policy affect consumption and output through their impact on interest rates. (23)

interest-rate risk   1. The risk that the interest rate will change, causing the price of a bond to change with it. (6) 2. The risk that changes in interest rates will affect a financial intermediary's net worth. It arises from a mismatch in the maturity of assets and liabilities. (12)

interest-rate spread   1. The difference between the interest rate a bank receives on its assets and the interest rate it pays to obtain liabilities. (12)   2. Can also be used as a synonym for *risk spread*. (7)

interest-rate stability   One of the objectives of the central bank is to reduce interest-rate fluctuations keeping it stable. (15)

interest-rate swap   A contract between two counterparties specifying the exchange of interest payments on a series of future dates. (9)

intermediate targets   Variables that are not directly under the central bank's control but lie somewhere between the tools policymakers do control and their objectives; the quantity of money is an example. (18)

internal rate of return   The interest rate that equates the present value of an investment with its cost. (4)

International Monetary Fund (IMF)   The international organization created to administer the Bretton Woods system of fixed exchange rates, provide technical assistance helping countries to design their financial and economic systems, and make loans to countries in crisis. (18)

inverted yield curve   When the term structure of interest rates slopes down. (7)

investment   Spending by firms for additions to the physical capital they use to produce goods and services. (21)

investment bank   A financial intermediary that issues (underwrites) stocks and bonds for corporate customers and advises customers. (3)

investment-grade bond   Bond with low default risk; Moody's rating of Baa or higher; and Standard & Poor's rating of BBB or higher. (3)

investment horizon   The length of time an investor plans on holding an asset. (6)

J

junk bond   A bond with a high risk of default. Also called a high-yield bond. (7)

L

lagged-reserve accounting   The procedure where a bank's reserve requirement is computed based on the level of deposits several weeks earlier. (18)

large certificates of deposit   Certificates of deposit that exceed $100,000 in face value. They can be bought and sold in financial markets. (12)

law of one price   The principle that two identical goods should sell for the same price regardless of location. (10)

lender of last resort   The ultimate source of credit to banks during a panic. A role for the central bank. (14, 18)

letter of credit   A financial guarantee provided for a fee, usually by a bank, that insures a payment by one of its customers. (12)

leverage   Borrowing to finance part of an investment; increases expected return and risk. (5)

liability   Something you owe. (3)

life insurance   Insurance that makes payment on the death of the policyholder; see *term life insurance* and *whole life insurance*. (13)

limited liability   The provision that even if a company fails completely, the maximum amount that shareholders can lose is their initial investment. (8)

liquidity   A measure of the ease with which an asset can be turned into a means of payment. (2)

liquidity premium theory of the term structure   The proposition that long-term interest rates equal the average of expected short-term interest rates plus a risk premium that rises with the time to maturity. (7)

liquidity risk The risk that a financial institution's liability holders will suddenly seek to cash in their claims; for a bank this is the risk that depositors will unexpectedly withdraw deposit balances. (12)

loan commitment A line of credit, similar to an individual's credit card limit, provided by a bank or other lender that gives a firm the ability to borrow whenever necessary. (12)

loan loss reserves A portion of a bank's capital that is set aside to cover potential losses from defaulted loans. (12)

London Interbank Offered Rate (LIBOR) The interest rate at which banks lend eurodollars to other banks. (13)

long futures position The position held by a buyer of a futures contract. (9)

long-run aggregate supply curve (LRAS) The quantity of output supplied in the long run at any level of inflation; the LRAS curve is vertical at potential output. (22)

long-run real interest rate The real interest rate that equates aggregate demand with potential output. (21)

Lucas critique Economist Robert Lucas's observation that changes in policymakers' behavior will change people's expectations, altering their behavior and the observed relationships among economic variables. (20)

M

M1 The narrowest monetary aggregate, which measures the most liquid means of payment available: currency, travelers' checks, demand deposits, and other checkable deposits. (2)

M2 The monetary aggregate most commonly used in the United States, it includes M1 plus somewhat less liquid financial instruments: small-denomination time deposits, savings deposits, money-market deposit accounts, and retail money-market mutual fund shares. (2)

M3 The broadest commonly used U.S. monetary aggregate, it includes M2 plus additional less liquid financial instruments: large-denomination time deposits, institutional money-market mutual fund shares, repurchase agreements, and eurodollars. (2)

margin 1. A minimum down payment legally required to purchase a stock. 2. A deposit placed by the buyer and seller of a futures contract with the clearing corporation. (9)

marked to market Accounting rule in which a financial instrument is repriced and funds transferred from the loser to the winner at the end of every day. (9)

market capitalization The total market value of a company; the price of a share of stock times the total number of shares outstanding. (8)

market federal funds rate The overnight interest rate at which lending between banks takes place in the market; differs from the federal funds rate target set by the FOMC. (18)

markets A virtual or physical place where goods, services, and financial instruments are purchased and sold. The basis for the fourth core principle of money and banking: Markets set prices and allocate resources. (1)

matched-sale purchase (reverse repo) A short-term arrangement in which the Federal Reserve's Open Market Trading Desk sells a security and agrees to repurchase it in the near future. (18)

maturity The time to the expiration of a debt instrument; the time until a bond's last promised payment is made. (4)

mean See *expected value*. (5)

means of payment Something that can be used to purchase goods and services; one of the functions of money. (2)

minimum bid rate The minimum interest rate that banks can bid for reserves in the ECB's weekly refinancing operation; the European equivalent of the Fed's target federal funds rate; also known as the target refinancing rate. (18)

monetary aggregates Measures of the quantity of money; M1, M2, and M3. (2)

monetary base The currency in the hands of the public plus reserves in the banking system; the central bank's liabilities. (17)

monetary policy The central bank's management of money, credit, and interest rates. (15)

monetary policy framework A structure in which central bankers clearly state their goals and the trade-offs among them. (15)

monetary policy reaction curve The relationship between the real interest rate set by the central bank and the level of inflation. (21)

monetary policy transmission mechanism The channels through which changes in the central bank balance sheet influence real economic activity. (23)

money An asset that is generally accepted as payment for goods and services or repayment of debt, acts as a unit of account, and serves as a store of value. (2)

money market A market in which debt instruments with a maturity of less than one year are traded. (3)

money multiplier The ratio between the quantity of money and the monetary base; the quantity of money (M) equals the money multiplier (m) times the monetary base (MB). $M = m \times MB$. (17)

money-market deposit accounts Accounts that pay interest and offer limited check-writing privileges; part of M2. (2)

money-market mutual fund shares Shares in funds that collect relatively small sums from individuals, pool them together, and invest them in short-term marketable debt issued by large corporations; retail shares are part of M2, shares held by corporations are part of M3. (2)

moral hazard The risk that a borrower or someone who is insured will behave in a way that is not in the interest of the lender or insurer; it is caused by asymmetric information. (11)

multiple deposit creation Part of the money supply process whereby a $1 increase in the quantity of reserves works its way through the banking system, increasing the quantity of money by more than $1. (17)

municipal bonds Bonds issued by state and local governments to finance public projects; the coupon payments are exempt from federal and state income taxes. (7)

mutual fund A fund that pools the resources of a large number of small investors and invests them in portfolios of bonds, stocks, and real estate; managed by professional managers. (8)

mutual fund company Financial intermediary that pools the resources of a large number of small investors and invests them in portfolios of bonds, stocks, and real estate. (3)

N

Nasdaq Composite Index The value-weighted index of over 5,000 companies traded on the over-the-counter (OTC) market through the National Association of Securities Dealers Automatic Quotations service; the index is composed mainly of smaller, newer firms and in recent years has been dominated by technology and Internet companies. (8)

National Central Banks (NCBs) The central banks of the countries that belong to the European Union. (16)

net exports Exports minus imports; it represents an addition to the demand for domestically produced goods. (21)

net interest income A bank's interest income minus its interest expenses. (12)

net interest margin A bank's interest income minus its interest expenses divided by total bank assets; net interest income as a percentage of total bank assets. (12)

net worth The difference between a firm's or household's assets and liabilities. (11)

nominal exchange rate The value of one unit of a country's currency in terms of another country's currency. (10)

Nominal Gross Domestic Product The market value of final goods and services produced in the economy during a year measured at current (dollar) prices. (20)

nominal interest rate An interest rate expressed in dollar terms; the real interest rate plus expected inflation. (4)

nondepository institution A financial intermediary that does not issue deposit liabilities. (12)

notional principal The amount upon which the interest payments in an interest-rate swap are based. (9)

O

off-balance-sheet activities Bank activities, such as trading in derivatives and issuing loan commitments, that are neither assets nor liabilities on the bank's balance sheet. (12)

open market operations When the central bank buys or sells a security in the open market. (17)

open market purchase The purchase of a security by the central bank. (17)

open market sale The sale of a security by the central bank. (17)

open market trading desk The group of people at the Federal Reserve Bank of New York who purchase and sell securities for the Fed's System Open Market Account. (18)

operating instruments The policy instruments that the central bank controls directly; the federal funds rate is an example. (18)

operational risk The risk a financial institution faces from computer hardware or software failure, natural disaster, terrorist attacks, and the like. (12)

option premium The price the buyer of an option pays to the seller in excess of the value of the option if it were immediately exercised. (9)

organized exchange See *centralized exchange*. (3)

out-of-the money option An option that would not yield a profit if exercised immediately. A call option is out of the money when the strike price is *more* than the current market price for the underlying instrument. (9)

output gap The difference between current output and potential output. (21)

overnight cash rate The overnight interest rate on interbank loans in Europe; the European analog to the market federal funds rate. (18)

over-the-counter (OTC) market A financial market in which trades occur through networks of dealers connected together electronically. (3)

overvalued currency A country's currency when it is worth more than purchasing power parity implies. (10)

P

par value See *bond principal value*. (4)

payments system The web of arrangements that allow for the exchange of goods and services, as well as assets, among different people. (2)

payoff The amount an investor receives in return for an investment. (5)

payoff method Where the Federal Deposit Insurance Corporation sells or pays off a failed bank's depositors and then sells the failed bank's assets in an attempt to recover the amount paid out. (14)

pension fund company Financial intermediary that invests individual and company contributions into stocks, bonds, and real estate (its assets) in order to provide payments to retired workers (its liabilities). (3)

perpetuity See *consol*. (6)

policy directive The instructions from the FOMC to the System Open Market Account manager specifying the federal funds rate target. (16)

portfolio A collection or group of investments held by a person or company. (3)

portfolio demand for money The theory of the demand for money based on the use of money as a store of value; the theory that treats money as an asset analogous to a bond. (20)

potential output What the economy is capable of producing when its resources are used at normal rates; also called sustainable output. (15, 21)

precautionary demand for money The theory of the demand for money based on the idea that people hold money to insure they have resources when faced with unexpected events. (20)

present discounted value See *present value*. (4)

present value The value today (in the present) of a payment that is promised to be made in the future. (4)

price stability One objective of the central bank is to keep inflation low so that prices are stable on average. (15)

price-weighted index An index based on the average price of a collection of individual stocks. Price-weighted averages give greater weight to shares with higher prices. (8)

primary credit The term used to describe short-term, usually overnight, discount loans made by the Federal Reserve to commercial banks. (18)

primary discount rate The interest rate charged by the Federal Reserve on primary credit; also known as the discount rate, it is usually 100 basis points above the target federal funds rate. (18)

primary financial market A financial market in which a borrower obtains funds from a lender by selling newly issued securities. (3)

prime-grade commercial paper Commercial paper with a low risk of default. (7)

probability A measure of the likelihood that an event will occur. (5)

prompt corrective action Regulators' closing of failing banks, mandated by bank regulations. (14)

property and casualty insurance Insurance against damage from events like automobile accidents, fire, and theft. (13)

purchase-and-assumption method Where Federal Deposit Insurance Corporation finds a firm that is willing to take over a failed bank. (14)

purchasing power parity (PPP) The principle that a unit of currency will purchase the same basket of goods anywhere in the world. (10)

pure discount bond See *zero coupon bond*. (6)

put option A contract that confers the right, but not the obligation, to sell a financial instrument at a predetermined price on or prior to an agreed upon date. (9)

Q

quantity theory of money The theory that changes in nominal income are determined by changes in the quantity of money. (20)

R

rating A measure of the default risk associated with a company's debt; normally a series of letters going from AAA for bonds with the lowest risk of default to D for bonds that have defaulted. (7)

rating downgrade When a bond-rating agency lowers the rating of a company, signaling that its bonds have an increased risk of default. (7)

rating upgrade When a bond-rating agency raises the rating of a company, signaling that its bonds have a reduced risk of default. (7)

real business-cycle theory The theory that prices and wages are flexible, so inflation adjusts rapidly, current output always equals potential output, and all business-cycle fluctuations arise from changes in potential output. (22)

real exchange rate The exchange rate at which one can exchange the goods and services from one country for goods and services from another country. (10)

real interest rate The interest rate measured in terms of constant (real) dollars; the nominal interest rate minus expected inflation. (4)

recession A decline in overall economic activity, as defined by the National Bureau of Economic Research. (22)

recessionary gap When current output is below potential output; the gap puts downward pressure on inflation. (21)

regulation A set of specific rules imposed by the government that the managers of financial institutions must follow. (14)

reinsurance company A very large company that provides insurance to insurance companies. (13)

repurchase agreement (repo) A short-term collateralized loan in which a security is exchanged for cash, with the agreement that the parties will reverse the transaction on a specific future date, as soon as the next day. (12, 18)

required reserve ratio The ratio of required reserves to demand deposit liabilities. (17)

required reserves Reserves that a bank must hold to meet the requirements set by regulators. In the United States, the requirements are established by the Federal Reserve. (12, 17)

reserve requirement Regulation obligating depository institutions to hold a certain fraction of their demand deposits as either vault cash or deposits at the central bank. (18)

reserves A bank's vault cash plus the balance in its account at the Federal Reserve. (12, 17)

residual claimant The final person to be paid. Stockholders are residual claimants; if the company runs into financial trouble, only after all other creditors have been paid will they receive what is left, if anything. (8)

return on assets (ROA) Bank net profits after taxes divided by total bank assets; a measure of bank profitability. (12)

return on equity (ROE) Bank net profits after taxes divided by bank capital; a measure of the return to the bank's owners. (12)

risk A measure of uncertainty about the future payoff to an investment, measured over some time horizon and relative to a benchmark. The basis for the second core principle of money and banking: Risk requires compensation. (1)

risk averse investor Someone who prefers an investment with a certain return to one with the same expected return but any amount of uncertainty. (5)

risk neutral investor Someone who is indifferent between investments with different risks but the same expected return. (5)

risk premium The expected return minus the risk-free rate of return; the payment to the buyer of an asset for taking on risk. (5)

risk sharing The ability of individuals to combine and share the financial risks that they face; one of the services provided by a financial intermediary. (11)

risk spread The yield over and above that on a low-risk bond such as a U.S. Treasury with the same time to maturity, it is a measure of the compensation investors require for the risk they are bearing. Also called a default risk premium. (7)

risk structure of interest rates The relationship among the yields of bonds with the same time to maturity but different levels of risk. (7)

risk-free asset An investment whose future value is known with certainty. (5)

risk-free rate of return The rate of return on a risk-free asset. (5)

rule of 72 The rule that allows you to find out how many years it will take for the value of an investment to double; divide 72 by the annual interest rate. (4)

S

savings deposits The general term used to describe interest-bearing deposits that may have limited withdrawal privileges, but have no expiration date. (2)

seasonal credit Discount lending made in response to local, seasonal liquidity needs; used primarily by small agricultural banks in the Midwest to help manage the cyclical nature of farmers' loans and deposits. (18)

secondary credit Discount lending to banks that are not sufficiently sound to qualify for primary credit. (18)

secondary discount rate The interest rate charged on secondary credit; it is usually 50 basis points above the primary discount rate. (18)

secondary financial market A financial market in which previously issued securities are bought and sold. (3)

secondary reserves Short-term U.S. Treasury securities held as bank assets. (12)

securities Financial instruments representing ownership or debt; stocks, bonds, and derivatives. (3)

short futures position The position held by the seller of a futures contract. (9)

short-run aggregate supply curve (SRAS) The quantity of output supplied in the short run at any level of inflation; the SRAS curve is horizontal at the current level of inflation. (22)

sovereign risk The risk that a foreign borrower will not repay a loan because its government prohibits it from doing so. (12)

specialists Individuals who oversee the trading of individual stocks in a centralized exchange. (3)

speculative attack A crisis in which financial market participants believe the government will become unable to maintain its exchange rate at the current fixed level, so they sell the currency, forcing an immediate devaluation. (19)

speculator Someone who takes risks for the purpose of making a profit. (9)

spot price The market price paid for immediate delivery of a commodity or financial instrument. (9)

spread over Treasuries The difference between the yield on a bond and that on a U.S. Treasury with the same time to maturity; a measure of the riskiness of the bond. (7)

spreading risk Reducing overall risk by investing in assets whose payoffs are unrelated. (5)

stability Steady and lacking in variation. The basis for the fifth core principle of money and banking: Stability improves welfare. (1)

stabilization policy Monetary and fiscal policies designed to stabilize output and inflation. (22)

Standard & Poor's 500 Index A stock-market index that is based on the value of 500 of the largest firms in the U.S. economy. (8)

standard deviation Square root of the variance measure of risk; measures the spread of possible outcomes. (5)

sterilized foreign exchange intervention A foreign exchange intervention that alters the composition of the central bank's assets but leaves the size of its liabilities unchanged. (19)

stock Ownership shares in a firm; also called *common stock* and *equity*. (3)

stock market The market where the prices of common stock are determined. (8)

stock-market indexes Index numbers that provide a sense of whether the value of the stock market is going up or down. (8)

store of value Allows movement of purchasing power into the future; one of the functions of money. (2)

stored-value card A card that can be used to make purchases after money is transferred from a cardholder's account. (2)

strike price See *exercise price*. (9)

stripped bond A bond whose principal and coupon payments are traded separately. (6)

(financial) supervision General government oversight of financial institutions. (14)

supply of dollars The number of dollars supplied in the foreign exchange market as a function of the nominal exchange rate. (10)

sustainable growth When the economy is growing at the rate dictated by potential output. (15)

swap A financial contract obligating one party to exchange one set of payments for a second set of payments made by a counterparty. (9)

swap spread The difference between the benchmark interest rate and the swap rate, it is a measure of risk. (9)

System Open Market Account (SOMA) The official name for the securities holdings of the Federal Reserve System. (18)

systematic risk Economywide risk that affects everyone and cannot be diversified. (5)

T

T-account A simplified balance sheet in the form of a T that shows the changes in assets on one side and the changes in liabilities on the other. (17)

taxable bonds A bond whose coupon payments are not exempt from income tax. (7)

Taylor rule A rule of thumb for explaining movements in the federal funds rate; the monetary policy rule developed by economist John Taylor. (18)

term life insurance Insurance that provides a payment to the policyholder's beneficiaries in the event of the insured's death at any time during the policy's term. (13)

term to maturity The length of time until a bond's final payment. (4)

theory of efficient markets The notion that the prices of all financial instruments, including stocks, reflect all available information. (8)

time A measurable period during which something can happen. The basis for the first core principle of money and banking: Time has value. (1)

time deposits Deposits that cannot be withdrawn before a specified date. Small-denomination time deposits are part of M2; large-denomination time deposits are part of M3. (2)

too-big-to-fail policy The idea that some financial institutions are so large that government officials cannot allow them to fail because their failure will put the entire financial system at risk. (14)

trading or market risk The risk that traders who work for a bank will create losses on the bank's own account. (12)

transactions costs The costs, including time, associated with buying and selling financial instruments, as well as goods and services. (3)

transactions demand for money The demand for money based on the use of money as a means of payment, for transactions purposes. (20)

transmission mechanism of monetary policy The way changes in central bank policy influence the real economy. (23)

transparency The central bank's communication of its policy decisions and how they are made clearly to the financial markets and the public. (15)

travelers' checks Issued by travel companies, banks, and credit card companies, they are guaranteed by the issuer and usually work just like cash; part of M1. (2)

Treasury Direct The system that allows individuals to purchase U.S. Treasury securities directly from the government without the use of a broker. (16)

U

underlying instrument A financial instrument used by savers/lenders to transfer resources directly to investors/borrowers; also known as a primitive security. (3)

undervalued currency A country's currency when it is worth less than purchasing power parity implies. (10)

underwriter A financial intermediary that sells a firm's stocks or bonds to the public, guaranteeing the price the issuer will receive. (11)

underwriting The process through which an investment bank guarantees the price of a new security to a corporation and then sells it to the public. (13)

unit bank A bank without branches. (13)

units of account The units (like dollars) used to quote prices and other financial quantities; one of the functions of money. (2)

universal bank An institution that engages in all aspects of financial intermediation, including banking, insurance, real estate, brokerage services, and investment banking. (13)

unsecured loan A loan that is not guaranteed by collateral. (11)

unsterilized foreign exchange intervention A foreign exchange intervention that both alters the composition and changes the size of the central bank's balance sheet. (19)

U.S. Treasury bill A zero-coupon bond in which the U.S. government agrees to pay the bondholder a fixed dollar amount on a specific future date; has a maturity of less than one year. (6)

U.S. Treasury bond A coupon bond issued by the U.S. Treasury to finance government activities. (6)

V

value at risk The worst possible loss over a specific time horizon at a given probability; a measure of risk. (5)

value-weighted index An index that is based on the value of the firms, like the S&P 500. Value-weighted indexes give greater weight to larger firms. (8)

variance The probability-weighted sum of the squared deviations of the possible outcomes from their expected value. (5)

vault cash Currency that is physically held inside a bank's vaults and automated teller machines (ATMs). (12, 17)

velocity of money The average number of times each unit of money is used per unit time. (20)

venture capital firm A financial intermediary that specializes in investing in risky new "ventures" in return for a stake in the ownership and a share of the profits. (11)

vested When the contributions your employer has made to the pension plan on your behalf belong to you. (13)

W

wealth The total value of all assets; the net worth of an individual. (2)

whole life insurance A combination of term life insurance and a savings account in which a policyholder pays a fixed premium over his or her lifetime in return for a fixed benefit when the policyholder dies. (13)

Wilshire 5000 The most broadly based value-weighted stock index in use. It covers the roughly 6,500 publicly traded stocks in the United States. (8)

Y

yen The currency used in Japan. (10)

yield The interest rate that equates the price of a bond with the present value of its payments. (6)

yield curve A plot showing the yields to maturity of different bonds of the same riskiness against the time to maturity. (7)

yield on a discount basis The return to holding a bond; differs from yield to maturity because it divides the difference between the face value and the price by the face value and because it uses a 360-day year. (6)

yield to maturity The yield bondholders receive if they hold the bond to its maturity when the final principal payment is made. (6)

Z

zero-coupon bond A promise to pay the face value of the bond on a specific future date, with no coupon payments.

zero nominal-interest-rate bound The fact that the nominal interest rate cannot fall below zero. (23)

Index

Commonly Occurring Symbols

Symbol	Definition	Introduced in:
M1	M1 monetary aggregate	Chapter 2
M2	M2 monetary aggregate	Chapter 2
M3	M3 monetary aggregate	Chapter 2
FV	Future Value	Chapter 4
i	Nominal interest rate (usually at an annual rate)	Chapter 4
PV	Present Value	Chapter 4
FV_n	Future Value in n years	Chapter 4
F	Final payment of a bond (principal, face value, par value)	Chapter 4
P_{BP}	Present Value of Bond Principle Payment	Chapter 4
P_{CP}	Present Value of Bond Coupon Payments	Chapter 4
C	Coupon payment	Chapter 4
P_{CB}	Price of a Coupon Bond	Chapter 4
r	Real interest rate	Chapter 4
π^e	Expected inflation	Chapter 4
St. Dev.	Standard Deviation	Chapter 5
VaR	Value-at-Risk	Chapter 5
i^e	Expected interest rate	Chapter 7
i_{nt}	Interest rate on a bond with n years to maturity at time t	Chapter 7
rp_n	Risk premium on an n-year bond	Chapter 7
D	Stock dividend payment	Chapter 8
P	Price of a stock	Chapter 8
g	Dividend growth rate	Chapter 8
rf	Risk-free return	Chapter 8
i^f	Foreign interest rate	Chapter 9
ROA	Return on assets	Chapter 12
ROE	Return on equity	Chapter 12
Δ	Change in a variable	Chapter 17
D	Checkable Deposits	Chapter 17
r_D	Required deposit reserve ratio	Chapter 17
RR	Required reserves	Chapter 17
M	Quantity of money	Chapter 17